Readings in
Social Psychology
Contemporary Perspectives

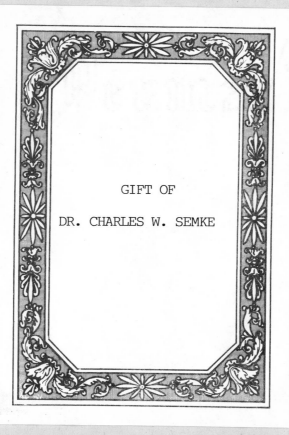

Harper & Row's
CONTEMPORARY PERSPECTIVES READER SERIES
Phillip Whitten, Series Editor

Readings in
Social Psychology
Contemporary Perspectives
second edition

Dennis Krebs <small>Simon Fraser University</small>

editor

68·1386

series editor Phillip Whitten

HARPER & ROW, PUBLISHERS, New York
Cambridge, Philadelphia, San Francisco,
London, Mexico City, São Paulo, Sydney

1817

Sponsoring Editor: Kathy Whalen
Project Editor: Pamela Landau
Senior Production Manager: Kewal K. Sharma
Compositor: Maryland Linotype Composition Co., Inc.
Printer and Binder: The Murray Printing Company

Readings in Social Psychology: Contemporary Perspectives
Second Edition

Library of Congress Cataloging in Publication Data
Main entry under title:
Readings in social psychology.
    (Harper & Row's contemporary perspectives reader
series)
    1. Social psychology—Addresses, essays, lectures.
I. Krebs, Dennis. II. Series.
HM251.R37 1982   302   81-6590
ISBN 0-06-043769-3   AACR2

Summary of Contents

Contents

evidence that they possessed capacities for empathy and altruism.

The anthropologist Irven DeVore describes recent revisions in Darwin's theory that launched the new field of sociobiology, and discusses some of the controversy surrounding this new gene-based model of evolution.

A philosopher criticizes sociobiology and ethology for assuming that similarities between nonhuman and human behavior signify similarities in underlying processes. Like Aesop's fables, Simon argues, the behavior of animals may supply lessons about how we ought to behave, but it says little about why we behave in the ways we do.

The authors examine the challenge presented by behaviors that appear to be altruistic to (a) the theory of evolution and (b) psychological theories of learning. They conclude that genetic similarity and empathy may supply the means for resolving the paradox of altruism.

Whether we consider ourselves male or female is one of the most essential aspects of our identity. It affects a vast array of social behavior. Are we born with a sexual identity, or do we learn to think of ourselves as male or female? This article reviews the evidence for both positions.

Humans are the most sexual of all animals. Almost all other mammals mate only when the female is in estrus. Why? The author of this article argues that sexuality evolved as a mechanism to induce the type of long-term male-female bonds necessary to insure the survival of vulnerable infants. Accompanying this, the author suggests, was a division of labor that gave rise to status differences between males and females.

This article evaluates the contribution of the anthropologist Margaret Mead's influential book on three preliterate New Guinea societies, in which she supplies evidence in support of the idea that most major differences between males and females are culturally, not biologically, determined.

Paula Stern lists stereotypes about women and conceptions about their nature that have appeared throughout history, especially those advanced by religion and social science. She reviews the images of women that appear in popular magazines, and implies that traditional feminine behavior is learned through cultural indoctrination.

A science writer interviews four leading researchers on nonverbal communication and face-to-face interaction: Ray Birdwhistell, Albert Sheflen, Adam Kendon, and Erving Goffman. Davis tells us a little bit about them and their work. In so doing, she supplies a readable introduction to the field.

When people talk, they communicate on both verbal and nonverbal levels. Language conveys both ideas and emotions. The pauses and timing of verbal communication convey information, as do the immediacy and distance of the words we use. The psychologist Albert Mehrabian describes studies on "paralanguage" and other varieties of nonverbal communication. He explores their implications for psychotherapy, interpersonal attraction, power relationships, and social class.

Loneliness, like love, has received very little attention from psychologists. This article reports the results of two of the first studies on the issue. The results contained a number of surprises. Taken together, they suggest that how people interpret their social relations (or lack of them) has a much greater impact on whether or not they feel lonely than the amount of social contact they actually have.

The family is the primary social group in all societies. Colleen Johnson outlines the nature and functions of families in cultures other than our own. She suggests that the emphasis on individuality and autonomy in modern societies creates casualties because it fails to satisfy basic emotional needs.

Encounter groups have a powerful effect on most of their participants. Eleanor Hoover reviews the practices of various encounter groups. She speculates about the source of their impact, wonders about the ethics that guide them, and raises some important questions about what they do to the people who take part in them.

What would induce street people who take drugs, drink, smoke, and engage in promiscuous sexuality to give these earthly pleasures up, toil six days a week, and spend most of the rest of the time reading the Bible? The same forces, apparently, that cause women who rejected traditional sex roles to accept them again with passion. The authors do not accept the Jesus People's explanation for their change, which is that they have "found Christ." The authors interpret the conversion in terms of thought reform and group dynamics.

How powerful a force is group approval? How difficult is it to oppose group consensus? Janis interprets various high-level decisions, such as the decisions that paved the way for the Bay of Pigs fiasco, the invasion of Pearl Harbor, and the escalation of the war in Vietnam in terms of "groupthink"—"a deterioration of mental efficiency, reality testing and moral judgment that results from ingroup pressures."

Involvement with a group of like-minded people—whether a weight-loss club, jury, political party, Alcoholics Anonymous, or class—often makes members adopt extreme positions on issues.

Competent authoritarian leaders get things done but make group members angry. Bad authoritarian leaders make poor decisions and make group members angry. Democratic leaders don't make much difference.

It seems obvious that there is a world external to our senses; yet, without our eyes and ears, we cannot perceive the world. It has been shown that what we perceive is determined by our past experience. Albert Rosenfeld explores the question, What happens when people with different past experiences and, indeed, different forms of perception perceive "reality" differently?

Hamachek reviews psychological research demonstrating ways in which people's needs, values, attitudes, beliefs, and self-concepts influence their perceptions, especially their perceptions of other people.

Is beauty in the eye of the beholder? Although we may resist the idea that anything so incidental and "skin-deep" as physical attractiveness would affect our impressions of people and our behavior toward them, two social psychologists show that people possess a

It makes sense to assume that people behave in ways that are consistent with their attitudes. However, a number of psychological experiments have found that people often appear to say one thing and do another. Ronald Dillehay undertakes a critical examination of the studies most frequently cited as indicating a discrepancy between attitude and behavior.

Sages have advised us for centuries to know ourselves. What is this "self" we are encouraged to know, and how have recent scientific discoveries affected its integrity? Does the specter of cloning, new life-maintaining techniques, organ transplants, sex-change operations, electrical stimulation of the brain, and the effects of drugs threaten the sense of self?

early ideas. Kohlberg describes his six stages of moral reasoning and the forces that foster moral maturity. Especially important in Kohlberg's theory is the development of role-taking abilities.

A *Psychology Today* editor traces the evolution of Kohlberg's theory of moral development and evaluates its contributions. Over the years Kohlberg has become increasingly practical, focusing his energy on promoting moral growth by creating "just communities" in schools and prisons. Criticisms of his basic theory and his community work have been severe.

The extent to which moral reasoning at each of Kohlberg's six stages is associated with or gives rise to political orientation, personality style, and moral behavior is an open question. Charles Hampden-Turner and Phillip Whitten explore the relationship between political attitudes and actions, and moral thinking.

To what extent is it justifiable to violate moral principles in order to contribute to knowledge? This question is especially significant in social psychological research. This article discusses the major ethical issues faced by researchers, the guidelines psychologists have developed, and the implications of various practices.

Preface

Several years ago, in the summer of 1975, my friend, Phillip Whitten, editor of this series, called me from Marblehead, Massachusetts, and asked me if I would be interested in putting together a book of readings in social psychology. My first response was to wonder why he wanted to publish another collection of readings in social psychology: there are so many on the market. Phil's response was that the existing books contain technical journal articles on topics mainly of concern to academics. He wanted a book that contained nontechnical selections on topics of interest to students.

The idea struck a sympathetic chord. Too often I had seen typical studies in social psychology turn off students, who, bogged down in a morass of numbers, missed the significance of such studies. More popular articles, oriented to the general reader, emphasize the implications of the findings rather than the results of controlled experiments. Students of social psychology bring years of personal experience to the academic study of the field. They arrive with implicit theories about human nature and social relations. Most students are interested in *practical* knowledge—ideas and information that will help them understand themselves and others better. These are legitimate concerns, and they guided, as much as possible, the selection of articles for the first edition of this book.

The volume is now in its second edition. In the preface of the first edition, I promised that the new edition would be revised in response to criticisms and suggestions from instructors and students, and to changes in the discipline. It has. All articles that received unfavorable reviews from a majority of students and instructors who filled out the response card in the back of the first edition have been dropped. In their place I have added some 21 new selections (most of which were published in the past few years). These include articles on sociobiology, altruism, sexual identity and sex roles, nonverbal communication, loneliness, group processes, the authoritarian personality, prejudice, the nature of the self, shyness, jealousy, love, happiness, moral development, and ethics in social psychology. At the same time, I have retained the best of the articles from the first edition. In addition, several sections of the reader have been reorganized to reflect new emphases in the field. Interestingly, and, perhaps hopefully, most of the major changes have entailed adding articles on positive social behaviors such as altruism, love, and moral development.

The selections contained in this volume do not reflect the field of social psychology as it is traditionally represented in textbooks. Rather, they are designed to complement and broaden it. I have always been uncomfortable with labels, such as *social psychology*; it is not always clear where social psychology begins and where sociology, personality psychology, biology, and other disciplines leave off. Some of the readings in this volume have been more closely identified with other fields—especially anthropology, sociology, and developmental psychology—than with social psychology. But their goal is to present an overview of the major forces that affect social behavior. Thus, they have important implications for social psychology.

I have tried to include in the book a varied and interesting selection of individual readings, but I also have tried to integrate them around a number of themes. The articles may be read and their ideas digested in any order; but I would hope that some students will read this book from beginning to end. The book's structure is hierarchical in the sense that it progresses from a discussion of processes that are evolutionarily most basic to those that are uniquely characteristic of rational humans. It is circular in the sense that it progresses from a methodological perspective that is defined by the naturalistic observations of animals, through the more traditional experimental methods of social psychology, into the holistic observations of individuals within the context of their life spans. Finally, it is dialectical: issues that are addressed from one point of view are explored from other points of view in other sections. Whenever possible I have attempted to present both sides of controversial issues. The readings hang together for me in an integrated fashion, which is why, I suppose, I organized them the way I did. But it is my hope that the overriding perspective to which the readings give rise—the working understandings of human nature and social relations—will contain within itself the seeds for growth and transformation. The readings, as a whole, should be accessible at several levels of understanding.

The articles in this book were carefully selected from a broad range of contemporary, as well as classical, sources: books, journals, and semipopular magazines. The work of many leading social psychologists and other social scientists has been included, for example, Leonard Berkowitz, Margaret Mead, Ray Birdwhistell, Albert Sheflen, Erving Goffman, Robert Zajonc, John Darley and Bibb Latané, Amitai Etzioni, Irving Janis, Elaine Walster, T. W. Adorno, Gordon Allport, Elliot Aronson, Kenneth Gergen, Philip Zimbardo, Robert Rosenthal, David L. Rosenhan, Seymour Epstein, Zick Rubin, Jonathan Freedman, Jean Piaget, and Lawrence Kohlberg. The range of issues covers virtually every topic taught in contemporary undergraduate courses in social psychology, and should provide a thorough and readable background introduction to the fascinating aspects of the discipline.

I would like to express my gratitude to Phillip Whitten for his friendship, editorial assistance, and patience; to his administrative assistant, Iris Stein; and to my secretary, Mrs. M. Hay, for her unremitting loyalty during the past five years. Finally, I'd like to express my appreciation to the more than 70 authors who generously allowed us to reprint their works, and without whom this book would not have been possible.

We will continue to revise *Readings in Social Psychology: Contemporary Perspectives* regularly—not only in response to changes in the discipline itself, but also as a result of the suggestions and criticisms of students and instructors who use it. For this reason, we have retained the Response Card, which can be located at the back of the book. Please take a moment to fill out the card and send it to the publisher after you have used the book. Your comments will be much appreciated and gratefully received.

DENNIS KREBS

Readings in
Social Psychology
Contemporary Perspectives

I. Roots of Human Nature: Selfishness and Aggression

In the 1960s a number of writers popularized the idea that humans are "naked apes," heir to the aggressive instincts of their "killer ape" ancestors. Robert Ardrey ("The Violent Way") presents a sample of this thought. It wasn't long, however, before writers such as Ardrey were soundly criticized—both for inaccuracies and selectiveness in their facts about primates and other nonhuman animals and for fallacies in their inferences (see "Simple Views of Aggression"). We can't all go out into the field to observe chimpanzees, but we can evaluate the plausibility of arguments about their behavior and its implications for understanding our own.

Robert Ardrey opens his article with a description of John Calhoun's study of the effects of overcrowding on rats. John Calhoun ("The Plight of the Ik and Kaiadilt Is Seen as a Chilling Possible End for Man") describes his experiment—which, according to Calhoun, involved mice not rats—and compares his findings with those of Colin Turnbull, an anthropologist who studied the effects of environmental disaster and overcrowding on the Ik, a mountain people from an isolated region in northeastern Uganda. Robert

Trotter ("Cities, Crowding & Crime") summarizes the results of other studies on the effects of overcrowding. Together these articles supply a case study in comparative social psychology. The authors emphasize the similarities between mice and men, but there are differences as well. For example, the Ik were undernourished and Calhoun's mice were not. Might overcrowding cause malnutrition that causes chemical changes in the body, which in turn cause antisocial behavior? Does violence in overcrowded quarters serve to regulate population growth? Or is it, as Ardrey suggests, "a by-product of social break-down, of the triumph of disorder over order, of aggression no longer subject to social channels spilling over without inhibition into monkey immorality"? The term *overcrowding* is not an explanation of violent behavior. It is a description of an environmental condition that *sometimes* precedes it.

We must be careful how we use words when we extrapolate from animals to humans. It is important to ask whether rats have a "class structure" in our sense of the term; whether the behavior of groups of rats can be described as "criminal," and whether rats "rape," as Ardrey implies. Obviously there are senses in which these descriptive labels are appropriate, but—and this is the critical issue—there are also senses in which they connote more similarity between humans and rats than actually exists. Rats have never organized a revolution nor has any rat ever been convicted of murder or rape. Only people have.

In "New Clues to the Causes of Violence," Gene Bylinsky reviews some of the evidence on the role played by (a) genes, hormones, and old brain mechanisms and (b) early experiences, modeling, and culture on various forms of violence. As much as we may wish it were different, we get angry, fearful, and sexually aroused in much the same way as other primates do. The structure of the old brain of a human and chimpanzee is essentially the same. However, humans possess a lot more cortex. By and large, this is beneficial; but it does have some unfortunate consequences. For example, one effect of intelligence is that something as abstract as a few unkind words, or the sight of a gun, may drive a human (but not a chimpanzee) to murderous rage. Indeed, there is considerable evidence that watching violence on TV increases the incidence of violence in many people (see "Television and Violence: Implications of the Surgeon General's Research Program" in Part V).

By now it has become a truism that all social behavior results from an interaction between heredity and environment. Bylinsky identifies some of the forms this interaction may take.

The Violent Way

by Robert Ardrey

In 1958 John Calhoun at Washington's National Institute of Mental Health decided to see what would happen to a rat population if he forced overcrowding. An experiment was conducted indoors, under controlled conditions, and its chief ingenuity was an arrangement of four interconnecting pens. The two end pens each had but one entrance which could be guarded by a strong male rat. But the middle pens, each with two entrances, could not be so guarded and so became the center of free social action. As the population rose, the action in these middle pens became such an animal nightmare that Calhoun was to describe it as a "behavioral sink."

In each pen was an abundance of food, water and nesting materials, along with artificial burrows for nesting mothers. And each was large enough to accommodate comfortably a group of 12 adult rats, the number that Calhoun had earlier learned was a normal size in a natural population. But as numbers rose and crowding took place, nothing like an even distribution of numbers occurred in the pens, just as nothing like equivalent behavior developed.

At the beginning of the experiment a natural status struggle took place among the males. The most powerful alphas—those individuals that rise to dominant roles in any animal population—each took possession of an end pen. Since there was but one entrance, each had only to take his position beside it to guard the pen and keep order within it. Here his harem of females made their nests undisturbed. Calhoun wrote, "In essence the dominant male established his territorial dominion and his control over a harem of females not by driving the other males out but by preventing their return." He slept by the entrance, paying no attention to the comings and goings of his females. If a male appeared, he was instantly alert, but he would tolerate the entrance of one who accepted his dominance. Such subordinates frequently slept in the pen. They never interfered with the females or attempted copulation. In general the harem females made good mothers, built proper nests, nursed and protected their young, and raised about half to weaning. But if there was order in the end pens, there was chaos in the middle.

As population rose, its weight fell on the unprotected middle pens. Here there was a class of dominant males, but they could hold no territories and fighting was frequent. Rank order shifted with victories and defeats. There emerged also a middle class frequently attacked by the alphas but rarely contending. They were sexually active but seemed unable to discriminate between estrous and nonestrous females, or even between females and juveniles. And then there were the inevitable losers, the last-in-line, the totally subordinated omegas who "moved through the community like somnambulists," who ignored all others and were ignored by all. To look at them, they seemed sometimes the fattest and sleekest, and they remained unscarred by combat. These were the dropouts.

So far, such a class structure in a crowded population might be expected. But with further crowding

a class quite beyond prediction emerged. Calhoun called them "the probers." They were subordinate but active, and it was an essentially criminal class. They moved sometimes in gangs. Attacked by a dominant, they never contended yet were never dis-

The rats loved the chaos of the crowded pens

couraged. They took no part at all in the status struggle, but they were the most active males in the colony. Hypersexual, they were also bisexual, and frequently cannibalistic too. Most astonishing was their tendency toward an action which can only be called rat rape. The normal male rat has a courtship ritual. If he pursues a female to her burrow he waits outside for her to emerge and accept. He never enters. But the probers dispensed with all courtship, chased females into burrows, sometimes trampling and killing the young with abandon. Following their sexual activity, if dead babies lay about, they ate them.

The disorder of the middle pens disrupted female life more than male. Nest-building suffered first, and throughout the last half of the experiment no nests were built at all. Infants were scattered, abandoned, eaten. Whereas infant mortality in the protected end pens was held to 50%, in the middle pens it rose to 96%. Half of the females themselves died of pregnancy disturbances or sexual assault.

Calhoun's experiment, with all its horrifying human implications, caused wide comment. Yet one observation has been little recorded. The rats enjoyed the behavioral sink. The females in particular seemed incapable of resisting the social excitement of the middle pens. Protected harem females sought the middle pens when in estrus, without interference from their overlords. Although food and water were available in the protected pens, almost all sought the middle-pen hoppers. Their behavior in the rat mob was no different from that of the nonharem females. The one advantage protecting their young was the peace and the order of the end pens, to which they could retreat. But while the end-pen alphas never left their estates, only a very small percentage of their females could resist the crowd.

Few will quarrel with the proposition that overcrowding has profound effects on human behavior.

As we consider the effect on animals, however, we may properly wonder whether Calhoun's behavioral sink presents a fair analogy. His subjects were domesticated rats responding to the artificial conditions of a laboratory. Could the same drastic consequences come about among wild animals, living in a state of nature? By good fortune we may turn to three independent studies of the langur, a member of our own primate family, living under varying conditions of population density in its native India and Ceylon.

The earliest observations of the langur were made by Phyllis Jay Dolhinow in certain forests of central India where the monkeys are fairly scarce. Each troop has a range of about two square miles and rarely comes into contact with another. While troops tend to avoid or ignore each other, there is no conflict if contact occurs. There are no defended territories, and no evident boundaries between groups. Within each troop's little society males have a rigid rank order in which every individual knows his place. They almost never quarrel.

The langurs of India's central forests seemed the ideal, sunny, nonaggressive creatures of legend, and Dolhinow's study, completed in 1959, did much to reinforce the arguments of those primate students that monkeys never fight, never defend territory, never do anything but behave themselves in a fashion rarely glimpsed in human schoolyards.

Then, however, Suzanne Ripley made her equally careful study of langurs in Ceylon. Her troops were of about the same size as those Dolhinow observed. But nowhere did there exist those infinite distances for the happy, wandering life. Instead of two square miles in India's central forests, a troop in Ceylon occupied only a half to as little as an eighth of a square mile. And here there were not only territories, with actively defended, unchanging borders, but groups sought combat.

It is important to note that for these leaf-eating monkeys no shortage of food inspired conflict. Even the most arid zones of forest could carry numbers well beyond the actual population. Neither was any great damage inflicted by the continual conflict. Despite what must be described as violent behavior, still in the best territorial tradition a maximum of excitement was generated with a minimum of physical harm. And finally, the aggression directed outward infected not at all relations within the group. Although all groups studied by Ripley contained at least two adult males, and one contained six, harmony and cooperation were near-perfect. Even females joined with their males in the territorial battles. This record of inner harmony was not to be duplicated in the third study.

Yukimaru Sugiyama of Kyoto University encountered in the Dharwar forest of western India the most extreme population density of langurs yet recorded. Dolhinow's had been less than 20 per square mile, Ripley's in Ceylon about 150. Sugiyama's was over 250. Whether density was the only factor contributing to social breakdown Sugiyama could not know, but disorder approached perfection. There were territories but borders were obscure and ill-defended. When troops met, leaders fought unassisted. Neither were there the rigid rank orders of dominance so characteristic of Dolhinow's widely separated groups. Perhaps as a consequence almost all troops had only one adult male, though there might be six or 10 adult females. Sugiyama speculated that without a hierarchy regulating the relationships of males, quarrels were so disruptive that only one male usually remained. The expelled males formed their own groups in the forest.

When the sexual season approached its peak an all-male gang, with no more inhibition than Calhoun's proberl rats, would descend on a troop containing females, kill or drive off the leader and any subadult males, and fight among themselves for sexual sovereignty. Far from mourning their departed overlord, the females would respond to the action with enhanced sexual stimulation and

copulate with the conqueror. The episode would reach its climax when the conqueror bit to death all the infants.

Here is violent behavior on a scale unprecedented in primate observation, and it seems a direct consequence of overcrowding. Of Sugiyama's nine troops under direct observation, such scenes of riot overwhelmed four troops in a season. It is true that the slaughter of the innocents provided a form of

Organized society is not a human invention

population control. But I doubt that this is more than a by-product of social breakdown, of the triumph of disorder over order, of aggression no longer subject to social channels spilling over without inhibition into monkey immorality.

Organized society, contrary to both common and academic assumption since the days of Jean Jacques Rousseau, is not a human invention. Whether we observe the langur or rat, the lion or elephant we observe species that are no different from us in the

inability of the individual to survive alone. As we face a common fact of life with these animal species, we accept with them the common necessity of group existence. Without the group we should all perish.

In such groups, animal and human, there is always a problem: to construct sufficient order so that the group may act as one in behalf of the individual, yet preserve sufficient disorder—what men would call freedom—so that diverse social partners may each fulfill their varying potentials. The problem is solved by an organizing principle which I term the social contract. This contract, which animals under normal conditions accept instinctively, provides a delicate balance between the necessary order and

Animals and men both fear strangers

the necessary disorder without which vulnerable beings could not survive.

Like the territorial imperative, the social contract is a biological mechanism of selective value, restraining yet enhancing individual capacities. Territory defends the individual through control of exclusive space; the social contract defends him through concert of numbers. But it is a fragile mechanism. As the social order contains and channels our innate aggressiveness, so with environmental change it may be an object itself of aggression until new balances are restored. Any rapid change in the circumstance of species may leave order and disorder grotesquely out of balance. Such has been the change throughout the last half century in man's relation to space.

What we are just beginning to learn about the human significance of space stems almost entirely from the observations of Heini Hediger, who first established the concept of individual distance. On a March day in 1938, in Zurich's Bellevue Square, he noticed black-headed gulls sitting on the lakeside parapet. The gulls had arranged themselves evenly, just two railings apart. His curiosity caught, Hediger began watching other species. Flamingos demand twice the distance, about two feet, whereas swallows will settle for six inches. All these and many others are "distance species," but there are also "contact/togetherness species" with quite opposite inclinations. Tortoises, some monkeys and lemurs, even owls and spiny hedgehogs will crowd together in an animal pile. But such species are a minority.

The master zoo keeper extended his observations to animal training. The distance an animal demands between himself and an enemy is of a special sort, a "flight distance." Small animals tend to demand less, large animals more. But flight distance will vary according to accustomed conditions. In a protected African reserve baboons normally may not move away until you have come within 20 yards, whereas in unprotected areas they will take flight at a hundred. It is the reduction of flight distance that is known as taming. When it reaches zero, the animal is a pet.

So new is scientific concern with the spacing of animals that discussion has not yet evolved reliable terminology with definitions agreed by all. Hediger's "individual distance" has become "personal space," and as we have seen may vary with individuals in its dimension. Likewise it is widely accepted that personal space may vary with seasons. The lapwing or

Urban life reveals the innate inequality of men

chaffinch may gather in quite tight little flocks in winter, but with the first sexual stirrings of the breeding season disperse to scattered, strenuously defended territories in which the demand for space is maxi-

mum. In our examination of the human crowd we have at least a language for individual contacts. But for the contacts of groups we have few such terms.

Besides individual distance Hediger gave us the term "social distance," to describe the farthest point that an animal will go as it strays from its group. The social distance of a group, in other words, may be expressed as a measure of its scatter. A baboon troop, scattering widely as it feeds, exhibits its maximum of social distance. But as dusk draws on, distance will rapidly shrink until all go to sleep in a few close trees. Social distance, then, is a measure of animal need for the familiar, and this too is a term we can agree on. But for the opposite and probably more powerful social force, the rejection of strangers, I can find no term in the literature.

I dislike and regard as an arrogance the contri-

bution of terms to established sciences. But since this discussion cannot proceed without such terms, I shall refer to this social rejection of strangers as animal xenophobia.

Animal xenophobia is as widespread a trait among social species as any single trait we can study. A limited group of familiars, many of them perhaps with kinship relation, know each other as individuals. Each has learned what to expect of his neighbor, and in such groups sufficient order comes easily. But the stranger presents a problem. Infrequently—most infrequently—his admission will be tolerated. If it occurs, however, normal procedure will probably condemn him to the bottom of the social rank where his potential for social disruption will be minimum. Xenophobia guarantees the integrity of the group, and the least possible chance of disorder.

Until the spectacular rise of the city, human social life in many ways bore reasonable resemblance to the life of normal animal species. Space sheltered us. Xenophobia between villages might be as marked as between animal groups, and as satisfying, but social space was abundant. Personal space was ample too, and if we did not like each other nothing compelled us to look at each other too closely. We competed, of course, as men will always compete for the conventional prizes of territory, wealth, alpha position. But as long as space was our abundant asset, the territory with a fence around it was a goal that all could seek.

For every territory there is a proprietor, an alpha who has won his conventional prize. Not even, of course, in the rural society of orchard and garden, small-town grocery store or dry-goods shop do all men become proprietors. Still, the alphas are many and the prizes remain real. But as urban concentration grows and competition shifts from dominance over a piece of space to dominance over fellow men, not only do we encounter the hierarchy of despotism from which territorial man was largely protected but we encounter a vanishment of alphas. Prizes grow fewer. And as we press farther into the ever-condensing mass we find ever-enlarging human organizations, be they corporations or labor unions, political groupings or taxpayers' protest meetings. And as organizations become larger alpha ranks become fewer.

In the United States of America the normal curve of genetic endowment would suggest that at least 10 million people are potential alphas competing as they must for a diminishing number of alpha slots. Their aggressive potentiality is uncontainable within a society of diminishing prizes. Equally stark, however, is the problem of the condemned omega. When men turned earth with a spade, moved coal with a shovel, cut hay with a scythe, carried hods on their backs, the body could support human dignity though the brain be inadequate. Such work in a highly organized, highly technological society is all but gone. As opportunity for the demanding alpha is withdrawn, so refuge for the condemned omega ceases to exist. The frustrations of urban society reveal in na-

kedness what our earlier rural societies modestly clothed: the innate, random inequality of men.

The city is a cultural invention enforcing on the citizen knowledge of his own nature. And this we do not like. That we are aggressive beings easily given to violence; that we get along together more because we must than because we want to, and that the brotherhood of man is about as far from reality today as it was two thousand years ago; that reason's realm is small; that we never have been and never shall be created equal; that if the human being is perfectible, he has so far exhibited few symptoms—all are considerations of man from which space tends to protect us.

And yet the city is not a concentration camp. Most of us go there not as slaves or prisoners, but as volunteers. Just as Calhoun's rats freely chose to eat in the middle pens, we freely enter the city. Overcrowding is a voluntary condition.

But overcrowding, as we saw in the langur studies, can lead to a breakdown in the social structure, which in turn calls forth urban disaster. No example is more illuminating than the violence and the regime of fear that invest American urban life. That regime is as perfect in a relatively uncrowded Kansas City as in the massed densities of a Chicago or New York. Were overcrowding the cause, then this could not be so. What we witness is the drunken tottering of a social structure supported by an inadequate philosophy. Tremors first may become evident where numbers are densest. But while overcrowding may test, advance and display a social weakness, it cannot be the ultimate cause.

Aggressiveness, by definition, is the determined pursuit of one's interests. Violence is the pursuit of such interests through force, or the threat of force. They are not the same.

Without aggression as an inborn force, survival throughout all the natural world would be impossible. But likewise survival dictates aggression's limits. Without traffic laws, aggression is a drunken driver in a lethal midnight. As no population could survive without sufficient numbers sufficiently aggressive, so no population could survive were competitions customarily carried to deadly conclusion. And so has evolved throughout the species that body of rules and regulations of infinite variety which while encouraging the aggressive discourages the violent. The problem of man is not that we are aggressive but that we break our own rules.

Any species must risk extinction when aggressiveness finds its fences in ruin and violence an ever-available entertainment. But the social species risk most. For beings who are biologically dependent on the group, whose existence is impossible without the cooperation of one's fellows, the violent solution of natural disagreement becomes a form of suicide.

There are two quite different expressions of human violence: the struggles within groups of social partners and the struggles between organized societies. The second is war, and I regard it as the lesser threat to our future. War today is either unwinnable or inconclusive, as the present stalemates in Vietnam and the Near East would indicate, or it is nuclear catastrophe. Neither kind is very satisfactory. So, human violence, once expressed on the battlefield, is today being transferred to the city's streets.

There is a paradox involved. Organized warfare, although an exercise exclusively human in the vertebrate world, received reinforcement from natural law, whereas civil violence breaks every rule of social species. Intolerable though the damage of warfare might be, still it united societies, strengthened social contracts and gave outlet for animal xenophobia. But war is technologically obsolete, and its civil substitute biologically unendurable. If we are to prepare ourselves for any profound understanding of sabotage, riot, political kidnappings and assassination, then we should first inspect carefully the concept of the stranger.

I have referred to the universality of animal xenophobia. The stranger is driven out of a group's social space and physically attacked if his attentions persist. The howling monkey roars, alerting his fellows in the clan; the spider monkey barks; the lion without ceremony attacks. However the animosity for strangers is expressed, whether through attack or avoidance, xenophobia is there, and it is as if throughout the animal world invisible curtains hang between the familiar and the strange.

We have in our genetic endowment the tendency

Throughout nature there is a force for order

to reject strangers and, if we are to read objectively the history of civilized man, a probable propensity for violence. War may be nearly abolished, but these tendencies are not. All that is vanishing from the human scene is the cultural institution that once provided satisfaction for both without damage to social integrity. We are faced with the question, "How do we get along without war?" Subconsciously we transform our cultural channel. We transfer energies once directed outward to the inward expression known as social violence. But such an expression presents an intriguing problem, for now we must invent strangers.

The invention of strangers must be the prime foundation for the future of civil violence. And the prime ingredient for the invention of strangers must be noncommunication between those who speak the same language, share the same territory.

Students and faculty, for example, could never have accomplished in our universities even their tentative scuffles of violence and destruction if either group had not been richly provided with noncomprehension concerning the other. The universities present an excellent example indeed, since here presumably the same language is spoken with fluency, authority and precision. Yet on many a campus the handicap has been overcome so overwhelmingly that noncommunication flourishes and the supply of strangers becomes as bountiful as the enticements of violence may demand.

The achievement of the universities admittedly has been nourished by the achievements of the floundering home. A few old-fashioned families may still cling to a degree of affection and toleration, but as we all know understanding between parents and children has been for long on the way out. What goes on in the parent becomes as mysterious to the young as what the young are up to remains a mystery to the parent.

One of the few flaws that I can see in the crystalline future of civil disorder is the improbability of organized violence between parents and young. While mutual noncomprehension may reach the most perfect level, while the creation of strangers has already attained conspicuous success, while hostility flourishes and conditions of downright enmity sometimes prevail, still something is lacking. And I believe it is because the young, organized into a legion by the peer-group, face in that stranger, the parent, too contemptible, too pathetic, too bewildered an object for worthy attack. Old battered shipwrecks floating on new seas, parents tempt few guns. And the aggressive energies of their offspring are redirected to such satisfying targets as the universities and the police.

In America blacks and whites, parents and young, students and faculties have demonstrated the workability of noncommunication, the creation of strangers, and the transformation of acceptable aggressiveness into unaccepted civil violence.

A touch of paranoia is inevitable if members of a subgroup are to test their strength against the weight of a majority. Any sense of injustice, however real, must be aggrandized to a point where risk becomes tolerable. Yet I find myself doubtful that such social scenes should be characterized as neurotic, since we neglect a prime fact: that the youth with a paving stone in his hand is enjoying himself.

We enjoy the violent, just as Calhoun's rats sought the middle pens. We hurry to an accident not to help; we run to a fire not to put it out; we crowd about a schoolyard fight not to stop it. For all the Negro's profound and inarguable grievances, there has not been a racial outbreak in America since the days of Watts in which a degree of carnival atmosphere has not prevailed. I myself may have no great taste for Molotov cocktails; it is because I am timid, not because I am good. Gerald Suttles, in his work with juvenile gangs in the Chicago slums, found that the reliability of gang members to join in an action could be analyzed: stealing might attract a fair number, but the prospect of a fight would enlist almost all.

Action and destruction are fun. The concerned observer who will not grant it indulges in a hypocrisy which we cannot afford. He who regards a taste for violent action as a human perversion will not likely make any great contribution to the containment of our violent way. Similarly, the observer who seeks nothing but earnest motivation in riot and arson, who looks only to environmental deprivation, neglect, or injustice to explain it—who in other words seeks wholly in the action of the majority the motivations of the minority—may flatter himself one day that he was violence's most dependable ally.

As one views the vistas of violent behavior rising before contemporary man, a conclusion comes with too great ease that we are finished. Since men can live neither with each other nor without, extinction seems in the cards. But any such conclusion is superficial. The social contract is an arrangement of biological validity. Like the sexual impulse or human diversity, it acts, in its balancing of order and disorder, to preserve the species with a power far beyond human predilection. What is at stake in our times is not the survival of man, but the survival of man's most rewarding invention, democracy, and the proposition that man can achieve social order through voluntary action.

There is visible throughout all nature a bias in favor of order. It is an explicable force that commands the orbits of planets about their sun, moons about their planets. Order invests all organic and inorganic processes, and while hindsight may exaggerate it, still order is there. Evolution and natural selection are no more than names for those orderly, long-term processions which any may observe in the history of species. That animal treaties are honored; that baboons do not commit suicide in wars of troop against troop; that kittiwakes successfully defend their cliff-hung properties and raise their young; that lions and elephants restrict their numbers so that a habitat will not be exhausted by too many offspring; that when species can no longer meet the challenge of environment they must quietly expire: all such transactions of animals furnish simple testimony to the prejudices of order in natural ways. The contract will provide order within human societies, whether through voluntary or involuntary means.

Violence thrills victims as well as violators

Humans share with other higher animals three innate needs which demand satisfaction. The first is identity, the opposite of anonymity, and it is the highest. The second is stimulation, the opposite of boredom. The lowest is security, the opposite of anxiety.

These innate needs—identity, stimulation and security—form a dynamic triad. Achievement of security and release from anxiety present us with boredom. It is the psychological process least appreciated by our social planners. Increasing affluence, and decreasing economic anxiety, is producing the bored society described by Desmond Morris in *The Human Zoo*.

The bored society could not be a reality, however, were we other than the anonymous society stripped in large part of our opportunity to search for identity. It is the most pressing of motives —to know who we are in our own eyes but even more in the eyes of our fellows. Territory satisfies it in animals, as does social rank. Egalitarianism, that most admired of human possibilities by the unsophisticated young, joins hands with the anonymity of enlarging organizations so despised by the young to contribute in equal measure to the defeat of identity's satisfaction. And so the frustration of the search for identity from above, just as much as the achievement of security from below, forces the member of a contemporary society into the unendurable area of boredom. Imprisoned by both affluence and anonymity, no way presents itself but stimulation.

Pornography and riot are of a piece. They are means of stimulation. By no coincidence at all have waves of shock and sensation arrived simultaneously on the scene of advanced contemporary societies. The exhibitions of demonstrators raising the blood pressure of their close-packed groups and the exhibitions of fashion of the female body hopefully raising the blood pressure of the passing male—their appeal is the same. The private titillations of the *voyeur* with his photographs from Denmark and the private hallucinations of the sense-stretching trip with its weeds from Mexico—these too are the same. Sexual adventures among adolescents, casual adultery among their jaded elders, the display of nudity and intercourse on the screen or stage, the robbing of houses by affluent burglars, the sense-assaulting decibels of electronic music paralyzing the brains of its listeners, the baring of waitresses' breasts for the excitement of timid gentlemen, the public display of illegitimacy in the obstetrical arrangements of the famous, the public display in the literary content of ancient, commonplace terms of the street by authors with larger vocabularies available—all provide stimulation for shocker and shocked alike in bored societies with nowhere else to go.

And violence, too, is stimulating. It carries excitement for both violator and violated, whether through the joyful hatreds of the one or the fearful rages of the other. A riot in Chicago is worth all the circuses that oldtime emperors could provide. And like any other form of sensual shock, violence to retain its stimulation must proceed to stronger or more novel levels of expression. That adaptable animal, the human being, habituates himself all too easily to any present situation.

I believe that, as we refer to the triad of innate needs—identity, stimulation, security—we shall glimpse more clearly the difference in actions seem-

Shall we glimpse the road to disaster in time?

ingly so much of a piece. We are pressed into stimulation by the flight from boredom which itself has been induced by both security and denial of identity. But novel sensory experiences satisfy only our need for stimulation. Violent experiences tend to satisfy not only stimulation but identity as well. The violent are applauded. Whether the applause be the praise of collaborators or the condemnation of antagonists, the little world of violence is recognized, identified, released from anonymity.

Such a cancerous world upholds its own values, defends its own territory, establishes its own rules, praises its own alphas, scorns or ignores its own omegas, punishes its own traitors. Whatever the nature of this little world of criminal or political conspirators, of the juvenile gang, or grim old dedicated members of the establishment of power, of rebellious militants whatever their sources of grievance or purpose, whatever indeed may be the long-term justification, still much the same processes of all the violent subgroups prevail: there is noncommunication, elimination of social compassion for the outsider. There is xenophobia, released by noncommunication to identify the majority of our social partners as the enemy. There is an illusion of central position, justifying one's own purposes as right and everybody else's as wrong, and providing a proper degree of paranoia. Righteous ends, thus proved, absolve of guilt the most violent means. And within this little world a new fellowship blooms, a new communication flourishes, anonymity vanishes, identity again becomes possible.

But the violent subgroup, even as it asserts itself, defeats itself. The student depends on the postman if he is to receive his check from home. The postman depends on the milkman if his infant children are to survive. The milkman depends on the dentist, unless he renounces toothaches. The dentist depends on the telephone system if the milkman is to make an appointment. The telephone system depends on God knows whom, black or white, if bells are to ring. And the black man depends on the ring of the telephone if he is to have hope of organizing any but an amateur riot. So it goes.

Violent subgroups now threaten our modern society. But at the same time the very intricacy of our social interdependence threatens the survival of these violent little worlds. The animal cannot stand alone, and least of all animals, modern man.

Long before total social disorder can take place, human foresight, combined with our biological need for order, should have taken command. The question we cannot now answer is when. Shall sufficient of us glimpse the road to disaster in time?

If we do, then with whatever pain we shall accept certain compromises, surrender certain rights which we believe sacred, provide prizes of identity which we now deny, contain our violent confrontations within such ritualized aggressions as negotiation, seek to correct those genuine injustices which lend respectability to violent arrangements and discourage social applause for the violator.

And if we do not? If we lack the will or the vision to see what waits for us?

A few years ago our eminent journalist and historian of the making of Presidents, Theodore H. White, published a play called *Caesar at the Rubicon.* While Rome sank deeply into anarchy, Julius Caesar by agreement stayed with his powerful army beyond the river. The play, of course, concerns his final reluctant decision to break the agreement, proceed to Rome and assume dictatorial power. And it closes with a simple comment worthy of being stamped on the coin of every democracy: "If men cannot agree on how to rule themselves, someone else must rule them."

If we have not the foresight, if we have not the will, then we shall discover one day who waits beyond our Rubicon. ■

Simple Views of Aggression

by Leonard Berkowitz

An essay review of:

THE TERRITORIAL IMPERATIVE,
by ROBERT ARDREY

ON AGGRESSION,
by KONRAD LORENZ

MAN & AGGRESSION,
Edited by M. F. A. MONTAGU

THE NAKED APE,
by DESMOND MORRIS

HUMAN AGGRESSION,
by A. STORR

THE THEME of this essay will be drawn from a dust jacket. On the back of the book *Human Aggression* by the British psychiatrist Anthony Storr, we find the following comment by Konrad Lorenz, widely renowned as the "father of ethology": "An ancient proverb says that simplicity is the sign of truth—and of fallacy . . . However, if the simple explanation is in full agreement with a wealth of data, and quite particularly, if it dovetails with data collected in altogether different fields of knowledge, simplicity certainly is indicative of truth." Four of the books reviewed here offer essentially simplistic messages. With the writers represented in the fifth work, I shall argue that the conceptual simplicity advocated by these volumes is definitely *not* "indicative of the truth." All of the books deal with man's capacity for violence, a problem deserving—no, demanding—careful and sophisticated consideration. The four volumes I shall concentrate on, those by Lorenz, Ardrey, Storr, and Morris—and especially the first three—provide only easy formulas readily grasped by a wide audience rather than the necessary close analysis. Being easily understood, their explanation of human aggression helps relieve the anxiety born of the public's concern with war, social unrest, race riots, and student protests, but is an inadequate, and perhaps even dangerous, basis for social policy.

All four voice essentially the same message: Much of human behavior generally, and human aggression in particular, must be traced in large part to man's animal nature. Aggression often arises for innately determined reasons, they say. The authors differ somewhat, however, in how they believe this nature leads to aggression. For Lorenz, Ardrey, and Storr (whom I shall refer to as the Lorenzians), a spontaneously engendered drive impels us to aggression, even to the destruction of other persons. Morris, on the other hand, views many of our aggressive acts as genetically governed responses to certain environmental conditions and to signals sent to us by other people. Nonetheless, over and above their similarities and differences, all four volumes present a highly simplified conception of the causes of and possible remedies for human aggression, and I think it would be well for us to look at a number of these misleading oversimplifications.

The Role of Learning in Human Aggression

Facing the writers at their own level, one misconception I shall not deal with here is their relative neglect of the role of learning in human aggression. Our behavior is influenced by our experiences *and* our inherited biological characteristics. I have argued elsewhere that innate determinants do enter into man's attacks on others, primarily in connection with impulsive reactions to noxious events and frustrations. These constitutionally governed impulsive responses can be modified by learning, however. The Lorenzians do not appear to recognize this kind of modification in these volumes. They draw a very sharp distinction between learned and innately determined responses, thus ignoring what is now known of the complex interplay between nature and nurture. Lorenz has admitted this on occasion, and the journalist, Joseph Alsop, has recently reported him as saying, "We ethologists were mistaken in the past when we made a sharp distinction between 'innate' and 'learned.'" Of course, there is also an experience-is-all imperialism at the opposite extreme. In sharp contrast to many ethologists and zoologists, social scientists typically have long ignored and even denied the role of built-in, biological determinants. Ashley Montagu's critical discussion of Lorenz in his introduction to *Man and Aggression* is illustrative. "The notable thing about human behavior," he says, "is that it is learned. Everything a human being does as such he has had to learn from other human beings."

Some book reviewers for the popular press, aware of these opposing stances, have approached the present volumes in terms of this kind of polarization. *If* human aggressiveness is learned, Lorenz, *et al.*, are obviously incorrect, but on the other hand, innate determinants to aggression presumably must operate as described by Ardrey, Lorenz, Morris, and Storr. Ardrey, Lorenz, and Storr pose the issue in these simple terms. Critics dispute their views, they maintain, primarily because of a misguided "American optimism"; American social scientists, psychologists and psychiatrists, having a liberal belief in the perfectability of man, want to attribute social ills—including violence—to environmental flaws which might be remedied rather than to intractable human nature. The critics certainly would recognize the existence of man's innate aggressive drive if they could only shed their honorable but mistaken vision of Utopia.

There are other alternatives, however. Some of human aggressiveness might derive from man's biological properties, characteristics which he shares to some degree with the other animals. He might even be innately "programmed" to respond violently to particular kinds of stimulation, much as other animals do. But his animal characteristics do not have to function the way Lorenz and his associates say they do. The

Lorenzian analysis of aggression can be criticized on a logical and empirical basis independently of any general assumptions about the nature of man.

The volume *Man and Aggression*, edited by Montagu, serves as a counterpoise to the Lorenzian books. A number of journalist-reviewers have assumed that Lorenz' views are shared by virtually all students of animal behavior. The Montagu volume clearly shows that there is not the unanimity of support that the laymen believe exists. Many eminent zoologists, as well as comparative psychologists, have taken Lorenz's analysis of aggression seriously to task. *Man and Aggression* is a compilation of generally damning criticisms of the Lorenz and Ardrey books by such authorities as S. A. Barnett, J. H. Crook, T. C. Schneirla, and Sir Solly Zuckerman, as well as Lorenz' old opponent, J. P. Scott. For those people who have read only the Lorenzian analyses, Lorenz may speak for all ethologists; Lorenz is equated with all of ethology in the Storr book, *Human Aggression*. Yet he is not all of the science of animal behavior, and there are many good reasons in the animal as well as human research literature to question the over-all thrust of Dr. Lorenz' argument on grounds besides the "overbold and loose" nature of the Lorenzian contentions generally recognized by many readers.

We need not here review the many objections to the Lorenz and Ardrey volumes that are summarized by the critics included in *Man and Aggression*. However, some of the oversimplifications and errors of reasoning and fact that are characteristic of these two books are also prevalent in the Storr and Morris works, and I think it is important to point out several of these common weaknesses in the extension of popular biology to human aggression.

The Use of Analogies

As nearly every critic of these Lorenzian books has pointed out, the writers are excessively free-wheeling in their use of analogies. They frequently attempt to explain various human actions by drawing gross analogies between these behaviors and supposedly similar response patterns exhibited by other animal species. Attaching the same label to these human and animal behaviors, the writers then maintain that they have explained the actions. For Lorenz, man is remarkably similar to the Greylag Goose. The resemblances (that occur to Lorenz but not necessarily to other observers) are supposedly far from superficial ones, and he believes that they can only be explained by the operation of the same mechanisms in man and goose. ". . .highly complex norms of behavior such as falling in love, strife for ranking order, jealousy, grieving, etc. are not only similar but down to the most absurd details the same. . ." and therefore, all of these actions must be governed by instincts.

The analogy emphasized by Ardrey, of course, is based on animal territoriality. Man's genetic endowment supposedly drives him to gain and defend property, much as other animals do, presumably because this territorial behavior provides identity, stimulation, and security. Basing part of his argument on a study of the lemurs of Madagascar, Ardrey contends that there are two types of societies, noyaux (societies said to be held together by the inward antagonism of the members) and nations (societies in which joint defense of territory has given rise to in-group leadership and cooperation). The examples of noyaux listed by Ardrey include, in addition to the Madagascar lemurs, herring gull colonies, certain groups of gibbons, and Italy and France.

Morris' analogy, needless to say, is between humans and apes. His theme is that "*Homo sapiens* has remained a naked ape. . .in acquiring lofty new motives, he has lost none of the earthy old ones." We cannot understand the nature of our aggressive urges, he says, along with Ardrey, Lorenz, and Storr, unless we consider "the background of our animal origins." Unlike the Lorenzians, however, he doubts the existence of an innate, spontaneous aggressive drive, and emphasizes, to the exclusion of such a drive, the genetically determined signals he believes both apes and people send to their fellows. All four authors make much of the control of aggression by supposedly innate appeasement gestures, although Morris seems to have greater confidence in their efficacy than do the others. He even tells us how we should respond to an angry traffic policeman on the basis of this analogy between human and animal behaviors: The policeman's aggression can (theoretically) be turned off automatically by showing abject submission in our words, body postures, and facial expressions. Moreover, it is essential to "get quickly out of the car and move away from it towards the policeman." This prevents the policeman from invading our territory (our car) and weakens feelings of territorial rivalry. The looks people give each other are very important signals, Morris maintains in accord with a rapidly growing body of experimental-social psychological research, but, in contrast to these investigators, he oversimplifies greatly. Morris contends that prolonged looking at another is an aggressive act. In reality, persistent eye-contact can also be a very intimate, even sexual, encounter, or may arise from a search for information or social support.

This type of crude analogizing is *at best* an incomplete analysis of the behavior the writers seek to explain. Important data are neglected and vital differences are denied. J. H. Crook's excellent paper in *Man and Aggression* (which should be read by every person who has written a favorable review of the Lorenz and Ardrey books) notes the many important considerations omitted by the Lorenzians in general and Ardrey's treatment of territoriality in particular. Where Ardrey, following Lorenz, maintains that territorial behavior is a highly fixed, species-specific action pattern produced by energy accumulating in certain centers in the nervous system, the truth cannot be packaged as easily as this. Many different conditions enter into animal territoriality. The outcome is a complex interaction of ecological and social conditions with internal states so that territorial behavior is far from inevitable as a species characteristic. Territorial maintenance, furthermore, involves different components, such as attack and escape. These components are probably governed by somewhat different, although often interrelated, mechanisms, and appear to be susceptible to different environmental and internal conditions. Given these complexities and the multiplicity of factors involved in the territoriality displayed by birds, we cannot make simple statements about the functions and causes of territoriality even in these species, and it is highly unlikely that human concern with property is controlled by the same processes. Crook's conclusion is certainly reasonable: "The likelihood that the motivation control of territorial behavior is at a different level from that of fishes and birds suggests that human resemblances to the lower animals might be largely through analogy rather than homology." Sixteen years ago, Daniel Lehrman remarked, in an outstanding critique of Lorenzian theory, "it is not very judicious, and actually is rash . . . to assume that the mechanisms underlying two similar response characteristics are in any way identical, homologous, or even similar," merely because the actions of different species or entities seem to resemble each other (in the eyes of the writer, we might add).

The Motion of Ritualization

The same comment can be made about the analogizing involved in Lorenz' and Storr's use of the notion of ritualization. Theorizing that there are evolutionary changes in behavior as well as structure, and that particular action patterns, such as appeasement gestures, have evolved from other behaviors, Lorenz argues that responses originally serving one function can undergo alteration in the course of evolution so that they come to have a different function as well. The drive or energy motivating the original action presumably still powers this altered behavior. According to Lorenz, the appeasement or greetings ceremonies performed by humans and animals alike have become ritualized in this manner through evolutionary developments but still make use of transformed aggressive motivation. Lorenz thinks that the smile of greeting, as an example, might have "evolved by ritualization of redirected threatening." Storr, adopting Lorenz' reasoning, also speaks of "ritualizing the aggressive drive in such a way that it serves the function of uniting" people. For both of these writers, diverted aggressive energy powers the social bonds which tie individuals together in affection and even love. Now, we must ask, is there really good reason to contend, as Lorenz does so authoritatively, that the human smile, the appeasement gesture of the macaques (baring the teeth), and the triumph ceremony of the geese must have evolved in the same way from some original aggressive display? The supposed similarity between the human, monkey, and goose behavior does not mean, as Lehrman pointed out, that the processes underlying these actions are "identical, homologous, or even similar." Elaborating further, in his essay in *Man and Aggression*, Barnett says there is no justification for the "confident, dogmatic assertions" Lorenz and his followers have made about the hypothetical process, 'ritualization.'" Harlow's observations regarding monkey development are also troublesome for the Lorenzian analysis of the genesis of social bonds. Affectional patterns generally emerge *before* aggressive ones in these animals, making it unlikely that the earlier, affectional-social acts are "driven" by aggressive motivation.

The dangers of unwarranted analogizing can also be illustrated by referring to another example of "ritualization" mentioned by Storr. It appears that the Kurelu, a primitive people in the heart of New Guinea, engage in frequent intertribal warfare. But instead of killing one another, the warriors shoot arrows at each other from a distance just beyond arrow range and rarely hit each other. Although this type of warfare seems to resemble the threat ceremonies exhibited by a number of animal species, we certainly cannot argue that the Kurelu behavior and animal threats have evolved in exactly the same manner or are based on similar biological mechanisms. Furthermore, both action patterns may ultimately lead to a cessation of attacks—but probably for very different reasons. It is also improper to insist, as the Lorenzians do, that competitive sports are the same type of ritual as the Kurelu warfare and animal threats merely because some writers have applied the same label to all three sets of phenomena; the surface resemblances do not guarantee that all have the same evolutionary causes and that all operate in the same or even in a similar way.

When we come right down to it, there seems to be a kind of "word magic" in this analogizing. The writers appear to believe that they have provided an adequate explanation of the phenomenon at issue by attaching a label to it: a person's smile is an *appeasement gesture;* athletic events are *rituals* comparable to certain animal displays, etc. Storr shows just this kind of thinking in the "proof" he offers for the notion of a general aggressive drive. Aggression is not all bad, Storr insists (in agreement with Lorenz); aggression is necessary to the optimal development of man. It is "the basis of intellectual achievement, of the attainment of independence, and even of that proper pride which enables a man to hold his head high amongst his fellows." The evidence he cites for this statement is word usage: "...the words we use to described intellectual effort are aggressive words. We *attack* problems, or *get our teeth* into them. We *master* a subject when we have *struggled with* and *overcome* its difficulties. We *sharpen* our wits ..." (Italics in the original.) Waving his words over the particular behavior (in this case, striving for independence and achievement), he has thus supposedly accounted for these actions—and has also swept aside the many studies of achievement motivation by McClelland and his associates suggesting that there is very little similarity between the instigation to aggression and achievement motivation.

Popular discussions of the role of evolution in behavior can also be criticized on this basis. Even if it can be shown that a given behavior pattern has "evolved," such a demonstration does not explain the performance of that action by a particular individual in a specific setting. The application of the word "evolution" does not really help us to understand what mechanisms govern the behavior in this individual or what stimulus conditions affect these mechanisms.

Instinctive Human Actions

The Lorenzians (and Morris as well) also display this same word magic in the ease with which they refer to human actions as instinctive. Without taking the trouble to specify the criteria they employ in making their designations, they go scattering the label "instinct" around with great relish. As an illustration, in his book *On Aggression*, Lorenz talks about people having an "instinctive need to be a member of a closely knit group fighting for common ideals," and insists that "there cannot be the slightest doubt that militant enthusiasm is instinctive and evolved out of a communal defense response." Doubts must exist, however. The Lorenzians offer neither a precise definition of what they mean by "instinct" nor any substantial evidence that the behavior in question, whether human aggression or militant enthusiasm, is innate even in their vague usage of this term. Several of the writers in *Man and Aggression* (e.g., Barnett and Schneirla), as well as other scientists such as Lehrman, criticize Lorenz severly for his excessively casual employment of the instinct concept. Lorenz elsewhere has acknowledged this imprecision in his popular utterances (see, for example, the previously mentioned article by Alsop), saying that he has used the word only in a shorthand sense.

Nevertheless, the over-simplification regarding "instincts" so prevalent in the Lorenz-Ardrey-Storr writings is difficult to excuse as only shorthand. To say this is not to deny the role of innate processes in human behavior; such determinants apparently exist. Psychologists, together with other students of behavior, have shown, as an example, that human babies have a built-in preference for certain visual stimuli, and do not start with blank neural pages, so to speak, in learning to see and organize complex visual stimulation. The difficulty is that ideas such as Lorenz' "instinctive need to be a member of a closely knit group fighting for common ideals" are, in actuality, extremely drastic departures from the more precise instinct concept found in technical ethological discussions. When they write for an audience of their peers, ethologists generally describe instincts, or better still, instinctive movements, as behavioral sequences culminating in "fixed action patterns." These patterns, which are at the core of the instinct concept, are thought of as rigid and stereotyped species-specific *consummatory* responses generally serving to end a chain of ongoing behavior. Can this definition be applied to "militant enthusiasm"? What is the rigid and stereotyped action that unerringly unfolds to consummate the hypothetical enthusiasm pattern?

Sports as Outlets for Aggression

We now come to the most important part of the Lorenzian instinct conception, and the feature that has the gravest social implications: the supposed spontaneity of the behavior. The stereotyped instinctive action is said to be impelled by a specific energy that has accumulated in that part of the central nervous system responsible for the coordination of the behavior. The energy presumably builds up spontaneously and is discharged when the response is performed. If the instinctive activity is not carried out for a considerable period of time, the accumulated energy may cause the response to "pop off" *in vacuo*. Aggression, according to Lorenz, Ardrey, and Storr—but not Morris—follows this formula. "It is the spontaneity of the (aggressive) instinct," Lorenz tells us, "that makes it so dangerous." The behavior "can 'explode' without demonstrable external stimulation" merely because the internal accumulating energy has not been discharged by aggressive actions or has not been diverted into other response channels as, for example, in the case of such "ritualized" activities as sports. If violence is to be lessened, suitable outlets must be provided. Lorenz believes that "present-day civilized man suffers from insufficient discharge of his aggressive drive," and together with Ardrey and Storr, calls for more athletic competitions—bigger and better Olympic games. (Denying the Lorenzian formulation, Morris maintains that we do not have an inborn urge to destroy our opponents—only to dominate them—and argues that the only solution is "massive de-population" rather than "boisterous international football.")

This conception can be discussed at various levels. Neurologically, for one thing, Lorenz bases his assertions on observations regarding cardiac and respiratory activities and simple motor coordinations. With such critics as Lehrman and Moltz we must question whether or not these findings can be extended to more complex neural organizations, to say nothing of human aggression. (The Lorenzian interpretation of these observations can also be disputed, as Moltz has shown in the 1965 *Psychological Review*.)

There are empirical difficulties as well as this problem of the long inductive leap. Basing their arguments on a number of studies, Hinde and Ziegler (the latter in an important 1964 *Psychological Bulletin* paper) have proposed that many apparent demonstrations of internally-driven spontaneity can be traced to external stimuli and the operation of associative factors. The responses evidently are evoked by environmental stimuli rather than being driven out by spontaneously accumulating internal excitation. Moltz has also summarized evidence disputing the Lorenzian notion that response performance is necessary if there is to be a reduction in the elicitability of the instinctive action pattern. As Hinde has suggested in several papers, stimulus satiation rather than a response-produced discharge of instinctive action-specific energy may cause a lessening in response elicitability.

Complex Aspects of Animal and Human Aggression

Going from the simple motor coordinations of the lower animals to the more complex aspects of animal and human aggression, the available data are even less kind to the Lorenzian formulation. Of course Lorenz maintains that his ideas are supported by a substantial body of observations. They are upheld, he says, by the failures of "an American method of education" to produce less aggressive children, even though the youngsters have been supposedly "spared all disappointments and indulged in every way." However, as I have pointed out elsewhere in discussing this argument, excessively indulged children probably expect to be gratified most of the time, so that the inevitable occasional frustrations they encounter are actually relatively strong thwartings for them. There is little doubt that these frustrations can produce aggressive reactions, and Lorenz' criticism of the frustration-aggression hypothesis is a very weak one. Belief in this hypothesis, by the way, does not necessarily mean advocating a completely frustration-free environment for children. Child specialists increasingly recognize that youngsters must learn to cope with and adapt to life's inescapable thwartings, and thus must experience at least some frustrations in the course of growing up. Nor do most contemporary psychologists believe that frustration is the only source of aggression. Violence can have its roots in pain as well as in obstacles to goal attainment, and can also be learned as other actions are learned.

Aggression, in other words, has a number of different causes, although the Lorenzians seem to recognize (or at least discuss) only one source. Here is yet another erroneous oversimplification: their notion of a unitary drive that is supposedly capable of powering a wide variety of behaviors from ritualized smiling to strivings for independence or dominance. This general drive conception is very similar to the motivational thinking in classical psychoanalysis, but is running into more and more difficulty under the careful scrutiny of biologists and psychologists. Indeed, contrary to Storr's previously cited argument, there is no single instigation to aggression even in the lower animals. Moyer recently has suggested (in the 1968 *Communications in Behavioral Biology*), on the basis of many findings, that there are several kinds of aggression, each of which has a particular neural and endocrine basis.

The Flow of Aggressive Energy

Also like the traditional psychoanalysts, the Lorenzians speak loosely of aggressive energy flowing from one channel of behavior to another. This hypothetical process, mentioned earlier in conjunction with "ritualization," must be differentiated from the more precisely defined response-generalization concept developed by experimental psychologists. Reinforcements provided to one kind of reaction may strengthen other, similar responses. Rewarding a child for making aggressive remarks can increase the likelihood of other kinds of aggressive reactions as well. The reinforcement influence generalizes from one kind of response to another because the actions have something in common. (The actor might regard both types of responses as *hurting* someone.) It is theoretically unparsimonious and even inadvisable to interpret this effect as an energy transfer from one response channel to another. The Lorenz-Storr discussion of ritualization, and the related psychoanalytic concept of sublimation as well, employs just this kind of energy-diversion idea. We cannot here go into the conceptual pitfalls of this analytical model. (The interested reader might wish to read Hinde's article on energy models of motivation in the 1960 *Symposia of the Society for Experimental Biology*.) But there is a fairly obvious flaw in the Lorenzian statement that pent-up aggressive energy can be discharged in competitive sports. Rather than lessening violence, athletic events have sometimes excited supporters of one or both of the competing teams into attacking other persons. This has happened in many countries: in England, as Crook points out and as Storr should have recognized, in this country at times when white and Negro high school basketball teams have competed against each other, and most dramatically, this past March in Czechoslovakia when the Czechs defeated the Russians in hockey. In these cases, the team supporters were so aroused, even when their team won, that they were extremely responsive to aggressive stimuli in the environment.

Experimental tests of the hostility catharsis hypothesis also argue against the energy-diversion idea inherent in both Lorenzian and psychoanalytic theorizing. This well-worn notion maintains, of course, that the display of aggressive behavior in fantasy, play, or real life, will reduce the aggressive urge. Although there is no explicit reference to a catharsis process in Storr's book, his belief that aggressive energy can be sublimated certainly is consistent with the catharsis doctrine. Lorenz comes much closer to a frank acceptance of this idea in his contention that "civilized man suffers from insufficient discharge of his aggressive drive," and in a bit of advice he offers to people on expeditions to the remote corners of the world. Members of socially isolated groups, he says in *On Aggression*, must inevitably experience a build-up of aggressive drive; outsiders aren't available to be attacked and thus provide an outlet for the accumulating aggressive energy. If a person in such an isolated group wishes to prevent the intra-group conflict that otherwise must develop (Lorenz insists), he should smash a vase with as loud and resounding a crash as possible. We do not have to attack other people in order to experience a cathartic reduction in our aggressive urge; it's enough merely to destroy inanimate objects.

Summary

Summarizing (and simplifying) a great many studies, research results suggest that angry people often do (a) feel better, and (b) perhaps even experience a temporarily reduced inclination to attack their tormentors, upon learning that these persons have been hurt. This phenomenon seems to be quite specific, however; the provoked individual is gratified when he finds that the intended target of his aggression has been injured, and does not appear to get the same satisfaction from attacks on innocent bystanders. Besides this, the apparent reduction in the instigation to aggression following an attack is probably often due to guilt- or anxiety-induced restraints evoked by the attack and/or the arousal of other, nonaggressive motives, and is not really the result of an energy discharge. Standard experimental-psychological analysis can do a far better job than the energy-discharge model in explaining the available data. Recent experiments indicate, for example, that the lessening of physiological tension produced by injuring the anger instigator comes about when the aggressor has learned that aggression is frequently rewarded. This tension reduction, or gratification, is evidently akin to a reinforcement effect, and is not indicative of any long-lasting decline in the likelihood of aggression; people who find aggression rewarding are more, not less, likely to attack someone again in the future. The reinforcement process can also account for the appetitive behavior Lorenz and Storr seem to regard as prime evidence for the existence of a spontaneous aggressive drive.

Provoked animals will go out of their way to obtain suitable targets to attack, while youngsters who are frequently aggressive toward their peers generally prefer violent TV. programs to more peaceful ones. But this search for an appropriate target or for aggressive scenes probably arises from the reinforcing nature of these stimuli rather than from some spontaneous drive, and again, does not mean that there has been an energy discharge when these stimuli are encountered. Quite the contrary. There is some reason to believe that the presence of such aggression-reinforcing stimuli as other people fighting can evoke aggressive responses from those who are ready to act aggressively—much as the sight of food (which is a reinforcement for eating) can elicit eating responses from those who are set to make such responses.

In the end, the Lorenzian analyses must be questioned because of their policy implications as well as because of their scientific inadequacies. Their reliance on casual anecdotes instead of carefully controlled, systematic data, their use of ill-defined terms and gross analogies, and their disregard of hundreds of relevent studies in the interest of an over-simplified theory warrant the disapproval generally accorded them by technical journals. But more than this, the Lorenz-Ardrey-Storr books can also have unfortunate social as well as scientific consequences by impeding recognition of the important roles played by environmental stimuli and learning in aggressive behavior, and by blocking awareness of an important social principle: Aggression is all too likely to lead to still more aggression.

Plight of the Ik and Kaiadilt is seen as a chilling possible end for Man

By John B. Calhoun

A commentary on the current work of two anthropologists contains a grim warning of debasement in our times

The Mountain—how pervasive in the history of man. A still small voice on Horeb, mount of God, guided Elijah. There, earlier, Moses standing before God received the Word. And Zion: "I am the Lord your God dwelling in Zion, my holy mountain."

Then there was Atum, mountain, God and first man, one and all together. The mountain rose out of a primordial sea of nothingness—Nun. Atum, the spirit of life, existed within Nun. In creating himself, Atum became the evolving ancestor of the human race. So goes the Egyptian mythology of creation, in which the Judaic Adam has his roots.

And there is a last Atum, united in his youth with another mountain of God, Mt. Morungole in northeasternmost Uganda. His people are the Ik, pronounced eek. They are the subject of an important new book, *The Mountain People*, by Colin M. Turnbull (Simon and Schuster, $6.95). They still speak Middle-Kingdom Egyptian, a language thought to be dead. But perhaps their persistence is not so strange. Egyptian mythology held that the waters of the life-giving Nile had their origin in Nun. Could this Nun have been the much more extensive Lake Victoria of 40 to 50 millennia ago when, near its borders, man groped upward to cloak his biological self with culture?

Well might the Ik have preserved the essence of this ancient tradition that affirms human beginnings. Isolated as they have been in their jagged mountain fastness, near the upper tributaries of the White Nile, the Ik have been protected from cultural evolution.

What a Shangri-la, this land of the Ik. In its center, the Kidepo valley, 35 miles across, home of abundant game; to the south, mist-topped Mt. Morungole; to the west the Niangea range; to the north, bordering the Sudan, the Didinga range; to the east on the Kenya border, a sheer drop of 2,000 feet into the Turkanaland of cattle herdsmen. Through ages of dawning history few people must have been interested in encroaching on this rugged land. Until 1964 anthropologists knew little of the Ik's existence. Their very name, much less their language, remained a mystery until, quite by chance, anthropologist Colin M. Turnbull found himself among them. What an opportunity to study pristine man! Here one should encounter the basic qualities of humanity unmarred by war, technology, pollution, over-population.

Turnbull rested in his bright red Land Rover at an 8,000-foot-high pass. A bit beyond this only "navigable" pass into the Kidepo Valley, lay Pirre, a police outpost watching over a cluster of Ik villages. There to welcome him came Atum of the warm, open smile and gentle voice. Gray-haired at 40, appearing 65, he was the senior elder of the Ik, senior in authority if not quite so in age. Nattily attired in shorts and woolen sweater—in contrast to his mostly naked colleagues—Atum bounced forward with his ebony walking stick, greeted Turnbull in Swahili, and from that moment on took command as best he could of Turnbull's life. At Atum's village a plaintive woman's voice called out. Atum remarked that that was his wife—sick, too weak to work in the fields. Turnbull offered to bring her food and medicine. Atum suggested he handle Turnbull's gifts. As the weeks wore on Atum picked up the

Dr. Calhoun and his controversial mouse "cities" appeared in SMITHSONIAN *of April 1970.*

parcels that Turnbull was supplying for Atum's wife.

One day Atum's brother-in-law, Lomongin, laughingly asked Turnbull if he didn't know that Atum's wife had been dead for weeks. She had received no food or medicine. Atum had sold it. So she just died. All of this was revealed with no embarrassment. Atum joined the laughter over the joke played on Turnbull.

Another time Atum and Lojieri were guiding Turnbull over the mountains, and at one point induced him to push ahead through high grass until he broke through into a clearing. The clearing was a sheer 1,500-foot drop. The two Iks rolled on the ground, nearly bursting with laughter because Turnbull just managed to catch himself. What a lovable cherub this Atum! His laughter never ended.

New meaning of laughter

Laughter, hallmark of mankind, not shared with any other animal, not even primates, was an outstanding trait of the Ik. A whole village rushed to the edge of a low cliff and joined in communal laughter at blind old Lo'ono who lay thrashing on her back, near death after stumbling over. One evening Iks around a fire watched a child as it crawled toward the flames, then writhed back screaming after it grasped a gleaming coal. Laughter erupted. Quiet came to the child as its mother cuddled it in a kind of respect for the merriment it had caused. Then there was the laughter of innocent childhood as boys and girls gathered around a grandfather, too weak to walk, and drummed upon his head with sticks or pelted him with stones until he cried. There was the laughter that binds families together: Kimat, shrieking for joy as she dashed off with the mug of tea she had snatched from her dying brother Lomeja's hand an instant after Turnbull had given it to him as a last token of their friendship.

Laughter there had always been. A few old people remembered times, 25 to 30 years ago, when laughter mirrored love and joy and fullness of life, times when beliefs and rituals and traditions kept a bond with the "millions of years" ago when time began for the Ik. That was when their god, Didigwari, let the Ik down from heaven on a vine, one at a time. He gave them the digging stick with the instruction that they could not kill one another. He let down other people. To the Dodos and Turkana he gave cattle and spears to kill with. But the Ik remained true to their instruction and did not kill one another or neighboring tribesmen.

For them the bow, the net and the pitfall were for capturing game. For them the greatest sin was to overhunt. Mobility and cooperation ever were part of them. Often the netting of game required the collaboration of a whole band of 100 or more, some to hold the net and some to drive game into it. Between the big hunts, bands broke up into smaller groups to spread over their domain, then to gather again. The several bands would each settle for the best part of the year along the edge of the Kidepo Valley in the foothills of Mt. Morungole. There they were once again fully one with the mountain. "The Ik, without their mountains, would no longer be the Ik and similarly, they say, the mountains without the Ik would no longer be the same mountains, if indeed they continued to exist at all."

In this unity of people and place, rituals, traditions, beliefs and values molded and preserved a continuity of life. All rites of passage were marked by ceremony. Of these, the rituals surrounding death gave greatest meaning to life. Folded in a fetal position, the body was buried with favorite possessions, facing the rising sun to mark celestial rebirth. All accompanying rituals of fasting and feasting, of libations of beer sprinkled over the grave, of seeds of favorite foods planted on the grave to draw life from the dust of the dead, showed that death is merely another form of life, and reminded the living of the good things of life and of the good way to live. In so honoring the dead by creating goodness the Ik helped speed the soul, content, on its journey.

Such were the Ik until wildlife conservation intruded into their homeland. Uganda decided to make a national park out of the Kidepo Valley, the main hunting ground of the Ik. What then happened stands as an indictment of the myopia that science can generate. No one looked to the Ik to note that their hunter-gatherer way of life marked the epitome of conservation, that the continuance of their way of life would have added to the success of the park. Instead they were forbidden to hunt any longer in the Kidepo Valley. They were herded to the periphery of the park and encouraged to become farmers on dry mountain slopes so steep as to test the poise of a goat. As an example to the more remote villages, a number of villages were brought together in a tight little cluster below the southwest pass into the valley. Here the police post, which formed this settlement of Pirre, could watch over the Ik to see that they didn't revert to hunting.

These events contained two of the three strikes that knocked out the spirit of the Ik. *Strike No. 1:* The shift from a mobile hunter-gatherer way of life to a sedentary farming way of life made irrelevant the Ik's entire repertoire of beliefs, habits and traditions. Their guidelines for life were inappropriate to farming. They seemed to adapt, but at heart they remained hunters and gatherers. Their cultural templates fitted them for that one way of life.

Strike No. 2: They were suddenly crowded together at a density, intimacy and frequency of contact far greater than they had ever before been required to experience. Throughout their long past each band of 100 or so individuals only temporarily coalesced into a whole. The intervening breaking up into smaller groups permitted realignment of relationships that tempered conflicts from earlier associations. But at the resettlement, more than 450 individuals were forced to form a permanent cluster of villages within shouting distance of each other. Suppose the seven million or so inhabitants of Los Angeles County were forced to move and join the more than one million inhabitants of the more arid San Diego County. Then after they arrived all water, land and air communication to the rest of the world was cut off abruptly and completely. These eight million people would then have to seek survival completely on local resources without any communication with others. It would be a test of the ability of human beings to remain human.

Such a test is what Dr. Turnbull's book on the Mountain People is all about. The Ik failed to remain human. I have put mice to the same test and they failed to remain mice. Those of you who have been following SMITHSONIAN may recall from the April 1970 and the January 1971 issues something about the projected demise of a mouse population experiencing the same two strikes against it as did the Ik.

Fate of a mouse population

Last summer I spoke in London behind the lectern where Charles Darwin and Alfred Wallace had presented their papers on evolution—which during the next century caused a complete revision of our insight into what life is all about and what man is and may become. In summing up that session of 1858 the president remarked that nothing of importance had been presented before the Linnean Society at that year's meeting! I spoke behind this same lectern to a session of the Royal Society of Medicine during its symposium on "Man in His Place." At the end of my paper, "Death Squared: The Explosive Growth and Demise of a Mouse Population," the chairman admonished me to stick to my mice; the insights I had presented could have no implication for man. Wonderful if the chairman could be correct—but now I have read about the Mountain People, and I have a hollow feeling that perhaps we, too, are close to losing our "mountain."

Turnbull lived for 18 months as a member of the Ik tribe. His identity transfer became so strong that he acquired the Ik laughter. He laughed at seeing Atum suffer as they were completing an extremely arduous journey on foot back across the mountains and the Kidepo Valley from the Sudan. He felt pleasure at seeing Lokwam, local "Lord of the Flies," cry in agony from the beating given him by his two beautiful sisters.

Well, for five years I have identified with my mice, as they lived in their own "Kidepo Valley"—their contrived Utopia where resources are always abundant and all mortality factors except aging eliminated. I watched their population grow rapidly from the first few colonizers. I watched them fill their metal "universe" with organized social groups. I watched them bring up a host of young with loving maternal care and paternal territorial protection—all of these young well educated for mouse society. But then there were too many of these young mice, ready to become involved in all that mice can become, with nowhere to go, no physical escape from their closed environment, no opportunity to gain a niche where they could play a meaningful role. They tried, but being younger and less experienced they were nearly always rejected.

Rejecting so many of these probing youngsters overtaxed the territorial males. So defense then fell to lactating females. They became aggressive. They turned against their own young and ejected them before normal weaning and before adequate social bonds between mother and young had developed. During this time of social tension, rate of growth of the population was only one third of that during the earlier, more favorable phase.

Strike No. 1 against these mice: They lost the opportunity to express the capacities developed by older mice born during the rapid population growth. After a while they became so rejected that they were treated as so many sticks and stones by their still relatively well-adjusted elders. These rejected mice withdrew, physically and psychologically, to live packed tightly together in large pools. Amongst themselves they became vicious, lashing out and biting each other now and then with hardly any provocation.

Strike No. 2 against the mice: They reached great numbers despite reduced conceptions and increased deaths of newborn young resulting from the dissolution of maternal care. Many had early been rejected by their mothers and knew little about social bonds. Often their later attempts at interaction were interrupted by some other mouse intervening unintentionally as it passed between two potential actors.

I came to call such mice the "Beautiful Ones." They never learned such effective social interactions as courtship, mating and aggressive defense of territory. Never copulating, never fighting, they were unstressed and essentially unaware of their associates. They spent their time grooming themselves, eating and sleeping, totally individualistic, totally isolated socially except for a peculiar acquired need for simple proximity to others. This produced what I have called the "behavioral sink," the continual accentuation of aggregations to the point that much available space was unused despite a population increase to nearly 15 times the optimum.

All true "mousity" was lost. Though physically they still appeared to be mice, they had no essential capacities for survival and continuation of mouse society. Suddenly, population growth ceased. In what seemed an instant they passed over a threshold beyond which there was no likelihood of their ever recouping the capacity to become real mice again. No more young were born. From a peak population of 2,200 mice nearly three years ago, aging has gradually taken its toll until now there are only 46 sluggish near-cadavers comparable to people more than 100 years old.

It was just such a fading universe Colin Turnbull found in 1964. Just before he arrived, *Strike No. 3* had set in: starvation. Any such crisis could have added the coup de grace after the other two strikes. Normally the Ik could count on only making three crops every four years. At this time a two-year drought set in and destroyed almost all crops. Neighboring tribes survived with their cultures intact. Turkana herdsmen, facing starvation and death, kept their societies in contact with each other and continued to sing songs of praise to God for the goodness of life.

By the beginning of the long drought, "goodness" to the Ik simply meant to have food—to have food for one's self alone. Collaborative hunts were a thing of the past, long since stopped by the police and probably no longer possible as a social effort, anyway. Solitary hunting, now designated as poaching, became a necessity for sheer survival. But the solitary hunter took every precaution not to let others know of his success. He would gorge himself far off in the bush and bring the surplus back to sell to the police, who were not above profiting from this traffic. Withholding food from wife, children and aging parents became an accomplishment to brag and laugh about. It became a way of life, continuing after the government began providing famine relief. Those strong enough to go to the police station to get rations for themselves and their families would stop halfway home and gorge all the food, even though it caused them to vomit.

Village of mutual hatred

The village reflected this reversal of humanity. Instead of open courtyards around each group of huts within the large compound, there was a maze of walls and tunnels booby trapped with spears to ward off intrusion by neighbors.

In Atum's village a whole band of more than 100 individuals was crowded together in mutual hostility and aloneness. They would gather at their sitting place and sit for hours in a kind of suspended animation, not looking directly at each other, yet scanning slowly all others who might be engaged in some solitary task, watching for someone to make a mistake that would elicit the symbolic violence of laughter and derision. They resembled my pools of rejected withdrawn mice. Homemaking deteriorated, feces littered doorsteps and courtyard. Universal adultery and incest replaced the old taboo. The beaded virgins' aprons of eight-to-

Australian Aborigines of the Kaiadilt tribe, like the Ik, have suffered debasement.

twelve-year-old girls became symbols that these were proficient whores accustomed to selling their wares to passing herdsmen.

One ray of humanity left in this cesspool was 12-year-old, retarded Adupa. Because she believed that food was for sharing and savoring, her playmates beat her. She still believed that parents were for loving and to be loved by. They cured her madness by locking her in her hut until she died and decayed.

The six other villages were smaller and their people could retain a few glimmers of the goodness and fullness of life. There was Kuaur, devoted to Turnbull, hiking four days to deliver mail, taunted for bringing food home to share with his wife and child. There was Losiké, the potter, regarded as a witch. She offered water to visitors and made pots for others. When the famine got so bad that there was no need for pots to cook in, her husband left her. She was no longer bringing in any income. And then there was old Nangoli, still capable of mourning when her husband died. She went with her family and village across Kidepo and into the Sudan where their village life turned for a while back to normality. But it was not normal enough to keep them. Back to Pirre, to death, they returned.

All goodness was gone from the Ik, leaving merely emptiness, valuelessness, nothingness, the chaos of Nun. They reentered the womb of beginning time from which there is no return. Urination beside the partial graves of the dead marked the death of God, the final fading of Mount Morungole.

My poor words give only a shadowy image of the cold coffin of Ik humanity that Turnbull describes. His two years with the Ik left him in a slough of despondency from which he only extricated himself with difficulty, never wanting to see them again. Time and distance brought him comfort. He did return for a

The debasement of overcrowding

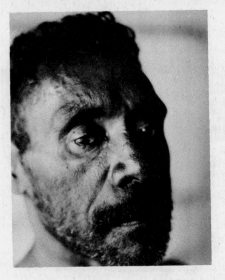

brief visit some months later. Rain had come in abundance. Gardens had sprung up untended from hidden seeds in the earth. Each Ik gleaned only for his immediate needs. Granaries stood empty, not refilled for inevitable scarcities ahead. The future had ceased to exist. Individual and social decay continued on its downward spiral. Sadly Turnbull departed again from this land of lost hope and faith.

Last summer in London I knew nothing about the Ik when I was so publicly and thoroughly chastised for having the temerity to suspect that the behavioral and spiritual death my mice had exhibited might also befall man. But a psychiatrist in the audience arose in defense of my suspicion. Dr. Geoffrey N. Bianchi remarked that an isolated tribe of Australian Aborigines mirrored the changes and kinds of pathology I had seen among mice. I did not know that Dr. Bianchi was a member of the team that had studied these people, the Kaiadilt, and that a book about them was in preparation, *Cruel, Poor and Brutal Nations* by John Cawte (The University Press of Hawaii). In galley proof I have read about the Kaiadilt and find it so shattering to my faith in humanity that I now sometimes wish I had never heard of it. Yet there is some glimmer of hope that the Kaiadilt may recover—not what they were but possibly some new life.

A frail, tenacious people, the Kaiadilt never numbered more than 150 souls where they lived on Bentinck Island in the Gulf of Carpentaria. So isolated were they that not even their nearest Aboriginal neighbors, 20 miles away, had any knowledge of their exist-

ence until in this century; so isolated were the Kaiadilt from their nearest neighbors that they differ from them in such heredity markers as blood type and fingerprints. Not until the early years of this century did an occasional visitor from the Queensland Government even note their existence.

For all practical purposes the first real contact the Kaiadilt had with Western "culture" came in 1916 when a man by the name of McKenzie came to Bentinck with a group of male mainland Aborigines to try to establish a lime kiln. McKenzie's favorite sport was to ride about shooting Kaiadilt. His helpers' sport was to commandeer as many women as they could, and take them to their headquarters on a neighboring island. In 1948 a tidal wave poisoned most of the freshwater sources. Small groups of Kaiadilt were rounded up and transported to larger Mornington Island where they were placed under the supervision of a Presbyterian mission. They were crowded into a dense cluster settlement just as the Ik had been at Pirre.

Here they still existed when the psychiatric field team came into their midst 15 years later. They were much like the Ik: dissolution of family life, total valuelessness, apathy. I could find no mention of laughter, normal or pathological. Perhaps the Kaiadilt didn't laugh. They had essentially ceased the singing that had been so much a part of their traditional way.

The spiritual decay of the Kaiadilt was marked by withdrawal, depression, suicide and tendency to engage in such self-mutilation as ripping out one's testes or chopping off one's nose. In their passiveness some of the anxiety ridden children are accepting the new mold of life forced upon them by a benevolent culture they do not understand. Survival with a new mold totally obliterating all past seems their only hope.

So the lesson comes clear, and Colin Turnbull sums it up in the final paragraph of his book: "The Ik teach us that our much vaunted human values are not inherent in humanity at all, but are associated only with a particular form of survival called society, and that all, even society itself, are luxuries that can be dispensed with. That does not make them any the less wonderful or desirable, and if man has any greatness it is surely in his ability to maintain these values, clinging to them to an often very bitter end, even shortening an already pitifully short life rather than sacrifice his humanity. But that too involves choice, and the Ik teach us that man can lose the will to make it."

Blind Lo'ono almost died in a fall on the mountain, to the glee of Ik neighbors. They abandoned her.

4 CITIES, CROWDING & CRIME

Recent studies strengthen the evidence that
crowding contributes to social problems and crime

by Robert J. Trotter

Sexual perversion, irrational and excessive aggression, increased mortality rates, lowered fertility rates, maternal neglect of young, withdrawal and other psychotic behavior—these are among the reactions of rats, monkeys, hares, shrews and fish that have been experimentally forced to live in overcrowded conditions. Are overcrowded human populations subject to this type of psychological and physiological disintegration? Can such reactions, for instance, explain or in part account for crime in the crowded cities?

At the recent meeting of the American Psychological Association, psychologists reported results of new studies on the effects of crowding on humans. One study was conducted in the Netherlands, one of the most densely populated countries in the world (323 persons per square kilometer). Leo Levy and Allen N. Herzog of the University of Illinois Medical Center in Chicago compared high-density areas to low-density areas and found that higher density appeared to be positively related to such things as deaths due to heart disease, admissions to hospitals and mental hospitals, juvenile delinquency, illegitimacy, divorce and infant mortality. In Honolulu density was related to adult and infant death rates, TB, VD and prison rates. In Chicago one measure of density, the number of people per room, was correlated with various types of social disintegration (SN: 4/15/72, p. 247). All of these findings tend to support some of the results of animal studies and suggest that human crowding is related to social disintegration and crime.

Arousal, stress, anxiety and frustration seem to be among the important results of crowding that can lead to personal and social degeneration. One thing that can sometimes lead to stress or anxiety, for instance, is infringement on personal space. Personal space or interpersonal physical distance (IPD) is defined as the area surrounding a person's body into which intruders may not come. Gay H. Price and James M. Dabbs Jr. of Georgia State University investigated the effects of age and sex on IPD. They found that personal space requirements become larger as children grow older. First grade boys and girls allowed another child to approach until a comfortable conversational distance was reported. Both boys and girls showed an IPD of 0.30 meters—about 12 inches. As children grow older, however, they need more personal space. Females in the 12th grade needed 0.45 meters and males the same age needed 0.60 meters. Other studies have shown cultural and racial differences in desired interaction distances. British and Germanic people prefer to interact at a greater distance than do Middle Eastern or Latin American people. Blacks tend to interact at greater distances than do whites. Maintaining this personal space is not always easy in a crowded city, and overly close contact with strangers can sometimes lead to psychological discomfort and may even be perceived as threatening. This, in turn, can lead to arousal, anxiety and stress that can be physically harmful and that can sometimes lead to antisocial activity.

Yokov M. Epstein and John R. Aiello of Rutgers University have made physiological measures of arousal caused by crowding. Skin conductance levels were used as a measure of arousal. The subjects were monitored as they sat quietly in either a crowded or noncrowded room. Arousal increased over time in both conditions, but arousal increased significantly under the crowded conditions. And arousal was higher under all conditions for men.

In another set of experiments Epstein and Robert A. Karlin examined some of the social and behavioral effects of crowding. According to their definition, social crowding exists when the distance between individuals is less than the expected appropriate distance for a particular setting. What is appropriate in the bedroom, for instance, is not appropriate in the subway. Whenever the appropriate distance is not maintained, say Epstein and Karlin, stress reaction can result. Such things as heat, odors, noise and bodily contact add to the perception of crowding.

What happens socially when crowding is perceived? Groups of men and women were subjected to crowded and noncrowded conditions. They were given various tests and tasks to complete while their reactions and interactions were monitored. In general, report Epstein and Karlin, crowded men concealed their distress from each other, became competitive and developed attitudes of distrust and hostility—all of which can lead to aggression, stress and crime. Women, in contrast, have usually been subjected to social norms and training that allow them to react quite differently. They tend to share their distress. In a number of crowding experiments women reacted as if they were in the same boat rather than becoming competitive. They formed cooperative groups. There were usually positive sentiments between individuals. When asked to evaluate other members of the group, the crowded women gave more positive evaluations than did the noncrowded women or any of the men's groups.

One reason for criminal activity and social breakdown, therefore, may be that when crowded, men feel more negatively about each other, become more competitive, fight with each other and even become more disposed to engage in criminal activity to achieve their own ends at each other's expense.

A slightly different explanation is the "overload theory." Stanley Milgram of the City University of New York has explained how the overload theory works. People in overcrowded cities, he suggests, are constantly bombarded by sensory stimuli (horns honking, phones ringing, lights flashing, people talking, etc., etc.) at such a rate that not all stimuli can be processed. To adapt to this sensory overload, city people tend to allocate less time to each input, disregard certain low priority inputs and decrease involvement with other people. These factors lead to a lower level of social responsibility and hence a lower rate of intervention in criminal activity. Where intervention is not expected, crime rates tend to increase.

Experiments conducted by Donna Gelfand of the University of Utah tend to confirm Milgram's theory. People raised in small towns reported shoplifting (done by an experimenter) at about twice the rate of people raised in large cities. Gelfand suggests that people raised in rural areas learn that they must rely on their neighbors while city dwellers learn to rely on municipal services. Therefore, an urbanite who sees a crime being committed is likely to let the police handle it rather than

get personally involved.

Frustration also affects criminal activity, and frustration has become almost an accepted fact of city life. Annoying interruptions, for example, often lead to frustration. Ineffective phone service, traffic and parking problems, transit strikes, construction noises and many other daily happenings interrupt life and lead to frustrations. And frustrations can lead to criminal behavior, says R. Lance Shotland of Pennsylvania State University.

Milgram and Shotland demonstrated experimentally how frustration can play a part in property crimes. They sent letters inviting people to come to a Manhattan theater to rate a television program. As a reward the subjects were to receive transistor radios. The subjects rated the program and were told where they could pick up their radios. They were sent to different offices that were fronts for the experiment. The offices looked real. They were furnished and each contained a charity display with about $14 in bills and change in it. There were no people in the offices and the subjects were monitored by closed circuit television.

In the high-frustration condition a rude message in the office said that no more free radios would be distributed until further notice. No reason was given for the empty office. In the low-frustration condition the message was apologetic. It explained that the workers were ill and that the radios could be picked up in another office. In the high-frustration condition 18.7 percent of the subjects stole something from the office including charity money, ash trays, plants, tools, etc. In the low-frustration condition only 2.9 percent of the subjects took anything.

The frustrations of life are increased for the lower class members of society. The Report of the National Advisory Commission on Civil Disorder stated that "middle-class citizens, although subject to many of the same frustrations and resentments in dealing with the public bureaucracy as ghetto residents, find it relatively easier to locate the proper agency for help and redress." Therefore, says Shotland, "One might expect and obtain more criminal activity from the lower class as they are more frustrated. They cannot use communication with a representative of government or a real or theoretical law suit as a substitute for aggression. They do not feel that they have any control over the annoyance."

With good evidence that crowding does contribute to social problems and increased criminal activity, is there any hope that crime rates can be lowered in the already overcrowded cities? Hong Kong is the most densely populated

area in the world (3,912 persons per square kilometer) yet its crime rate is only half that of the United States (22 persons per square kilometer). So crowding need not always be a great contributing factor to criminal activity. Cultural attitudes are involved. The people of Hong Kong react differently to crowding than do the people of the United States. Similarly, women react differently to crowding than do men. But changing the cultural patterns, even if possible, would be only a long-range solution to the problems caused by crowding. It will be as difficult to achieve as eliminating poverty.

Architectural design, some have suggested, is a possible and more immediate solution to some of the problems caused by crowding. "Architecture will not eliminate poverty or other conditions surrounding it," says Shotland. But there are certain conditions that architecture can effect. Movable walls and ceilings can lend flexibility to a setting and allow people to increase personal space when necessary. Other architectural strategies can help make crime and criminals more visible and easier to report. But in areas where there is a high turnover of residents, says Shotland, intruders cannot be easily identified. All neighbors begin to look like strangers, and architectural design is not much help.

New York's Chinatown has traditionally had a low crime rate. But in recent years street crime has increased in Chinatown. Indications are that this may be due to an increase in population and immigration from the Orient. Little Italy, adjacent to Chinatown, has comparatively little crime. Architecturally, both neighborhoods are the same, a grid pattern of tenements. Little Italy, however, has a stable population and has not had a great influx of strangers. The residents know each other, says Shotland, and can and do recognize and challenge strangers. Correct architecture cannot guarantee a knowledge of one's neighbors but it can, he says, foster this knowledge by designing so there are only a small number of neighbors to be recognized. Increased contact between neighbors leads to friendships and raises the rate of bystander intervention. In conclusion, Shotland says, architectural design can only contribute toward the lowering of crime rates. It is not a panacea and is no guarantee of reduced crime rates.

A total solution to the many problems caused by crowding is not in sight. Ongoing and future research on human crowding should, however, continue to offer additional clues to the solution of crime in the crowded cities.   ◻

5 NEW CLUES TO THE CAUSES OF VIOLENCE

Scientists studying over-aggressive behavior are now implicating brain damage from hitherto hidden sources.

by Gene Bylinsky

Assassinations, vicious muggings, and the high and rising U.S. murder rate have pushed the subject of violence to the forefront among American concerns. At times, the nation appears to be oddly fascinated by the phenomenon. Consider, for example, the recent proliferation of grisly movies, some of which seem to glorify violence as a cult. We have been hearing an abundance of theories about the causes of violence, which variously attribute it to the war in Vietnam, to permissiveness, to drug addiction, to racial frustrations, and even to the legacy of the wild frontier.

Now science is venturing into this area of speculation and dispute. A broad interdisciplinary effort is getting under way to explore the biological nature and origins of violence. Biologists, biochemists, neurophysiologists, geneticists, and other natural scientists are probing with increasingly precise tools and techniques in a field where supposition and speculation have long prevailed. Their work is beginning to provide new clues to the complex ways in which the brain shapes violent behavior. It is also shedding new light on how environmental influences, by affecting the brain, can trigger violence. In time, these insights and discoveries could lead to practical action that may inhibit violent acts—perhaps, for example, a change in the way children are brought up, or treatment with "anti-violence" drugs. Such preventive steps might in the long run be more effective in controlling violent crime than either "law and order" or social reform.

By tradition, students of aggression and violence have been divided into two separate camps that hardly ever communicated with each other. On one side stood the ethologists, students of animal behavior in the wild, many of whom held that man is biologically fated to violence. At the other extreme were social scientists, who knew, or cared, little about biology. They argued that violent crime is strictly a social phenomenon, best dealt with by eliminating slums, urban crowding, and racial discrimination, and by alleviating poverty and improving the prison system.

An imprint on the brain

The most recent research suggests that the biological and environmental causes of violence are so closely intertwined as to require a less fragmented search for remedies. The research is showing, among other things, that the environment itself can leave a physical imprint on a developing brain. The wrong kind of upbringing can make a young animal, and probably a child too, more inclined to violent behavior as an adolescent or an adult. The hopeful augury of this research is that such behavior can be prevented if steps are taken to assure that young brains develop properly.

Until a few years ago, scientists knew comparatively little about the intricate inner mechanisms of the brain that initiate and control violence. These mechanisms lie deep in an inaccessible area called the limbic system, wrapped around the brain stem, as shown in the drawing on page 136. In the limbic system, the hypothalamus stands out as the single most important control center. Regulating many of man's primitive drives, its networks of nerve cells, or neurons, direct not only aggressive and violent behavior but also the states of sleep and wakefulness, as well as sexual and feeding behavior. The front part of the hypothalamus contains networks of nerve cells that promote calmness and tranquillity. The back part regulates aggression and rage.

Restraining the hypothalamus

Nearby lies the almond-shaped amygdala, which restrains the impulses from the hypothalamus. Another close-by structure, the septum, seems to inhibit messages from both the hypothalamus and the amygdala. The cerebellum, the large structure at the back of the brain, filters sensory impulses. The hippocampus, a short-term memory bank in front of the cerebellum, is importantly involved in ways that brain researchers do not yet adequately understand.

All these structures are functionally as well as anatomically interrelated. Electrical signals, arising in response to sensory or internal cues (e.g., sight or thought), speed along nerve pathways to activate or block the function of other nerve cells. Chemicals such as noradrenaline and dopamine, which are normally present in the brain and are known as neurotransmitters, apparently ferry these electrical signals across the tiny gaps between nerve cells, called synapses, to such control centers as the hypothalamus. At the same time, the neurons are constantly bathed in waves of background electrical activity. In still unknown ways, this background "music" apparently conveys information, too.

So complex are the organization and function of the human brain that some of its estimated 10 billion nerve cells may have

Research associate: Bro Uttal

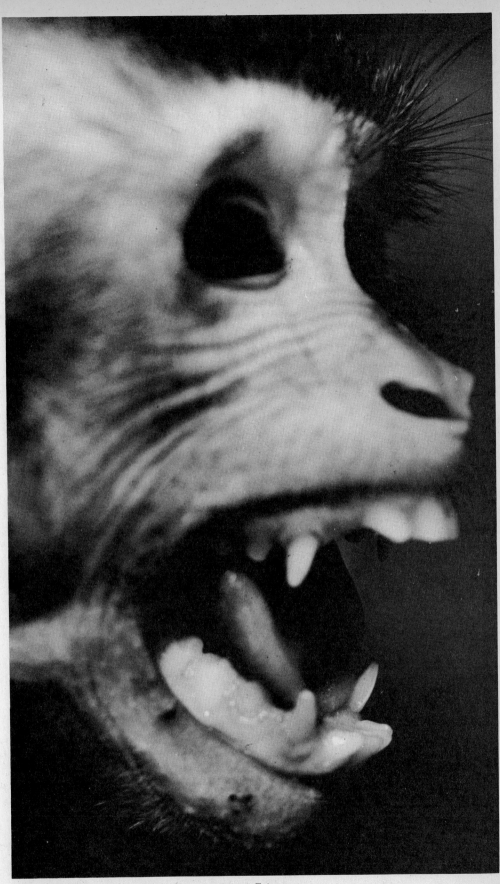

Enraged animals, such as this rhesus monkey at Tulane University, are helping scientists to shed new light on how the brain governs violent behavior. Reared in isolation, the monkey attacks other animals, and even the researchers working with it, at the slightest provocation. It has been established that raising monkeys and other animals in isolation alters the biochemistry, and perhaps the circuitry, of their brains. Somewhat similar changes may affect improperly raised children who grow up to be violent.

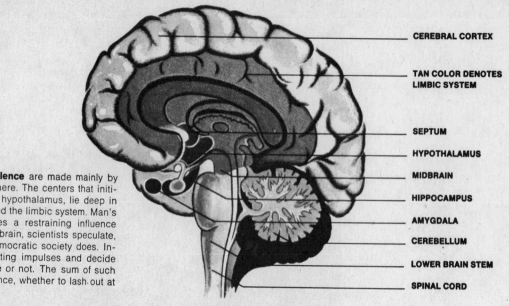

The brain's decisions about violence are made mainly by some of the structures depicted here. The centers that initiate aggressive acts, such as the hypothalamus, lie deep in the primitive part of the brain called the limbic system. Man's more intellectual cortex exercises a restraining influence over the lower brain regions. The brain, scientists speculate, reaches decisions much as a democratic society does. Individual neurons sort out conflicting impulses and decide whether to fire an electrical pulse or not. The sum of such decisions tells a person, for instance, whether to lash out at an enemy or to remain calm.

CEREBRAL CORTEX

TAN COLOR DENOTES
LIMBIC SYSTEM

SEPTUM

HYPOTHALAMUS

MIDBRAIN

HIPPOCAMPUS

AMYGDALA

CEREBELLUM

LOWER BRAIN STEM

SPINAL CORD

as many as 100,000 connections to adjoining cells. When an aggressive act escalates into a violent one, apparently more and more of these neurons are recruited to create bigger pathways for the flow of pulses. Thus violence, as some scientists define it, is aggression gone awry.

The case of the enraged cat

Fortunately for the advance of knowledge about human aggression, the limbic systems of animals have recently been found to bear an amazing functional resemblance to that of man. So laboratory experiments with animals (notably monkeys, cats, and mice) underpin the still limited investigations of aggression systems in the human brain.

Using fine electrodes inserted into animal brains, researchers have induced a fascinating range of aggressive behavior. Cats that normally do not attack rats, for instance, will stalk and kill a rat when stimulated in a certain area of the hypothalamus. On the other hand, a cat stimulated in another nearby region of the hypothalamus may ignore an available rat and attack the experimenter instead. Destruction of the nucleus of the amygdala will turn a friendly cat into a raging beast that claws and bites without provocation, because the signals from the hypothalamus are no longer dampened by the amygdala.

Similarly, a tumor in the hypothalamus or the amygdala can turn a peaceful person into a violent one. Such tumors occur infrequently. Corrective brain surgery remains highly controversial, however, mainly because surgeons lack precise knowledge of the aggression systems and know little about the risk of unwanted side effects from such operations. A surgical lesion—a scar-producing cut, freeze, or burn intended to destroy tissue—can increase or decrease hostile behavior, depending on its location.

Similar gaps in medical information inhibit manipulation of aggressive behavior with drugs that structurally mimic the

neurotransmitter chemicals. Recent experiments by Peter Bradley, a British neuropharmacologist, show that a brain cell can be affected in different ways by the same neurotransmitter, depending on the state of the cell, the amount of neurotransmitter, and how often the chemical is administered. It also appears that during an aggressive act a general arousal of the physiological system occurs—the same type of arousal that can be produced by such peaceful activities as jogging or even a concentrated mental effort.

Dynamite in the genes?

The complex anatomical and biochemical systems of the brain get their "orders" from the genes that determine behavior. Recent studies suggest that males have more brain cells that specialize in aggression than do females. This means that boys are more likely than girls to inherit aggressive tendencies. Very little is yet known, though, about the relationship between specific genetic defects and violence, how many such defects exist, and how frequently they might be inherited. Among the handful of anomalies discovered so far that some scientists have connected with violent behavior is the famous extra Y chromosome, which luckily appears to be inherited by fewer than two men in a thousand. (X and Y are sex chromosomes, with a normal male having an X and a Y, and a normal woman two X's.)

The Y chromosome leaped from the quiet of the laboratory four years ago and landed with a splash in newspaper headlines and courtrooms. The XYY males, usually tall, were said to have a natural propensity for violent crime. Some lawyers tried to gain reduced sentences or acquittal for their clients on the basis of their real or imagined extra Y chromosome. In France, at least, one attorney succeeded.

Some imaginative work now in progress at the University of Connecticut suggests that the Y chromosome story isn't all that simple. Researchers in the department of biobehavioral sciences, led by Benson E. Ginsburg, a noted geneticist, have designed animal breeding techniques that allow them to "tease out," as Ginsburg puts it, the contributions of individual genes and chromosomes to behavior. Their findings strongly hint that an XYY male's tendency to aggressiveness depends on whether he inherited his extra Y chromosome from a peaceful or aggressive father. The Y chromosome may act on the brain through the male sex hormones. Ginsburg and other scientists are trying to find out how this process works.

Elevating genetic probing to a new level of precision, Ginsburg and his colleagues have also shown that a Y chromosome from an aggressive father can combine with another genetic anomaly to make an animal twice as aggressive as it would be with just one genetic defect. They worked with an inbred strain of mice known as DBA 1. These mice are genetically susceptible to epileptic-type seizures that can be initiated by a high-frequency sound from a buzzer, or a bell, or even a jangling set of keys. The sound activates an enzyme system, controlled by a gene as all enzymes are, and located in the hippocampus. In a mouse, the network of neurons involved makes up an area the size of a pinpoint. The enzyme activated by sound, nucleoside triphosphatase, generates epileptic-like brain waves that can be recorded.

Stormy weather in the hippocampus

The DBA mice, particularly males, are abnormally aggressive, apparently because of the defect in their hippocampus. In such mice, complex chemical reactions are superimposed on abnormal electrical activity in their hippocampal neurons. "You whip up an electrical storm in that region of the brain," says Ginsburg, describing his work with a touch of poetic license. Chemicals in the brain intensify the storm, he says, "as if you poured gasoline on a fire—and it went whoosh!"

The same type of storm, and in the same spot, rages in the brains of certain humans. They are either pathologically aggressive or have been made aggressive by hippocampal stimulation. This suggests, of course, that Ginsburg and his colleagues have found a genetic anomaly underlying aggression in both mice and men. In recent years, surgeons in some hospitals have been stimulating different parts of the brains of cancer patients in an effort to find an area that might block unbearable pain. In a number of instances, where doctors have stimulated the hippocampus by administering a very mild electrical shock through an electrode, patients showed the type of rage that Ginsburg and his associates found in those DBA mice. One mild-mannered patient in his fifties suddenly brandished his bedpan as a weapon against the nurses and whoever else happened to be around. He later felt quite embarrassed and contrite.

The discovery of the consequences of these anomalies and of other types of brain damage shatters the assumption made by criminologists and sociologists that the vast majority of cases of violent behavior involve people with completely normal brains. Studies of criminals who have repeatedly committed violent offenses show that they have a higher incidence of brain

Investigating violent behavior in children, James W. Prescott and Albert Bandura have developed widely differing, but not necessarily conflicting, theories to explain the phenomenon. Prescott, a neurophysiologist at the National Institute of Child Health and Human Development, holds that much violence has biological underpinnings, specifically brain damage caused by improper upbringing. His theory covers both monkeys and people. Bandura, a psychologist at Stanford University, is a prominent proponent of social learning theory. He contends that whether a person responds violently to stress depends greatly on what he has seen or been taught. For his experiments, Bandura used large, inflated plastic dolls, one of which can be seen in the background, being walloped by a boy who had watched a doll beaten in a demonstration.

James W. Prescott

Albert Bandura

damage than the general population. Moreover, recent research is uncovering subtle forms of brain damage, unrecognized until now. No one knows for sure how many people in the U.S. suffer from brain damage, but some doctors place the number at 10 million to 20 million. Not all of them are violent, of course, but in addition there are many thousands who suffer from delusions or other forms of mental disturbance that make them dangerous. David Hamburg, head of the psychiatry department at Stanford University Medical School, estimates that the nation harbors some 200,000 potential presidential assassins. "Many manage their delusions on the fantasy level," says Hamburg. "Others engage in other forms of violent behavior."

What many people with brain abnormalities may have in common are pathways in the brain that failed to develop properly in infancy because of faulty upbringing, just as visual nerve pathways fail to develop properly in animals deprived of light. The fault, especially during the first two years of life when the brain is growing the fastest, lies in lack of physical affection, which an infant needs as much as nourishment. Earlier researchers had usually blamed emotional, social, or learning deficiencies for behavioral disturbances in infants raised in a foundling home. But James Prescott, a young neuropsychologist at the U.S. National Institute of Child Health and Human Development, suggests that there is a more fundamental biological reason. He maintains that normal pathways in the brain do not fully develop in children deprived of such expressions of affection as touching, cuddling, and being carried about. Instead, he says, this "somatosensory deprivation" leaves them with damaged central nervous systems.

A chicken-wire mother

In a dramatic series of experiments, Harry F. Harlow, a University of Wisconsin psychologist, has demonstrated what happens when baby rhesus monkeys are deprived of their mothers. Harlow placed an infant monkey in a cage with two inanimate mother substitutes. One, covered with terry cloth and equipped with bicycle-reflector eyes, was designed to feel and look somewhat like a real rhesus mother but had no apparatus for feeding the infant. The other "mother," made of unadorned chicken wire, was unattractive to touch but contained a baby's bottle from which the infant could drink milk. Harlow found that the infant rhesus clearly preferred to spend all of its time with the nonfeeding surrogate. Even when feeding from the chicken-wire "mother," the infant would cling to his terry-cloth favorite. Harlow concluded that in infant-mother love, holding and cuddling are even more important than feeding. He also found that female monkeys who grew up with mother surrogates failed to develop maternal affection: they all seemed indifferent to their own children. Like parents who abuse their children, these monkey mothers frequently attacked, and sometimes even killed, their infants. Other researchers have recently traced three generations of human parents who batter and abuse their children. The only common characteristic of such parents, regardless of social or economic class, was that they themselves had suffered from lack of mothering and affection. Harlow wryly concluded a recent paper:

Hell hath no fury like a woman spurned.
With love not given, love is not returned.
The loveless female, human or macaque,
In place of love will substitute attack.

Can such deprived, aggressive monkeys be restored to normalcy? Experiments in Harlow's laboratory indicate that rehabilitation is possible if it is done early enough. Young monkey mothers reared in isolation sometimes regain most of their normal maternal behavior when locked in a cage with their own babies. The infant clings to the mother so persistently, despite her efforts to push it away, that eventually the baby monkey begins to serve as a therapist. Similarly, some young male monkeys reared in isolation become less aggressive when forced to play with monkeys their own age or younger.

Research into the brains of monkeys raised in isolation is just beginning, but indirect evidence already hints that such treatment induces brain damage. In humans, brain waves with abnormal, jagged "spikes" are often a telltale sign of damage. Robert G. Heath and Bernard Saltzberg, researchers at Tulane University, have recorded such spikes in the brain waves of monkeys reared by Harlow. The spikes reflect abnormal electrical activity, particularly in the cerebellum.

Why Ding feared Dong

Further evidence of the cerebellum's role in violence comes from the work of A. J. Berman, a neurosurgeon at Mount Sinai Medical School and the Jewish Hospital in Brooklyn. He has successfuly modified autistic and aggressive behavior in isolation-reared monkeys by removing presumably abnormal sections of cerebellum that deal with the reception of sensory signals. In one experiment, Berman performed similar surgery on two monkeys called Ding and Dong, who had fought viciously and continuously. The operation turned Ding into a submissive animal, while Dong remained as aggressive as ever. Berman attributes the difference to the location of the surgery. Some tissue was removed from the midline section of Ding's cerebellum while the excision on Dong was microscopically closer to the side of that brain structure.

Berman suggests that his findings may one day be relevant to treating humans. "Walk into the back wards of any mental institution," he says, "and you'll find children whose behavior is identical with that of Harlow's monkeys."

All these and many other experiments have led a number of scientists to conclude that people who behave overaggressively may have an abnormality in the mechanism by which they perceive pleasure. In animals reared in isolation, as in pathologically violent people, the impulses resulting from the stimulation of movement and skin sensations may not be reaching their normal destinations in the brain. The feeling of pleasure may thus be experienced only partially or not at all.

This may explain, among other things, why both institutionalized children and monkeys brought up in isolation generally rock back and forth for hours on end and respond violently if touched. Adults with damaged pleasure systems similarly may be trying to derive pleasure from the rough physical contact involved in violent acts; they may, in effect, be seeking an additional stimulus. Researchers have also found that electrical stimulation of pleasure centers in the brain eliminates feelings of rage, because the brain seems to contain rival nerve systems that suppress opposing emotions chemically and electrically.

The scientist plays victim

Aggressive behavior doesn't necessarily have to arise as a result of damaged networks of nerve cells; it can be easily learned, too. Albert Bandura, a pioneering psychologist at Stanford University, demonstrated almost a decade ago how effectively aggression can be taught through the power of example. He used as "victims" large, inflated plastic figures known as Bobo dolls. Small children watched both real-life and filmed attacks on the dolls, then were given an opportunity to act aggressively themselves.

In study after study, researchers discovered that boys, especially, easily learn and retain aggressive behavior. They readily act out what they have learned not only on Bobo dolls but on other children and even adults. In one typical and recent experiment, conducted by psychologist Robert M. Liebert and his associates at New York State University at Stony Brook, kindergarten children watched a short film. Later they spontaneously attacked a scientist who had appeared in the film dressed up as a hard-luck clown and had been beaten up by another researcher. Many studies show that televised violence affects children in similar ways.

Violent behavior can be set off by many other environmental conditions. For instance, Leonard Berkowitz, a University of Wisconsin psychologist, showed that the mere presence of firearms can stimulate aggressive action. He tested groups of students who were provoked and insulted by one of his colleagues. Later, the groups had a chance to administer electric shocks to their tormentor. Students in a room where a gun was casually displayed gave the investigator about 25 percent more shocks than those in a room containing no weapons. The findings suggest to Berkowitz and others that easy access to lethal weapons—about 65 percent of homicides in the U.S. are committed with guns—not only facilitates the commission of crimes but creates an atmosphere in which violence is more likely to occur.

As in the laboratory, violence in real life often begets more violence. Marvin E. Wolfgang, a noted criminologist at the University of Pennsylvania, has coined the term "subculture of violence" to describe the cluster of values, attitudes, and life styles prominent among the poor living in the slums. Violence in that setting is so common as a problem-solving mechanism, says Wolfgang, that there is no shortage of real-life models for the young to imitate.

Many other factors—frequent absence of fathers, low income, unstable employment, poor living conditions—also bend the behavior of underprivileged youths toward violence, according to Wolfgang. Under all these pressures, plus in some cases a lack of physical affection at home, adolescent blacks have the highest homicide rate of any group in the U.S.

To complicate matters, they, like other adolescents, undergo a hormonal upheaval. Boys in particular become more aggres-

sive as the amount of sex hormones in their bodies increases. Electron microscopy at Oxford University has recently begun to reveal structural differences between males and females in such control centers of aggression as the hypothalamus, for which sex hormones have a particular affinity.

Are men stronger than mice?

The still mysterious workings of hormones on the brain constitute only a small part of the enormous gap between what scientists have discovered and what remains to be learned about the physiology and biochemistry of violence. For example, says Benson Ginsburg, the University of Connecticut geneticist, scientists should find out whether men, through conscious control and training, can override the physiological changes involved in aggression much more effectively than, say, mice can. Another unknown is whether genetic instructions are so strong in some people as to completely mold their behavior. Answers to such questions could open the way to far more specific therapies. More effective antiviolence drugs, for instance, could be developed if we could delineate the particular enzymatic mechanisms in the brain that affect aggression.

Treatment with existing drugs, many scientists feel, is something like using a shotgun where a rifle is needed. Even so, some investigators propose that methadone-type clinics be set up to dispense drugs available now to persons prone to violence. Lithium might be useful because it appears to speed up the release of serotonin, a brain chemical that seems to inhibit aggression. Michael H. Sheard, a Yale neuropharmacologist, has had some success in modifying the behavior of violent prisoners with lithium.

Other novel approaches may emerge from studies that are under way. For example, development of a vastly improved brain-wave recording machine, now in progress at Tulane, would enable doctors to detect signals of trouble from deep in the brain without surgically implanting recording electrodes there. It may also become possible to treat damaged deep-nerve networks ultrasonically, thereby avoiding surgery.

It is clear that much more specific therapies than those in use today are needed for people who have brain damage. Vernon H. Mark and Frank R. Ervin observe in their recent book, *Violence and the Brain:* "Hoping to rehabilitate such a violent individual through psychotherapy or education, or to improve his character by sending him to jail or by giving him love and understanding—all these methods are irrelevant and will not work. It is the malfunction itself that must be dealt with, and only if this fact is recognized is there any chance of changing his behavior."

No trouble in Tahiti

To prevent brain damage that may lead to violence, some new tactics could be tried now. "Changing child-rearing practices is probably the most important single thing we can do as a society," says Prescott. "We have to make sure that the children we have are wanted children." Prescott and others also suggest that it might be a good idea to evaluate and treat children as early as age five if they show a tendency to brutalize other children or animals or have episodes of uncontrolled rage. Such youngsters, scientists say, are good candidates for violent behavior later.

Anthropologists have gained some intriguing clues about child rearing by studying peaceful societies. Prescott surveyed data from forty-nine primitive cultures and found in thirty-six of them an amazingly strong correlation between physical affection toward infants and lack of violence. In societies where infants were treated cruelly, violence prevailed. Robert Levy, an anthropologist at the University of California at San Diego who has studied tranquil Tahiti, found that parents on the island seldom punish children by hitting them. Thus the children have no aggressive models to emulate.

Another deterrent to violence may be the habit of arguing it out. Societies that have developed highly elaborate ways of verbalizing violence are quite peaceful. In Tahiti and other Polynesian islands, people engage in "talking out acute anger, rather than taking physical action," says Levy. Similarly, Italians sometimes sound violent, but according to scientists who have studied Italy, there is far less incidence of violent offenses there than in the U.S.

This nation leads the advanced industrialized countries of the world in homicide and other violent crimes. Assaults in the U.S. occur nearly twice as often per capita as in England and Wales, and robberies are ten times as common. In 1971, the latest full year for which figures are available, 17,630 people in the U.S. were murdered. In England and Wales, West Germany, France, and Italy, which have a combined population about 3 percent larger than ours, there were only 1,948 murders—a rate almost ten times lower than that in the U.S.

By contrast with the U.S., these other industrial countries have more homogeneous populations, exert greater control over firearms, and operate with somewhat more rigid social structures. These differences may explain some, though not necessarily all, of the disparities in the rates of violence. In any case, it is clear that our methods of dealing with the problem have not proved particularly effective. Scientific investigation at last is beginning to provide surprising insights into why this is so. In time, the new research may lead to a much broader understanding of violent behavior, and, eventually, to effective means of discouraging it.   END

II. Roots of Human Nature: Altruism and Sociobiology

It is commonly assumed that people are born essentially bad (possessed by "original sin"), and that the primary task of culture is to make them good, or to *socialize* them. The contention of writers like Robert Ardrey— that we are born with aggressive instincts—fits well with this conception. However, the assumption that biology is bad and culture is good is limited in at least two ways. First, as the last articles in the previous section showed, people *learn* to behave aggressively. Second, there is considerable evidence suggesting that humans are *born* with socially *desirable* instincts. As Robert Claiborne points out ("How Homo Sapiens Learned to Be Good"), observations of primates contain more evidence of caring, sharing, and cooperating than of violence and aggression. Claiborne suggests that the survival value of communal hunting caused cooperative and altruistic dispositions to be selected in early humans. In an interesting twist, he cites the selfish behavior of the preliterate Ik people (see "Plight of the Ik and Kaiadilt Is Seen as a Chilling Possible End for Man" in Part I) not as evidence that humans are innately bad but as evidence that "people forced to live under grossly abnormal and dehumanizing conditions are likely to behave in grossly abnormal and dehumanized ways."

Popularly interpreted, Darwin's theory of evolution implies that all

Artwork by Martin Riskin.

surviving species must be essentially selfish and competitive. Yet there is compelling evidence of altruism, if not among humans, then surely among ants, bees, and termites. The problem of altruism in the theory of evolution spurred the development of the new, controversial field of sociobiology ("The New Science of Genetic Self-Interest"). Sociobiology embraces most of Darwin's theory of evolution, except that it focuses on the propagation of genes rather than the propagation of individuals. This seemingly small switch in focus has profound implications for the explanation of altruism and a wide array of other social behaviors. Helping people who are genetically related may, under many circumstances, be more adaptive (get more replicas of your genes into succeeding generations) than helping yourself.

With its emphasis on genetic determinism, it is not surprising that sociobiology has evoked vehement criticism ("Sociobiology: The Aesop's Fables of Science," by Michael A. Simon). While raising some valid points, some critiques confuse important issues. For example, in the "Aesop's Fables" critique, Simon equates sociobiology and ethology, criticizing the former for faults of the latter. Second, he appears to imply that sociobiology assumes that some traits are universal, across all environmental conditions, whereas one of the central assumptions in sociobiology is that the environment selects traits. Aggression may be adaptive when resources are scarce but maladaptive when they are not.

Not only is the apparent existence of altruism problematic in the theory of evolution, it also raises problems for learning theory. Can you teach someone to be altruistic? If learning involves reinforcement, and if altruism is defined as behavior that conveys reinforcements to others but not to the self, it would appear not. The paradox of altruism in the theory of evolution and in learning theory is examined by Dennis Krebs and Mark Holder in "Evolution, Altruism, and Reinforcement," where it is argued that empathy may provide a resolution.

HOW HOMO SAPIENS LEARNED TO BE GOOD 6

Like his kinfolk the chimps and baboons, man has *had* to help his fellows—if only to survive

By ROBERT CLAIBORNE

Wisdom begins with asking the right questions. A recurrent question in recent years has been. Why is man a killer? To answer it, the commentators I have termed biotheologians (see "Man the Peaceable Primate" in HORIZON, Spring, 1973) have devised various schemes of evolution as dubious as they are hypothetical. The question itself rests on a false premise. Men—even in the narrow sense, excluding women and children—are typically *not* killers. In our own culture—not widely known for its abhorrence of violence—the proportion of adult men who have deliberately killed another human being is probably one in ten or less; if one excludes those who have killed as soldiers, under threat of death from the enemy or court-martial from their officers, the proportion drops to something under one in a hundred. Inevitably, then, attempts to explain this far from universal human trait by the universal processes of human evolution have not been satisfactory.

If one is looking for a really widespread human characteristic, a far more eligible candidate is altruism, for man helps his fellows much oftener than he kills or even injures them. We feed and clothe our children, bandage their hurts, soothe their fears—even though the best-behaved kids can at times be little monsters. If a friend goes broke, we are more likely than not to offer a loan. If a housewife is disabled, her relatives and neighbors turn out to lend a hand with the children and housework. If a blind man asks for help in negotiating a busy intersection, he is not often ignored. And beyond these direct and personal services to our fellows, millions of us contribute money to help people we have never seen and almost certainly never will —starving Bengalis, earthquake-shocked Nicaraguans, hurricane refugees along our own southern coasts.

I am not claiming that we do not sometimes perform generous acts under social compulsion—just as some of us kill under compulsion—still less that all of us are generous all the time. Yet it seems to me incontestable that nearly all of us do act generously at least some of the time. In fact, it can be argued—and I shall so argue —that without this pervasive web of mutual help and concern no human society could long endure, and that for this if for no other reason we must seek the roots of altruism in the basics of human nature.

Note that I say the *roots* of altruism, not altruism itself. Altruistic behavior, like all other kinds of human behavior except for a few reflex actions such as sneezing, is learned, not innate. How we care for our children and succor our neighbors—and when, and how often—is governed by our personal experiences and by the cultures in which we have grown up. But the fundamental biases and potentialities of human nature that encourage us to learn these things, in particular the human capacity for *empathy*—for deriving pleasure from other people's pleasure and distress from their distress—cannot be taught; they are bred in the bone.

In tracing the evolution of altruism we can obtain only limited help from studying the behavior of our primate relatives, which is presumed to resemble that of our primate ancestors. For altruism is a peculiarly human kind of behavior. Other primates gather food, mate, squabble, and fight among themselves, engage in mutual back scratching, and band together for mutual defense, but very few of them *give* to their adult fellows. Nonetheless it is among the primates that we must begin, since it is in them that we can observe what appears to be the prototype of man's concern for his fellows: the mother's concern for her child.

A good primate to start with is the Indian langur monkey. Its life style is basically arboreal, as was that of our ancestors twenty million years ago, but the langur also spends a good deal of time on the ground, as those ancestors may already have begun doing. Around 1960 primatologist Phyllis Jay spent nearly a thousand hours observing langurs; she concluded, among other things, that "the mother-newborn infant relationship is the strongest and most intense bond in the life of a langur." And for good reason. Langur babies, though by no means as helpless as human babies, are at birth totally dependent on their mothers, not only for food but also for transport—the latter being important because a foraging langur troop may cover more than a mile a day. The infant langur must cling to its mother "so tightly . . . that she can run on the ground or make long jumps through the air without dislodging it."

As we know from Harry F. Harlow's famous experiments, infant monkeys cling to their mothers essentially because they find the physical contact comforting and reassuring. But why does the mother allow herself to be clung to, or tend her baby at all? From Jay's observations, a major reason is that she, too, finds the physical contact pleasurable: "The mother inspects, licks, grooms and manipulates the infant from the hour of its birth"; even when it is quietly resting "she grooms and strokes it softly without disturbing or waking it." In fact, *all* female langurs, says Jay, "are intensely interested in newborn infants." As soon as the troop's females notice the arrival of a new baby, all of them, from juveniles on up, "immediately cluster closely around its mother. She is surrounded by a group of from four to ten females, all reaching out gently and trying to touch, lick and smell" the newcomer. Within a few hours the mother begins allowing other females to handle it. One of them "takes the infant from the mother's arms and holds it. . . . She inspects it minutely, gently manipulating, nudging, licking and smelling the infant. . . . At the first sign of discomfort in the newborn it is taken by another of the waiting females, although if the mother is sitting nearby she often reaches out and intercepts the infant. . . . As many as eight females may handle the infant during the first day of life."

From Jay's observations we can draw three conclusions:

1. Female langurs enjoy physical contact with infants.

2. They find babies intrinsically interesting.

3. They have *some built-in need, or propensity, to respond to the infant's needs* "at the first sign of discomfort. . . ."

There is no reason to suppose that the langur female, any more than her human counterpart, possesses any instinctive knowledge of *how* to go about soothing an uncomfortable or fractious baby. These things she learns—by watching other females and by "practicing" on their infants. Some langur mothers learn the techniques better than others, Jay reports; a few barely learn them at all. But the motive underlying the learning is, quite clearly, an unlearned, built-in capacity to sense the needs of another creature and a desire to satisfy those needs. And that, in essence, is what altruism is about.

Thus far I have said nothing about langur fathers and their reactions to infants—the reason being that there is little to say. Langur males take no interest in babies, their own or anyone else's (to a langur male, of course, it's the same thing), apart from threatening or chasing them when their play becomes too noisy.

Matters are different, however, among another much-observed group of monkeys, the baboons. Baboon males, reports primatologist Irven De Vore, are not mere disciplinarians; they also show intense interest in the troop's infants and enjoy playing with them. The basic reason for this difference, De Vore believes, is the animals' habitat. Langurs, though they may spend much time on the ground, never venture far from trees—and thus can escape into them at the first sign of danger. Baboons, by contrast, frequently live in open savannas and grasslands where such refuges may be far off. Accordingly the adult males have necessarily evolved the motivations to assume the role of group defenders—a job that the females, encumbered with their young, are in no position to undertake. And among these motivations, evidently, is a concern with babies; as De Vore states, "an animal is hardly likely to risk its life to save an infant for whom it feels no emotion."

These observations are relevant to man because our species and its ancestors have also long dwelt in open country (for more than five million years), and thus the males must have evolved similar motivations for protecting females and their young. The principle of "women and children first" when danger threatens obviously goes back a long way! Indeed, one need not be overly imaginative to see in the baboon or protohuman male, defending the lives of his females and young at the risk of his own, a foreshadowing of those tribal kings in the ancient Mediterranean world whose duty, in dire emergency, was to sacrifice themselves for their people—or of Christ, who many believe gave His life for mankind.

We can make other inferences about altruism among our far-off grassland ancestors from the remarkable chimpanzee studies of Jane Van Lawick-Goodall. Chimps, to be sure, are not grassland animals, but in every other respect—physical, biochemical, and mental—they are much closer to man than the baboon. Interestingly, the mother-child bond persists far longer among chimpanzees than it does among langurs. A female chimp will defend her adolescent son against the attack of an adult male, or, if the latter is too formidable, will linger in the background making threatening noises. Goodall has also observed adolescent males defending their mothers against attacks or threats from other females.

Part of the reason for the persistence of this bond is undoubtedly that the animals mature relatively slowly, and so presumably need maternal protection longer. But this is clearly not the whole answer, since the mother-child bond continues long after it could play any direct role in survival. Male chimps, too, in addition to playing with infants, show a certain capacity to empathize with adolescents. Goodall several times observed male adolescents, frightened by the presence of mature males—who are often short-tempered with "teen-age boys"—being reassured by a pat from their elders.

One probable reason for the evolution of this sort of behavior is the fact that chimps are more intelligent and more complex than any monkey. One indication of this is the chimp's comparatively large vocabulary of noises, gestures, and grimaces, which suggests that he has more to "say" to other chimps—and more to

> We can thus visualize our Australopithecine ancestors
> of perhaps five million years ago as a psychological
> blend of chimpanzees—which they resembled in intelli-
> gence—and baboons—which they resembled in habitat.

understand. Given an animal of this complexity, an enhanced sensitivity to others of its species is surely necessary if conflict within the group is not to reach disruptive levels. (Like higher primates, including man, chimps are very much group animals, dependent upon their fellows for the social contacts they evidently value and, while young, for information—by example—on how to survive as adults.)

We can thus visualize our protohuman Australopithecine ancestors of perhaps five million years ago as a psychological blend of chimpanzees—which they resembled in intelligence—and baboons—which they resembled in habitat. The females would be preoccupied with the infants and younger children, while retaining close ties with their grown sons and daughters. The adult males would also be concerned with the young, romping and playing with them on occasion. The leaders among the males—presumably the largest, toughest, and cleverest—would have had the job of keeping the group orderly and together, so that stragglers did not get picked off by leopards, wild dogs, and hyenas. If predators became aggressive, the males would gang up on them, throwing rocks and wielding bone clubs or stout sticks, fighting, if need be, to the death. Finally, we may infer that both sexes had by this time evolved at least a rudimentary capacity to sense the emotional needs of their fellows and to convey some of the reassurances and gestures of affection that are the lubricants of life among us today.

But all this is far from the systematic mutual aid and concern we see within human groups. These far-off ancestors very likely possessed the primitive altruistic capacities of chimps—but chimps, as Goodall remarks, "usually show a lack of consideration for each other's feelings which in some ways may represent the deepest part of the gulf between them and us."

What bridged that gulf in human evolution, I am convinced, was hunting—an activity that is often accused, ironically, of having transformed man from an amiable vegetarian into a "predator" and "killer."

This could have come about in two ways. First, we can safely assume that almost from the beginning our ancestors hunted in groups at least part of the time. Even chimps do this, albeit in a rudimentary way. As a human trait, group hunting would have survived because it yielded more food. But our ancestors of five million years ago knew nothing of efficiency; having no language, they could not reason or plan their hunting forays rationally. For group hunting to develop under these conditions it must have involved some payoff to the hunters: all members of the group must have shared in the rewards.

We can see how this may have come about from reports on hunting among baboons and chimps. Baboons are strictly individual hunters, each pursuing its chosen prey. The payoff is no less individual: each baboon eats what it catches, if some higher-ranking baboon doesn't grab it from him. As we have seen, however, chimps hunt in a crudely co-operative fashion—and the payoff is likewise co-operative. According to Geza Teleki, an associate of Goodall's, as soon as the prey has been seized all the chimps within reach "are free to grab a part of the carcass without risk of retaliation from the . . . captors." Obviously, sharing of this sort did not develop for logical reasons, along the lines of "if I don't give him a share now, he won't help me hunt next time." It must have been the other way around: without a willingness to share, there would have been no payoff to any but the actual captors—and group hunting would not have developed. A chimp does not share because he hunts co-operatively; he hunts co-operatively because he has learned by experience that he will get a share. Thus we can hardly doubt that as group hunting became routine among our ancestors, so did sharing.

But as hunting became a major source of food, it must have promoted altruism in another way. The systematic pursuit of game, particularly large game, would often have involved tracking it for distances of several miles. This would have been a job for the adult and near-adult males; children and females with infants could not have kept up. But if the band had come to rely on meat, the hunters could not simply share their kill on the spot; some of it would have to be taken home for the females and children. The hunters must, then, have evolved some awareness of the needs of these absent ones—and a capacity to derive satisfaction from ministering to those needs, even if this meant eating less meat themselves.

And we see evidence of such empathy among chimps in another type of food-sharing situation—one occurring *after* the initial division of the prey. At this point all the chimps gather in "sharing clusters" around those that have seized a chunk of meat and "beg" for a piece of the highly valued food. And, as often as not, they get it. There is, I must stress, no "practical" reason for this type of behavior in terms of the group's nutritional needs. The sharers share out of what Teleki calls "social considerations": evidently they derive some satisfaction from responding to the begging of their fellows.

This sort of sharing among chimps for reasons of what must be called good fel-

A chimp does not share because he hunts co-operatively; he hunts co-operatively because he has learned he will get a share. Thus we can hardly doubt that as group hunting became routine among our ancestors, so did sharing.

lowship is typical rather than exceptional: Teleki says categorically that "no chimpanzee . . . has ever been observed to capture and privately consume a mammal, however small, if other adult chimpanzees were present to form a sharing cluster." And if this is true of chimps, how much more true it must have been of our hunting ancestors, for whom sharing food with the nonhunting members of the tribe was not merely a matter of sociability, but often a stark necessity. Thus we, their descendants, routinely respond to the needs of others—sometimes, indeed, in hope of reward, sometimes in fear of what people will say if we don't, but often *because satisfying the needs of others, and thereby sharing their satisfaction, is intrinsically rewarding.*

The foregoing reconstruction of the evolution of altruism is admittedly conjectural, but it is nevertheless extremely plausible. Though we have no direct evidence that our early hunting ancestors shared food, how could they have survived had they not done so? As it happens, however, we also have fairly direct evidence of prehistoric altruism, albeit from much later—among the Neanderthals of perhaps fifty thousand years ago.

The Neanderthals were originally visualized as stooped, shambling figures more like apes than men, a picture derived from studies of the first complete Neanderthal skeleton to be unearthed. More careful examination of these bones made clear that what ailed their owner was not apeishness but arthritis: he was a man of about sixty, who for years prior to his death had been so crippled that he could not stand upright. He could not conceivably have hunted or otherwise contributed to the well-being of his tribe or family—yet they had continued to provide him with food. Fifty thousand years

ago these creatures—who may have lacked even the ability to speak except in grunts—were looking after their own.

Let us now, for the moment, abandon evolution and look at some laboratory evidence on the nature of altruism. As reported in 1971, experimenters at the University of Oklahoma decided to see whether altruism could function as a reward in the classic type of "instrumental conditioning" made famous by B. F. Skinner, where learning is "reinforced" by a positive stimulus (such as food) or by the cessation of a negative stimulus (such as an electric shock). They knew that they could not test the effect of altruistic "reinforcement" openly, since the subjects' responses could be biased by the general conviction that altruism is praiseworthy. Accordingly, they engaged in a bit of deception. The subjects were told that they were evaluating responses of some other individual to stress. This person—actually a confederate of the experimenters—had to hold a metal stylus steady in a tunnel while supposedly receiving an electric shock from which he visibly "suffered." The subject was to evaluate the confederate's performance by setting pointers on three dials; then, at a signal, he pressed a button to record his evaluations on tape, at which point the confederate was granted a ten-second break and heaved a loud sigh of "relief." Control experiments were run in the same way, except that the confederate received no "shock" and showed neither suffering nor relief.

What the experimenters were interested in was not, of course, the subject's evaluation of the confederate's theatrics, but rather his response to them—as measured by how quickly he pressed the button after receiving the "record" signal. From the beginning there was a significant

difference between the experimental and control subjects: the former, confronted by the confederate's apparent suffering, averaged 1.06 seconds between the signal and the button pressing that ended the "shock," while the latter averaged more than 1.3 seconds. Moreover, the experimental subject's performance improved much more than the control's. Additional experiments established that altruism functioned just like other rewards. The experimenters concluded that "the roots of altruistic behavior are so deep that people not only help others" without reward, but find the help rewarding in itself.

Of course this experiment does not prove that the psychological rewards of altruism are innate; that most of us like money is hardly evidence that we are born liking it. But taken together with the other facts I have cited, it makes the case for an innate human propensity to help others very convincing indeed. We *know* that female langurs—and baboons, and chimps—are from an early age interested in babies and attentive to their needs. And if this prototypical capacity for altruism is learned rather than innate, it must be learned in such a way that the males acquire it to a far less marked degree, or not at all—which seems ridiculous.

We *know* that our hunting male ancestors must have shared their kills, and also carried meat home to the women, children, and elders—if only from the fact that we, their descendants, are here to argue the point. Finally, we *know* that empathy—the capacity to laugh when others laugh, rejoice when they rejoice, suffer when they suffer—is present to some degree in

Set up a social framework in which men are encouraged to be altruistic and most will rise to the occasion; set up one that encourages them to be selfish and most will sink to it.

most if not all humans, supplying the psychological payoff for altruistic behavior.

Looking at the question from another standpoint, we know that very nearly all the things that men do, in any culture, are learned. But we also know that what men learn, and how easily they learn it, is partly determined by innate incentive systems that encourage us to learn whatever is essential for survival. Sexual pleasure, for one example, insures that we will learn those delightful activities without which our species would die out; likewise, our pain-sensitive nerves insure that we will learn to avoid harmful objects.

Evolution, in other words, has arranged that we will be guided by what I have called a "psychological payoff" in the form of pleasure or the "negative payoff" of pain. If, then, caring for our young is essential to our survival—as it obviously is and has been for tens of millions of years—and if a concern for other adults has been essential at least since we began relying on hunting as a food source, we should expect to find innate payoffs in the pleasure we derive from others' pleasure and in the pain we suffer from others' pain. And from all the evidence I have cited, that is exactly what we do find.

I must stress that the existence of a psychological payoff does not of itself *guarantee* that we will learn the activities that bring that payoff, still less that we will engage in them. All a payoff does is make it *more likely* that we will learn the actions that produce it and, having learned them, repeat them. Evolution does not insure that we will learn to behave with generosity and concern for others; the payoff of such behavior merely makes it probable that we will. And in fact the great majority of us do.

Let us conclude with a look at how the biotheologians—who have managed to attribute to our species almost every discreditable motive imaginable, from an impulse to murder to an impulse to imperialism—have dealt with man's more generous impulses. Lionel Tiger and Robin Fox, in *The Imperial Animal*, correctly see the act of giving as "perhaps the most basic step on the road to truly human social relationships." But they find its prototype not (as I have) in the relationship between the primate mother and child, but in that between debtor and creditor. Giving "implies an obligation to return the gift." "If a human being gives something, real or incorporeal, to another, something will be given back. Even the Spanish beggar gives his blessing in return for alms."

One might expect this generalization to be supported by comprehensive evidence, but in fact, the authors cite but one study, dating from 1925. And, in fact, one finds their argument is based on false premises. Primates other than man, they say, "do not share." This is simply not true; moreover, if Tiger and Fox actually read Goodall's chimpanzee studies cited in their bibliography, they must have known it was not true. Giving among chimps does not imply any "obligation" to return the gift. Even less is any obligation implied when the female langur cares for an infant. Our ancestors were giving—first to their young, later to their fellows—long before they were engaging in the wheeling and dealing these anthropologists say is basic to human gift giving. Beyond this, Tiger and Fox simply duck the question of motive, or "payoff," i.e., the satisfaction derived from altruistic actions.

Instead of further belaboring the unlikelihood of this in evolutionary terms, let us take a look at some actual givers: 3,800 unpaid British blood donors, studies of whom were reported by Richard Titmuss in his recent book *The Gift Relationship.* Asked why they gave blood, the donors naturally gave very different answers. But if we group the answers by type, we find that nearly two-thirds of the reasons must be classed as altruistic, while only about one donor in twelve gave blood for "selfish" reasons, or to meet an obligation (e.g., a transfusion to a member of his family).

A young woman factory worker was eloquent on the subject: "You cant get blood from supermarkets and chaine stores. People them selves must come forword, sick people cant get out of bed to ask you for a pint to save theier life so I came forword in hope to help somebody who needs blood." A more literate factory foreman was more succinct: "No man is an island." And these donors, I must stress, were no gallery of "English eccentrics"; the British blood-bank system depends entirely on such voluntary gifts, involving well over a million givers a year.

Technically, of course, the British blood donors fell within Tiger and Fox's "reciprocity arrangement"; all of them received—or at least were offered—a cup of tea for their trouble, thereby presumably entering into a "deal" along the lines of "I give blood, they give tea, and we're all square." Personally, I find "I came forword in hope to help somebody" far more credible.

A more recent biotheological assault on altruism has been leveled by the anthropologist Colin Turnbull in his hair-raising book *The Mountain People,* an account of the Ik tribe of eastern Uganda. The Ik, says Turnbull, are "as unfriendly, un-

> The remedy is not to belabor human nature. . . . The soured romantics who say man is basically selfish are no less child- ish than the romantics who proclaim him basically altruistic.

charitable, inhospitable and generally mean as any people can be." Instead of caring for their children, they toss them out of the hut at the age of three; instead of caring for the aged and feeble, they literally snatch food from their mouths; instead of feeling distress at the misfortunes of their fellows, they are apt to show amusement.

So far, so good—or bad. But Turnbull then makes this tribe of near-monsters the text for an elaborate sermon on human nature; the Ik, he claims, prove that altruism is a "myth," that our much vaunted human values "are not inherent in humanity at all"; their dog-eat-dog society shows "how shallow is man's potential for goodness."

Turnbull might better have spent more time discussing how the Ik got to be so nasty. As he tells us, they were originally seminomadic hunters on the borderland between Uganda, Kenya, and the Sudan. They were quite as honest, generous, and compassionate as hunting peoples (according to Turnbull) generally are. But then their lands were circumscribed by the national boundaries set up by the new East African states and next seized by the Ugandan government, which converted their prime hunting ground into a national park and told the Ik to become farmers—just like that.

This was bad enough; worse still, the "farm" land they were given was steep, rocky, and, even in a good year, dry. Turnbull did not visit them in a good year: he met them in the midst of a drought when crops withered in the ground and even drinking water sometimes had to be fetched from scummy water holes five miles away. Nearly all the Ik were hungry and thirsty; many literally starved to death. What the Ik prove is simply that people forced to live under grossly abnor-

mal and dehumanizing conditions are likely to behave in grossly abnormal and dehumanized ways. Their tragic story tells us nothing about the nature of altruism—except that the degree of altruism men show depends rather heavily on circumstances. Turnbull, however, like some other biotheologians, is arguing that if man isn't a good guy all the time, he must be a bad guy all the time.

he story of the Ik proves more than its author realized. For his selfish, conniving, mean-minded tribe is, as he himself intimates, a vanishing tribe. If the wages of sin is death, the Ik are rapidly getting paid off: within a generation or so they seem doomed to disappear.

I am not, let me emphasize, claiming that man is "innately good" or any such oversimplified and romantic folderol. If a chimp is a complex creature compared with a langur, man is far more complex as compared with a chimp: his actions are governed by the most intricate and variable combinations of motives. But among those motives is a capacity to empathize with others, to share their pleasures and pains, and so derive satisfaction from that of others.

Obviously, if altruism and self-interest conflict, self-interest is more likely to win. But if altruism is sometimes less powerful than other motives, it is not less real; that a thirsty man may reach for a glass of water in preference to a beautiful woman is no reflection on his virility.

Whether our behavior at a given moment is governed by our concern for our fellows will obviously depend on the choices open to us, and on the rewards attached.

Titmuss, in discussing the implications of his blood-bank study, emphasizes that the altruism of the British, compared to other people's, is not due to any inherent moral superiority, but to the fact that in this area British society has institutionalized generosity. Set up a social framework in which men are encouraged to be altruistic and most of them will rise to the occasion; set up one that encourages them to be selfish and most of them will sink to it. If a society offers special rewards to those who pursue the strategies of dog-eat-dog and "I'm all right, Jack," then many people are, of course, going to use those strategies.

But the remedy is not to belabor human nature, misrepresenting man as a selfish beast. The soured romantics who say man is basically selfish are no less childish than the romantics who proclaim him basically altruistic. Nature has made him both. And she also seems to have arranged matters so that societies fostering selfishness have a short life expectancy: along with the obscure Ik we have the better known example of a society that, having institutionalized inhumanity, expired in a Berlin bunker after twelve years, though it had been advertised to last for a thousand. If, then, we are concerned with the survival of *our* society, we might well inquire whether, in fact, its institutions foster our selfish impulses rather than our altruistic ones—and if so, how they can be changed to give the latter greater scope. "We crave to be more kindly than we are," wrote Bertolt Brecht; given the chance, we will be.

Robert Claiborne's "Man the Peaceable Primate," which appeared in HORIZON *a year ago, and this article are based on his book* God or Beast: Evolution and Human Nature, *to be published by W.W. Norton.*

The New Science of Genetic Self-Interest

An Interview with Irven DeVore

Sociobiologist Irven DeVore talks with Scot Morris
about the selfishness built into our genes.
It is not the survival of the fittest that humans
and other animals strive for, it is for
the reproduction of the individual's genes.

Scot Morris: The evolution of behavior has become a hot issue lately. The conference you organized at the American Anthropological Association last November caused quite a stir: huge attendance, radical protest, even an attempt to pass a resolution condemning social biology.

Irven DeVore: The hullabaloo is because many people oppose the notion that human behavior is in any way directed by our genes or that our destinies may be somewhat preordained by our biology.

Morris: Is this theory really something new and important, or is it just a repetition of the same old argument that biologists and environmentalists get into every few years?

DeVore: Yes it *is* new: we're still calling it by several names: sociobiology, behavioral biology, psychobiology, and so on. And it *is* important, probably the most important development in understanding behavior since Darwin. It has already revolutionized the understanding of animal behavior and is well on its way to revolutionizing the social sciences.

Morris: Psychology and ethology have gotten along pretty well without it up to now, though. Why do you say it's so important now?

DeVore: Because it's a complete "paradigm shift," in Thomas Kuhn's terminology. It's a whole new way of looking at behavior, especially the most puzzling behaviors that defy traditional explanations.

Morris: Like what, for example?

DeVore: Like murder and infanticide.

Systematically killing other members of your own species. Lorenz and others had convinced people that aggressive animals stop short of killing their own kind—or if they do, it's because of some breakdown in their ritualized fighting system caused by some unusual stress; or even that the killing was somehow for the good of the species as a whole.

Morris: As a means of population control, for example?

DeVore: Yes. But we now know that it occurs in species that aren't overpopulated, or may even be on the verge of extinction. Male lions sometimes eat lion cubs, for instance. Murder is a comparatively rare event in *any* species, so no one had reported it in lions and other animals until recently, after field studies that had been running continuously for eight or 10 years. Reports on animals killing their own kind are now coming in so fast that it's almost routine. I was just reading about some studies on the murder rates in bears and mountain lions. But we've heard similar reports about many species: chimpanzees, gorillas, baboons, elephant seals, wild dogs, hyenas, hippos, gulls, you name it.

Morris: What happened to the "Peaceable Kingdom"?

DeVore: It was an illusion, apparently. Contrary to what the popular writers were saying a few years ago—that humans are the most aggressive, vicious animals on earth, the "killer ape" with the mark of Cain—we may turn out to be one of the most pacific animals of all, warfare aside.

Morris: What kind of killing has been

observed?

DeVore: There are many instances of adult males killing each other, but even more revealing is the wide-spread infanticide. Not just leaving the young to die, but deliberate killing, usually by a male who has just taken over a group of females and young after driving out the resident male. And the new male continues to kill any young born in the next few weeks or months—that's true in lions and in the langur monkeys of India, for example. One would have to construct a very tortured argument to show how this behavior is "good for the species as a whole." It is manifestly *bad* for the young who are killed, of course, and it's bad for the females who lose all the time and energy they have invested in their offspring. But that's not to say it isn't good for the males who do the killing; those offspring aren't his. Infanticide can increase the male's *own* reproductive success and help him leave more offspring.

Morris: For instance?

DeVore: Female langur monkeys, for example, ordinarily come into estrus about every two years. But if a nursing mother loses her infant, she comes into estrus and conceives within two months, instead of six to eight months. So the killer male comes out ahead of the game if he can get the females pregnant and keep out other males until his infants grow big enough to avoid being killed by the next invading male.

Morris: What about human beings? Is there any comparable kind of behavior in human societies?

DeVore: Oh yes. It's rare, but it does happen. Most often the parents will kill a newborn because there's another infant that's not yet old enough to be weaned. But the other kind occurs too. An anthropologist among the Eskimo recently reported an incident in which a man married a woman who already had a nursing infant by her former husband. The new husband decided to kill the infant, explaining matter-of-factly to the astonished anthropologist that "the child had another father."

You need go no further than the Bible to find examples of this. In Matthew is the account of King Herod's "slaughter of the innocents," and in Numbers, 31, there's the story of the Israelites' conquest of the Midianites, and Moses' instructions about treatment of the P.O.W.s: "Now kill every male dependent," he said, "and kill every woman among them who has had intercourse with a man but spare for yourselves every woman among them who has not had intercourse."

Morris: These observations may contradict the recent view of evolution that Lorenz, Ardrey, and others have put forth—that aggressiveness ultimately benefits the species as a whole—but I don't see that it puts Darwin himself in jeopardy.

DeVore: It doesn't, Scot. Darwin would have had no difficulty understanding why one male would kill another, or an infant, if this increased the male's reproductive success. But we're learning about many other kinds of behavior that could not be explained without an understanding of adaptation, including a genetic theory of inclusive fitness which Darwin couldn't have known about: essentially, any behavior that leads an individual to leave fewer offspring. Why are there sterile castes of bees and ants, for example? Why would any animal risk its life to help another? Why, when a predator approaches, would an animal give a warning cry to other animals, attracting the predator's attention to itself, rather than just fleeing quietly? Why do people adopt babies? Altruistic behavior, self-sacrifice, generosity—these bones have been sticking in the throats of evolutionary biologists for over a century now. These are some of the troublesome questions

---

A SKETCH OF IRVEN DEVORE
A MAN IN THE MIDDLE

It is hard to say whether Irven DeVore is more of an expert on people or animals. He is interested in social behavior wherever it may be found, and in understanding how it evolved. He makes no sharp distinctions between species, drawing examples from Eskimos and langur monkeys to make one point, or from American suburbanites and red-wing blackbirds to make another. At 42, he is a pioneer in the budding science called sociobiology, the study of how social systems are genetically programed in all species.

DeVore's interest in people and animals goes back a long way. He was born in Joy, Texas, population eight, the son of a Methodist minister. For a time he was a preacher himself and, as his father put it, "had authority to bury the dead and marry the afflicted." He kept animals in the back yard of the parsonage, and at one time during junior high school had about 30 different species: "great horned owls, pigeons, chickens, rabbits, chipmunks, squirrels, ducks. could leave my home and walk to the park with a string of ducklings behind me, an owl on each shoulder, and a crow circling overhead. I was called 'Nature Boy' around town because Nat 'King' Cole had a hit song, Nature Boy, that year."

The University of Texas served as a decompression chamber from

Nick Passmore

DeVore's early Methodist upbringing. He graduated with a double major in philosophy and anthropology, the one a remnant of his early intentions to become a minister, the other a reflection of his newer interests in the social sciences. He enrolled at the University of Chicago to study social anthropology, and worked with American Indians in Iowa as part of his training. Then, near the beginning of his second graduate year, two things changed his life. "The first was reading Tinbergen's Study of Instinct and his little book on ethology. The second was working with Sherwood Washburn. A few weeks after I met him I was convinced that he was the most

creative, challenging and alive anthropologist I had ever encountered." While most of his graduate-student colleagues were off studying one primitive culture or another, DeVore joined Washburn on an expedition to Kenya to study the social behavior of baboons. There was some grumbling around the department about "the proper study of mankind," but finally DeVore became the first person at the University of Chicago to receive a Ph.D. in social anthropology for a thesis on animals.

DeVore's mixed interests continued through his postgraduate years. He alternated between studies of baboons and orangutans and that have led to this new science.

Morris: And the answers...?

DeVore: The answers began to come out of a theoretical approach to behavior that was emerging independently from the study of social insects. First developed by W.D. Hamilton in 1965 and quickly picked up by other biological theorists like John Maynard Smith, G.C. Williams, Robert Trivers, E.O. Wilson, and Richard Alexander, it pointed out what Darwin could never have seen; namely, that it is misleading to focus a theory of evolution on individuals or even clusters of individuals. What you are really interested in is the *genes*, because it is only the genes that

are passed on to future generations. You've heard Samuel Butler's aphorism that the chicken is only an egg's way of making another egg. Well, in the same sense, the individual organism is just the genes' way of making more genes.

Morris: So where does Darwin stand in all this? Is he in or out?

DeVore: He's very much in, but updated with the knowledge we've gained about the mechanism of inheritance—the gene.

Morris: So the basic unit of natural selection is not survival of the fittest individuals or species, but survival of the fittest genes?

DeVore: Yes. Individuals die, and only

the gene can reproduce itself exactly. So we are ultimately concerned not with individuals, but with individual genes and their replicas in other members of the species—what we call an individual's inclusive fitness.

Morris: Why do you say inclusive?

DeVore: Because the fundamental insight about your genes is that you aren't the only one who can reproduce them. You have to include all your relatives who share genes in common with you, and consider how well *they* are reproducing, too. That's why some call it "kin-selection" to distinguish it from "individual selection."

Morris: You mean my sister can pass on some of *my* genes?

DeVore: Sure. By common descent, there is a 50 percent chance that your sister will have the same gene as yourself, and a 25 percent chance that her children will also have that gene. So natural selection would be expected to provide you with behaviors that help your relatives reproduce, and the closer the relative, the more you should be willing to help. If your sister and her husband die, their children come to live with you—or with one of the husband's relatives. It's in your own genetic interest to see that your nieces and nephews survive. Around the world, adoption by close kin is by far the most common form.

Morris: But in America and other Western cultures, many people adopt unrelated children and thereby help someone else's genes to survive. How can you explain that? Is it just a case of the parental instincts misfiring?

DeVore: Not necessarily. Misfiring surely occurs, but I can also think of several ways this behavior could be passed along by selection, and there are probably more. In rare cases an adoption may actually add to the status of the whole family, and thereby enhance the reproductive success of the real offspring. Sometimes people are paid to adopt children. In still other societies, parents may adopt a girl who grows up to be the wife or concubine of one of their sons.

Then there's the story of the couple who've tried for years to have a baby and can't. So they finally adopt a child and, lo and behold, six months later the wife is pregnant. You hear of so many families where it's happened that there must be something to it.

Morris: It's almost as if the reproductive plumbing is clogged and having a baby in the house is like a shot of Drano.

---

research on the !Kung Bushmen. He was coauthor of The Primates for the Time-Life Nature Series, and coeditor of Primate Behavior, Man the Hunter, and, most recently, Kalahari Hunter-Gatherers.

"For the first 10 years of my professional life," DeVore says, "I spent an inordinate amount of time trying to explain to colleagues whether I was a physical or social anthropologist. When I finally got an appointment at Harvard I got them to make it just 'professor of anthropology' without specifying which." In time, he became chairman of both departments.

In 1969, DeVore switched gears again. Robert Trivers, a Harvard biologist, called him one Sunday afternoon to discuss some new ideas he'd had about behavior. One was a genetic interpretation of "you scratch my back, I'll scratch yours" behavior (which was later refined into reciprocal-altruism theory); the other was a genetic approach to the question of why men and women seem to react differently when their mates commit adultery. That idea evolved into the concept of parental investment. They reasoned that because of the greater investment a human female makes in having a child, she would be more sensitive to desertion than to adultery. The human male, on the other hand, would be most disturbed by cuckoldry, because raising another man's child would delay the reproduction of his own genes. "Trivers' ideas were so far removed from the way I had thought about these things that at first I thought he was crazy. It didn't take him

long to convince me otherwise," DeVore says.

For the next two years, the DeVore kitchen table was the site of countless hours of conversation between the anthropologist and the biologist. "For a couple of months we talked virtually every night, often late into the night, giving each other examples of unusual behavior in different human cultures and animal species, trying to reconcile them with this new genetic view of behavior." For Robert Trivers' part, the collaboration with DeVore brought new insights into the variety and function of social behavior. "Irv is an acute observer of all kinds of social phenomena," Trivers told me, "in baboons, humans, dogs, anything... even lice, if he ever studied them."

The kitchen-table talks covered some of the most exciting and controversial aspects of sociobiology: the theories of reciprocal altruism and parental investment, genetic approaches to understanding sex differences, the conflicts between parents and children, and the evolutionary significance of female choice of mates. Irven DeVore, the preacher/animal-trainer who turned into an anthropologist who turned into a primatologist found himself turning again, this time into a behavioral biologist. Nature Boy had found his niche: the new science of sociobiology, a science that attempts to understand all social behavior in terms of one currency, the natural selection of the genes that most promote the individual's success in reproduction.

—Scot Morris

"Your reproductive future is vested in your grandchildren and their heirs, not in the klutz your son or daughter chose to marry."

DeVore: Scot, that's terrible! Let's call it "priming the pump" if we must. Anyway, you see how this kind of adoption could be self-perpetuating.

Morris: Natural selection would keep it going through the natural children.

DeVore: Right.

Morris: Are there any other kinds of adoption?

DeVore: Well, this is another one that I don't really have any data on. It's the classic story of the old farmer whose sons are grown, so he goes to the orphanage to take in a couple of boys to give them a home. And he does give them a good home, but he also works their tails off to build up his farm, and then when he dies most of the estate goes to his natural children. In the ethologist's terminology he has created a "helper at the nest."

Morris: But doesn't the farmer occasionally give his money to the "good" adopted son rather than to the wayward natural one?

DeVore: Occasionally, and this conflict is a typical Western plot. The profligate son is out spending all Dad's money and the ranch foreman is the "helper at the nest," who behaves like the responsible son the old man always wanted. It's one of the oldest plots in history. The most common way out of it, of course, is to have the foreman marry the rancher's daughter. The ranch still goes to the grandchildren, but through the daughter.

Morris: And if the old man dies without leaving a will, the courts see to it that the estate goes to his natural children.

DeVore: Yes, the laws for dividing up estates read as if they were written by geneticists. Adopted children are excluded, half-siblings get half as much as full-sibs, and so on. Also, if you're wealthy and getting on in years, you may tie up your estate in trust for your grand-

children. It's a common practice and very sensible, in terms of your inclusive fitness. Your reproductive future is vested in your *grandchildren* and their heirs, not in the klutz your son or daughter chose to marry.

We tend to favor our full-siblings over half-siblings—that's probably true all over the world. Throughout European history, this has led to some of the bloodiest court battles. Everyone found it despicable if you killed a brother, but if you killed a half-brother who was a pretender to the throne, well, that wasn't so bad—it was almost expected. The stepchild is worst off; he's not related to the new parent at all, and in European folklore the cruel treatment by the stepmother is a cliché—Cinderella, Hansel and Gretel.

Morris: This is beginning to sound awfully selfish. It seems to imply that the legend of the wicked stepmother may have some basis in our DNA.

DeVore: But we expect people to favor their own children, don't we? Sure, there are exceptions, and then the neighbors will say, "Isn't it nice, how they treat the adopted child just like a real one." In our society, the couple may actually treat an adopted child *better*, but notice how often other people feel called upon to comment on this. Perhaps they are reflecting deep feelings that adopted children will not always be treated equally.

Morris: You seem to be saying that we're genetically predisposed to be nice to people in proportion to how closely related they are. Doesn't that lead to all kinds of conflicts?

DeVore: Yes. At the theoretical level, all imperfectly related organisms are in conflict. You are in conflict with all organisms except an identical twin, including your own parents or children. Individuals will view a situation differently if they have different amounts

of genetic investment in it. My mother, for example, has an equal genetic investment in both me and my brother, so she wants me to help him whenever the benefit to him is greater than the cost to me. But we don't look at it that way at all. I, as Ego, have 100 percent of my own genes, of course, but I only share 50 percent of these with my brother. So for me to perform an altruistic act for my brother, I want the benefit to him to be twice, or more, what the cost is to me.

Now, it becomes even more interesting when you look at cousins, because I'm only related to my cousins by one-eighth, but my mother is related to them—her nieces and nephews—by one-fourth. So in terms of the mother's internal equation, here's what she's saying: "My son has half my genes, my niece (or nephew) has one-fourth. Therefore, any time my son can do something for my niece, which only costs him half as much as the benefit to her, I want him to do it." As my mother sees it, any time the cost/benefit ratio is 1:2, she wants me to bear the cost and help the cousin. But from *my* point of view, my cousin is only related to me by one-eighth so I shouldn't be happy about doing it unless the ratio is 1:8 or better. So my mother and I are going to disagree by 400 percent over how nice I should be to my cousins.

Morris: What do you mean by "cost" and "benefit" in this case?

DeVore: Ultimately, they're always measured in terms of reproductive success, the number of genes that a person will reproduce. The factors in that calculation will include lots of things—the amount of biological energy expended, the use of calories for one purpose rather than another, the risk to your life and limb, the depletion of your resources, and so on.

Morris: Are there simple, everyday cost/benefit decisions that you could

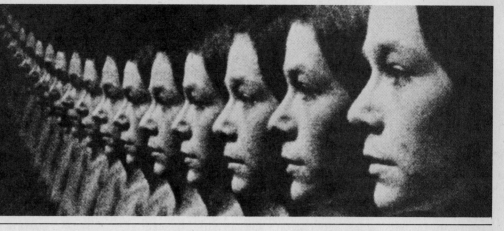

"We are left with emotions—love, friendship, gratitude—that are entirely natural expressions of our deepest biological nature."

use to illustrate what you mean?

DeVore: My family is constantly acting out such calculations. If my children are both at the dining-room table and Greg says, "Claire, I'm already late so will you go upstairs and throw my coat down to me?" Claire would be quite likely to tell him to shove off. The cost of the act is the same for either one, but the benefit goes only to Greg. But if Claire is already upstairs, she doesn't mind dropping the coat down to him; the cost to her is small and the benefit to him is great. She doesn't mind doing it, and she has been *selected* not to mind doing it. But if the cost to her is the same as it is to him, she should say, "Go get your own coat." This kind of trivial calculation enters into family relations all the time. People come to expect that certain requests are reasonable and others aren't.

Morris: When you say calculation, do you really mean a conscious strategic decision? Are we all cynical Machiavellis wandering around computing costs and benefits?

DeVore: Not at all. The reason your mouth waters when you sit down to Christmas dinner, and not when you see a plate of hay, is not because you're saying to yourself that your dinner will increase your inclusive fitness while the hay will not. It is simply that millennia of evolution have equipped you with a whole complex of motivations, inclinations, propensities, emotions—what we call proximate mechanisms—that guide your behavior appropriately. The fact that love, friendship, anger, or jealousy usually occur when they have adaptive consequences is not to belittle these emotions. The individual might even be aware of the ultimate causes that underlie his behavior, but the whole point is that while these emotions are authentic, they also serve the interests of one's genes. Various aspects

of these systems might be quite conscious; for example, the mother scheming to arrange the best marriage for her daughter. But in most instances, the sources of these emotions are beyond the limits of our ordinary awareness. What counts is that we are left with emotions—love, friendship, gratitude—that are expressions of our deepest biological nature, entirely natural and adaptive. Natural-selection theory tells us that cooperation and altruism are natural, but it also tells us competition is natural. What it says is that each will occur in conditions that are adaptive from the point of view of the genes someone bears.

Morris: You talk as if genetic strategies underlie everything we do. But surely there are cultural norms and traditions that influence us too.

DeVore: Yes, of course, but we often assume a cultural explanation is adequate when it may not be. Take a widespread cultural pattern: cousin marriage. It's the preferred form of marriage in hundreds of societies, from Pacific-island tribes to European monarchies. Even in this country you find it encouraged in the elite classes—the Boston Brahmins or the Philadelphia Main Line. But anthropologists often find that the actual number of cousin marriages, in a society that insists that this is the most preferred form, may be very small. How can such a cultural value persist generation after generation when so few persons are adhering to it?

Remember what we said earlier about the disagreement a person will have with his or her parents over how to treat a cousin? If my parents are convinced that, from the point of view of *their* inclusive fitness, I should marry my cousin to keep the family estates together, they may try to convince me that this is a long-standing cultural norm. But if I

think *I* can do better from my point of view, I will resist such a match, perhaps successfully. But once I am a parent, with a child ready to marry, the whole situation is repeated. Now, from genetic considerations, it is *I* who will be insisting that "cousin marriage is one of the deepest, most important values in our society." And this fascinating persistence of a "cultural value" can be predicted from the genetic consequences alone. It doesn't require assumptions about socialization of the child, cultural experiences, or other intervening variables that are usually worked out.

Morris: When you talk about how one person will act toward another, you use business terms—cost/benefit ratios, investments, and payoffs—that sound terribly impersonal. It seems to dehumanize the kinds of behavior that we like to call altruistic.

DeVore: That's true. But up to now I've been talking about a type of altruism—kin altruism—that is not particularly human. It runs along strict kinship lines, so it has evolved in many mammals that live in close kin groups. Among the primates and the social carnivores like wolves, lions, and hyenas, you'll sometimes see one animal make a kill and share it with other adults and their young. A cat or a mouse would never do that.

There are times when one animal will give a warning signal to others in a way that puts itself in danger. You can bet that this kind of behavior most often evolves when the warned animals are close relatives of the animal doing the warning; otherwise the behavior of giving a signal when you see a predator—rather than running like hell—would have died out rather quickly. The behavior isn't truly altruistic in the way we typically use the term; ultimately the actor is *selfishly* promoting the welfare of its own genes.

In my research on baboons I found that the male leader of a troop—the alpha male—may do 80 percent of the fighting, which altruistically protects the whole troop. But he's also doing about 80 percent of the copulating. His energy investment is in direct proportion to the probability that the young who benefit by his actions are his own. But a male who has just joined the troop is rarely willing to risk his neck for other troop members.

Morris: Most people think of altruism as one of the qualities that separates us from the beasts. How do you get away with using the word in connection with other animals?

DeVore: Biologists are very specific about what they mean by altruism, and the crucial test is always reproductive success. It's when one animal does something that benefits another animal's chances to survive and reproduce offspring, in the Darwinian sense, which has some cost to its *own* chances to survive and reproduce. The most altruistic animals of all are the social insects, such as bees and ants. A bee that stings an intruder at the hive almost always dies, sacrificing itself for the welfare of the colony. An ant may die simply to help form a bridge for other ants to walk across. You don't find this degree of altruism in other animals, including humans, except in very rare circumstances. Kamikaze pilots, for instance.

But you normally don't find altruism even in the most idealistic communes. The reason you find this altruism in these insects is because they reproduce by a sexual process called haplodiploidy, which produces a whole colony of sisters who are more closely related to each other than they would be to their own daughters. So a social insect should not object to helping her mother take care of sisters, rather than choosing to have daughters of her own.

Morris: So if she sacrifices herself for the benefit of her sisters, it ultimately leads to more reproduction of her own genes, including the genes that led to such a sacrifice in the first place.

DeVore: Exactly.

Morris: Are people really so callous and calculating when they dole out favors? Generosity isn't always reserved for kinfolks; we do nice things for friends who are not related at all.

DeVore: That's very true, and this is what I was referring to earlier when I said that there wasn't anything particularly human about directing good deeds toward one's kin. It appears that human beings, especially, have evolved another level of altruism. It's what my colleague Robert Trivers has called "reciprocal altruism." It had probably evolved by the time of the agricultural revolution, when human beings began living in long-term communities. If you have every reason to believe that you and your descendants will be living in a peasant village for many years to come, you can set some of the cost/benefit calculations aside, temporarily. You don't have to expect an immediate return benefit for any act you perform, because you can build up "credits," so to speak, in people's minds. And these may never accrue to you, but to your children, your relatives, or just to your good name. As long as everyone participates in the system it will equalize out.

Morris: You mean if I pull you out of a river to save your life, then I will expect you to do a favor for me sometime in the future?

DeVore: That's not what was on your mind at the moment you helped, of course, but I think people in any culture would think of that as a reasonable expectation. The other side of the coin is that I will feel a strong obligation to repay you in some way, or if you die in the act of saving me, I'll feel an obligation to be nice to your relatives, especially your children. It's both of these emotions—the expectation of repayment and the feeling of indebtedness—that make the system work. We have both been selected to experience those feelings because we're both descendants of people who played the game.

Morris: What about the guy who doesn't reciprocate? You go out of you way to help him and he says, "Thanks, sucker," and goes on his way.

DeVore: That, to me is the most interesting part of reciprocal-altruism theory. While it's good for most people, most of the time, to be in a reciprocal system, one can also predict that natural selection will favor a certain amount of cheating. There are likely to be situations in which it pays to take advantage of the system, to receive assistance but not to give any in return. But you expect people to evolve defenses against this, ways of identifying whether a person is likely to reciprocate or not, feelings of moral outrage that come when a cheater is detected, and the righteous indignation that can be shammed if one wants to make a public point of it. If someone cuts ahead of us in line at the theater, or pulls into a parking space that we were maneuvering for, the amount of rage we feel is all out of proportion to the act. Such feelings seem to be tapping some basic human expectation of reciprocity. In a society where mutual trust is expected, people should have evolved to detect very subtle hints that they are being lied to or cheated. To overcome that, we also evolve ways to convince others that we are sincere and won't cheat them.

Gratitude, indebtedness, contrition, supplication, revenge, apology, forgiveness, are uniquely human behaviors that apparently evolved as functional parts of the uniquely human system of reciprocal altruism.

Morris: It's almost as if we carry a genetic representation of the Golden Rule.

DeVore: It's surely no accident that every major religion teaches some variation on the Golden Rule. It makes such intuitive sense to us that it's hard to imagine a stable society existing without legal or moral codes, yet there's no reason to expect chimps or dogs or horses to live by it.

Morris: So you're saying that one kind of altruism, based along kinship lines, developed in many group-living species, including man, but that reciprocal altruism is something uniquely human.

DeVore: In a sense, yes, because conditions that favor kin altruism are very widespread, but reciprocal altruism would only evolve under special conditions. While it exists in other species, human beings have developed reciprocal altruism out of all proportion. We have been living in long-term groups in which each individual and his kinship ties and history of reciprocity are publicly known. Without such conditions, the expectation of being paid back couldn't exist, and the willingness to help nonrelatives wouldn't evolve.

Morris: But who lives in a permanent settlement any more? If you help a stranger in New York City you'll probably never see him again. Will the Good Samaritan become extinct?

DeVore: That may be where we're heading, sad to say. I think you can see this already in urban indifference, the desire not to get involved with persons you don't know.

Morris: And by your own description, doesn't even reciprocal altruism turn out to be just a more subtle and complex form of selfish behavior?

DeVore: Yes. Over the long pull, natural selection will always favor the genes of individuals who, by their behavior, have increased the reproductive success of themselves and their relatives. Obviously there are many other advantages to group life in a social species like ours, and hence many reasons why individuals will want to keep social relations as harmonious as possible. But if this were the whole story, why would every society spend such enormous energy on social and religious institutions that constantly remind everyone to remember their mutual obligations?

Morris: Has behavioral biology changed the way we look at other social species?

DeVore: Very much so. When I did my first field study of baboons, in 1959, I was very impressed by the body size, canine teeth, and complete dominance of the adult males; they were clearly in charge, and I said so. But many recent, long-term field studies of monkeys and apes lead to a very different conclusion. In fact, not only primates, but all mammalian social groups—with only two documented exceptions—turn out to be *female* groups. Elephants, lions, monkeys, and so on always seem to center around a group of close female relatives—sisters, daughters, nieces, cousins. Males pass through these groups, usually dominating things for a time and perhaps leaving their genetic imprint, but the continuing heart of the social group is entirely female. It's a true sisterhood. In many ways the two sexes lead separate careers. Among most langur monkeys, for example, the male is primarily engaged in fighting off other males; the females join to dispute territorial boundaries with the neighboring female groups. I believe that as we put primate male dominance in better perspective, we will come to see that the basic social system of these species is largely determined by the females. If they choose to be solitary, like the orangutan; monogamous, like the gibbon; in a small group, like the gorilla; or a loose community, like the chimp, there is little the males can do about it. Basically, males must adjust their reproductive strategies to whatever social setting the females and young provide.

Morris: You said there were two exceptions?

DeVore: Yes, interestingly enough, ourselves and our nearest living relative, the chimpanzee. Chimps are the only social primates where the males stay home and some (but not all) females change groups. The males also patrol and defend the territory as a group, and do almost all of the hunting.

There are many ways in which chimps seem to illustrate the primal horde that philosophers once postulated as the first stage of human society.

Morris: And what about human males?

DeVore: I have little difficulty in comparing a lot of male behavior to the competitive, status-seeking, political maneuvers common to all primates. In the broadest sense, political struggles are the heritage of all males, and inevitably many of them are losers. But human males, by language and their symbols of power, have a knack for turning the situation upside-down and assuming that what they are up to is what's *really* important.

Morris: I can see that you feel the application of behavioral biology to the human sciences is almost endless, but I know that many social scientists are hostile to this form of reasoning. They see it as a re-emergence of the same Social Darwinism they fought at the turn of the century.

DeVore: I think that is an impulsive, gut-level reaction. There really is no similarity at all to Social Darwinism, which might better have been called Social Anti-Darwinsim, because it was based on a complete and probably deliberate distortion of Darwin's concept of fitness. Social Darwinists defined fitness in a peculiar way. They looked at a social order dominated by feudal barons and captains of industry, looked upon their own gracious way of life, compared it to that of the workers in the factories, and said, "Clearly, we cannot be held accountable for exploiting our laborers, because we're the fittest and they aren't, and our very success proves that. We're just following a natural law."

From a pure Darwinian point of view they had turned the argument on its head. Darwin meant only one thing by fitness: reproductive success. So, to put a fine point on it, if the poorest, weakest, least-educated portion of the population is producing the most children who survive and reproduce again, then these people are the fittest by Darwin's definition. Arguing that the privileged class was fittest because it had all the money, was transparently self-serving and from a Darwinian point of view irrelevant. Karl Marx wasn't misled by that argument; if fact, he asked permission to dedicate Das Kapital to Darwin.

Morris: That's interesting. Aren't people charging that behavioral biology will be used as a defense of capitalism?

DeVore: That charge is based on some superficial similarities between classical economic models that purport to explain capitalism, and natural-selection models that purport to explain behavior. The similarities are not because sociobiologists have projected capitalist ideology onto nature, but because many systems, including capitalism and natural selection, share similar mechanisms. Such systems operate by feedback, for example. In capitalism, it is the return of capital for capital invested; in behavioral biology, it is the spread of successful genes. But the similarities are shallow. One of the most important differences is that classical economics doesn't account for the social constraints that limit individual choices, particularly the effects of concentrating power in one segment of society. Sociobiology is a theoretical framework from which we can begin to ask questions about the origins of systems of social constraint in which economic behavior takes place.

It is one thing to contend that individuals seek the power to manipulate their society to their own advantage. But it doesn't follow that such competition in a capitalistic society, or any other, is somehow good for the society. Evolutionary theory *does* view specifics as necessarily competitve, but there is no right or wrong about it. If you maintain that capitalism is natural and good because people are expected to compete, you are making the fallacious argument that what *is* determines what *ought* to be. Actually, it would be just as logical, if not more so, to oppose capitalism on the grounds that it exacerbates a number of predictable but undesirable human tendencies.

Morris: Surely the differences between these new theories and Social Darwinism will soon be obvious. Is that really the reason so many scientists are upset?

DeVore: Oh no. Equating sociobiology with Social Darwinism or genetic capitalism is probably just an initial, reflexive response. I think people are wary of any argument that smacks of biological reductionism, and rightly so. Having scarcely rid ourselves of the killer ape/naked ape image, we now confront a far more powerful theory on the biological basis of human behavior. I am astonished and saddened to see my colleagues dumping inclusive-fitness theory into the ragbag of naive and discredited attempts at biological reductionism.

Morris: You have also been accused of being a "genetic determinist" and lumped with Shockley and Jensen. What is that all about?

DeVore: It's basically a matter of confusion and misrepresentation. My position about the contribution of genes and environment to the phenotype, the whole individual, is essentially the same as any other scientist's. All traits, including behavioral traits, are the results of 100 percent genetic causes and 100 percent environmental causes.

Morris: Doesn't that add up to 200 percent?

DeVore: Right. The individual is the product of the interaction between his genes and his environment. Sociobiologists carry this well-known fact one step further. They maintain that natural selection will act to insure that the result of the interaction is adaptive in the very precise biological sense—the behavior contributes directly or indirectly to inclusive fitness. To call us genetic determinists is silly. We believe that the action of the environment on the genes will tend to produce an individual who is behaving adaptively. There is no similarity between the type of theorizing done by sociobiologists and that done by someone like Shockley. Sociobiology doesn't need recourse to genetic differences between individuals to explain behavioral differences. The primary thrust is to explain behavioral differences as adaptive responses to environmental differences. The major message of behavioral biology for the social sciences would be unchanged even if one assumed that all human beings were genetically uniform.

Morris: But I sense an even more immediate, personal reaction to the theory. As if it were telling people things they'd rather not hear.

DeVore: I think many scientists find themselves uncomfortable with the new interpretation of human nature that behavioral biology implies. No one, including myself, is likely to welcome a view that suggests that much of our behavior has a calculating, selfish, deceitful quality. We erect elaborate religious, social, and linguistic networks to mask underlying manipulative motivations. We often deceive ourselves in the process; self-deception is surely the first step in successfully hiding our strategies from others. If you really have deceived yourself, you can be very convincing to others. It's the phenomenon of righteous indignation. I think that Richard Nixon really believes he was unjustly accused, that he

never really did anything untoward. But the layers of deception and self-deception can often lead people to the psychiatrists to help them sort everything out.

Morris: When people play strategies, it makes them very uncomfortable to see those strategies exposed, and to talk about them.

DeVore: Undoubtedly. On the other hand, to me, it ultimately lends a certain dignity to behaviors that one might otherwise consider aberrant or animalistic. A couple at the bottom of an economic system that has as many kids as they can is playing a strategy—unconscious, I presume. Middle-class, high-investment parents may resent such behavior, but this is because they are simply playing one reproductive strategy against another.

Morris: But won't people use your theory as a justification of their resentment of welfare freeloaders?

DeVore: Depending on your view of other people, you could use it to justify many things. On one hand, you could use it to urge that we scrap the welfare system. But I would argue that if we increased welfare to a decent living wage for everyone, we might encourage people to switch to a strategy of higher investment in fewer offspring—who would then have more opportunity to escape dependence on the welfare system.

Morris: Would this only work in the United States?

DeVore: Not necessarily. All over the world demographers have noticed for the last 20 years that as soon as a country becomes industrialized, its population goes down; sometimes below-zero-population-growth rate. They've called it a secular trend, but have essentially treated it as a magical effect. They have said—correctly, by one set of criteria—that if we could just industrialize the underdeveloped countries, the population problem would be solved. Forget about trying to get them to use condoms and pills, just industrialize them.

What they have not seen is that historically, industrialization has gone hand-in-hand with the availability of higher, steady incomes but with relatively scarce jobs. This has encouraged parents to equip their children to compete for these jobs. This means parents invest heavily in a small number of children, rather than invest a bare minimum in many offspring. But that doesn't mean that in the real world, where there are serious obstacles to in-

dustrialization in many countries, that you have to tie the shift in strategy to Western-style industrialization. The important task is to open opportunities to social mobility for the poorest workers, to make the payoff greater for high-investment strategies than for large-family, low-investment strategies. The demographers have been floundering for years because they've noticed a correlation, but have no idea what's behind it. This is just one instance of the way sociobiology can revolutionize the way we think about the issues raised by social sciences.

Morris: One of the strongest arguments against sociobiology comes from those who fear that the theories will be used as the latest ideological weapon in the battle to justify the status quo, including all the injustices of race, sex, and class.

DeVore: I'm painfully aware of that, but people who argue that way are committing the old "naturalistic fallacy." They equate the study of what has been with what will be or should be. That's nonsense. It's tantamount to believing that the many studies of the rise of the Third Reich can be used as a justification for Nazi atrocities or that communists should condemn Marx because he studied capitalistic systems.

In the second place, just suppose that some of the insights from biology do indeed reveal important ideas about human beings. Do we call a halt to the studies because we find our new self-image uncomfortable? Such a reaction has dogged Darwinian theory from the beginning. The Bishop of Worcester once returned from a debate at the British Association for the Advancement of Science to explain "the terrible theories of Mr. Darwin" to his scandalized wife. On hearing the claim that we might be descended from apes, the good woman is reported to have exclaimed, "Oh dear, let us pray that is not so. But if it is so, let us hope that it does not become generally known."

I guess those who shrink from inclusive-fitness theory without understanding it have a more optimistic view of the present state of social theory than I. But it seems to me we are still very far from a powerful, integrated theory of the psyche, social behavior, and culture; indeed, I see the behavioral and social sciences stymied, floundering, searching rather desperately for better approaches to understanding human behavior.

Morris: Do you think behavioral biology is the answer? How can we hope to explain human behavior biologically when we see it shaped this way and that by the multitude of cultures in the world?

DeVore: I am interested in what's universally human more than what's culturally variable. I am intrigued by the human biogram, the enormous areas of human behavior that are the same the world over. Among the thousands of possible ways of categorizing our relatives by blood or marriage, most human societies use only one of about five basic kinship systems. That tells me something about the limits of human nature. Anthropologists always talk about crosscultural diversity, but that's the icing on the cake. The cake itself is remarkably panhuman. Different cultures turn out only minor variations on the theme of the species—human courtship, our mating systems, child care, fatherhood, the treatment of the sexes, love, jealousy, sharing. Almost everything that's importantly human—including behavorial flexibility—is universal, and developed in the context of our shared genetic background. The critics who constantly point to our cultural diversity actually help to prove the sociobiologist's point; how else can we explain the remarkable panhuman similarities across the enormous variety of cultural contexts?

Morris: I still have the feeling that your view of human nature leaves us trapped by powerful evolutionary forces over which we have no control. Do you agree? If so, what hope can we have for the future?

DeVore: I do agree, with qualifications. Natural selection is blind, amoral, merciless, without goal or direction. Almost no single species survives long. We pity the extinct dinosaurs, but they were around for more than 100 million years; our species has evolved over a scant five percent of that time. Yet, except for Divine Creation, no one can imagine life on this, or any other planet, except by evolution through natural selection. I take the current state of the world as evidence that we are no less subject to natural selection than any other species. Our growing population problem, the overexploitation of natural resources, the increasing gap between the industrial nations and the Third World, the enormous defense budgets of the wealthy nations are ample evidence that our competitive strategies are bungling things badly. Under the circumstances, I don't think we should dismiss lightly a powerful body of theory that has revealed the basis of aggression, competition, indeed, the very nature of the social system in hundreds of species from insects to birds to primates. How can we ignore, for example, the deep drive for reproductive success when making population policy? Indira Gandhi recently admitted that between 50 and 150 persons were killed while rioting against an enforced sterilization program.

Morris: But can we escape our evolutionary heritage? Can we control our own evolution?

DeVore: Well, Scot, it's obvious we won't have any control until we understand the problem. But it is clear that we can't afford to bumble along simply following the path of least resistance. I devoutly hope that we will be the one species that understands evolutionary processes enough to control our own destinies. But this certainly won't happen until we understand the psychology of our species, the proximate mechanisms we have inherited by natural selection. Only then can we begin to change the world in ways that offer hope for human survival and development.

But such understanding will require the courage to view ourselves objectively. Too often we have been told that we must believe only the best or only the worst about ourselves. That's foolish. We are not innately depraved, but we're not the best of all products of evolution, either. I do know that we will survive only if we have the courage to discover our own, human nature. Ω

Scot Morris, born in Kalamazoo, Michigan, received his M.A. and Ph.D. in clinical psychology from Southern Illinois University. He is a  free-lance writer with interests in science and humor. He has written for many publications, including Psychosources, The Sports Book, and Psychology '73/'74. Morris is a former editor of Psychology Today and is working on a book about sociobiology. For further information, read:

Dawkins, Richard. The Selfish Gene; Oxford, 1976, $8.95.

Williams, G.C. Adaptation and Natural Selection; Princeton, 1966, $12.50, paper, $3.45.

Wilson, E.O. Sociobiology: The New Synthesis; Harvard, 1975, $20.00.

Charles H. Bennett's (1903) illustration of the Aesop's fable in which the lion is elected king of the beasts.

Sociobiology:
The Aesop's Fables of Science

by Michael A. Simon

How relevant is biology to understanding human behavior?

Is there such a thing as "human nature"? If biological research can help to discover what it is, biology would prove itself extremely valuable as a means to understanding how human societies work. If we could discover what is natural for the human species, what people are really like—independent of cultural influences—we would then know what is fixed by biology and what needs to be explained as a result of our environment.

If we knew what sorts of human social patterns could be expected to remain stable, regardless of major cultural changes, and if we knew what sorts might be modifiable, we would have a powerful social tool. If we knew how deeply (or shallowly) rooted human aggressive or territorial behavior is, for instance, we might have a better idea as to whether certain social institutions could maintain peace.

Given the apparent desirability of obtaining an adequate biological conception of human nature, what have the ethologists and sociobiologists achieved thus far? Their results have been extremely meager or, at best, highly controversial. Apart from those aspects of human behavior that are trivial or uninteresting from the point of view of social science, such as eating, sleeping and excreting, there seems to be no human behavior sufficiently invariable to count as instinctive or which can be established as fully heritable. The problem is not that animal behavior has not been adequately investigated but rather that what has been discovered has not shed much light on humans. Nobel laureate Konrad Lorenz' studies of geese, wolves and rats, for example, have definitely not succeeded in demonstrating the presence of an instinctive aggressive drive in humans, nor have the studies by George Schaller on gorillas and Jane Goodall on chimpanzees, indicat-

Michael Simon, associate professor of philosophy at the University of Connecticut, is currently visiting associate professor at the State University of New York at Stony Brook. He is the author of THE MATTER OF LIFE: PHILOSOPHICAL PROBLEMS OF BIOLOGY *(Yale, 1971) and is nearing completion of a book on the philosophy of the social sciences. This article is based on a chapter from that book.*

ing a lack of aggression in the higher primates, proven that humans are *not* innately aggressive. Sociobiologists have speculated that behavior such as human altruism, social conformity, and even creativity and entrepreneurship is controlled by genetic factors, but there appears to be no direct scientific evidence for these claims.

What would we have to do to establish that a human behavioral trait is based on genetic inheritance? First, we would have to become convinced that the trait is universal. A way of discovering whether a trait is universal is to make cross-cultural comparisons. But would this show that the trait is genetically based, rather than a result of common environmental influences? E.O. Wilson, in his book, *Sociobiology* (Harvard, 1976), suggests we can make the assumption of universality, especially when the trait is found in all, or nearly all, other primates. Although he allows for the possibility that some traits that are present throughout the rest of the primates "might nevertheless have changed [i.e. mutated] during the origin of man," he does not seem to consider seriously the possibility that they may be environmentally induced in humans. The fact that Wilson says of qualities that are "distinctively ineluctably human," that "they can be safely classified as genetically based," indicates that he simply *assumes* that whatever is universal in humans must be fixed in their common genotype.

Another possibility—not ruled out by the evidence—is that what is most distinctive in humans, beyond their "distinctively ineluctably human" traits, is their adaptability, their capacity to learn what in other animals is already programmed into the genes. Humans have no instinct to eat only edible food or to drink only safe water, but must acquire these tendencies on an individual basis in order to survive. It is very likely true that whatever is universal in humans is biologically significant, in the sense of contributing to the perpetuation of the species, but it does not follow that any of these qualities must be determined genetically.

One of the features of social behavior in humans, and at least certain other animals, is its susceptibility to modification. Almost any kind of social behavior can be inhibited or provoked by means of sufficiently drastic manipulation of the creature's environment. Dogs can be domesticated, ordinarily peaceful monkeys can be trained in aggressiveness, and birds can be made to ignore their young.

We cannot justly characterize as instinctive or as rooted in human nature any kind of social behavior for which exceptions are known, unless we are prepared to explain away the exceptions as results of abnormal or unnatural conditions. We are able to justify calling eating instinctive, but only because we recognize as extraordinary the conditions under which a person will voluntarily starve to death. We could not, on the other hand, maintain that human aggression is innate, in the face of evidence indicating the existence of nonaggressive tribes.

Universal Traits

A number of cross-cultural universals have been suggested by sociobiologists. Male-male competition, for example, is something that has not been specified as absent in any culture that has been studied. Another universal seems to be the avoidance of incest by taboo. Others that have been mentioned include sexual inhibition and shyness, play, male dominance, and territoriality. There is no evidence that any of these characteristics is genetically based, but neither is there any evidence that they are not.

Let us assume, nevertheless—perhaps on the grounds that no alternative assumption is any better supported—that these patterns are genetically based and reveal certain characteristics of human nature.

Consider human *territoriality*: such behavior is not simply a matter of turning away unwanted visitors by means of a pattern of signals and responses common to the whole species. Rules regarding property are culturally determined and vary widely among different societies, and it is these variations that are ordinarily of primary interest to us. If one group is blatantly territorial and has elaborate legal institutions concerning private property, and another group is nomadic, it is hardly enlightening to insist, as Wilson seems to, that even the latter group is territorial as well, but merely in a subtle and extended sense.

And what about *altruism?* When Wilson defines an act of altruism as what occurs "when a person or animal increases the fitness of another at the expense of his own fitness," he ignores the distinction between acts that are performed with the intention and for the purpose of benefiting others and acts that *turn out* to have this effect. It is this definition that allows Wilson to label as cases of altruism, not only the behavior of dolphins in cooperating to rescue their wounded, but also the labors of sexually neuter workers among the social insects, the warning calls of small birds, the defense of a colony by the soldier caste of termites, and even the case of bees that lose both their stings and their lives when attacking a predator, thereby leaving a chemical deposit to summon additional defenders.

Wilson, in a popular presentation of this example, refers to these as "Kamikaze attacks." One would, I think, be unlikely to call an *actual* Kamikaze attack a case of altruism unless the mission were a *voluntary* one. By disregarding what makes the creature do the beneficial acts it performs—its reasons, if you will—the biologist is likely to miss the entire point of designating a piece of behavior as altruistic. We would hardly be willing to accredit a putative study of suicide that failed to distinguish it from accidental death.

One way—perhaps the only way—that human biology could influence voluntary behavior, other than by setting the limits that fix capacities, would be through the determination of certain feelings and inclinations. The idea is that what people do in any given situation depends on their natural urges, their inborn desires, and the tastes and preferences that are part of their biological makeup. All of these features are supposed to be fixed by the genotypes; the genotypes are the result of natural selection; and natural selection is based on the adaptive advantages that the genotypes confer, or did confer at an earlier time, either on the individuals who perform the actions to which these genotypes lead or on populations in which these actions occur.

What the theory—if that is what it may be called—implies is that social practices that persist do so not because they are adaptive or because of the weight of cultural tradition but because of propensities that reside in the genes. The theory also seems to require that when people opt for what their tradition and their cultural inputs encourage them to do, it is because of their innate tendencies. Not only is such a proposition unsupported by evidence, but it is entirely gratuitous, especially when other explanations, notably cultural ones, are readily available.

We do not need to invoke innate tendencies to account for racism, for example, especially when we already have available to us equally well-supported explanations in terms of social and economic factors. The problem with explanations of social practices in terms of innate preferences and propensities is that, whenever one is confronted with a counterinstance, either one must suppose that the tendency can be overridden, in which case the factor in question is too weak to have explanatory force, or else one must make an *ad hoc* postulation of a genetic difference in order to account for the exception.

Incest Taboo

These considerations apply to the attempt to provide a biological explanation of the apparently ubiquitous *incest* taboo. There is evidence, albeit indirect, that the avoidance of the dangers of excess homozygosity—physical and mental defects—might very well be the basis of the taboo, but this, the giving of a biological reason, would not show that incest avoidance has a genetic basis. At the very least, what would be needed is knowledge of a biological mechanism, one that works through natural preferences, to make individuals not *want* to mate with kin. As the wags have pointed out, if incest avoidance were instinctive, incest would not have to be illegal.

Wilson has suggested that the way a cultural tradition may become established is by means of social reinforcement of natural tendencies that have been selected for the adaptive advantages they confer. With regard to the incest taboo, a mechanism that has been supposed to operate involves what has been called "the precluding of bonds": kinship relationships such as between fathers and daughters, mothers and son, and brothers and sisters seem to exclude the possible formation of other types of bonds.

Evidence cited for this hypothesis include studies in Israeli kibbutzim, where it was found that, among unrelated members of the same kibbutz peer group who had been together since birth, there were no recorded instances of heterosexual activity, despite the absence of formal or informal pressure, and that all of the marriages that occurred were with persons outside the kibbutz. The inference drawn is that social prohibitions on incest may have arisen as a result of evolved natural inhibitions, inhibitions that have persisted because those who have them tend to leave a larger number of fertile offspring than do those who lack them.

The problem with this model—apart from the fact that it lacks direct empirical support—is that these preferences, since they are known to be overridable, are too weak to provide any significant explanatory power. As many anthropological studies have shown, human beings are capable of internalizing a number of quite different norms. Innate preferences of the sort invoked are clearly not strong enough to prevent some tribes from drawing the incest line between cross-cousin and parallel-cousin marriages, for example. It is very tempting to try to derive norms from natural tendencies; but it is impossible to say which norms *must* be so derived. A norm is something that governs *voluntary* behavior, and there is no norm that is not capable of being replaced by a substitute.

Or consider the matter of the *sexual division of labor*. As Wilson puts it, "women and children remain in the residential area while the men forage for game or its symbolic equivalent in the form of barter of money." Wilson has suggested that the basis for this division of labor, which he takes as revealing a genetic bias, may lie in the fact that males are, on the average, demonstrably more aggressive than females from the beginnings of social play in infan-

cy, and that they tend to show less verbal and greater mathematical ability.

These facts, if true, may help to explain why some people dominate others, and also why certain professions have a disproportionate number of men in them. They do not explain the extent to which the social patterns that are actually observed reveal polarizations that are much more pronounced than the essentially statistical findings would dictate. A basketball team may dominate another team whose members are on the average shorter than those of the first team, but only because each team is organized as a unity for the sake of demonstrating its collective dominance. You cannot derive a culture of male/female dominance, or deduce a strict or nearly strict sexual division of labor, from a set of statistical differences between classes of males and females.

Reliance on Analogy
What the biologist who seeks a basis for understanding human social behavior in the study of nonhuman animals is trying to show is that some of what we know about animals is also true of human beings. Since human behavioral traits, unlike anatomical features, cannot, for the most part, be established as homologous—based on common phylogenetic descent—the ethologist is forced to rely on analogy. But analogies which concern patterns of human social behavior and similar displays among animals are unconvincing. The behavior typically is either disanalogous or not known to be analogous just at the point where analogy is the most crucial: the way the behavior is mediated. If behavior that is rigidly determined by a specific releaser that triggers off an internal mechanism has, as its counterpart in human beings, behavior that is subject to nothing like such rigid causal determination, we are not licensed to infer anything whatever concerning the biological basis of the behavior in question.

If what is true of animal societies is also true of human societies, this can be established only by studying human beings on their own. We cannot *assume* that animals in different species will behave in similar ways under similar circumstances, nor can we assume that behavior that is common to two or more species and has a genetic basis in one is equally heritable in the others. We simply do not know what to make of our observations of animals, nor are we able to show these data to be relevant to a scientific understanding of the human species. There is not enough force in any conclusion that could be reached regarding nonhuman animals to give its extension to human beings a significantly higher likelihood of being true than could be given to the proposition that people are exceptions.

Because discoveries about the way animals behave are often so *interesting*, it is tempting to believe that there must be something that we can learn about humans as a result of these studies. One can readily be impressed by seeing the way monkeys or wolves avoid destructive intraspecies fighting by means of dominance hierarchies, or by observing the effects of crowding on social harmony among rats and hippopotamuses. By telling us a lot about animals that we did not know, it seems that animal behaviorists can help us to discover that we are more like animals than we thought we were.

Aesop's Fables

Nothing that is a possible source of ideas deserves to be summarily dismissed, of course, and animal behavior studies may be a particularly rich source. They may be a no better source of ideas about human behavior than might be afforded by travel to foreign lands or by reading imaginative fiction. I suspect that what makes animal societies a particularly attractive source is not so much the wealth of illustrations they afford as is the unsupported notion that what is true of animals and can be applied to humans is likely to be true of them.

Citing ethological discoveries in the context of considering human social behavior has an effect that is largely rhetorical. Like Aesop's fables, facts about the ways animals behave are often thought to provide us with "lessons" as to how we ourselves might behave, quite apart from whether or not they reveal the way we actually do behave. Specific findings

with regard to animals, like stories or myths, neither establish nor refute assertions concerning what human behavior is or ought to be; the most they can do is serve to counter other claims that have been made based on other examples. Finding that higher primates seem to lack intraspecies aggression does not lead to any reliable conclusion concerning humans, but it may serve as an antidote to the claim, based on analogies between humans and certain animals that do fight, that human beings are innately given to fighting. The popularity of books by Konrad Lorenz, Desmond Morris, and Robert Ardrey is mainly due to these rhetorical effects.

There is in these accounts a definite undercurrent that suggests that people do what they do, not for reasons or as a result of conditions that are brought about by other people or by cultural influences, but because of internal forces that we have all inherited from our remote animal ancestors and which cannot easily be resisted. Thus Lorenz suggests that the reason "why reasonable beings . . . . behave so unreasonably," is that human social behavior "is still subject to all the laws prevailing in all phylogenetically adapted instinctive behavior." The lesson being taught is that we ought to resign ourselves to accepting a non-rational basis to our social behavior.

Scientific inference need not be regarded as the sole vehicle of truth. Myths and fables, as well as true stories

about other people and other animals, often are repositories of truths of a very important sort. What I deny is that what can be learned about people from observing animals has any more credibility, is any more proven by evidence, than are the insights of Aesop's fables.

Consider an example from the work of Lorenz. One of the things that he found in studying pair-formation in ravens is that it is the sex of a newly introduced prospective sexual partner that determines whether an individual that has been raised in isolation will act like a male or a female: regardless of its own biological sex, the isolated bird will adopt the courting behavior appropriate to the sex opposite to that of the introduced bird. Lorenz' finding offers no basis for inference concerning a potentially analogous human situation—any suggestiveness is merely implicit, that being part of the rhetorical effect of the example—though it could very well express something that is true of human beings. The suggestion is not altogether dissimilar to one that is found in D. H. Lawrence's story, "The Fox," in which the role that a young woman has assumed in a homosexual relationship is seen abruptly to change from that of a male to that of a female when a young man enters the scene. The writer and the ethologist are both in the position of being able to point out, but not to prove, something significant about the way the human creature behaves.   □

9

Evolution, Altruism, and Reinforcement

by Dennis Krebs and Mark Holder

Most of us have engaged in arguments about altruism. These arguments follow a predictable pattern. One person takes the position that humans are essentially selfish, and provides supporting examples. The other person disagrees, and cites examples of human benevolence. Soldiers who smother grenades with their own bodies to save their buddies is a favorite. Germans who risked their lives to save Jews during the Second World War, the Good Samaritan, and philanthropists such as Albert Schweitzer and Mother Theresa are others.

Of course, examples of human unselfishness do not convince the more cynical, who respond by demonstrating how acts that appear to be altruistic could be determined by selfish forces: the soldier may not have believed that the grenade would go off; he may have wanted to commit suicide; he may have gone crazy; or he may have been trying for sick leave. "Scratch an altruist," so the saying goes, "and you will see a hypocrite bleed." Philosophers such as Hobbes, Machiavelli, and Nietzsche have supplied rich descriptions of the ingenious devices fashioned by selfish people to disguise their self-interest.

Arguments about altruism usually end up unresolved. The problem is that they are based on external observations of behavior rather than information about the internal forces that motivate it—on *how* a person acts, rather than *why*. In order to determine whether an act is altruistic, we must discover what forces determined it. Why did the soldier smother the grenade? Why did the boy scout help the old lady? One obvious place to search for such explanations is in theories of behavior.

At first glance what must be considered the two most influential theories of behavior appear to suggest that people are essentially selfish. Darwin's theory of evolution assumes that behaviors that enhance the fitness of individuals are naturally selected, and behaviors that do not become extinct. If altruism is defined as behavior that enhances another's fitness at some cost to one's own, it would appear to be doomed to extinction

through natural selection. Thus, at a basic biological level, all surviving species, humans included, ought to be selfish by nature.

But it could be argued that humans differ from other animals because they *learn* to behave altruistically. Humans are not locked into biological evolution like other animals. The idea that the positive influences of culture override the negative influences of nature is a popular one. This "original sin" type of assumption pervades many religions and most theories of socialization. Psychoanalysis is a clear case in point. Donald Campbell endorsed it recently in his presidential address to the American Psychological Association:

> Social evolution has had to counter individual selfish tendencies which biological evolution has continued to select as a result of . . . genetic competition (Campbell, 1975, p. 1115).

However, there is a significant problem with the idea that people can be taught to behave altruistically. The central principle of learning theory, the principle of reinforcement, dictates that only acts followed by positive reinforcement or the omission of negative reinforcement—that is, acts that result in net gains—are perpetuated. By most definitions, there can be no gain for the self in altruism; or, at least, the costs of the act (e.g., smothering a grenade) outweigh its gains. Therefore, it would seem that the learning of altruism in individuals violates the principle of reinforcement in much the same way that the evolution of altruism in a species violates the principle of natural selection.

For those who believe in altruism, the phenomenon presents a major challenge to the principles of natural selection and reinforcement. To these people, the onus is on advocates of evolutionary and reinforcement theory to explain how altruism could evolve and how it could be learned. Interestingly, Darwin (1859) found himself in this camp. Commenting on the extreme altruism displayed by social insects, Darwin wrote that it presented "one special difficulty, which at first appeared to me insuperable, and actually fatal to my whole theory" (p. 236). Darwin came up with an explanation for such altruism—one that left his theory intact. However, in ensuing years his explanation was

EVOLUTION, ALTRUISM, AND REINFORCEMENT, by Dennis Krebs and Mark Holder, was published as an original essay, 1981. Reprinted by permission.

called into question, again raising the problem of explaining altruism. This problem remained until the early 1960s when another biologist, W. D. Hamilton, offered another type of solution. The implications of Hamilton's ideas proved revolutionary to many and were instrumental in launching the new, controversial field of sociobiology. Let us examine the problem of altruism in Darwinian theory. Then we will return to the problem of the principle of reinforcement.

ALTRUISM AND EVOLUTION

Group Selection. One way to account for the evolution of altruism is to suggest that altruism enhances the fitness of *groups* of individuals. For example, if one group contained individuals who were willing to sacrifice their lives to save everyone else, and another group did not, more individuals in the altruistic group than in the nonaltruistic group might survive. Darwin attempted to explain self-sacrificial helping in this manner. He hypothesized that social dispositions for the good of the community had evolved in humans. These dispositions, strengthened by habit and group encouragement, resulted in cooperation.

Many years later a Scottish ethologist, Wynne-Edwards, published a major elaboration of Darwin's solution to the problem that altruism presented to the theory of evolution. Wynne-Edwards argued that natural selection operated at the group level, not just at the individual level. He suggested that if maximizing one's own reproductive success was the only motivating force, then organisms would selfishly exploit as many natural resources as possible to attain this goal. This strategy would deplete the limited vital resources, such as food, resulting in the starvation and, therefore, the extinction of the selfish populations. Thus, he inferred, in order to prevail, a species must evolve unselfish, cooperative dispositions to protect and conserve its resources.

There is at least one crucial flaw in Wynne-Edwards theory of "group selection." Imagine a cooperative society that distributed its resources equally. Inevitably, through genetic variation some of the individuals within the society would possess more selfish dispositions than others. These individuals would have an advantage over the more altruistic individuals because they would selfishly use more resources, sacrifice less, and, therefore, end up with a better chance of surviving and producing offspring. Through this process, more and more selfish individuals would evolve in succeeding generations, eventually superseding the altruists (leading, perhaps, to the destruction of the group). Today, it is generally accepted among biologists that the conditions that would need to prevail in order to enable the between-group benefits of altruism to surpass the within-group benefits of selfishness are exceedingly rare.

Cooperation. Although Darwin's theory is popularly portrayed as implying that all individuals single-mindedly pursue their own interests, competing with one another "red in tooth and claw," there is nothing in his theory that precludes the evolution of non-altruistic helping behaviors. In fact, it is quite clear that animals of many species help one another. Explaining many, if not most, of these acts of helping presents no problem at all for Darwinian theory, because in many situations the most effective means for an individual to enhance his or her fitness is through helping others. Indeed, this is the essence of behaviors commonly covered by the concept of cooperation. Cooperation customarily involves helping others as a necessary condition of helping yourself. Two or more small animals who possess the dispositions to cooperate may fend off a larger predator or kill a larger prey, while those with more individualistic dispositions perish. Considering the relative physical vulnerability of the human species, it is easy to see that the capacity to cooperate would be particularly adaptive.

Reciprocity. Personal benefits for engaging in cooperative behavior do not have to be realized immediately. A mathematical model, developed by Robert Trivers, shows how helping behaviors that involve relatively small costs would be selected for if they eventually resulted in a substantial benefit. This concept is illustrated by the idiom, "I'll scratch your back if you'll scratch mine," where the benefits of being scratched are greater than the cost of scratching. This "reciprocal altruism" can be clearly seen in humans remembering and paying off debts, and forming complex social contracts.

Groups that depend on cooperation or "reciprocal altruism" must control selfish individuals who attempt to receive the benefits of the systems without paying the cost. These individuals, called "cheaters," can be controlled by the evolution of strategies such as helping only those individuals who have helped you or whom you have seen help others, and by attaching sanctions to individuals' reputations.

Though cooperation and "reciprocal altruism" are helping behaviors, they do not meet the criterion of altruism based on evolutionary theory. These behaviors are initiated only if the potential overall benefits to one's own fitness outweigh the costs. Thus, they do not show how altruistic behavior, behavior that enhances another's fitness while reducing one's own, could have an adaptive advantage.

Kin Selection. The solution to the problem of altruism in evolutionary theory that has gained credence and proven most influential was introduced by W. D. Hamilton in 1964. Whereas Darwin had focused on individual selection, and Wynne-Edwards on group selection, Hamilton focused on *kin selection*.

The basic idea behind kin selection is that natural selection will favor any strategy that maximizes the absolute number of an individual's *genes* in future generations. Although the most straightforward way of accomplishing this is through individual survival and the propagation of offspring, this is not the only means. Because some of the genetic makeup of your relatives and their offspring is common to you, you can increase the probability of these common genes prevailing by helping these individuals. In some situations, such as, for example, when an individual cannot reproduce, helping relatives is the only way to increase his or her genetic representation in succeeding generations. It is not, therefore, just an individual's fitness that is important but also the fitness of all those who share that individual's genes: his or her *inclusive fitness*.

The unusual genetic composition of ants nicely illustrates inclusive fitness. Female workers share three-quarters of their genes with their sisters. Workers tend to be sterile for most of their lives, but those who reproduce share only one-half of their genes with their offspring, as do most species, including our own. The most efficient way for a worker ant to propagate her genes is to help ensure the survival of her potentially fertile sisters, rather than producing her own offspring. And this is exactly what the ants do. They are among the most altruistic of all species.

Of course, human females do not share three-quarters of their genes with their sisters, but this is not the point. They also do not behave more altruistically toward them than they do toward their own offspring. The point is that the refinements in the principle of natural selection derived from the behavior of ants have implications for human altruism. Humans, as well as all other animals, will be favored by natural selection for employing behaviors that maximize their inclusive fitness. Though these behaviors are often directed at propagating their own genes directly, and therefore are selfish behaviors, dispositions to behave altruistically toward others can evolve if the effect is to increase the proportion of an individual's altruistic genes in succeeding generations carried by those who share them—that is, his or her relatives.

Inclusive fitness not only explains how altruism may have evolved, but it predicts who will be altruistic to whom and to what degree. To understand these predictions, keep in mind that there is a whole continuum of relatedness ranging from virtually 100 percent common genes between identical twins to almost 0 percent common genes between you and a fourth cousin or any nonrelative. In general, the more closely related two

people are, the more altruistically they should behave toward each other. The model predicts that parents will help their children more than their neighbors' children, and that siblings will help each other more than they will help their cousins. Though examples supporting these particular predictions are easily found, parents typically are more altruistic toward their children than vice versa, even though they each share 50 percent of their children's genes. Strictly speaking, it is not just the degree of relatedness that is important but also the expectation that the relative will reproduce. By the time children are able to help their parents in any appreciable way, their parents are unlikely to continue reproducing. The expectation of future reproduction is even less for grandparents. Therefore, because one's siblings and offspring are more likely to reproduce than one's parents and grandparents, the give-and-take of altruism will not be mutual.

Though kin selection supplies an explanation for altruistic dispositions toward relatives, it does not, at least directly, account for altruism directed at non-relatives—a phenomenon that is rare in the animal kingdom but apparently is characteristic of humans. Although no one has offered a complete explanation of how the disposition to behave altruistically toward nonrelatives could evolve in humans, two related possibilities have been suggested. First, early in their history, humans are believed to have lived in groups of relatives. Thus, behaving altruistically toward the group may have increased the inclusive fitness of all individuals. Second, characteristics of people such as familiarity, proximity, and physical similarity that are associated with their degree of relatedness may elicit altruistic behavior because it used to be a more dependable index of relatedness than it is now. Social psychological research has shown that people are usually more willing to help people who possess these characteristics than those who do not.

When Darwin developed his theory of evolution, he did not know about genetic transmission. Recognizing that it is genes, not individuals, that evolve helps supply one solution to the paradox of altruism. Although genes are always "selfish"—that is, those that prevail in the process of evolution have propagated themselves—individuals may behave altruistically in the service of their "selfish" genes. Kin selection supplies a means through which altruistic dispositions could have evolved in individuals.

In summary, the concept of inclusive fitness supplies at least a partial solution to the problem of altruism in evolutionary theory. The matter is important because it concerns the roots of human nature—our basic biological dispositions. However, to many people altruism involves more than the sacrifice of reproductive fitness, and to speak of altruism in ants is ridiculous. To such people, altruism is a uniquely human response, and it is acquired through learning.

THE PARADOX OF ALTRUISM IN LEARNING THEORY

The most popular definitions of altruism characterize it as behavior that serves to enhance the pleasure of others at some cost to the self. But how, if the consequences of a behavior determine whether or not it is learned, can people learn to behave altruistically? If the costs of altruistic behaviors outweigh their rewards, these behaviors should extinguish.

Two centuries ago, the philosophers Adam Smith and David Hume suggested one solution to this paradox of altruism. In recent years, contemporary psychologists have rediscovered and refined this solution. It goes like this: humans are born with (or acquire after birth) the disposition to *empathize* with others—to feel good when others feel good, and to feel badly when they feel badly. When a person who is empathizing with another behaves altruistically and thereby enhances the other's emotional state, the helper also will feel better. Thus, the altruistic behavior will be reinforced through the vicariously experienced changes in the way the other feels. This behavior can be considered altruistic for two reasons: (1) because the primary goal of the behavior is to make someone else feel better, and (2) because the altruist experiences pleasure or reinforcement by identifying with another.

In recent years, psychologists have conducted a number of interesting investigations on empathy and its relationship with altruism. Evidence that humans experience empathy has come from a number of sources. Some investigators have found that people tend to move their lips when watching stutterers and to blink their eyes when watching eye-blinkers. Other investigators have found that young children and adults emit strong emotional responses and display empathic facial expressions while watching movies. Still other psychologists have found that newborn infants cry when they hear other infants cry. Although this crying could reflect an adverse reaction to noise, there is apparently something uniquely upsetting about signs of distress in another: newborn infants cry much less to equally loud noises and even computer-simulated crying.

In 1975 one of the present writers conducted a study that tested the idea that empathic emotional responses mediate altruistic behavior. Krebs (1975) induced each of the members of one group of subjects to believe that they were similar to another person who appeared to experience pain and pleasure. A second group believed that they were dissimilar. Krebs monitored psychophysiological reactions of the subjects such as heart rate and

blood pressure as they observed the other person. He found that the subjects who believed they were similar to the other reported identifying with him to a greater extent than other subjects, and that they expressed stronger emotional reactions to signs that the person with whom they were identifying was experiencing pain and pleasure. Finally, making the connection between empathy and altruism, Krebs found that the subjects who had experienced the most empathy also volunteered to give the person they had empathized with the most help (at expense to themselves) when given a chance.

This experiment supplies quite strong evidence that people who react most strongly to the pains and pleasures of others are most prone to help them. But, you might argue, the helping was not altruistic because its goal was to make the *observer* feel better. Subsequent experiments have investigated this possibility. Two researchers, C. D. Bateson and J. S. Coke (1981) have distinguished between the egoistic "personal distress" component of vicarious emotional arousal (made up of emotions such as shock, alarm, disgust, and fear) and the altruistic "empathic concern" component (made up of emotions such as compassion, concern, warmth, and softheartedness). In a number of experiments, they have found that while people may help others in order to reduce personal distress, they also help others out of empathic concern. For example, in one study they led subjects to believe that the personal distress they experienced while watching a person suffer was caused by a drug, but that their empathic concern was caused by the suffering of the other. They found that these subjects volunteered to help the suffering person. Because it did not make sense for the subjects to assume that helping the other would relieve their personal distress, the investigators concluded that the goal of the behavior was to relieve the suffering of the other and, therefore, that it was altruistic.

We have considered the challenge of altruism to two grand theories of behavior. Although one theory is biological and the other psychological—although one concerns heredity and the other concerns environment or culture—it is interesting to note the parallels between the two positions. Both the principle of natural selection and the principle of reinforcement assume that behavior is determined by its consequences—in the former case to the genes and in the latter case to a person's hedonic state. Both theories explain behavior in terms of its adaptiveness. In both theories the environment exerts a selective influence on the development of behaviors. At one level, both theories are circular, or tautological. Evolutionary theory asserts that characteristics will survive if they are adaptive, and we know that they are adaptive because they have survived. Similarly, the principle of reinforcement asserts that the probability of a behavior occurring is changed by a reinforcing event, and we know when an event is reinforcing because it has caused a change in the probability of a behavior. And, finally, the explanations for altruism offered by each theory imply that individuals are far more at one with each other than they usually assume; people overlap with one another genetically because they possess replicas of identical genes, and they overlap with one another emotionally because they empathize.

The view that we have advanced here indicates that biology and culture may not always be in opposition, as those who subscribe to "original sin" assumptions assume. Basic biological dispositions toward altruism may have evolved through the evolution of empathy. Although humans are able to control their destinies in a manner unparalleled in the animal kingdom, they bear the biological legacy of millions of years of evolution. The thrust of our analysis is that while humans may inherit selfish and aggressive instincts, they are more than civilized "killer apes." Through genetic and emotional sharing, they also can be altruistic.

References

Bateson, C. D., and Coke, J. S. Empathic motivation for helping: egoistic or altruistic. In P. Rushton and R. M. Sorrentino (Eds.) *Altruism and Helping Behavior II*. Hillsdale, N. J.: Erlbaum, 1981.

Campbell, P. On the conflicts between biological and social evolution and between psychology and moral tradition. *American Psychologist*, 1975, *30*, 1103–1120.

Darwin, C. *On the origin of species by means of natural selection, or the preservation of favored races in the struggle for life*. London: Murray, 1859.

Krebs, D. Empathy and altruism. *Journal of Personality and Social Psychology*, 1975, *32*, 1134–1146.

III. Sexual Identity and Sex Roles

The feeling that we are male or female is an integral part of our identity. But how do we acquire this feeling? Are we born with it, or do we learn it as we develop? Milton Diamond ("Sexual Identity and Sex Roles") considers the evidence on both sides of the issue and concludes that while both heredity and environment contribute to this feeling, biological factors are more important than many people think.

Considering yourself male or female has strong implications for how you behave—the sex role you adopt. Do males behave differently than females in all societies? Is the form of sex-typed behaviors the same everywhere? What causes the sex differences that do occur? Are dispositions to behave in masculine or feminine ways inherited, or are they acquired through learning? These are the central questions that guide this section.

Males and females are different. Anyone who attempts to deny this simple fact is foolish. However, it is far from clear exactly how males and females differ, and whether the differences that exist are results primarily of biological or of cultural factors. From the perspective of evolution, it makes sense for males and females to have specialized in different activities and, thus, to have developed different characteristics. One of the most essential differences between the sexes is that women bear children. Pregnancy and childbearing make women less mobile and more vulnerable than men. For this and perhaps other reasons males came to specialize in hunting and females in gathering and childrearing. This, according to many experts, is the primary reason why males and females are different. Boyce Rensberger ("Our Sexual Origins") suggests that there is a high correlation between bringing home the meat and status in preliterate societies (although the reasons for this association remain somewhat unclear). Rensberger goes on to speculate about why humans have become such a sexually oriented species, and how human sexuality ties in with pairbonding, foodsharing, childrearing, and even bipedalism!

Quite a different tack is taken by the anthropologist Margaret Mead. In her early book, *Sex and Temperament* (1935), Mead attempts to show that sex roles are variable across culture and, therefore, acquired through learning. Paula Stern carries this argument even further in "The Womanly Image: Character Assassination Through the Ages," leaving little doubt that however biologically based the differences between the sexes may be, women have been systematically subjugated in our society. And it is not only men who subjugate women. Women are also guilty (see article 41 in Part VIII).

10

Sexual Identity and Sex Roles

by Milton Diamond

The recent prominence of people like Dr. Renée Richards and author Jan Morris and movies like "Dog Day Afternoon" have brought to public attention a situation that might seem bizarre to most people—an individual is born and raised as a male, yet considers himself to be a female; or the individual may have been born and raised a female, yet consider herself to be male. Such individuals are transsexuals.

How can anyone grow up in our American society as a male and, as if in disregard of "all that is holy," effect such a complete switch in sexual identity and gender role? Even if it is possible to make the switch, why would one want to? In our society isn't it better to be a male physician, male writer, or male whatever than to be a female? Understanding the motivation behind such changes has developed only in the last two dozen years. While these cases are intriguing because of their novelty, the underlying question of much broader interest is, How does anyone come to "know" he or she is male or female?

One of the first tasks of those interested in the issues is to agree on definitions of terms. An individual's *sex*—male or female—is determined by the presence of testes or ovaries. Therefore, sex is biological and fixed. *Sexual identity* refers to the private and personal *assessment* of one's sex; in effect, the individual says inwardly, "I am a male," or "I am a female."

Milton Diamond is professor of reproductive biology at the University of Hawaii School of Medicine and research professor of psychiatry and behavioral science at the State University of New York at Stony Brook. He is the author of Perspectives in Reproduction and Sexual Behavior.

SEXUAL IDENTITY AND SEX ROLES, by Milton Diamond. This article first appeared in THE HUMANIST, March/April 1978, and is reprinted by permission.

This assessment may or may not be in concert with the gonads one possesses. A person's *gender* or *gender identity* is the life style that he or she chooses and projects to the public. *Gender roles* for males and females are those appropriate sex-related behavior patterns accepted by society. Patterns that are most often displayed by men are considered *masculine*, and those that are most often displayed by women are considered *feminine*. The interrelationship of these three factors assumes more complexity when one restates the original question: What effect does society's institutionalizing of a gender role have on a person's sexual identity, and vice versa? How does society's ordering or structuring of gender roles affect our sexual identity, and vice versa?

Research originally considered significant in understanding sexual identity was the study of hermaphrodites and pseudohermaphrodites. These individuals were treated in clinics for various reproductive, fertility, endocrine, and genetic problems. According to researchers John Money, Joan G. Hampson, and John L. Hampson, despite disparities among an individual's genetic sex, hormonal sex, internal and external genitalia, and rearing, in the vast majority of cases, the individual assumed the gender role consistent with the sex of rearing. They said:

> In the light of hermaphroditic evidence, it is no longer possible to attribute psychologic maleness or femaleness to chromosomal, gonadal, or hormonal origins, nor to morphological sex differences of either the internal or external genitalia. . . . From the sum total of hermaphroditic evidence, the conclusion that emerges is that sexual behavior and orientation as male or female does not have an innate, instinctive basis. In place of a theory of instinctive masculinity or femininity which is innate, the evidence of hermaphroditism lends support to a conception that psychologically, sexuality is undifferentiated at birth and that it becomes differentiated as masculine or feminine in the course of the various experiences of growing up.—"An Examination of Some Basic Sexual Concepts: The Evidence of Human Hermaphroditism," (*Bulletin*, Johns Hopkins Hospital, 97: 301-309.)

During the period between 1955 and 1965, this view represented the prevailing opinion of most American clinicians and psychologists—that is, that newborns were psychosexually neutral at birth and developed their sexual identity and behaviors through learning and modeling influences.

During this same period, two other sets of laboratory experiments were conducted that had wide-ranging repercussions. In the laboratories of William C. Young and his collaborators, experiments proved conclusively that the adult sexual behavior of animals could be programmed (organized) simply by treating them with hormones prenatally. Females subjected to male hormones before birth by injections given to the mother did not show typical female behaviors. Instead, they displayed male-like sexual activities. The extent of this atypical adult behavior could be regulated by the amount of hormone, the timing, and the duration of the prenatal treatment. (The mothers showed no effects from the injections.)

The second series of experiments from several laboratories demonstrated that the nervous systems of animals are programmed to be male or female essentially from birth, particularly in regard to sexual behavior and reproduction. It is relatively simple to tamper with this system. The hypothalamus can "switch effective sex" from a single hormone injection. For example, a female given an injection of male hormone the first week of her life never would ovulate or exhibit typical sexual receptivity.

The implication of these laboratory experiments—that animals indeed come into the world sexually programmed—was obviously at odds with the clinical observations mentioned above. There were at least two attempts to reconcile the disparate reports: an article by this writer in the *Quarterly Review of Biology* in 1965, and *The Development of Sex Differences*, edited by Eleanor Maccoby, in 1966. These works pulled together material from different studies and disciplines in an attempt to understand the nature and development of sexual behavior. My article and subsequent work did several things simultaneously. First, they challenged the prevailing opinion on psychosexual development by placing the biological studies on animals into human perspective and showing them on an evolutionary continuum. All other species are sexually programmed, the extent varying with the species. Humans may be the least programmed, but there is no evidence for believing there is a complete divestiture of evolution in this regard. Second, they reviewed the rapidly accumulating research on animals, showing how relatively simple it is to alter adult sexual behavior patterns permanently through prenatal treatment. Third, they showed that the conclusions drawn from the work with hermaphrodites and pseudohermaphrodites were hasty, since these individuals are particularly flexible and liable to postnatal experiences because of their biological abnormalities. Fourth, and most crucial, they reported that many clinical cases revealed individuals who had emerged with sexual identities and behaviors completely at odds with their upbringing. The sexually-neutral-at-birth theory was revised. As I stated in the article:

> Primarily owing to prenatal genetic and hormonal influences, human beings are definitely predisposed at birth to a male or female gender orientation. Sexual behavior of an individual and thus gender role are not neutral and without initial direction at birth. . . . We are dealing with an interaction of genetics and experience; the relative contribution of each, however, may vary with the particular individual concerned. . . . It is the genetic heritage of an individual which predisposes him to react in a particular manner so that the learning of a gender role can occur.

This was probably the first major statement to claim that sexuality was significantly dependent upon biological heritage. This inherent sexuality was seen as a built-in "bias" that determined how the individual interacted with the environment. This was not a theory that denied the effects of learning or experience, but rather one that suggested how this interaction most probably was organized. In this article, I also gave support to the clinical aspect by recommending that individuals, particularly transsexuals and hermaphrodites, be allowed to select their own gender roles rather than have them imposed by others.

The Maccoby book had a greater influence in the social sciences. Theories of psychological sexual development, including "social learning" and "role-modeling," were presented. In addition, a relatively new theory was offered by Lawrence Kohlberg:

> Sexual development starts directly with neither biology nor culture, but with cognition . . . by the child's cognitive organization of his social world along sex-role dimensions. . . . This patterning of sex-role attitudes is essentially "cognitive" in that it is rooted in the child's concepts of physical things—the bodies of himself and others—concepts which he relates in turn to a social order that makes functional use of sex categories in quite culturally universal ways.

With this cognitive-theory base, learning is influenced by reward in the following way. The child first somehow conceives of himself as a boy or girl and internally says to himself something like this: "I am a boy; therefore I want to do boys' things, and doing them is rewarding." The inner identity of the boy determines what will be rewarding. Research findings provided support for this theory. For example,

---

"Experiments from several laboratories demonstrated that the nervous systems of animals are programmed to be male or female essentially from birth, particularly in regard to sexual behavior and reproduction. It is relatively simple to tamper with this system."

---

kindergarten children were found to hold strongly to their "masculine" or "feminine" values regardless of punishment or reward. These values actually help determine the worth of situational rewards. With these findings, the cognitive theory of identity is seen as a cause, rather than as a product, of social learning and modeling.

If one were to ask rhetorically where a child's self-concept comes from, since all behavior must somehow be rooted in the nervous system the answer would have to be, "Biological heritage." Is it a chicken-and-egg puzzle? I don't think so. We have a good idea where we humans come from. We have evolved from other species in which mammalian biology preceded the human socialization processes. But invariably, in order for the individual to be adaptive, they must interact in concert.

Another significant book is Harry Benjamin's *The Transsexual Phenomenon*, published in 1966. It focuses on the clinical condition, which, by its very nature, gives immense

support to the sexuality-at-birth thesis. The book reviews numerous cases of transsexuals who were brought up in accordance with their unambiguous gonads and yet as adults considered themselves to be members of the opposite sex. Despite their rearing as males, for example, men *claimed* to be (not just to *want* to be) females. The transsexual says, "I am a female, but for some unknown reason I have the body of a male. I am wrongly imprisoned." In the overwhelming majority of cases, investigators found little or no conditioning in childhood that would propel the individual in this direction. Certainly the findings call into question the usual view of social learning and role modeling.

A significant volume of work sympathetic to the understanding of transsexualism appeared in 1969. Edited by Richard Green and John Money, *Transsexualism and Sex Reassignment* explored transsexualism from social, psychological, clinical, and legal aspects. It attempted to support the position of transsexuals and help the medical profession understand them. Most psychologists and sociologists, however, were unaware of its publication and its implications for comprehending the wider area of sexual identity and gender roles.

Man and Woman, Boy and Girl, by John Money and Anke Ehrhardt and *Sexual Conduct,* by John Gagnon and William Simon, appeared in 1972 and 1973. These two books strengthened the arguments of the social-learning and "nurture" advocates, who place significance on environmental forces as a determinant of human sexual behavior. Money and Ehrhardt appeared to repeat and expand the material presented in 1965 regarding the biased-interaction-at-birth theory of sexuality. Even though they took into account the force of biology, they concluded that postnatal rearing has the final say in organizing an individual's sexual identity and gender role.

One new report included in *Sexual Conduct* has become a

classic and has been influential in maintaining the importance of these two elephantine questions: How does anyone come to know he or she is male or female? and What organizes behavior? The report described a set of male twins who were circumcised by cautery. Because of an accident, the penis of one of the twins was burned off. In the belief that sex is primarily a social phenomenon and that identity is learned, the decision was made to raise the penectomized boy as a girl. The experimental stage was set to test the hypothesis that if the boy was reared as a female he would overcome the biology of being a male. Money and Ehrhardt reported that when he was six years old, the twin raised as a girl, aside from some tomboyish behaviors, identified with, generally behaved as, and accepted the role of a female. The twin brother raised as a boy identified and behaved as a normal boy. This situation was seen as good evidence for the power of rearing and social forces over biology. But is it?

Instead of letting rearing compete with biology in a true test, the penectomized twin was subsequently castrated to remove the androgen source, and he was placed on a schedule for female hormones. Indeed, while the wisdom of the original decision might be questioned, these practices were consistent with it, and humanitarian motives took precedence over experimental niceties. It must be emphasized that as much as possible was done to defeat the male biological realities and enhance female biological maturation.

Sexual Conduct provided a theory that supported the force of social experience in organizing sexual behavior. This theory of "sexual scripts" reinforced the twin study report and continues to have a significant impact, particularly on learning theorists, psychologists, and sociologists. A sexual script is an internal rehearsal that describes sexual behavior. It defines the situation, the actors, and the plot. "Scripts are involved in learning the meaning of internal states, organizing the sequences of specifically sexual acts, decoding novel situations, setting the limits on sexual responses, and linking meanings from nonsexual aspects of life to specifically sexual experience." According to the theory's proponents, these scripts are learned and provide "the ordering of bodily activities that will release these internal biological states. Here, scripts are the mechanisms through which biological events can be potentiated." The script, a product of learning what is and is not appropriate in our society, not only provides a social reference for each actor in a sexual situation, but provides an intrapsychic motivating force to produce arousal, or at least a commitment, to a sexual activity.

If 1972 and 1973 were good for environmental theorists, the next year went to the biologists. An experiment of nature was reported in 1974 by J. Imperato-McGinley and co-workers.

"This was probably the first major statement to claim that sexuality was significantly dependent upon biological heritage. This inherent sexuality was seen as a built-in 'bias' that determined how the individual interacted with the environment."

In its own way it is a classic. For those who were keeping score, it reinforced the predictive value of the "biased-interaction" theory and cast doubts on the "twin experiment" and the theory of "sexual scripts." In a small community in the Dominican Republic, due to a genetic endocrine problem a large number of males were born who at birth appeared to be females. These males had a blind vaginal pouch instead of a scrotum and, instead of a penis, a clitoris like phallus. They thus looked more "female" than did the penectomized twin. The uneducated parents were unaware of anything unusual, and these males were raised as typical females in the community. There was no reason to do otherwise. At puberty a spontaneous change in their biology induced a penis to develop and their psychological orientation to change. They gave up living as females and assumed life as males. The medical researchers reached the following conclusion:

Psychosexual orientation (post-pubertal) is male, and this is of considerable interest, since the sex of rearing in 18 of the affected males was female. Despite the sex of rearing, the affected were able to change gender identity at the time of puberty. They consider themselves as males and have a libido directed toward the opposite sex. Thus, male sex drive appears to be endocrine related, and the sex of rearing as female appears to have a lesser role in the presence of two masculinizing events, testosterone exposure in utero and again at puberty with development of male phenotype. (J. Imperato-McGinley, L. Guerrero, T. Gautier, and R. E. Peterson, "Steroid 5α Reductase Deficiency in Man: An Inherited Form of Male Pseudohermaphroditism," *Science*, 186: 1213-1215.)

These individuals obviously did not totally respond to the gender roles assigned by rearing, since they assumed their own inner sexual identity and preferred roles. Any "scripting" obviously was not potent enough to organize the biological events relative to sexual identity and sexual preferences.

These individuals, despite being raised unambiguously from birth to puberty as females, saw themselves as males and found females to be their erotic choice.

Of equal importance in 1974 was another review of sexual identity and gender roles—the impressive *Psychology of Sex Differences*, by Eleanor E. Maccoby and Carol N. Jacklin, which became a major reference work on the psychological and social aspects of sexual behaviors. The book didn't address the question of sexual identity or present a new theoretical approach to its study. However, it did ask the basis for psychological sex differences and provided a valuable review of scores of studies pertinent to the popular theories of role-modeling and social learning.

This review contradicted many impressions and stereotypes with respect to sex-typing of behavior and organization of gender roles. For example, it was discovered that mothers didn't treat their sons or daughters differently in encouraging cooperation or dependency or in discouraging aggression. However, fathers punished their sons more than they did their daughters for being aggressive. Aggression was not encouraged as a way of resolving disputes. Mothers didn't choose toys on the basis of sex. The children *themselves* behaved or chose according to sex. Sons and daughters were given equal punishment or acceptance in response to frank sexual behavior, such as masturbation, display of nudity, genital play with peers, and questions asked about sex. Maccoby and Jacklin conclude:

Our analysis of the arguments concerning the role of modeling in sex-typing and our review of the research on selective imitation have led us to a conclusion that is very difficult to accept, namely, [that] modeling plays a minor role in the development of sex-typed behavior. This conclusion seems to fly in the face of common sense and to conflict with many striking observations of sex-typed role playing on the part of children.

When seen *in toto*, the bulk of evidence seems to argue that an inner biological "voice," an "innate feeling" of being male or female develops quite early. Many find that this is an unacceptable concept, or at least argue that it has not yet been proven. The research and reviews of 1974 provided greater assurance that humans develop sexually in accordance with a "biased-interaction" theory. At the same time, reflecting on the penectomized twin referred to earlier, I became convinced that at puberty his innate male bias may provide him with a male sexual identity incompatible with the assigned female gender role. In 1965 I had predicted this possible outcome of such cases.

I would like to offer a theory that synthesizes the above findings, in an attempt to answer our original question about sexual identity and sex roles. The test of this theory, as of any other, is how well it takes past findings into account and allows prediction of future ones.

An individual is born with a biased predisposition to interact with the world in certain ways. Part of this bias leads to a cognitive frame that provides a preprogrammed standard against which possible behavior choices will be considered. The basic feature is sexual identity—an internal and personal conviction of being male or female. Different male and female forces influence which behaviors are modeled and which are learned from the environment. Experiences may be viewed as

"The healthiest environment for sexual growth is one that provides the richest possible banquet of experiences and models from which the individual can learn without fear of social censure."

a smorgasbord from which certain things will be chosen and others left, according to one's individual taste. The forces of rearing are crucial in providing reinforcement of or challenge to one's concept of self even though they are normally not deterministic. Rearing and experiences will provide social and cultural models and scripts from which the individual might choose and order future behavior. An individual who is reared in ways contrary to his or her sense of sexual identity will manifest the incongruity by not accepting impositions or sex roles that are out of character. The smorgasbord of experience must include the possiblity of free choice.

For normal individuals in open societies the "smorgasbord"
of choice is wide. Many different sex roles and gender roles are possible and can be seen cross-culturally. Therefore, both masculine and feminine behavior patterns may appear mixed in normal males and females. Many families or situations do not allow free choice and stifle attempts at individual expression. "Deviance" is often severely repressed. The fact that many so-called sexual aberrations (that is, behavior patterns usually seen in females that are demonstrated by males, and vice versa) appear in families where there is an absent or "weak" parent would, according to this theory, not be due to the absence of a proper role model but rather to the absence of strong influences *inhibiting* deviance. In permissive families a child's basic natural tendencies (to have gender identity conform to sexual identity) would be allowed to develop even if deviant. The presence of overly rigid forces (parents or others) would prevent free choice and thwart the emergence of these natural tendencies.

The healthiest environment for sexual growth is one that provides the richest possible banquet of experiences and models from which the individual can learn without fear of social censure. If each individual is free to act according to his or her sense of sexual identity, preference, and role, then men and women will be truly able to express who they are.   ●

11 OUR SEXUAL ORIGINS

Sudden evolutionary development made us sensual so that we would survive.

BY BOYCE RENSBERGER

Why, of all animals, can only humans be classed as truly erotic?

Why did human beings become the most sensual species known to science?

Why is it that people engage in a wider range of sexual behaviors, and do them all much more frequently, than any other known creature?

Is our preoccupation with sex more than a modern phenomenon?

How deep are the roots of our sensuality?

Anthropology is shedding fascinating new light on all these questions, and there is indeed growing evidence that sexuality or eroticism is among the oldest and most distinguishing features of the human species, dating back more than three and a half million years.

Even more fascinating is the fact there appears to have been a number of very specific ancient events that altered our minds and bodies in ways that turned us into the sexual creatures we are today.

The story begins just before the dawn of human history. In the African forests, a species of apelike creatures dwelt in a climate that was evenly warm and moist, and consistently abundant with food. These four-legged apelike animals probably lived something like chimpanzees, foraging the forest floor and the small, lush meadows for fruits and tender stems. Like the chimpanzees of today, our forest ancestors may also have grabbed the occasional bit of animal food—insects or bird eggs or small mammals.

Beginning about 25 million years ago, the African climate started to change. It became more strongly seasonal, and periods of concentrated rain alternated with long dry spells. As a result, the great forests shrank. As fingers of grassland penetrated forest, a new ecological niche was created. During this time the

OUR SEXUAL ORIGINS, by Boyce Rensberger, is reprinted by permission from SCIENCE DIGEST, SPECIAL EDITION, Winter. Copyright © 1979 by The Hearst Corporation.

During a Nigerian wedding celebration, unmarried Miango women dance to display their beauty to the unmarried men of the village. Their cord girdles decked with leaves signify their single status as well as their role as farmer-gatherers in this primarily agrarian society.

apelike creatures in the forest would have been under severe pressure to sustain their way of life. Food was often scarce. Habitable territory was diminishing. The shrinking of the forests continued relentlessly into the Pliocene Epoch (10 million to 2 million years ago) and is, in fact, continuing today.

It would have been a crucial time for evolution. Faced with the right combination of circumstances a species can undergo virtual evolutionary explosions. Anthropologists have no direct evidence of what happened, but they do have incontrovertible fossil evidence of one extraordinary fact: by 3.6 million years ago, the savannah grasslands of eastern Africa were inhabited by at least one species of hominid, or humanlike creature, that walked fully erect on two legs, yet retained a brain the size of a chimp's.

Partial skeletons of these creatures have been found in Ethiopia and in Tanzania. The fossil bones, including pelvises and knee joints, indicate clearly that these hominids—the earliest known to science—walked exactly as do people today, although they stood only around 4 feet tall at maturity.

Striking confirmation that a fully de-

veloped, striding bipedal form of locomotion had evolved by then has come from the recent discovery by Dr. Mary Leakey and Dr. Tim White, of the University of these creatures. Found in a layer of volcanic ash that has been dated reliably to 3.6 million years of age—the same as that of the fossil bones—the prints are the oldest known marks of humanlike creatures on the face of the earth.

Those footprints and fossils have rekindled interest in an old question: why did bipedalism arise in the first place? Current scientific thinking is fascinating. It suggests that walking on two legs had very much to do with the origins of the human family as a social unit and with specialized roles played by men and

---

In order to survive, early hominids, who had become bipedal, evolved a way of life in which sex and love both played crucial roles.

women in that family.

There have been many theories about the origin of two-legged walking. Some say it enabled our ancestors to see over tall grass to spot predators such as lions or hyenas. Many have linked it to freeing the hands for tool-making, which many scientists think is related to brain enlargement. The latest discoveries seem to clash with this theory, since they link fully developed bipedalism with a brain not at all enlarged. This, anthropologists say, suggests that there must be some other explanation for the origin of this distinctively human trait.

Dr. Owen Lovejoy, professor of anthropology at Kent State University, believes nothing less than survival itself could have caused bipedalism to arise. This is because it is so radically different from quadrupedalism—requiring wholesale changes in anatomy and behavior.

PROMISCUOUS CHIMPS

If our ancestors were anything like the chimpanzee, they must have faced extraordinary demographic pressures. Lovejoy observes that a female chimp

Photographs from the Museum of African Art

must live more than 20 years just to produce two offspring—the minimum needed to keep the population alive. A female chimp does not become sexually mature until she is about 9 or 10 years old, and chimp mothers have only one baby at a time. Like human mothers in many primitive societies, they suckle their young for about four years, during which time they do not become pregnant again.

Childrearing is left to the chimp mother. Since chimpanzees are completely promiscuous, there is no pair bond or social role of father. The mother provides food for herself and her young one. This is why she can raise only one infant at a time.

If her species is to prosper, the chimp mother must have three or more youngsters. In fact, however, chimpanzee populations do not really thrive. It is well known that chimps are declining in Africa today as a result of their severely reduced habitat. Many scientists also suspect that chimpanzees are incapable of reproducing fast enough to get far ahead of natural mortality in the wild.

The receding forests of the Miocene Epoch (25 million to 10 million years ago), had a similar effect on our hominid ancestors, Lovejoy believes. Their fossils suggest that many died quite young— hardly out of their 20s. What was needed was a new system of social organization that would permit faster reproduction. It was crucial that parents be able to replace themselves and increase their numbers before they died. The solution, Lovejoy holds, was the human way of life, which made it possible to raise more than one infant at a time.

PAIRING AND SHARING

Just what is meant by "the human way of life"? First, there is pair bonding—a male and female who share food with one another and with their young. Among primates, only human beings, gibbons (small Asian apes) and marmosets (squirrel-sized monkeys from South America) share food, and only these three are monogamous. To share food, one must carry it from the source to a meeting place. This, Lovejoy suggests, was the primary purpose of bipedalism. By walking on two legs, the hands and arms became free to carry food back to a home base. The home base itself is another trait, distinctively human, that must have arisen at the same time.

Dramatic evolutionary changes were now possible.

With two adults pooling their resources, a hominid couple could have a second child before the first became independent. Indeed, this would have been absolutely necessary, in view of the lengthening period of infant dependence. Chimp mothers need to look after their

DIVISION OF LABOR BY SEX

In primitive societies around the world, hunting is almost always a male job, gathering a female one. Water carrying is strictly for females. Making weapons is an all-male occupation. In 18 percent of primitive societies, men share in the cooking. Making jewelry is nearly an equal-opportunity employment. The following statistics on divisions of labor are culled from an unusual reference work, the *Ethnographic Atlas.*

Activity	Exclusively Female	Shared	Exclusively Male
Weapon making	0	1.1	98.9
Musical instrument making	1.1	5	94
Leatherwork	38.5	19.5	42
Jewelry & Ornament making	20.2	52.2	27.5
Cooking	78.9	18	2.7
Water carrying	86.4	8	5

young for only four or five years. Human children require parental care at least twice as long. Only with a nuclear family could there be this long period of infant dependence. It is part of the bargain that comes with a larger brain and a longer opportunity for education.

But how did pair bonding come about? For physiological reasons, mothers are obliged to care for their young. But what can make a father take up a share of the burden? The answer seems to be: sex.

Like virtually all other animals, our apelike ancestors were undoubtedly interested in copulating only when the female was in oestrus and exuding the odors that arouse the male's ardors. A female chimp's genitalia, usually inconspicuous, swell and redden during oestrus, providing males an unmistakeable visual signal as

well. Sex is cyclic in all mammals except human beings, gibbons and marmosets. When the female is not fertile, not ovulating, neither she nor any males are interested in mating. Somewhere along the evolutionary line, however, hominids' cyclic sex changed to continuous sexual availibility.

In the human way of life, women rarely have any clear idea of when they are fertile and capable of conceiving, much less their mates. Both men and women are capable of sexual arousal at any time during the woman's largely hidden ovulatory cycle. Furthermore, human beings have acquired a number of sexually arousing traits that may be displayed at any time.

The most obvious is the permanent female breast. All other mammalian fe-

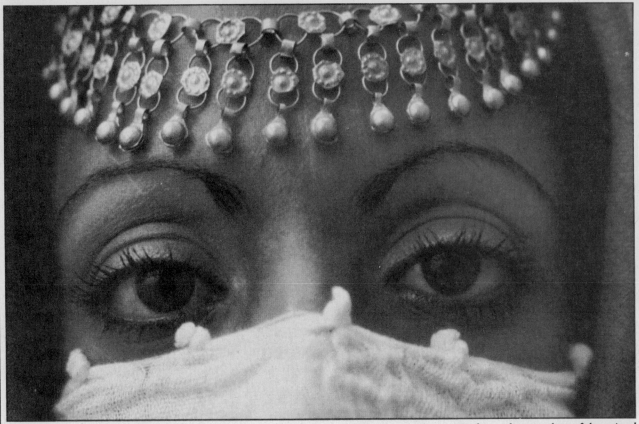

Men and women have several sexually alluring traits in their physical make-up that set them apart from other members of the animal kingdom. In every society, distinctive differences between the sexes are enhanced by costumes, hairstyles, jewelry and body makeup.

males develop conspicuous breasts only when the organs are needed to suckle their young. Thus, male interest in female breasts, mainly fat deposits, is not entirely a product of Hollywood hype. Quite likely it is based on instincts that are millions of years old. Furthermore, the nipple has become erotically sensitive, taking on a role unknown for the female breast in any other animal.

A comparable hypertrophy in males is the penis. Human penises are extraordinarily large by comparison with those of other primates. The largest living primate, for example, is the gorilla but its penis, when erect, is only 2 inches long. The distribution of hair and hairless areas is also likely to have evolved to be sexually attractive. Furthermore, the simple fact of general hairlessness is thought to enhance the sensations of close physical contact. Erect posture itself makes human genitalia more conspicuous, a point Sigmund Freud noted many years ago. In fact, Freud anticipated some of the current thinking by suggesting that the high degree of overt sexuality in human beings naturally drew them into couples and, therefore, into nuclear families, which he held to be the basic units of civilization.

FULL-TIME LOVERS
This is, in fact, quite close to Lovejoy's

thesis: "It is this more or less continuous sexual attraction between men and women that creates and maintains the pair bond." The primary purpose of the human way of sex, then, is not reproduction (That can be done by cyclic sex) but pair bonding or, in other words, love.

By being full-time sexual partners, hominid females and males cemented a personal bond that kept them coming back to the home base after each day's foraging and hunting. Sexual intercourse evolved into "making love," and deep emotional attachment between a man and a woman became one of the distinctive features of the human way of life. As significant is the attachment between parents and children, a consequence of the long and extremely dependent childhood and the parents' long term investments in their children.

Male chimps, like our promiscuous apelike ancestors, never know which

> In those human societies where sex is promiscuous and paternity is unknown, men select their sisters' children as their heirs.

youngsters in the troop are theirs. Females do know their babies and care for them. Thus, the mothers' efforts represent good genetic sense, for their actions improve the survival prospects of their own genes. Ape males, by contrast, have no idea where to invest any paternal behavior and, as a result, invest none at all. More correctly, no paternal instinct can even evolve under such a system.

"Confidence in paternity is required for a male parental role to evolve," according to Dr. Martin Daly and Dr. Margo Wilson of McMaster University in Hamilton, Ontario. "Any male who expends much time and energy rearing unrelated young must be at a selective disadvantage," they wrote in a new book called *Sex, Evolution and Behavior.*

In other words, an individual who diverts some of his efforts to the survival of others, thereby reducing his contributions to the welfare of his own descendents, is enhancing the survival of individuals who do not bear his genes. He is reducing his own genetic fitness and enhancing that of others. The result is that his descendents will be less likely to survive than those of someone else. Evolution, thus, will *not* favor his descendents and his instincts to care for the children of others would not be passed on.

In species where males help care for the young, they commonly take steps to

As full-time sexual partners, hominid females and males cemented a bond to the home base after each day's foraging and hunting. Sexual intercourse evolved into "making love," and so deep emotional attachments became a distinctive feature of the human way of life.

ensure that their females do not mate with other males. Such measures include sequestering the female, as some birds do, or vigorously fighting off rival males. The goal—though, of course, it is never consciously perceived—is to assure knowledge of paternity, to assure that the male's efforts will be directed only toward his own offspring.

This behavior, Daly and Wilson contend, is at the root of the human male's traditional fear of being cuckolded. The term derives from "cuckoo," a bird that lays its eggs in another species' nest. The cuckold, a man deceived by an adulterous wife, risks being put in the position of investing his efforts in behalf of another man's children. "In a sense," Daly and Wilson wrote, "it is for the parasitizing of his parental investment that the cuckolded man is ridiculed or pitied." The anthropologists go on to suggest that the biological disadvantage imposed on the man by an adulterous wife (but not on the wife herself since she would always be raising her own child) is at the root of the traditionally greater penalties for adultery imposed on women. As James Boswell put it in the 18th century, "There is a great difference between the offense of infidelity in a man and that of his wife." Samuel Johnson concurred: "The difference is boundless. The man imposes no bastards on his wife."

POLYGAMY TOP CHOICE

Thus, in the human family there is a biological incentive for the husband to prevent his wife's mating with other males. The wife's incentive to prevent her husband's mating with other women is much weaker, at least in purely biological terms, because that act imposes no biological burden on the wife.

What biology predicts, anthropology confirms. In those few human societies where sex is promiscuous and paternity is unknown, men select their sisters' sons as heirs; thereby investing in known kin.

Pair bonding, it should be noted, does not rule out polygamy. The reproductive ideal is one man bonded to several wives. Of the 849 societies cataloged in the *Ethnographic Atlas*, only 137 practiced monogamy. Of the 712 that were polygamous, nearly all (708) practiced polygyny (the man taking more than one wife). Polyandry (more than one husband) is al-

---

While cultural expressions may endlessly change, our sexuality is apt to go on, since human eroticism is more than Hollywood hype.

most nonexistent.

Another human characteristic is a division of labor by gender. In virtually every known primitive society, the men hunt and scavenge meat and the women gather plant foods. This way of making a living, commonly called "hunting and gathering," was undoubtedly the base of the human economic system from the earliest days of hominids. It persisted, with various refinements, through all the major phases of human evolution.

Until a mere 10,000 years ago, we were hunters and gatherers. Modern human beings, *Homo sapiens*, emerged at least 200,000 years ago. *Homo sapiens sapiens*, the subspecies of which all people today are members, emerged about 150,000 years later. Not until the invention of agriculture did the hunting and gathering way of life begin to decline. Today about 300,000 people still live this way. The best known are the San (once called "bushmen") of the Kalahari Desert, the "aborigines" of Australia and the Eskimos of the North Polar region.

Surprisingly, the way of the hunter-gatherer is not harsh or difficult. One striking example is the !Kung San (the ! stands for a click sound that is part of their language), one of several ethnic groups within the San. These primitive people manage to work only about 20 hours a week to get all the food they need. Men spend about two and a half days a week—averaging six hours per working day—on hunting trips. Women forage enough plant food in one day to last about three days. Those under 20 and over 60 need not work. The diet is varied, averaging 56 grams of protein a day, sufficient by American standards.

The time that is not spent working is largely devoted to socializing—playing with children, receiving visitors, and listening to the old people tell stories, dancing, playing any of the complex games the San people traditionally enjoy. Progress consists not of accumulating possessions but of building a more harmonious relationship between one's self and others. In short, the !Kung way of life is what anthropologist Marshall Sahlins calls "the original affluent society."

STATUS SYMBOL

One point of great interest to many anthropologists is how men achieved more status than women. The hunter-gatherer division of labor between men and women, many anthropologists believe, holds the roots of male domination in modern society. There is good reason to make men hunters and women gatherers. For most of their adult lives women have infant children to suckle. It would be foolish to expose children to the hazards of hunting, and even more so women, who are more biologically precious than men.

There is a striking and fascinating correlation of meat with status and male dominance. Among the San people, where meat amounts to only one-third of

the dietary intake, men have higher social status than women, but it is only a moderate degree of dominance. Among the Eskimos, who rely almost entirely on hunted meat for food (there being no edible plants in the far north), women are virtually chattel.

At the other extreme, with male dominance at a low, are the Hadza people of Tanzania. Hadza hunters get very little meat and eat much of it themselves before returning to their families. The plant food gathered by the women provide the vast bulk of the diet and, accordingly, the social status of women is very nearly equal to that of men. Among the Ice Age hunters of Europe who, if we can judge from the prominence of game animals depicted in their cave paintings, relied heavily on hunting, male dominance must have been quite marked.

The social role of hunter can remain a powerful tradition even when a hunter-gatherer culture has adopted many of the ways of agricultural societies. Not long ago, for example, the Eskimos of Alaska were prohibited from hunting endangered bowhead whales, one of their dietary mainstays. Eskimo leaders argued with the International Whaling Commission that this would destroy their culture because the tradition of a hunter distributing the whale meat throughout his community was the ancient basis of Eskimo social structure. A compromise was reached, permitting the Eskimos to kill a limited number of whales.

In most other primitive societies as well, hunters win the recognition and ac-

claim of their neighbors via the ceremonial distribution of meat throughout the community. Women, by contrast, gather food for their families without such opportunities for triumphal displays.

Meat. Prestige. Thus did men gain political and economic power. There can be little doubt that hunting and gathering began early in the original human way of life, and that it is to this way of life that human beings are biologically adapted.

Today, men rarely hunt and women rarely gather. Yet because human culture evolved slowly from hunter-gatherer times, traditions such as male dominance retain a strong influence. Most anthropologists agree, however, that there is no practical or innate reason that male dominance needs to be continued.

EROTICISM'S FUTURE

But while cultural expressions may change endlessly, it is much less likely that man will lose any of his innate sexuality. Human eroticism is much more than a product of Madison Avenue hype, even though that interest is easily exploited. Our capacity for continuous sexual receptivity and pair bonding are built into human beings as permanently as upright posture—part of a complex system of adaptations that arose in the very earliest days of human existence, well before any substantial expansion of the brain. The social structure in which men and women live today is not a recent cultural development but among the most ancient elements of our biological heritage. ∎

Reconsideration: Sex and Temperament in Three Primitive Societies

12

by Shirley Lindenbaum

Sex and Temperament in Three Primitive Societies
by Margaret Mead
Harper & Row, 1935;
William Morrow, 1963, paper, $3.95

Reconsidered by Shirley Lindenbaum

Between 1931 and 1933 Margaret Mead lived in three different societies in New Guinea. She went there intending to define the way in which culture stylizes the roles of men and women because, as she later said, "until one had got out of the way the problem of the effects of cultural stylization on feminine and masculine personalities, it seemed futile to raise questions about biologically-given sex differences."

The temper of the period of the New Deal and the Soviet experiment favored the view that human nature is inherently flexible. Under the direction of Columbia University Professor Franz Boas, Mead along with Ruth Benedict and others gathered data that argued against biological determinism. In 1939 Mead reflected, "It was a simple—a very simple—point to which our materials were organized in the 1920s, merely the documentation over and over of the fact that human nature is not rigid and unyielding . . . but that it is extraordinarily adaptable, that cultural rhythms are stronger and more compelling than the physiological rhythms which they overlay and distort." By drawing on the most fantastic and startling examples they could muster, Mead and Benedict set out to demonstrate the plasticity of human nature.

With *Sex and Temperament* Mead turned to the question of the malleability of sex-linked behavior. She asked whether the differences in temperament that we regard as "natural" are indeed innate or are culturally determined. With no previous knowledge of the cultures she had chosen nor of the contrasts they would present, Mead found three New Guinea societies within a 100-mile area, which, she acknowledged, some readers considered too good to be true. In two societies, the Arapesh and the Mundugumor, no distinctions in temperament appeared to exist between men and women; in the third, the Tchambuli, the sex roles were the reverse of those in our own culture. Arapesh men and women both displayed a personality that "we would call maternal in its parental aspects, and feminine

Margaret Mead in 1928, during field work among the Manus of New Guinea. Her second book, Growing Up in New Guinea, *was based on this research.*

in its sexual aspects." Men and women were cooperative, unaggressive, and responsive to the needs and demands of others. Mundugumor men and women both approximated the personality type "that we in our culture would find only in an undisciplined and very violent male." Women in the third society, the Tchambuli, were dominant, impersonal managers who manufactured mosquito bags, and caught and marketed fish. Tchambuli men were artists who created dances, carvings, and paintings for ceremonial use. The men played "an emotionally subservient role, dependent upon the security given them by the women."

The conclusion Mead drew from these three examples is that "if those temperamental attitudes which we have traditionally regarded as feminine—such as passivity, responsiveness, and a willingness to cherish children—can be so easily set up as the masculine pattern in one tribe, and in another be outlawed for the majority of women as well as for the majority of men, we no longer have any basis for regarding such aspects of behavior as sex-linked. [The evidence] is overwhelmingly in favour of the strength of social conditioning."

The book evoked strong and contradictory reactions despite the apparent simplicity of the message and its beautifully lucid style. Some feminists took it to mean that women did not "naturally" like children, and recommended that little girls not be given dolls to play with. Others accused the author of not recognizing the existence of sex differences. "This," Mead wrote in the preface to the 1950 edition, "is my most misunderstood book."

Reviews by fellow anthropologists were notably acerbic. Bronislaw Malinowski, who was professor of anthropology at the London School of Economics, commented that under her deft touch "the women of one tribe appear masculine, while in another males develop feminine qualities almost to the verge of parturition." He compared the book unfavorably with Raymond Firth's *We, the Tikopia,* which he said was "an unaffected piece of genuine scholarship, based on real experience of a culture and not on a few hypostasized impressions." Richard C. Thurnwald, a German anthropologist who taught at the University of Berlin, suggested that "a clear separation of the factual information from the author's hypotheses would have been useful." The most sympathetic early review was provided by a woman, anthropologist Camilla Wedgwood, who took the time to tell the reader what the book was about, although she too had reservations about the data. By 1939, Reo Fortune, who had worked with Mead in New Guinea, had disavowed Mead's interpretation of their joint field data, saying that "as far as we know, the Arapesh do not expect a similar temperament in both sexes." He quoted an Arapesh proverb, "Men's hearts are different; women's hearts are different," and drew attention to the existence of a class of men called "women male," effeminate men who were assigned an inferior social position.

Despite this bombardment, the book flourished. Forty-two years later, it has reached a third edition and is regularly cited in essays on sex and gender. The public's attraction to the book appears to derive from the mixture of edifying and exotic information that Mead offered. She is a kind of evangelist, educating her American audience in the potential for human variation.

As for the issue of biological determinism, Mead judged that the idea of a fixed human nature had been put to rest. In 1939 she wrote, "The battle which we once had to fight with the whole battery at our command . . . is now won," a point of view that ethnologists and anthropologists including Mead herself subsequently altered. By the late 1960s, anthropologists were again disputing the position that human social behavior is mostly or wholly determined by genes.

In spite of the book's apparent

Tchambuli males instruct young men in the art of warfare during initiation rites that take as long as three months to complete.

association with feminism, Mead has stated that it is not a treatise on the rights of women nor an inquiry into the basis of feminism. She was concerned rather with the waste to society that results from the creation of male and female stereotypes. The result of rigid sex roles is a sacrifice of complexity, a loss of diversity, an impoverishment of culture, but not an injustice. Her sights were on the plasticity of human nature, not on differences in social status. The recent reinterpretation of the book as a feminist tract emerged during the general struggle for civil rights when women's groups read it with new eyes.

From the perspective of the hypothesis-oriented anthropology of the 1960s and 1970s, Mead's work has been criticized for its methodology and for its simplistic assumptions about the relationship between culture and personality. Like many anthropologists of the 1930s, Mead perceived personality to be an aspect of culture. Both "culture" and "personality" referred to configurations of behavior that were manifested

and carried by individuals and were characteristics of a group. Since there was no conceptual distinction between personality and culture, there was no attempt to search out causes, to tie personality types to technology, economics, history, or to any conditioning factors other than socialization.

In hindsight we can also see the limitations of research methods that rely on data from only one or two informants, instead of on a statistical sample from many informants. As an informant the individual is fallible, and as a representative of the culture the person selected is a transformer as well as a mirror. Mead's data would be more acceptable to other anthropologists had she validated the descriptions that came from isolated informants by checking with a larger cross section of the society.

New intellectual currents in anthropology have also passed *Sex and Temperament* by. The trend has been away from a preoccupation with cultural differences to an interest in psychological and intellectual universals, and to the merging of biology and culture. As anthropologist Eric Wolf notes, World War II marked a shift in the way American anthropologists approached and interpreted their subject matter, a move away from the view of the culturally constituted personality as a bearer of common values toward a model of the problem-solving "organization man." The emphasis on the uniqueness and diversity of world cultures gave way to an interest in the evolution of larger and more encompassing social and cultural systems.

As the book passes from an active to a historical position in psychological anthropology and as it disappears from the bibliographies of the feminists, it seems headed toward rebirth in yet another form. Another generation of anthropologists has begun to work in the Sepik District of New Guinea, pursuing new theoretical interests with new technologies. In her introduction to Donald Tuzin's study *The Ilahita Arapesh,* a subgroup of the Plains Arapesh, Mead describes the immense differences between the ethnologist of 40 years ago and today. In addition to linguistic texts and pidgin-speaking informants, the modern field worker has the assistance of computers, tape recorders, and movie and still cameras, as well as aerial photographs provided by the Australian government; charter planes and helicopters provide low-altitude reconnaissance of villages and their surrounding areas. Where Mead's mobility was limited by narrow native paths along which she traveled laced into a hammock slung from a pig-carrying pole, anthropologists can now travel easily on motorbikes. Mead was confined to one village for the entire Arapesh study, but Tuzin divided his research time into three field periods, organizing his results during breaks in Canberra, Australia, and using a computer to turn his observations into a data bank.

The image of the anthropologist interrupting field work to talk with colleagues on another continent while feeding data into a computer seems an appropriate index of the shift that has taken place in anthropology over the past generation. Recent studies have focused on interactions that transcend local groups, viewing primitive villages not as isolated societies but as components of a larger social system. The flow of people, genes, information, objects, disease, and cultural symbols is the new object of study. Computers are used to analyze data from blood groups to estimate the genetic distance between villages affiliated by history or language. By matching this information with genealogical and ecological data from the same populations, anthropologists can examine patterns of relationships that have persisted for centuries.

The emphasis on complex networks that go beyond local groups may be seen as part of the profound change in our perceptual and behavioral frames of reference. It reflects our declining sense of community in the West as we participate in an exploding world order. We have a new sense of space, and we have rediscovered history.

For this new historically based anthropology, Mead's work is particularly useful. Her method, despite theoretical weaknesses, allowed her to sketch the overall picture as well as the significant detail. There is a grand sweep to the data from the 1920s and 1930s that is missing from the general anthropological literature of subsequent decades. It is possible to return to *Sex and Temperament* to trace a set of connections with which the author was not primarily concerned.

The deference shown by the Mountain Arapesh, for example, may be a

---

Among the Plains Arapesh, as among the Mountain Arapesh studied by Mead, men enjoy caring for their children.

product of trade relations. The Mountain Arapesh participate in a complex trade network involving the Coastal and Plains Arapesh, their neighbors to the north and the south. Many items, including stone axes, bows and arrows, ornaments, tobacco, feathers, pots, net bags, and shell rings move back and forth. The Mountain Arapesh are the middlemen in this system. Producing nothing themselves, their profits and survival perhaps depend on a proper show of emotion in two directions—respect toward the Coast and fear toward the Plains. Economic and political vulnerability may lead both men and women to be cooperative, unaggressive, and deferential to the needs of others, a temperament that may not be a permanent state of affairs.

Although Mead's framework did not lead her to explain the historical development of cultural configurations, *Sex and Temperament* is a provocative record of some of the best-known ethnographic subjects by one of the best-known anthropologists. It will stimulate future historically based studies of the Arapesh, the Tchambuli, the Mundugumor, and their neighbors. Its influence is already well recognized. As Marvin Harris, an anthropologist at Columbia University, notes, the artful presentation of cultural differences to a wide professional and lay public by Mead and Benedict must be reckoned among the important events in the history of American intellectual thought.   □

Shirley Lindenbaum *is an assistant professor of anthropology at the New School for Social Research, the Graduate Faculty. She has done field research in symbolic and medical anthropology among the Fore of the eastern highlands of New Guinea.*

13 The Womanly Image

Character assassination through the ages
by Paula Stern

I had a job interview several weeks ago. Friends warned me not to be too aggressive. During the interview, I tried to present myself as a competent candidate, able to "think like a man" and yet not to be a "masculine" female. After fielding several questions relevant to the job, I suddenly heard, "Miss Stern, are you in love?"

Do you think they asked my competition—seven men—the same question? No, for a cultureful of reasons. Jacqueline Kennedy Onassis was quoted once as saying. "There are two kinds of women: those who want power in the world and those who want power in bed." And the majority seem to agree with Jackie that the latter is socially more acceptable. That's how many women in America have been taught to think. And that's how many men think women ought to think.

Children are taught sexual stereotypes early, as well as the appropriate behavior for a sex-determined role in life. Asking a little boy, "What do you want to be when you grow up?" implies to him unlimited possibilities in his future. But most often we ask a little girl, "Where did you get that pretty dress," suggesting she has only one real option open to her. If we do ask her what she wants to be, she's likely to give the conditioned female response—"A mother." Why? So she can replace her dolls with real babies.

The inspiration for teaching girls to expect less than boys comes from a range of cultural sources, religious, literary, psychiatric, and pop. Even in the Bible, exceptional, independent women like Rebecca, Sarah, Deborah, or Ruth are practically "unknowns" compared with infamous Eve or Delilah.

Eve was made from one of Adam's spare parts, almost as an afterthought, to help him out on earth: "And the Lord God said: 'It is not good that the man should be alone; I will make him a help-meet for him.' "

There is a contrary legend of the first female, Lilith, who was equal to man.

> When the Lord created the world and the first man, he saw that man was alone, and quickly created a woman for him, made like him from the earth, and her name was Lilith. Right away, they began to quarrel. He would say "You sleep on the bottom," and she would say "No, you sleep on the bottom, since we are equals and both formed from the earth. . . ." When Lilith saw what the situation was, she pronounced the Ineffable Name and disappeared into thin air.

But Eve, not Lilith, is the prototypal woman—man's little helper, and his temptress.

Today the heirs to the Bible in America—Jews and Christians—have formalized biblical biases in laws and cere-

monies and thereby elevated folklore to religious truths. Among the Orthodox Jews, for example, discrimination against women is so blatant that they are forced to sit segregated behind a curtain or in a balcony. The rationale is that women will distract men from their prayers. It is no wonder that men thank God every morning in their ritual prayer "that Thou has not made me a woman."

A Jewish wife is less subservient to her husband than a gentile wife; so say comparative studies on the subject. That's somewhat understandable since Christianity owes much to a prominent classical heritage, that held the second sex in even lower esteem. Utopia for the male chauvinist is Demosthenes' description of Hellenic male-female arrangements: "We have herairae for the pleasure of the spirit, concubines for sensual pleasures, and wives to bear our sons."

Aristotle's definition of feminity was "a certain lack of qualities; we should regard the female nature as afflicted with a natural defectiveness." And his disciple Saint Thomas Aquinas echoed him religiously: ". . . a female is something deficient and by chance."

Contempt for women helps explain why they can't become Catholic priests, and why theologians, religious education courses, and Catholic marriage manuals highlight the supposedly inferior and passive qualities of women, who "naturally" subordinate themselves to men.

Traditional Protestant marriage services also perpetuate the attitude that the female is a second-class human being. Like a piece of property, the bride is "given" by her father to the groom, whom she promises to "obey." (Although formally removed from the liturgy, this vow still persists in the popular image of the wedding ceremony.) The clergyman reminds her of her proper place when he says, "I pronounce that they are man and wife." Not husband and wife. Not man and woman. The man keeps his status, while she takes on a new one. Her identity vanishes when she sheds her maiden name for his identification. (Blackstone's *Commentaries* on the law strips a married woman of her rights altogether as she legally dies on her wedding day and becomes "incorporated and consolidate with her husband." Accordingly, "A man cannot grant anything to his wife for the grant would be to suppose her separate existence.")

Although reputedly "progressing" beyond the attitudes of antiquity and the Middle Ages, our enlightened European ancestors continued furnishing us some not too enlightened guidelines on a woman's place—or lack of it—in the world.

High school English students learn from Shakespeare that "Frailty, thy name is woman." Rousseau's contribution to the ideas of man's equality and natural goodness makes one exception: "Woman was made to yield to man and put up with his injustice."

Samuel Johnson's word to the wise woman is that "a man is in general better pleased when he has a good dinner upon his table, than when his wife talks Greek." Honoré de Balzac adds, "A woman who is guided by the head and not the heart is a social pestilence: she has all the defects of a passionate and affectionate woman with none of her compensations: she is without pity, without love, without virtue, without sex."

When in 1776 in America, Abigail Adams asked her husband, John Adams, to "be more generous and favorable to them [women] than your ancestors" and to see to it that the new government not "put such unlimited power into the hands of the husbands," John reportedly chuckled. The Continental Congress ignored her. Two hundred years later Spiro Agnew said: "Three things have been difficult to tame —the ocean, fools, and women. We may soon be able to tame the ocean; fools and women will take a little longer."

America's twentieth-century gospel is the work of Freud. Although Freud supposedly has altered the entire course of Western intellectual history, many of his ideas about women are simply male chauvinism. Letters he wrote his fiancée reveal that he, too, wanted his woman kept relatively docile and ignorant so she couldn't compete with him.

His theories have given scientific status to prejudice. The Freudians—psychiatrists, clinical psychologists, psychiatric social workers, marriage counselors, pastoral counselors, educators, writers, literary critics, historians, anthropologists, sociologists, criminologists, and just plain subway psychiatrists in the newspapers, magazines, and on TV—all subscribe to the belief that "anatomy is destiny." In other words, biological differences between the sexes determine personality differences; standards of mental health depend on the sex of the sick.

How? Dr. Judd Marmor, clinical professor of psychiatry at UCLA, has summarized Freud's views on feminine psychology:

> The most significant of the biological factors . . . is the lack of the penis, which inevitably leads to "penis envy" in the woman. Freud considered penis envy to be a dominant theme in all feminine life, and one that inevitably causes women to feel inferior to men. These deep seated feelings of inadequacy can be compensated for only partially by giving birth to a male child. . . .
>
> Masochism and passivity . . . are natural aspects of normal femininity and whenever a woman behaves in non-passive or aggressive ways or competes with men, she is being neurotically unfeminine. . . .
>
> The most complicated sequence of personality development that women are subject to . . . leads inevitably . . . to less adequate superego formation than in men. This presumably is reflected in women having a poorer sense of justice and weaker social interests than men have.

The myths of marriage counselor G. C. Payetter (from his book *How To Get and Hold a Woman*) have been praised by a number of psychiatrists, and he is consulted in earnest by troubled people. Payetter counsels:

> Feelings, moods, and attitude . . . rule a woman, not facts, reason, nor logic.
>
> By herself woman is all mixed-up but superb as an auxiliary (Genesis: helper).
>
> Woman is inanimate or on the defensive until you create a feeling such as a praise. Then she goes all out.
>
> Never scold or explain when she is angry, remember she is feeling not thinking. . . .
>
> Stop bossing; just manipulate her in her feelings. . . .
>
> The acquisition of knowledge or responsibilities does not lessen women's need for support, guidance, and control. Quite the contrary.
>
> Why ask women when they only need to be told? Why ask women when they hope to be taken?

Any resemblance between woman and pet dogs or mute concubines is purely coincidental. No doubt, Payetter's

model woman is the runner-up to this year's Miss America, who said women shouldn't try to run things "because they are more emotional and men can overcome their emotions with logic."

Even more objectionable are psychiatrist-authors who pronounce final judgment on the mental health of thousands of women reading books like *The Power of Sexual Surrender*. Featured in the book, which has had at least ten paperback printings and been excerpted in *Pageant* magazine, is "The Masculine Woman." (Doctor, how can a woman be a female and be masculine simultaneously?) She's "frigid"— "a driving, competitive woman who was very successful in the business world, having graduated from a leading woman's college." "Clean thinking and logical mind, her emotionless almost masculine forthrightness in expressing herself belied her softly feminine appearance." Surrendering to her "real nature," the doctor's cure, is the only way she can be mentally healthy. Then miraculously

> . . . those details of life that once seemed so difficult become simple. And because they are feminine tasks, household work, planning and getting dinners, keeping the children busy or in line—whatever life demands—soon lose their irksome and irritating quality and become easy, even joyful. . . . At this juncture, or closely following on it, a woman begins to feel her full power, the power that comes to her for her surrender to her destiny.

The spuriously Freudian vision of a truly "feminine" female serves the purposes of admen who woo women to spend millions on clothes and cosmetics in vain pursuit of their "real nature." To sell a new product, industry need only simultaneously make the product and manufacture anxiety in gals, pressing them to consume or be consumed in a female identity crisis. For example, featured in every women's magazine, including those for teen-agers, are the latest advertising campaigns for vaginal deodorants, a "female necessity." One called Cupid's Quiver comes in four flavors—Orange Blossom, Raspberry, Champagne, or Jasmine. Madison Avenue courts the female, even seducing minors. Teenform, Inc., manufacturers of bras for teen-agers, estimates that nine-year-olds spend $2 million on bras annually.

Ingenue magazine pushes teenagers into adult posturing. The format is peppered with advertisements for engagement rings, pictures of desirable adolescent boys, and occasionally a plan of attack such as dinners for two. The ads for cosmetics and clothes are practically identical to those in magazines designed for their mothers. Typical of women's magazines, *Ingenue* includes at least one psychologically centered article. Recently, it explained in "The Hardest Thing About Growing Up" that "inevitably, relationships with boys affect relationships with girls." It condoned the statement, "I don't trust other girls in the same way anymore. They become rivals." This is how girls learn the platitudes: women can't work with other women when men are around, and never work for a woman.

If a girl manages to survive *Ingenue* without succumbing to marriage, *Glamour* picks her up. ("How Five Groovy Men Would Make You Over Into Their Dream Girls") Where the boys are is where it's at for the reader who is shunted from high school to college to career to marriage to motherhood—"Find Your New Look. College Into Career Make-over. Job Into Mother Make-over."

The lucky gal who's made the grade by landing a man is promoted to *Modern Bride,* which induces her to buy "utterly feminine" wedding gowns, bride-and-groom matching wedding rings, silver, china, furniture, ad nauseam. The wedding itself is big business; Wediquette International, Inc., offers total planning—the place, time, invitations, gown, caterers, florist, photographer . . .

Ah, then conjugal bliss—and of course, a magazine for mothers. *Redbook* boasts its biggest year because it knows "Young Mamas Spend More Than Big Daddies" and so talks "to that 18–34 year old the way she wants to be talked to," which means in baby talk or kitchen chatter.

McCall's claims 16 million matrons who "buy more than the readers of any other woman's service magazine." Its reader "buys more cosmetics and toiletries, more prepared foods, owns more life insurance, more automobiles . . ."

Although *Cosmopolitan* says its reader is the career woman who desires success in her own right, it is pitched to the gal who missed the marriage boat the first time around. Female passivity is still the accepted mode of behavior. She can be assertive in the office, but when man-hunting after five, she must be seductively submissive. Who knows? She might hook a divorced man or married man looking for an affair.

Cosmo repeats an old tip from Jackie and Delilah—sex is a woman's hidden arsenal. Under a pseudonym, "a well-known American gynecologist" instructs readers "How to Love Like A Real Woman." If your man bawls at you and you know you are in the right, what should you do?" "You should take your clothes off. Sex is a woman's strongest weapon. It is her proper weapon."

Taking a cue from *The Power of Sexual Surrender,* the expert explains, "Women must give and give and give again because it is their one and only way to obtain happiness for themselves." Further, "To argue is a male activity. To fight is a male activity. I say to women: "Don't become a man in skirts. Don't fight. Don't argue. . . .' " Any female who would practice this advice must be masochistic—typical of a "normal" female, according to Freudian thought.

A popular misconception is that in time education will erase all the ill effects of thinking in stereotypes. But the educational system takes over where cultural myths, Freudian folklore, and the media leave off in depressing a girl's aspirations and motivations. All along, she's taught to accept a double standard for success and self-esteem: It's marriage and motherhood for girls, while it's education and career for boys. She's pushed to be popular, date, and marry young (more than half of all American women are married before the age of twenty-one). Success in school only inhibits her social life. Intellectual striving, a necessity for academic success, is considered competitively aggressive; that is unnatural and unladylike behavior, since the essence of femininity, she has learned, is repressing aggressiveness. Telling her she thinks like a man is a backhanded compliment, which is discouraging if she has tried to be a woman using her brains, not sex, in the classroom and office.

While girls outperform boys intellectually in prepuberty, attrition in IQ sets in during adolescence when they learn from new, extracurricular lessons that looks, not brains, are what counts. After high school, achievement in terms of productivity and accomplishment drops off even more. More than 75 percent (some say as high as 95 percent) of all qualified high-schoolers not entering college are girls. Those who go attend more for husband-hunting than for educational self-advancement: one study at a Midwestern university revealed 70 percent of the freshmen women were there for an MRS. Women BA's are less than half as likely to try for a graduate degree as equally qualified men.

Women should not be given an even break in education and careers, says a clichéd argument, because they will get married and quit anyway. But that's because they are given an arbitrary, unfair option which men aren't forced to accept—either career or marriage. Career opportunities and salary levels for women are so poor that a calculating female would figure marriage is a better bargain. Once married, she can stop fighting the stereotypes and start teaching them to her children.

IV. Nonverbal Communication

Nonhuman mammals communicate nonverbally—through facial expressions, body positions, emotional vocalizations, eye contact, and gestures. When we think of human communication, we usually think of symbolic language. However, humans also communicate nonverbally.

It is easy to underestimate the force and significance of the nonverbal components of human communication. I don't know whether I would go as far as Ray Birdwhistell (see "The Way We Speak 'Body Language,'" by Flora Davis), who claims that words contribute only about 30–35 percent to meaning, or as far as Albert Mehrabian ("Communication Without Words"), who claims that verbal communication contributes only 7 percent to the communication of feelings (with facial expression contributing 55 percent and vocal expression—tone of voice, pauses, etc.—38 percent). But I would argue that the nonverbal channel is often taken for granted.

Research on nonverbal communication is relevant to some of the controversies addressed by research in the previous sections. Systematic similarities in systems of nonverbal communication in humans and nonhumans may serve as a basis for insight about our evolutionary heritage. The investigation of similarities and differences in body language across cultures may supply a basis for deciding whether dispositions are learned or inherited.

Albert Mehrabian and Flora Davis review evidence that nonverbal communication serves a number of basic purposes in social interaction. It helps regulate conversations; it supplies definitions of dominance, power, and status; it indicates anxiety and security; and it affects sexual reactions. In a

Artwork by Martin Riskin.

fascinating set of observations, the investigator Albert Scheflen suggests that nonverbal indices of sexual arousal, which he calls "quasicourtship behavior," create a tension and excitement that energize social interactions.

In many cases, the verbal and nonverbal channels of communication work together and complement one another. In others, they send quite different messages. A red-faced shout of "I'm *not* angry!" is a common example. We have more control over the messages we give than the messages we "give off," to use sociologist Erving Goffman's phrase. Indeed, there is evidence that even in the nonverbal channels, aspects of our demeanor of which we are least aware—our hands and feet, for example—supply a better indication of whether we are lying than our facial expressions. Albert Mehrabian reports research suggesting that certain psychological disorders, such as schizophrenia, are frequent among children whose parents communicate negative messages nonverbally. The interesting article, "Perfidious Feminine Faces," by Bugental, Love, and Gianetto, explores the implications of the finding that mothers smile at their children more indiscriminately and in more inappropriate circumstances than do fathers.

Eye contact is one of the most perplexing forms of nonverbal communication. Staring at people (and nonhuman primates) may evoke anger, or it may evoke sexual arousal. Eye contact is a sign of dominance—powerful people look at subordinates more than vice versa. It is also a sign of love; the social psychologist Zick Rubin validated his love scale (see Article 58) by assessing the amount of time people spend gazing into one another's eyes. According to Michael Argyle ("The Laws of Looking"), there is a universal tendency for people who gaze too much to be considered threatening and disrespectful, and people who gaze too little to be regarded as submissive and untrustworthy.

Although many aspects of eye-to-eye communication are universal, other aspects vary across cultures. For example, northern Europeans maintain relatively little eye contact, whereas Arabs look at one another a great deal. The biological basis and cultural variation of communications through the eyes is typical of all forms of nonverbal communication.

14

INACCESSIBLE: *When a woman tightly crosses her arms and legs, she generally indicates she is not accessible to any approach. But Scheflen and other researchers warn that whether this is specifically true will depend on circumstances: what the woman is doing with the rest of her body and what people are around her.*

The Way We Speak 'Body Language'

By FLORA DAVIS

A NUMBER of the country's top-flight psychiatrists have taken their patients on a trip to Philadelphia in recent years for a visit to a research lab at the Eastern Pennsylvania Psychiatric Institute. There, psychiatrist and patient hold a therapy session while movie cameras purr in the background. Psychotherapy is perhaps the most verbal of all 20th-century experiences. Yet what the film-makers are primarily interested in is nonverbal communication: shifts of posture and muscle tone, gestures, eye movements, and the like. They are looking for recurring patterns, the constellations of body movement which they see as a kind of subliminal language that can be translated by the trained interpreter.

For example, in one particular film the psychiatrist was seeing a family — mother, father, daughter, grandmother—together for the first time. Again and again during the interview, the mother turned flirtatiously to the therapist. She would extend her legs

FLORA DAVIS, a freelance writer, is working on a book about body talk for McGraw-Hill.

and delicately cross her ankles. Resting one hand on her hip, she would lean forward and talk with great animation for perhaps 20 or 30 seconds. Then, quite suddenly, she would subside, sink back in her chair, pull in her legs, drop her hands to her sides. The withdrawal was so complete that she looked almost autistic.

So much one can see with the naked eye. But when the film is run through slow motion, a whole constellation of movement suddenly becomes clear. Each time the mother set out to charm the psychiatrist, her husband would begin to jiggle one foot nervously. At this, both daughter and grandmother — who were sitting on either side of the mother — would cross their knees so that their shoe tips almost met and their legs boxed her in. It was after this that she subsided. The sequence occurred 11 times in just 30 minutes of the film.

It is hardly a surprise, then, to learn that the mother's flirtatiousness was a family problem. Experts in kinesics—the study of communication through body motion—cite this fragment of nonverbal drama as a neatly documented example of the way people sometimes use body language to keep others who may be misbehaving in line. Kinesicists believe

that all families have similar systems, though they are almost never conscious of having them.

In the past few years, hundreds of researchers across the country have turned to the study of nonverbal language, convinced that what people do with their bodies communicates as importantly as the words they use. No single discipline has a monopoly on this new field, and each researcher brings to it the jargon and biases of his own particular science. The great mass of the new data is being produced by psychologists who are doing classic psych-lab experiments on minute body movements, such as those of the face. There are also psychiatrists working in the field who hope to apply what they learn in psychotherapy, sociologists studying body language in actual social situations and anthropologists doing cross-cultural comparisons.

People speak and move, and you and I respond, and we never stop to think that most of the time words express only the smallest part of our meaning — just 30-35 per cent of it, according to Ray Birdwhistell, who is senior research scientist at the Eastern Pennsylvania Psychiatric Institute and director of the Studies in Human Communication project there. How does a man know when a woman is a possible pickup? How do we know when another person is listening to us or if he really means what he is saying? Sometimes the signs are unmistakable, but often we rely on "intuition." Scientific research is now giving a clearer understanding of what lies behind our institutions. A lot of the work going on merely serves to confirm common sense, but much of it is both subtle and surprising.

DR. ALBERT E. SHEFLEN, a psychiatrist-turned-kinesicist, has demonstrated, for instance, that people in a group often mirror each other's posture. In a large gathering, as many as half a dozen may sit or stand with limbs arranged in an identical—or mirror-imaged way—and if one member of the set then shifts his body, the others quickly do the same. Where two different postures have been adopted by a gathering, those who share a posture usually turn out to share a viewpoint as well. When three people are together, most often one will arrange himself so that his upper body is congruent with one companion and his lower body with the other—making himself into a kind of human link between the two.

Some gestures have a conscious, understood meaning (psychologist Paul Ekman of the Langley Porter Neuropsychiatric Institute in San Francisco calls them "emblems"). The hitchhiker's thumbing is an example that comes easily to mind. Every culture has its own repertoire of these, and they vary from culture to culture. Catching sight of a pretty girl, an Italian will signal his appreciation by pulling one of his ear lobes, an Arab will stroke his beard, but the Englishman will assume an overly casual stance and elaborately look away.

These observations are Birdwhistell's, but he cautions that it is often a mistake to interpret such gestures in isolation. The individual's facial expression or stance—or what he is saying—can give a gesture an ironic twist; as everyone knows, an Army private, when he salutes, can convey everything from blind obedience to complete contempt, depending upon the speed and duration of the gesture and what he does with the rest of his body.

Sociologist Erving Goffman of the University of Pennsylvania speaks of another sort of body language which is not communication but a means of relieving inner tension. "Creature releases," as he calls them, are brief rebellions against the social roles that we are all forced to play ("Fleeting acts slip through the individual's self-control and momentarily assert his 'animal nature.'"). Some samples: "At one extreme are the minor releases such as scratching, momentary coughing, rubbing one's eyes, sighing, yawning, and so forth; at the other extreme are such acts as flatulence, incontinence, and the like; in the middle ranges of the continuum are dozing off, belching, spitting, nose picking or loosening one's belt."

Nonverbal language, when understood, offers psychiatrists valuable clues to their patients' emotions, but most researchers in this new field shun broad theorizing about feelings and motivations. As behavioral scientists, they prefer to isolate, classify and analyze the interaction of *observable* physical acts. Really hard-nosed behavioral scientists actually deny that there is any inner-man to study ("According to some psychologists," says Dr. Scheflen, "the head is populated with all sorts of little people —id, ego, super ego. They emit communication, transmit messages, cause things to happen. It's a kind of animism, like the primitives who thought trees were alive.")

I talked to four pioneers in the field of body language— Birdwhistell, Scheflen, Goffman and Dr. Adam Kendon, a colleague of Scheflen's at the Bronx State Hospital. Significantly, none of the four refer to it as nonverbal communication. Kendon prefers the term "visible behavior"; his fellow kinesicists, Scheflen and Birdwhistell, who refuse to segregate words from gestures, define their field simply as "communication." (Bristling at the phrase non-verbal communication, Birdwhistell cracked: "That's like saying 'noncardiac physiology.'") Goffman speaks of his specialty as "face-to-face interaction"; he is interested in how the unwritten body codes help people to get along with each other in public.

WRITERS, artists and psychiatrists have long known that body motions have significance, and the psychologists' first studies of facial expressions were done early in the century. But it was anthropologists such as Franz Boas, Edward Sapir and, in the 1940's, Weston LaBarre and David Efron, who first put forward the notion that body motions are actually a code that can be cracked.

However, sustained, systematic Kinesics research really began with the publication of Ray Birdwhistell's book, "Introduction to Kinesics," in 1952. Tall, 51 years old, with crisp grey hair, Birdwhistell is an anthropologist born and educated in the Midwest. His interest in body language dates back to a field study he did of the Kutenai Indians of western Canada in 1946. While he was living among the Kutenai, he noticed that they looked quite different when speaking English from the way they looked when speaking Kutenai: their gestures their facial expressions changed. It seems that some people are bilingual in body language as well as in spoken language!*

Birdwhistell's work is elusive. His book is now long out of print, although a new

---

*One of the best examples of this was the late Fiorello La Guardia, the popular New York Mayor, who delivered campaign speeches in Italian and Yiddish as well as English —and was a master of the gestures appropriate to each language. His gesturing was so clear, in fact, that Birdwhistell, who has seen films of the speeches, says he could tell what language "The Little Flower" was speaking even with the sound track turned off.

one, "Kinesics and Context," will be published in the fall. His papers, appearing mostly in professional journals, are properly dense and scholarly but short on the mass of documentation that other researchers expect. The man himself is a surprise, then: not at all the dry-voiced scholar, but tweedy, relaxed, with a face that creases easily into a smile and a voice that's resonantly basso profundo.

THE day of our interview, Dr. Birdwhistell met my train at North Philadelphia and during the drive over to his lab filled me in on the early history of kinesics research. He started out, he explained, with a search for universal gestures, that is, for body language common to all cultures. He now states flatly:

"There are no universal gestures. As far as we know, there is no single facial expression, stance, or body position which conveys the same meaning in all societies."

This is a controversial statement, hotly disputed by others in the field, including psychologists such as Dr. Ekman of the Langley Porter Neuropsychiatric Institute, who has done cross-cultural research. In one study, armed with photographs of happy faces, sad faces, angry faces, surprised, disgusted and fearful faces, Ekman asked people in half a dozen different parts of the world to name the emotions portrayed in each one. And he concluded that the people in all the places selected, even those in isolated, primitive cultures, associated each photo with the same emotion. If people all over the world smile when they are happy, and recognize a happy face, is not the smile, then, a universal expression of emotion —part of our biological heritage (as no less an authority than Darwin said it was)? Birdwhistell concedes that all humans smile—even blind babies do—for we all have the same face muscles. However, he contends that the *meaning* of the smile is not universal. Even in the United States he has found that there are

"high-smile" areas, such as the South, where people do a lot of smiling, and "low-smile" areas, such as western New York State, where they do not (this is not a sign that Southerners are happier). In the South someone who does not often smile may be asked if he is angry, but in the Great Lakes region someone who does smile a lot may be asked what is so funny. It is culture, according to Birdwhistell, that supplies the meaning of the smile, and it cannot be said to be a simple pleasure reflex.

This is the old nature-nurture argument again, of course: heredity vs. environment. In this case, the two sides are not quite so far apart as they at first sound, since those who believe in universal gestures admit that smiles are culture-modified, and Birdwhistell admits that, anatomically speaking, they *are* universal.

AT this point, we arrived at the laboratory, which, with its sunny offices and quiet corridors, is actually nothing at all like a lab but more like the premises of some sedate, suburban firm with an interest in the movie-film business. Birdwhistell took me directly to the room where he does kinesic analysis using a slow-motion projector. The film he showed me there was as undramatic as anything you could find: just two people, therapist and patient, sitting opposite each other, talking. The segment he was working on was only a few seconds long, but for each second there were 24 frames of the film, and for each frame he was making a record, using an ingenious shorthand system he has devised, of every body motion of both therapist and patient.

Dr. Birdwhistell approaches the stream of body motion the same way the descriptive linguists approach the stream of speech. The first time you hear a strange language, it makes no sense at all. But if you go on listening, soon you can pick out distinct, recurr-

ing units, which may or may not be whole words, and eventually you can hear them combining in regular ways with other "words" into sentences. And if you repeat one of these units to yourself, you find it breaks down into smaller units called sounds.

In the same manner, Birdwhistell hunts through the stream of body motion for repeated movements. Each position of the head, brows, chin, eyes and other parts of the body has a shorthand symbol: these are the basic units that he calls "kines," which combine into larger patterns. He records the direction of movement of each "kine" with another set of symbols. Then, he analyzes what happens to the meaning of the message when one kine is removed from the context and everything else stays the same. The meaning, he said, is always in the context, never in any particular, isolated body motion. One case in point is Birdwhistell's and Scheflen's assertion that a woman who tightly crosses her arms or legs is relatively inaccessible to any approach. Whether this is correct, both affirm, depends upon such circumstances as what other people are around, what else she does with her body, and so on.

Kinesic stress is one way people reduce verbal ambiguities. As everyone knows, an eyebrow lift often accompanies a question. However, it is also a way to stress a word in the speech stream. There are other ways to signal a question, too, such as an upward tilt of the head or hand, and one can as easily stress something with a nod of the foot or a blink of the eyelids.

Small movements of the head, eyes, hands, fingers or even the shoulders that accompany specific pronouns, verbs or phrases Birdwhistell describes as "markers." With the pronouns "I," "me," "we" and "us" as well as words such as "this" and "how," a hand "marker" would be a motion toward the speaker's body, while the shoulders would be squeezed, or hunched, in the direction of an imaginary vertical line through the center of the body. With future-tense verbs the marker motion is forward; with the past tense, it is backward. All this seems so logical to Americans that it is a surprise to learn that other peoples, for example some American-Indian cultures, sometimes find these markers confusing or even insulting when combined with their language.

FROM the projection room we went on to the studio where psychotherapy sessions are filmed, a big, quiet room furnished with a semicircle of chairs, a closed-circuit TV and one small camera on a tripod that poked its snout unobtrusively through a gap in some curtains. Birdwhistell was interested in filming psychotherapy because it provides an accessible, natural context within which to study body motion. "Natural" is the key word, for he does not believe you can learn much that's valid about communication in the artificial environment provided in psych-lab experiments. "I don't take a fish out of water to learn how it swims," he said.

One of the things Birdwhistell has learned from the psychotherapy project is that even the best therapists usually cannot explain what it is that they do right. In fact, sometimes they do the opposite of what they think they do. A man who believes in being completely nonauthoritative, for example, can be seen conducting a group session as firmly as a conductor leads an orchestra, telling one person to speak and another to stop with a glance or a flick of the fingers.

OVER lunch that day, Dr. Birdwhistell explained his concept of "gender signals" to me. In every culture he has studied people can distinguish feminine body behaviors from masculine ones. Birdwhistell speculates that because in the human species the secondary sexual characteristics, such as breasts and body hair, are not

that dramatically different, body-motion differences function as "tertiary sexual characteristics" to help humans distinguish male from female. Gender in our society determines such simple matters as who gets up to do the dishes after dinner or who goes through a door first. What is defined as masculine or feminine, furthermore, varies from one culture to the next.

"We think of male Arabs as effeminate and seductive because of the way they close their eyelids—very slowly—in contrast to the speed with which American males do it. We find the way Latin males cross their legs feminine in contrast to the broken-four spread typical of American males." Birdwhistell leaned back in his chair and indicated his own legs: four-shaped, with one ankle propped on the other knee.

When sending gender signals, American women hold their thighs close together, according to Birdwhistell's studies. They walk with upper arms against their bodies and tilt their pelvises forward slightly. In contrast, American men sending gender signals stand with thighs somewhat apart. They hold their arms away from their bodies and swing them as they walk, and they carry their pelvises rolled slightly back.

Birdwhistell denies that these varying walking styles can be attributed to anatomical differences. Otherwise, he argues, they would be the same in all cultures—which they are not. In Eastern European countries, for instance, a man is much less likely to walk with the broad carriage and arm-swinging that we label "masculine," says Birdwhistell.

INEVITABLY, when Birdwhistell explains gender signals, people leap to the conclusion that what they signal is sexual attraction. Though this is sometimes true, very often it is not. Though gender emphasis may lead to a sexual relationship sometimes, at other times it is actually a way of preventing one from developing. A woman can pro-

tect herself from getting involved by sending inappropriate gender signals. "She sends them so strongly that they exclude all incoming messages. They're an insistence, not a response. That's the difference between a sexy woman and a sexual woman," Dr. Birdwhistell explained.

The belle of the cocktail party, the siren in the low-cut dress who is surrounded by men, is — according to Birdwhistell—surrounded primarily by the men who do not like women or simply do not want to get involved. For them, she is the safest woman in the room to be around, just because she is not in any real sense responsive. Men simply do not turn her on—they cannot, because her volume is already on "high." The sexual woman, on the other hand, may stand on the sidelines looking pretty uninteresting until a man comes along. Then she will respond to him in dozens of subtle, nonverbal ways, perhaps by sending gender signals, perhaps with "courting behavior."

RELEGATED in the Birdwhistell scheme of things to a category called "parakinesics" are all kinds of fascinating things that he feels are definitely part of the communication system. They include stance and posture; the way skin varies from pale to flushed, dry to oily, flaccid to rigid. Then there are general categories such as beauty and ugliness, gracefulness and awkwardness.

How can being ugly be communicative? Birdwhistell refuses to see ugliness as an inborn characteristic. To begin with, he says, attractiveness may be a very transitory quality, which comes and goes like sunshine on a cloudy day. Everyone recognizes that people sometimes become quite beautiful when they fall in love, or ugly in moments of hate and anger. And on a more long-term basis, looks are one way in which society sorts people out, and being attractive is not necessarily good for a person if it means that too much is expected of him. Some people feel safer being part of the minority group of the unattractive. The point is that culture presents us with certain definitions, and we behave accordingly. If culture says that fat is ugly, then the fat person is saying something with his obesity about how he wants to be treated.

IN the presence of Birdwhistell and other kinesicists, for whom every movement has a message, one cannot help being somewhat self-conscious about making dramatic gestures. By the time I interviewed Dr. Albert Scheflen, in fact, I was practically sitting on my hands. He told me that people often react this way: "But their fear is predicated on the idea that body behavior often reveals one's inner dirty work." Again, he reassured me that this is not what kinesicists are looking for.

Scheflen is a towering, white-bearded scientist whose slangy, drawling style of speech sits oddly with his rather formidable qualifications. Born in New Jersey in 1920, he got his M.D. in the nineteen-forties, became a neurologist, then in the nineteen-fifties a psychiatrist. He began private practice and went on to become involved in psychotherapy research. "We weren't getting anywhere with it, though," he recalls, "and then, just as I was looking around for something new to learn, I met Ray [Birdwhistell]. And he had it."

For 10 years, Scheflen shared the trials and triumphs of kinesic research with Birdwhistell. In the division of labor worked out between the two men, Birdwhistell did "microanalysis" — that is, he concentrated on mini-movements that are over in a fraction of a second or 10 seconds at most—while Scheflen tackled the longer stretches of behavior. In 1967, Scheflen moved to New York, where in his own lab, he is now studying day-long and even week-long sequences of body motion. This new Project on Human Communication — Scheflen is project director— is sponsored by the Albert

Einstein College of Medicine, the Bronx State Hospital and the Jewish Family Service, and supported by state funds. Lab space is provided by the hospital in an erstwhile nurses' residence.

Scheflen's current project centers on a ghetto neighborhood in the Bronx and involves televising families in their own homes with a camera mounted high on a living room or kitchen wall. The camera is simply left in place for six to ten weeks and family members, self-conscious at first, after about a week seem to forget that it is there. The video signal is recorded in a nearby apartment and researchers work with the tapes of it.

He is not primarily concerned with the personalities of the people whose daily lives he studies. What he is mainly interested in is territoriality: he studies body behavior by which an individual indicates that he is—or is not —on his own "turf."

I sat with Dr. Scheflen in a room crowded with bulky equipment, while he worked on a videotape of a family. The monitor showed a kitchen. A woman wearing an overcoat drifted into the room, then drifted out again. A moment later she was back and an eddy of small children came with her. It was early morning and she was about to leave for work.

Just then, Scheflen saw something he had been watching for and aimed a Polaroid camera at the screen. He explained that he had spotted an instance of face-to-face confrontation, a phenomenon that he is studying apart from his work on territoriality. So far, he has not found many cases of it in his videotapes. A colleague of Scheflen's, Dr. William Stewart, has a hunch that in poor black families, people look directly at each other less often than people do in middle-class white families. This is a small difference, but it may account for the fact that blacks meeting whites sometimes feel stared at, while whites feel that blacks are avoiding their eyes.

Really documenting such cultural differences, though, can be a lengthy, painstaking process. Dr. Scheflen, for example, will have to do comparison studies of black families and white families before he can back up Dr. Stewart's hunch about face-to-face confrontations with proof, and all that will take one or two years.

(Without new developments in audio-visual equipment, the kind of research the kinesicists are doing would not be possible—and sometimes their need has been mother of an invention. Until just about 10 years ago, for example, it was impossible to get a film projector that could be slowed to less than two-thirds normal speed; beyond that point, the image flickered badly. Partly because of the kinesicists' needs, some one finally invented a projector that could be run without flicker at any speed down to one frame a minute.)

With Birdwhistell and Kendon, Scheflen has done a lot of research on courting behavior. Everyone knows that when two people are attracted to each other, they show it in subtle ways. Some of the symptoms are well known; others are not. Scheflen has reported that readiness to court is visible first of all as heightened muscle tone. The individual holds himself, or herself, erect; legs have tighter tone and even the face changes — sagging, jowliness and pouches under the eyes all decrease. Eyes seem brighter and skin may become either flushed or pale. And often the person preens. Feminine preening is easy to recognize. Some of the male preening gestures —hair-grooming, tie-preening, sock-preening—usually go unrecognized.

Courting couples, of course, exchange long looks. They cock their heads and roll their pelvises. A woman may cross her legs, slightly exposing one thigh, place a hand on her hip, or protrude her breasts. She may slowly stroke her own thigh or wrist or present a palm. Anglo-Saxon women ordinarily show their palms hardly at all, says Scheflen,

PREENING: *A woman preening for a man is easy to recognize, but male preening is harder to spot. The man adjusting his tie is probably in what scientists call, quaintly, a "courting state." Smoothing the hair or straightening the socks may also be tipoffs that a man is courting a woman.*

but in courting they palm all over the place, even smoking or covering a cough with palm out.

"From that," says Scheflen, "you could perhaps derive a cheap rule: whenever a woman shows you her palm, she's courting you, whether she knows it or not." But in fact, he went on, people show palms in all sorts of relationships. "Showing the palm is an invitation to an encounter, and not necessarily sexual at all. It doesn't even mean one person necessarily likes the other, it just means they're coming together in some way, perhaps only on business. The whole thing is the context, again."

Scheflen has also discovered a phenomenon he calls quasi-courting, which can occur in practically any situation and need not signal sexual attraction at all. In the American middle class, quasi-courting may happen between parent and child, doctor and patient, at business meetings and at cocktail parties, even between people of the same sex. It is courting with a dif-

ference, with subtle qualifiers added that indicate that it is not to be taken seriously. A couple may momentarily seem to be courting, but closer observation will show that their bodies are turned slightly aside from each other, or their voices are a shade too loud for an intimate twosome. One or both may keep glancing about the room, or one person may extend an arm as if to include a third party, or drape the arm across his lap as a kind of barrier. Whatever the signal, it changes the whole significance of the behavior.

Quasi-courting apparently has a social function. In the group therapy films, it appeared regularly as a way to reinvolve someone who was becoming withdrawn. For example, in one film of family therapy, the daughter at first flashed courtship signals at the therapist. When he did not respond, she "decourted," meaning that she lost all that alert muscle tone and began to look uninterested and remote. Soon afterward, the therapist began a quasi-courting sequence: he locked

glances with the girl and for a while they dragged on their cigarettes in perfect synchrony. Then, perhaps becoming a little self-conscious about this intimacy, she looked sharply away and placed her arm across her lap as a barrier. Again she began to decourt, and she adopted her mother's posture and smoking rhythm. However, she did not, this time, dissociate herself from the group.

THESE days, while Dr. Scheflen concentrates on his televised families other members of his research team are involved in their own projects. For example, there is Dr. Adam Kendon, 36 years old, an Englishman with a luxuriant auburn beard, who likes to think of kinesics as a branch of zoology, a kind of human ethology. Dr. Kendon's current project, with Dr. Andrew Ferber as a collaborator, is a study of how humans greet one another.

"There are films of chimpanzee greetings," he says, "where you see two chimps approach each other. They shake hands, they embrace, they slap each other on the back. I can show you human greetings that look very similar."

Dr. Kendon's office is dominated by a film projector that has a hand crank added, to make frame-by-frame analysis easier. His greetings film, made at a backyard birthday party, shows a whole series of people crossing the yard to the host, who greets them with open arms.

"Watch now," Dr. Kendon told me, running through a particular sequence with the hand crank. "You'll see that the host moves forward with his neck extended and lifts his arms out and away from his body. Now look at the guest. His trunk is erect, his neck is not extended, and when he puts his arms up for the embrace, they are on the inside, with the host's arms outside. There are several other greetings in the film where you see the same things. These are just some observations we've made lately, but we wonder whether this is a particular greeting posture that you will see in males being greeted on their own territory, a sort of dominant-greeter's posture."

Kendon hopes eventually to do a "typology" of greetings, describing those that take place at the edges of territories and in public places, between close acquaintances and strangers, formal greetings and informal. Then, since animals greet, too, it should be possible to do a comparative anaylsis— to spot similarities and differences between human and other primate greetings, for example.

The kinesicists are all given to quoting Erving Goffman, as are many of the other researchers in the field. In a sense, he supplies the framework and they fill in the behavioral details. I talked to Professor Goffman at his beautiful old Philadelphia town house, in a living room the size of a small ballroom with a ceiling so high that it gradually vanished that day in the late-afternoon dusk. He is a small man, a 47-year-old Canadian with a ruggedly intelligent face whose interest in nonverbal communication dates back to the nineteen forties when he took a course taught by Birdwhistell at the University of Toronto.

Goffman does not have a lab. What he has instead is a filing system. When he writes, he puts together things he has read, bits of novels, items from books of etiquette, and what he gleaned from a year he spent studying the social structure of a mental institution. To this he adds his own systematic observation in social situations, from cocktail parties to public meetings, which he has recorded in voluminous detail. (Goffman dislikes being photographed for publication, perhaps, as he jokes, because he will lose anonymity, and thus his ability to do research in social gatherings.)

The results, in cool, precise and measured prose, are his books on face-to-face interaction. He has described, for example, what constitutes proper involvement in a conversation, as opposed to underinvolvement or overinvolvement, and how people accord each other "civil inattention" in public places. By this he means, for example, that a person passing a stranger in the street does not, under the rules, make gestures that indicate too much interest in the other; if he does, his behavior is likely to be interpreted as nosy or threatening.

Reading about Goffman's rules of public order, one gets a sense of just how vulnerable human beings really are. We simply assume that when we are out in public no one will attack us or block our way to suddenly start up a conversation; we depend on each other to behave properly. In recent years, though, the free and easy use of public and semipublic places has become subject to question. "What happens in confrontation politics," says Goffman, "is that persons in each other's presence decline intentionally to sustain one or more of the fundamental rules of order. Mental patients use the same strategies for different reasons."

Goffman has written that everything an individual does in the presence of others is made up of tacit threats and promises: indications that he knows his place and will stay in it, that he knows it but will not stay in it, or that he does not and may not. Mental symptoms are often simply evidence that he is not prepared to keep to his place. "In a hospital setting," he explained, "patients will in a conversation put to you a question much more candid, delicate and probing than would anyone but your analyst. They will, when you address them, not answer back. They will be exquisitely slovenly in their dress or withdrawn in their manner or when you're talking will come and lean into the conversation or interrupt it physically. These are all devices aimed at the rules of order."

Young radicals also attack the rules—and signify their refusal to know their place— when they occupy a building, seize the microphone at a public meeting or address a dean by his first name. Goffman cites the story of what happened when, during the student demonstrations at Columbia two years ago, Mark Rudd was invited to discuss the issues with some faculty members in a professor's apartment. After coffee was brought in on a silver service, Rudd took off his boots and socks, complaining that his feet were sweating.

THIS kind of pantomime is not hard to understand—it was an obvious attempt to shock others—but will you and I some day be able to read more obscure motives in a person's body behavior? Certainly some of us will try, though probably with marginal accuracy, since body language is subtle and complex. Most of the time, people simply use the motions prescribed by their culture as suitable in the context—which is actually the best way to conceal their true feelings. More important, we may learn to depend more on our intuitions, realizing that they are often based on actual body signals from other people which we perceive on a subliminal level.

As to the future uses of the field, most of the men working in it are not primarily concerned about that. They are doing pure science, not applied science; they study human communication because it is there. But there are, of course, numerous possibilities. Someday language specialists will probably be taught the kinesics of a foreign language along with its grammar and vocabulary. Kinesics should prove a handy tool for the study of child development. And research on intercultural differences could clear up some of the small but alienating misunderstandings between men of different cultures that come about just because they speak different body languages.

Birdwhistell, who has taught his science of kinesics to young psychiatrists in the past, now wants to concentrate on working with educators. He wants to do basic behavioral research on what makes a teacher good, how children learn to be good students, what is an optimum teaching situation.

Individual psychotherapy will not last long, he thinks, because it is too expensive and reaches only a small number of people: "No society in the world has ever been rich enough before so that one person—apart from a king or an emperor—could afford to take up so much of another person's time. A small number of therapists treat a small number of people, but it's a fraction of the population. On the other hand, a very large proportion of the population goes through our school system."

His most ambitious goal, however, is that men—at least some men—will learn to "communicate on purpose," that they will become aware of their own body motions and of what they communicate, and will then exercise the same control over their kinesic behavior that they already do over their words.

But the study of human communication is still in its infancy and it is hard to get a really clear idea of what it might grow up to be. Birdwhistell says that it is only about as far along as microbiology was when the microscope was first invented and people went around wearing face masks to protect them-selves from germs. One thing seems certain, though: men will no longer be able to assume that when two people meet, all that is communicated is the words they speak. As Dr. Birdwhistell told me:

"Years ago I started with the question: How do body motions flesh out words? Now I ask instead: When is it appropriate to use words? They're very appropriate to teach or to talk on the telephone, but you and I are communicating on several levels now and on only one or two of them have words any relevance whatsoever. These days I put it another way: Man is a multi-sensorial being. Occasionally, he verbalizes." ■

communication
WITHOUT WORDS

By Albert Mehrabian

SUPPOSE YOU ARE SITTING in my office listening to me describe some research I have done on communication. I tell you that feelings are communicated less by the words a person uses than by certain nonverbal means—that, for example, the verbal part of a spoken message has considerably less effect on whether a listener feels liked or disliked than a speaker's facial expression or tone of voice.

So far so good. But suppose I add, "In fact, we've worked out a formula that shows exactly how much each of these components contributes to the effect of the message as a whole. It goes like this: Total Impact = .07 verbal + .38 vocal + .55 facial."

What would you say to *that?* Perhaps you would smile good-naturedly and say, with some feeling, "Baloney!" Or perhaps you would frown and remark acidly, "Isn't science grand." My own response to the first answer would probably be to smile back: the facial part of your message, at least, was positive (55 per cent of the total). The second answer might make me uncomfortable: only the verbal part was positive (seven per cent).

The point here is not only that my reactions would lend credence to the formula but that most listeners would have mixed feelings about my statement. People like to see science march on, but they tend to resent its intrusion into an "art" like the communication of feelings, just as they find analytical and quantitative approaches to the study of personality cold, mechanistic and unacceptable.

The psychologist himself is sometimes plagued by the feeling that he is trying to put a rainbow into a bottle. Fascinated by a complicated and emotionally rich human situation, he begins to study it, only to find in the course of his research that he has destroyed part of the mystique that originally intrigued and involved him. But despite a certain nostalgia for earlier, more intuitive approaches, one must acknowledge that concrete experimental data have added a great deal to our understanding of how feelings are communicated. In fact, as I hope to show, analytical and intuitive findings do not so much conflict as complement each other.

It is indeed difficult to know what another person really feels. He says one thing and does another; he seems to mean something but we have an uneasy feeling it isn't true. The early psychoanalysts, facing this problem of inconsistencies and ambiguities in a person's communications, attempted to resolve it through the concepts of the conscious and the unconscious. They assumed that contradictory messages meant a conflict between superficial, deceitful, or erroneous feelings on the one hand and true attitudes and feelings on the other. Their role, then, was to help the client separate the wheat from the chaff.

The question was, how could this be done? Some analysts insisted that inferring the client's unconscious wishes was a completely intuitive process. Others thought that some nonverbal behavior, such as posture, position and movement, could be used in a more objective way to discover the client's feelings. A favorite technique of Frieda Fromm-Reichmann, for example, was to imitate a client's posture herself in order to obtain some feeling for what he was experiencing.

Thus began the gradual shift away from the idea that communication is primarily verbal, and that the verbal message includes distortions or ambiguities due to unobservable motives that only experts can discover.

Language, though, can be used to communicate almost anything. By comparison, nonverbal behavior is very limited in range. Usually, it is used to communicate feelings, likings and preferences, and it customarily reinforces or contradicts the feelings that are communicated verbally. Less often, it adds a new dimension of sorts to a verbal message, as when a salesman describes his product to a client and simultaneously conveys, nonverbally, the impression that he likes the client.

A great many forms of nonverbal behavior can communicate feelings: touching, facial expression, tone of voice, spatial distance from the addressee, relaxation of posture, rate of speech, number of errors in speech. Some of these are generally recognized as informative. Untrained adults and children easily infer that they are liked or disliked from certain facial expressions, from whether (and how) someone touches them, and from a speaker's tone of voice. Other behavior, such as posture, has a more subtle effect. A listener may sense how someone feels about him from the way the person sits while talking to him, but he may have trouble identifying precisely what his impression comes from.

Correct intuitive judgments of the

feelings or attitudes of others are especially difficult when different degrees of feeling, or contradictory kinds of feeling, are expressed simultaneously through different forms of behavior. As I have pointed out, there is a distinction between verbal and vocal information (vocal information being what is lost when speech is written down—intonation, tone, stress, length and frequency of pauses, and so on), and the two kinds of information do not always communicate the same feeling. This distinction, which has been recognized for some time, has shed new light on certain types of communication. Sarcasm, for example, can be defined as a message in which the information transmitted vocally contradicts the information transmitted verbally. Usually the verbal information is positive and the vocal is negative, as in "Isn't science grand."

Through the use of an electronic filter, it is possible to measure the degree of liking communicated vocally. What the filter does is eliminate the higher frequencies of recorded speech, so that words are unintelligible but most vocal qualities remain. (For women's speech, we eliminate frequencies higher than about 200 cycles per second; for men, frequencies over about 100 cycles per second.) When people are asked to judge the degree of liking conveyed by the filtered speech, they perform the task rather easily and with a significant amount of agreement.

This method allows us to find out, in a given message, just how inconsistent the information communicated in words and the information communicated vocally really are. We ask one group to judge the amount of liking conveyed by a transcription of what was said, the verbal part of the message. A second group judges the vocal component, and a third group judges the impact of the complete recorded message. In one study of this sort we found that, when the verbal and vocal components of a message agree (both positive or both negative), the message as a whole is judged a little more positive or a little more negative than either component by itself. But when vocal information contradicts verbal, vocal wins out. If someone calls you "honey" in a nasty tone of voice, you are likely to feel disliked; it is also possible to say "I hate you" in a way that conveys exactly the opposite feeling.

Besides the verbal and vocal characteristics of speech, there are other, more subtle, signals of meaning in a spoken message. For example, everyone makes mistakes when he talks—unnecessary repetitions, stutterings, the omission of parts of words, incomplete sentences, "ums" and "ahs." In a number of studies of speech errors, George Mahl of Yale University has found that errors become more frequent as the speaker's discomfort or anxiety increases. It might be interesting to apply this index in an attempt to detect deceit (though on some occasions it might be risky: confidence men are notoriously smooth talkers).

Timing is also highly informative. How long does a speaker allow silent periods to last, and how long does he wait before he answers his partner? How long do his utterances tend to be? How often does he interrupt his partner, or wait an inappropriately long time before speaking? Joseph Matarazzo and his colleagues at the University of Oregon have found that each of these speech habits is stable from person to person, and each tells something about the speaker's personality and about his feelings toward and status in relation to his partner.

Utterance duration, for example, is a very stable quality in a person's speech; about 30 seconds long on the average. But when someone talks to a partner whose status is higher than his own, the more the high-status person nods his head the longer the speaker's utterances become. If the high-status person changes his own customary speech pattern toward longer or shorter utterances, the lower-status person will change his own speech in the same direction. If the high-status person often interrupts the speaker, or creates long silences, the speaker is likely to become quite uncomfortable. These are things that can be observed outside the laboratory as well as under experimental conditions. If you have an employee who makes you uneasy and seems not to respect you, watch him the next time you talk to him—perhaps he is failing to follow the customary low-status pattern.

Immediacy or directness is another good source of information about feelings. We use more distant forms of communication when the act of communicating is undesirable or uncomfortable. For example, some people would rather transmit discontent with an employee's

work through a third party than do it themselves, and some find it easier to communicate negative feelings in writing than by telephone or face to face.

Distance can show a negative attitude toward the message itself, as well as toward the act of delivering it. Certain forms of speech are more distant than others, and they show fewer positive feelings for the subject referred to. A speaker might say "Those people need help," which is more distant than "These people need help," which is in turn even more distant than "These people need our help." Or he might say "Sam and I have been having dinner," which has less immediacy than "Sam and I are having dinner."

Facial expression, touching, gestures, self-manipulation (such as scratching), changes in body position, and head movements—all these express a person's positive and negative attitudes, both at the moment and in general, and many reflect status relationships as well. Movements of the limbs and head, for example, not only indicate one's attitude toward a specific set of circumstances but relate to how dominant, and how anxious, one generally tends to be in social situations. Gross changes in body position, such as shifting in the chair, may show negative feelings toward the person one is talking to. They may also be cues: "It's your turn to talk," or "I'm about to get out of here, so finish what you're saying."

Posture is used to indicate both liking and status. The more a person leans toward his addressee, the more positively he feels about him. Relaxation of posture is a good indicator of both attitude and status, and one that we have been able to measure quite precisely. Three categories have been established for relaxation in a seated position: least relaxation is indicated by muscular tension in the hands and rigidity of posture; moderate relaxation is indicated by a forward lean of about 20 degrees and a sideways lean of less than 10 degrees, a curved back, and, for women, an open arm position; and extreme relaxation is indicated by a reclining angle greater than 20 degrees and a sideways lean greater than 10 degrees.

Our findings suggest that a speaker relaxes either very little or a great deal when he dislikes the person he is talking to, and to a moderate degree when he likes his companion. It seems that extreme tension occurs with threatening addressees, and extreme relaxation with nonthreatening, disliked addressees. In particular, men tend to become tense when talking to other men whom they dislike; on the other hand, women talking to men *or* women and men talking to women show dislike through extreme relaxation. As for status, people relax most with a low-status addressee, second-most with a peer, and least with someone of higher status than their own. Body orientation also shows status: in both sexes, it is least direct toward women with low status and most direct toward disliked men of high status. In part, body orientation seems to be determined by whether one regards one's partner as threatening.

The more you like a person, the more time you are likely to spend looking into his eyes as you talk to him. Standing close to your partner and facing him directly (which makes eye contact easier) also indicate positive feelings. And you are likely to stand or sit closer to your peers than you do to addressees whose status is either lower or higher than yours.

What I have said so far has been based on research studies performed, for the most part, with college students from the middle and upper-middle classes. One interesting question about communication, however, concerns young children from lower socioeconomic levels. Are these children, as some have suggested, more responsive to implicit channels of communication than middle- and upper-class children are?

Morton Wiener and his colleagues at Clark University had a group of middle- and lower-class children play learning games in which the reward for learning was praise. The child's responsiveness to the verbal and vocal parts of the praise-reward was measured by how much he learned. Praise came in two forms: the objective words "right" and "correct," and the more affective or evaluative words, "good" and "fine." All four words were spoken sometimes in a positive tone of voice and sometimes neutrally.

Positive intonation proved to have a dramatic effect on the learning rate of the lower-class group. They learned much faster when the vocal part of the message was positive than when it was neutral. Positive intonation affected the middle-class group as well, but not nearly as much.

If children of lower socioeconomic groups are more responsive to facial expression, posture and touch as well as to vocal communication, that fact could have interesting applications to elementary education. For example, teachers could be explicitly trained to be aware of, and to use, the forms of praise (nonverbal or verbal) that would be likely to have the greatest effect on their particular students.

Another application of experimental data on communication is to the interpretation and treatment of schizophrenia. The literature on schizophrenia has for some time emphasized that parents of schizophrenic children give off contradictory signals simultaneously. Perhaps the parent tells the child in words that he loves him, but his posture conveys a negative attitude. According to the "double-bind" theory of schizophrenia, the child who perceives simultaneous contradictory feelings in his parent does not know how to react: should he respond to the positive part of the message, or to the negative? If he is frequently placed in this paralyzing situation, he may learn to respond with contradictory communications of his own. The boy who sends a birthday card to his mother and signs it "Napoleon" says that he likes his mother and yet denies that he is the one who likes her.

In an attempt to determine whether parents of disturbed children really do emit more inconsistent messages about their feelings than other parents do, my colleagues and I have compared what these parents communicate verbally and vocally with what they show through posture. We interviewed parents of moderately and quite severely disturbed children, in the presence of the child, about the child's problem. The interview was video-recorded without the parents' knowledge, so that we could analyze their behavior later on. Our measurements supplied both the amount of inconsistency between the parents' verbal-

vocal and postural communications, and the total amount of liking that the parents communicated.

According to the double-bind theory, the parents of the more disturbed children should have behaved more inconsistently than the parents of the less disturbed children. This was not confirmed: there was no significant difference between the two groups. However, the *total amount* of positive feeling communicated by parents of the more disturbed children was less than that communicated by the other group.

This suggests that (1) negative communications toward disturbed children occur because the child is a problem and therefore elicits them, or (2) the negative attitude precedes the child's disturbance. It may also be that both factors operate together, in a vicious circle.

If so, one way to break the cycle is for the therapist to create situations in which the parent can have better feelings toward the child. A more positive attitude from the parent may make the child more responsive to his directives, and the spiral may begin to move up instead of down. In our own work with disturbed children, this kind of procedure has been used to good effect.

If one puts one's mind to it, one can think of a great many other applications for the findings I have described, though not all of them concern serious problems. Politicians, for example, are careful to maintain eye contact with the television camera when they speak, but they are not always careful about how they sit when they debate another candidate of, presumably, equal status.

Public relations men might find a use for some of the subtler signals of feeling. So might Don Juans. And so might ordinary people, who could try watching other people's signals and changing their own, for fun at a party or in a spirit of experimentation at home. I trust that does not strike you as a cold, manipulative suggestion, indicating dislike for the human race. I assure you that, if you had more than a transcription of words to judge from (seven per cent of total message), it would not.

16

PERFIDIOUS FEMININE FACES [1]

DAPHNE E. BUGENTAL,[2]

LEONORE R. LOVE,

AND ROBERT M. GIANETTO

University of California, Los Angeles

Ratings were made of videotaped verbal and nonverbal (smiling) behavior of parents in interaction with their children. The sample included 20 families containing a disturbed child and 20 normal control families. An interaction was predicted and confirmed ($p = .05$) between parent sex and facial expression; that is, when a father smiled, he was making a friendlier or more approving statement than when he was not smiling; for mothers, there was no difference in the evaluative content of verbal messages when she was smiling versus when she was not smiling. This pattern was found to be unrelated to child disturbance. The findings were, however, limited to middle-class families because the majority of lower-class mothers in this sample did not smile at all.

This study explored the evaluative connotations of smiles in parental communications to their children, as part of a continuing analysis of communication within families (Bugental, 1966; Bugental, Kaswan, & Love, 1970; Bugental, Kaswan, Love, & Fox, 1970; Bugental, Love, Kaswan, & April, 1971). The experimental portions of our research have included analyses of the meanings ascribed to communications containing systematically varied channel inputs; the findings obtained suggested that children respond differently to male and female smiles. In the present investigation, an analysis was made of spontaneous parent-child communication in order to measure parental sex differences in the relationship between smiling behavior and associated verbal content. It was predicted that the smile is more closely related to positive verbal evaluation (friendliness, approval, or consideration) for male encoders than for female encoders.

The smiling face stereotypically represents friendliness in our culture. And there is little question that a heavy reliance is placed on facial expressions in estimating the evaluative connotation of a message. Mehrabian and Ferris (1967) found that adults give greater weight to facial expressions than to vocal intonation in decoding conflicting messages; Bugental, Kaswan, and Love (1970) found that adults give greater weight to facial expression than either verbal content or vocal intonation in interpreting conflicting messages. But it is obvious that a smile may be used without sincerity or without a truly positive evaluative connotation. It may be used as part of socially prescribed role behavior. Strangers smile as a polite gesture in casual, nonevaluative interaction. A woman smiles in response to a baby. A smile may be used as a facade when a person is nervous; experimental subjects have been found to give "forced smiles" in response to a variety of emotion-provoking situations (Landis, 1924). Additionally, it has been found to have a stronger relationship with approval seeking than with actual subsequent approval (Rosenfeld, 1966). From a phylogenetic standpoint, it has been observed that apes use a rudimentary smile as an appeasement gesture (Andrew, 1965). Cross-culturally, the smile or laugh has been observed to be used by the Japanese to mask sorrow (Klineberg, 1935). Some question may be raised then as to just how reliably friendly a smile is, and whether, in fact, everyone responds to a smile as positive. There are indications from recent research that there are developmental differences in response to facial expressions. Levy-Schoen (1964) found that although young children do respond to facial expressions, these cues do not become *dominant* in impression formation until children are at least 8 years old. Bugental, Kaswan, Love, and Fox (1970) found that young children (5–8 years old) respond to women's smiles, in comparison with men's smiles, as relatively neutral. In a second study (Bugental, Kaswan, & Love, 1970), it was found that children (5–12 years old), in contrast with adults, respond to "kidding" messages (a negative statement accompanied by a smile) as negative; this negative interpretation was stronger if the speaker was a woman.

The question which arises from the observed developmental trend is: To what extent do children perceive adult communication accurately, and to what extent is the perception and integration of facial expressions an emergent skill which is not fully developed until somewhere between the ages of 8 and 12? It was predicted here that the young child's differential response to men and women reflects true sex differences in adult communication patterns. A general developmental trend in perceptual skills, although potentially a contributing factor, would not account for the differential response to male and female smiles.

It was anticipated that fathers are more likely than mothers to use the smile in nonverbal conjunction with friendly, approving statements. Women—in particular, mothers—may use the smile as a part of their culturally prescribed role. The traditional female role demands warm, compliant behavior in public situations; the smiling facial expression may provide the mask to convey this impression. If the smile serves this function for women, there may be little or no relationship between smiling and the evaluative content of verbal messages. For her, the smile may be situationally or role defined, rather than being relevant to the immediate verbal interchange.

In this study, the videotaped interactions of 20 "disturbed" and 20 normal control families were analyzed for parental facial expressions and verbal content. The main prediction was concerned with the differential relationship between smiles and verbal content for fathers versus mothers. An interaction was anticipated between parent sex and smiling: fathers (but not mothers) communicate more positive verbal connotations when smiling than when not smiling.

A second prediction was made with respect to the verbal messages accompanying parental smiles. It was predicted that this relationship would vary as a function of child disturbance. In a previous study (Bugental et al., 1971), it was found that the mothers of disturbed children were more likely than normal control mothers to demonstrate evaluative conflict between communication channels. For this reason, it was predicted that there would be more verbal-visual conflict for this group.

METHOD

Sample

The original group from which we drew samples was composed of 91 disturbed and 30 matched normal control families (samples are described in Kaswan & Love, 1969). The disturbed group included children (ages 8–12) referred by their teachers as chronically demonstrating behavior or emotional disturbances in the school setting. Families varied widely in socioeconomic level. Eighty-one percent of the disturbed children and 86% of the normal control children were boys.

For this study, 20 disturbed and 20 normal control families were selected from the total sample for analysis of their videotaped interaction. The two groups were matched for socioeconomic composition, which we believed to be of major concern as a potentially interacting variable. Families were restricted to those containing both a mother and a father. Beyond these selection factors, families were chosen on the basis of the technical quality of their videotapes.

Videotaped Interaction

All families were videotaped from an adjacent room in a standardly equipped waiting room; all knew they would be observed and recorded at some point during their visits to the clinic. Videotaped material included free interaction between family members while they were waiting (about 20 minutes) and a problem-definition period, in which the family discussed what they would like changed in their family (about 5 minutes).

Visual Ratings

Each videotape was rated for visual content by showing judges the TV picture with the sound turned off. Two judges watched the tapes independently and recorded any instances in which a parent smiled or demonstrated negative facial expressions or gestures.[3] Although three judges[4] were used in making picture ratings, only two were used for any given tape. Judges included one male and two female undergraduate students.

[1] This study was supported by United States Public Health Service Grant 1R01-MH-14770; computing assistance was obtained from the Health Sciences Computing Facility, University of California, Los Angeles, sponsored by National Institites of Health Grant FR-3.

[2] Requests for reprints should be sent to Daphne E. Bugental, Department of Psychology, University of California, Los Angeles, California 90024.

[3] "Scenes" containing negative visual content were relatively infrequent (only 40% of the mothers and 28% of the fathers had any "negative picture" scenes) and were not used in this study.

[4] The three judges had known interjudge reliability, based on previous ratings of the evaluative components of the visual content of videotaped messages (rs = .85, .86, and .87).

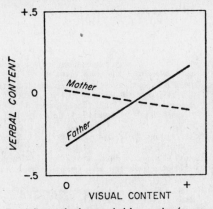

Fig. 1. Interaction between facial expression (presence or absence of smiling) and parent sex.

Verbal Ratings

Typescripts were made of all parent-child messages in which the parent speaking was visible. The total set of typescripts was subdivided into 10 subsets, each of which was rated by five male and five female introductory psychology students (10 groups of subjects). Subjects rated scripts on a 5-point evaluative scale from positive (friendly, approving, or considerate) to negative (unfriendly, disapproving, or inconsiderate).

Scene Selection

Messages were retained for analysis only if (a) both judges agreed on the visual rating (smiling versus not smiling) and (b) 8 out of 10 script judges made ratings within a 2-point range.[5] Scripts given more variable ratings were excluded. There were no significant differences (or trends) in the proportion of scenes eliminated for mothers versus fathers, or normal versus disturbed families. The final sample included 417 scenes.

RESULTS

For each parent, mean ratings were computed on parent-child scripts accompanied by smiles and parent-child scripts accompanied by neutral faces. The predicted relationships were tested by a mixed-design analysis of variance, which included two between-subjects comparisons (normal versus disturbed families; mothers versus fathers) and one within-subjects comparison (smiles versus neutral faces). The final analysis was based on 13 disturbed and 13 normal mothers and 12 disturbed and 12 normal fathers; 30 parents were excluded because they did not produce *both* smiling and nonsmiling messages (required for a within-subjects comparison in the analysis of variance).

The predicted interaction between parent sex and facial expression was obtained ($F = 4.75$, $df = 1/46$, $p = .05$). The interaction is shown graphically in Figure 1. No other F tests approached statistical significance. As predicted, fathers made more positive statements when smiling than when not smiling ($t = 2.39$, $p = .05$). Mothers' verbal messages, on the other hand, were no more positive (or were even slightly more negative) when they were smiling than when they were not smiling. It should be noted that this sex difference cannot be explained on the basis of smaller variability of the evaluative content of mothers' verbal statements; in actuality, mothers' verbal messages were more variable than fathers' verbal messages (for both positive-face and

[5] The median interjudge reliability in a sample of raters ($n = 10$) was low ($r = .49$). Consequently the final scene selection was restricted to scripts with agreed-upon ratings.

neutral-face scenes). The trend for fathers' smiles to accompany friendlier statements than did mothers' smiles was in the expected direction. The trend for fathers' neutral faces to accompany more negative statements than did mothers' neutral faces was not anticipated. The exact pattern of interaction observed would require replication before it could be interpreted exactly.

No significant main effects or interactions were found as a function of child disturbance. Thus, our prediction was not confirmed with respect to verbal-visual conflict within parental messages to disturbed children.

The sample used in this study included eight families from lower-class schools; six of these families were black and two were Mexican-American (none of the middle-class families were black or Mexican-American). Because of this confounding, it is impossible to make any clear socioeconomic or racial comparison. However, it is of interest to note that only 13% of the lower-class mothers smiled more than once, whereas 75% of the middle-class mothers smiled more than once.[6] The difference between groups on frequency of smiling was significant at the .01 level of confidence ($X^2 = 7.09$). This difference in smiling frequency is not an artifact of number of scenes: lower-class mothers had slightly (but not significantly) more neutral-face scenes than did middle-class mothers. Because of the small number of lower-class mothers who smiled at all ($n = 3$), no meaningful comparison could be made of the "sincerity" of lower-class versus middle-class smiles.

DISCUSSION

As predicted, smiling was found to be differentially related to verbal communication for male and female encoders. When fathers smiled at their children, they were saying something relatively friendlier or more approving than if they were not smiling. When mothers smiled at their children, their verbal message was no more positive in evaluative content than if they were not smiling. This parental sex difference was observed within both disturbed and normal families. Our evidence was based on videotaped observations, but the same parental sex trend was found in a pilot study of spontaneous, non-videotaped communications to children (based on eavesdropping of public interaction between family members).[7] It was very apparent to

[6] There was no significant difference between lower-class and middle-class fathers in smiling frequency.

[7] Comparisons were made of the first statement made with a smile and the first statement made with a neutral face in natural parent-child interaction. Fathers' statements were friendlier when they were smiling ($+.63$ on a scale from $+2$ to -2) than when they were not smiling ($-.01$; $t = 1.48$, $df = 26$, $p = .10$, one-tailed test); fathers' smiling statements were also friendlier than mothers' smiling statements ($t = 1.47$, $df = 26$, $p = .10$, one-tailed test). There was, however, no difference in the ratings of mothers' "smiling" statements ($+.04$) and mothers' "neutral face" statements ($-.03$). This pilot data supports our principal finding with respect to the friendliness of fathers' smiles, but fails to replicate our initial observation that fathers' neutral faces accompanied somewhat negative messages. All interactions observed were limited to intrafamily interaction under low-observation conditions, that is, others around them were engaged in their own activities and conversations, and there was little reason for them to suspect surveillance.

observers that parents (in particular, mothers) smiled a great deal when observed (videotaped) and very little when supposedly unobserved; but the *differential* sincerity of the smile (fathers versus mothers) held for both observational conditions. All situations measured were public, of course, but within this constraint, it does appear that fathers' smiles are more sincere (i.e., more likely to be associated with verbal friendliness or approval) than mothers' smiles. Consequently, support is given for our expectation that children are, in fact, perceiving adults accurately when they attribute greater friendliness to a male than a female smile (Bugental, Kaswan, Love, & Fox, 1970).

Significant differences occurred in maternal smiling behavior as a function of social class. White middle-class mothers smiled significantly more than lower-class mothers (all of whom were black or Mexican-American). The confounding of race and social class does not allow us to make any secure generalizations about group differences in the use of the smile; however, the differences in the use of this facial expression were striking and would appear to be of importance in any observational measures made of families which differ in socioeconomic and/or racial composition. It was noted anecdotally that there was a consistent focus among lower-class mothers on controlling their children closely. They visually "tracked" every movement the child made, and were constantly concerned that the child behaved properly. To the extent that it may be assumed that parents were trying to present a good impression, this behavior may have represented the lower-class mother's idea of a "good mother." This restrictive, controlling behavior has classically been observed among lower-class mothers (Sears, Maccoby, & Levin, 1957; Waters & Crandall, 1964). Additionally, it may reasonably be posited that lower-class families are more uncomfortable within a university clinic (under semiexperimental conditions) than a middle-class family would be. This discomfort could in turn influence the observed communication patterns.

No significant differences were found between the mothers of normal and disturbed children in the relative sincerity of their smiles. Normal and disturbed mothers produced an equivalent number of conflicting messages, that is, negative verbal messages accompanied by smiles. This type of channel conflict appears to be widespread in mother-child messages, rather than being unique to communication patterns where a disturbance is present.

The question arises as to the meaning of the middle-class mother's public smile. The most obvious interpretation is that she was trying to meet middle-class expectations of the good mother role. To enact the part of a "loving mother" (for the benefit of possible observers), she should not express negativity openly; thus, she may have used the smile not only with positive messages but also with critical verbal statements as a concomitant "softener." Smiling behavior may also connote submissiveness or compliance. Women, in meeting generalized sex-role expectations, may use a smile as socially ingratiating behavior, rather than as an indicator of friendliness or approval. The submissive or compliant expectations of the female role may not be completely known to the young child (as indicated by the absence of sex differences in persuasibility; Janis & Field, 1959; King, 1959) but are learned by adolescence (Abelson & Lesser, 1959). The submissive female smile thus would have little positive value for the young child, but might be expected to be seen as "good" behavior by adolescents and adults. There would be little disagreement that the dominant woman is negatively evaluated in our culture as a whole. The young child's response to a woman's smile could then be understood as accurate, in the sense that her smile does not directly signal friendliness toward or approval of him. Any social ingratiation connotations of a woman's smile would not be interpreted by the child as good (or bad); not only are these connotations likely to be poorly understood by the child, but they are more likely to be directed toward potential adult observers than toward the child himself.

Our observations provide a start toward a systematic individual and intracultural analysis of the differential use made of one type of nonverbal behavior. Further research will be needed to separate out the social class and racial aspects of our observed differences between middle-class and lower-class mothers.

To better understand the meaning of smiling behavior, additional information is needed about (*a*) differential qualitative features of smiles (duration, eye involvement, etc.), (*b*) nonevaluative connotations (e.g., submissiveness) of the smile, and (*c*) contextual factors in the use of smiles.

REFERENCES

ABELSON, R. P., & LESSER, G. S. The measurement of persuasibility in children. In I. L. Janis & C. I. Hovland (Eds.), *Personality and persuasibility.* New Haven: Yale University Press, 1959.

ANDREW, R. J. The origins of facial expressions. *Scientific American,* 1965, **213,** 88–94.

BUGENTAL, D. E. Characteristics of interpersonal messages in families. In D. J. Kincaid (Chm.), Communication patterns in the family and school as related to child adjustment. Symposium presented at the meeting of the American Psychological Association, New York, September 1966.

BUGENTAL, D. E., KASWAN, J. W., & LOVE, L. R. Perception of contradictory meanings conveyed by verbal and nonverbal channels. *Journal of Personality and Social Psychology,* 1970, 16, 647–655.

BUGENTAL, D. E., KASWAN, J. W., LOVE, L. R., & FOX, M. N. Child versus adult perception of evaluative messages in verbal, vocal, and visual channels. *Developmental Psychology,* 1970, 2, 367–375.

BUGENTAL, D. E., LOVE, L. R., KASWAN, J. W., & APRIL, C. Verbal-nonverbal conflict in parental messages to normal and disturbed children. *Journal of Abnormal Psychology,* 1971, 77, 6–10.

JANIS, I. L., & FIELD, P. B. Sex differences and personality factors related to persuasibility. In C. I. Hovland & I. L. Janis (Eds.), *Personality and persuasibility.* New Haven: Yale University Press, 1959.

KASWAN, J. W., & LOVE, L. R. Confrontation as a method of clinical intervention. *Journal of Nervous and Mental Disease,* 1969, 148, 224–237.

KING, B. T. Relationships between susceptibility to opinion change and child rearing practices. In C. I. Hovland & I. L. Janis (Eds.), *Personality and persuasibility.* New Haven: Yale University Press, 1959.

KLINEBERG, O. *Racial differences.* New York: Harper & Row, 1935.

LANDIS, C. Studies of emotional reactions: II. General behavior and facial expression. *Journal of Comparative Psychology,* 1924, 4, 447–509.

LEVY-SCHOEN, A. *L'image d'autrui chez l'enfant.* Paris: Presses Universitaries de France, 1964.

MEHRABIAN, A., & FERRIS, S. R. Inference of attitudes from nonverbal communication. *Journal of Consulting Psychology,* 1967, 31, 248–252.

ROSENFELD, H. M. Approval-seeking and approval-inducing functions of verbal and nonverbal responses in the dyad. *Journal of Personality and Social Psychology,* 1966, 4, 597–605.

SEARS, R. R., MACCOBY, E. E., & LEVIN, H. *Patterns of child-rearing.* Evanston, Ill.: Row, Peterson, 1957.

WATERS, E., & CRANDALL, V. J. Social class and observed maternal behavior from 1940 to 1960. *Child Development,* 1964, **35,** 1021–1032.

17

The Laws of Looking

by Michael Argyle

Human gaze can convey a threat,
entice a lover, direct a conversation,
or express personality.

Residents of big cities quickly learn the laws of looking. Never make eye contact with a panhandler, or you will be pursued for handouts; with a religious fanatic, or you will be caught in a diatribe; with a belligerent loner, or you will become the object of a menacing tirade; with a lost visitor, or you will feel responsible to help. Never stare back at a stranger who stares relentlessly at you, or your life may be in danger.

There are happier laws, of course. Ovid, wise in the ways of sexual seduction, advised the lover to "Let your eyes gaze into hers, let the gazing be a confession: Often the silent glance brings more conviction than words." The woman was to keep her eyes "gentle and mild, soft for entreating of love. . . . If he is looking at you, return his gaze, and smile sweetly." Ovid understood that gaze is a sensual signal of sexual intention.

What poets suspected, researchers have demonstrated. Patterns of gaze are neither arbitrary nor accidental, but follow definite rules—some apparently innate and others specific to culture. We use vision not just as a channel for collecting information about the world around us, but also as a signal that directs

conversation, conveys silent messages, and expresses personality. Gaze is closely coordinated with speaking and listening; it provides feedback, for example, that tells a speaker when to be quiet and the listener when to start talking. You will know from your companion's sullen glare that she is peeved, or from her misty gaze that she is smitten.

Gaze emerged as a social signal early in evolutionary time, as soon as vision developed. Eyes and eyelike designs often acted as protective coloration or a warning to predators. Some butterflies have eye designs on their wings, for instance, and if these patterns are experimentally removed, the butterflies are more likely to be attacked by birds. Some fish have eye spots that expand during attack; small eye spots apparently provoke attack and large ones inhibit it. In primates, eye patterns such as eyebrows and eye rings may play a similar role. Many human societies have believed in the power of the eye to inflict harm (the evil eye), and tribal masks with elaborate eye displays are common devices to ward off danger and assert authority.

The most common meaning conveyed by gaze is a threat signal. Ralph Exline and Absalom Yellin found that if an experimenter stared at a caged monkey, the monkey attacked or threatened to attack on 76 percent of the trials; if the experimenter looked away almost at once, the monkey responded aggressively about half the time. We have much of the monkey in us. Phoebe Ellsworth and her colleagues found that when they got motorcyclists or pedestrians to stare at car drivers stopped at intersections, the drivers moved off more rapidly from stoplights. Peter Marsh found that a

Large, staring eyes are often prominent in tribal masks, like this one from the Gere of Liberia. Many such masks are used as a defense against evil spirits.

mere glance from a member of a rival group of football supporters is enough to start a fight; the recipient of the glance justifies his attack with cries of "He looked at me!"

Conversely, to avoid or break a stare has a shared meaning among many animal species—appeasement. During battle or courtship, gaze cutoffs reduce the opponent's aggression or the urge to flee. I heard of one man who discovered the appeasement meaning of gaze cutoff just in time. He was riding a New York subway one afternoon when he inadvertently caught the eyes of a large, nervous man sitting opposite, reading about the art of self-control. At once they were locked in a deadly stare-down. My friend soon capitulated, smiled, broke the gaze and offered the V sign. The nervous giant laughed, strode across the aisle and, magnanimous victor he, embraced my friend warmly.

The further a species travels up the evolutionary ladder, the greater the range of significance of the eye. Reptiles, birds, and mammals use their eyes and eye rings (such as the raccoon's mask) for many social purposes: territoriality, courtship, dominance, withdrawal. At the primate level, however, gaze takes on a unique capacity to indicate attachment. Only primates— monkeys, apes, and human beings—use gaze to attract as well as attack, to make friends as well as enemies, to seduce as well as repel.

Primates *can* use gaze to threaten, but they are just as likely to gaze fondly. Psychologists have found that couples in love and individuals who are mutually attracted gaze longer at each other than couples who are indifferent. This may not be news to songwriters and lovers, but it is a special talent of primates that should be celebrated.

My colleague Mansur Lalljee suggests that the reason primates use gaze for affiliation is that primate infants and mothers are able to look at each other during breast-feeding. Human babies,

for example, are able to focus to a distance of 20 to 30 cm, roughly the proximity of the mother's face when she holds the infant to nurse. Primates are the only mammals in which nursing fosters eye-to-eye contact.

Gaze emerges as a social signal early in the life of infants. By the third week of life babies smile at a nodding head, and by the fifth week they can exchange mutual gazes. Further, babies respond positively to eyes and eye patterns—they smile and their pupils dilate, indicating that they are attending to the stimulus. During the infant's first year, parent and child typically play many mutual-gaze games, such as peekaboo, that seem to delight both players and are among the first forms of social communication.

The physiological underpinning of the meaning of gaze has been established mainly by studies with monkeys. We know, for instance, that one effect of staring eyes is arousal. Various measures of physiological arousal—galvanic skin response, EEG, brain-stem activity— show that organisms can tolerate a certain amount of stimulation and find it interesting, but that overstimulation becomes unpleasant. Too much arousal

is unsettling and causes the animal— wolf, bird, or human being—to avoid the prying eyes by fleeing, fighting, or threatening. This is true whether the eyes are those of one's natural predator or those of a stranger on a subway.

When two people like each other there is more gaze and more mutual gaze. Too much gaze, however, is uncomfortable. Janet Dean and I postulated that there are tendencies to approach or to avoid other people, to look or not to look, resulting in an equilibrium level of intimacy. This balance is based on a combination of proximity, gaze, smiling, and other affiliative signals. It would follow that if two people moved away from each other, they would maintain their intimacy level by increasing their gaze, and a number of experiments have confirmed this. Mark Patterson has extended the theory, proposing that signals a person interprets favorably lead him to respond in kind; if he finds the same signals unpleasant or disquieting, he will retreat or look away, thereby restoring equilibrium.

Human beings are able to use the additional cues of context and body language to interpret a gaze. Most people find a steady gaze to be pleasant if they like the gazer and want to be liked by him; the same gaze will be irritating if they think the gazer has undue sexual interests or is seething with anger. If the gazer's stare seems meaningless and vacant, and no other cues allow one to interpret his intentions, the gaze will be even more disturbing.

Usually, though, people within a culture show an excellent ability to decode the message sent in a look. They can readily distinguish affectionate gazes that say "I like you," worried gazes that request help, or threatening gazes that say "Lay off." Although the specific meaning of a look may shift across cultures, people everywhere recognize that a gaze means that the other person is attending, and therefore requires a reac-

The function of eye spots and eye rings

Eyes function as social signals early on the evolutionary scale. Fish, birds, moths, and butterflies often have eye spots, imitation eyes that appear on various parts of the body and may help to ward off predators. Although some birds will peck at eye spots, in these cases the spots appear to deflect attack from the insect's vulnerable body to its wings. In some fish, eye spots expand during battle; in others, eye spots appear on the male during courtship and attract the female.

Eye rings, like those of the raccoon, are widespread in the animal kingdom. Their significance is unknown, although a number of theories have been advanced to account for them. It has been suggested that they act as threats to establish dominance, to space animals out over a territory, or to repel predators. However, some believe they may simply be recognition signals to other members of the species.

insulting, or supercilious; a person who looks too little is regarded as impolite, inattentive, dishonest, or submissive.

But apart from these universal aspects of gaze, each culture tends to have its own specific variations on the main rules. Sometimes the lessons are taught specifically: "Don't stare, it's impolite," or "Don't look back at him, dear, you'll only encourage him." More often the lessons are indirect, acquired in the course of experience; they remain subtle but strong influences on action.

For example, Navaho children learn not to gaze directly at another person during a conversation. Among the Wituto and Bororo Indians of South America, both the speaker and the listener look at irrelevant objects during conversation, and a storyteller turns *away* from his audience to face the back of the hut. Japanese speakers focus on the listener's neck rather than the eye. A Luo man of Kenya must not look at his mother-in-law. The Mende of Sierra Leone believe that the dead reappear in human guise—but that the dead can be recognized because they never look a live person in the face. Naturally, the Mende are suspicious of people who avert their eyes during a conversation; a Mende would think that America and England are nations of zombies.

The language of the eye is, of course, only one part of a culture's communication system. Variations occur depending on the other communication channels a culture has adopted. Among the Tuareg of North Africa, gaze is an especially important way to send and receive messages, partly because the whole body, apart from the eyes, is covered with clothes and veils. Tuaregs stare steadily at each other while they are conversing in order to glean as much information as possible. In contrast, the Japanese make little use of the facial-visual channel, either to send or receive information; much of their communication takes place through nuances of spoken

tion. The experience of being looked at has a special subjective quality—the feeling of being observed, of being an object of interest for another. Mutual gaze also has such a quality—based on the realization that each person is open to signals from another.

Some meanings and rules of gaze seem to be universal, possibly a result of our biological heritage or the nearly universal experience of being held

closely while being fed. Generally, people convey positive attitudes and emotions, such as affection and happiness, with more and longer gazes; they convey negative feelings, such as dislike or depression, with less gazing. In all cultures people notice if a look or stare is done incorrectly. Too much or too little gaze creates an unfavorable impression. A person who gazes too much is usually regarded as disrespectful, threatening,

language and body position. (Possibly the Japanese pay less attention to eyes because Japanese infants are carried on their mothers' backs much of the time, and thus have less visual contact with the mother's face.)

An extensive study of cultural variations in the rules of gaze comes from O. Michael Watson, who worked with male foreign students at the University of Colorado. The students participated in the experiment in pairs, talking about anything they wanted to in their native language while the researchers observed them behind a one-way mirror. Each man's visual style was scored on a scale from one (sharp focusing directly on the other person's eyes) to four (no visual contact at all; looking down or gazing into space). Watson found that young men from contact cultures, where people typically stand close together and frequently touch each other, were far more likely to make eye contact and gaze at each other directly than the men from noncontact cultures:

	Number of men	Average score
Contact cultures:		
Arabs	29	2.57
Latin Americans	20	2.47
Southern Europeans	10	2.19
Noncontact cultures:		
Asians	12	3.25
Indians-Pakistanis	12	3.59
Northern Europeans	48	3.51

Watson also found that these cultural differences in gaze held up no matter how much time each student had spent in the United States or in big cities. Apparently styles of gaze, once learned in childhood, are relatively unaffected by later experience.

Roger Ingham observed how 22 pairs of Swedes and 22 pairs of Englishmen conversed with each other. The Swedish speakers looked at their listeners less often than the English did, with longer glances, and the Swedish pairs had a greater amount of mutual gaze. Swedes, Ingham found, dislike being looked at if they can't look back. This custom differs sharply from other traditions. Indeed,

Greek friends have told me that Greeks traveling in Europe feel rejected and ignored because, they say, people do not look at them enough.

Such cultural clashes can provoke unexpected problems when a person from one society moves to another that has different rules. Anthropologist Judith Herbstein explains that in Latin America it is considered rude and disrespectful to gaze too long at one's superior. When a Puerto Rican child in an American school is admonished by a teacher, the child will lower his eyes as a sign of respect and obedience. But what do American teachers and parents demand of the child they are scolding? "Look at me! Pay attention!"

Researchers have found individual differences within cultures as well as broad differences across them. Everyone knows the hearty salesman who looks you in the eye and the shy violet who can barely raise his head high enough to look at your nose. Some people look directly at their companions and

Poetry has long celebrated the mutual gaze of lovers. Psychological experiments confirm the poets' finding that couples in love gaze into each other's eyes longer than couples who are indifferent.

prefer a few long gazes to frequent darting glances; their characteristic style transcends situation. Individual differences are related to personality traits, though a given person will vary his gaze patterns in different situations.

Richard Christie devised a scale some years ago to measure a person's "Machiavellian" qualities—skepticism about human nature, willingness to use deceit to get one's way, belief in manipulation. In an ingenious experiment on the connections between cheating, lying, and gaze, Ralph Exline and his colleagues arranged to get students implicated in cheating on a project. They managed this by having another subject, who was actually a confederate, pretend to cheat. Then Exline questioned them about the cheating. He found that low-Machiavellian students looked away when lying to protect the subject who cheated; the high Machiavellians looked squarely at him, as much when lying as when telling the truth. Other studies show that most people will look down and otherwise avoid eye contact when they feel guilty or embarrassed, but not psychopaths, high Machiavellians, or, we infer, some used-car dealers. One explanation is that these exceptions do not feel as guilty about lying as most people do, and they probably realize that gaze avoidance indicates lying.

Individual styles can be quite distinctive. Gerhard Nielsen observed pairs of students in conversation and found, as is typical, that people look at their partners less when they are speaking than when they are listening. But individuals varied considerably. Some students looked at their partners only 8 percent of the time, others as much as 73 percent. Extroverts gaze more than introverts, women more than men, adults more than adolescents. Some experiments find that the gaze levels of adolescents may reflect the lower self-esteem or uncertain self-im-

age of many teenagers. It should be emphasized again that a person's gaze level is quite different in different situations. For instance, people tend to look most at people they like, when they are some distance away, and when there is nothing else to look at.

People at the atypical extremes— those who stare too much or who avoid eye contact altogether—may have serious psychological problems. Schizophrenics and depressives tend to avert their gaze (at least when interviewed about their problems), as do some neurotics. Autistic children gaze least. In fact, they are so fearful of looking at others that gaze aversion is one criterion of diagnosis. Autistic children peek at others in abrupt glances, only one half second long, often through their fingers. Or they avoid looking at people by turning their backs or pulling hats over their heads. They avoid looking at eyes and faces, but they do not shun all social contact; they will sit on an adult's lap but avert their gaze.

Corinne Hutt theorizes that autistic children have an abnormally high level of cortical arousal, possibly caused by a genetic defect. Because mutual gaze is arousing, they avoid eye contact to keep their high levels of arousal tolerable. Other researchers, however, think that the overarousal is a consequence, not a cause, of the autism.

At the other end of the spectrum, people with certain psychiatric problems may stare inappropriately for extended minutes. One consequence of the research on gaze is that patients can be taught how to look at other people properly without making them feel uncomfortable or threatened. The patient role-plays an encounter with the therapist. The scene is videotaped and played back

to the patient, while the therapist comments on what was correct or incorrect about the patient's gaze level. Practice ensures that the patient learns to get the visual information that he or she needs without excessive staring.

So far I have discussed general patterns of gaze, but in fact we have identified gaze rules to a precise degree. The glances exchanged during a conversation are used to send and to collect information; they are central to the encounter. In conversation, the gazes of speaker and listener are closely linked to the spoken words, and aid in the timing and synchronizing of speech.

We look at people primarily to collect information, to open a channel for observing their expressions and other cues. But the act of looking also becomes a signal for others, and the same glance may serve two purposes. For example, the long glance at the end of an utterance collects feedback and also serves as a full-stop signal to the listener.

The earliest studies of gaze required an observer to watch two speakers through a one-way mirror, recording on a stopwatch how many seconds each participant gazed at the other during a three-minute conversation. Technology has relieved the experimenter of this tedious task. Today we can keep a permanent record of the interaction by using two video cameras, one trained on each speaker, that shows us precisely how gaze is synchronized with speech. Pen recorders keep track, on a moving strip of paper, of continuous gaze sequences—how often speaker A looks at speaker B, how many seconds mutual gazes last, who gazes most, and so on. The reliability of these recordings is very high; two observers agree with each other on the timing and length of gaze sequences virtually all the time.

*When speculating which member of the
pair below will break off the mutual
gaze, consider that both personal
discomfort and implied criticism make
people look away, and that status
affects how people make eye contact.*

Gaze provides feedback to the speaker when it is most needed—at the ends of long statements, at grammatical breaks. Adam Kendon studied the timing of gaze in relation to speech for 10 people. He found that the speaker gazes at the listener before the end of an utterance, and the listener looks away. The speaker seeks feedback on whether the listener understands, agrees, is paying attention, or daydreaming. If the speaker does not end an utterance with a full-stop gaze, there is likely to be an awkward delay before the listener realizes it is time to reply. The listener's gaze, in turn, indicates interest, acknowledgment, or impatience. Thus, while the speaker is sending verbal signals, the listener is returning nonverbal signals. This balance of communication permits the conversation to continue with a surprising minimum of overlap and interruption.

Other studies show that there are many nonverbal ways a speaker can keep (or yield) his turn. A raconteur who wants to hold the spotlight does not pause at the end of a sentence, gives no terminal gaze, and keeps a hand in mid-gesture. If interrupted he speaks more loudly, drowning out the interrupter.

The speaker uses gaze for purposes other than feedback and full stops. As Walker recently found, speakers may emphasize a point with an eye flash, a sudden widening of the eye. The speaker can even direct which of several listeners should speak next, simply by a steady look at his choice. Conversely, a listener can get the speaker's attention and good will by looking at him supportively, smiling, and nodding.

If gaze is so important in social ex-

Although the specific meaning of a look may vary across cultures, people within a single society generally have little trouble decoding the message. Glances that convey affection, worry, or anger are easy to read.

change, what happens when people do not see each other? If negotiators cannot read visual messages between the spoken lines, what difference does it make? Dozens of experiments have compared face-to-face communication with communication by television video and by voice only (telephone). By and large, the loss of visual signals is not as disastrous as people think. People *prefer* to meet face to face; they prefer videophone to telephone; but the phone is not the antisocial creature that many people think it is. With practice,

speakers have adapted beautifully to the nonvisual disadvantage. Most of our phone conversations are well synchronized because we have learned to replace visual signals (gaze, head nods, facial expressions) with audible ones (uh-huhs and hmmms). For the exchange of factual information, the telephone is no worse than face-to-face exchange. Its only disadvantage is that one cannot convey spatial material, such as maps, graphs, and spiral staircases.

There are, in fact, some situations in which the telephone is the best medium.

John Short, in a series of studies, showed that it is easier to change someone's opinions over the phone than face to face, especially if the opinion is not a personal attitude but based on official policy or factual data. Ian Morley and Geoffrey Stephenson carried out a series of management-union bargaining simulations to see whether face-to-face or telephone encounters were the more effective. They gave one side or the other a clearly stronger case to defend, and indeed the stronger case was much more likely to win — *but only when it was*

In Arabian cultures, people look more, face each other more directly, and stand closer together than in Britain or the United States. Arabs in conversation generally stand close enough to detect each other's breath.

presented on the telephone! If the negotiators could see each other, the weaker side won quite often, probably because the participants became more concerned about being thought well of by the opposition. Telephone encounters allow a person to ignore the distracting information of gaze and other nonverbal signs and concentrate on business. This result augurs well for potential negotiators: Keep to the telephone if you are in a strong position, or your strength may be dissipated by the blandishments of an attractive opponent.

However, face-to-face communication is better for making friends than the telephone is. All things being equal, people who are meeting for the first time will like each other more and be more cooperative if they meet in person than if they meet on the telephone. We know this from experiments that required people to play the Prisoner's Dilemma Game, a task that offers players a choice of competitive or cooperative strategy, either face to face or over the telephone. When the players could see each other, they were much more likely to cooperate and come to early agreement.

Such research has produced a wealth of practical applications. The development of the picture-phone, for instance, may be regarded not just as an extravaganza on the part of Bell Telephone, but as an important aid to diplomacy,

business relationships, friendships, and love affairs. Telephones will still do nicely for most business dealings, but people want the benefits of nonverbal language for first contacts, for negotiations when they have a weaker case, for the social signals that make routine conversation work smoothly.

Architects, decorators, and designers are becoming more aware of the subtle ways in which the design of a room or building, and the location of chairs and

desks, affect how and whether people interact, even how they feel about each other. Care should be taken, for example, to arrange office furniture so that workers are not forced to stare at each other every time they look up. Otherwise, much time will be wasted in provoked but irrelevant conversation, or in unexpected seductions.

Training in gaze rules is not useful simply for psychiatric patients. Teachers, interviewers, social workers, managers, diplomats, and people who move to another culture have all benefited from learning the cultural rules of the people they meet. Englishmen who learn Arabian gaze customs, for example, do better and are better liked by Arabs than Englishmen who unconsciously follow their own customs.

Looks speak as clearly as the voice. Like speech, gaze is part of our biological heritage, yet wears many cultural disguises. For all the emphasis on spoken words, we would do well to pay more attention to the messages of gaze. The eyes, as often as not, have it.   □

For further information:
Argyle, Michael, and Mark Cook. *Gaze and Mutual Gaze.* Cambridge University Press, 1976.
Exline, R. V. "Visual Interaction: the Glances of Power and Preference." *Nebraska Symposium on Motivation.* Vol. 19. University of Nebraska Press, 1972, pp. 163-206.
Hinde, R. A. *Non-Verbal Communication.* Cambridge University Press, 1972.

Michael Argyle *is a reader in social psychology at Oxford University and a fellow of Wolfson College. He helped found the* British Journal of Social and Clinical Psychology *and for three years was chairman of the British Psychological Society's social psychology section. He has been a fellow at the Center for Advanced Study in the Behavioral Sciences, Palo Alto, California, and visiting lecturer or professor at universities in Canada, Ghana, and the United States. His books cover various aspects of social psychology, including work and religion. His present research centers around nonverbal communication; he is author of* Bodily Communication *and co-author, with Mark Cook, of* Gaze and Mutual Gaze.

V. The Influence of Others

I can still remember one of the questions on the final exam of my first course in psychology: "What is the definition of psychology?" The correct answer was "the *science* that studies the *prediction* and *control* of behavior." (It was correct with or without the italics.) I received one point for a correct answer on the exam, but I'd get it wrong today. I now believe that the goal of psychology is to understand people. The study of social influence is mainly concerned with the prediction and control of social behavior. It has been guided by the "practical" concern of regulating what people do—of increasing socially desirable behavior and decreasing socially undesirable behavior.

The review of research on social facilitation by Zajonc ("Social Facilitation") outlines one of the most basic ways in which people influence others— by their mere presence. The idea that the presence of people affects emotional reactions such as anxiety is consistent with some of the findings on over-crowding reported in Part I. People also influence the behavior of others by rewarding and punishing them. However, interestingly, it is not the straight-forward types of rewards and punishments that influence people the most (see Gray's "Little Brother is Changing You"). In addition, people influence others by what they do. Social learning theorists have shown that models may affect

Artwork by Martin Riskin.

both antisocial behavior ("Television and Violence: Implications of the Surgeon General's Research Program," by John P. Murray) and prosocial behavior ("The Subway Samaritan" and "Helpers and Nonhelpers"). Indeed, as Darley and Latané show ("When Will People Help in a Crisis?"), people's disposition to model the behavior of others often takes on an interesting twist in emergencies—everyone copies everyone else's lack of action, and no one does anything. Finally, people influence others by telling them what to do. Although you may feel that people are distinctly immune to your commands, a classic study by Stanley Milgram suggests that most people are frighteningly susceptible to the commands of authorities ("If Hitler Asked You to Electrocute a Stranger, Would You? Probably." by Philip Meyer).

Most of the selections in this section suggest that people are easy to influence. However, this conclusion must be tempered. Although countless studies have shown that the average behavior of subjects who are exposed to social influence in social psychological experiments is more conforming than the average behavior of subjects in control groups, it is nevertheless frequently the case that many subjects in the experimental group don't conform at all, or that they conform very little. In addition, it is fair to ask how relevant the laboratory findings generated by experimental social psychology are to real life. This question becomes particularly pointed when we look at the millions of dollars spent by governments on various people-improvement programs ("Human Beings Are Not Very Easy To Change After All" by Amitai Etzioni).

Social Facilitation

Robert B. Zajonc

18

Most textbook definitions of social psychology involve considerations about the influence of man upon man, or, more generally, of individual upon individual. And most of them, explicitly or implicitly, commit the main efforts of social psychology to the problem of how and why the *behavior* of one individual affects the behavior of another. The influences of individuals on each other's behavior which are of interest to social psychologists today take on very complex forms. Often they involve vast networks of interindividual effects such as one finds in studying the process of group decision making, competition, or conformity to a group norm. But the fundamental forms of interindividual influence are represented by the oldest experimental paradigm of social psychology: social facilitation. This paradigm, dating back to Triplett's original experiments on pacing and competition, carried out in 1897 (1), examines the consequences upon behavior which derive from the sheer presence of other individuals.

Research in the area of social facilitation may be classified in terms of two experimental paradigms: audience effects and co-action effects. The first experimental paradigm involves the observation of behavior when it occurs in the presence of passive spectators. The second examines behavior when it occurs in the presence of other individuals also engaged in the same activity. We shall consider past literature in these two areas separately.

Audience Effects

Simple motor responses are particularly sensitive to social facilitation effects. In 1925 Travis (2) obtained such effects in a study in which he used the pursuit-rotor task. In this task the subject is required to follow a small revolving target by means of a stylus which he holds in his hand. If the stylus is even momentarily off target during a revolution, the revolution counts as an error. First each subject was trained for several consecutive days until his performance reached a stable level. One day after the conclusion of the training the subject was called to the laboratory, given five trials alone, and then ten trials in the presence of from four to eight upperclassmen and graduate students. They had been asked by the experimenter to watch the subject quietly and attentively. Travis found a clear improvement in performance when his subjects were confronted with an audience. Their accuracy on the ten trials before an audience was greater than on any ten previous trials, including those on which they had scored highest.

A considerably greater improvement in performance was recently obtained in a somewhat different setting and on a different task (3). Each subject (all were National Guard trainees) was placed in a separate booth. He was seated in front of a panel outfitted with 20 red lamps in a circle. The lamps on this panel light in a clockwise sequence at 12 revolutions per minute. At random intervals one or another light fails to go on in its proper sequence. On the average there are 24 such failures per hour. The subject's task is to signal whenever a light fails to go on. After 20 minutes of intensive training, followed by a short rest, the National Guard trainees monitored the light panels for 135 minutes. Subjects in one group performed their task alone. Subjects in another group were told that from time to time a lieutenant colonel or a master sergeant would visit them in the booth to observe their performance. These visits actually took place about four times during the experimental session. There was no doubt about the results. The accuracy of the supervised subjects was on the average 34 per cent higher than the accuracy of the trainees working in isolation, and toward the end of the experimental session the accuracy of the supervised subjects was more than twice as high as that of the subjects working in isolation. Those expecting to be visited by a superior missed, during the last experimental period, 20 per cent of the light failures, while those expecting no such visits missed 64 per cent of the failures.

Dashiell, who in the early 1930s carried out an extensive program of research on social facilitation, also found considerable improvement in performance due to audience effects on such tasks as simple multiplication or word association (4). But, as is the case in many other areas, negative audience effects were also found. In 1933 Pessin asked college students to learn lists of nonsense syllables under two conditions, alone and in the presence of several spectators (5). When confronted with an audience, his subjects required an average of 11.27 trials to learn a seven-item list. When working alone they needed only 9.85 trials. The average number of errors made in the "audience" condition was considerably higher than the number in the "alone" condition. In 1931 Husband found that the presence of spectators interferes with the learning of a finger maze (6), and in 1933 Pessin and Husband (7) confirmed Husband's results. The number of trials which the isolated subjects required for learning the maze was 17.1. Subjects confronted with spectators, however, required 19.1 trials. The average number of errors for the isolated subjects was 33.7; the number for those working in the presence of an audience was 40.5.

The results thus far reviewed seem to contradict one another. On a pursuit-rotor task Travis found that the presence of an audience improves performance. The learning of nonsense syllables and maze learning, however, seem to be inhibited by the presence of an audience, as shown by Pessin's experiment. The picture is further complicated by the fact that when Pessin's subjects were asked, several days later, to recall the nonsense syllables they had learned, a reversal was found. The subjects who tried to recall the lists in the presence of spectators did considerably better than those who tried to recall them alone. Why are the learning of nonsense syllables and maze learning inhibited by the presence of spectators? And why, on the other hand, does performance on a pursuit-rotor, word-association, multiplication, or a vigilance task improve in the presence of others?

There is just one, rather subtle, consistency in the above results. It would appear that the emission of well-learned responses is facilitated by the presence of spectators, while the acquisition of new responses is impaired. To put the statement in conventional psychological language, performance is facilitated and learning is impaired by the presence of spectators.

This tentative generalization can be reformulated so that different features of the problem are placed into focus. During the early stages of learning, especially of the type involved in social facilitation studies, the subject's reponses are mostly the wrong ones. A person learning a finger maze, or a person learning a list of nonsense syllables, emits more wrong responses than right ones in the early stages of training. Most learning experiments continue until he ceases to make mistakes—until his performance is perfect. It may be said, therefore, that during training it is primarily the wrong responses which are dominant and strong; they are the ones which have the highest probability of occurrence. But after the individual has mastered the task, correct responses necessarily gain ascendancy in his task-relevant behavioral repertoire. Now they are the ones which are more probable —in other words, dominant. Our tentative generalization may now be simplified: audience enhances the emission of dominant responses. If the dominant responses are the correct ones, as is the case upon achieving mastery, the presence of an audience will be of benefit to the individual. But if they are mostly wrong, as is the case in the early stages of learning, then these wrong responses will be enhanced in the presence of an audience, and the emission of correct responses will be postponed or prevented.

There is a class of psychological processes which are known to enhance the emission of dominant responses. They are subsumed under the concepts of drive, arousal, and activation (8). If we could show that the presence of an audience has arousal consequences for the subject, we would be a step further along in trying to arrange the results of social-facilitation experiments into a neater package. But let us first consider another set of experimental findings.

Co-action Effects

The experimental paradigm of co-action is somewhat more complex than the paradigm involved in the study of audience effects. Here we observe individuals all simultaneously engaged in the same activity and in full view of each other. One of the clearest effects of such simultaneous action, or co-action, is found in eating behavior. It is well known that animals simply eat more in the presence of others. For instance, Bayer had chickens eat from a pile of wheat to their full satisfaction (9). He waited some time to be absolutely sure that his subject would eat no more, and then brought in a companion chicken who had not eaten for 24 hours. Upon the introduction of the hungry co-actor, the apparently sated chicken ate two-thirds again as much grain as it had already eaten. Recent work by Tolman and Wilson fully substantiates these results (10). In an extensive study of social-facilitation effects among albino rats, Harlow found dramatic increases in eating (11). In one of his experiments, for instance, the rats, shortly after weaning,

were matched in pairs for weight. They were then fed alone and in pairs on alternate days. Figure 1 shows his results. It is clear that considerably more food was consumed by the animals when they were in pairs than when they were fed alone. James (12), too, found very clear evidence of increased eating among puppies fed in groups.

Perhaps the most dramatic effect of co-action is reported by Chen (13). Chen observed groups of ants working alone, in groups of two, and in groups of three. Each ant was observed under various conditions. In the first experimental session each ant was placed in a bottle half filled with sandy soil. The ant was observed for 6 hours. The time at which nest building began was noted, and the earth excavated by the insect was carefully weighed. Two days afterward the same ants were placed in freshly filled bottles in pairs, and the same observations were made. A few days later the ants were placed in the bottles in groups of three, again for 6 hours. Finally, a few days after the test in groups of three, nest building of the ants in isolation was observed. Figure 2 shows some of Chen's data.

There is absolutely no question that the amount of work an ant accomplishes increases markedly in the presence of another ant. In all pairs except one, the presence of a companion increased output by a factor of at least 2. The effect of co-action on the latency of the nest-building behavior was equally dramatic. The solitary ants of session 1 and the final session began working on the nest in 192 minutes, on the average. The latency period for ants in groups of two was only 28 minutes. The effects observed by Chen were limited to the immediate situation and seemed to have no lasting consequences for the ants. There were no differences in the results of session 1, during which the ants worked in isolation, and of the last experimental session, where they again worked in solitude.

If one assumes that under the conditions of Chen's experiment nest building *is* the dominant response, then there is no reason why his findings could not be embraced by the generalization just proposed. Nest building is a response which Chen's ants have fully mastered. Certainly, it is something that a mature ant need not learn. And this is simply an instance where the generalization that the presence of others enhances the emission of dominant and well-developed responses holds.

If the process involved in audience effects is also involved in co-action effects, then learning should be inhibited in the presence of other learners. Let us examine some literature in this field. Klopfer (14) observed greenfinches—in isolation and in heterosexual pairs—which were learning to discriminate between sources of palatable and of unpalatable food. And, as one would by now expect, his birds learned this discrimination task considerably more efficiently when working alone. I hasten to add that the subjects' sexual interests cannot be held responsible for the inhibition of learning in the paired birds. Allee and Masure, using Australian parakeets, obtained the same result for homosexual pairs as well (15). The speed of learning was considerably greater for the isolated birds than for the paired birds, regardless of whether the birds were of the same sex or of the opposite sex.

Similar results are found with cockroaches. Gates and Allee (16) compared data for cockroaches learning a maze in isolation, in groups of two, and in groups of three. They used an E-shaped maze. Its three runways, made of galvanized sheet metal, were suspended in a pan of water. At the end of the center runway was a dark bottle into which the photophobic cockroaches could escape from the noxious light. The results, in terms of time required to reach the bottle, are shown in Figure 3. It is clear from the data that the solitary cockroaches required considerably less time to learn the maze than the grouped animals. Gates and Allee believe that the group situation produced inhibition. They add, however (16, p. 357):

> The nature of these inhibiting forces is speculative, but the fact of some sort of group interference is obvious. The presence of other roaches did not operate to change greatly the movements to different parts of the maze, but did result in increased time per trial. The roaches tended to go to the corner or end of the runway and remain there a longer time when another roach was present than when alone; the other roach was a distracting stimulus.

The experiments on social facilitation performed by Floyd Allport in 1920 and continued by Dashiell in 1930 (4, 17), both of whom used human subjects, are the ones best known. Allport's subjects worked either in separate cubicles or sitting around a common table. When working in isolation they did the various tasks at the same time and were monitored by common time signals. Allport did everything possible to reduce the tendency to compete. The subjects were told that the results of their tests would not be compared and would not be shown to other staff members, and that they themselves should refrain from making any such comparisons.

Among the tasks used were the following: chain word association, vowel cancellation, reversible perspective, multiplication, problem solving, and judgments of odors and weights. The results of Allport's experiments are well known: in all but the problem-solving and judgments test, performance was better in groups than in the "alone" condition. How do these results fit our generalization? Word association, multiplication, the cancellation of vowels, and the reversal of the perceived orientation of an ambiguous figure all involve responses which are well established. They are responses which are either very well learned or under a very strong influence of the stimulus, as in the word-association task or the reversible-perspective test. The problem-solving test consists of disproving arguments of ancient philosophers. In contrast to the other tests, it does not involve well-learned responses. On the contrary, the probability of wrong (that is, logically incorrect) responses on tasks of this sort is rather high; in other words, wrong responses are dominant. Of interest, however, is the finding that while intellectual work suffered in the group situation, sheer output of words was increased. When working together, Allport's subjects tended consistently to write more. Therefore, the generalization proposed in the previous section can again be applied: if the presence of others raises the probability of dominant responses, and if strong (and many) incorrect response tendencies prevail, then the presence of others can only be detrimental to performance. The results of the judgment tests have little bearing on the present argument, since Allport gives no accuracy figures for evaluating performance. The data reported only show that the presence of others was associated with the avoidance of extreme judgments.

In 1928 Travis (18), whose work on the pursuit rotor I have already noted, repeated Allport's chain-word-association experiment. In contrast to Allport's results, Travis found that the presence of others decreased performance.

The number of associations given to his subjects was greater when they worked in isolation. It is very significant, however, that Travis used stutterers as his subjects. In a way, stuttering is a manifestation of a struggle between conflicting response tendencies, all of which are strong and all of which compete for expression. The stutterer, momentarily hung up in the middle of a sentence, waits for the correct response to reach full ascendancy. He stammers because other competing tendencies are dominant at that moment. It is reasonable to assume that, to the extent that the verbal habits of a stutterer are characterized by conflicting response tendencies, the presence of others, by enhancing each of these response tendencies, simply heightens his conflict. Performance is thus impaired.

Avoidance Learning

In two experiments on the learning of avoidance responses, the performances of solitary and grouped subjects were compared. In one, rats were used; in the other, humans.

Let us first consider the results of the rat experiment by Rasmussen (19). A number of albino rats, all litter mates, were deprived of water for 48 hours. The apparatus consisted of a box containing a dish of drinking water. The floor of the box was made of a metal grille wired to one pole of an electric circuit. A wire inserted in the water in the dish was connected to the other pole of the circuit. Thirsty rats were placed in the box alone and in groups of three. They were allowed to drink for 5 seconds with the circuit open. Following this period the shock circuit remained closed, and each time the rat touched the water he received a painful shock. Observations were made on the number of times the rats approached the water dish. The results of this experiment showed that the solitary rats learned to avoid the dish considerably sooner than the grouped animals did. The rats that were in groups of three attempted to drink twice as often as the solitary rats did, and suffered considerably more shock than the solitary subjects.

Let us examine Rasmussen's results somewhat more closely. For purposes of analysis let us assume that there are just two critical responses involved: drinking, and avoidance of contact with the water. They are clearly incompatible. But drinking, we may further assume, is the dominant response, it is enhanced by the presence of others. The animal is therefore prevented, by the facilitation of drinking which derives from the presence of others, from acquiring the appropriate avoidance response.

The second of the two studies is quite recent and was carried out by Ader and Tatum (20). They devised the following situation with which they confronted their subjects, all medical students. Each subject is told on arrival that he will be taken to another room and seated in a chair, and that electrodes will be attached to his leg. He is instructed not to get up from the chair and not to touch the electrodes. He is also told not to smoke or vocalize, and is told that the experimenter will be in the next room. That is all he is told. The subjects are observed either alone or in pairs. In the former case the subject is brought to the room and seated at a table equipped with a red button which is connected to an electric circuit. Electrodes, by means of which electric shock can be administered, are attached to the calf of one leg. After the electrodes are attached, the experimenter leaves the room. From now on the subject will receive ½ second of electric shock every 10 seconds unless he presses the red button. Each press of the button delays the shock by 10 seconds. Thus, if he is to avoid shock, he must press the button at least once every 10 seconds. It should be noted that no information was given him about the function of the button, or about the purpose of the experiment. No essential differences are introduced when subjects are brought to the room in pairs. Both are seated at the table and both become part of the shock circuit. The response of either subject delays the shock for both.

The avoidance response is considered to have been acquired when the subject (or pair of subjects) receives less than six shocks in a period of 5 minutes. Ader and Tatum report that the isolated students required, on the average, 11 minutes, 35 seconds to reach this criterion of learning. Of the 12 pairs which participated in the experiment, only two reached this criterion. One of them required 46 minutes, 40 seconds; the other, 68 minutes, 40 seconds! Ader and Tatum offer no explanation for their curious results. But there is no reason why we should not treat them in terms of the generalization proposed above. We are dealing here with a learning task, and the fact that the subjects are learning to avoid shock by pressing a red button does not introduce particular problems. They are confronted with an ambiguous task, and told nothing about the button. Pressing the button is simply not the dominant response in this situation. However, escaping is. Ader and Tatum report that eight of the 36 subjects walked out in the middle of the experiment.

One aspect of Ader and Tatum's results is especially worth noting. Once having learned the appropriate avoidance response, the individual subjects responded at considerably lower rates than the paired subjects. When we consider only those subjects who achieved the learning criterion and only those responses which occurred *after* criterion had been reached, we find that the response rates of the individual subjects were in all but one case lower than the response rates of the grouped subjects. This result further confirms the generalization that, while learning is impaired by the presence of others, the performance of learned responses is enhanced.

There are experiments which show that learnings is enhanced by the presence of other learners (21), but in all these experiments, as far as I can tell, it was possible for the subject to *observe* the critical responses of other subjects, and to determine when he was correct and when incorrect. In none, therefore, has the co-action paradigm been employed in its pure form. That paradigm involves the presence of others, and nothing else. It requires that these others not be able to provide the subject with cues or information as to appropriate behavior. If other learners can supply the critical individual with such cues, we are dealing not with the problem of co-action but with the problem of imitation or vicarious learning.

The Presence of Others as a Source of Arousal

The results I have discussed thus far lead to one generalization and to one hypothesis. The generalization which organizes these results is that the presence of others, as spectators or as co-actors, enhances the emission of dominant responses. We also know from extensive research literature that arousal, activation, or drive all have as a consequence the enhancement of dominant responses (22). We now need to examine the hypothesis that the presence of others increases the individual's general arousal or drive level.

The evidence which bears on the relationship between the presence of others and arousal is, unfortunately, only indirect. But there is some very suggestive evidence in one area of research. One of the more reliable indicators of arousal and drive is the activity of the endocrine systems in general, and of the adrenal cortex in particular. Adrenocortical functions are extremely sensitive to changes in emotional arousal, and it has been known for some time that organisms subjected to prolonged stress are likely to manifest substantial adrenocortical hypertrophy (23). Recent work (24) has shown that the main biochemical component of the adrenocortical output is hydrocortisone (17-hydroxycorticosterone). Psychiatric patients characterized by anxiety states, for instance, show elevated plasma levels of hydrocortisone (25). Mason, Brady, and Sidman (26) have recently trained monkeys to press a lever for food and have given these animals unavoidable electric shocks, all preceded by warning signals. This procedure led to elevated hydrocortisone levels; the levels returned to normal within 1 hour after the end of the experimental session. This "anxiety" reaction can apparently be attenuated if the animal is given repeated doses of reserpine 1 day before the experimental session (27). Sidman's conditioned avoidance schedule also results in raising the hydrocortisone levels by a factor of 2 to 4 (26). In this schedule the animal receives an electric shock every 20 seconds without warning, unless he presses a lever. Each press delays the shock for 20 seconds.

While there is a fair amount of evidence that adrenocortical activity is a reliable symptom of arousal, similar endocrine manifestations were found to be associated with increased population density (28). Crowded mice, for instance, show increased amphetamine toxicity—that is, susceptibility to the excitatory effects of amphetamine—against which they can be protected by the administration of phenobarbital, chlorpromazine, or reserpine (29). Mason and Brady (30) have recently reported that monkeys caged together had considerably higher plasma levels of hydrocortisone than monkeys housed in individual cages. Thiessen (31) found increases in adrenal weights in mice housed in groups of 10 and 20 as compared with mice housed alone. The mere presence of other animals in the same room, but in separate cages, was also found to produce elevated levels of hydrocortisone. Table 1, taken from a report by Mason

Table 1. Basal Plasma Concentrations of 17-hydroxycorticosterone in Monkeys Housed Alone and in Same Room

Subject	Time	Conc. of 17-Hydroxycorticosterone in Caged Monkeys (μg per 100 ml of plasma)	
		In Separate Rooms	In Same Room
M-1	9 A.M.	23	34
M-1	3 P.M.	16	27
M-2	9 A.M.	28	34
M-2	3 P.M.	19	23
M-3	9 A.M.	32	38
M-3	3 P.M.	23	31
Mean	9 A.M.	28	35
Mean	3 P.M.	19	27

From Leiderman and Shapiro (35, p. 7).

and Brady (30), shows plasma levels of hydrocortisone for three animals which lived at one time in cages that afforded them the possibility of visual and tactile contact and, at another time, in separate rooms.

Mason and Brady also report urinary levels of hydrocortisone, by days of the week, for five monkeys from their laboratory and for one human hospital patient. These very suggestive figures are reproduced in Table 2 (30). In the monkeys, the low weekend traffic and activity in the laboratory seem to be associated with a clear decrease in hydrocortisone. As for the hospital patient, Mason and Brady report (30, p. 8).

> he was confined to a thoracic surgery ward that bustled with activity during the weekdays when surgery and admissions occurred. On the weekends the patient retired to the nearby Red Cross building, with its quieter and more pleasant environment.

Table 2. Variations in Urinary Concentration of Hydro-cortisone over a Nine-Day Period for Five Laboratory Monkeys and One Human Hospital Patient

Amounts Excreted (mg/24 hr)

Subjects	Mon.	Tues.	Wed.	Thurs.	Fri.	Sat.	Sun.	Mon.	Tues.
Monkeys	1.88	1.71	1.60	1.52	1.70	1.16	1.17	1.88	
Patient		5.9	6.5	4.5	5.7	3.3	3.9	6.0	5.2

From Leiderman and Shapiro (35, p 8).

Admittedly, the evidence that the mere presence of others raises the arousal level is indirect and scanty, And, as a matter of fact, some work seems to suggest that there are conditions, such as stress, under which the presence of others may lower the animal's arousal level. Bovard (32), for instance, hypothesized that the presence of another member of the same species may protect the individual under stress by inhibiting the activity of the posterior hypothalamic centers which trigger the pituitary adrenal cortical and sympathetico-adrenal medullary responses to stress. Evidence for Bovard's hypothesis, however, is as indirect as evidence for the one which predicts arousal as a consequence of the presence of others, and even more scanty.

Summary and Conclusion

If one were to draw on practical suggestion from the review of the social-facilitation effects which are summarized in this article he would advise the student to study all alone, preferably in an isolated cubicle, and to arrange to take his examinations in the company of many other students, on stage, and in the presence of a large audience. The results of his examination would be beyond his wildest expectations, provided, of course, he had learned his material quite thoroughly.

I have tried in this article to pull together the early, almost forgotten work on social facilitation, and to explain the seemingly conflicting results. This explanation is, of course, tentative, and it has never been put to a direct experimental test. It is, moreover, not far removed from the one originally proposed by Allport. He theorized (33, p. 261) that "the sights and sounds of others doing the same thing" augment ongoing responses. Allport, however, proposed this effect only for *overt* motor responses, assuming (33, p. 274) that "*intellectual* or *implicit responses* of thought are hampered rather than facilitated" by the presence of others. This latter

conclusion was probably suggested to him by the negative results he observed in his research on the effects of co-action on problem solving.

Needless to say, the presence of others may have effects considerably more complex than that of increasing the individual's arousal level. The presence of others may provide cues as to appropriate or inappropriate responses, as in the case of limitation or vicarious learning. Or it may supply the individual with cues as to the measure of danger in an ambiguous or stressful situation. Davitz and Mason (34), for instance, have shown that the presence of an unafraid rat reduces the fear of another rat in stress. Bovard (32) believes that the calming of the rat in stress which is in the presence of an unafraid companion is mediated by inhibition of activity of the posterior hypothalamus. But in their experimental situations (that is, the open field test) the possibility that cues for appropriate escape or avoidance responses are provided by the co-actor is not ruled out. We might therefore be dealing not with the effects of the mere presence of others but with the considerably more complex case of imitation. The animal may not be calming *because* of his companion's presence. He may be calming *after* having copied his companion's attempted escape responses. The paradigm which I have examined in this article pertains only to the effects of the mere presence of others, and to the consequences for the arousal level. The exact parameters involved in social facilitation still must be specified.

References

1. N. Triplett, *Am. J. Psychol.*, 1897, 9, 507.
2. L. E. Travis, *J. Abnorm. Soc. Psychol.*, 1925, 20, 142.
3. B. O. Bergum, & D. J. Lehr, *J. Appl. Psychol.*, 1963, 47, 75.
4. J. F. Dashiell, *J. Abnorm. Soc. Psychol.*, 1930, 25, 190.
5. J. Pessin, *Am. J. Psychol.*, 1933, 45, 263.
6. R. W. Husband, *J. Genet. Psychol.*, 1931, 39, 258. In this task the blindfolded subject traces a maze with his finger.
7. J. Pessin, & R. W. Husband, *J. Abnorm. Soc. Psychol.*, 1933, 28, 148.
8. See, for instance, E. Duffy, *Activation and behavior*, New York: Wiley, 1962; K. W. Spence, *Behavior theory and conditioning*, New Haven: Yale Univ. Press, 1956; R. B. Zajonc, & B. Nieuwenhuyse, *J. Exptl. Psychol.*, 1964, 67, 276.
9. E. Bayer, *Z. Psychol.*, 1929, 112, 1.
10. C. W. Tolman, & G. T. Wilson, *Animal behav.*, 1965, 13, 134.
11. H. F. Harlow, *J. Genet. Psychol.*, 1932, 43, 211.
12. W. T. James, *J. Comp. Physiol. Psychol.*, 1953, 46, 427; *J. Genet. Psychol.*, 1960, 96, 123; W. T. James, & D. J. Cannon, *ibid.*, 1956, 87, 225.
13. S. C. Chen, *Physiol. Zool.*, 1937, 10, 420.
14. P. H. Klopfer, *Science*, 1958, 128, 903.
15. W. C. Allee, & R. H. Masure, *Physiol. Zool.*, 1936, 22, 131.
16. M. J. Gates, & W. C. Allee, *J. Comp. Psychol.*, 1933, 15, 331.
17. F. H. Allport, *J. Exptl. Psychol.*, 1920, 3, 159.
18. L. E. Travis, *J. Abnorm. Soc. Psychol.*, 1928, 23, 45.
19. E. Rasmussen, *Acta Psychol.*, 1939, 4, 275.
20. R. Ader, & R. Tatum, *J. Exptl. Anal. Behav.*, 1963, 6, 357.

21. H. Gurnee, *J. Abnorm. Soc. Psychol.,* 1939, 34, 529; J. C. Welty, *Physiol. Zool.,* 1934, 7, 85.
22. See K. W. Spence, *Behavior theory and conditioning,* New Haven: Yale Univ. Press, 1956.
23. H. Selye, *J. Clin. Endocrin.,* 1946, 6, 117.
24. D. H. Nelson, & L. T. Samuels, *ibid.,* 12, 519.
25. E. L. Bliss, A. A. Sandberg, & D. H. Nelson, *J. Clin. Invest.,* 1953, 32, 9; F. Board, H. Persky, & D. A. Hamburg, *Psychosom. Med.,* 1956, 18, 324.
26. J. W. Mason, J. V. Brady, & M. Sidman, *Endocrinology,* 1957, 60, 741.
27. J. W. Mason, & J. V. Brady, *Science,* 1956, 124, 983.
28. D. D. Thiessen, *Texas Rep. Biol.* 1964, 22, 266.
29. L. Lasagna, & W. P. McCann, *Science,* 1957, 125, 1241.
30. J. W. Mason, & J. V. Brady, in P. H. Leiderman, & D. Shapiro, (Eds.), *Psychobiological approaches to social behavior,* Stanford, Calif.: Stanford Univ. Press, 1964.
31. D. D. Thiessen, *J. Comp. Physiol. Psychol.,* 1964, 57, 412.
32. E. W. Bovard, *Psychol. Rev.,* 1959, 66, 267.
33. F. H. Allport, *Social psychology,* Boston: Houghton-Mifflin, 1924.
34. J. R. Davitz, & B. J. Mason, *J. Comp. Physiol. Psychol.,* 1955, 48, 149.
35. P. H. Leiderman, & D. Shapiro, Eds., *Psychobiological approaches to social behavior,* Stanford, Calif.: Stanford Univ. Press, 1964.

19

Central to the nervousness over behavior modification is the question of who shall modify whom, and when. Here, a group of junior-high-school students set to work on their teachers and friends, and find that behavior shaping works fine for those near the bottom of the power structure.

LITTLE BROTHER IS CHANGING YOU

by Farnum Gray with Paul S. Graubard
and Harry Rosenberg

JESS'S EIGHTH-GRADE TEACHERS at Visalia, California, found him frightening. Only 14 years old, he already weighed a powerful 185 pounds. He was easily the school's best athlete, but he loved fighting even more than he loved sports. His viciousness equaled his strength: he had knocked other students cold with beer bottles and chairs. Jess's catalog of infamy also included a 40-day suspension for hitting a principal with a stick, and an arrest and a two-and-a-half-year probation for assault.

Inevitably, Jess's teachers agreed that he was an incorrigible, and placed him in a class for those with behavioral problems. Had they known that he had begun secret preparations to change *their* behavior, they would have been shocked.

The New Jess. His math teacher was one of the first to encounter his new technique. Jess asked for help with a problem, and when she had finished her explanation, he looked her in the eye and said, "You really help me learn when you're nice to me." The startled teacher groped for words, and then said, "You caught on quickly." Jess smiled, "It makes me feel good when you praise me." Suddenly Jess was consistently making such statements to all of his teachers. And he would come to class early or stay late to chat with them.

Some teachers gave credit for Jess's dramatic turnaround to a special teacher and

his rather mysterious class. They naturally assumed that he had done something to change Jess and his "incorrigible" classmates.

Rather than change them, the teacher had trained the students to become behavior engineers. Their parents, teachers and peers in the farm country of Visalia, California, had become their clients.

A Reward System. Behavior engineering involves the systematic use of consequences to strengthen some behaviors and to weaken others. Jess, for example, rewarded teachers with smiles and comments when they behaved as he wanted; when they were harsh, he turned away.

People often call reward systems immoral because they impose the engineer's values upon those he conditions. But the Visalia Project turns things around, according to Harry Rosenberg, head of the project and Director of Special Education for the school district. "The revolutionary thing here is that we are putting behavior-modification techniques in the hands of the learner. In the past, behavior modification has been controlled more-or-less by the Establishment. It has been demanded that the children must change to meet the goodness-of-fit of the dominant culture. We almost reverse this, putting the kid in control of those around him. It's kind of a Rogerian use of behavior modification."

Rosenberg was born and reared in Visalia and has been teacher and principal in

a number of schools in that area. He began using behavior modification nine years ago, and he has kept experimentation going in the district with modest grants, mostly Federal. His proposals have emphasized that Visalia is an isolated district that, to avoid provincialism, needs contact with innovative educators from around the country. The grants have paid a variety of consultants to work with Visalia schools over the years.

Reinforcing Opponents. The idea of training kids as behavior engineers arose from a single incident with a junior-high-school student. He was in a behavior-modification program for the emotionally disturbed. His teacher told Rosenberg that although the boy was responding fairly well to the class, he was getting into fights on the playground every day. As they discussed ways of helping the boy, the teacher suggested that they identify the kids with whom he was fighting and teach him to reinforce those kids for the behaviors that he wanted. The process worked.

Rosenberg mentioned the incident to Paul Graubard of Yeshiva University who was a consultant to the district. The incident intrigued him and he thought that training students as behavior engineers could have widespread implications in education, answering some philosophical objections to the use of behavior modification in schools.

Rosenberg had long believed that many students who were segregated in special-education classes should be reintegrated into regular classes. Graubard agreed. He designed an experiment to help children diagnosed as retardates, or as having learning or behavior problems, change their teachers' perceptions of them. This, predicted Graubard, would enable the child to be reintegrated into regular classes.

Special Classes: Incorrigibles and Deviants. For the pilot project, Rosenberg selected a local junior high school with an unfortunate but accurate reputation. It was the most resistant in the district to the integration of special-education students; it had a higher percentage of students assigned to special classes than any other in the district. Classes for those labeled incorrigible held 10 percent of the school's 450 students; Rosenberg saw this as a disturbing tendency to give up on pupils too easily. He also found that minority children were more likely to be labeled incorrigible or tagged with some other form of deviancy. Directives from the principal and supervisors to treat all children alike regardless of race or ability had failed. To make matters worse, the school also had the highest suspension and expulsion rates in the district.

Graubard and Rosenberg selected seven children, ages 12 to 15, from a class for children considered incorrigible, to be the first behavior engineers. Jess and one other child were black, two were white, and three were Chicanos. A special-education teacher gave the seven students instruction and practice in behavior modification for one 43-minute class period a day. He then moved them into regular classes for two periods each day. The teachers of these classes became their clients. The teachers ranged in age from 26 to 63, and had from two to 27 years of teaching experience.

Shaping Teachers' Behavior. Stressing the idea that the program was a scientific experiment, the special teacher required each student to keep accurate records. During the experiment, they were to record daily the number of both positive and negative contacts with their clients. The students would not try to change the teachers' behavior during the first period; instead, they would keep records only to determine the norm. For the next phase, the students were to work at shaping the teachers' behaviors and to continue to keep records. For the last phase the students were not to use any of the shaping techniques.

Rosenberg had estimated that record-keeping could begin after two weeks of training students to recognize and to record teachers' positive and negative behavior. But this preliminary training took twice as long as he expected. While the

> Learning to praise teachers with sincerity was difficult for the children. They were awkward and embarrassed at first, but they soon became skillful.

students quickly learned to score negative behavior, they were seldom able to recognize positive behavior in their teacher-clients. Without the knowledge of the teachers or of the student-engineers, trained adult aides also kept records of teacher behavior in classes. Rosenberg compared their records to those of the students to determine accuracy; he found that the aides recorded substantially more instances of positive teacher behavior than did the students. For example, an aide reported that a teacher had praised a child, but the child reported that the teacher had chewed him out. Rosenberg determined through closer monitoring that the aides were more accurate. He speculated that students were unable to recognize positive teacher behavior because they were accustomed to failure and negative treatment.

The students learned to identify positive teacher behavior accurately by role playing and by studying videotapes. This eventually brought about a high correlation between their records and those kept by adult teacher aides.

Building a New Smile. Rosenberg and Graubard taught the students various reinforcements to use in shaping their

teachers' behavior. Rewards included smiling, making eye contact, and sitting up straight. They also practiced ways of praising a teacher, for example, saying, "I like to work in a room where the teacher is nice to the kids." And they learned to discourage negative teacher behavior with statements like, "It's hard for me to do good work when you're cross with me."

Each student studied techniques for making himself personally more attractive. One of the hardest tasks for Jess, for example, was learning to smile. Through use of a videotape, he learned that instead of smiling at people, he leered at them menacingly. Although he thought the process was hilarious, he practiced before the camera, and eventually developed a charming smile.

Learning to praise teachers with sincerity was difficult for the children. They were awkward and embarrassed at first, but they soon became skillful. Rosenberg said that the teachers' responses were amazing, and added that "the nonverbal cues make the difference between being a wise guy and being believable. They had to *sincerely* mean it so it would be accepted by the teacher as an honest statement of a kid's feelings, not as smarting off." Besides learning to praise and to discourage teachers, they also learned to make small talk with them. This was a new skill for these students and, after considerable training, they excelled at it.

Ah Hah! The students enjoyed using a device that Fritz Redl, a child psychologist, has called "the Ah-Hah reaction." When a pupil was sure that he already understood a teacher's explanation, he would say that he did not understand. When the teacher was halfway through a second explana-

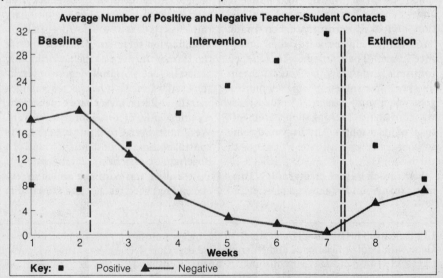

tion, the pupil would exclaim, "Ah hah! Now I understand! I could never get that before." Unlike some of the other reinforcements used, this one does not directly help the teacher improve his teaching, and it is less than honest. But it does encourage the teacher to like the student who gave him a feeling of accomplishment, and it is hoped, will lead to a better relationship between them.

Rosenberg recorded the results of the project on a graph. It showed that during each of the five weeks of shaping, the number of positive comments from teachers increased while the number of negative comments decreased. The seven students in Jess's group felt that they had succeeded in engineering their teachers' behavior more to their liking. The "extinction" period proved to be a good indicator of the effects of this engineering. During those two weeks, there was a sharp drop in positive comments, but a marked rise in negative comments. The engineering had indeed caused the changes in teacher behavior. As the extinction period showed, the teachers were like other people. Most were backsliders and they needed persistent reinforcement to maintain their new behavior.

When the project was over, the students resumed conditioning of the teachers, but they no longer kept formal records. Positive behavior increased once again, they reported; and in many cases, the negative comments ceased entirely. Rosenberg stressed the importance of requiring the children to keep data while teaching them reinforcement techniques. Projects that do not require data have failed. A student's success with a full, formal project, on the other hand, increases his ability to continue informal use of the behavior-engineering techniques that he has learned.

Who Really Changed? The teacher-clients were enthusiastic about the project, and Rosenberg reported that so far, none had expressed hostility or displeasure. Some teachers did question the right of aides to observe and to record their teaching methods. But Rosenberg pointed out that it was "justified by the necessity for scientific validation of the procedure." He assured them that the district did not use data from the project for evaluation of their abilities, and so, it would not affect their careers. When he explained the project to teachers afterwards, two or three said that it did change them. They admitted that they had be-

---

Through systematic use of praise and other conditioning techniques, the girl made her mother into a much better homemaker.

---

come more positive toward their engineers. It is interesting to note, however, that most teachers tended to think of the projects as having changed the *children* rather than themselves.

Children, especially those in special-education classes, often suffer feelings of impotence when they encounter the school environment. The crucial goal of the project was to instill within the student a feeling of power, the ability to control the controllers, i.e., his teachers and the school. As a result of their training in behavior engineering, the students reported feeling more power in their relationships with their teachers and the school than ever before. And with that feeling of power came a new feeling of self-confidence.

Parents As Clients. When children shape the behaviors of their parents, procedures are much the same as they are in the teacher-training projects. One difference, however, is that Rosenberg first asks the parents to let him work with the child. He does not tell them, though, that their children will be shaping them.

After the parents grant permission, the student decides what he wants to change in their behavior. Then, Rosenberg or a special teacher will help him to design a project to bring about that change. After the child completes his project, Rosenberg talks with the parents in their home, and tells them what the child has been trying to accomplish. For example, one girl's mother seldom had meals on time, nor did she wash or iron the girl's clothes. Through systematic use of praise and other conditioning techniques, the girl made her mother into a much better homemaker. After more than a year, the mother had maintained her improvement and gained new self-respect.

Rosenberg cited other examples of adolescents who have shaped their parents to be less restrictive. But the critical result of each of these parent-shaping projects was the parents' increased awareness of their

child's needs as a person. One father said that the project had really helped them with their child; for the first time the child talked to them about the different ways that they could help him.

Switch, Don't Fight. Since children have problems with each other as well as with adults, the students at Visalia have used the same conditioning techniques on their classmates.

"We can teach kids systematically how to make friends, how to get along with other students," Rosenberg said. "If they're being teased, we can teach them how to extinguish that permanently. If they're getting in fights, we can teach them to use basic learning principles to get the same thing they were trying to get by fighting."

He cited the example of Peggy, an attractive, intelligent girl who nevertheless encountered extreme problems in school. Her sixth-grade teachers sent her to the office frequently, and she was unable to make friends with the other students, whose hostility towards her made her miserable. She was gifted academically, but apparently because of her unhappiness in school, she had never achieved even an average report card.

The special teacher helped her to design and to carry out a project to change her classmates' attitudes towards her. She was spectacularly successful. She spoke of the experience later: "They told me it was a scientific experiment, but I really didn't know what that meant. At first I was confused, and I really didn't think it would help me. But then I thought I might as well try it. At least I would get out of the classroom for part of the time."

The teacher asked Peggy to name three people whom she would like to have as friends. She named Arthur, Elwyn and Doris, all of whom frequently insulted her. For two weeks, she and her teacher recorded both positive and negative contacts with them. Then they discussed how they could increase the number of nice things that those students said to her. She began to apply the behavior-modification theory and techniques that her teacher had taught her. "I ignored Doris if she said anything bad to me. But when she said anything nice to me, I'd help her with her work, or compliment her, or sit down and ask her to do something with me. She's been increasing saying the nice things about me and now we can ride on the bus together, and she'll sit by me in the class. I'll tell you that really helps me a lot."

She engineered Elwyn's behavior in much the same manner; she would turn her back on him whenever he said something bad to her. But the first time he walked past her without saying something bad, she gave him a big smile and said, "Hi, Elwyn, how are you today?" After he recovered from his initial shock at Peggy's overtures, he eventually became her friend.

Arthur proved to be a much tougher subject than the other two. As Peggy stated, "He calls *everybody* names. I don't think anybody likes Arthur." She attempted to ignore him whenever he called her names, but with Arthur, this tactic was unsuccessful. If the other children laughed, it just gave Arthur more encouragement. As she discussed her shaping of Arthur, Peggy showed her grasp of behavioral learning theory. She realized that the reward of the other children's laughter far outweighed her attempts to extinguish Arthur's teasing by ignoring it. They, not she, were reinforcing Arthur. She came up with a clever solution. "If Arthur was standing around with some kids, I tried to stay away from him. I'd wait until Arthur was by himself, and then I'd walk up to him, say "Hi" and smile. He just didn't know what to do! The first time, though, he still called me a name, because he thought I was being mean to him...I'd never said anything nice to Arthur...hardly anybody ever does. I guess the only way [he] ever gets anybody's attention is by calling people names...being mean, and fighting."

Arthur was a small sixth-grader and apparently, his stature caused him a great deal of self-consciousness. Peggy continued her positive reinforcement of Arthur, who is now friendly and no longer calls her names.

Peggy's social difficulties disappeared with dramatic speed as she made use of behavior-modification techniques. The teachers who once reported her attitude as disagreeable, now found her charming and delightful. Her grade average rose to B, and the following year, she was elected president of the seventh grade.

Gifted Students. Rosenberg also instructed a class of gifted children in the use of behavior engineering; each child chose as a client a classmate, an adult, or a sibling. The children met frequently to discuss ways of handling problems and to report on the progress of their projects.

Rosenberg estimates that the students are doing about as well in exercising control over human behavior as professionals who charge 50 dollars an hour.

One student related how he had modified the disruptive behavior of a fellow math student. "I compliment him when he's not disruptive, and when he is, I say things to him like, 'You know, you could be a real bright student, and I like you a lot more when you don't disrupt the class.' He doesn't do it so much now, and he makes good grades."

One student was near despair over her efforts to change a teacher who, the other students agreed, was a difficult person. This teacher seemed impervious to any type of conditioning technique. "His latest thing is to send everybody out to sit under a table," she reported. "The first minute you open your mouth, he sends you out, and he doesn't really give you a chance." She had tried unsuccessfully to tell him that she was not learning math while sitting under the table, or she would apologize for saying something she should not have. But his response was usually, "You're not sorry, you're *ignorant*!" or "You're a knothead!"

The special-education teacher asked the girl to name the behavior she most wanted to change. "Sending me out without a chance," the girl replied. "That's what bothers me most. I'm out in the *first 10 minutes* of the class!"

The special teacher then suggested that she say to the problem teacher, "I'd really appreciate it if you'd give me a warning before sending me out of the room, because I have trouble about talking anyway." It was necessary for her to repeat this several times, but it wasn't long before the teacher stopped sending kids out of the room.

Dignity & Worth. In *Beyond Freedom and Dignity*, B.F. Skinner points out that "Any evidence that a person's behavior may be attributed to external circumstances seems to threaten his dignity or worth. We are not inclined to give a person credit for achievements over which he has no control."

The people at Visalia are very con-

cerned with maintaining the dignity of their clients. They believe that dignity is lost if the reinforcements given in behavior engineering are insincere. The individual must feel that he has earned rewards by his own actions, not because the engineer is using a technique. Otherwise the gesture lacks dignity and worth.

A junior-high-school boy drew agreement from his fellow students when he said, "If the person knows you're doing it, it won't work. At least not very well. He'll figure, 'Oh, he's trying to do it on me. He's not going to change the way I am!' " The boy cited his little brother as an example. He was trying to condition him not to curse, but the child found out about the conditioning techniques, and said, "Oh, you dumb little psychologist!"

Sincerity is also an integral part of instruction in behavior engineering. Rosenberg recalled with amusement that the teachers working with him on the experiment have at times doubted each other's sincerity. "One person compliments another, who says, 'You're just reinforcing me!' And the response is, 'Oh, the hell if I am! I really mean it.' With the kids, and with our own staff," Rosenberg said, "we've had to continually stress being sincere. You should really want the other person to change."

Many of the teachers felt that the engineering by the students created a more positive working environment; it eliminated the ever-present cutting and sarcasm. It also eliminated the meanness that is so often characteristic of junior-high-school students, according to a humanities teacher. He found that children of that age often conform by being meaner than they would really like to be. "I feel these projects are very effective in giving kids an *excuse* to be positive. At this age, that seems very helpful to them."

The Visalia project revived the issue of whether it is *moral* for people to condition each other. Certainly, behavior engineering could appear to be a harbinger of *A Clockwork Orange*, or *Brave New World*. But Rosenberg, Graubard, and other behaviorists believe that people are always conditioning each other, and that often, in their ignorance, they strengthen behaviors that no one wants. Proponents believe that to make really *constructive* changes in behavior, people should be conscious of what they are doing.

Future Projects. Rosenberg envisions another three or four years of research on this project before its techniques are disseminated in the school district. The current research is to provide information for the effective matching of the student with the technique for behavioral conditioning. In the future, this "prescription" will aid the counselor in helping the student.

Additional experiments planned will compare the teacher-training effectiveness of a single child to that of two or three children working as a team. And in some projects, teachers will know that the students are trying to change them. In this instance, Rosenberg wants to find out if that will make a difference in the effectiveness of the conditioning.

Having students train teachers is inexpensive and effective. Since the students spend more time with their teachers than does any professional supervisor, they have more opportunity to change them. Students also have the most to gain or to lose from the quality of teaching. Rosenberg estimates that the students are doing about as well in exercising control over human behavior as professionals who charge 50 dollars an hour. ∩

20

Television and Violence

Implications of the Surgeon General's Research Program

JOHN P. MURRAY   *National Institute of Mental Health* [1]

The magnitude of television's involvement in our daily lives is rather impressive. Recent census figures estimate that 96% of the households in the United States contain at least one television set; many have two or more. In families where there are young children, the television ownership rate approaches total saturation—99%. Moreover, the data available from broadcast rating services indicate that American television sets are turned on for an average of approximately six hours each day. The obvious implication of these rather dry statistics is that virtually every person in the United States has access to television, and some are watching for a considerable length of time. These facts, coupled with the common observation that our youngest citizens are among the heaviest users, have fostered serious concern about television's potential impact on the attitudes, values, and behavior patterns of this vast audience. This concern has been expressed not only by legislators but also by parents, teachers, and a wide range of mental health professionals involved with the growth and development of children.

Throughout television's quarter-of-a-century broadcast history, various commissions and committees have questioned its impact. In the early

[1] This article was presented at the Current Issues in Mental Health Forum sponsored by the Mental Health Association of Oregon, Portland, May 17, 1972. Some of this material was also presented at a symposium, "Violence in Our Society," sponsored by the Washington Association for Mental Health, Seattle, May 16, 1972. The author wishes to acknowledge the contribution of his colleagues at the National Institute of Mental Health, especially Eli A. Rubinstein. Opinions expressed are those of the author and do not necessarily reflect the opinions or official policy of the National Institute of Mental Health.

1950s, the National Association of Educational Broadcasters surveyed the program content of stations in four major cities (Los Angeles, New York, New Haven, and Chicago) and reported that "crime and horror" drama accounted for 10% of all programming broadcast in these cities.

The first Congressional inquiry was launched in 1954 by Senator Estes Kefauver, Chairman of the Subcommittee to Investigate Juvenile Delinquency. As a result of testimony presented to this committee, it was concluded that televised crime and brutality could be potentially harmful to young children. Broadcasters were then urged to take appropriate action to reduce the level of violence portrayed in their programming. A subsequent survey of program content, undertaken by the same Senate subcommittee in 1961, indicated an increase in the level of televised violence over that observed in the 1950s. An additional survey conducted in 1964 again indicated no diminution in the level of portrayed violence. As Chairman of these later hearings, Senator Thomas Dodd noted:

Not only did we fail to see an appreciable reduction of violence in the new shows, but we also found that the most violent shows of the 1961–62 season have been syndicated and are now being reshown on independent networks and stations [U.S. Senate, 1964, p. 3731].

The committee concluded that, despite its laudable achievement in the fields of education and entertainment, television has also functioned as "a school for violence."

In 1969, the Mass Media Task Force of the National Commission on the Causes and Prevention of Violence concluded, on the basis of a review of existing research, that there was sufficient justification to call for a general reduction in the level of televised violence. The Commission particularly stressed the need to eliminate violence portrayed in children's cartoon programming. The Violence Commission also recommended continued evaluation of television programming, research on the long-term cumulative effects of viewing televised violence, and an analysis of the broad range of television's impact on society (Baker & Ball, 1969).

In response to this mounting concern, Senator John O. Pastore, Chairman of the Subcommittee on Communications of the Senate Commerce Committee, asked the Secretary of Health, Education, and Welfare to request the Surgeon General to conduct a study of the impact of televised violence. In requesting the Surgeon General's participation, Senator Pastore noted the recent success of the Smoking and Health Study and indicated that he considered television violence to be a similar public health question. As a result of this request, the Surgeon General's Scientific Advisory Committee on Television and Social Behavior, composed of 12 behavioral scientists, was appointed in June 1969. At the same time, $1 million was allocated for research funds, and a staff at the National Institute of Mental Health was appointed to coordinate the research program. During the following two years, a total of 23 independent research projects were conducted by scholars at a number of universities and research institutes. The resulting set of approximately 60 reports and papers was reviewed by the Advisory Committee during the late summer and fall of 1971, and the Committee's report, entitled "Television and Growing Up: The Impact of Televised Violence," was presented to the Surgeon General on December 31, 1971. The Advisory Committee report and five volumes of research reports were published early in 1972.

The studies in this program were focused on three major research questions concerning (*a*) the characteristics of television program content; (*b*) the characteristics of the audience (Who watches what? For how long?); and (*c*) the potential impact of televised violence on the attitudes, values, and behavior of the viewer. Within this framework, let us turn first to the research findings that bear on the nature of the stimulus—the characteristics of television programs viewed in American homes.

Television Content

One study, conducted by George Gerbner (1972) at the Annenberg School of Communications, was addressed to an analysis of the content of prime time (7:30–10:00 p.m. on weekdays and 9:00–11:00 a.m. on Saturday) television programming broadcast during one week in October for the years 1967, 1968, and 1969. Observers recorded all instances of violence defined by "the overt expression of physical force against others or self, or the com-

pelling of action against one's will on pain of being hurt or killed." The results indicated the following:

1. The level of violence did not change from 1967 to 1969. In each of the three years, violent episodes occurred at the rate of five per play or eight episodes per hour, with 8 out of every 10 plays containing some form of violence.
2. Lethal violence (killing) *did* decline over the measured years from 2 in 10 leading characters involved in killing in 1967; to 1 in 10 in 1968; to 1 in 20 in 1969.
3. The level of violence portrayed in programs especially designed for children—cartoons (already the leading violent program format in 1967)—became increasingly violent in 1969. As Gerbner (1972) pointed out: "Of all 95 cartoon plays analyzed during the three annual study periods, only two in 1967 and one each in 1968 and 1969 did not contain violence [p. 36]."

On the average, in 1967, one hour of cartoons contained *three* times as many violent episodes as one hour of adult programming. However, in 1969, one hour of cartoons contained *six* times as many violent episodes as an adult hour.

A more recent study, conducted by F. Earle Barcus (1971) at Boston University, was focused on the content of Saturday morning children's programs during the 1971 season. Barcus reported findings that parallel Gerbner's: 71% of all segments had at least one instance of human violence and 3 out of 10 dramatic segments were "saturated" with violence.

In one sense, these statistics are merely body counts, significant perhaps, but to "understand" televised violence one must look at the qualitative aspects: the time, place, or setting and the characteristics of the aggressors and victims. In the world of television, violence tends to occur in the past or future; in places other than the United States; and frequently in remote, uninhabited, or unidentifiable areas. The means to commit violence are usually weapons, with guns being the most favored weapon. The agents of this violence are usually humans; however, the prevalence of non-human agents has increased each year from 1967 to 1969. The consequences of all this violence are almost negligible. Punching, kicking, biting, even shooting, do not seem to result in much suffering. As Gerbner (1972) pointed out:

Pain and suffering were so difficult to detect that observers could not agree often enough to make the results acceptable. There was no doubt that no painful effect was shown in over half of all violent episodes [p. 41].

Who commits all this mayhem? And who are the unlucky recipients? We noted earlier that the agents of most of the violence are humans—so, too, are the victims. But the aggressors and the victims, the powerful and the weak, the killers and the killed, do not share many common characteristics. Indeed, as Gerbner lyrically indicated: "The shifting sands of fate have piled a greater burden of victimization on women [p. 50]." The aggressors are more likely to be male, American, middle–upper class, unmarried, and in the "prime of life."

Approximately 70% of all leading characters studied by Gerbner were involved in some form of violence (either as an aggressor or a victim). Of those involved in killing, the odds are two to one in favor of the leading character being a killer rather than being the one killed. Moreover, the odds were also seven to one that the killer would *not* be killed in return.

How "real" is this violence? Some researchers have suggested that, in a statistical sense, it is very *un*real. For example, content analyses show that violence in the *television* world occurs between total strangers, but crime statistics indicate that lethal violence in the *real* world is likely to be perpetrated by persons known to the victim. A study conducted by David Clark and William Blankenburg (1972) at the University of Wisconsin failed to find a clear relationship between the level of televised violence broadcast each year and an environmental crime index based on the FBI Uniform Crime Reports. What they were able to demonstrate is that the level of broadcast violence has fluctuated from 1953 to 1969 and seems to run in cycles reaching a peak every four years. In addition, if the audience applauded violent television programs during one season, the viewers were likely to receive an increased dosage during the following season. Thus, Clark and Blankenburg were able to demonstrate a significant correlation between the number of high-violence programs available during a given season and the average Nielsen rating of that type of program during the preceding season.

What are the implications of these content analyses? Foremost is that violence is inherent in television drama and, according to Gerbner (1972), appears to be used to define power and status. In another study, conducted by Cedric Clark (1972) at Stanford University, the author concludes that some members of our society are regularly denied power and status by being continually cast in the role of the helpless victim. Indeed, Clark suggests that the portrayal of specific groups, such as blacks or women, in powerless roles is a form of violence against society.

The overwhelming conclusion that can be drawn from these content analyses is that violent behavior is a common theme in many of the television programs viewed in American homes. Keeping this fact in mind, let us turn next to the topic of viewing.

Viewing Patterns

Who watches television? Virtually everyone does. It was noted earlier that some studies have estimated that the television set is turned on for an average of more than six hours each day. However, it would be a mistake to leave the impression that everyone views extensively. True, almost every home has a television set, but the patterns of use vary according to age, sex, and the family's socioeconomic level. There are, of course, some general guidelines concerning the extent of viewing, such as younger children view more than older children; women more than men; and persons from lower income homes more than middle and upper income families. With regard to children, the developmental pattern is one of onset of television viewing at $1\frac{1}{2}$–2 years of age, followed by extensive television viewing during preschool and early elementary school years, which is followed by a sharp decline in viewing as the youngster approaches adolescence. Indeed, the extent and duration of viewing remain low from adolescence to early adulthood. For adults, the peak life-span viewing periods occur for persons in their late twenties through early thirties and the elderly.

An idealized curve demonstrating the extent of television viewing across all ages would identify three primary clusters of viewers: young children, young adults, and elderly persons. The most parsimonious explanation for these clusters is the lack of alternative activities: young children have limited physical mobility outside the home; young adults are more likely to be married and have families with young children; and elderly persons frequently report a restricted range of outside activities due to physical limitations.

Our research program has been focused on only one of these three groups: young children. Although this seemed reasonable in terms of limited resources, future research should not neglect the elderly viewer. At present, one can only speculate about the experiences of a person who is physically separated from his or her family, alone and lonely, whose only regular visitor is Johnny Carson.

With regard to children's viewing, we have already suggested that they are among the heaviest users of television. Indeed, several studies (Lyle & Hoffman, 1972a, 1972b; Murray, 1972) have demonstrated that young children spend between two and three hours watching television each day, and they watch more on weekends than during the week. On the average, preschoolers spend approximately half of an adult's workweek sitting in front of the television set.

What kinds of programs do they watch? Universally, the youngest children prefer cartoons and situation comedies to other types of television fare. There is a definite sequence of change in preference patterns during childhood, beginning with cartoons and shifting to situation comedies (e.g., *I Love Lucy*) and child adventure (e.g., *Lassie*), and then to action/adventure programs (e.g., *Hawaii Five-O* and *Mod Squad*). It should *not* be assumed, however, that very young children are only exposed to relatively nonviolent programming. Indeed, we have already noted that cartoons are among the most violent programs on television. Moreover, the three studies cited above, which asked parents to keep a diary of the programs viewed by their children, indicated that even preschoolers spent almost half of their viewing time watching action/adventure programs such as *Mannix, Mod Squad*, and the *FBI*.

Impact of Televised Violence

Given the fact that there is a considerable amount of violence portrayed on television and that large segments of our society are routinely exposed to such material, one may legitimately question the impact of such programming. In this regard, a considerable body of prior research on imitative behavior (Bandura, 1969), as well as accumulated folk wisdom, has led to the conclusion that children *can* learn from observing behavior of others. The "others" may be their fellow playmates, parents, teachers, or the repairman who visits the child's home. Thus, the boy or girl who mimics the teacher's voice and the youngster who pretends to be the plumber who repaired the family's kitchen sink yesterday are generally considered living proof of this thesis. Can one extend this line of reasoning to include television as one of the "others" from whom a child is likely to learn specific behaviors? (For recent reviews, see Murray, Nayman, & Atkin, 1972; Weiss, 1969.) We know that there have been isolated incidents in which a child has attempted to replicate behavior he has just observed on television—occasionally with tragic consequences. But what about the youngster who is merely surly or inconsiderate toward his brothers and sisters, excessively aggressive or disruptive on the playground, or hostile and cynical about the

value of trust and love in interpersonal relationships? Can these, too, be related to the behaviors the child has observed on the television screen? Perhaps. However, the basic question to which several studies in this program were addressed was, Are children who view televised violence more aggressive than those who do not view such fare? With this question in mind, let us look at some of the findings.

One study, conducted by Aletha Stein and Lynette Friedrich (1972) at the Pennsylvania State University, assessed the effect of exposing preschool children to a "diet" of either antisocial, prosocial, or neutral television programming. The antisocial programs consisted of *Batman* and *Superman* cartoons; prosocial programs were composed of segments of *Misteroger's Neighborhood;* and neutral programming consisted of children's travelogue films. The children were observed throughout a nine-week period which consisted of two weeks of previewing, four weeks of television exposure, and three weeks of follow-up. All observations were conducted while the children were engaged in their daily activities in the nursery school. The observers recorded various forms of behavior that could be described as prosocial (i.e., helping, sharing, cooperative play, tolerance of delay) or antisocial (i.e., arguing, pushing, breaking toys). The overall results indicated that children who were adjudged to be initially somewhat more aggressive became significantly more aggressive as a result of viewing the *Batman* and *Superman* cartoons. On the other hand, the children who viewed 12 episodes of *Misteroger's Neighborhood* became significantly more cooperative, willing to share toys and to help other children.

In another study, Robert Liebert and Robert Baron (1972), at the State University of New York at Stony Brook, assessed young children's willingness to hurt another child after viewing either aggressive or neutral television programming. The aggressive program consisted of segments drawn from *The Untouchables*, while the neutral program featured a track race. The main findings indicated that the children who viewed the aggressive program demonstrated a greater willingness to hurt another child. The experimental setting provided a situation in which a child could press a button that would either HELP or HURT a child in another room. The youngest children who had viewed the aggressive program pressed the HURT button earlier and for a longer period of time than did their peers who had viewed a track race. Moreover, when the children were later observed during the free-play period, those who had viewed *The Untouchables* exhibited a greater preference for playing with weapons and aggressive toys than did the children who had watched the neutral programming.

In a related study, Paul Ekman (1972) and his associates at the Langley Porter Neuropsychiatric Institute filmed the facial expressions of the children in the Liebert and Baron study and attempted to relate the child's emotional expression while viewing to later hurting or helping behavior. The results indicated that young boys whose facial expressions depicted positive emotions of happiness, pleasure, interest, or involvement while viewing *The Untouchables* were more likely to make hurting responses than were the boys whose facial expressions indicated displeasure or disinterest in such television fare.

An additional series of studies conducted by Aimee Leifer and Donald Roberts (1972) at Stanford University further explored the impact of televised violence in relation to the child's understanding of the motivations and consequences for the portrayed violent acts. The results indicated that as the child grows older, he is more likely to understand the portrayed motives and consequences, but such increased understanding does not seem to modify his postviewing aggressive behavior. Indeed, when a number of variables were assessed, the best predictor of subsequent aggressive behavior was the amount of violence portrayed in the program viewed: children who had viewed the more violent programs produced significantly more aggressive responses.

The several studies we have discussed thus far have demonstrated some immediate, short-term effects of viewing televised violence. But one may justifiably question the long-range cumulative impact of viewing violence. In this regard, a number of studies in this research program attempted to relate the child's program preference and viewing patterns to the viewer's perception of violence and attitudes concerning the use of violence or force to resolve conflicts. Bradley Greenberg and Thomas Gordon (1972) have suggested, on the basis of a series of studies conducted at Michigan State University, that watching violence on television sensitizes the viewer to perceive more violence in the world around him and increases the likelihood that the viewer will espouse attitudes favorable toward the use of violence as a means of resolving conflicts. Moreover, Steven Chaffee and his associates (Chaffee & McLeod, 1971; McLeod, Atkin, & Chaffee, 1972a, 1972b) at the University of Wisconsin and Jennie McIntyre and James Teevan (1972) at the University of Maryland have noted that there is a consistent and reliable relationship between prefer-

ence for and viewing of violent television programs and engaging in aggressive or delinquent acts.

Perhaps the most crucial study in this regard was one conducted by Monroe Lefkowitz and his colleagues (Lefkowitz, Eron, Walder, & Huesmann, 1972) at the New York State Department of Mental Hygiene. This study is of particular importance because it was designed to investigate the development of aggressive behavior in children by studying the same boys and girls over a 10-year period, at ages 8 and 18. Ten years ago, the investigators obtained several measures of each child's aggressive behavior and related these to his or her preference for violent television programs (see Eron, 1963). Now, 10 years later, when the subjects were one year out of high school, the investigators obtained similar measures of program preferences and aggressive behavior. For boys, the results indicated that preference for violent programs at age 8 was significantly related to aggressive and delinquent behavior at age 18. For girls, this relationship was in the same direction but was less strong. Thus, one general interpretation of the results of this study is that preferring violent television at age 8 is at least one cause of the aggressive and antisocial behavior these young men displayed 10 years later.

The conclusions that can be drawn from the results of this series of studies are threefold. First, there is considerable violence portrayed on the television screen. And such violence tends not to mirror societal violence, but rather is used as a dramatic punctuation mark—a definer or arbiter of power and status among the performers in each dramatic episode. Second, young children view a considerable amount of television, in the course of which they are exposed to a considerable amount of televised violence. Third, there are a number of studies which point to the conclusion that viewing televised violence causes the viewer to become more aggressive. Indeed, the Surgeon General's Scientific Advisory Committee on Television and Social Behavior (1972) summarized its interpretation of this point as follows:

Thus, there is a convergence of the fairly substantial experimental evidence for *short-run* causation of aggression among some children by viewing violence on the screen and the much less certain evidence from field studies that extensive violence viewing precedes some *long-run* manifestations of aggressive behavior [p. 10].

Thus, the major implication of the results of this research program is the clear need for a reduction in the level of violence portrayed on television. At the same time it is equally important to encourage broadcasters to modify the balance of programming in favor of prosocial content. Indeed, the recommendations stemming from this research program are not merely negative sanctions against televised violence but rather a plea for more beneficial and useful forms of television content.

REFERENCES

BAKER, R. K., & BALL, S. J. *Mass media and violence: A staff report to the National Commission on the Causes and Prevention of Violence.* Washington, D.C.: U.S. Government Printing Office, 1969.

BANDURA, A. Social learning theory of identificatory processes. In D. A. Goslin (Ed.), *Handbook of socialization theory and research.* Chicago: Rand McNally, 1969.

BARCUS, F. E. *Saturday children's television: A report of TV programming and advertising on Boston commercial television.* Boston: Action for Children's Television, 1971.

CHAFFEE, S., & McLEOD, J. Adolescents, parents, and television violence. Paper presented at the annual meeting of the American Psychological Association, Washington, D.C., September 1971.

CLARK, C. Race, identification, and television violence. In G. A. Comstock, E. A. Rubinstein, & J. P. Murray (Eds.), *Television and social behavior.* Vol. 5. *Television's effects: Further explorations.* Washington, D.C.: U.S. Government Printing Office, 1972:

CLARK, D. G., & BLANKENBURG, W. B. Trends in violent content in selected mass media. In G. A. Comstock & E. A. Rubinstein (Eds.), *Television and social behavior.* Vol. 1. *Media content and control.* Washington, D.C.: U.S. Government Printing Office, 1972.

EKMAN, P., LIEBERT, R. M., FRIESEN, W., HARRISON, R., ZLATCHIN, C., MALMSTROM, E. J., & BARON, R. A. Facial expressions of emotion while watching televised violence as predictors of subsequent aggression. In G. A. Comstock, E. A. Rubinstein, & J. P. Murray (Eds.), *Television and social behavior.* Vol. 5. *Television's effects: Further explorations.* Washington, D.C.: U.S. Government Printing Office, 1972.

ERON, L. Relationship of TV viewing habits and aggressive behavior in children. *Journal of Abnormal and Social Psychology,* 1963, **67,** 193–196.

GERBNER, G. Violence in television drama: Trends and symbolic functions. In G. A. Comstock & E. A. Rubinstein (Eds.), *Television and social behavior.* Vol. 1. *Media content and control.* Washington, D.C.: U.S. Government Printing Office, 1972.

GREENBERG, B. S., & GORDON, T. F. Children's perceptions of television violence: A replication. In G. A. Comstock, E. A. Rubinstein, & J. P. Murray (Eds.), *Television and social behavior.* Vol. 5. *Television's effects: Further explorations.* Washington, D.C.: U.S. Government Printing Office, 1972.

LEFKOWITZ, M., ERON, L., WALDER, L., & HUESMANN, L. R. Television violence and child aggression: A follow up study. In G. A. Comstock & E. A. Rubinstein (Eds.), *Television and social behavior.* Vol. 3. *Television and adolescent aggressiveness.* Washington, D.C.: U.S. Government Printing Office, 1972.

LEIFER, A. D., & ROBERTS, D. F. Children's responses to television violence. In J. P. Murray, E. A. Rubinstein, & G. A. Comstock (Eds.), *Television and social behavior.*

Vol. 2. *Television and social learning.* Washington, D.C.: U.S. Government Printing Office, 1972.

LIEBERT, R. M., & BARON, R. A. Short-term effects of televised aggression on children's aggressive behavior. In J. P. Murray, E. A. Rubinstein, & G. A. Comstock (Eds.), *Television and social behavior.* Vol. 2. *Television and social learning.* Washington, D.C.: U.S. Government Printing Office, 1972.

LYLE, J., & HOFFMAN, H. R. Children's use of television and other media. In E. A. Rubinstein, G. A. Comstock, J. P. Murray (Eds.), *Television and social behavior.* Vol. 4. *Television in day-to-day life: Patterns of use.* Washington, D.C.: U.S. Government Printing Office, 1972. (a)

LYLE, J., & HOFFMAN, H. R. Explorations in patterns of television viewing by preschool-age children. In E. A. Rubinstein, G. A. Comstock, & J. P. Murray (Eds.), *Television and social behavior.* Vol. 4. *Television in day-to-day life: Patterns of use.* Washington, D.C.: U.S. Government Printing Office, 1972. (b)

McINTYRE, J., & TEEVAN, J. Television and deviant behavior. In G. A. Comstock & E. A. Rubinstein (Eds.), *Television and social behavior.* Vol. 3. *Television and adolescent aggressiveness.* Washington, D.C.: U.S. Government Printing Office, 1972.

McLEOD, J., ATKIN, C., & CHAFFEE, S. Adolescents, parents, and television use: Adolescent self-report measures from Maryland and Wisconsin samples. In G. A. Comstock & E. A. Rubinstein (Eds.), *Television and social behavior.* Vol. 3. *Television and adolescent aggressiveness.* Washington, D.C.: U.S. Government Printing Office, 1972. (a)

McLEOD, J., ATKIN, C., & CHAFFEE, S. Adolescents, parents, and television use: Self-report and other-report measures from the Wisconsin sample. In G. A. Comstock & E. A. Rubinstein (Eds.), *Television and social behavior.* Vol. 3. *Television and adolescent aggressiveness.* Washington, D.C.: U.S. Government Printing Office, 1972. (b)

MURRAY, J. P. Television in inner-city homes: Viewing behavior of young boys. In E. A. Rubinstein, G. A. Comstock, & J. P. Murray (Eds.), *Television and social behavior.* Vol. 4. *Television in day-to-day life: Patterns of use.* Washington, D.C.: U.S. Government Printing Office, 1972.

MURRAY, J. P., NAYMAN, O. B., & ATKIN, C. K. Television and the child: A comprehensive research bibliography. *Journal of Broadcasting,* 1972, **26**(1), 21–35.

STEIN, A., & FRIEDRICH, L. K. Television content and young children's behavior. In J. P. Murray, E. A. Rubinstein, & G. A. Comstock (Eds.), *Television and social behavior.* Vol. 2. *Television and social learning.* Washington, D.C.: U.S. Government Printing Office, 1972.

SURGEON GENERAL'S SCIENTIFIC ADVISORY COMMITTEE ON TELEVISION AND SOCIAL BEHAVIOR. *Television and growing up: The impact of televised violence.* Washington, D.C.: U.S. Government Printing Office, 1972.

UNITED STATES SENATE, Committee on the Judiciary. *Effects on young people of violence and crime portrayed on television. Part 16. Investigation of juvenile delinquency in the United States, July 30, 1964.* Washington, D.C.: U.S. Government Printing Office, 1964.

WEISS, W. Effects of the mass media of communication. In G. Lindzey & E. Aronson (Eds.), *The handbook of social psychology.* (2nd ed.) Reading, Mass.: Addison-Wesley, 1969.

21

The Subway Samaritan

A man slumps in a doorway and lies there unattended as pedestrians scurry past. A child is beaten unconscious while residents in adjoining apartments turn a deaf ear to his shrieks. Six years ago, Kitty Genovese, 28, was stabbed to death in New York City while 38 of her neighbors, roused by her screams, watched or listened and did nothing. Such incidents feed the popular notion, especially in big cities, that the average citizen is not prepared to go to the aid of his fellow man.

Now this pessimistic view has been challenged in a recently published study, "Good Samaritanism: An Underground Phenomenon?" by Psychologists Irving M. and Jane Allyn Piliavin of the University of Pennsylvania and Judith Rodin of Columbia University Based on experiments conducted by four teams of Columbia students in that grimy citadel of public indifference, the New York City subway system, the study finds that "people do, in fact, help with rather high frequency." The experiments, carried on over a period of 73 days, sought to determine in a realistic setting how a captive audience reacts to a person obviously ill, and another plainly drunk, and whether these responses differ with the victim's race.*

A team composed of a "victim," a model who was to come to the victim's aid if there was no response, and two women observers boarded an Eighth Avenue express. The victim, wearing an Eisenhower jacket and old slacks, stood near a pole in the center of the coach. He carried a cane if he was playing an invalid; if feigning drunkenness, he

* Of the four victims repeatedly used, three were white.

smelled of liquor and carried a bottle tightly wrapped in a brown paper bag. After the train departed the station, the victim suddenly staggered, collapsed and lay on the floor.

Sticky Problem. "The frequency of help received by the victims was impressive," write the psychologists. "The victim with the cane received spontaneous help on 62 of the 65 trials. Even the drunk received help on 19 of 38 trials." In fact, some passengers were so solicitous in helping the victim out of the train, remaining with him at the station or insisting on finding him an ambulance, that getting on with the next trial became a sticky problem.

Help for the ill man was offered about evenly from blacks and whites, but those who risked trouble to come to the aid of the drunk tended most often to be of his race. Only 10% of those offering spontaneous help were women, who tended to rationalize their inaction with comments like "I'm not strong enough."

In at least one important respect, the findings of this study collide with the now classic report by John M. Darley of Princeton and Bibb Latané of Ohio State. Working under carefully controlled laboratory conditions, Darley and Latané found that a bystander is less likely to help in a group than when he is alone. A crowd, they concluded, tends to diffuse responsibility and makes it easier for the individual to do nothing. The Piliavins and Mrs. Rodin cautiously dispute this theory. They contend that under real-life conditions the average person—even in a group—will act when he clearly sees that another human being is in trouble.

God may help those who help themselves, but if He should happen to be busy elsewhere while you're fighting off six vicious muggers, just try getting a substitute to help you help yourself.

Whether asking a favor or crying out in obvious distress, it's not easy to get results. But now, helpful behavior has turned into a social science: at least three sets of investigators have recently probed the anatomy of "Good Turns and How to Painlessly Extract Them."

Planned Approach. First of all, advise Yale psychologists Ellen J. Langer and Robert P. Abelson, the granting of a favor depends to a large extent on how the request is worded. There are two rather fundamental approaches, they helpfully explain. The first is referred to as "victim oriented," and depends on the target person's sympathy for the victim—who may variously cry out, "I'm hurt," or "I'm suffering" or even "What a mess I'm in."

In "target-oriented" appeals, sympathy is unnecessary, since emphasis is placed on the target person's duty and responsibility to the victim. Examples of such appeals are "Do something for me," "Can you give me a hand?" or "Would you do me a favor?"

The right appeal depends upon the desired favor. If it is legitimate, empathy will be easy to evoke and the victim-oriented appeal will probably wring out tears and Christian charity. But if the favor is presumptuous or illegitimate, you'd best depend on the clarion call to duty and the target-oriented approach.

Careful Wording. Langer and Abelson devised some tricky situations—one in which a lady shopper in distress (with a feigned knee injury) called for help. A request to make a phone call was phrased four different ways. Half the passersby were asked to call her husband to pick her up (a legitimate request); the others were requested to call her employer to tell him she would be late (an illegitimate one). Both calls were designed to evoke either sympathy or responsibility.

Another female confederate alternately moaned that she might miss her train (legitimate) or that she needed to get to a Macy's sale (illegitimate) or asked passersby if they would mail a package for her, in victim- or target-oriented pleas.

Overall in the two experiments, 75 percent of the passersby complied to a legitimate victim-oriented appeal; when it was illegitimate, less than 28 percent assisted. But when the appeal was target-oriented, say Langer and Abelson, legitimacy made very little difference, since the decision to help has little to do with the victim but a lot to do with the target person's own considerations about whether going out of the way will benefit her.

Thus, Rule One for a guaranteed favor is to invoke empathy and not make outlandish demands.

Uncertainty Immobilizes. Or make sure your situation is not ambiguous, emphasize psychologists Russell D. Clark III and Larry E. Word of Florida State University. It's not apathy that prevents people from coming to the rescue, they say. It's indecision. While bystanders are deciding whether they are witnessing a true emergency, each one looks to the others for guidance. That hesitation is seen by everyone as a lack of concern, and therefore no one thinks the situation is serious. Individuals, free of crowd influence, are likely to act—if they're sure it is an emergency.

While filling out a questionnaire on sexual attitudes, Clark and Word's bystanders witnessed an "accident" —either alone, with an equally naive stranger, with a stranger who was the investigator's accomplice, with a naive friend or with a friend who had been clued to what was going on. A workman carrying a ladder and a venetian blind walked past the subjects into the next room. A loud crash was heard three minutes later, followed by groans, grunts and an exclaimed "Oh, my back—I can't move," then a definite cry for help. Finally, silence.

In all informed situations, the investigators' accomplice maintained complete neutrality. He didn't voice an opinion or make a move until the subject did. There was 75 seconds from the time of the first crash until termination of the experiment.

At least one subject in every group took helpful action long before the time was up, even though action was delayed among uninformed friends and strangers, and especially when

one friend had been briefed to ignore the situation.

Befuddled Bystanders. The 100 percent charitable average contradicted previous experiments, but Clark and Word had neglected the previously omnipresent ambiguity. Their bystanders never doubted there had been a serious accident. So they repeated the experiment, this time adding larger groups and ambiguity: up to five persons heard nothing more than the crash of a ladder. Helping behavior dropped 70 percent. In the unambiguous situation, subjects took an average of only eight seconds to react; when the situation became confused, 56 seconds was the median reaction time.

Another tip: happy people are generally helpful people. Those who feel the world has just given them the raspberries are likely to return the favor with sour grapes.

Duke University psychologist David Aderman subjected 120 students to a series of tests linking mood and helpful behavior—after they read a list of either 50 elation or depression statements. Elation statements reached a high of "I'm full of energy," and "God, I feel great"; depression statements sunk to a low of "All of the unhappiness of my past life is taking possession of me," and "I want to go to sleep and never wake up."

When Aderman asked subjects to do him a favor, depression subjects saw those requests as threats to their freedom, while elation subjects felt they needed to grant the favor since they had been given so much (their good mood) for so little (reading the 50 mood statements). But elation subjects felt freer to turn down requests for help, while depression subjects felt the request was a demand, and therefore performed the task reluctantly.

All of the investigators would probably agree that to find a good Samaritan, you'd best brush up on your semantic powers; leave no doubt in a bystander's mind that your very life is ebbing rapidly; and, above all, don't call on someone who just had a fight with his wife.

23

WHEN WILL PEOPLE HELP IN A CRISIS?

by John M. Darley and Bibb Latané

Kitty Genovese is set upon by a maniac as she returns home from work at 3:00 a.m. Thirty-eight of her neighbors in Kew Gardens come to their windows when she cries out in terror; none come to her assistance even though her stalker takes over half an hour to murder her. No one even so much as calls the police. She dies.

An 18-year-old switchboard operator, alone in her office in the Bronx, is raped and beaten. Escaping momentarily, she runs naked and bleeding to the street, screaming for help. A crowd of 40 passersby gathers and watches as, in broad daylight, the rapist tries to drag her back upstairs; no one interferes. Finally two policemen happen by and arrest her assailant.

Andrew Mormille is stabbed in the stomach as he rides the A train home to Manhattan. Eleven other riders watch the 17-year-old boy as he bleeds to death; none come to his assistance even though his attackers have left the car. He dies.

Eleanor Bradley trips and breaks her leg while shopping on Fifth Avenue. Dazed and in shock, she calls for help, but the hurrying stream of executives and shoppers simply parts and flows past. After 40 minutes a taxi driver helps her to a doctor.

The shocking thing about these cases is that so many people failed to respond. If only one or two had ignored the victim, we might be able to understand their inaction. But when 38 people, or 11 people, or hundreds of people fail to help, we become disturbed. Actually, this fact that shocks us so much is itself the clue to understanding these cases. Although it seems obvious that the more people who watch a victim in distress, the more likely someone will help, what really happens is exactly the opposite. If each member of a group of bystanders is aware that other people are also present, he will be less likely to notice the emergency, less likely to decide that it is an emergency, and less likely to act even if he thinks there is an emergency.

This is a surprising assertion—what we are saying is that the victim may actually be less likely to get help, the more people who watch his distress and are available to help. We shall discuss in detail the process through which an individual bystander must go in order to intervene, and we shall present the results of some experiments designed to show the effects of the number of onlookers on the likelihood of intervention.

Since we started research on bystander responses to emergencies, we have heard many explanations for the lack of intervention. "I would assign this to the effect of the megapolis in which we live, which makes closeness very difficult and leads to the alienation of the individual from the group," contributed a psychoanalyst. "A disaster syndrome," explained a sociologist, "that shook the sense of safety and sureness of the individuals involved and caused psychological withdrawal from the event by ignoring it." "Apathy," claimed others. "Indifference." "The gratification of unconscious sadistic impulses." "Lack of concern for our fellow men." "The Cold Society." All of these analyses of the person who fails to help share one characteristic; they set the indifferent witness apart from the rest of us as a different kind of person. Certainly not one of us who reads about these incidents in horror is apathetic, alienated or depersonalized. Certainly not one of us enjoys gratifying his sadistic impulses by watching others suffer. These terrifying cases in which people fail to help others certainly have no personal implications for us. That is, we might decide not to ride subways any more, or that New York isn't even "a nice place to visit," or "there ought to be a law" against apathy, but we needn't feel guilty, or re-examine ourselves, or anything like that.

Looking more closely at published descriptions of the behavior of witnesses to these incidents, the people involved begin to look a little less inhuman and a lot more like the rest of us. Although it is unquestionably true that the witnesses in the incidents above did nothing to save the victims, apathy, indifference and unconcern are not entirely accurate descriptions of their reactions. The 38 witnesses of Kitty Genovese's murder did not merely look at the scene once and then ignore it. They continued to stare out of their windows at what was going on. Caught, fascinated, distressed, unwilling to act but unable to turn away, their behavior was neither helpful nor heroic; but it was not indifferent or apathetic.

Actually, it was like crowd behavior in many other emergency situations. Car accidents, drownings, fires and attempted suicides all attract substantial numbers of people who watch the drama in helpless fascination without getting directly involved in the action. Are these people alienated and indifferent? Are the rest of us? Obviously not. Why, then, don't we act?

The bystander to an emergency has to make a series of decisions about what is happening and what he will do about it. The consequences of these decisions will determine his actions. There are three things he must do if he is to intervene: *notice* that something is happening, *interpret* that event as an emergency, and decide that he has *personal responsibility* for intervention. If he fails to notice the event, if he decides that it is not an emergency, or if he concludes that he is not personally responsible for acting, he will leave the victim unhelped. This state of affairs is shown graphically as a "decision tree" (*see illustration, right*). Only one path through this decision tree leads to intervention; all others lead to a failure to help. As we shall show, at each fork of the path in the decision tree, the presence of other bystanders may lead a person down the branch of not helping.

Noticing: The First Step

Suppose that an emergency is actually taking place; a middle-aged man has a heart attack. He stops short, clutches his chest, and staggers to the nearest building wall, where he slowly slumps to the sidewalk in a sitting position. What is the likelihood that a passerby will come to his assistance? First, the bystander has to *notice* that something is happening. The external event has to break into his thinking and intrude itself on his conscious mind. He must tear himself away from his private thoughts and pay attention to this unusual event.

But Americans consider it bad manners to look too closely at other people in public. We are taught to respect the privacy of others, and when among strangers, we do this by closing our ears and avoiding staring at others—we are embarrassed if caught doing otherwise. In a crowd, then, each person is less likely to notice the first sign of a potential emergency than when alone.

Experimental evidence corroborates this everyday observation. Darley and Latané asked college students to an interview about their reactions to urban living. As the students waited to see the interviewer, either by themselves or with two other students, they filled out a preliminary questionnaire. Solitary students often glanced idly about the room while filling out their questionnaires; those in groups, to avoid seeming rudely inquisitive, kept their eyes on their own papers.

As part of the study, we staged an emergency: smoke was released into the waiting room through a vent. Two-thirds of the subjects who were alone when the smoke appeared noticed it immediately, but only a quarter of the subjects waiting in groups saw it as quickly. Even after the room had completely filled with smoke one subject from a group of three finally looked up and exclaimed, "God! I must be smoking too much!" Although eventually all the subjects did become aware of the smoke, this study indicates that the more people present, the slower an individual may be to perceive that an emergency does exist and the more likely he is not to see it at all.

Once an event is noticed, an onlooker must decide whether or not it is truly an emergency. Emergencies are not always clearly labeled as such; smoke pouring from a building or into a waiting room may be caused by a fire, or it may merely indicate a leak in a steam pipe. Screams in the street may signal an assault or a family quarrel. A man lying in doorway may be having a coronary or be suffering from diabetic coma—he may simply be sleeping off a drunk. And in any unusual situation, Candid Camera may be watching.

A person trying to decide whether or not a given situation is an emergency often refers to the reactions of those around him; he looks at them to see how he should react himself. If everyone else is calm and indifferent, he will tend to remain calm and indifferent; if everyone else is reacting strongly, he will become aroused. This tendency is not merely slavish conformity; ordinarily we derive much valuable information about new situations from how others around us behave. It's a rare traveler who, in picking a roadside restaurant, chooses to stop at one with no other cars in the parking lot.

But occasionally the reactions of others provide false information. The studied nonchalance of patients in a dentist's waiting room is a poor indication of the pain awaiting them. In general, it is considered embarrassing to look overly concerned, to seem flustered, to "lose your cool" in public. When we are not alone, most of us try to seem less fearful and anxious than we really are.

In a potentially dangerous situation, then, everyone present will appear more unconcerned than they are in fact. Looking at the *apparent* impassivity and lack of reaction of the others, each person is led to believe that nothing really is wrong. Meanwhile the danger may be mounting, to the point where a single person, uninfluenced by the seeming calm of others, would react.

A crowd can thus force inaction on its members by implying, through its passivity and apparent indifference, that an event is not an emergency. Any individual in such a crowd is uncomfortably aware that he'll look like a fool if he behaves as though it were—and in these circumstances, until someone acts, no one acts.

In the smoke-filled-room study, the smoke trickling from the wall constituted an ambiguous but potentially dangerous situation. How did the presence of other people affect a person's response to the situation? Typically, those who were in the waiting room by themselves noticed the smoke at once, gave a slight startle reaction, hesitated, got up and went over to investigate the smoke,

hesitated again, and then left the room to find somebody to tell about the smoke. No one showed any signs of panic, but over three-quarters of these people were concerned enough to report the smoke.

Others went through an identical experience but in groups of three strangers. Their behavior was radically different. Typically, once someone noticed the smoke, he would look at the other people, see them doing nothing, shrug his shoulders, and then go back to his questionnaire, casting covert glances first at the smoke and then at the others. From these three-person groups, only three out of 24 people reported the smoke. The inhibiting effect of the group was so strong that the other 21 were willing to sit in a room filled with smoke rather than make themselves conspicuous by reacting with alarm and concern—this despite the fact that after three or four minutes the atmosphere in the waiting room grew most unpleasant. Even though they coughed, rubbed their eyes, tried to wave the smoke away, and opened the window, they apparently were unable to bring themselves to leave.

These dramatic differences between the behavior of people alone and those in a group indicate that the group imposed a definition of the situation upon its members which inhibited action.

"A leak in the air conditioning," said one person when we asked him what he thought caused the smoke. "Must be chemistry labs in the building." "Steam pipes." "Truth gas to make us give true answers on the questionnaire," reported the more imaginative. There were many explanations for the smoke, but they all had one thing in common: they did not mention the word fire. In defining the situation as a nonemergency, people explained to themselves why the other observers did not leave the room; they also removed any reason for action themselves. The other members of the group acted as nonresponsive models for each person—and as an audience for any "inappropriate" action he might consider. In such a situation it is all too easy to do nothing.

The results of this study clearly and strongly support the predictions. But are they general? Would the same effect show up with other emergencies, or is it limited to situations like the smoke study involving danger to the self as well as to others—or to situations in which there's no clearly defined "victim"? It may be that our college-age male subjects played "chicken" with one another to see who would lose face by first fleeing the room. It may be that groups were less likely to respond because no par-

---

THE DECISION TREE. In an emergency, a bystander must: 1) notice something is happening; 2) interpret it as an emergency; 3) decide that he has a personal responsibility for intervention.

ticular person was in danger. To see how generalizable these results are, Latané and Judith Rodin set up a second experiment, in which the emergency would cause no danger for the bystander, and in which a specific person was in trouble.

Subjects were paid $2 to participate in a survey of game and puzzle preferences conducted at Columbia by the Consumer Testing Bureau (CTB). An attractive young woman, the market-research representative, met them at the door and took them to the testing room. On the way, they passed the CTB office and through its open door they could see filing cabinets and a desk and bookcases piled high with papers. They entered the adjacent testing room, which contained a table and chairs and a variety of games, where they were given a preliminary background information and game preference questionnaire to fill out. The representative told subjects that she would be working next door in her office for about 10 minutes while they completed the questionnaires, and left by opening the collapsible curtain which divided the two rooms. She made sure the subjects knew that the curtain was unlocked, easily opened and a means of entry to her office. The representative stayed in her office, shuffling papers, opening drawers, and making enough noise to remind the subjects of her presence. Four minutes after leaving the testing area, she turned on a high fidelity stereophonic tape recorder.

If the subject listened carefully, he heard the representative climb up on a chair to reach for a stack of papers on the bookcase. Even if he were not listening carefully, he heard a loud crash and a scream as the chair collapsed and she fell to the floor. "Oh, my God, my foot....I...I...can't move it. Oh...my ankle," the representative moaned. "I...can't get this...thing...off me." She cried and moaned for about a minute longer, but the cries gradually got more subdued and controlled. Finally she muttered something about getting outside, knocked over the chair as she pulled herself up, and thumped to the door, closing it behind her as she left. This drama lasted about two minutes.

Some people were alone in the waiting room when the "accident" occurred. Seventy per cent of them offered to help the victim before she left the room. Many came through the curtain to offer their assistance, others simply called out to offer their help. Others faced the emergency in pairs. Only 20 per cent of this group—eight out of 40—offered to help the victim. The other 32 remained unresponsive to her cries of distress. Again, the presence of other bystanders inhibited action.

And again, the noninterveners seemed to have decided the event was not an emergency. They were unsure what had happened but whatever it was, it was not too serious. "A mild sprain," some said. "I didn't want to embarrass her." In a "real" emergency, they assured us, they would be among the first to help the victim. Perhaps they would be, but in this situation they didn't help, because for them the event was not defined as an emergency.

Again, solitary people exposed to a potential emergency reacted more frequently than those exposed in groups. We found that the action-inhibiting effects of other bystanders works in two different situations, one of which involves risking danger to oneself and the other of which involves helping an injured woman. The result seems sufficiently general so that we may assume it operates to inhibit helping in real-life emergencies.

Diffused Responsibility

Even if a person has noticed an event and defined it as an emergency, the fact that he knows that other bystanders also witnessed it may still make him less likely to intervene. Others may inhibit intervention because they make a person feel that his responsibility is diffused and diluted. Each soldier in a firing squad feels less personally responsible for killing a man than he would if he alone pulled the trigger. Likewise, any person in a crowd of onlookers may feel less responsibility for saving a life than if he alone witnesses the emergency.

If your car breaks down on a busy highway, hundreds of drivers whiz by without anyone's stopping to help; if you are stuck on a nearly deserted country road, whoever passes you first is apt to stop. The personal responsibility that a passerby feels makes the difference. A driver on a lonely road knows that if he doesn't stop to help, the person will not get help; the same individual on the crowded highway feels he personally is no more responsible than any of a hundred other drivers. So even though an event clearly is an emergency, any person in a group who sees an emergency may feel less responsible, simply because any other bystander is equally responsible for helping.

This diffusion of responsibility might have occurred in the famous Kitty Geno-

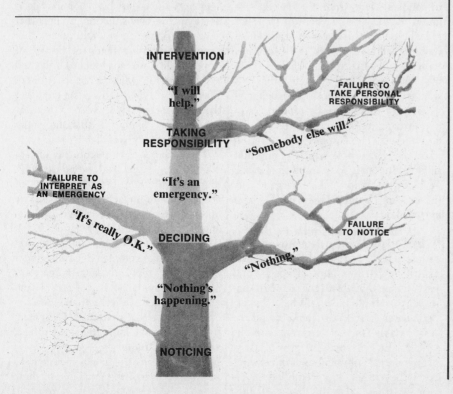

INTERVENTION

"I will help."

FAILURE TO TAKE PERSONAL RESPONSIBILITY

TAKING RESPONSIBILITY

"Somebody else will."

FAILURE TO INTERPRET AS AN EMERGENCY

"It's an emergency."

"It's really O.K."

DECIDING

FAILURE TO NOTICE

"Nothing."

"Nothing's happening."

NOTICING

vese case, in which the observers were walled off from each other in separate apartments. From the silhouettes against windows, all that could be told was that others were also watching.

To test this line of thought, Darley and Latané simulated an emergency in a setting designed to resemble Kitty Genovese's murder. People overheard a victim calling for help. Some knew they were the only one to hear the victim's cries, the rest believed other people were aware of the victim's distress. As with the Genovese witnesses, subjects could not see each other or know what others were doing. The kind of direct group inhibition found in the smoke and fallen-woman studies could not operate.

For the simulation, we recruited male and female students at New York University to participate in a group discussion. Each student was put in an individual room equipped with a set of headphones and a microphone and told to listen for instructions over the headphones. The instructions informed the participant that the discussion was to consider personal problems of the normal college student in a high-pressure urban university. It was explained that, because participants might feel embarrassed about discussing personal problems publicly, several precautions had been taken to insure their anonymity: they would not meet the other people face to face, and the experimenter would not listen to the initial discussion but would only ask for their reactions later. Each person was to talk in turn. The first to talk reported that he found it difficult to adjust to New York and his studies. Then, very hesitantly and with obvious embarrassment, he mentioned that he was prone to nervous seizures, similar to but not really the same as epilepsy. These occurred particularly when he was under the stresses of studying and being graded.

Other people then discussed their own problems in turn. The number of other people in the discussion varied. But whatever the perceived size of the group —two, three or six people—only the subject was actually present; the others, as well as the instructions and the speeches of the victim-to-be, were present only on a pre-recorded tape.

When it again was the first person's turn to talk, after a few comments he launched into the following performance, getting increasingly louder with increasing speech difficulties:

"I can see a lot of er of er how other people's problems are similar to mine because er er I mean er it's er I mean some of the er same er kinds of things that I have and an er I'm sure that every everybody has and er er I mean er they're not er e-easy to handle sometimes and er I er er be upsetting like er er and er I er um I think I I need er if if could er er somebody er er er er er give me give me a little er give me a little help here because er I er I'm er h-h-having a a a a a real problem er right now and I er if somebody could help me out it would it would er er s-s-sure be sure be good be . . . because er there er er a cause I er *uh* I've got a a one of the er seiz—er er things coming *on* and and and I c-could really er use er some h-help s-so if somebody would er give me a little h-help uh er-er-er-er-er c-could somebody er er help er uh uh uh (choking sounds) . . . I'm gonna die er er I'm . . . gonna . . . die er help er er seizure er er . . ." (chokes, then quiet).

While this was going on, the experimenter waited outside the student's door to see how soon he would emerge to cope with the emergency. Rather to our surprise, some people sat through the entire fit without helping; a disproportionately large percentage of these nonresponders were from the largest-size group. Eighty-five per cent of the people who believed themselves to be alone with the victim came out of their rooms to help, while 62 per cent of the people who believed there was one other bystander did so. Of those who believed there were four other bystanders, only 31 per cent reported the fit before the tape ended. The responsibility-diluting effect of other people was so strong that single individuals were more than twice as likely to report the emergency as those who thought other people also knew about it.

The Moral Dilemma Felt by Those Who Do Not Respond

People who failed to report the emergency showed few signs of apathy and indifference thought to characterize "unresponsive bystanders." When the experimenter entered the room to end the situation, the subject often asked if the victim was "all right." Many of these people showed physical signs of nervousness; they often had trembling hands and sweating palms. If anything, they seemed more emotionally aroused than did those who reported the emergency.

Their emotional arousal was in sharp contrast to the behavior of the nonresponding subjects in the smoke and fallen-woman studies. Those subjects were calm and unconcerned when their experiments were over. Having interpreted the events as nonemergencies, there was no reason for them to be otherwise. It was only the subjects who did not respond in the face of the clear emergency represented by the fit, who felt the moral dilemma.

Why, then, didn't they respond? It is our impression that nonintervening subjects had not decided *not* to respond. Rather, they were still in a state of indecision and conflict concerning whether to respond or not. The emotional behavior of these nonresponding subjects was a sign of their continuing conflict; a conflict that other people resolved by responding. The distinction seems an academic one for the victim, since he gets no help in either case, but it is an extremely important one for arriving at an understanding of why bystanders fail to help.

The evidence is clear, then, that the presence of other bystanders and the various ways these other bystanders affect our decision processes, make a difference in how likely we are to give help in an emergency. The presence of strangers may keep us from noticing an emergency at all; group behavior may lead us to define the situation as one that does not require action; and when other people are there to share the burden of responsibility, we may feel less obligated to do something when action is required. Therefore, it will often be the case that the *more* people who witness his distress, the *less* likely it is that the victim of an emergency will get help.

Thus, the stereotype of the unconcerned, depersonalized *homo urbanis*, blandly watching the misfortunes of others, proves inaccurate. Instead, we find a bystander to an emergency is an anguished individual in genuine doubt, concerned to do the right thing but compelled to make complex decisions under pressure of stress and fear. His reactions are shaped by the actions of others—and all too frequently by their inaction.

And we are that bystander. Caught up by the apparent indifference of others, we may pass by an emergency without helping or even realizing that help is needed. Aware of the influence of those around us, however, we can resist it. We can choose to see distress and step forward to relieve it.

If Hitler Asked You to Electrocute a Stranger, Would You? *Probably*

by Philip Meyer

24

In the beginning, Stanley Milgram was worried about the Nazi problem. He doesn't worry much about the Nazis anymore. He worries about you and me, and, perhaps, himself a little bit too.

Stanley Milgram is a social psychologist, and when he began his career at Yale University in 1960 he had a plan to prove, scientifically, that Germans are different. The Germans-are-different hypothesis has been used by historians, such as William L. Shirer, to explain the systematic destruction of the Jews by the Third Reich. One madman could decide to destroy the Jews and even create a master plan for getting it done. But to implement it on the scale that Hitler did meant that thousands of other people had to go along with the scheme and help to do the work. The Shirer thesis, which Milgram set out to test, is that Germans have a basic character flaw which explains the whole thing, and this flaw is a readiness to obey authority without question, no matter what outrageous acts the authority commands.

The appealing thing about this theory is that it makes those of us who are not Germans feel better about the whole business. Obviously, you and I are not Hitler, and it seems equally obvious that we would never do Hitler's dirty work for him. But now, because of Stanley Milgram, we are compelled to wonder. Milgram developed a laboratory experiment which provided a systematic way to measure obedience. His plan was to try it out in New Haven on Americans and then go to Germany and try it out on Germans. He was strongly motivated by scientific curiosity, but there was also some moral content in his decision to pursue this line of research, which was, in turn, colored by his own Jewish background. If he could show that Germans are more obedient than Americans, he could then vary the conditions of the experiment and try to find out just what it is that makes some people more obedient than others. With this understanding, the world might, conceivably, be just a little bit better.

But he never took his experiment to Germany. He never took it any farther than Bridgeport. The first finding, also the most unexpected and disturbing finding, was that we Americans are an obedient people: not blindly obedient, and not blissfully obedient, just obedient. "I found so much obedience," says Milgram softly, a little sadly, "I hardly saw the need for taking the experiment to Germany."

There is something of the theatre director in Milgram, and his technique, which he learned from one of the old masters in experimental psychology, Solomon Asch, is to stage a play with every line rehearsed, every prop carefully selected, and everybody an actor except one person. That one person is the subject of the experiment. The subject, of course, does not know he is in a play. He thinks he is in real life. The value of this technique is that the experimenter, as though he were God, can change a prop here, vary a line there, and see how the subject responds. Milgram eventually had to change a lot of the script just to get people to stop obeying. They were obeying so much, the experiment wasn't working—it was like trying to measure oven temperature with a freezer thermometer.

The experiment worked like this: If you were an innocent subject in Milgram's melodrama, you read an ad in the newspaper or received one in the mail asking for volunteers for an educational experiment. The job would take about an hour and pay $4.50. So you make an appointment and go to an old Romanesque stone structure on High Street with the imposing name of The Yale Interaction Laboratory. It looks something like a broadcasting studio. Inside, you meet a young, crew-cut man in a laboratory coat who says he is Jack Williams, the experimenter. There is another citizen, fiftyish, Irish face, an accountant, a little overweight, and very mild and harmless-looking. This other citizen seems nervous and plays with his hat while the two of you sit in chairs side by side and are told that the $4.50 checks are yours no matter what happens. Then you listen to Jack Williams explain the experiment.

It is about learning, says Jack Williams in a quiet, knowledgeable way. Science does not know much about the conditions under which people learn and this experiment is to find out about negative reinforcement. Negative reinforcement is getting punished when you do something wrong, as opposed to positive reinforcement which is getting rewarded when you do something right. The negative reinforcement in this case is electric shock. You notice a book on the table, titled, *The Teaching-Learning Process*, and you assume that this has something to do with the experiment.

Then Jack Williams takes two pieces of paper, puts them in a hat, and shakes them up. One piece of paper is supposed to say, "Teacher" and the other, "Learner." Draw one and you will see which you will be. The mild-looking accountant draws one, holds it close to his vest like a poker player, looks at it, and says, "Learner." You look at yours. It says, "Teacher." You do not know that the drawing is rigged, and both slips say "Teacher." The experimenter beckons to the mild-mannered "learner."

"Want to step right in here and have a seat, please?" he says. "You can leave your coat on the back of that chair . . . roll up your right sleeve, please. Now what I want to do is strap down your arms to avoid excessive movement on your part during the experiment. This electrode is connected to the shock generator in the next room.

"And this electrode paste," he says, squeezing some stuff out of a plastic bottle and putting it on the man's arm, "is to provide a good contact and to avoid a blister or burn. Are there any questions now before we go into the next room?"

You don't have any, but the strapped-in "learner" does.

"I do think I should say this," says the learner. "About two years ago, I was at the veterans' hospital . . . they detected a heart condition. Nothing serious, but as long as I'm having these shocks, how strong are they—how dangerous are they?"

Williams, the experimenter, shakes his head casually. "Oh, no," he says. "Although they may be painful, they're not dangerous. Anything else?"

Nothing else. And so you play the game. The game is for you to read a series of word pairs: for example, blue-girl, nice-day, fat-neck. When you finish the list, you read just the first word in each pair and then a multiple-choice list of four other words, including the second word of the pair. The learner, from his remote, strapped-in position, pushes one of four switches to indicate which of the four answers he thinks is the right one. If he gets it right, nothing happens and you go on to the next one.

If he gets it wrong, you push a switch that buzzes and gives him an electric shock. And then you go to the next word. You start with 15 volts and increase the number of volts by 15 for each wrong answer. The control board goes from 15 volts on one end to 450 volts on the other. So that you know what you are doing, you get a test shock yourself, at 45 volts. It hurts. To further keep you aware of what you are doing to that man in there, the board has verbal descriptions of the shock levels, ranging from "Slight Shock" at the left-hand side, through "Intense Shock" in the middle, to "Danger: Severe Shock" toward the far right. Finally, at the very end, under 435- and 450-volt switches, there are three ambiguous X's. If, at any point, you hesitate, Mr. Williams calmly tells you to go on. If you still hesitate, he tells you again.

Except for some terrifying details, which will be explained in a moment, this is the experiment. The object is to find the shock level at which you disobey the experimenter and refuse to pull the switch.

When Stanley Milgram first wrote this script, he took it to fourteen Yale psychology majors and asked them what they thought would happen. He put it this way: Out of one hundred persons in the teacher's predicament, how would their break-off points be distributed along the 15-to-450-volt scale? They thought a few would break off very early, most would quit someplace in the middle and a few would go all the way to the end. The highest estimate of the number out of one hundred who would go all the way to the end was three. Milgram then informally polled some of his fellow scholars in the psychology department. They agreed that very few would go to the end. Milgram thought so too.

"I'll tell you quite frankly," he says, "before I began this experiment, before any shock generator was built, I thought that most people would break off at 'Strong Shock' or 'Very Strong Shock.' You would get only a very, very small proportion of people going out to the end of the shock generator, and they would constitute a pathological fringe."

In his pilot experiments, Milgram used Yale students as subjects. Each of them pushed the shock switches, one by one, all the way to the end of the board.

So he rewrote the script to include some protests from the learner. At first, they were mild, gentlemanly, Yalie protests, but, "it didn't seem to have as much effect as I thought it would or should," Milgram recalls. "So we had more violent protestation on the part of the person getting the shock. All of the time, of course, what we were trying to do was not to create a macabre situation, but simply to generate disobedience. And that was one of the first findings. This was not only a technical deficiency of the experiment, that we didn't get disobedience. It really was the first finding: that obedience would be much greater than we had assumed it would be and disobedience would be much more difficult than we had assumed."

As it turned out, the situation did become rather macabre. The only meaningful way to generate disobedience was to have the victim protest with great anguish, noise, and vehemence. The protests were tape-recorded so that all the teachers ordinarily would hear the same sounds and nuances, and they started with a grunt at 75 volts, proceeded through a "Hey, that really hurts," at 125 volts, got desperate with, "I can't stand the pain, don't do that," at 180 volts, reached complaints of heart trouble at 195, an agonized scream at 285, a refusal to answer at 315, and only heart-rending, ominous silence after that.

Still, sixty-five percent of the subjects, twenty- to fifty-year-old American males, everyday, ordinary people, like you and me, obediently kept pushing those levers in the belief that they were shocking the mild-mannered learner, whose name was Mr. Wallace, and who was chosen for the role because of his innocent appearance, all the way up to 450 volts.

Milgram was now getting enough disobedience so that he had something he could measure. The next step was to vary the circumstances to see what would encourage or discourage obedience. There seemed very little left in the way of discouragement. The victim was already screaming at the top of his lungs and feigning a heart attack. So whatever new impediment to obedience reached the brain of the subject had to travel by some route other than the ear. Milgram thought of one.

He put the learner in the same room with the teacher. He stopped strapping the learner's hand down. He rewrote the script so that at 150 volts the learner took his hand off the shock plate and declared that he wanted out of the experiment. He rewrote the script some more so that the experimenter then told the teacher to grasp the learner's hand and physically force it down on the plate to give Mr. Wallace his unwanted electric shock.

"I had the feeling that very few people would go on at that point, if any," Milgram says. "I thought that would be the limit of obedience that you would find in the laboratory."

It wasn't.

Although seven years have now gone by, Milgram still remembers the first person to walk into the laboratory in the newly rewritten script. He was a construction worker, a very short man. "He was so small," says Milgram, "that when he sat on the chair in front of the shock generator, his feet didn't reach the floor. When the experimenter told him to push the victim's hand down and give the shock, he turned to the experimenter, and he turned to the victim, his elbow went up, he fell down on the hand of the victim, his feet kind of tugged to one side, and he said, 'Like this, boss?' Zzumph!"

The experiment was played out to its bitter end. Milgram tried it with forty different subjects. And thirty percent of them obeyed the experimenter and kept on obeying.

"The protests of the victim were strong and vehement, he was screaming his guts out, he refused to participate, and you had to physically struggle with him in order to get his hand down on the shock generator," Milgram remembers. But twelve out of forty did it.

Milgram took his experiment out of New Haven. Not to Germany, just twenty miles down the road to Bridgeport. Maybe, he reasoned, the people obeyed because of the prestigious setting of Yale University. If they couldn't trust a center of learning that had been there for two centuries, whom could they trust? So he moved the experiment to an untrustworthy setting.

The new setting was a suite of three rooms in a run-down office building in Bridgeport. The only identification was a sign with a fictitious name: "Research Associates of Bridgeport." Questions about professional connections got only vague answers about "research for industry."

Obedience was less in Bridgeport. Forty-eight percent of the subjects stayed for the maximum shock, compared to sixty-five percent at Yale. But this was enough to prove that far more than Yale's prestige was behind the obedient behavior.

For more than seven years now, Stanley Milgram has been trying to figure out what makes ordinary American citizens so obedient. The most obvious answer—that people are mean, nasty, brutish and sadistic—won't do. The subjects who gave the shocks to Mr. Wallace to the end of the board did not enjoy it. They groaned, protested, fidgeted, argued, and in some cases, were seized by fits of nervous, agitated giggling.

"They even try to get out of it," says Milgram, "but they are somehow engaged in something from which they cannot liberate themselves. They are locked into a structure, and they do not have the skills or inner resources to disengage themselves."

Milgram, because he mistakenly had assumed that he would have trouble getting people to obey the orders to shock Mr. Wallace, went to a lot of trouble to create a realistic situation. There was crew-cut Jack Williams and his grey laboratory coat. Not white, which might denote a medical technician, but ambiguously authoritative grey. Then there was the book on the table, and the other appurtenances of the laboratory which emitted the silent message that things were being performed here in the name of science, and were therefore great and good.

But the nicest touch of all was the shock generator. When Milgram started out, he had only a $300 grant from the Higgins Fund of Yale University. Later he got more ample support from the National Science Foundation, but in the beginning he had to create this authentic-looking machine with very scarce resources except for his own imagination. So he went to New York and roamed around the electronic shops until he found some little black switches at Lafayette Radio for a dollar apiece. He bought thirty of them. The generator was a metal box, about the size of a small footlocker, and he drilled the thirty holes for the thirty switches himself in a Yale machine shop. But the fine detail was left to professional industrial engravers. So he ended up with a splendid-looking control panel dominated by the row of switches, each labeled with its voltage, and each having its own red light that flashed on when the switch was pulled. Other things happened when a switch was pushed. Besides the ZZUMPHing noise, a blue light labeled "voltage energizer" went on, and a needle on a dial labeled "voltage" flicked from left to right. Relays inside the box clicked. Finally, in the upper left-hand corner of the control panel was this inscription, engraved in precise block letters:

SHOCK GENERATOR TYPE ZLB
DYSON INSTRUMENT COMPANY
WALTHAM, MASS.
OUTPUT: 15 VOLTS—450 VOLTS

One day a man from the Lehigh Valley Electronics Company of Pennsylvania was passing through the laboratory, and he stopped to admire the shock generator.

"This is a very fine shock generator," he said. "But who is this Dyson Instrument Company?" Milgram felt proud at that, since Dyson Instrument Company existed only in the recesses of his imagination.

When you consider the seeming authenticity of the situation, you can appreciate the agony some of the subjects went through. It was pure conflict. As Milgram explains to his students, "When a parent says, 'Don't strike old ladies,' you are learning two things: the content, and, also, to obey authority. This experiment creates conflicts between the two elements."

Here is a partial transcription from one of the experiments. The naïve "teacher" is a heavyset, worried-looking man with prematurely grey hair. He is wearing a polo shirt. He is very polite. He has just pushed the 180-volt lever. A hidden camera is recording the performance.

LEARNER (*who, from the teacher's point of view is heard but not seen, an offstage voice*): Ow, I can't stand the pain. Don't do that . . . .

TEACHER (*pivoting around in his chair and shaking his head*): I can't stand it. I'm not going to kill that man in there. You hear him hollering?

EXPERIMENTER: As I told you before, the shocks may be painful, but—

TEACHER: But he's hollering. He can't stand it. What's going to happen to him?

EXPERIMENTER (*his voice is patient, matter-of-fact*): The experiment requires that you continue, Teacher.

TEACHER: Aaah, but, unh, I'm not going to get that man sick in there . . . know what I mean?

EXPERIMENTER: Whether the learner likes it or not, we must go on, through all the word pairs.

TEACHER: I refuse to take the responsibility. He's in there hollering!

EXPERIMENTER: It's absolutely essential that you continue, Teacher.

TEACHER (*indicating the unused questions*): There's too many left here, I mean, Geez, if he gets them wrong, there's too many of them left. I mean who's going to take the responsibility if anything happens to that gentleman?

EXPERIMENTER: I'm responsible for anything that happens to him. Continue please.

TEACHER: All right. (*Consults list of words.*) The next one's "Slow—walk, truck, dance, music." Answer, please. (*A buzzing sound indicates the learner has signaled his answer.*) Wrong. A hundred and ninety-five volts. "Dance." (*Zzumph!*)

LEARNER: Let me out of here. My heart's bothering me! (*Teacher looks at experimenter.*)

EXPERIMENTER: Continue, please.

LEARNER (*screaming*): Let me out of here, you have no right to keep me here. Let me out of here, let me out, my heart's bothering me, let me out! (*Teacher shakes head, pats the table nervously.*)

TEACHER: You see, he's hollering. Hear that? Gee, I don't know.

EXPERIMENTER: The experiment requires. . . .

TEACHER (*interrupting*): I know it does, sir, but I mean—hunh! He don't know what he's getting in for. He's up to 195 volts! (*Experiment continues, through 210 volts, 225 volts, 240 volts, 255 volts, 270 volts, delivered to the man in the electric chair, at which point the teacher, with evident relief, runs out of word-pair questions.*)

EXPERIMENTER: You'll have to go back to the beginning of that page and go through them again until he's learned them all correctly.

TEACHER: Aw, no. I'm not going to kill that man. You mean I've got to keep going up with the scale. No sir. He's hollering in there. I'm not going to give him 450 volts.

EXPERIMENTER: The experiment requires that you go on.

TEACHER: I know it does, but that man is hollering in there, sir.

EXPERIMENTER (*same matter-of-fact tone*): As I said before, although the shocks may be painful. . . .

TEACHER (*interrupting*): Awwww. He—he—he's yelling in there.

EXPERIMENTER: Start with "Blue," please, at the top of the page. Continue, please, Teacher. Just go ahead.

TEACHER (*concentrating intently on list of words in front of him, as if to shut everything else out*): "Blue—boy, girl, grass, hat." (*Buzz indicates answer.*) Correct. "Night—day, sky, job, chair. (*Buzz*) Wrong. The answer is "day." Two hundred and eighty-five volts. (*Zzumph!*)

LEARNER: Ohhhuhhoohhh!

EXPERIMENTER: Continue, please.

TEACHER: "Fat—man, lady, tub, neck." Answer, please. (*Buzz*) Wrong. The answer is "neck." Three hundred volts. (*Zzumph!*)

LEARNER: Ohhh. I absolutely refuse to answer any more. (*Shouting urgently, now*) Let me out of here. You can't hold me here. Get me out. Get—me—out—of—here.

EXPERIMENTER: Continue. The next word is "Green," please.

TEACHER: "Green—grass, hat, ink, apple." (*Nothing happens. No answering buzz. Just gloomy silence.*)

TEACHER: I don't think he is going to answer.

EXPERIMENTER: If the learner doesn't answer in a reasonable time, about four or five seconds, consider the answer wrong. And follow the same procedures you have been doing for wrong answers. Say "Wrong," tell him the number of volts, give him the punishment, read him the correct answer. Continue, please.

TEACHER: "Green—grass, hat, ink, apple." Answer, please. (*More silence. Teacher just sits there.*)

EXPERIMENTER: Go on with the procedure, please, Teacher.

TEACHER: Three hundred and fifteen volts. The answer is "ink." (*Zzumph!*)

LEARNER: Ohh. Ooohh.

TEACHER (*relieved to hear response*): Next one. . . .

LEARNER: I absolutely refuse to answer.

TEACHER: You got to. You get a shock if you don't answer. (*Experiment continues with learner refusing to answer, and, finally, failing even to grunt or groan. At 375 volts, the teacher stands up. Has he had enough? Will he break off the experiment? Will he disobey?*)

TEACHER: I think something's happened to that fellow in there. I don't get no answer. He was hollering at less voltage. Can't you check in and see if he's all right, please?

EXPERIMENTER (*same detached calm*): Not once we've started. Please continue, Teacher.

TEACHER (*sits down, sighs deeply*): "Cool—day, shade, water, paint." Answer, please. Are you all right in there? Are you all right?

EXPERIMENTER: Please continue, Teacher. Continue, please. (*Teacher pushes lever. Zzumph!*)

TEACHER (*swiveling around in his chair*): Something's happened to that man in there. (*Swiveling back*) Next one. "Low—dollar, necklace, moon, paint." (*Turning around again*) Something's happened to that man in there. You better check in on him, sir. He won't answer or nothing.

EXPERIMENTER: Continue. Go on, please.

TEACHER: You accept all responsibility.

EXPERIMENTER: The responsibility is mine. Correct. Please go on. (*Teacher returns to his list, starts running through words as rapidly as he can read them, works through to 450 volts.*)

TEACHER: That's that.

EXPERIMENTER: Continue using the last switch on the board, please. The four-fifty switch for each wrong answer. Continue, please.

TEACHER: But I don't get no anything!

EXPERIMENTER: Please continue. The next word is "White."

TEACHER: Don't you think you should look in on him, please.

EXPERIMENTER: Not once we've started the experiment.

TEACHER: But what if something has happened to the man?

EXPERIMENTER: The experiment requires that you continue. Go on, please.

TEACHER: Don't the man's health mean anything?

EXPERIMENTER: Whether the learner likes it or not. . . .

TEACHER: What if he's dead in there? (*Gestures toward the room with the electric chair.*) I mean, he told me he can't stand the shock, sir. I don't mean to be rude, but I think you should look in on him. All you have to do is look in the door. I don't get no answer, no noise. Something might have happened to the gentleman in there, sir.

EXPERIMENTER: We must continue. Go on, please.

TEACHER: You mean keep giving him what? Four hundred fifty volts, what he's got now?

EXPERIMENTER: That's correct. Continue. The next word is "White."

TEACHER (*now at a furious pace*): "White—cloud, horse, rock, house." Answer, please. The answer is "horse." Four hundred and fifty volts. (*Zzumph!*) Next word, "Bag—paint, music, clown, girl." The answer is

"paint." Four hundred and fifty volts. (*Zzumph!*) Next word is "Short—sentence, movie. . . ."

EXPERIMENTER: Excuse me, Teacher. We'll have to discontinue the experiment.

(*Enter Milgram from camera's left. He has been watching from behind one-way glass.*)

MILGRAM: I'd like to ask you a few questions. (*Slowly, patiently, he dehoaxes the teacher, telling him that the shocks and screams were not real.*)

TEACHER: You mean he wasn't getting nothing? Well, I'm glad to hear that. I was getting upset there. I was getting ready to walk out.

(*Finally, to make sure there are no hard feelings, friendly, harmless Mr. Wallace comes out in coat and tie. Gives jovial greeting. Friendly reconciliation takes place. Experiment ends.*)

© *Stanley Milgram 1965.*

Subjects in the experiment were not asked to give the 450-volt shock more than three times. By that time, it seemed evident that they would go on indefinitely. "No one," says Milgram, "who got within five shocks of the end ever broke off. By that point, he had resolved the conflict."

Why do so many people resolve the conflict in favor of obedience?

Milgram's theory assumes that people behave in two different operating modes as different as ice and water. He does not rely on Freud or sex or toilet-training hang-ups for this theory. All he says is that ordinarily we operate in a state of autonomy, which means we pretty much have and assert control over what we do. But in certain circumstances, we operate under what Milgram calls a state of agency (after agent, n . . . one who acts for or in the place of another by authority from him; a substitute; a deputy. —*Webster's Collegiate Dictionary*). A state of agency, to Milgram, is nothing more than a frame of mind.

"There's nothing bad about it, there's nothing good about it," he says. "It's a natural circumstance of living with other people . . . . I think of a state of agency as a real transformation of a person; if a person has different properties when he's in that state, just as water can turn to ice under certain conditions of temperature, a person can move to the state of mind that I call agency . . . the critical thing is that you see yourself as the instrument of the execution of another person's wishes. You do not see yourself as acting on your own. And there's a real transformation, a real change of properties of the person."

To achieve this change, you have to be in a situation where there seems to be a ruling authority whose commands are relevant to some legitimate pur-

pose; the authority's power is not unlimited.

But situations can be and have been structured to make people do unusual things, and not just in Milgram's laboratory. The reason, says Milgram, is that no action, in and of itself, contains meaning.

"The meaning always depends on your definition of the situation. Take an action like killing another person. It sounds bad.

"But then we say the other person was about to destroy a hundred children, and the only way to stop him was to kill him. Well, that sounds good.

"Or, you take destroying your own life. It sounds very bad. Yet, in the Second World War, thousands of persons thought it was a good thing to destroy your own life. It was set in the proper context. You sipped some saki from a whistling cup, recited a few haiku. You said, 'May my death be as clean and as quick as the shattering of crystal.' And it almost seemed like a good, noble thing to do, to crash your kamikaze plane into an aircraft carrier. But the main thing was, the definition of what a kamikaze pilot was doing had been determined by the relevant authority. Now, once you are in a state of agency, you allow the authority to determine, to define what the situation is. The meaning of your action is altered."

So, for most subjects in Milgram's laboratory experiments, the act of giving Mr. Wallace his painful shock was necessary, even though unpleasant, and besides they were doing it on behalf of somebody else and it was for science. There was still strain and conflict, of course. Most people resolved it by grimly sticking to their task and obeying. But some broke out. Milgram tried varying the conditions of the experiment to see what would help break people out of their state of agency.

"The results, as seen and felt in the laboratory," he has written, "are disturbing. They raise the possibility that human nature, or more specifically the kind of character produced in American democratic society, cannot be counted on to insulate its citizens from brutality and inhumane treatment at the direction of malevolent authority. A substantial proportion of people do what they are told to do, irrespective of the content of the act and without limitations of conscience, so long as they perceive that the command comes from a legitimate authority. If, in this study, an anonymous experimenter can successfully command adults to subdue a fifty-year-old man and force on him painful electric shocks against his protest, one can only wonder what government, with its vastly greater authority and prestige, can command of its subjects."

This is a nice statement, but it falls

short of summing up the full meaning of Milgram's work. It leaves some questions still unanswered.

The first question is this: Should we really be surprised and alarmed that people obey? Wouldn't it be even more alarming if they all refused to obey? Without obedience to a relevant ruling authority there could not be a civil society. And without a civil society, as Thomas Hobbes pointed out in the seventeenth century, we would live in a condition of war, "of every man against every other man," and life would be "solitary, poor, nasty, brutish and short."

In the middle of one of Stanley Milgram's lectures at C.U.N.Y. recently, some mini-skirted undergraduates started whispering and giggling in the back of the room. He told them to cut it out. Since he was the relevant authority in that time and that place, they obeyed, and most people in the room were glad that they obeyed.

This was not, of course, a conflict situation. Nothing in the coeds' social upbringing made it a matter of conscience for them to whisper and giggle. But a case can be made that in a conflict situation it is all the more important to obey. Take the case of war, for example. Would we really want a situation in which every participant in a war, direct or indirect—from front-line soldiers to the people who sell coffee and cigarettes to employees at the Concertina barbed-wire factory in Kansas—stops and consults his conscience before each action. It is asking for an awful lot of mental strain and anguish from an awful lot of people. The value of having civil order is that one can do his duty, or whatever interests him, or whatever seems to benefit him at the moment, and leave the agonizing to others. When Francis Gary Powers was being tried by a Soviet military tribunal after his U-2 spy plane was shot down, the presiding judge asked if he had thought about the possibility that his flight might have provoked a war. Powers replied with Hobbesian clarity: "The people who sent me should think of these things. My job was to carry out orders. I do not think it was my responsibility to make such decisions."

It was not his responsibility. And it is quite possible that if everyone felt responsible for each of the ultimate consequences of his own tiny contributions to complex chains of events, then society simply would not work. Milgram, fully conscious of the moral and social implications of his research, believes that people should feel responsible for their actions. If someone else

had invented the experiment, and if he had been the naïve subject, he feels certain that he would have been among the disobedient minority.

"There is no very good solution to this," he admits, thoughtfully. "To simply and categorically say that you won't obey authority may resolve your personal conflict, but it creates more problems for society which may be more serious in the long run. But I have no doubt that to disobey is the proper thing to do in this [the laboratory] situation. It is the only reasonable value judgment to make."

The conflict between the need to obey the relevant ruling authority and the need to follow your conscience becomes sharpest if you insist on living by an ethical system based on a rigid code—a code that seeks to answer all questions in advance of their being raised. Code ethics cannot solve the obedience problem. Stanley Milgram seems to be a situation ethicist, and situation ethics does offer a way out: When you feel conflict, you examine the situation and then make a choice among the competing evils. You may act with a presumption in favor of obedience, but reserve the possibility that you will disobey whenever obedience demands a flagrant and outrageous affront to conscience. This, by the way, is the philosophical position of many who resist the draft. In World War II, they would have fought. Vietnam is a different, an outrageously different, situation.

Life can be difficult for the situation ethicist, because he does not see the world in straight lines, while the social system too often assumes such a God-given, squared-off structure. If your moral code includes an injunction against all war, you may be deferred as a conscientious objector. If you merely oppose this particular war, you may not be deferred.

Stanley Milgram has his problems, too. He believes that in the laboratory situation, he would not have shocked Mr. Wallace. His professional critics reply that in his real-life situation he has done the equivalent. He has placed innocent and naïve subjects under great emotional strain and pressure in selfish obedience to his quest for knowledge. When you raise this issue with Milgram, he has an answer ready. There is, he explains patiently, a critical difference between his naïve subjects and the man in the electric chair. The man in the electric chair (in the mind of the naïve subject) is helpless, strapped in. But the naïve subject is free to go at any time.

Immediately after he offers this distinction, Milgram anticipates the objection.

"It's quite true," he says, "that this is almost a philosophic position, because we have learned that some people are psychologically incapable of disengaging themselves. But that doesn't relieve them of the moral responsibility."

The parallel is exquisite. "The tension problem was unexpected," says Milgram in his defense. But he went on anyway. The naïve subjects didn't expect the screaming protests from the strapped-in learner. But they went on.

"I had to make a judgment," says Milgram. "I had to ask myself, was this harming the person or not? My judgment is that it was not. Even in the extreme cases, I wouldn't say that permanent damage results."

Sound familiar? "The shocks may be painful," the experimenter kept saying, "but they're not dangerous."

After the series of experiments was completed, Milgram sent a report of the results to his subjects and a questionnaire, asking whether they were glad or sorry to have been in the experiment. Eighty-three and seven-tenths percent said they were glad and only 1.3 percent were sorry; 15 percent were neither sorry nor glad. However, Milgram could not be sure at the time of the experiment that only 1.3 percent would be sorry.

Kurt Vonnegut Jr. put one paragraph in the preface to *Mother Night*, in 1966, which pretty much says it for the people with their fingers on the shock-generator switches, for you and me, and maybe even for Milgram. "If I'd been born in Germany," Vonnegut said, "I suppose I would have *been* a Nazi, bopping Jews and gypsies and Poles around, leaving boots sticking out of snowbanks, warming myself with my sweetly virtuous insides. So it goes."

Just so. One thing that happened to Milgram back in New Haven during the days of the experiment was that he kept running into people he'd watched from behind the one-way glass. It gave him a funny feeling, seeing those people going about their everyday business in New Haven and knowing what they would do to Mr. Wallace if ordered to. Now that his research results are in and you've thought about it, you can get this funny feeling too. You don't need one-way glass. A glance in your own mirror may serve just as well.   ☷

25

HUMAN BEINGS ARE NOT VERY EASY TO CHANGE AFTER ALL

An unjoyful message and its implications for social programs

BY AMITAI ETZIONI

A while back there was a severe shortage of electricity in New York City, and Columbia University tried to help out in two ways: A card reading "Save a watt" was placed on everyone's desk, and janitors removed some light bulbs from university corridors. The ways in which this shortage was made up for illustrate two major approaches to social problem solving. One approach is based on the assumption that people can be taught to change their habits, that they can learn to remember to switch off unused lights. The second approach assumes that people need not, or will not, change and instead alter their environment so that, even if they leave light switches on, watts are saved.

The prevalent approach in the treatment of our numerous and still-multiplying social problems is the first. Imbedded in the programs of the federal, state, and city governments and embraced almost instinctively by many citizens, especially liberal ones, is the assumption that, if you go out there and get the message across—persuade, propagandize, explain, campaign— people will change, that human beings are, ultimately, quite pliable. Both political leaders and the general public believe that advertising is powerful, that information campaigns work, and that an army of educators, counselors, or rehabilitation workers can achieve almost everything if they are sufficiently numerous, well trained, and richly endowed.

But can they? We have come of late to the realization that the pace of achievement in domestic programs ranges chiefly from the slow to the crablike—two steps backward for every one forward—and the suspicion is growing that there is something

basically wrong with most of these programs. A nagging feeling persists that maybe something even more basic than the lack of funds or will is at stake. Consequently, social scientists like myself have begun to re-examine our core assumption that man can be taught almost anything and quite readily. We are now confronting the uncomfortable possibility that human beings are not very easily changed after all.

Take smoking, for instance. Since 1964, when the surgeon general began calling attention to the dangers of cigarettes, a vast and expensive campaign has been waged, involving press releases, lectures, television advertisements, pamphlets, and notations on the cigarette package. The positive re-

sult of all this activity, however, has been slight. At first there was no effect at all; actual cigarette smoking continued to rise until 1967. Then it dropped from 11.73 cigarettes per day per person aged eighteen years and over to 10.94 in 1969. More recently the level has risen again.

The moral? If you spend $27 million, you may get enough people to switch from Camels to Kools to make the investment worthwhile for the Kool manufacturers. However, if the same $27 million is used to make nonsmokers out of smokers—that is, to try to change a basic habit—no significant effect is to be expected. Advertising molds or teases our appetites, but it doesn't change basic tastes, values, or preferences. Try to advertise desegregation to racists, world government to chauvinists, temperance to alcoholics, or—as we still do at the cost of $16 million a year—drug abstention to addicts, and see how far you get.

In fact, the mass media in general have proved to be ineffectual as tools for profoundly converting people. Studies have shown that persons are more likely to heed spouses, relatives, friends, and "opinion leaders" than broadcasted or printed words when it comes to deep concerns.

Another area in which efforts to remake people have proved glaringly inefficient is that of the rehabilitation of criminals. We rely heavily on re-educational programs for prisoners. But it is a matter of record that out of every two inmates released, one will be rearrested and returned to prison in short order. Of the 151,355 inmates in state prisons on December 31, 1960, there were 74,138, or 49 per cent, who had been committed at least once to adult penal institutions. Reformatories come off no better. A study of 694 offenders released by one well-known institution reports 58.4 per cent returned within five years. The study concludes self-assuringly: "But this is no worse than the national average."

What about longer, more sustained educational efforts? Mature people can be taught many things—speed reading, belly dancing, Serbo-Croatian—usually with much more pain, sweat, cost, time, and energy than most beginning pupils suspect. When we turn, though, to the modification of ingrown habits, of basic values, of personality traits, or of other deep-seated matters, the impact is usually much less noticeable.

What is becoming increasingly apparent is that to solve social problems by changing people is more expensive and usually less productive than approaches that accept people as they are

Solving social problems by changing people is apparently less productive than accepting people as they are and changing their circumstances instead.

and seek to mend not them but the circumstances around them. Just such a conclusion was implicit, for instance, in an important but widely ignored study of automobile safety done by the Department of Health, Education, and Welfare. Applying cost-effectiveness measurements to efforts to cut down the horrendous toll on American highways—59,220 Americans were killed in 1970—the HEW study noted that driver education saves lives at the cost of $88,000 per life. New automobile accessories, as simple as seat belts, proved more than a thousand times as effective; saving a life this way, it was computed, costs a mere $87. Yet we continue to stress driver education as the chief preventive measure; the laws regarding the redesign of autos are moderate in their requirements and are poorly enforced. Similarly, we exhort people not to drive while under the influence of liquor, even not to drink in excess to begin with. But these are rather monumental, perhaps impossible, educational missions. However, a simple device that measures the level of intoxication by breath analysis and that is widely used by highway patrols in Great Britain has tended to scare drunken drivers off the roads in that country. It could be applied to a rapid reduction of traffic fatalities in this country. Educate drinkers later.

The problem of educating against drug addiction in general offers parallel lessons. Acting on the belief that per-

sonality predispositions yield fairly rapidly to such approaches, we have tried a variety of informational, persuasive, personal, and group-therapeutic techniques in the battle against addiction. However, these approaches have rehabilitated only a few addicts. Much more promising are counter-drugs. For example, Antabuse, which if taken makes a person feel quite uncomfortable when he drinks, is more effective than psychotherapy in dealing with alcoholics. It takes so much less effort to decide each day to take medication than to decide, all the time, to refrain from drinking. True, Antabuse

so far is a little-known remedy, and many who do know of it are skeptical, because early experiments in which a high dosage was administered seem to have resulted in some fatalities. Now, though, smaller dosages are being given, and Antabuse is slowly regaining serious consideration.

The failure of educational and therapeutic approaches to help most heroin addicts has led, finally, to the wide use of a substitute, methadone, which is usually referred to as a blocking drug because it is said to curb the craving for heroin. Let's not ask here if methadone is the most suitable drug for the purpose, to what extent it is different from heroin, or even if it actually blocks out heroin. For our purpose, it is sufficient to say that, unlike the educational and therapeutic approaches to heroin addiction, methadone is effective. That is, people taking methadone work, study, are satisfied, function as human beings and citizens, and have a much lower criminality record. Thus, of a group of 990 men

carefully examined, those employed or attending school rose from 27 per cent at admission to the methadone program to 65 per cent after one year on the program, to 77 per cent after two years, and to 92 per cent in the third year. A report by the director of the District of Columbia narcotics treatment division shows that as the number of addicts on methadone increased, the level of crimes that addicts tended to commit fell almost proportionally. Thus, with about 20 per cent of the addicts on such treatments, robberies in Washington, D.C., fell from 12,432 in 1969 to 11,222 in 1971. There is no evi-

dence that any educational program has ever had such an effect.

Though there seem to be no similarly effective drugs to help food addicts (or persons afflicted with obesity), we have recently been informed by medical researchers that serious weight problems seem to arise, *not* from faulty will power, character, or motivation—qualities subject to educability—but from different rates of metabolism and divergent nutritional pathways. These pathways are established early in childhood and may be either set for life or altered by medication, but exhortation or other educational efforts can alter them little.

Again medication has proved to be more promising than education in dealing with mental patients. After year upon year of increase, the number of patients in mental hospitals declined sharply in 1956. This turning point came about, not because therapy was expanded or intensified or a new procedure found, but because tranquilizers were widely introduced. Most of those discharged now live on medications at home.

Technological devices and medication are not the sole approaches we may rely upon more heavily once we understand the limits of adult educability and allow ourselves to see the full extent and implications of these limits. Improved matching of persons and jobs may go a long way toward reducing the need for job training. Here the two alternative assumptions about the pliability and perfectibility of human nature come into sharp focus. Few educators are quite willing to assume, as it was once put rather

extremely, that "given time and resources, we can make a piano player out of anybody." Yet whole job-training programs are still based on such an assumption. For instance, the scores of training programs for the unemployed or the to-be-employed that are run or supported by the Department of Labor assume that people can be changed, and quite fundamentally.

The Department of Labor stresses, in its discussion of "social-psychological barriers" to employment, the need to modify "attitudes, aspirations, motivation (especially achievement motivation), ability or willingness to defer gratification, and self-image." And the 1968 Manpower Report suggests "the necessity of direct efforts to modify the attitudes of the disadvantaged before introducing them to job situations." One major training program aims at providing "needed communication skills, grooming and personal hygiene, the standards of behavior and performance generally expected by employers."

In a study I conducted with three of my colleagues for the Center for Policy Research, we found that persons have deep-seated preferences in their work behavior that are very difficult to change, and we concluded that it may be unethical to try to change them. Thus, if a person prefers to engage in nonroutine work of the more creative type, at an irregular pace, training him or her to be a "good" assembly-line worker—which entails teaching not only how to turn bolts but also how to be a more "uptight" person—may be both ineffective and morally dubious, especially if we are correct in suggesting that people's existing preferences can be readily analyzed so that they can be helped to choose jobs compatible with their personalities. It is also much less costly to test and assist people than it is to train and mold them. If we run out of compatible jobs, jobs may be changed to suit people rather than people to suit jobs.

One of the few effective and efficient ways in which people can be basically remade lies in a total and voluntary reconstruction of their social environment. Thus, when students withdraw from the campus into a rural commune, or Jews emigrate from the U.S.S.R. and Eastern Europe to found a new Israeli kibbutz, life can be deeply recast. The creation of a whole new environment for addicts—indeed, a new social community—on a voluntary basis, as achieved by Synanon, is highly effective, and Alcoholics Anonymous seems to provide a cure as effective as or better than Antabuse. Many alcoholics and mental patients who are integrated into therapeutic communities are reported to recover well.

This total-change approach is very appealing to a radical New Left perspective, which suggests that new persons cannot evolve except in a new society and that a new society will emerge only from the deep efforts of people in the crisis of reshaping their world. At the same time one must note that effective total-change groups work only for those who join voluntarily. Most addicts, mental patients, prison inmates, and others in need of change don't volunteer to join. Hence, the total-change approach is considerably less applicable to social problems than some would have it be.

Much of what I have said is primarily concerned with adult educability. It also holds true, albeit to a lesser degree, for children. While children, especially younger ones, are more educable than adults—who must often first be disabused of the education they have acquired as youngsters

—most Americans, both the general public and the policy-makers, still enormously overestimate what the education of children can achieve.

The schools, which are still the main institutions of education for children aged six through eighteen, cannot carry out many of the missions assigned to them. Most schools do not build character, open the mind, implant an appreciation of beauty, or otherwise serve as the greater humanizer or the social equalizer as educators would wish them to do. In desperation it is suggested now that the schools concentrate on teaching the three Rs, and

it is common knowledge that they have a hard time doing even that.

Probably the greatest disappointment educators have encountered in recent years, and have not quite come to terms with, is the failure of intensive educational campaigns to help children from disadvantaged backgrounds catch up with their more advantaged peers. As has already been widely reported, virtually all of the 150-odd compensatory education schemes that have been tried either have not worked at all or have worked only marginally or only for a small proportion of the student population. The Coleman Report makes this point, and the same conclusion comes from another source. Professor Jesse Burkhead of Syracuse University found that differences in the achievements of high school students in large-city schools are almost completely conditioned by the students' social backgrounds and environments, including the incomes and occupations of the parents (class), housing conditions, and ethnicity.

The reasons for this inability to bridge the distance between the educational achievements of disadvantaged and better off children are hotly debated. It seems to me that the key reason for the failure of compensatory education lies in the fact that the disadvantaged children are locked into total environments, which include home, neighborhood, parental poverty, discrimination, and inhibiting models of behavior. We cannot hope to change one without changing the others. Education will become more effective when it works together with other societal changes—which, of course, means that, by itself, it is not half so powerful as we often assume.

The contention that personal growth and societal changes are much harder to come by than we had assumed, especially via one version or another of the educationalist-enlightenment approach, is not a joyful message, but one whose full implications we must learn to accept before we can devise more effective social programs. Once we cease turning to ads, leaflets, counselors, or teachers for salvation, we may realize that more can be achieved by engineers, doctors, social movements, and public-interest groups; and the educators will find new and much-needed allies. □

VI. Groups

Perhaps the most basic conflict people experience in their social lives is the conflict between self and other: between the individual and society, independence and dependence, selfishness and altruism, being with other people and being alone. We need other people. Our social nature is one of our most adaptive characteristics. However, we also sometimes need to be alone. Being alone is not tantamount to loneliness, one of the most devastating of all psychological states. Loneliness is much more closely associated with how people *interpret* their solitude than with how much time they spend alone—with the discrepancy between the type of life people actually have and the type of life they want to have (see "Loneliness," by Rubinstein, Shaver, and Peplau). The determining power of how people interpret their condition, rather than the condition itself, is a theme that runs through many areas in social psychology.

The primary social group is the family. Some social scientists believe that the emphasis on individuality in the western world is interfering with the ability of the family to fulfill the social needs of its members. The plight of the aged is a dramatic case in point. The function of the family can be seen quite clearly by examining the structure of families in other cultures (see "The Family as Source of Security," by Colleen Johnson).

North Americans create groups almost as fast as they create breakfast cereals, perhaps in reaction to the absence of strong and extended familial bonds. For a few years encounter groups were the rage. When I was in graduate school on the East Coast, I was invited to participate in encounter groups of various sorts. These groups presented a paradox to me. The guiding idea was to "be natural," "be yourself," and "let go." But somehow this always seemed to mean doing what the group wanted you to do. Eleanor Links Hoover discusses encounter groups ("The Age of Encounter") and voices some compelling reservations. She makes the point that encounter groups *can* have a powerful effect on their members, but the effect may be powerfully destructive.

I don't have any stories about grassroots religious groups because I've never been in one; but I find them fascinating. No group therapist, or any psychotherapist for that matter, can lay claim to inducing the type of personality change that is precipitated by religious conversion. The "Jesus People" article by Harder, et al., does not explain religious conversion, but it does describe some of the forces that make a cohesive community.

Most of the social psychological research on groups has investigated group processes such as the effectiveness of autocratic versus democratic leaders, and the dynamics of decision making. Some years ago there was a spate of research on "brainstorming" that tested whether a free exchange of ideas in groups would produce more creative ideas than individuals working alone. In general, groups failed to prove more effective. Two articles ("Group-think," by Irving Janis, and "How Groups Intensify Opinions," by David Myers) discuss the dangers of group decision making. Members reinforce one another's biases and produce an artificial consensus that may give rise to the worst possible decisions. In general, discussing issues in groups results in an intensification of members' opinions. Other research has shown that more gets done more efficiently when an authoritarian leader takes control than when members of the group are permitted to take part in the decision-making process ("Testing Leaders").

Loneliness

26

CARIN RUBINSTEIN, PHILLIP SHAVER,
AND
LETITIA ANNE PEPLAU

Almost everyone is lonely sometimes,
but this common feeling arises not from a person's circumstance,
but from how he decides to interpret his situation.

God says in the Book of Genesis, "It is not good that man should be alone," and decides to make a fitting companion for him. The Old Testament discourses at length about the benefits of fruitful multiplying, and about the intricate attachments and intrigues between men and women, parents and children, friends and kin.

Modern evolutionary biologists, who have developed their own creation story, also emphasize the need for human beings to be together. They offer evidence for the genetic advantages of sexual reproduction, the adaptive benefits of prolonged attachment to parents in childhood, and the survival benefits of belonging to complex groups. The human ability to form strong emotional attachments has a long evolutionary history, which is why people can be seriously hurt if their attachments are disrupted by rejection, separation, or death.

The Bible and biologists share a major premise: It isn't good for people to be alone. This evaluation bodes ill for modern industrial societies, especially the United States, where the divorce rate is soaring, geographic and social mobility are high, and an unprecedented number of adults of all ages are choosing or being forced by events to live by themselves.

Many social commentators and popular writers have inferred from these statistics that *alone* means *lonely* and use the terms interchangeably. In *The Broken Heart: The Medical Consequences of Loneliness*, psychologist James Lynch argued that people who live alone (and are, he assumed, lonely) are especially susceptible to serious illnesses and may even die prematurely. Sociologist Philip Slater's *The Pursuit of Loneliness*, based primarily on armchair analysis, denounced the American commitment to individualism and competition, which, he said, frustrate the basic human desires for community, engagement, and dependence. "The competitive life is a lonely one," Slater concluded.

Like these writers, many social scientists arrive at conclusions without putting much stock in people's own interpretations of their feelings or actions. Once researchers begin talking to individuals, however, they quickly learn that "alone" is an objective term—indicating whether a person lives with someone else, how many friends he or she has, and so on—but that "lonely" is subjective, a matter of what goes on in a person's head. As we have learned, the two experiences occasionally but by no means always over-

Carin Rubenstein *is completing her dissertation for her Ph.D. in social psychology at New York University.* **Phillip Shaver** *is chairman of the doctoral program in personality and social psychology at NYU. Rubenstein and Shaver are* *writing a book based on their work, tentatively titled* What It Means To Be Lonely, *to be published by Delacorte Press.* **Letitia Anne Peplau** *is an assistant professor of psychology at the University of California at Los Angeles.*

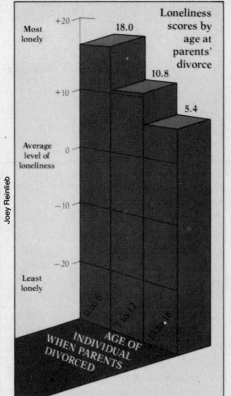

Loneliness scores by age at parents' divorce

The older a child is when his or her parents divorce, the less lonely he is likely to be as an adult. In an NYU survey, people who were younger than six years of age when their parents separated got the highest scores on the loneliness scale; people who were in middle childhood got lower scores; but people who were adolescent or older were the least lonely as adults.

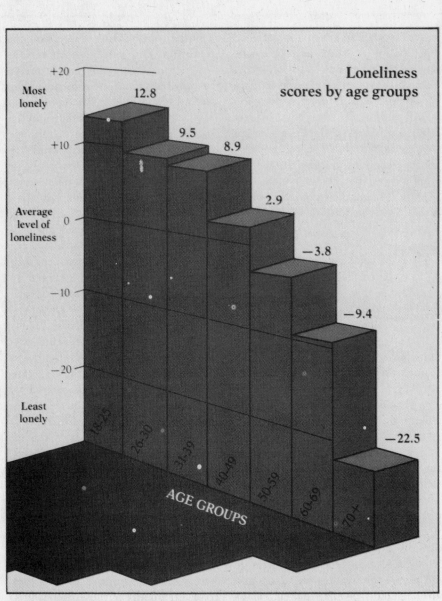

Loneliness scores by age groups

Senior citizens are not the loneliest people in America: Young people are. NYU surveys found a steady decline in loneliness as people get older. The researchers believe that young adults sense an impossible gap between romantic expectations and reality; older people interpret things more realistically.

lap. Feelings of loneliness do not inevitably follow from solitude or circumstance; they depend on how people view their experiences and whether they decide to call themselves lonely.

Among us, we have conducted two independent programs of research on loneliness, one at New York University (Rubenstein and Shaver) and one at the University of California at Los Angeles (Peplau). The NYU research was based on a carefully pretested questionnaire that was published in the Sunday magazine sections of several East Coast newspapers in the spring of 1978. More than 25,000 people responded, a large sample of adults of all ages, races, and income levels. The research at UCLA by Peplau and her co-workers is developing a model of loneliness that emphasizes the thought processes of lonely people. This work is based primarily on college students, who answer questions about their own experiences with loneliness and their impressions of lonely people. So far, nearly 1,000 undergraduates have participated. These different methods and the diversity of people interviewed offer the first coherent picture of adult loneliness based on data rather than on speculation.

Although newspaper surveys are subject to the bias of people who choose

Old people are less lonely, on the average,
than young adults; they even
complain less about physical and psychological symptoms.

to fill out the questionnaire, we believe that the results are valid and representative of most of the population. Regardless of city size and location (for example, small town or metropolis, northern or southern city), the findings within each sample remained virtually the same. And although a few people noted that "only a lonely person would bother to fill this out," we received thousands of questionnaires from people who said they were not lonely. Only 15 percent of those who replied said they felt lonely most or all of the time, and only 6 percent said they never felt lonely. The majority, as one would expect, felt lonely on occasion.

The survey results dispelled many of the popular assumptions about loneliness and confirmed others. One common prediction favored by sociologists turned out *not* to be true. The American fondness for moving—for changing jobs, partners, cities, and social networks—has long been considered a cause of psychological distress. In *A Nation of Strangers*, Vance Packard described the chronic rootlessness of Americans, which he believed to be at the heart of the country's social problems. The NYU surveys included a number of questions to test Packard's claims, such as how often people had moved during childhood and adulthood, the length of time they have lived at their present locations, and whether, if they were lonely, moving too often was responsible.

But none of these questions was connected with current feelings of loneliness; people who had moved frequently and those who had never strayed from their birthplace had equal chances of feeling lonely. People who change cities often have just as

many friends and are just as satisfied with their friendships as people who remain rooted in one spot. We recognize, of course, that moving is often fraught with difficulty; separation from friends often causes bouts of loneliness. But the NYU data suggest that such feelings, for most people, are temporary reactions during the adjustment phase. People who move frequently, it seems, learn quickly how to make friends and put down roots in a new community.

The sociologists turned out to be correct in predicting that the loneliest people are likely to be poor, uneducated, and of minority groups; we found too that an even stronger companion of loneliness is unemployment. But none of these conditions, however adverse, was as strongly related to feelings of loneliness as a person's perception of reality—to feeling a painful mismatch between *actual* life and *desired* life.

A good example of this comes from the surprising but reliable finding that old people are less lonely, on the average, than young adults. This pattern has turned up in other large surveys as well as the NYU study, and directly counters the cliché of the lonely senior citizen. Although more old people than young live alone, and although older people see their friends less often than young adults do, the elderly are more satisfied with their friendships, have higher self-esteem, and feel more independent. They join social and civic groups more often, and get drunk far less often than the young. Old people even complain less than young folks do about physical and psychological symptoms—such as head-

aches, poor appetite, depression, irritability, and poor concentration.

We think that young people are so susceptible to loneliness because they feel most sharply the discrepancy between the search for intimacy and the failure to find it. Young people are romantic and idealistic; they think it is more important to find a "romantic or sexual partner" than older people do.

Because loneliness is more in one's mind than one's circumstances, living alone does not by itself foster the feeling. The NYU researchers tested the notion that living alone produces serious medical problems, but found no differences in the mental and physical health of people who live alone and those who live with others. Lonely people do have more medical and psychological problems than their less lonely peers, even though the lonely are as likely to be living with roommates, or spouses, or families, or on their own.

The NYU questionnaire included a number of items about a person's social life, which showed that although lonely people do have fewer friends and contacts, on the average, than less lonely people, their dissatisfaction with the ties they have is what makes them feel lonely. Lonely people are dissatisfied with everything about their lives: their living arrangements (whether solo or with others), the number of friends they have, the quality of those friendships, their marriages or love affairs, the number of conversations they have each day, and their sex lives.

We cannot say for sure, yet, whether dissatisfactions create feelings of separation and loneliness, or whether loneliness turns the whole world sour. But we did glean evidence that some causes of adult loneliness have their origin in

Lonely people remember their parents as being disagreeable, remote, and untrustworthy; the loneliest people of all were those whose parents had divorced.

childhood. Psychiatrist John Bowlby has argued persuasively that separation from parents can have lasting detrimental effects on children, and Bowlby's thesis was supported in the survey. Lonely people tended to remember their parents as being disagreeable, remote, and untrustworthy; individuals who said they were not lonely described their parents as close, helpful, and warm. (Current feelings of loneliness, though, may color one's memory of events.) But the loneliest people of all were those whose parents had divorced. As one man commented, "My mom was married twice and my father and stepfather have been nothing but pure hell for me. I have lost all of my confidence and feel not worth anything to anyone."

If their parents did divorce, people fared better the later the separation occurred. People who were less than six years old when their parents split up were by far the loneliest as adults; people who were older than six were lonelier than those who were adolescents; and so on. This is disturbing, for the Census Bureau predicts that 45 percent of all children born in 1977 will spend a significant period of their lives with only one parent.

The loss of either parent by divorce is more detrimental, in terms of later loneliness, than loss by death. Whether a parent dies when a person is a child, a teenager, or an adult has no effect on later feelings of loneliness. It is as if children regard divorced parents as having *chosen* to reject them and are tormented by the parent's inaccessibility. But most children come to understand that a parent's death is not their responsibility. It is thus not the event of parental separation itself but *how children perceive it* that will affect their later adjustment.

People who have had unhappy childhood experiences, who feel that their parents neglected or rejected them, may grow up with fragile self-esteem. Psychological research has shown that people who dislike themselves also tend to dislike or be less tolerant of others, possibly because a hostile stance protects a vulnerable person from the risk of rejection. We suspected that this defensiveness is part of a self-fulfilling prophesy: A guarded lonely person is hard to get to know and is therefore likely to remain isolated.

Recent experiments by Warren Jones at the University of Tulsa find that lonely students do tend to be self-focused and difficult to talk to. Jones observed college students who said they were lonely conversing with students who were not. Lonely people, he noted, talked more about themselves, asked fewer questions of their partners, and changed the topic more frequently than their socially adept peers did. Jones concluded that many lonely students simply do not know how to behave in social situations, so their encounters tend to be superficial and emotionally unsatisfying to them.

In the NYU surveys, too, lonely people had lower self-esteem than people who were not lonely. They also tended to dislike others more readily, to have fewer friends, to be less busy during the week and on weekends, to join social groups less frequently, and to say they feel bored.

Loneliness does not feel the same to everyone. The NYU surveys asked people how they usually feel when they are lonely, and found four different sets of feelings. For some people, the largest group, loneliness feels like desperation; words they use to describe the sensation include "desperate," "panic," "helpless," and "afraid." Such individuals feel cut off from others when they are lonely—abandoned and frightened. Another cluster of feelings, which we label "impatient boredom," represents a milder loneliness, the kind that people may feel when they are unexpectedly left alone on a Saturday night, or when they are stuck in a boring hotel room on a business trip. This temporary feeling of loneliness includes such emotions as "bored," "uneasy," and "desire to be elsewhere."

The last two factors, self-deprecation and depression, are common reactions to prolonged feelings of loneliness. Self-deprecation is anger at oneself: "I am alone, unattractive, and stupid; I deserve to be lonely." Depression is a more resigned and passive state marked by self-pity: "I am isolated, cut off, sorry for myself."

The four meanings of loneliness suggest a progression from occasional dissatisfaction with one's social situation, to chronic and more intense dissatisfaction, and finally, if things do not get better, to self-hatred and self-pity.

The NYU surveys were deliberately broad and exploratory, making up in coverage of many issues what they lost in clinical detail. The UCLA studies aimed at constructing a theoretical model of the conditions and interpretations that go into the self-label "lonely." Researchers at UCLA have worked primarily with college students, and this is one topic for which it makes good sense

Attributions for loneliness are important because they determine how a person will feel and how he or she will behave in the future.

to use them. As we mentioned earlier, the young are far more likely than the old to report feeling lonely—college students and high-school seniors most of all. (In one UCLA study, more than 70 percent of all undergraduates thought loneliness was an important problem.)

The UCLA research started off with the importance of the explanations people give for being lonely—in social-psychological terms, their causal attributions. One young woman blamed her environment, for example, noting that "UCLA is such a big impersonal factory that it's hard to meet people." But another student blamed himself: "I'm just too shy to get to know people or ask a girl for a date." Many previous studies of the attribution process had suggested that people would ask themselves three basic questions about why they are lonely: Who's to blame? Can it change? What control do I have over my feelings?

In a series of five studies, the UCLA researchers found that the answers to these questions can be arranged along three dimensions: *locus of causality* ("Am I to blame for my loneliness, or is it something in my environment?"); *stability* over time ("Is my loneliness transitory, or is it likely to be permanent?"); and *controllability* ("Is there anything I can do about being lonely, or is it out of my hands?").

Some students blamed external causes, emphasizing elements of the university situation that led to loneliness (the immense size of the university, the impersonal classes, the lack of opportunities to meet people, or the existence of social cliques). Others gave internal attributions, focusing on lack of social skills, shyness, physical unattractiveness, or fear of trying. One stu-

dent wrote, "The fault, I believe, always lies in the individual who is lonely. If a person is lonely it is because he or she has not taken the initiative in attempting to meet people."

The students regarded some causes of loneliness as more stable than others. They thought shyness was a temporary quality that could change with effort, but they regarded unattractiveness or an unpleasant personality as causes that would be very hard to change. Students felt that they had the most control over causes that were internal (such as lack of effort) and unstable (such as being shy). UCLA undergraduates are, by and large, an optimisitc group. They were reluctant to blame loneliness on looks or personality; the single most common explanation for loneliness was that a person was not trying hard enough, a matter relatively easy to remedy, in their view. Many students, of course, recognized the complexity of the problem, assuming some personal responsibility for feeling lonely but also noting the difficulties imposed by the large university.

Attributions for loneliness determine how a person will feel (depressed, accepting, optimistic, angry), and how he or she will behave in the future. The man whose attributions are internal and stable is saying, in effect, "The fault is in me, and I am unlikely to change." The woman whose attributions are internal and unstable is saying, "The fault was in me, but next time I will try harder and make it work."

The attribution process is linked to self-blame or blame of others. The NYU surveys found that lonely people are less friendly to others, which under-

standably would exacerbate their social isolation. But on closer inspection of the UCLA studies, it appears that hostility and anger are marks only of people who believe they are lonely for external reasons—such as being excluded by ingroups. Several of the NYU interviewees expressed hostility toward people for rejecting or ignoring them. "You can't do anything for people," a middle-aged woman said. "Everyone is ungrateful." (In a study by Bernard Weiner of reactions to success and failure, people who felt they failed because of other people's efforts or motives tended to feel "revengeful," "furious," "bitter," and "fuming.")

When people aim attributions at themselves, the resulting emotion is not usually anger, but disappointment, shame, or embarrassment ("Why didn't I try harder?" "How could I have been such a stupid clod?"). Their behavior in turn depends on whether they view the problem as unchangeable or fixable. Attributions are of pivotal importance in explaining why some lonely people become depressed and withdraw socially, and others ward off depression and actively work to improve their social lives. Depression occurs primarily when people account for loneliness in stable, internal terms ("I am hopelessly fat, ugly, and unlovable; there's nothing I can do about it"); other attributions may galvanize them into effective action ("I won't find fellow skiers in a place this big unless I advertise in the school newspaper"). The longer a spell of loneliness lasts, the more likely a person is to think the reasons are permanent rather than temporary, to lose the hope that life will improve.

Of course, the particular precipitat-

Young single people and the recently divorced were most likely to say they are lonely because they are unattached, longing for "one special person."

ing causes of loneliness that are relevant to a college student undoubtedly differ from the explanations that a recently divorced 35-year-old, an unemployed factory worker, or a disabled 80-year-old might have, but their attributions still fall along the same three dimensions of internality, stability, and control. In the NYU studies, young single people and the recently divorced were most likely to say they are lonely because they are unattached, longing for "one special person." Young adults also linked loneliness to alienation—not being understood, not having close friends, not being needed. Among older people who felt lonely, the main reason was forced isolation (being housebound or handicapped), not the lack of friends or lovers.

Another key influence on a person's experience of loneliness is expectations: People want to know when their feelings of loneliness are "normal," and typically decide by watching how other people react in the same situation. If everyone else seems to be suffering, one's own problems are tolerable. But if everyone else seems to be happy, one's own suffering becomes unbearable. One of the NYU researchers (Rubenstein) interviewed a young black woman who expressed this sentiment well: "When I'm lonely, I don't know what to do for myself . . . I just sit in the house with my two kids and look out the window and see everybody else going by and having a good time." As social psychologist Stanley Schachter put it, "Misery doesn't just love company. It loves *miserable* company."

Past experiences also shape expectations. As psychologist Marjorie Lowenthal showed, elderly people who have lived most of their lives with minimal

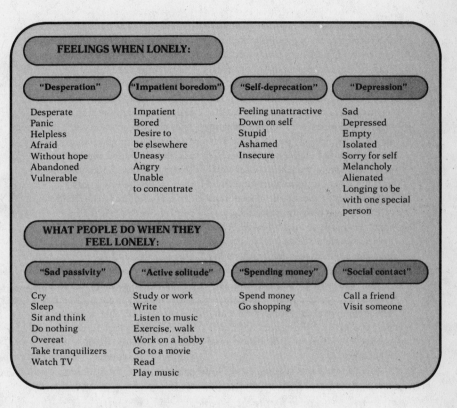

FEELINGS WHEN LONELY:

"Desperation"	"Impatient boredom"	"Self-deprecation"	"Depression"
Desperate	Impatient	Feeling unattractive	Sad
Panic	Bored	Down on self	Depressed
Helpless	Desire to	Stupid	Empty
Afraid	be elsewhere	Ashamed	Isolated
Without hope	Uneasy	Insecure	Sorry for self
Abandoned	Angry		Melancholy
Vulnerable	Unable		Alienated
	to concentrate		Longing to be with one special person

WHAT PEOPLE DO WHEN THEY FEEL LONELY:

"Sad passivity"	"Active solitude"	"Spending money"	"Social contact"
Cry	Study or work	Spend money	Call a friend
Sleep	Write	Go shopping	Visit someone
Sit and think	Listen to music		
Do nothing	Exercise, walk		
Overeat	Work on a hobby		
Take tranquilizers	Go to a movie		
Watch TV	Read		
	Play music		

NYU studies uncovered four clusters of feelings that people have when they say they feel lonely. Some people associate the experience of loneliness with desperation and abandonment; others feel bored; others sink into self-deprecation or depression. What people do when they are lonely depends on how they feel about their loneliness. The severely depressed and most lonely individuals fall into "sad passivity." People who are only mildly or rarely lonely prefer to attack the mood with vigorous strategies: They work, exercise, write letters, read books, or call or visit a friend.

social contact are content with few friends and do not feel deprived or especially lonely. But elderly people who suddenly face a change in the number of friends and activities they are used to *do* feel lonely. Likewise, a person who has had an unusually good relationship may feel lonely if he or she cannot duplicate it. A woman wrote the NYU researchers: "It is possible to be

alone and never be lonely. It is also possible to be lonely and never be alone. Since the death of my first husband, there has been a core of loneliness within me, a void that is never filled, despite the fact that I remarried less than a year after his death."

Our studies suggest that people can benefit from understanding the multiple causes of loneliness, and from rec-

People want to know when their feelings
of loneliness are "normal," and typically decide by watching how other
people react in the same situation.

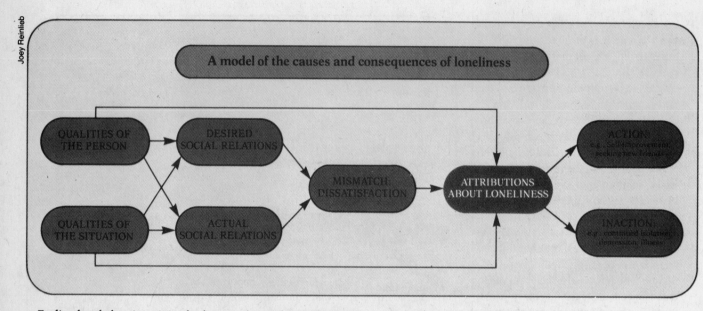

Feeling lonely has its origins both in qualities of the individual (sensitivity to rejection, shyness, physical appearance) and in qualities of the situation (unemployment, recent divorce or loss, large lecture classes, moving to a new city). The intersection of these two factors in turn affect a person's desired and actual social life—whether the person expects to have many friends, finds them, is satisfied with them. When a gap occurs between expectation and reality, the individual feels unhappy and frustrated, and is motivated to account for the discrepancy. Depending on the explanation (attribution) he makes, he will take action to overcome loneliness, or become depressed, ill, bitter, and further isolated.

ognizing their own role in perpetuating or extinguishing it. Research has long demonstrated that people tend to underestimate the effects of situations on their behavior; they overemphasize personality factors. The trick is to understand which causes of loneliness are under one's control, and which are not; which events *precipitated* the lonely feelings (such as the death of a spouse, forced retirement) and which ones *maintain* it (refusal to find new friends or interests, shyness).

The phenomenon of loneliness is both a personal and a social one. Therapy may be appropriate for people whose parents rejected them (or who feel rejected by their parents), and for lonely souls whose self-esteem is low.

Therapy usually won't help people made lonely by loss of work, racial discrimination, or competition.

While collaborating coast-to-coast on this article, we discovered that we had unintentionally developed different opinions about the prospects for treating loneliness. Rubenstein and Shaver, after surveying thousands of adults of all ages and occupations (residing mostly in gray northeastern cities) and interviewing middle-aged people who have been lonely for years, felt pessimistic about reversing many of the social and personal forces that cause loneliness. Peplau and her colleagues, working with college students (in sunny California), were much more optimistic. By nipping negative attri-

butions in the bud, she argues, severe loneliness and depression can be prevented or overturned. The three of us agree on one thing: The earlier loneliness is dealt with the more likely it is to be dispelled. □

For further information:

Gordon, Suzanne. *Lonely in America.* Simon and Schuster, 1976.

Peplau, L., D. Russell, and M. Heim. "An Attributional Analysis of Loneliness." *Attribution Theory: Applications to Social Problems*, ed. by I. Frieze, D. Bar-Tal, and J. Carroll. Jossey-Bass, forthcoming.

Rubenstein, C., and P. Shaver. "Loneliness in Two Northeastern Cities." *The Anatomy of Loneliness*, ed. by J. Hartog and J. Ralph Audy. International Universities Press, 1979.

Weiss, Robert S. *Loneliness* M.I.T. Press, 1974.

THE FAMILY AS A SOURCE OF SECURITY

27

Some cross-cultural contrasts

Colleen Leahy Johnson

In contrast to the past, the family today has been described as a unit with reduced functions, particularly specialized in fulfilling the emotional needs of its members. However, increases in divorce rates, juvenile delinquency, child abuse, and the loneliness of the elderly lead many observers to question just how adaptive the family is in this respect. We see a proliferation of specialists in the helping professions, trained to assist the family in those few tasks left to it. Marriage counselors, psychiatrists, and gerontologists stand ready to prop up the slender resources remaining to this most basic and fragile unit.

Philip Slater makes a great deal of sense when he identifies the source of the pervasive problems of our time as a frustration of the individual's basic need for dependence, community, and engagement. Some alternatives sought by the new generation of adults also center on a search for the intimacy and relatedness presumably missing from the families of their childhood. This search usually leads us back to family forms that were discarded in the processes of industrialization and urbanization. The "back to basics" approach found in some rural communes involves extended-family households, plural mating, and communal economic enterprise, which essentially replicate the dominant family form found in simpler, preliterate societies.

It is common to use cross-cultural material today to justify innovative changes in life-styles. However, most writing on new family forms appears to borrow the sexual-freedom mores of numerous primitive societies without viewing the social system in its entirety. For example, proponents may use Bronislaw Malinowski's *Sexual Life of Savages* as a model for today's sexual freedom, but they do not examine the other side—the excessive rigors of reciprocity and support built into nonsexual institutional areas. Although both male and female Trobrianders can be promiscuous from prepuberty until marriage, they must be prepared for onerous duty-bound exchanges throughout their adult life. Sex is controlled in all societies, and where promiscuity is allowed, it is allowed because this freedom does not interfere with meeting more-basic social requirements.

Another proposal freely borrowed from ethnographic material is that of plural forms of marriage. "Why not have group marriage or plural matings to relieve the monotony of monogamy—it's not uncommon in simpler societies." Such proposals ignore the fact that plural marriages have evolved over innumerable generations in integration with other institutions in a system as intricate as the gears of a clock. If marriage has become impermanent, it is because other provisions have been made for the care of dependent family members. Such proposals ignore the fact that our nuclear family is more or less detached from the kinship system, so that any change in marriage forms seriously jeopardizes the socialization of children and the fulfillment of security needs. Consequently

THE FAMILY AS A SOURCE OF SECURITY, by Colleen Leahy Johnson. This article first appeared in THE HUMANIST May/June 1975 issue and is reprinted by permission.

it is worthwhile restating the raison d'être of the family, however prosaic the facts may be.

In the course of evolution, as the human species lost its instinctual forms of defense, sex had to be brought under social control to ensure the survival of the species. This survival came to rely upon the development of permanent social groupings that could develop a cooperative enterprise based on a division of labor and a clearly defined system of rights and obligations. The greatest survival problems were posed by the extended period of infantile dependency. In contrast to the prehominid, the human infant was born as an exquisitely helpless neonate who required years of nurturing and enculturation. This protracted period of dependency, which drastically limited the autonomy of the mother, had important consequences.

It formulated the universal institution of the family, which was designed to fulfill basic prerequisites for survival. These included the care and protection of the mother and infant and, in fact, was extended to all dependent individuals—notably the aged and infirm. Other functional necessities included the provision of food and shelter, satisfaction of sexual needs, protection from enemies, and the education of new members into the culture. As the male became increasingly important as a provider of food and protection, the human family began to evolve.

The nuclear family can be identified in all societies, with only a few exceptions, which are at the "believe it or not" level of discourse. However, its functional importance in meeting the needs of individuals is by no means universal and causes one to conclude that the nuclear family of Western nations is an unusual form of organization. In fact, the variations and embellishments of the nuclear family in most societies are so complex that the study of kinship in anthropology is a highly sophisticated specialty. In many societies, the kinship relationships reach such importance that the nuclear family, as we know it, has minimal functional significance. Furthermore, in most simpler societies, day-to-day activities occur only with kin, so that if strangers are to participate, an imaginary kinship relationship must be created, a kinship term must be assigned, and appropriate behaviors must be initiated. We have then a network of relationships created by the social recognition of kinship that is sharply differentiated to exclude the world of strangers.

The nuclear family in the majority of other societies is generally submerged and obscured by the generational links between parent and child. The emphasis is usually on the solidarity of blood relatives, whereby the marrying spouses are incidental. Permanent corporate groups, based on blood ties, ensure the enduring protection of members, intergenerational continuity of statuses, and consequently high status for aged family members. Marriage may be more fragile simply because it is less important. In contrast, family systems that stress the solidarity of husbands and wives, as we do, and place relatives on the periphery of importance, are less frequent around the world. When the core of the system is the marital pair, there is inevitably less permanence, great vulnerability, and greater discontinuity between generations. Hence, the position of aged parents is particularly tenuous, for the family is less able to incorporate them into its core. In a hierarchy of obligations, those to aged parents come only after obligations to one's spouse.

Frequently customs, taboos, and clearly defined rules have been developed to regulate relationships within the family. Although these practices may be repugnant to the contemporary belief system, they do provide a stabilizing function. For example, certain customs serve to build estrangement into the nuclear family so that greater cohesion can be established with the wider kinship group. A young wife depends not so much on her husband for happiness as upon his parents and other relatives with whom she is living. Conflict between a man's and a woman's interests and allegiances can be institutionalized so that romantic love, as we know it, does not generally exist. If a man is too devoted to his wife and neglects his duties to his kin, some tribes accuse the wife of having used a love potion to bewitch him. They can then evoke sorcery or taboos to drive a wedge into the relationship. In these ways, conflict is built into the marriage relationship, so that the priorities to kin are not forgotten.

Another means of lubricating the operation of a family system is the use of avoidance rules. Most frequently, this takes the form of mother-in-law avoidance, where a purposeful social distance is demanded in this potentially stressful relationship. Rather than fluid, changing rules for relating, complete avoidance or the use of highly conventionalized rules of etiquette is required in order to prevent conflict and permit innumerable family members to live together in comparative harmony. A society can also invoke rules for a joking relationship, where familiar, even disrespectful, behavior is permitted. This pattern, often occurring between grandparent and grandchild, has a friendliness and familiarity that softens the strains of other hierarchical relationships—such as the respectful, asymmetrical relationship between parent and child.

In most cases, relationships within a family system are bound by an orderly set of rules that establishes a predictability in everyday life. We have also minimized another important social function— the rites of passage to signify transitions into new statuses. These rituals are often occasions for spectacular ceremonies that recognize and elaborate upon the transformation of the individual from birth through maturity, betrothal, marriage, assumption of parenthood, and death. The birth of a child requires social recognition of the new member and elaboration of the requirements of parenthood. When a child approaches adulthood, puberty rites provide a transition mechanism that educates the individual for the responsibilities of adult status. Betrothal and marriage rituals legitimize a union between two individuals and alert them to a new set of obligations to affinal relatives. The passage of individuals from adulthood to old age is given ceremonial recognition in some cultures, while death ceremonies convey the deceased to the next world and serve to repair the morale of the surviving kin. In sum, a system of ritually recognized age-grading maps out an orderly transition from one status to the next in the life cycle.

Hence, a particular family system evolves because it is efficient in exploiting the environment and providing for the individual's basic needs. Although all presumably provide food, shelter, and protection to its members, we cannot stake universal claims on its efficiency in providing security to all. Although the family in the United States is efficient in facilitating the exploitation of the environment, all too often it fails in providing for one's emotional contrasts between most primitive

societies and modern industrialized nations. One finds in even superficial reading of the cross-cultural literature that whatever form the family takes in other societies, it is practically unheard of that any individual is ever alone or without familial supports. An individual's birthright and lifelong expectation is his membership in a stable group from which he will never be excluded or abandoned. Only in cases of extreme environmental stress does the system of reciprocity, mutual aid, and concern fragment basic social ties.

In reading descriptions of primitive societies, one comes away with a highly nostalgic impression of the security and integration that has supposedly been irretrievably lost in more complex societies. In contrast to members of modern society, the primitive lives in a small, homogeneous community, enveloped in an all-embracing kinship system, with a strong sense of group solidarity, where sex, age, and family are the major status determinants. Such a structure creates a highly direct system of social relationships where most transactions take place within a network of intimate, mutually supportive relations.

There is a tendency to idealize primitive society as a direct antithesis to the fragmentation and alienation of our modern society. Whether such a sharp dichotomy can bear up under close scrutiny of empirical data can be seriously questioned. We can, however, make broad generalizations in regard to the markedly different nature of the individual's relationship to the primary group. In other words, the patterns of social integration and the style of interpersonal relationships in most primitive cultures are qualitatively different from those in our society. That is, an individual in a simpler society adheres to a sociocentric orientation to the world, whereby his primary group, the family, takes precedence over individualistic desires.

This immersion of the individual into the group at the expense of personal autonomy, independence, and egoism is a factor at every stage of the life cycle. The infant, the adolescent, and the elderly are incorporated into family activities and given significant roles to play. All individuals are expected to be dependent upon the group for the satisfaction of their needs for sociability and security. Means are provided to prevent an individual's separation from the primary group. For example, some societies prescribe widow remarriage to the brother of the deceased in order to reincorporate her into the group. To illustrate this point, it is useful to compare the position of the aged in simpler societies with their status in our country today. We can see that this general orientation of interdependency, rather than independence, minimizes certain problems arising from the inevitably increasing dependency of the aged. Since no one is expected to be independent of the primary group, the dependency of the aged is an acceptable human condition to which the family system can readily accommodate.

The claim is often made that societies with low technologies have no problems with the elderly, simply because the rigors of life prevent most individuals from living that long. There is justification in this conclusion if one defines old age in terms of an arbitrary change of status at a given age. In this sense, fewer individuals reach our arbitrary milestone age of sixty-five. However, if old age is defined as a stage in the life cycle, such as the event of grandparenthood, a movement to the next status, which resembles our old age, takes place. However, it rarely means a decline in status, as is common in our society; on the contrary, it can mean an elevation to a higher status with more prestige and power.

One important explanation for the esteemed position of the elders in simpler societies relates to the slow rate of change. If a society is relatively isolated from the outside world or resistant to the acceptance of new cultural traits, the major area of change comes principally from the cyclical processes of birth, maturation, and death. Such societies have been called repetitive social systems, where there is little change in the statuses or in the content of the roles but merely change in the personnel who occupy them. Among the Zulu, the past has been described as encapsulated into the present, to the extent that when one recounts the history of his family, he uses first person, present tense. What all this means is that in rather static societies the aged are not made obsolete by social change but instead become guardians of tradition and repositories of most knowledge. In societies without a written language, the memories of the elders constitute a sort of reference library that holds the store of knowledge of that culture. From this vast storehouse, the elders are qualified to be teachers, lawmakers, arbitrators, and historians. Although it is impossible to decelerate the rate of change today, this fact deserves more attention in dealing with the problems of the aged.

Frequently the elevation of the aged to a high status occurs in those societies that elaborate a body of beliefs centering on ancestor worship. Ancestors play an important role, not only as objects of devotion and rituals, but also as links in the endless cyclical nature of life. An interdependence pervades the relationships between child, adult, the aged, and even the deceased. On one hand, filial piety is the parents' unquestioned moral right. But it is not merely a one-way street. A person becomes an ancestor not just because he is dead but because he leaves a successor to worship him. Hence, a parent may not reject his child, regardless of what he does, but rather is tied to him by reciprocal duties and sentiments. Children, in this case, are not merely an insurance policy for one's old age but for one's status in perpetuity.

Such an interdependence is quite foreign to our modern way of thinking. For example, Austin J. Shelton tells us that disengagement and senility are quite rare among the Ibo. The aged not only enjoy high status but also continue to be involved in prestigious affairs. They are the closest link to the ancestors and in this position can fulfill collective superego functions for the group. They are the most revered and important people in the villages. But such a secure position does not come full blown at the onset of old age. Throughout the life cycle, dependence is seen as a virtue to be reinforced and rewarded. Parents show excessive indulgence toward their children, on the grounds that they will be dependent upon their children for support and status both in old age and in the world after death. Children grow up participating in the adult world and in this sphere learn to conform to the community and to avoid the danger of isolation from the group. The Ibo have a saying, "He who goes alone dies like a chicken."

This kind of interdependence exists among some modern groups. My own research among Japanese-Americans in Hawaii indicates that a reciprocity is built into relationships throughout life, which makes loneliness and disengagement quite foreign to the experiential world of most individuals. However, such a pattern is more prevalent in simpler societies and is quite unusual in modern Western nations, where the freedom of the individual is a sacred tenet.

Probably our society or the society of the future should pay heed to the Ik, another African tribe, who were studied by Colin Turnbull. In the face of extreme environmental stress, the Ik have discarded their culture, their values, and their sense of responsibility, somewhat as did the young boys in William Golding's *Lord of the Flies*. As the food supply diminished, the Iks forgot the norm of reciprocity and the patterns of cooperation inherent in the family.

It is the "survival of the fittest" as their daily struggles become a Darwinian nightmare. The very old and the very young are the dispensable members of this culture in decay. At three years of age, the child is turned out of the family to forage for himself. The old are treated with scorn and derision: food is literally grabbed from their mouths and they are left alone to die of starvation. They are even fortunate if they can command a perfunctory burial. A sense of humanity goodness, and mutuality has been replaced by a system of unutual exploitation and fanatical individualism.

Although there are few parallels in the anthropological literature to this extreme of cultural breakdown, one must conclude that traditionally morality regarding mutual responsibility is not inherent in the nature of man. However, most cultures have mechanisms that operate at various levels of efficiency to protect most members. If environmental stress poses a threat to the survival of the group, some members are sacrificed so that the group can survive. Generally it must be the nonproductive members, the very young and the very old. The elderly Eskimo might be put out on the ice to die if he threatens the mobility of the group. This desperate last resort usually results from inadequate technology for exploiting the means of subsistence—never because these helpless individuals lack social significance.

In attempting to make generalizations from this brief overview of the enormously varied patterning of family life in the primitive world, we can make some statements that can be placed in the perspective of our own culture. First, the family structure, however it is defined, does not usually take the form of the isolated nuclear family. Instead, individuals are submerged in a wider collective of kin to whom they are bound by a pattern of interdependence and reciprocity. This network of relationships generally meets security and sociability needs far more efficiently than a smaller unit based on the solidarity of husband and wife. Second, a prominent characteristic of simpler societies is the existence of mechanisms to regulate relationships in order to reduce tensions and conflict and to produce an orderly transition from one status to the next in the life cycle. Third, although premarital sexual freedom and plural forms of marriage are quite common, they exist within a kinship group that fulfills the functions we usually assign to the institution of marriage. Hence, greater freedom in mating does not threaten the basic functional necessities.

In regard to the security provided, one might conclude that our modern society is inimical to the well-being of human beings, while primitive society is a primeval Garden of Eden. Evidence from both levels of development would certainly contradict such a sentimental conclusion. Nevertheless, there are qualitatively different levels of social integration between the two extremes of cultural development that center on the individual's attachment to the group and the extent to which he or she is either submerged in an interdependent network or freed for autonomous pursuit of self-interest.

I am not suggesting that we can radically change the structure of our family in order to alleviate the current social malaise. We should, however, recognize the costs involved in an overemphasis upon individual freedom and independence. Despite the rewards accruing from the autonomy and self-actualization inherent in our nuclear family, some individual needs must be sacrificed, for this small, vulnerable group cannot provide the necessary props. Perhaps the experimenters with alternatives will produce in time new family forms that can be integrated into the system and can recapitulate the functions that initially made the survival of humanity possible. •

28 The Age of Encounter

ELEANOR LINKS HOOVER

Eleanor Links Hoover is an experienced observer and reporter on the group encounter movement. She attended Reed College and has an M.A. in psychology from the University of Iowa. Before becoming a writer, she did several years of graduate work in psychology and anthropology at New York University, UCLA and Yale University.

Charlie pounds the sofa cushion, screaming: "I hate you . . . you bitch . . . you never loved me, never, never . . . never!", his voice trailing off as his tears and flailing arms subside. Mary rushes across the room, tears streaming down her cheeks, and throws her arms around him. "We know," she says, "what you are feeling." She sobs. "We've all felt it sometime, about someone . . . if it wasn't mother, it was someone else." The group, in various stages of commiserative tears, stoic recall, or crushed empathy, nods and mumbles collective assent. For a moment, it is as one, united in the common human agony of an unpent scream. . . of anguished, forbidden words actually spoken, finally uttered . . . "O woe is me, to have seen what I have seen, see what I see," Ophelia had moaned. The group knows . . . it "feels" the woe . . . its compassion laves over each member like warm milk. There is silence. Then the Leader softly asks: "Stephen, how do you really feel about what is happening to Charlie?"

By now, they have been satirized, televised, filmed and acculturated as close as your neighborhood growth center, or perhaps your very own living-room: if not "encounter" itself, then the "gut-level," "here-and-now," "open," "honest" totally frank, anything-goes jargon and ethos of the "Encounter Group." If anyone exists who does not yet know that we are well into the throes of the Age of Encounter, he has simply not been listening.

Those that have may realize that the encounter groups which first sprouted like yuccas on the California landscape six years ago are now flourishing in the East with much success. All in all, psychologist Warren Bennis estimates that more than 6,000,000 people have now participated in one kind of encounter or another and this includes all kinds of middle and upper-middle-class Americans: lawyers, policemen, clergymen, housewives, addicts, businessmen, teachers, doctors — everyone.

Since its Eastern debut has made it a certifiable nation-wide phenomenon even its severest critics do not deny that it is here to stay nor that there are many good things to be said about it. Certainly, more and more, the movement mirrors stresses and strains in the American personality, and obviously it is answering — in one fashion or another — pressing social needs. But a big difference between now and six years ago is the professional reception encounter is receiving. Earlier, when encounter was just a California scene, no one was ready — or willing — to evaluate the strange hybrid: the suddenness of its emergence and the sheer drama of its impact took everyone by surprise. Now, however, the psychiatrist and psychologist establishmentarians of the tradition-bound, still Freudian-dominated East have their guns loaded and are rolling them out post-haste.

"Critiques" and serious articles on the so-called "casualties" of encounter — people who for one reason or another couldn't take all that intimacy and either cracked up or had negative responses — began appearing in professional and intellectual journals. New York psychologist Emanuel Schwartz has written about the coming of encounter in these utterly damning terms, "When their leaders (Esalen) barnstormed New York, advance publicity heralded the coming of the Esalen circus. The appellation is apt. The psychological dimensions of the circus include a negation of reality followed by feelings of omnipotence. The relationship between real and symbolic objects is not integrated. The tempo is maniacal. Magic is everywhere. Scoptophilic relations with objects are central. Primary processes press to break through. There is an upsurge of bisexuality; that is, an increasing loss of sexual differentiation takes place. Many marathons and encounter workshops are like circuses in these and other ways."

The criticism is not just professional but social and political as well — some of it from surprising sources. The Birch Society has a serious campaign going against encounters as hand-maiden to sex education, the breakdown of the family and Communist brainwashing. Even professionals who admit to some of the positive aspects of encounters have called them "a kind of fascism of the emotions that tyrannically imposes the will of the group on the individual."

Encounterers dismiss Birch charges as nonsense: sex education is here to stay and the institution of the family is in flux and upheaval, encounter or no. As for Communist or Fascist brainwashing, the answer to that was summed up by a devotee of the Synanon "game" (a particularly rough and tumble "karate chop" encounter developed by ex-addicts at

Synanon for general use) when she said, "Sure, the group is tough but you can still oppose them. If you can hold your own with the group, you've earned the right to your ideas."

Those are noble sentiments, but group pressure being what it is, very few ever try, or succeed. There was little opposition when about 1,000 or more people — psychologists, students and guests — went through a sensitivity awareness session at the opening of the Association for Humanistic Psychology in Washington, D.C. last September. The scene was the grand ballroom at the Statler-Hilton and everyone was lined in a great rectangle facing inward like a huge square dance, as a psychologist "caller" intoned instructions over a loud speaker:

"Look across the room and experience the mass over there ... got it? ... now focus on one person ... take a head trip ... analyze the feelings that person arouses in you ... now, slowly walk to that person ... fantasize doing something to that person (try to feel the action in your muscles) ... now get a little space for yourself ... experience your territory, close your eyes, and settle in...." At this point some people are sprawling on the rug stretching, most are sitting and groping in one direction or another and a few are standing in a brooding trance. The voice continues: "Now with your hands try to work around your boundaries ... now close your eyes and do a real head trip ... analyze your neighbors and take a trip into your past ... think what it will be like in the year 2001 and take a trip into the future ... let a word happen, move to the feeling of that word ... now let a sentence, a poem happen and move to it as you say it out loud ... open your eyes and if you can see someone you'd like to tell your poem to ... now tell them the poem ... come on and skip!"

The spectacle of 1,000 people moving trancelike as one, readily, avidly in fact, responding to every nuance of mass suggestion, is indeed a sobering sight. And much as one may wish to rejoice at the notion of people bypassing the strait-jacket of conventional behavior for even a moment, the mind reels at the alacrity with which people willingly suspend judgment and submit to the will of the leader or a group. One psychologist who reluctantly went through a similar warm-up even commented on

the beguiling quality of the experience. "After a while, you feel you would follow *anywhere*" he said.

Encounter actually seems to perform an equalitarian function — a societal tension release — in providing perhaps the only place in our society where one can appear as oneself and be evaluated for that alone, utterly free from the supports and bolsters of rank, title, education, sex and money. Everyone is equal in an encounter group — democracy really works — if only for a little while. In providing such humane services, in defusing the social, economic and personal frustrations of the very frustrated affluent middle class, it is just conceivable that encounter may be providing a saving social grace. Max Lerner thinks so; he sees encounter as a positive force — one that may defray "our" decline and fall. Social historian William Irwin Thompson in "At the Edge of History," sees encounters as nothing less than a "rehearsal for the complete transformation of basic human nature and civilization." Clearly, encounter is more than a fad or social aberrance as some once thought — or hoped. It is a way of life, and a recognized movement that sees man in a totally different way from anything before in history.

In any case, pioneering Esalen, its many supporters and the hundred or more "growth centers" across the nation where encounter has now settled down as a "staple" of the curriculum, accepts the waves of criticism philosophically. Says Bill Schutz, author of "Joy" and a leader in sensory awareness at Esalen, "The so-called 'casualties' have been greatly exaggerated ... On the whole, in every way, encounter has been an overwhelmingly good experience. It has merged with other things into a revolution that is really going to change the way we feel about ourselves."

Encounter is basically much the same now as it has always been: an anguished, teary, drop-that-mask, tote-that-candor, shout-it-like-it-is, total, "gut-level" person-to-person confrontation for 12 to 20 people, mostly or often strangers (though less and less so), and for a period of time ranging from two hours to two days to two weeks — the livelier, angrier and more "loving" the better. Beyond that, there is considerable variability in encounter. It depends probably on the temperament and style of the

"facilitator" (encounterers insist on the word — in this brave new world, no one, God forbid, is a therapist or leader), the particular "school" of encountering being employed (Gestalt, Bioenergetics, etc.) and whether the encounter takes place in a group-therapy center, a growth center like Esalen or in a juvenile hall lounge between young addicts and probation officers.

The big change, as Dr. Thomas Greening, head of the Topanga Center for Human Development, sees it, is that "Encounter is settling down to be more a part of the culture.... It is now 'built-in,' less of a special event, less sensational and more 'institutionalized'." You now find encounter, he points out, as a regular part of the school system, various medical and social programs, youth and rehabilitation work, police department activities, very much in church work, club work and university programs. Many West Coast churches have been swamped with encounter activities. In fact, professional churchmen have expressed open concern about the number of ministers who have thrown off their ministerial robes to become full-time encounter facilitators. Obviously these apostates find the communal confession aspect of encounter a revitalizing religious force among parishioners.

Encounter is the closest most people will ever come to a "therapeutic" learning situation for economic reasons alone. The usual minimum fees of most psychiatrists and clinical psychologists—about $35.00 an hour —obviously eliminate much of the population, while a workshop in encounter or Rolfing and Gestalt at $20 for the day which is about what most growth centers charge, is well within the reach of many. The tab is even lower—maybe $5 a session—for students, and campus bulletin boards and underground papers abound with group announcements, while for middle-class affluents $125 for a 40-hour non-stop week-end marathon with a psychologist is not too much, considering what the alternatives would run. The recession has certainly not done business any good, but marathon facilitators are not likely to complain that their former $2000 or so weekend take has fallen off by a few hundred dollars.

A visible index of encounter's acceptance is the rapid proliferation of "growth centers" around the country.

Modeled more or less after Big Sur's Esalen, there are now more than 100 of these—Aureon Institute in New York City with a retreat in Woodstock; "Quest" in Washington, D.C.; The Center of the Whole Person in Philadelphia; and the Athena Center for Creative Living (with intimacy labs in Mexico and Aliquippa), to name a few. There are now certainly half as many such centers now in Canada, and workshops led by American facilitators are turning up in Holland, Germany (where encounter methods are used regularly in the Armed Forces) and Japan. It may well be, as social historian William Irwin Thompson says in his book, that encounter is one of the social forces leading to the coming "planetization of man."

What is happening to encounter is that it is sifting down into the culture —our social institutions, theater, and the arts. it is also "rising up," as it were, to merge with other techniques in the Human Potential Movement— all moving toward a revolutionary new break-through in our conception of man. At centers like Esalen now, encounter is like English 1A. It is a pre-requisite to all upper division courses. Once you have had it, you can go on to other things, but it is doubtful that you would want to repeat 1A again. The things you go on to are called Rolfing, Bio-energetics, Alexander technique, Gestalt therapy, psychosyntheses, maybe T'ai Chi— and a host of other exotic-sounding activities.

In other words, in addition to encounter talk-outs, you may now choose sensory wake-ups, meditational cool-offs, fantasy role-plays, Wilderness camp-outs, mystical psyche-ins, Gestalt act-outs, massage pummel-offs and nude dip-ins or cope-outs, depending on your point of view. During a recent typical week at Kairos, a leading Los Angeles growth center, the following potpourri of one-day workshops was offered: Rolfing and Gestalt; Opening to Feeling—a Neo-Reichian Workshop; Breaking Through—A marathon; An exploration of Inner Space with Alpha Bio-feedback; Gestalt Encounter; Sexuality Revisited; Parameters of Change—Revising your Lifestyle; and Meditation for the Western Man. As the Beatles' song used to say, "It's a long day's night" keeping up with the new psychology.

Irresistibly, some of the grandiose terms and descriptions of encounter seem a little humorous, as do all new movements, cults, revolutions or religions. Often those closest to it seem the most serious and humorless, weary perhaps with the defensive effort of trying to make themselves understood in an uptight world. But even they may smile a little at the undeniable humor of Esalen running "an encounter for people who have been to too many encounters"... or the importing of a rational psychotherapist (rational or reality psychotherapy is a totally different approach) from New York with the express purpose of helping participants adequately "close up" again — a task, the brochure admits, unfortunately often neglected in the hurly burly of all that "opening up, risk taking and creativity-enhancing experience."

The important point, encounterers feel, is not the humor, the "so-called casualties," or the question of whether to encounter or not to encounter; the Human Potential Movement, of which encounter is now just a part, is bigger than all that. The important thing they say is what encounter has already taught us about ourselves. Americans as a group are desperate. Whether they know it or not they have become so alienated from themselves, each other and the world of nature, there is an atrophy of feeling as serious as any physical dysfunction. They agree with Dr. R. D. Laing, a British psychoanalyst who writes in his book, "The Politics of Experience":

"As adults, we have forgotten most of our childhood, not only its contents but its flavor; as men of the world, we hardly know of the existence of the inner world; we barely remember our dreams, and make little sense of them when we do; as for our bodies, we retain just sufficient proprioceptive sensations to coordinate our movements and to insure the minimal requirements for biosocial survival—to register fatigue, signals for food, sex, defecation, sleep; beyond that, little or nothing. Our capacity to think, except in the service of what we are dangerously deluded in supposing is our self interest and in conformity with common sense is pitifully limited; our capacity even to see, hear, touch, taste and smell is so shrouded in veils of mystification that an intense discipline of unlearning is necessary for anyone before one can begin to experience the world afresh, with innocence, truth and love."

This passionate view may seem overdone to anyone who has never been to an encounter, particularly an encounter-marathon, but to anyone who has (this writer included) there is no denying the searing shock of what one sees and feels once the mask of everyday polite behavior peels away: the smooth and powerful business executive finally cracking and confessing in wracking sobs that he has never had a friend, never really "talked" to his wife, is a stranger to his children; the "successful" housewife and clubwoman gasping out the tragedy of what she really feels is "a wasted life;" the smart young junior executive, his tie askew, grimacing in anguish as he confesses aloud for the first time in his life the humiliation and anguish of being a closet homosexual; the beautiful young bride admitting through silent tears that she feels nothing—absolutely nothing— for anyone or anything.

It is not so easy to dismiss all these people as dilettantes, faddists or weak-willed neurotics who should be in proper therapy somewhere and not messing around with the time-bomb called encounter—they remind us too much of ourselves and people we know.

Quite aside from any therapeutic consideration, the encounter is frequently a stunning memorable event —what some psychologists call "a peak experience" in and of itself— and therefore one that can be valuable and significant just as *human experience*, if for no other reason. We learn for all time the truth of Bertrand Russell's remark, "to know a person is to know his tragedy." In other words, there is probably a case to be made for the encounterers' view that the distinction between who is sick and who is well is not so easily (or sometimes even properly) made in this society. Even for their view that the built-in, instinctive healing powers of the group may sometimes be trusted perhaps more than some neurotic Ph.D. who just happened to make it through the degree mill to collect what he contemptuously refers to as his "union card." Perhaps.

In any case, it is clear that the encounter movement is an out and out revolution that sees man, his nature and the meaning of his life in a totally different way than ever before. By its very existence, it indicts psychology, psychoanalysis and all the so-called therapeutic disciplines for being obtuse, smug, insensitive, banal, venal, uncaring, untrained, arrogant and ineffectual.

The time has certainly come to seriously evaluate what is real and what isn't about the encounter movement. What do encounters actually do for their participants? What don't they do? As critics dash in to attack and defenders rush out to support, it seems appropriate to ask if encounter groups really know what they have gotten into despite their brave words. Is it therapy they offer or just an extraordinary or heightened experience or a little of both?

A serious charge against the movement is the doctrinaire, almost nihilistic, anarchic view they take toward the notion of psychotherapy—precarious a discipline though it be. They are dedicated to the idea that they are dispensing "therapy for the well" if it may be called "therapy" at all—they see it as closer to re-education; that there is no distinction between the so-called "therapist" and the so-called "patient;" that neither really exists and that no one, in fact, is really "sick" (except those poor unfortunates who misguidedly end up with psychiatrists). As we are our own executioners, we are presumably our own therapists as well. The group *knows* — it *heals*. The group is all.

But is it? Students of group process know that while the group can dispense a powerful cohesive and communal power, a "magic" in fact—it can also be tyrannical, abrupt, abusive and unwise: as unauthentic and distorted in its way as any individual. The group experience which is deified as the only true, spontaneous one, is often actually a "manipulated" milieu with a harsh set of rules not always in an individual's best interest. In a sense, the encounter is "rigged" from the start by dictums requiring participants behave in a certain way. The group is absolutely ruthless when participants do not. Individual personal style does not matter nor is it tolerated. Intimacy is the thing—and everyone must dive into intimacy in the same uninhibited way, even though it is known that individuals seem to differ significantly in the amount of intimacy they can stand. The group is not supportive if one does not play by its rules, no matter how much "show" it makes of trying to be.

Almost every encounter seems to turn up an Edna. Frustrated, bitter, very delicately balanced, Edna, a 54-year-old divorcee, works as a secretary and only came to a 40-hour marathon because she thought it might help her be more successful at work and in an affair she is having with a younger man. She speaks little during the early part of the encounter and then with great caution when she does: clearly the marathon with all its gutsy frankness is more than she bargained for and she tries to cope by acting aloof and using the same coy, devious mannerisms she has always hidden behind. "Aw, come off it," a man finally shouts at her. "You're such a sour apple, I doubt anything would please you . . . if you dropped dead tomorrow, nobody would care." The woman grabs her things and runs out sobbing. An hour later she is back, taking a seat in the corner and quietly listening. Occasionally she makes a small show of being "with it" but clearly she is not. At the end, she confides to a friend that it was a "ridiculous experience" and that she only came back "to get my money's worth." Not everyone drops his guard (even if he seems to) or cozies up to the warming intimacy of encounter.

The marathon especially illustrates how artifice is built in the very structure of encounter making it anything but the pure spontaneous "happening" people like to say it is. After 20 or more hours of uninterrupted talk without sleep, facades do indeed crumble but so can other things as well—like judgment, rational thought, perspective, maybe even "sanity" if we may be allowed this archaic word. Now sometimes this may be a valuable thing in its way if it is recognized for what it is and called by its rightful name: perhaps those who speak of "peak experience" or "heightened . . ." or "altered states of consciousness" are closer to the truth. These can indeed occur in encounter, and often do. But the same or similar conditions also can be re-created in the psychology laboratory after prolonged sleep deprivation, or on the highway after a long, non-stop trip, in solitary confinement or when emerging from anesthetic. It is not a true mystical experience although it may seem like one. In our alienated, sexually-repressed society, just the simple experience of being physically and psychologically close to other people—even or especially strangers —for an extended period of time can constitute an intoxicated turn-on of major proportions. It is probably just that—a turn-on; for some, maybe nothing more. As Alvin Toffler points out in *Future Shock*, the relatively short, temporary encounter seems exactly to fit the sense of impermanence in modern life: a transient world can offer little more than transient friendships.

So there is no question that encounters turn people on. Most encounters leave the group in a state of euphoria, calling it a good and positive experience of lasting value —a few even call it the greatest experience of their lives. But it is significant that very few evaluate it the same way a month, or six months later. A study by Drs. Irvin D. Yalom, Morton Lieberman and Matthew Miles shows that while 75% of the Stanford undergraduates who attended an encounter thought the results were positive and lasting, this was not matched by the percentage of actual change that took place. While such a formal study may actually miss the heart of the matter, the fact remains that those traditional follow-up reunions that group members plan for a month to six weeks later are notoriously badly-attended. We know of one case where—out of 20 ardent participants who parted after a 40-hour marathon amidst much tears and avowals of undying love and devotion—only three turned up for a reunion a month later.

The mock-equalitarian view that no one has the right to presume that he might "help" or "treat" someone else because since we are all sick in the same way we are therefore all well (or as well as we are likely to be for the time being) has led to a complete abdication of any real authority or responsibility on the part of many so-called trained facilitators. Rebellion against the obvious inequalities of the academic world that frequently awards its degrees in psychology and psychiatry to people patently ill-equipped by reasons of temperament, personality and sometimes training, for dealing with people in-trouble or out, the humanist revolt has catapulted to the other extreme: there are no distinctions, no one is better or more expert at this business of "helping" than anyone else (but one notices that facilitators still persist in charging for their services).

This viewpoint reached rather absurd proportions during a seminar titled "Should a Professional Therapist Go To Bed With His Patient If Mutually Attracted?" at the meetings in Washington, D.C., last September of the Association for Humanistic Psychology. Two "therapists" on the panel, after ascertaining by a show of hands that at least 10 or so of their colleagues had done likewise, allowed that they had slept with certain patients, found the experience valuable for the patient (and presumably the therapist as well) and speculated on whether, in some cases, this might be a valuable therapy. In any case, they felt the whole question should come out of the shadows and be openly discussed. Someone in the audience wanted to know, if, with the same impartiality, these therapists would sleep with old, homely female patients or, say, a male patient "who needed it." If not, how could they honestly say that their behavior was motivated by anything but sex? An honest question. And since honesty was the order of the day, a well-known therapist in the audience dropped his mask and candidly admitted what so many of these practitioners really feel. "I don't want any more patients," he said. "They want to act like patients. If someone tells me 'I don't want to get up in the morning'—I can only say 'That's how I feel too sometimes.' I only want to work with friends."

Interestingly, the only words of caveat and restraint came from Dr. Albert Ellis, head of a school of therapy known as rational-emotive, and author of innumerable books on sex, whose views are usually thought to be free-wheeling. He cautioned the obvious: intercourse with patients could interfere with their getting well, vitiate totally the therapeutic situation and easily be exploitive on the part of the therapist. He debunks, incidentally, the whole reification of feeling on the part of the humanists. "The whole point of therapy is having to grow up and face reality," he says. "Feeling will only get you so far. Hitler felt great." As for encounters, Ellis thinks they will be around for awhile because they are "pleasant and people are pleasure-seeking." But he dismissed the notion that weekenders at Esalen and other growth centers are just casual shoppers in a psychic supermarket. "These are people actively seeking help—and needing it—whether they know it or not," he observes.

In the last analysis there does not seem to be any satisfactory substitute for either good old-fashioned ethics or solid substantial training for group leaders, whatever they call themselves. In a reaction against the narrow, formal rubrics the academic world traditionally uses to admit a few anointed into the sacred world of psychotherapy, the movement has overturned the whole caboodle with a nihilistic whoop. But salvation is not that easy—either for an individual or an institution, or as psychologist William Blanchard says, "Ecstasy without agony is baloney." Comments psychiatrist Louis Gottschalk, "Like it or not, you have to ask what are the qualifications of the 'leaders' although they hate that word. Who are the people leading groups? The answer now is anybody and everybody. Everyone wants some of the action. There is as yet no professional school, a code of ethics nor any well-organized group to take responsibility. At least with new surgery or new drugs, there is someone to stand whatever risk is being taken."

Even when group leaders are psychologists with formal university degrees, it frequently turns out that these credentials are in fields other than clinical. In other instances they are ill-equipped in personal ways for the work they do. Nonetheless, their colleagues in the humanist movement close ranks behind them in as traditional a cloture as practiced by MDs. One famous group leader for example, is notorious in and out of his field for his totally bizarre personal and professional behavior. In several articles in national publications, where writers describe him as openly fondling and caressing women patients during encounters, he meets group protest by saying, "That is the way I am . . . I like touching people, I like girls . . . I will try to control my nature . . . I'm sorry. I'm not sorry for myself, I can't help that . . . But why is the group focusing on such a trivial matter?" His wife who frequently "co-leads" although she is not a psychologist, rejoins, "I don't mind seeing you kiss other women, but when you put your hands on their breasts and bottoms, I think it is disgusting."

Feedback in his groups reveals that newcomers especially are confused and often repelled by his actions. But the point made tacitly, and this to people who can least afford to learn it, is one of license (although he would call it creativity). Anything goes, he is saying—if I can do what I do, say what I say, so can you—just stop being so uptight. A valuable lesson perhaps for a tough world but hardly in the best tradition of the "healing arts."

What then do we know about "healing" or "growing" or "feeling"—whatever it is that happens or is supposed to happen in encounters? Fortunately, thanks to the Yalom, Lieberman and Miles study, we have a little more to go on than our intuition and experience, quintessentially important though they may be.

We know that encounter leaders who are warm and supportive (sometimes called "love-leaders") have more *lasting* positive effects on their groups than leaders characterized as "Aggressive Stimulators." These "aggressive" charismatic leaders produce more so-called "peak experiences" but also more (44%) of the casualties as well. We know that people tend to go to encounter groups when they are considering major personal or occupational changes or undergoing life crises involving major decisions. Interaction with a group seems to be particularly helpful to people at this time—a key perhaps to their appeal with the young. Encounters, when successful, also seem to affect styles of "coping" with personal issues. A person, may learn, for example, that paying more attention to his inner life aids "coping," or he may learn that expressing his feelings more frequently eases the way. Each person, after a good encounter, comes away with a little cachet of new ideas about himself and improved ways of "coping." In some cases, they also come away with increased self-esteem—a difference that persists in long-term follow-ups. It seems we like ourselves better when we have won through to something.

Apparently catharsis per se is not enough to effect lasting change in a person. We sob after all at a good movie or a play; we are deeply touched for awhile but who can say we have really changed. Neither does confession—even communal confession — seem the magic ingredient in the "healing" experience. We expiate our fear, guilt and separateness by "baying at the moon," to use Yeats' phrase, but it certainly does not bay back despite our relief, release and purgation. Confession may be the start of something but it is hardly ever the end—or all confession booths would be analysts' couches at less than half the price. Mere acting out or verbalizing of feeling without understanding or insight does not rid us of these feelings—as therapists have long known. Nor, necessarily, does mere "regressing"—(in some of the nude groups participants act out childhood fears and fantasies with nursing bottle, blanket and crib). What we need, in addition to the words is a profound integration, a deep understanding of what we have poured forth. But this may not happen in the anti-intellectual context of encounter where "thinking" and "cognition" are suspect and shouted down. It *may* happen afterwards—if one is lucky. Freud said, "The voice of the intellect is a soft one, but it does not rest until it has gained a hearing. Ultimately, after endlessly repeated rebuffs, it succeeds."

Growth centers need to decide what the main service is they are dispensing—recreation, expanded consciousness, excitement, mystery, theater, the sense of being alive, instant camaraderie, or a serious attempt at changing people—especially people in trouble. If it is change we are after, encounter in all its forms may be too strong for some (studies sharply disputed by Esalen people, put those having psychotic depression and episodes after encounters at around 9% and suicides linked to encountering are not unknown) and not strong enough or deep enough for others. In any case real inner progress is frequently a slow, anguished, unspectacular road with many ego-shattering pitfalls and cliffs that fall off to the night. The rewards of traversing it are not to be bought for a few easy tears and sobs, no matter how painful. It is also frequently a solitary road. (Is this why Esalen is trying out a new workshop called "On Being Alone"?) For some—perhaps the most sophisticated (Esaleners would say they need it most)—encounter is mostly banal. Encounterers talk a lot about risk-taking, but perhaps they haven't taken enough of their own—in facing up to what their goals really are in relation to the people who come to them. At the very least they owe these people, in addition to the moon (which they are all too eager to promise them), a little solid professional responsibility and guidance before they lead them into a hazardous experience that's been described as "verbal sky-diving."

As for the rest of us, however we view encounter with all its imperfections, good, bad or indifferent, we shall probably never be the same again because of it. Like it or not, the vitality of the encounter movement has touched all our lives and made changes in human relations. We are franker now and more willing to show our emotions. Once we have tasted such freedom we can never wholly give it up again. As Thoreau wrote after leaving Walden, "I did not wish to take a cabin passage, but rather to go before the mast and on the deck of the world, for there I could best see the moonlight amid the mountains. I do not wish to go below now."

29

NO DRUGS • NO LIQUOR • NO TOBACCO
NO PREMARITAL SEX • NO HOT PANTS • NO POSSESSIONS

They're young, tireless, devout, dogmatic, evangelical and terribly earnest on this fundamentalist farm in a Western state. And it's a man's world: the women know their place.

by Mary White Harder, James T. Richardson, and Robert B. Simmonds

"I know God created us equal. And we're just helpmates for the man. I know that our souls and spirits are equal. But I know that we're weaker vessels. We just have different ministries to fulfill." —a sister at Christ Commune

THE YOUNG MEN ("brothers"), long-haired and bearded, were hoeing the field. A few young women ("sisters") worked alongside them. One sister, wearing a dress with a loose-fitting top, bent over and inadvertently allowed a brother to glimpse her breasts. Later in the day the brother complained to a pastor that the sister had "stumbled" him—she had caused him to have fleshly desires. The hoeing continued; later the brothers and sisters congregated as usual for dinner, the sisters who were not serving food took places at the end of the line, behind the men. That evening after dinner the sisters had a special meeting.

As part of our ongoing study of Christ Commune, one of our female interviewers was permitted to attend the meeting. Sisters who were "older in the Lord" explained that it was necessary for women to dress in a manner that revealed neither ankle nor curve. Cosmetics and jewelry were discouraged for the same reason; sisters were to avoid drawing attention to their bodies. The justification given for these rules was that the male's God-given nature automatically causes him to "stumble" at the sight of certain parts of the female body. The male has little or no control over this, so it becomes the female's responsibility to avoid sexually charged situations. It is also a mark of vanity and pride for the female to call attention to herself through flirtation or dress.

Sexism. This justification, of course, absolves males of responsibility and puts females in the position of agreeing that their bodies cause sin. The episode helped delineate for us the place of women in the group, as well as the sexism that we believe is inherent in fundamentalist theology.

Our interest in sex roles of the young Christian converts is part of our general interest in the religious organization that operates the commune. Christ Commune is a pseudonym for one branch of what is probably the best-organized, most rapidly growing sect in the so-called Jesus movement. It appears to us the group is more viable than even the much-publicized Children-of-God sect.

The commune is two years old, located in a Western state. During the summer of 1971, and again last summer, its leaders allowed us to visit for several weeks on three different occasions and to interview members. The approximately 100 persons living there during the summers were drawn from the group's year-round houses strung out along the West Coast. At the end of both summers the members returned to their original houses, or continued on to others where they would be trained for leadership and groomed for work in evangelical teams formed to open houses.

Sect. The organization that runs Christ Commune has been in existence four years; it operates, in addition to the commune branch we studied, other agricultural activities, a small fishing fleet, and about 35 other houses across the country. We estimate that the sect has between 600 and 800 members overall, and financial assets of about a million dollars.

In addition to studying sex roles at Christ Commune, and the structure and history of the group, we gathered information about members' backgrounds and personalities, about the theology and values of the sect, and about the techniques used to win conversions and keep com-

> ## "I do love my brothers, and I do want the house to be nice for them, but I clean it for the Lord."

mitment. We investigated changes in persons before and after they joined the group, and changes in the operation of the group itself.

Blessing. Among the noticeable changes in the operation of Christ Commune over two summers was a perceptible redefinition of sex roles. During our 1971 visit we often heard sisters exchange comments that summed up woman's role in the group—such as, "Isn't it a blessing to know your place!"

The following summer, although basic sex roles remained intact, there were changes indicating that some sisters were less than satisfied with their "place." The ankle-length, loose-fitting dresses of 1971 had given way to more formfitting and stylish clothes. An occasional sister even wore knee-length shorts. Some sisters had begun to work in the fields, and teams of brothers volunteered to help with the dishes in the evening. We have found no evidence that changed sex-role behavior has meant any change in the group's theology of sex roles.

Submission. Today as in 1971 the women of the group know their place: one of submission to men, just as men are in submission to the Lord. Theoretically, men and women in the group are equal. According to the Word of God as revealed in the scriptures—so goes the group's official theology—all Christians are equal in the eyes of the Lord. But also rooted in the scriptures is the idea that God has provided an appropriate place for all His children, and in order to be a good Christian, one must accept that place.

Sisters recognize their subservience to brothers, but they define themselves in terms of their relationship with God. They appear to gain neither status nor identity through their relationships with men, but instead evaluate themselves in terms of fulfilling their duties as required by the Lord.

One sister explained to us: "At two of the houses I've lived at I've been the only sister the majority of the time, besides the married wife whose ministry is to her husband. So, my ministry was to like patch up the brothers' pants when they tore out. And cook—always cook—breakfast, lunch and dinner. And keep the house clean. 'Cause it's the Lord's house, 'cause I always know that Jesus could come at any time. And I don't want Him to see the house being a mess. Like I'm not on a self-righteous-worker trip, praise God, 'cause I fall into that sometimes. But I just like to keep the house presentable to the Lord, and clean it for the Lord. I do love my brothers, and I do want the house to be nice for them, but I clean it for the Lord. I do it for Him, not for the 10 different brothers that are in the house. It's just the Lord."

Trials. As a result of this male-female hierarchy, no woman at Christ Commune in 1972 is included in the farm's decision-making process. One woman has the title of deaconess, but her authority is limited to other women, primarily to their kitchen duties. Women bow to the authority of all men in the group, especially their fiancés or husbands. Some of the sisters have difficulty accepting their roles. They have had to reject their former life-styles, which often included sexual relations with men, employment and independence, and have had to assume submissive positions. One newly engaged sister we interviewed was having "trials" accepting the authority of her fiancé. She talked with the other sisters about her problems, and they advised her to search her heart for the strength to follow the Lord's will, or to take her trial to the Lord. The older sisters counseled

From the Bible—WOMAN'S PLACE

For after this manner in the old time the holy women also, who trusted in God, adorned themselves, being in subjection unto their own husbands:

Even as Sarah obeyed Abraham, calling him lord: whose daughters ye are, as long as ye do well, and are not afraid with any amazement.

Likewise, ye husbands, dwell with them according to knowledge, giving honor unto the wife, as unto the weaker vessel, and as being heirs together of the grace of life; that your prayers be not hindered.
—I PETER, 3:5-7

And Adam said, This is now bone of my bones, and flesh of my flesh: she shall be called Woman, because she was taken out of Man.
—GENESIS 2:23

Also thou shalt not approach unto a woman to uncover her nakedness, as long as she is put apart for her uncleanness.
—LEVITICUS 18:19

A gracious woman retaineth honor; and strong men retain riches.
—PROVERBS 11:16

A virtuous woman is a crown to her husband: but she that maketh ashamed is as rottenness in his bones.
—PROVERBS 12:4

Who can find a virtuous woman? For her price is far above rubies.
—PROVERBS 31:10

And I find more bitter than death the woman, whose heart is snares and nets, and her hands as bands: whoso pleaseth God shall escape from her; but the sinner shall be taken by her.
—ECCLESIASTES 7:26

Be ye followers of me, even as I also am of Christ.

Now I praise you, brethren, that ye remember me in all things, and keep the ordinances, as I delivered them to you.

But I would have you know, that the head of every man is Christ; and the head of the woman is the man; and the head of Christ is God.

Every man praying or prophesying, having his head covered, dishonoreth his head.

But every woman that prayeth or prophesieth with her head uncovered dishonoreth her head: for that is even all one as if she were shaven.

For if the woman be not covered, let her also be shorn: but if it be a shame for a woman to be shorn or shaven, let her be covered.

For a man indeed ought not to cover his head, forasmuch as he is the image and glory of God: but the woman is the glory of the man.

For the man is not of the woman; but the woman of the man.

Neither was the man created for the woman; but the woman for the man.

For this cause ought the woman to have power on her head because of the angels.

Nevertheless neither is the man without the woman, neither the woman without the man, in the Lord.

For as the woman is of the man, even so is the man also by the woman; but all things of God.

Judge in yourselves: is it comely that a woman pray unto God uncovered?

Doth not even nature itself teach you, that, if a man have long hair, it is a shame unto him?

But if a woman have long hair, it is a glory to her: for her hair is given her for a covering.
—I CORINTHIANS 11:1-15

Let the woman learn in silence with all subjection.

But I suffer not a woman to teach nor to usurp authority over the man, but to be in silence.

For Adam was first formed, then Eve.

And Adam was not deceived, but the woman being deceived was in the transgression.

Notwithstanding she shall be saved in childbearing, if they continue in faith and charity and holiness with sobriety.
—I TIMOTHY 2:11-15

For by means of a whorish woman a man is brought to a piece of bread: and the adulteress will hunt for the precious life.
—PROVERBS 6:26

And if they will learn any thing, let them ask their husbands at home: for it is a shame for women to speak in the church.
—I CORINTHIANS 14:35

Even as Sodom and Gomorrha, and the cities about them in like manner, giving themselves over to fornication, and going after strange flesh, are set forth for an example, suffering the vengeance of eternal fire.
—JUDE 7

Nevertheless, to avoid fornication, let every man have his own wife, and let every woman have her own husband.
—I CORINTHIANS 7:2

"Courtship is encouraged, but closely regulated. Close chaperoning guarantees that taboos on petting and premarital sex will be honored."

her in the familiar words: "What a blessing when you finally find your place!"

Women's conversations seem to focus on knowing that "place," instead of on such topics as men, dating and dress. It is assumed that sisters who were "new" in the Lord would experience many trials in their relationships with men. The group encourages these sisters to share their trials with "older" sisters or with pastors (all males). "Older" sisters anticipate these problems and serve as strong intentional socializing agents. They sympathize with the trials but never challenge the correctness of the rules.

We hope to return to Christ Commune next summer to investigate further changes in sex-role definitions, and in the group's operation. We interpret the changes to date in dress and work roles as part of an effort by the group's leaders to attract and keep more females. More sisters mean more brothers. No group without enough females can expect to maintain the interest and commitment of all its male members, especially ones the age of Christ Commune members (average, 21). "Nonbelieving" females would attract males from the group, even though this is strongly discouraged by the social isolation and by directives from pastors in the group.

Courtship. Indirect evidence supporting this interpretation comes from the emphasis that the group places on courtship and marriage. Such emphasis intensifies interpersonal relationships *within* the sect, which is a crucial factor in group maintenance.

Courtship is encouraged, but closely regulated. When a brother or sister develops an interest in a fellow member, he or she is expected to communicate this at first in subtle ways. One sister said that one good way to let a brother know of your interest was to give him extra-large servings of food, or just to smile at him. After the initial hints, the brother or sister openly confesses his or her interest to the other.

If the interest is mutual, the couple talks to a pastor. Then, if they have the pastor's permission, they are engaged for a six-month period that must include a three-month separation. The couple may separate immediately, or they may postpone the parting until the last three months of their engagement.

Separation. The separation is real; one of the two must leave the commune, and go to live at another of the group's houses or farms. During their time apart, each "searches the heart" to discern God's will in the matter. Engaged couples are expected and permitted to spend their free time together during the other three months. There is some hand-holding at Christ Commune, but no other overt signs of affection. Close chaperoning guarantees that taboos on petting and premarital sex will be honored. Members told us that married members interact more and more with engaged couples, thus preparing them for their future roles. Some of the engaged females we interviewed were very conscious that they were being taught the "place" of a woman. After six months, if the couple still wants to marry, one of the pastors, who has counseled them at length on sex relations and family life, performs the ceremony.

After marriage the couple might stay on at Christ Commune (the original farmhouse was used as a couples' building, with a separate bedroom for each couple), or they might go to another house or farm. Most couples move to one of the houses designated by the sect as "couples' houses."

Contraception. The concern for group maintenance evident in courtship and marriage rules carries over to procreation. Married women are expected to have children "as God wills." Even so, we found some sisters very interested in birth-control techniques. The pill is taboo, as is abortion, but the all-male leadership approve other methods including foam, condoms, rhythm, and "trusting the Lord."

At least for the time being, the group seems to have worked out a successful compromise between its theology and the rights of its female members. On our first visit the disproportionate sex ratio at Christ Commune was apparent. Only about 15 percent of the members were female. We concluded that the generally low status of women in the group contributed to this disparity. (Of course, the population from which membership is drawn [street people] has a disproportionately high number of males.) The proportion of females at Christ Commune has increased, perhaps a reflection of relaxed dress and work codes. Early this summer about 25 percent were female, and by late summer female members had increased to about 35 percent.

The members of Christ Commune usually rise at 4:30 a.m. and go to bed at 11 p.m. They meet for meals in a plain room furnished with rough benches and tables. In the room is a bookcase, in which the youthful eaters place their Bibles, and a large, wood-burning stove. In response to a gong, the sisters and the brothers file in quietly and sit at the tables. Then, with no apparent direction, some of them start singing. The songs, nearly always minor-key spirituals, are picked up by the group, which sings them in a subdued, haunting way. After several songs a person stands and offers a long and thoughtful prayer, praising God for the accomplishments of the day, thanking Him for the food (usually soup and homemade bread) and always asking that others (including the observers) be "led to accept Christ." Then the food line forms.

Satisfaction. The brothers and sisters are satisfied with their simple fare (little meat, water to drink, only peanut-butter sandwiches for lunch) and with the strenuous

"There is no talk of football games, dating and sex, politics, drugs, school, or other topics common among 21-year-olds. The talk is of God."

work. For the entire summer they work hard six days a week, hoeing and harvesting crops, repairing machinery, and keeping the profitable agricultural operation going. They do it without complaint and with praise to God for giving them the work. Nearly all the members always have their Bibles at hand. They read their Bibles during brief breaks from work and talk among themselves about the marvelous things that God, through Christ, had done for them. There is no talk of football games, dating and sex, politics, drugs, school, or other topics common among 21-year-olds. The talk is of God.

One day a week is designated as a day of rest. This day was Monday during the past summer. Members relaxed, spent time in prayer, Bible study or just visiting. Occasionally when work on the farm demanded it, teams of "volunteers" work on this day of rest. No special services are held, except for the usual daily evening Bible study.

Who are these young Christian fundamentalists? For two years we have worked with the members of Christ Commune to find out. Leaders in the commune have been extremely cooperative throughout our research, taking our appearance as "God's will." They gave us access to members and, because of the group's authority structure, they could encourage members to cooperate in interviews. As a result, we interviewed between 95 and 100 percent of available members during each of our three trips to the farm, and we have nearly 250 interviews.

Interview teams lived in the group during visits, sharing food, entering into conversations, attending nightly Bible study and prayer groups, and taking a close look at life in the group. All members of the interview teams felt extreme pressure to convert. Many members made attempts to convert us during interviews and mentioned interviewers in their extemporaneous prayers at meals and in Bible-study periods. The members were genuinely glad that we were there and went out of their way to help us with our research, even though we plainly did not share the fundamentalist Christian beliefs of the group and were gathering personal data on its members.

Education. We interviewed 88 members during the summer of 1971. Most were between 18 and 24, and the average age was 21. The youngest member was a 15-year-old girl, while the oldest was a 30-year-old male. All were Caucasian. (There was one black male who declined to be interviewed.) Sixty-seven of them had completed at least 12 years of school; the average was 12.2 years. A few had had as little as three years of formal education, while a handful had studied at graduate-school level. Twenty of the 74 males had served in the armed forces. In the two years before he joined the organization that operates Christ Commune, the typical

member had held a variety of low-paying, boring jobs.

The average member comes from a fairly affluent, fairly large family. Although 32 did not know their parents' income, 16 reported that their parents' incomes were $20,000 or more. The average reported family income was over $17,000. Nearly half of the members said that their fathers were professionals, managers, officials, or self-employed businessmen.

Thirteen members said there were six or more children in their families, and only two were only children. The average member's family had about four children. The majority said that they got along well with their mothers, but not so well with their fathers. Only 15 percent said that they felt closer to their fathers than to their mothers, and most of these were females.

Twenty-five percent reported that their parents were divorced or separated. When they were asked how their parents got along together, only 16 percent reported good relationships. Thus there emerges a pattern of fairly affluent, but unhappy homes.

Religion. As a child, the average member attended church regularly, but religion apparently did not play an integral part in his life. Eighty of the 88 reported that their families did not read the Bible at home; 76 said that their families took no part in religious observances except at Christmas and Easter; and 48 said that their parents did not turn to God when they faced crises. Members were most likely to come from Baptist or Roman Catholic homes, although many had been Methodists, Lutherans and Pentecostals.

The beliefs and practices—life-styles—of most members are different today from what they were on the outside. To demonstrate this change, we compared members' behavior and attitudes on drugs, alcohol, tobacco and sex before and after they joined the group. We understand the pitfall in attributing all changes in behavior and beliefs to group influence. For example, some members we interviewed "found Christ" before they joined the group, and their behavior changes may date from their conversion. Others gave up tobacco some time before they joined because they had turned to other drugs. Some had left drugs to go on nature trips. Even with these qualifications, the data are impressive and represent a fundamental shift in behavior.

Drugs. Although 85 percent of the members formerly had used alcohol and 67 percent had used tobacco, only two reported that they continued to use tobacco, and only one said that he used alcohol. None reported using drugs, although 90 percent said they had had previous experience with drugs. Among the former drug users, 45 percent had taken drugs daily for some time. We coded a person according to the hardest drug he or she admitted using. Twenty-one of the 79 users said they had taken opiates or cocaine; 43 others said they had

"Drugs played an important part in the former lives of 51 of the 88 we interviewed."

used hallucinogens. Only seven reported that they used only marijuana.

Drugs played an important part in the former lives of 51 members, and 65 said that most of their friends on the outside were drug users. Many said that they had started using drugs because their friends used them.

Attitudes toward premarital sex also changed dramatically. Eighty-six percent of the members we interviewed said that before joining the group they had approved of premarital sex; today only five percent approve. This change, while it is consistent with fundamentalism's belief that pleasures of the flesh are sinful, has led to difficulties. Members of both sexes say that "marriage trials" (sexual desires) are a major problem.

Sex, Use of Alcohol, Tobacco, and Drugs Before and After Joining Christ Commune (First Visit)		
	before	after
premarital sex	76(86%)	5(6%)
alcohol	75(85%)	1(1%)
tobacco	59(67%)	2(2%)
drugs	79(90%)	0(0%)

Mission. Many, for good reason, have applauded the Jesus movement for its success in changing attitudes and behavior concerning drugs, alcohol, sexual promiscuity, and other components of the counterculture. It is apparent that Christ Commune and other segments of the movement have built viable alternative life-styles, which many in our society still seek. The "new life" of the commune members deeply impressed all who worked on the project. Members had been transformed from purposeless, cynical, and self-destructive persons into loving, concerned, productive individuals with a sense of mission. The fellowship and sense of community that we encountered at Christ Commune is rare in today's world. One member summed up the sentiments of many when he said, "If I had not come to the Lord, I would either be in jail or in an institution, or maybe dead by now."

This seems to indicate that Christ Commune (and the Jesus movement in general) may serve a useful function for individuals and for society. At worst it is a deterrent to self-destruction and may often serve as a halfway house on the road back into society. But many, particularly intellectuals, continue to pass negative judgment on the entire Jesus movement. At least some of the bias is, we feel, simply irrational, antireligion sentiment. Some want nothing to do with religion on any terms, and they seem to resent the fact that religion can do some good. However, we would readily admit that some of our findings could substantiate a negative evalu-

ation of the movement and of Christ Commune in particular. Those opposed to the movement could point to the members' political interest, alienation, and personality assessment.

Politics. Before they joined the group, 42 of the members we interviewed in 1971 said they were radicals or liberals (although only two had led political demonstrations). Another 14 claimed to be moderates or conservatives. Only 27 said they had no interest in politics when they lived on the outside. When we asked them to categorize themselves at the time of the interview, only four claimed to be liberals or radicals, and 71 said "nothing" or that they had lost all interest in politics.

We asked them how one could change society if he took no part in politics, and they gave us replies consistent with religious fundamentalism. "The only way to change society is to change men's hearts," said one. "Politics is man's way not God's way, and it (politics) has failed," said another. We often heard references to the Second Coming of Christ, which most members believe to be imminent, making energy spent on politics a waste of time. Our second visit to the group was during the hotly contested 1972 California primary, but not a single member mentioned this crucial contest. No one was interested.

Political Self-Characterization Before and After Joining Christ Commune (First Visit)			
Characterize self as:	before joining	after joining	change
conservative	8	6	−25%
moderate	6	5	−17%
liberal	19	1	−95%
radical	23	3	−87%
nothing, don't care	27	71	+163%
total	83*	86	

*Totals differ because some information was not ascertained. Eighty eight were interviewed.

Alienation. Such political apathy puts the group (and most other segments of the Jesus movement) in the position of indirectly supporting the political status quo. Members' responses to some items in a preliminary alienation scale (based on Peter Berger's *The Sacred Canopy*) that we used during our first visit confirmed this indirect support.

When we asked, "Do you think that God has a hand in the nomination and election of our country's leaders?" 77 said yes, or yes with some qualifications. Only five said no, or qualified a no answer. When asked, "Do you think that the leaders of our country are guided by God in making decisions?" they gave 50 yes or qualified-yes

" 'I am confident in the Lord, but I am not confident in myself. Therefore I do not have self-confidence.' "

responses, and 27 no or qualified-no responses. When we asked members, "Do you think it is a sin to break a law of the land?" 75 said yes or qualified yes, and only seven said no, or qualified no. When we asked, "Do you think the U.S. generally is an instrument of God in the area of world politics?" 38 said yes or qualified yes, and 43 said no or qualified no. Berger's theory about the alienating effects of religious beliefs predicts that the members of Christ Commune would be likely to answer these questions with a strong yes.

But we found it surprising that so many agreed to this last question, which relates closely to the Vietnam conflict. It is difficult to assess data from the alienation scale. It is possible, of course, that the members were alienated from the institutional structure *before* they joined the Jesus movement, and that their joining simply gave a religious flavor to their alienation. This is information we hope to concentrate on in the future.

Personality. The data that we gathered on the personality patterns of members run into the same objections. We have no way of knowing whether members' personalities changed when they joined, or whether the patterns they reported had been established before they joined the group.

At an evening prayer meeting during our first visit, we administered Gough's Adjective Check List (ACL) which asks a person to choose from a list of 300 adjectives, both positive and negative, those words that he feels best describe him.

We compared our data from Christ Commune with ACL data from a sample of 1,600 college students of similar age, education, and past socioeconomic circumstances. Comparison of standard scores from the two groups suggests that members of Christ Commune are significantly less defensive and less self-confident than their college counterparts. The Christ-Commune group also scored significantly lower on personal adjustment and on all these needs: for achievement, dominance, endurance, order, intraception (a low scorer tends to become bored or impatient when direct action is impossible), affiliation, heterosexuality and change. Group members scored significantly higher than college students on readiness to submit to counseling and on the need for succor and abasement. Per-

sons in the religious group also checked significantly fewer favorable adjectives and more unfavorable adjectives than persons in the college sample did.

Prophecy. Some might say that those ACL results indicate that life in Christ Commune (or in the Jesus movement) leads to maladaptive and deficient personality patterns; however, the results may reflect a greater honesty and frankness in self-evaluation by the commune members than the comparison group showed. Also, the ideology of Christian fundamentalism explicitly suggests that man is sinful and degraded. Thus the commune respondents may have tried to evaluate themselves "the way they were supposed to be," instead of the way they saw themselves. Such attempts at negative self-definition would probably function as self-fulfilling prophecy.

This process seemed to be operating in an interview that took place on the first day of our second visit. An interviewer described one sister's struggle to respond to a question on one of the inventories:

"The first person I interviewed was a girl named May Woods. She had an extreme amount of difficulty with one question on the questionnaire: 'I feel self-confident.' She kept talking to herself, trying to figure out what to do about this question. She kept saying things like, 'I'm confident in the Lord, but I'm not confident in myself.' She said this over and over, and she circled and erased her answer several times. Twice she looked up and spoke to me and said something to this effect, 'This is really a tough question. This is really a hard question. I'm having trouble with this question.' And finally she worked it out in a very logical fashion after at least five minutes of fretting over it by saying audibly as she talked to herself, 'I am confident in the Lord, but I am not confident in myself. Therefore I do not have self-confidence.' She circled 'not at all' with reference to that question."

Cooperation. Besides the usual problems of data interpretation another substantial issue must be raised. Some would accept the ACL results as valid and go on to criticize the commune for producing such personality patterns. These same critics propose life-styles that differ from the competitive, aggressive, achievement orientation of our society. We suggest that the Christ Commune might have developed a viable life-style that differs remarkably from what our culture ex-

pects. Perhaps we should congratulate them for developing a way of life that encourages cooperation and self-abasement instead of competition and dominance. We are not ready at this time to take a stand on the issue. The question of the value of such personality patterns is still open. On our two visits there this past summer we again gave members the Adjective Check List and added other personality inventories, but we have not completed analyzing this data.

Mechanism. If, as seems apparent, the brothers and sisters do experience profound changes of personality when they join the sect that operates Christ Commune, interesting questions arise about how the changes occur. We found the thought-reform research of Robert Jay Lifton and others very helpful in understanding the mechanisms of personality change. Lifton's studies of the reform of Chinese intellectuals seem particularly apropos. He developed a three-step model:

1 the great togetherness: group identification;
2 the closing in of the milieu: the period of emotional conflict; and
3 submission and rebirth.

Lifton's analysis comes from an examination of what went on at the Chinese revolutionary universities that were set up between 1948 and 1952. These "universities" were quite large, sometimes involving up to 4,000 persons in highly organized, authoritarian situations. At the start of a session (which lasted approximately six months) administrators warmly greeted participants and told them to spend several days getting to know members of their small groups of about six to 10 persons. Lifton points out that a high *esprit de corps* developed as members openly exchanged personal information and discussed why they were attending the "university."

Thus, we see the development of a new reference group for the persons involved—something similar to what happens upon first contact with some Jesus-movement groups, including Christ Commune. Such groups are friendly and open, and members express genuine concern for the visitor who crashes at the group's residence—they treat him as an important person.

Step 1. Close personal ties begin to develop between prospects and members,

"The prospect either leaves or he submits to group pressures and accepts the group's world view."

strengthening the great "togetherness." Many prospects have come from the dog-eat-dog world of drug-oriented communities or have been moving around the country. Such situations prevent close relationships from developing and the close ties become meaningful. Our data indicate that prospects often stay on at Christ Commune because of the primary relationships that develop; in order to stay successfully, they *must* begin to show interest in the group's ideology.

A prospect begins by studying the Bible, attending prayer groups, and working with the members in the fields. These activities allow him to demonstrate his interest in the group. They also teach him how to act and believe if he wants to remain in the group. The activities affect the prospect as the formal courses and group discussions in the revolutionary universities affected the Chinese intellectuals. In both situations group leaders present acceptable views and help others to rationalize them during the group discussions.

Step 2. The prevailing harmonious situation soon changes drastically. In Lifton's terms, there is a "closing in of the milieu." The group expects the prospect to make progress toward becoming a "committed Christian," and progress follows a fairly rigid timetable. The group brings pressure, both subtle and overt, on the novice, letting him know what kind of belief and behavior the group expects. The leaders at Christ Commune allow an outsider to remain for three or four days without indicating that he is "accepting Christ." After this period, if he still shows no sign that he seriously considers "taking Jesus," they ask him to leave. Commune leaders say that their goal is to bring people to Christ, and that the nonaccepting person would feel uncomfortable unless he shared the beliefs of the others.

Group members explain over and over the value in taking Christ (happiness and, implicitly, acceptance), and the reasons for the difficulty (pride, sinfulness, pleasures of this world, etc.). When a prospect responds there is celebration and the group offers social rewards (warmth, acceptance, addressing the person as "brother" or "sister").

Pressure. The pressure often is successful because the prospect places a high value on the primary relationships that he has developed among the members. The high value members place on such relationships showed up when 84 percent of members we interviewed on our first visit said that if they had to leave the commune they would miss most the fellowship of the brothers and sisters.

All of us who interviewed members came under such pressure that we felt the need to withdraw at least once a day in order to reaffirm our own world views. If trained and fairly objective observers began to succumb to the group influences, then the effect on participants without strong personalities or alternative reference groups must be great.

A simple way of describing the step of closure is to say that the prospect, after a certain length of time, no longer occupies the privileged newcomer status. He must occupy a new role of interested person which he may hold for an indeterminate period and which eventually leads to the role of "convert."

Step 3. Conversion comes about through "submission and rebirth." The prospect either leaves or he submits to group pressures and accepts the group's world view. This world view contains many elements that aid him in making a proper self-definition and in knowing what actions to take and beliefs to hold as a consequence of his conversion. The new member publicly confesses—submits. (Perhaps he watches members demonstrate the ritual first.) After denying his past and his old self, he commits himself to the future and a new self. This is his rebirth. For some members at Christ Commune, conversion seems to have been a going home—more a reaffirmation of earlier-held values than a learning of things completely new. For these members who have grown up in conservative or fundamentalist churches, the thought-reform process is particularly effective.

Winning converts is the first step.
Keeping them is the second.

Here again the organization that runs Christ Commune has been successful. The disaffiliation rate is low; even though the work at the commune is difficult and boring only about 10 percent of the members drop out.

Christ Commune's emphasis on community is a major element in the group's success. Members must make a total commitment and give up all material things, never to reclaim them. The group encourages members to break their outside ties, and members may not leave or even make a phone call without receiving a pastor's permission.

The physical isolation of the farm (five miles from a small town) reinforces the social isolation.

Disruption. Communal living and working also builds community. Group leaders structure the daily work so that brothers and sisters toil side by side, never alone. The courtship and marriage rules give needed structure in the troublesome area of sex relations, which might cause group disruption. The organization also has established two schools—kindergarten and elementary—for the 50 to 100 children of members. Thus the group plans to educate their children in the ways of the sect.

While it has developed much elaborate structure, Christ Commune also has shown a willingness to make necessary changes. It has relaxed rules governing sex roles. It has branched out into unknown areas such as farming or fishing as opportunities arose or—they say—"as God guides us."

Recognition. Christ Commune is a successful farming operation that fills its contracts and buys the supplies it needs. The Federal Government has declared it eligible for commodity foods (homemade bread at every meal is made from these). It is a county labor camp (which means that members get free medical care); it is a state-designated conscientious-objector alternative-service center; it has Government-approved nonprofit status, with attendant privileges. The state courts recognize Christ Commune and occasionally remand juvenile delinquents to its custody.

The successful agricultural operation of Christ Commune is a major reason for our confidence in the group's future. It provides a solid financial basis and furnishes money for missionary work. As funds come in, teams go into new areas to establish houses, which serve as recruitment centers.

Another reason Christ Commune will last is the members themselves. They are alienated from institutional society, and are disinterested in it (except as a pool of potential converts). They are noncompetitive, anti-intellectual, and otherworldly. In short, either by accident or design they are unlikely to drift back into ordinary society. Christ Commune and the group it serves will be around for a long time.

30

GROUPTHINK

by Irving L. Janis

The idea of "groupthink" occurred to me while reading Arthur M. Schlesinger's chapters on the Bay of Pigs in *A Thousand Days*. At first I was puzzled: How could bright men like John F. Kennedy and his advisers be taken in by such a stupid, patchwork plan as the one presented to them by the C.I.A. representatives? I began wondering if some psychological contagion of complacency might have interfered with their mental alertness.

I kept thinking about this notion until one day I found myself talking about it in a seminar I was conducting at Yale on the psychology of small groups. I suggested that the poor decision-making performance of those high officials might be akin to the lapses in judgment of ordinary citizens who become more concerned with retaining the approval of the fellow members of their work group than with coming up with good solutions to the tasks at hand.

When I re-read Schlesinger's account I was struck by many further observations that fit into exactly the pattern of concurrence-seeking that has impressed me in my research on other face-to-face groups when a "we" feeling of solidarity is running high. I concluded that a group process was subtly at work in Kennedy's team which prevented the members from debating the real issues posed by the C.I.A.'s plan and from carefully appraising its serious risks.

By now I was sufficiently fascinated by what I called the "groupthink" hypothesis to start looking into similar historic fiascoes. I selected for intensive analysis three that were made during the administrations of three other American presidents: Franklin D. Roosevelt (failure to be prepared for Pearl Harbor), Harry S. Truman (the invasion of North Korea)

Irving L. Janis, professor of psychology at Yale, teaches courses in attitude change, decision-making, leadership and small-group behavior. This material is adapted from his "Victims of Groupthink: A Psychological Study of Foreign Policy Decisions and Fiascoes," just published by Houghton Mifflin.

and Lyndon B. Johnson (escalation of the Vietnam war). Each decision was a group product, issuing from a series of meetings held by a small and cohesive group of government officials and advisers. In each case I found the same kind of detrimental group process that was at work in the Bay of Pigs decision.

In my earlier research with ordinary citizens I had been impressed by the effects—both unfavorable and favorable—of the social pressures that develop in cohesive groups: in infantry platoons, air crews, therapy groups, seminars and self-study or encounter groups. Members tend to evolve informal objectives to preserve friendly intra-group relations, and this becomes part of the hidden agenda at their meetings. When conducting research on groups of heavy smokers, for example, at a clinic established to help people stop smoking, I noticed a seemingly irrational tendency for the members to exert pressure on each other to increase their smoking as the time for the final meeting approached. This appeared to be a collusive effort to display mutual dependence and resistance to the termination of the sessions.

Sometimes, even long before the final separation, pressures toward uniformity subverted the fundamental purpose. At the second meeting of one group of smokers, consisting of 12 middle-class American men and women, two of the most dominant members took the position that heavy smoking was an almost incurable addiction. Most of the others soon agreed that nobody could be expected to cut down drastically. One man took issue with this consensus, arguing that he had stopped smoking since joining the group and that everyone else could do the same. His declaration was followed by an angry discussion. Most of the others ganged up against the man who was deviating from the consensus.

At the next meeting the deviant announced that he had made an important

decision. "When I joined," he said, "I agreed to follow the two main rules required by the clinic—to make a conscientious effort to stop smoking, and to attend every meeting. But I have learned that you can only follow one of the rules, not both. I will continue to attend every meeting but I have gone back to smoking two packs a day and I won't make any effort to stop again until after the last meeting." Whereupon the other members applauded, welcoming him back to the fold.

No one mentioned that the whole point of the meetings was to help each person to cut down as rapidly as possible. As a psychological consultant to the group, I tried to call this to the members' attention and so did my collaborator, Dr. Michael Kahn. But the members ignored our comments and reiterated their consensus that heavy smoking was an addiction from which no one would be cured except by cutting down gradually over a long period of time.

This episode—an extreme form of groupthink—was only one manifestation of a general pattern that the group displayed. At every meeting the members were amiable, reasserted their warm feelings of solidarity and sought concurrence on every important topic, with no reappearance of the unpleasant bickering that would spoil the cozy atmosphere. This tendency could be maintained, however, only at the expense of ignoring realistic challenges—like those posed by the psychologists.

The term "groupthink" is of the same order as the words in the "newspeak" vocabulary that George Orwell uses in *1984*—a vocabulary with terms such as "doublethink" and "crimethink." By putting "groupthink" with those Orwellian words, I realize that it takes on an invidious connotation. This is intentional: groupthink refers to a deterioration of mental efficiency, reality testing and moral judgment that results from in-group pressures.

A Yale psychologist isolates the disease that caused our worst foreign policy fiascoes: a compulsion by the decision-makers to have each other's approval, even at the cost of critical thinking.

form of morality. That loyalty requires each member to avoid raising controversial issues, questioning weak arguments or calling a halt to soft-headed thinking.

Paradoxically, soft-headed groups are likely to be extremely hard-hearted toward out-groups and enemies. In dealing with a rival nation, policy-makers constituting an amiable group find it relatively easy to authorize dehumanizing solutions such as large-scale bombings. An affable group of government officials is unlikely to pursue the difficult issues that arise when alternatives to a harsh military solution come up for discussion. Nor are they inclined to raise ethical issues that imply that this "fine group of ours, with its humanitarianism and its high-minded principles, could adopt a course that is inhumane and immoral."

The greater the threat to the self-esteem of the members of a cohesive group, the greater will be their inclination to resort to concurrence-seeking at the expense of critical thinking. Symptoms of groupthink will therefore be found most often when a decision poses a moral dilemma, especially if the most advantageous course requires the policy-makers to violate their own standards of humanitarian behavior. Each member is likely to become more dependent than ever on the in-group for maintaining his self-image as a decent human being and will therefore be more strongly motivated to maintain group unity by striving for concurrence.

Although it is risky to make huge inferential leaps from theory to practice, we should not be inhibited from drawing tentative inferences from these fiascoes. Perhaps the worst mistakes can be prevented if we take steps to avoid the circumstances in which groupthink is most likely to flourish. But all the prescriptive hypotheses that follow must be validated by systematic research before they can be applied with any confidence.

The leader of a policy-forming group should, for example, assign the role of critical evaluator to each member, encouraging the group to give high priority to airing objections and doubts. He should also be impartial at the outset, instead of stating his own preferences and

When I investigated the Bay of Pigs invasion and other fiascoes, I found that there were at least six major defects in decision-making which contributed to failures to solve problems adequately.

First, the group's discussions were limited to a few alternatives (often only two) without a survey of the full range of alternatives. Second, the members failed to re-examine their initial decision from the standpoint of non-obvious drawbacks that had not been originally considered. Third, they neglected courses of action initially evaluated as unsatisfactory; they almost never discussed whether they had overlooked any non-obvious gains.

Fourth, members made little or no attempt to obtain information from experts who could supply sound estimates of losses and gains to be expected from alternative courses. Fifth, selective bias was shown in the way the members reacted to information and judgments from experts, the media and outside critics; they were only interested in facts and opinions that supported their preferred policy. Finally, they spent little time deliberating how the policy might be hindered by bureaucratic inertia, sabotaged by political opponents or derailed by the accidents that happen to the best of well-laid plans. Consequently, they failed to work out contingency plans to cope with foreseeable setbacks that could endanger their success.

I was surprised by the extent to which the groups involved in these fiascoes adhered to group norms and pressures toward uniformity, even when their policy was working badly and had unintended consequences that disturbed the conscience of the members. Members consider loyalty to the group the highest expectations. He should limit his briefings to unbiased statements about the scope of the problem and the limitations of available resources.

The organization should routinely establish several independent planning and evaluation groups to work on the same policy question, each carrying out its deliberations under a different leader.

One or more qualified colleagues within the organization who are not core members of the policy-making group should be invited to each meeting and encouraged to challenge the views of the core members.

At every meeting, at least one member should be assigned the role of devil's advocate, to function like a good lawyer in challenging the testimony of those who advocate the majority position.

Whenever the policy issue involves relations with a rival nation, a sizable block of time should be spent surveying all warning signals from the rivals and constructing alternative scenarios.

After reaching a preliminary consensus the policy-making group should hold a "second chance" meeting at which all the members are expected to express their residual doubts and to rethink the entire issue They might take as their model a statement made by Alfred P. Sloan, a former chairman of General Motors, at a meeting of policymakers:

"Gentlemen, I take it we are all in complete agreement on the decision here. Then I propose we postpone further discussion until our next meeting to give ourselves time to develop disagreement and perhaps gain some understanding of what the decision is all about."

It might not be a bad idea for the second-chance meeting to take place in a relaxed atmosphere far from the executive suite, perhaps over drinks. According to a report by Herodotus dating from about 450 B.C., whenever the ancient Persians made a decision following sober deliberations, they would always reconsider the matter under the influence of wine. Tacitus claimed that during Roman times the Germans also had a custom of arriving at each decision twice—once sober, once drunk.

Some institutionalized form of allowing second thoughts to be freely expressed might be remarkably effective for breaking down a false sense of unanimity and related illusions, without endangering anyone's reputation or liver.

Pearl Harbor: Geniality and Security

On the night of Dec. 6, 1941—just 12 hours before the Japanese struck—Admiral Husband E. Kimmel (Commander in Chief of the Pacific Fleet) attended a dinner party given by his old crony, Rear Admiral H. Fairfax Leary, and his wife. Other members of the in-group of naval commanders and their wives were also present. Seated next to Admiral Kimmel was Fanny Halsey, wife of Admiral Halsey, who had left Hawaii to take his task force to the Far East. Mrs. Halsey said that she was certain the Japanese were going to attack. "She was a brilliant woman," according to Captain Joel Bunkley, who described the party, "but everybody thought she was crazy."

Admiral Leary at a naval inquiry in 1944, summarized the complacency at that dinner party and at the daily conferences held by Admiral Kimmel during the preceding weeks. When asked whether any thought had been given to the possibility of a surprise attack by the Japanese, he said, "We all felt that the contingency was remote . . . and the feeling strongly existed that the Fleet would have adequate warning of any chance of an air attack." The same attitude was epitomized in testimony given by Captain J. B. Earle, chief of staff, Fourteenth Naval District. "Somehow or other," he said, "we always felt that 'it couldn't happen here.'"

From the consistent testimony given by Admiral Kimmel's advisers, they all acted on the basis of an "unwarranted feeling of immunity from attack," though they had been given a series of impressive warnings that they should be prepared for war with Japan.

Most illuminating of the norm-setting behavior that contributed to the complacency of Kimmel's in-group is a brief exchange between Admiral Kimmel and Lieutenant Commander Layton. Perturbed by the loss of radio contact with the Japanese aircraft carriers, Admiral Kimmel asked Layton on Dec. 1, 1941, to check with the Far East Command for additional information. The next day, discussing the lost carriers again with Layton, he remarked jokingly: "What, you don't know where the carriers are?

Do you mean to say that they could be rounding Diamond Head [at Honolulu] and you wouldn't know it?" Layton said he hoped they would be sighted well before that.

This exchange implies an "atmosphere of geniality and security." Having relegated the Japanese threat to the category of laughing matters, the admiral was making it clear that he would be inclined to laugh derisively at anyone who thought otherwise. "I did not at any time suggest," Layton later acknowledged at a Congressional hearing, "that the Japanese carriers were under radio silence approaching Oahu. I wish I had."

But the admiral's foolish little joke may have induced Layton to remain silent about any vague, lingering doubts he may have had. Either man would risk the scornful laughter of the other—whether expressed to his face or behind his back—if he were to express second thoughts such as, "Seriously, though, shouldn't we do something about the slight possibility that those carriers might *really* be headed this way?" Because this ominous inference was never drawn, not a single reconnaissance plane was sent out to the north of the Hawaiian Islands, allowing the Japanese to win the incredible gamble they were taking in trying to send their aircraft carriers within bombing distance of Pearl Harbor without being detected.

That joking exchange was merely the visible part of a huge iceberg of solid faith in Pearl Harbor's invulnerability. If a few warm advocates of preparedness had been within the Navy group, steamed up by the accumulating warning signals, they might have been able to melt it. But they would certainly have had a cold reception. To urge a full alert would have required presenting unwelcome arguments that countered the myth of Pearl Harbor's impregnability. Anyone who was tempted to do so knew that he would be deviating from the group norm: the others were likely to consider him "crazy," just as the in-group regarded Mrs. Halsey at the dinner party on the eve of the disaster when she announced her deviant opinion that the Japanese would attack.

A Perfect Fiasco: The Bay of Pigs

Why did President Kennedy's main advisers, whom he had selected as core members of his team, fail to pursue the issues sufficiently to discover the shaky ground on which the faulty assumptions of the Cuban invasion plan rested? Why didn't they pose a barrage of penetrating and embarrassing questions to the representatives of the C.I.A. and the Joint Chiefs of Staff? Why were they taken in by the incomplete and inconsistent answers they were given in response to the relatively few critical questions they raised?

Schlesinger says that "for all the utter irrationality with which retrospect endowed the project, it had a certain queer logic at the time as it emerged from the bowels of government." Why? What was the source of the queer logic" with which the plan was endowed? If the available accounts describe the deliberations accurately, many typical symptoms of groupthink can be discerned among the members of the Kennedy team: an illusion of invulnerability, a collective effort to rationalize their decision, an unquestioned belief in the group's inherent morality, a stereotyped view of enemy leaders as too evil to warrant genuine attempts to negotiate, and the emergence of self-appointed mind-guards.

Robert Kennedy, for example, who had been constantly informed about the Cuban invasion plan, asked Schlesinger privately why he was opposed. The President's brother listened coldly and then said: "You may be right or you may be wrong, but the President has made his mind up. Don't push it any further. Now is the time for everyone to help him all they can."

Here is a symptom of groupthink, displayed by a highly intelligent man whose ethical code committed him to freedom of dissent.

Robert Kennedy was functioning in a self-appointed role that I call being a "mind-guard." Just as a bodyguard protects the President and other high officials from physical harm, a mind-guard protects them from thoughts that might damage their confidence in the soundness of the policies which they are about to launch.

Escalation in Vietnam: How Could It Happen?

A highly revealing episode occurred soon after Robert McNamara told a Senate committee some impressive facts about the ineffectiveness of the bombings. President Johnson made a number of bitter comments about McNamara's statement. "That military genius, McNamara, has gone dovish on me," he complained to one Senator. To someone on his White House staff he spoke even more heatedly, accusing McNamara of playing into the hands of the enemy. He drew the analogy of "a man trying to sell his house while one of his sons went to the prospective buyer to point out that there were leaks in the basement."

This strongly suggests that Johnson regarded his in-group of policy advisers as a family and its leading dissident member as an irresponsible son who was sabotaging the family's interest. Underlying this revealing imagery are two implicit assumptions that epitomize groupthink: We are a good group, so any deceitful acts that we perpetrate are fully justified. Anyone who is unwilling to distort the truth to help us is disloyal.

This is only one of the many examples of how groupthink was manifested in Johnson's inner circle.

31

HOW GROUPS INTENSIFY OPINIONS

Associating with like-minded people may help you lose weight
or stop smoking, but it can also increase your prejudices.

DAVID G. MYERS

We live our lives within small groups. From infancy through old age we move in congenial groups whose attitudes and interests we generally share. Their influence is powerful. Several years ago Yale psychologist William McGuire concluded that the mass media have less impact on opinion than do informal conversations with family, friends, neighbors, and co-workers.

Recently, the inclination toward forming small groups has become less casual. The act of people coming together to discuss issues and solve problems seems increasingly integral to our existence. Alcoholics, dieters, and educators draw on the presumed power of mutual assistance typical of a small group, and individual psychotherapy moves more and more in the direction of various group therapies. Group-oriented management methods are displacing authoritarian control.

It is no secret that people associate with others whose attitudes and values are similar to their own. Most of us need only look at our circle of friends to illustrate this point. When people come together in a group, whether it be to

David G. Myers *is professor of psychology at Hope College in Holland, Michigan. A longer version of this article recently won the Gordon Allport Prize, awarded for the best paper of the year on intergroup relations. Myers' book* The Human Puzzle *was published by Harper & Row in 1978.*

combat a drinking problem, to lose weight, or to make a decision regarding management policy, members are apt to carry certain shared inclinations. In the case of losing weight, they have a mutual desire to stop their excessive eating.

When group members share common attitudes, does discussion do anything more than converge their opinions? Social psychologists have found that it does. As members of diet groups discuss their mutual problem, their shared desire to cut their food consumption may strengthen. In commu-

Bill Longcore

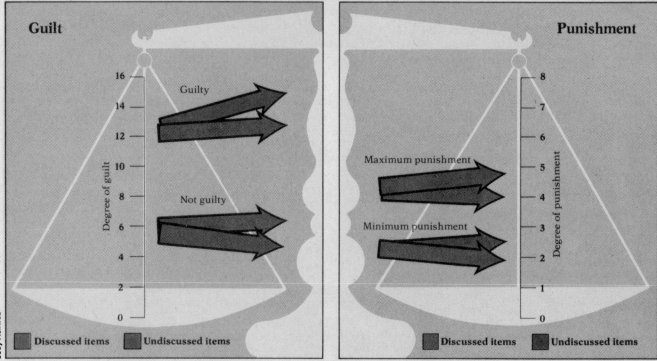

Joey Reinlieb

Discussion by juries magnifies the jurors' initial judgments. When simulated juries were asked to discuss traffic cases in which the defendants were obviously guilty, deliberation increased the jurors' certainty of guilt and led them to recommend harsher punishment. When the defendant was obviously innocent, the opposite occurred.

nity controversies, according to sociologist James Coleman, like-minded people increasingly associate with one another as a conflict evolves, amplifying their shared tendencies. The President's Commission on Campus Unrest noted the same dynamic at work during the evolution of the radical student movement in the 1960s. Similarly, investigators of gang delinquency have observed a process of mutual reinforcement within neighborhood gangs whose members have a common socioeconomic and ethnic background. Shakespeare portrayed the polarizing power of the like-minded group when he described Julius Caesar's followers:

Antony: Kind souls, what weep you when you but behold
Our Caesar's vesture wounded? Look you here,
Here is himself, marr'd, as you see, with traitors.
First Citizen: O piteous spectacle!
Second Citizen: O noble Caesar!
Third Citizen: O woeful day!
Fourth Citizen: O traitors, villains!
First Citizen: O most bloody sight!

Second Citizen: We will be revenged!
All: Revenge! About! Seek! Burn! Fire! Kill!
Slay! Let not a traitor live!

Observations of small groups, together with recent experiments in social psychology, have provided insights concerning the effects of talking in small groups. Researchers now realize that discussion generally strengthens the average inclination held by group members before the discussion. To test this theory of group polarization, researchers have asked individuals to discuss statements that most people like themselves either favor or oppose.

In France, Serge Moscovici and Marisa Zavalloni observed that discussion enhanced French students' initially positive attitude toward de Gaulle and negative attitude toward Americans. Likewise, Willem Doise found that discussion magnified negative attitudes that some French architectural students had toward their school. Martin Kaplan and I studied the effect of simulated jury deliber-

ations in an attempt to find out whether decisions following jury deliberations differed in any predictable way from the average initial opinions of individual jury members. We asked people to discuss traffic cases in which the defendant obviously appeared either guilty or innocent. In cases where the defendant appeared not guilty, the "jurors," after deliberation, became even more definite in their judgments of innocence and more lenient in their recommended punishments. In cases where the defendant seemed guilty, deliberation moved the jurors toward harsher judgments.

Another research strategy has been to pick issues where opinion is mixed and then isolate those who share attitudes in common. Once each person's opinion is established, he or she is assigned to a group of like-minded people, where the statement is discussed. The purpose is to see whether discussion with similarly minded people polarizes the attitude gap between the two groups.

In one of my own experiments studying polarization, I separated college students into "chauvinist" and "feminist" groups. I then introduced topics on the role of women and asked each group to discuss them—for instance, the argument that women with children should not work outside the home if they are not required to for financial reasons. After each group discussed such topics, their attitudes on them were even further apart than they were before. Apparently the discussion among the liberal, feminist-oriented groups served as a consciousness-raising session.

George Bishop and I set up groups of relatively prejudiced and unprejudiced high-school students and asked them to respond—both before and after discussion—to issues involving racial attitudes, such as property rights versus open housing. We found that discussion among like-minded students increased the initial gap between the two groups.

The reliability of these experiments established, we were prompted to examine group polarization outside the laboratory. It is difficult to disentangle cause and effect when observing natural occurrences, but I believe there are many parallels between the laboratory situation and everyday life. Kenneth Feldman and Theodore Newcomb have found, for example, that initial differences among students in attitudes and intellectual ability become accentuated as they progress through college. Likewise, attitude differences between those who belong to a fraternity and those who do not are modest at the freshman level and more pronounced in the senior year. This effect seems at least partly a result of the tendency of group members to reinforce their shared dispositions.

One discouraging example of the power implicit in group polarization is its potential for producing destructive governmental decisions. In situations fraught with possible conflict, individuals tend to justify their behavior, especially after discussion within their group. The resulting group-enhanced

self-justification is part of the "group-think" process that Irving Janis proposed could help explain the failure of certain political and military decisions, namely the escalation of the Vietnam War.

Robert Riley and Thomas Pettigrew have observed that dramatic events can polarize attitudes also. Surveys of white Texans—before and after the 1957 desegregation of the Little Rock, Arkansas, schools, the assassination of Martin Luther King, Jr., and the subsequent civil disorders in 1968—revealed that the opinions of various groups tended to polarize following the dramatic events. When measuring attitudes before the events, for instance, Riley and Pettigrew found that lower-class groups tended to be more segregationist than middle-class ones, and that East Texans favored segregation more than West Texans. After the assassination and the civil disorders, these group differences became even greater as each group became more convinced of what it believed before the events.

Riley and Pettigrew also found that the forms of racial contact most acceptable prior to these events, such as riding the same bus, were even more acceptable after the turmoil and that the least acceptable realms of contact, such as rooming together in college, became even less so. Dramatic events apparently stimulate discussions that intensify the locally dominant point of view. In the absence of dramatic events and the accompanying group discussion, influences common to all groups, such as television or economic and international events, may reduce polarization at a local level.

Religious fellowship provides another example of group polarization; it heightens religious identity, especially when members of a religious body concentrate their interaction among themselves. A chief feature of many religious movements is the mutual strengthening provided by small, interacting groups. An example of this goes back to early Christianity. The apostles Peter and Paul, freed from jail, met with their fellow believers and then went out to proclaim their mes-

sage with even greater boldness. Whether the religious group consists of born-again Christians or members of a Catholic religious order, the ardor and devoutness of the group often enhances that of its individual members.

Why polarization takes place at all has become a tantalizing puzzle for a number of social psychologists. Why do groups of people seem to adopt stances more exaggerated than those held by their average individual members? The answer might provide new insights into how people influence one another.

It has been suggested that the role of the strong leader is the source of group polarization. The reasoning is that one person in a group probably emerges as the most forceful member and sways the others. Although it is indeed true that some members of a group are more verbal and assertive than others, this argument assumes that those who emerge as leaders express the exaggerated view that the group will later reach. Yet we have found that leaders are not always extreme in their views.

Among several other possible explanations, two have survived critical scrutiny. One of these has to do with the arguments presented during a discussion, the other with how members of a group view themselves vis-à-vis other members during a discussion. In the former, group discussion permits a pooling of ideas, most of which favor the dominant viewpoint. These arguments may include persuasive points that some group members had not previously considered.

To examine this theory, researchers have tried to discover what importance arguments play in a discussion. They have done this both by controlling the introduction of arguments and by analyzing their content. When a person says "I feel so-and-so about this," the statement typically combines information about the person's arguments regarding the issue with information about the person's position on the issue. Disentangling these two factors, it has been found that when people hear relevant arguments but gain no informa-

People are so eager to be seen in a favorable light that they will change the opinions they express—especially if others share their inclinations.

tion about the stands that other people assume, they still shift their positions. Arguments are apparently the principal factor in polarizing attitudes.

Researchers have also examined the content of the arguments. Studies by Amiram Vinokur, Eugene Burnstein, and our own laboratory confirm that the arguments presented in a group mostly favor the group's initial preference. The amount of shift can be predicted by mathematical models that combine the direction, cogency, and novelty of the expressed arguments. New arguments, for example, tend to have more influence over a group than typical ones.

The models also explain why a group that is already quite extreme in its views before discussion will often not show as much polarization as a less extreme group. A well-polarized group has less to learn because members already share the most persuasive arguments. On the other hand, less polarized groups have more to learn from exchanging arguments.

Researchers have also found that active participation in discussion elicits more attitude change than does passive eavesdropping. Both participants and observers hear the same ideas, but when participants must put them into their own words, the resulting verbal commitment seems to magnify the impact of the discussion. This finding parallels attitude research done by Anthony Greenwald showing that people who actively reformulate a persuasive message in their own words are most influenced by it.

In the second explanation of polarization, social comparison plays an important role. People want to be perceived favorably and will modify their expressed opinions to this end, especially if they discover that other people share their inclinations. In several experiments, we have shown people either the true average response or the distribution of others' responses, some-

times providing them with a peek at "early returns" from a survey. This simple exposure to others' positions stimulates a small polarization. Instead of simply joining the crowd, as many conformity experiments have found, the people in our experiments responded with statements slightly more extreme than the average.

Perhaps this dynamic has contributed to the tax revolt that has gained momentum in recent months. As a result of California's Proposition 13, many people have found that their antitax sentiments are shared more widely than they previously imagined. This new information about others' attitudes seems to have magnified antitaxation opinions and emboldened people to express them more openly.

The tendency to "one-up" the observed norm may reflect the fact that people want to view and present themselves as better than the average person. National surveys show that most business people perceive the average business person as less ethical than themselves. Most community residents see their friends and neighbors as more racially prejudiced than themselves. These beliefs are, of course, distorted—the average person is not better than the average person. In a group situation, the same thing may be true. After sensing the predominant inclination of a group, a member may attempt to get away from the average inclination but still be looked upon favorably by espousing an opinion a bit more extreme than the consensus.

This shift allows people to differentiate themselves within a group, but only to a small extent—and in the approved direction. As experiments by Howard Fromkin have shown, people feel better when they see themselves as being unique, and they will act in ways that create a sense of individuality.

Researchers have obtained interest-

ing results from several discussion experiments that show an accentuation of the average response is not inevitable. When people are given a choice between behaving selfishly and altruistically, group interaction often brings out their selfish inclinations, even if these have not surfaced before the discussion. But most of these results are consistent with the explanation of group polarization; even if social inhibitions cause people to conceal their private leanings, discussion may accentuate such inclinations.

Social comparison and information processing can explain group polarization and its variants. Group interaction affects responses when people want to act in a given way but are restrained from doing so by their perception of a social norm. When several such people find themselves in a group, they soon learn that they are not alone in their feelings, and as they express their shared inclinations in discussion, arguments become polarized. As a result, discussion with similarly inclined people generally magnifies the internal preferences of people who feel a conflict between what they ought to do and what they want to do. □

For further information:

Burnstein, Eugene, and Amiram Vinokur. "Persuasive Argumentation and Social Comparison as Determinants of Attitude Polarization." *Journal of Experimental Social Psychology*, Vol. 13, 1977, pp. 315-332.

Lamm, Helmut, and David G. Myers. "Group-Induced Polarization of Attitudes and Behavior." *Advances in Experimental Social Psychology, Vol. II*, ed. by Leonard Berkowitz. Academic Press, 1978.

Moscovici, Serge, and Marisa Zavalloni. "The Group as a Polarizer of Attitudes." *Journal of Personality and Social Psychology*, Vol. 12, 1969, pp. 125-135.

Myers, David G., and Helmut Lamm. "The Polarizing Effect of Group Discussion." *American Scientist*, Vol. 63, 1975, pp. 297-303.

32

Testing Leaders

Many a group has been torn apart by a brassy, bossy leader who polarizes the membership into warring camps. The lubrication of tact and compromise is supposed to bring groups together, insuring a leader's viability. But whether soft sell works best may depend on the group's purpose and the relative position of power enjoyed by a leader.

Five researchers from the United States Air Force Academy recently gauged the influence of leaders under four specific conditions. Both authoritarian and democratic leaders can be effective, but in different group situations, according to the work of Joseph Cammalleri, Hal Hendrick, Wayne Pittman, Jr., Harry Blout and Dirk Prather of the academy's Department of Life and Behavioral Sciences.

An initial study involved 48 four- or five-man groups, male sophomores and juniors from the Air Force Academy. A duplicate experiment, which turned up similar results, used 32 groups of four or five cadets. Each young man was issued an individual copy of the *National Aeronautic Space Administration (NASA) Decision-Making Problem.* The problem entailed ranking the worth of survival items for a ship crew stranded on the moon 200 miles from its mother vehicle. Students worked alone for 10 minutes, then were randomly assigned to groups. Leaders of the groups had been briefed beforehand, half instructed to use an authoritarian style, the others asked to employ more democratic techniques. Within each style of leadership, half argued for a predetermined correct ranking of the survival tools and the remaining leaders tried to sway their groups to the least accurate solution.

Pushy and Right. The highest accuracy scores came out of the groups with dictatorial leaders who were trying to push a correct ranking of survival tools. Interestingly, the two democratically run units emerged with comparable accuracy despite the fact that one leader was asked to favor the right ranking and the other a wholly inaccurate one. Leader opinion just didn't seem to make that much difference in the group's successful performance. Making the least accurate judgments of all were units led by an authoritarian person who was determined to shove false conclusions down everyone's throat.

When group leaders were bossy, members displayed considerable aggression and verbal hostility. Even when they were right, the high-accuracy dictatorial leaders generated harsh interpersonal clashes. Such groups seemed to pay a price in ill will for getting the right "answer." The pushy leader may be most destructive when good vibes and pulling together of members are crucial for the group's success. Authoritarian leadership seems most effective under conditions similar to those in the study—good leader-member relations to start, a structured task and strong leader-position power (conferred here by public appointment of facilitators). Task-oriented organizations that do not rely upon personal rapport for achieving collective goals perhaps may hit the bull's-eye more often with a firm leader in charge. But if it's a wrong-headed dictator, even such no-nonsense groups could be better off using democratic consensus to make decisions.

VII. Person Perception

It is easy to assume that when you perceive objects, your eye works in much the same way as a camera: you look at something and snap a print of it in your mind. However, psychological research on perception indicates that this assumption is incorrect. Perception is far from a passive, receptive process (see "How Real is Our Reality?" by Albert Rosenfeld). This is especially true when it comes to perceiving people. Indeed, it would be more exact to say that people "construct" their impressions of others than to say that they perceive others. The constructs we use to describe people—constructs such as "warm," "kind," "generous," and "shy"—have no tangible physical existence. They are inferences that summarize a vast amount of information. For this and other reasons, the same person is often perceived differently by different people or even by the same person at different times (see "The Self and Perceptual Processes," by D. E. Hamachek). Indeed, some research suggests that if you ask one person to describe another, you can learn more about the person doing the describing than the person he or she describes.

Recently, social psychologists have become interested in the effect of physical attractiveness on person perception. It might seem that a superficial attribute such as physical attractiveness would exert a relatively minor effect on impression formation. However, this clearly is not the case (see "Beauty and the Best," by Ellen Berscheid). How other people look is generally one of the first things we confront when we meet them. It often serves as the basis for subsequent inferences about them. People tend to infer that good-looking people are good people, and unattractive people are bad; and they generally agree on how physically attractive others are.

Because we have some control over how we look, we can manage the initial impression we make. We can style our hair, bathe, trim our nails, wear makeup if we are female, and, probably most importantly, we can choose how we dress. In many senses, our clothes are uniforms. They advertise the identity we seek to display, and they demonstrate our taste. The article "You Are What You Wear" describes an experiment that tests one relationship between people and their clothes.

But what about aspects of our identity over which we have no control, such as our names? Studies have shown that people with unusual names are more likely to display signs of maladjustment in later life than people with common names (see "Funny, You Don't Look Cecil," by James Bruning and William Albott). It is not clear, however, whether the unusual names or the unusual parents who gave the names have caused the problems.

Sometime in my teenage years, a recreation director told me that he could "analyze" my personality. I invited him to do so. He gave me a test of some sort, then said something like, "You are happy most of the time, but sometimes you have spells of unhappiness. You like people, but sometimes feel the need to be alone. You have hidden creative potential. You sometimes feel insecure." Well, I was astonished. The counsellor didn't seem like a very smart guy, but he had captured me exactly! I believed in the powers of the counsellor and his test for about three weeks, until I overheard him do exactly the same thing to someone else. It turned out that he was using a trick that is probably employed by fortune-tellers of various persuasions—supplying the categories and letting you fill in the content (see Bertram R. Forer's "The Fallacy of Personal Validation").

How Real Is Our Reality?

by ALBERT ROSENFELD

I am haunted by one of the experiments described in Roger Lewin's article, "Observing the Brain Through a Cat's Eyes." Two groups of kittens are trained in separate, carefully controlled environments. One group can perceive only horizontal lines while the other sees only vertical. When both groups move out into the real world, we are treated to the disquieting spectacle of two sets of intelligent animals, both of the same species (they could even be siblings), both perfectly normal (within the definition of their upbringing); each sharing the same reality, yet experiencing that reality in a radically different manner—each, in fact, quite blind to important segments of the other's universe.

One can easily imagine a society where the horizontal-oriented cats were in the overwhelming majority and in unequivocal political ascendancy. Their view of the world would of course represent the norm. Those few cats who perceived vertically would be "hallucinating." They might be adjudged insane and put away in the crazy-cage. Verticality might even be considered subversive or heretical.

"What is reality?" is a question as old as philosophy. Even ancient sages understood, long before scientific insight made it explicitly clear, that our reality is closely related to our biology (especially to our neurobiology), to the ways in which we perceive.

Suppose 10 of us are in a room, and I take a dose of LSD. In a short time I will be seeing and sensing all kinds of bizarre and distorted visions—all very real to me. But inasmuch as your view of the world remains unchanged, I am hallucinating. The electrochemistry of my brain cells and fluids has been scrambled in such a way as to distort all my "normal" perceptions. But suppose it were possible to scramble the brains of all 10 of us simultaneously in precisely the same detailed manner, so that we were all hallucinating together. Might our hallucinations then be identified as real—especially if we didn't suspect that our brains had been meddled with?

Through the centuries philosophers have grappled with the problem of a reality we can count on—the "something-I-know-not-what" that John Locke was sure must underlie our perceptions. Or could reality be, as Bishop Berkeley argued, merely an idea in the mind of God? If a hypnotist can put 10 people into a trance simultaneously and suggest to them an event—thus making it real for them, even though we "know" it "didn't really happen"—why couldn't an omnipotent mind, if one existed, similarly impose its own reality on the minds of a whole population or of a whole species?

We do of course realize, even if only by analogy, that perception has limits. We know that the mole and the dragonfly see a different world from the one we see. (They may not see at all, in the strict human sense.) We know, too, that reality exists beyond the reach of our senses—sound waves past the threshold of our audibility, electromagnetic radiations stretching far on both sides of the narrow spectral slit visible to our eyes.

We also recognize that we can't always accept the evidence of our senses. To us, the earth appears flat; the stars are pinpoints of light fixed on the dark roof of night; a rock is a dense, motionless solid rather than a mostly empty space sparsely populated by dancing atoms, seemingly "at rest" on a round, unresting earth, itself a speck of cosmic dust lost in the unimaginable vastnesses of galaxies in non-stop flight.

"What is reality?" is, then, a question difficult to answer in any absolute way. On a commonsense, everyday level, we don't usually need to trouble ourselves with such abstruse considerations. As a practical matter, we settle for what our senses report—as long as the senses of others report the same things. Ordinary reality, then, is consensual reality—reality by consensus.

Let's go back to the 10 of us in a room and skip the LSD. If I point to a table, a book, a chandelier, and you all see these objects, their reality will not be questioned. If I say I saw a bird fly through the room, and if no one else saw it, you will think that I am either lying or hallucinating. If a bird really does fly through the room, and if I succeed, through hypnosis, in erasing the event from your minds—though your testimony outweighs mine by nine to one, I am the one who knows what really happened. On the other hand, if I could hypnotize you into accepting a totally imaginary bird flight, you would all swear to the reality you had "seen."

Sheer sophistry? Maybe so. After all, who would have any *reason* to be playing the cosmic jokester, to be tricking us this way all the time? Besides, there must be very few people in the world who have such hypnotic powers (I surely have not). Nevertheless, these are good, instructive "thought games" to play as a reminder of how plastic and suggestible are our minds and our perceptions.

The most pertinent questions that the horizontal and vertical cats give rise to are: how much of our reality is imprinted on us by our culture? And how much is denied us? We are taught what we are taught when we are at our most pliant, long before we have anything to say about it. In the process, what worlds are lost to us? Many creative people in the contemporary human-potential movements are convinced that (just as Don Juan is supposed to have demonstrated to Carlos Castaneda) other realities exist beyond our usual perceptions—realities we could have access to if only we could learn to open ourselves up to them.

Like the horizontally deprived cats, do we blunder around the world, never seeing beautiful places where we might stretch out and ease our souls? Like the missing verticals, do we keep knocking ourselves silly against obstacles we can't see are there?

34 The Self and Perceptual Processes: Theory and Theorists

by D. E. Hamachek

The Nature of Perceptual Processes

Combs and Syngg have developed the idea that each person behaves in a manner consistent with his "perceptual field," which is a more or less fluid organization of personal meanings existing for every individual at any given instant in time. Perceptual field has also been called one's private or personal world, one's psychological field or life-space, or one's phenomenal field. The last term, which is appearing more frequently in psychological circles these days, is derived from the Greek, *phainesthai,* which means "to appear," or "to appear so," or "as it appears." In its original usage, a phenomenon was "that which is known through the senses and immediate experience" rather than through deductions. This is still the case. That is, to a phenomenologist, reality lies not in the event but in the phenomenon, which is to say, in a person's *perception* of the event. The idea of how perception can influence behavior is nicely illustrated in the following example cited by Combs:

Several years ago a friend of mine was driving in a car at dusk along a Western road. A globular mass, about two feet in diameter, suddenly appeared directly in the path of the car. A passenger screamed and grasped the wheel attempting to steer the car around the object. The driver, however, tightened his grip on the wheel and drove directly into the object. The behavior of both the driver and the passenger was determined by his own (perceptions). The passenger, an Easterner, saw the object in the highway as a boulder and fought desperately to steer the car around it. The driver, a native Westerner, saw it as tumbleweed and devoted his efforts to keeping his passenger from overturning the car.

Each person in the car behaved according to what he "saw." The behavior of each was determined not by what the "objective" facts were, but by their "subjective" interpretations of the facts. It turned out that the driver was correct: it wasn't a boulder, but the passenger, at the instant of behaving, responded in terms of what he *thought* the facts were and not what they *actually* were. In other words, when the passenger grabbed the wheel, *he* was right, and he behaved accordingly. Our perceptions usually have the feeling of "being right" at the instant of behaving. This may not be true in retrospect as we look back over things we did yesterday, or last week, or five years ago, but at the time we acted it very likely seemed to us that the things we did, the thoughts we had, and the feelings we felt were legitimate, valid, and rational. For example, consider the following incident reported by Shlien about a twenty-eight-year-old sociology graduate student who was wearily on his way home by bus after midterm examinations. In the graduate student's own words, this is what happened:

> After an hour or so, the bus stopped in a small town, and a few passengers got on. One of them was a blonde girl, very good looking in a fresh but sort of sleazy way. I thought that she was probably a farm girl, and I wished she'd sit by me. By God, she did. She was really comely, if you know what I mean, and she smiled a bit so I felt sure she'd be approachable. Oh boy, what luck. I didn't want to be too eager, and I was still exhausted so we just smiled then I sort of dozed off for a little while, hoping to recuperate by the time the driver turned out the lights and meanwhile enjoying my fantasies about the prospects for the rest of the trip. The last thing I remember was smiling at her and noticing that when her skirt slipped up on her knee as she reached up to the back of the seat, she didn't pull it down. Wow! About four hours later we were pounding along the road in complete darkness when I opened my eyes. Her leg, the outside of it, was against mine, and the way it pressed and moved with the motion of the bus woke me up. This was more than I'd dreamed of. I was terribly excited, and when I stirred a little the steady pressure of leg didn't move away. By this time, I had a terrific erection, and the more I thought about this cute little babe pressing against me, the worse it got. I was just about to reach out and touch her when we pulled into a gas station for a stop, and when the light came through the window, *she* wasn't there at all! She must have left while I was asleep. A fat man with a growth of beard and a dead cigar dropping ash on his vest was sprawled next to me, sound asleep. It was *his* leg pressing against me, and he was so fat and slovenly that even when I drew myself away, his sloppy flesh stayed against me. I was so dumbfounded—disappointed too, and the funny thing—I lost that erection almost immediately, got up and moved to another seat. What a letdown.

Just as it is true that we may find our perceptions (hence, our behavior) in error as we review them in retrospect, we may also discover that our most carefully considered plans for the future can also be inaccurate. That is, looking forward at this moment to the situation we will be in next week or next year, we may plan very carefully what will be first and appropriate to do and even feel confident about the outcome. When the time comes, however, we may end up behaving very different

at the moment. The exam you take today, for example, that you "saw" yourself prepared for yesterday, may radically change your perceptions of how ready you actually may be. So, behavior has to be revised to be consistent with new perceptions.

We organize, we "see" our environment—initially a physical, then a sensory environment—in such a way so that it has personal meaning for us. It is full of objects, circumstances, and events that are perceived as beautiful or ugly, good or bad, positive or negative, experiences to be approached or avoided. The perceptual world of each of us is organized in ways that are dictated not only by the construction of our central nervous systems, but also in accordance with the symbolic backgrounds and self-concepts which each of us brings to our perception of "reality."

INFLUENCE OF NEEDS AND VALUES

Each of us is continually motivated to maintain and enhance how we feel about ourselves. Whether we are successful or not depends on the sort of perceptions we're able to make in the course of our lifetime. Our perceptions enable us to be aware of the world around us and to behave in ways which result in the satisfaction of our fundamental needs for personal adequacy. We might expect then, that an individual's needs and values would strongly influence his perceptions. This is exactly what proves to be so.

Out of all the phenomena we might perceive, we usually perceive what is meaningful to us and consistent with the needs we feel at the moment. For example, experiments on food deprivation in which participants were kept off food for varying periods of time have shown repeatedly that as hunger increases, so, too, do erroneous perceptions of food. In classes you may have had which lasted into the lunch hour, have you noted how your mind sometimes flashes more and more food images across your mental screen? Osgood describes this nicely from his own personal experience as follows: "An office that I pass each day is numbered 400D; inevitably, when the hour is near mealtime, I perceive this as FOOD. The car I used to drive had the euphemistic label SILVER STREAK on its dashboard; inevitably when the hour was near mealtime, I would read this as SILVER STEAK." And of course we're all familiar with the common desert scene of the parched, dehydrated man pulling himself across the hot sands toward some watery illusion created in answer to a desperate need for body fluid.

The influence of needs on perceptions has also been demonstrated under more rigorous laboratory conditions. For example, Levine and others presented food-deprived subjects with pictures of various objects distorted behind a ground-glass screen and found that those who had gone three to nine hours without eating saw more food objects than did those who had eaten forty-five minutes to two hours before the experiment. McClelland and Atkinson deprived Navy men of food for periods ranging from one to sixteen hours. The investigators then pretended to flash food pictures on a screen, but actually projected nothing. All of the subjects were unaware of the relation between their hunger and the perceptual test they were taking. Under the general set to see objects, the hungrier men had a greater frequency of food perceptions than the less hungry ones. The differences in the number of food responses were particularly large between the one-hour and sixteen-hour groups. The experimenters also found that as the hours of food deprivations increased so, too, did the apparent size of the perceived food objects.

Rogers has emphasized that a person's need for self-consistency also influences perception. If, for example, a person has learned to regard homosexual behavior as an abnormality "too disgusting to even think about" then any feeling within himself which could possibly be construed as homosexual (because "normal people just don't feel that way") has to be adjusted so it is consistent with how he sees himself. A young man, who had recently been confronted by a homosexual, told me during one of our counseling sessions: "I don't know whether I was frightened by his proposition or my feelings of maybe going along with it. All I know is that it makes me nervous to even think about being a queer, so I told him to get the hell out of my room."

Even psychologists, who should know about such things, are not immune to the effect of needs on perception. In a study of the evaluations of other people by clinical psychologists, Weingarten found that psychotherapists saw more problems in their clients in those areas in which the clinicians themselves had problems. Even when the purpose of the investigation was brought to their attention, they persisted in seeing in the clients they examined the problems they wrestled with themselves!

Similarly, values are determinants of our perceptions and behavior. We more readily perceive those things, experiences, and people we value, prize, and esteem. For example, have you ever noticed your ability to spot the person you care for in a crowd of people, or your ability to quickly see *your* name on an entire page of names. Or have you noticed your inclination to buy more food than you really need when exceptionally hungry? The need for something, in this case food, seems to have the effect of increasing its value potential.

The influence of one's values on perceptions has also been demonstrated in research. A case in point is Vroom's findings which suggest that an individual tends to perceive his own values and attitudes in persons for whom he has a negative attitude. Apparently we do not like to see characteristics we value in ourselves as being part of a disliked individual's personality. Could it be that if we see certain of our own values exhibited in a person we do not like, that these same values seem to us less important or less real or less good in ourselves?

Postman and others have been able to demonstrate that personal values are determinants of an individual's perceptual selectivity. First they measured the value orientation of twenty-five students with a value scale. Then they flashed words representing the six values one at a time on a screen with increasingly longer exposures

until they were recognized by each student. Their general finding was that the more closely a given word reflected a value already held by the student, the more rapidly he was able to recognize it. For example, subjects with dominant religious values would recognize on very brief exposure such words as "priest" or "minister" while taking longer to perceive economic words such as "cost," "price," or "bonds." In other words, there seemed to be a predisposition, or readiness, to see more quickly words reflecting one's personal values. In another study, Bruner and Goodman found that values exert other kinds of influence on perception. They asked ten- and eleven-year-old boys from wealthy and poor families to guess the size of various denominations of coins (1, 5, 10, 25, 50 cents) by having them vary the diameter of a circle of light to the size of a specified coin. When asked to adjust the light to the size of a remembered nickel or dime or half dollar, all the children tended to overestimate the size of the coins, with the overestimation increasing with the increased value of the coin. The poorer boys, however, overestimated to a greater extent than boys from more prosperous families. The hunch here is that perhaps because perceived size is related to perceived value, the personal value of the coins was greater for the poorer boys.

A very lifelike example of how social values influence perception was reported by Hastorf and Cantril and dealt with the perceptions of Princeton and Dartmouth students to a rough and tense football game between the two schools. Each group of students was asked questions about which side was responsible for the "roughness" or "dirtiness" of the game. When asked which team "started it," only 36 percent of the Dartmouth students said Dartmouth did, while 86 percent of the Princeton students blamed Dartmouth; 34 percent of the Dartmouth students saw the game as "rough and fair"; while only 3 percent of the Princeton students could make the same judgment, tending almost unanimously to see it as "rough and dirty" with the Dartmouth team responsible for the dirt. When later shown the complete movie for the game, Princeton players "saw," on the average, about 10 rule infractions by Dartmouth players. On the other hand, Dartmouth players "saw" less than half that much foul play on the part of their own team. (Alas, the report failed to mention who won.)

INFLUENCE OF BELIEFS

By and large, people tend to behave in a manner which is consistent with what they believe to be true. In this sense, seeing is not only believing. seeing is behaving! A fact is not what is; a fact is what one believes to be true. When man believed that the earth was flat he avoided its edges; when he believed that blood-letting would drain out the evil spirits and cure a patient he persisted in this practice despite the fact that people died before his very eyes. When man believed that phrenology could help him, he had his head examined (literally). There is even evidence to suggest that when a researcher believes that his hypothesis is true, he is more apt to find evidence supporting that hypothesis than if he didn't believe it was true. And so it goes.

Kelley conducted an experiment which very clearly shows the influence of beliefs on behavior. Students in a college class were presented with brief written descriptions of a guest lecturer prior to his appearance in class. The descriptions were almost the same except for one phrase, which in one case described him as a "rather cold" person and in the other case as a "very warm" person. Some students received the "warm" and some the "cold" description. They did not know that two different descriptions had been distributed.

After hearing his lecture the students who had received the "warm" description rated the lecturer as more considerate of others, more sociable, more popular, better natured, more humorous, and more humane than did students who had received the "cold" description. The findings directly reflect how implicit beliefs regarding what traits go with warmth and coldness can influence what one "sees" in another person.

Kelley also found that the warm-cold variable affected the amount of interactions that the students engaged in with the guest lecturer. Fifty-six percent of the students who received the "warm" description participated in class discussion, but only thirty-two percent of the students who received the "cold" description did so. This was the case even though the students were sitting in the same room hearing the same lecture. Thus do our beliefs about people sway our reactions to them and influence the course of interpersonal behavior.

Bills and McGehee found that the students who learned and retained the most in a psychology experiment were inclined to believe things such as, "Psychology experiments are useful and will eventually help us to completely understand people," and "Psychology, in general, is a valuable, quantitative science with many practical aspects." On the other hand, students who quickly forgot the material were those who held beliefs such as "Psychological experiments are a total waste of time," and "Psychology, in general, is nothing but a witch hunt."

Our beliefs influence our perceptions, nurture our assumptions, and to a large extent determine our behavior. We do not easily give up that which we believe to be true. The church of our youth and the first political party to which we gave our allegiance usually continue to be our choices. Perceptions of one person by another person can be as varied as the assumptions on which the perceptions are based. An interesting example of how different beliefs can influence different perceptions was reported by Stachnik and Ulrich in a paper in which they described the divergent perceptions of Barry Goldwater by psychiatrists after he received the 1964 Republican nomination for President. *Fact* magazine sent a questionnaire to all 12,356 psychiatrists registered in the American Medical Association asking, "Do you believe Barry Goldwater is psychologically fit to serve as President of the United States?" Not all answered, but of the 2,417 who did reply, 571 said they did not know enough about him to answer, 657 said they thought him psy-

chologically fit, and 1,189 said he was not. Consider some examples of how dramatically the perceptions of Goldwater differed. One psychiatrist said, "I not only believe Barry Goldwater is psychologically fit to serve as President, but I believe he is a very mature person." On the same subject, however, another psychiatrist observed, "I believe Mr. Goldwater is basically immature . . . He has little understanding of himself or why he does the things he does." It is also interesting to note that diametrically opposing views regarding Goldwater's fitness were defended with rock-like conviction. For example, a Connecticut psychiatrist concluded:

I believe Goldwater is grossly psychotic . . . he is a mass murderer at heart and a suicide. He is amoral and immoral, a dangerous lunatic. Any psychiatrist who does not agree with the above is himself psychologically unfit to be a psychiatrist.

A Georgia psychiatrist was just as adamant, but had a different belief about Goldwater:

I value my reputation as a psychiatrist, but I am willing to stake it on the opinion that Barry Goldwater is eminently qualified—psychologically and in every other way—to serve as President of the United States.

The authors suggested, tongue-in-cheek(?), that among other things "A Republican seeking psychiatric counsel should be sure to see a Republican psychiatrist since this apparently enhances the probability of receiving a favorable diagnosis. . . ."

Beliefs are difficult to change. This is even more true for persons who have strong prejudices, which, after all, are nothing more than beliefs which have become so fixed as to become permanent props in one's personality structure. Perhaps the point that beliefs change slowly can be illustrated by the yarn about the man who believed he was dead. His psychiatrist, after hearing his story, suggested that during the next week he repeat thrice daily, "Dead men don't bleed." When the man returned the next week the psychiatrist asked the man if he had followed his advice. Assured that he had, the psychiatrist took a needle and pricked the man's finger and squeezed out a drop of blood. "Well," said the psychiatrist, "What do you think about that?" The man regarded his finger with some care, looked up at the psychiatrist with a puzzled expression and answered, "I'll be darned. Dead men *do* bleed!"

INFLUENCE OF SELF-CONCEPT

Perception is a selective process and the picture that one has of himself is a vital factor in determining the richness and variety of perceptions selected. It makes a great deal of difference how one perceives, let's say, the Pope if one sees himself as a Jew, Protestant, or Catholic. Depending on one's concept of self, an exam is perceived as either something to avoid failing or something to pass with as high a grade as possible; a class discussion is viewed as either something to actively engage in or something to sit quietly through for fear of saying the wrong thing; front seats of classrooms are seen as either vantage points for better seeing and hearing or as potentially dangerous spots where one could be more easily seen and, heaven forbid, called on! It depends on how one perceives himself.

There is another consideration related to the impact of self-concept on perception and that is connected to its possible boomerang effect. For example, a student who views himself as poor in math not only internalizes that perception, but he is also likely to *project* it in his behavior. That is, he "projects" the "I can't do math" perception outside of himself by either, (1) avoiding math courses, and/or (2) by being so tense in the math courses he does take that he trips over his own anxiety trying to work problems he doesn't think he can solve in the first place. Through either course of action it is possible to perpetuate a negative self-image. By avoiding math, the student is in effect saying, "I'm too dumb to take math," which serves to reinforce the negative attitude with which he started. By taking math with the "I can't do it," feeling he is apt to increase the likelihood of overstimulating his anxiety to the point of not being able to think clearly when it counts. Naturally enough this usually leads to poor performance and ultimately leads to further evidence to support his negative self-concept. This is what is meant by the boomerang effect. The very process of *beginning* with a negative attitude usually guarantees that it will be projected in behavior in such a way as to "bring back" to the person evidence that he really cannot do what he thought he couldn't do in the first place. It ends up being a self-fulfilling prophecy. Of course, the boomerang effect can also work in the other direction. It is possible to start with a more positive attitude and accumulate evidence to support and maintain a more favorable self-perception.

I am not for a moment suggesting that how one performs or behaves is a simple matter of saying "I can" or "I can't" and therefore it will be true. Behavior is far more complex than that. Each of us has certain aptitudes and skills which equip us to do a few things a little better than some and some things a little better than most. The task before any person desiring to grow more competent is to keep himself as open as possible to experiences and opportunities which could broaden and expand his perception of self. By sampling new experiences and by testing one's self in as wide a variety of ways as possible, one not only increases the possibility of discovering those things which he does a little better than most, but he also decreases the possibility of being deflated by things he's not particularly good at. Most of us are better than we give ourselves credit for being and taking on new challenges now and then is one good way to find that out.

THINGS ARE NOT ALWAYS WHAT THEY SEEM

When we look at things from our own point of view they don't always square with how they may be perceived by another person. For example, I recall an incident involving a youthful art teacher who admonished one of her first-grade pupils for drawing a cow the way he did because, after all, "Cows just don't look like that." The little boy frowned a bit, examined his cow closely, looked up at the teacher and said, "Maybe they don't, but I bet if you were down here with me they would."

Shlien has reported a story about a psychologist which perhaps best illustrates some of the things about perception we have been talking about: influence of needs, impact of self-concept, behavior which is consistent with perceptions, the possibility of misinterpreting behavior if we examine it only from our point of view, etc. It goes like this.

The parents of a small boy were worried. He was quiet, sensitive, lonely, and acted afraid of other children. The parents wanted some professional advice before the child entered school and so invited a psychologist friend of theirs to the house for an afternoon and dinner so he could observe the boy under more natural conditions. Upon arriving, the psychologist asked all the appropriate questions about history and behavior and then took a spot on the balcony where he watched, unseen, the boy play in a garden by himself. The boy sat pensively in the sun, listening to the neighborhood children shout. He frowned, rolled over on his stomach, kicked the toes of his white shoes in the grass, sat up and looked at the stains. Then he saw an earthworm. He stretched it out on a flat stone, found a sharp edged chip, and proceeded to saw the worm in half. Many impressions were taking shape in the psychologist's mind, and he made some tentative notes to the effect: "Seems isolated and angry, perhaps over-aggressive, or sadistic, should be watched carefully when playing with other childen, not have knives or pets." Then he heard the boy talking to himself. He leaned forward and strained to catch the words. The boy finished his separation of the worm, his frown disappeared, and he said, "There. Now you have a friend."

PERCEPTIONS CAN BE MODIFIED

As difficult as it is to change perceptions once they are acquired and incorporated into one's self-system, there nonetheless is abundant evidence to suggest that perceptions toward one's self and others can be modified. For example, studies in psychotherapy have shown us that if a therapist is genuine, accepting, and empathically understanding of a client's private world, then the client is better able to alter his self-perceptions in the direction of becoming more confident and self-directing, more mature and socialized, more healthy and integrated.

On the other hand, clinical studies of "brainwashing" techniques used by the Chinese communists on American prisoners during the Korean conflict have shown that it is possible to break down a man's confidence, destroy the concept he has of himself, and, in general, disintegrate his personality structure to the point of apathetic resignation.

As another illustration, research has demonstrated that some members of a group will report perceptions which are contrary to the evidence of their senses. They will, for example, report that Figure A covers a larger area than Figure B, when their visual perceptions *plainly indicate that this is not true*. Experiments by Asch, later refined and improved by Crutchfield, have shown that when a person is *led to believe* that other members in a group see B as larger than A, then he is inclined to go along with this judgment. More than that, he frequently does so with a real belief in his false perception.

Perception can be dramatically altered by setting up conditions which produce vivid hallucinations and other abnormal reactions in a thoroughly normal, awake individual. For example, in sensory deprivation experiments at McGill University it was discovered that if all sensory input was cut off or reduced, abnormal perceptions resulted. If healthy subjects lie relatively motionless, to reduce kinesthetic stimuli, with eyes covered to eliminate light, with hearing muffled by foam-rubber pillows as well as being in a quiet cubicle, and with tactile sensations reduced by cuffs over the hands, then within forty-eight hours many subjects experience weird perceptual processes and hallucinations resembling that of a psychotic individual.

Anyone who has ever had a drink or two (or three or four) at a party has first-hand evidence of how perceptual processes can be temporarily modified via the introduction of alcohol into the blood. For example, recent research indicates that when an individual has had a given amount to drink, he is inclined to distort the subjective probability of success and begin to perceive various alternatives as less serious than they really are. What would normally be regarded as high risk-taking behavior is no longer perceived as such at all. As actual ability decreases, the feeling of competency increases. Interesting to note in regard to risk-taking is how the party behavior of imbibing individuals is inclined to get more socially daring and aggressive as the evening wears on. From alcohol to "truth serum" to chemotherapy practiced in psychiatric wards to drugs for the normal person, there are many ways of changing psychological and perceptual states. We may take a drug to mobilize our anxiety to cram for an exam or a drug to reduce our anxiety before an exam. And of course drugs such as marijuana, heroin, LSD, and its many variants are known to have enormous effects on one's perceptual processes—many times very destructive effects.

Perceptions can be modified or changed by conditions both inside and outside the self. The changes can be for better or for worse and they can be either temporary or permanent. What we see may be real or imagined and whether we perceive when we are drunk or sober, manic or depressed, anxious or tranquil, we persist in behaving in a manner which, at the moment of behaving, is consistent with what we perceive to be true.

35

Beauty and the Best

"We're all of us sentenced to solitary confinement inside our own skins, for life."

ORPHEUS DESCENDING
—TENNESSEE WILLIAMS

For all the talk about character and inner values, we assume the best about pretty people. And from grade school on, there's almost no dispute about who's beautiful.

by Ellen Berscheid
& Elaine Walster

A BILLION-DOLLAR cosmetics industry testifies that the severity of the sentence may depend upon the quality of the skin. We can cold-cream it, suntan it, bleach it, lift it, and paint it—but we cannot shed it. And, unless we are willing to adopt the tactics of the Oregon State student who enclosed himself in a large black bag, our physical appearance is our most obvious personal characteristic.

For the past few years we have investigated the impact of one aspect of appearance—physical attractiveness—upon relationships between persons. Our initial interest in attractiveness was negligible. We shared the democratic belief that appearance is a superficial and peripheral characteristic with little influence on our lives. Elliot Aronson has suggested that social scientists have avoided investigating the social impact of physical attractiveness for fear they might learn just how powerful it is. It may be, however, that we have simply given too much credence to collective assertions that internal attributes are more important determinants of who wins or loses our affections than external appearance is.

Impact. The results of our research suggest that beauty not only has a more important impact upon our lives than we previously suspected, but its influence may begin startlingly early.

Nursery-school teachers often insist that all children are beautiful, yet they can, when they are asked, rank their pupils by appearance. The children themselves appear to behave in accordance with the adult ranking.

This finding resulted from a study of nursery-school records. Some schools collect information on how students view each other. A teacher will ask a child to select from photographs of his classmates the person he likes most and the person he likes least. The teacher also asks such questions as, *Who is teacher's pet?*, *Who is always causing trouble in the class?*, and *Who is most likely to hit other kids?*

The children in our nursery-school sample ranged in age from four to six. We thought that the older nursery-school children, who had had more time to learn the cultural stereotypes associated with appearance, might be more influenced by their classmates' attractiveness than the younger children. To examine this hypothesis, we divided the sample into two age groups. We then studied the children's reactions to their classmates who had been judged to be attractive or unattractive by adults.

We found that boys who had been judged by adults to be relatively unattractive were not as well liked by their classmates as the more attractive boys. This was true regardless of the age of the boy. In contrast, the unattractive girls in the younger group were more popular than the attractive girls. With age, however, the unattractive girls declined in popularity, while the attractive girls gained favor with their classmates.

Fight. We also examined how the children described their classmates' behavior. We found that unattractive boys were more likely to be described by their classmates as aggressive and antisocial than were attractive boys. Children said that the less-attractive boys were more likely to fight a lot,

hit other students, and yell at the teacher.

The nursery-school children also thought that their unattractive peers, regardless of sex, were less independent than attractive children. They were seen to be afraid, unlikely to enjoy doing things alone, and as needing help from others.

When the children were asked to name the one person in their class who scared them, they were more likely to nominate an unattractive classmate than an attractive one.

Type. The available data did not re-

> *"Beauty has more impact than we suspected. Its influence may begin startlingly early."*

veal whether the unattractive children actually did misbehave more than the attractive children. We do not know if the students opinions of their classmates were based on factual observation of the behavior, or on adherence to social stereotypes.

It is possible that physical-appearance stereotypes have already been absorbed at this early age. We know that nursery-school children can differentiate among various body types and prefer some to others. For example, fat bodies are already disliked at this age. If a child assumes that nice children are handsome and naughty ones are unattractive, he may notice only those episodes that fit this image.

Whether or not attractive and unattractive children really do behave differently, their classmates think they do and they doubtless act accordingly. Physical attractiveness thus may become a major factor in the social development of the child. It could affect his self-concept and his first social relationships.

Bias. What if the children's reports of behavioral differences are not the result of distorted perception to fit their stereotype, but are accurate descriptions of their classmates' behavior? What if unattractive nursery-school boys are indeed more

aggressive and hostile than handsome boys? Research suggests that such differences might be caused by discriminatory treatment at the hands of parents, teachers and babysitters.

A study by Karen Dion indicates that adults may have a stereotyped image of the moral character of attractive and unattractive children. She found that this image may affect the way adults handle a matter such as discipline for misconduct.

Dion asked young women to examine reports of disturbances created by schoolchildren. To each report she attached a paper that gave a child's name and age, and a photograph that other adults had judged to be attractive, or unattractive. The women believed that the descriptions came from teachers' journals reporting classroom and playground disturbances. Dion asked each woman to evaluate the disturbance and to estimate how the child behaved on a typical day.

Dion hypothesized that the women would interpret the same incident differently depending on whether the naughty child was attractive, or unattractive. The data supported her hypothesis. When the supposed misconduct was very mild in nature, the women did not distinguish between the everyday behavior of unattractive and attractive children. When the disturbance was severe, however, the women assumed that the unattractive boys and girls were chronically antisocial in their everyday behavior.

Cruelty. One young woman made this comment after reading about an attractive girl who had supposedly thrown rocks at a sleeping dog: "She appears to be a perfectly charming little girl, well-mannered, basically unselfish. It seems that she can adapt well among children her age and make a good impression . . . she plays well with everyone, but like anyone else, a bad day can occur. Her cruelty . . . need not be taken too seriously."

When a less-attractive girl committed the identical act, another young woman concluded: "I think the child would be quite bratty and would be a problem to teachers. . . . She would probably try to pick a fight with other children her own age. . . . She would be a brat at home. . . . All in all, she would be a real problem."

To a significant degree, the young women expressed the ominous expectation that the unattractive child would be more likely to commit a similar disturbance in the future. To a lesser, nonsignificant degree the women suspected the unattractive child of having misbehaved in the past.

Who. These findings suggest that in cases in which there is some question about who started the classroom disturbance, who broke the vase, or who stole the money (and with children it always seems that there is the question of *who did it?*) adults are likely to identify an unattractive child as the culprit. The women in Dion's study also believed that unattractive children were characteristically more dishonest than their attractive classmates.

Thus, if an unattractive child protests his innocence, his pleas may fall on deaf ears. The long march to the principal's office starts early, and physical unattractiveness may be a silent companion for the marcher. Often the only possible justice is blind justice.

Grades. Contrary to the popular belief that "beauty and brains don't mix," there is evidence that physical attractiveness may even influence which students make the honor roll. In collaboration with Margaret Clifford, we asked 400 fifth-grade teachers to examine a child's report card. The report card itemized the student's absences during the school year, his grades (for six grade periods) in reading, language, arithmetic, social studies, science, art, music, and physical education. It also reported his performance in healthful living, his personal development, and his work habits and attitudes.

Pasted in the corner of the report card was a photograph of a child, one of six boys and girls who previously had been judged to be relatively attractive, or one of six boys and girls judged to be less attractive.

Future. We asked the teachers to evaluate the student's I.Q., his parents' attitudes toward school, his future educational accomplishment, and his social status with his peers. We predicted that the child's appearance would influence the teacher's evaluation of the child's intellectual potential, despite the fact

that the report cards were identical in content. It did.

The teachers assumed that the attractive girl or boy had a higher I.Q., would go to college, and that his parents were more interested in his education. Teachers also assumed that the attractive student related to his or her classmates better than did the unattractive student.

Prophecy. Other researchers have shown that a student is likely to behave in the way a teacher expects him to behave. Robert Rosenthal and Lenore Jacobson gave an I.Q.

> *"Physical attractiveness may even influence which students make the honor roll."*

test to students in grades one through six. They told the teachers that the test identified children who were likely to show marked intellectual improvement within the year. The researchers then, at random, chose 20 percent of the children and announced that test scores had identified these children as the special students.

A year later, Rosenthal and Jacobson gave the same I.Q. test to the same children—all of them. The results of the second test revealed that the supposed bloomers showed more improvement in I.Q. than the other youngsters did. The gains were most pronounced for first- and second-graders. Rosenthal and Jacobson speculated that teachers probably were more encouraging and friendly toward those children identified as bloomers. Their expectations acted as a self-fulfilling prophecy.

These studies suggest that physical attractiveness in young children may result in adult evaluations that elicit special attention. In turn, special attention may confirm teacher predictions of individual accomplishment.

Dating. The preceding findings, which indicate that a child's physical attractiveness may affect a variety of his early social and educational experiences, were somewhat unexpected. That beauty affects one's social rela-

tionships during the adolescent dating years comes as less of a surprise. What is disconcerting, however, is the apparently overwhelming importance of appearance in opposite-sex dating.

Physical attractiveness may be the single most important factor in determining popularity among college-age adults. In a series of studies of blind dates, we found that the more physically attractive the date, the more he or she was liked. We failed to find additional factors that might predict how well a person would be liked. Students with exceptional personality features or intelligence levels were not liked more than individuals who were less well endowed.

Match. In these studies of the factors that influence courtship, we tested the hypothesis that persons of similar levels of social desirability tend to pair off in courtship and marriage. Erving Goffman described this matching process in 1952: "A proposal of marriage in our society tends to be a way in which a man sums up his social attributes and suggests to a woman that hers are not so much better as to preclude a merger or a partnership in these matters." To test the matching hypothesis we sponsored a computer dance for college students. We obtained a rough estimate of each student's social attributes from scores on personality, social skill, and intelligence tests. In addition, we rated each student's physical appearance at the time he or she purchased a ticket.

The participants assumed that the computer would select their dates on the basis of shared interests. But we paired the students on a random basis, with only one restriction—the cardinal rule of dating that the man be taller than the woman.

Gap. At intermission we handed out a questionnaire to determine how the students liked their dates. If the matching hypothesis is true, we would expect that students paired with dates from their own levels of social desirability would like each other more than those paired with dates from levels inferior or superior to their own. The results did not confirm the hypothesis. The most important determinant of how much each person liked his or her date, how much he or she wanted to see the partner again, and (it was determined later) how often the men actually did ask their computer partners for subsequent dates, was simply how attractive the date was. Blind dates seem to be blind to everything but appearance.

Subsequent blind-date studies, however, did provide some support for the hypothesis that persons of similar social-desirability levels pair off. Although a person strongly prefers a date who is physically attractive, within this general tendency he or she does seek a person who is closer to his or her own attractiveness, rather than a person who is a great deal more or less attractive. Apparently, even in affairs of the heart, a person is aware of a credibility gap.

We thought at first that the blind-date studies had exaggerated the importance of physical attractiveness as a determinant of popularity for, after all, blind-date situations do not allow the dates much opportunity to get to know one another. Subsequent evidence indicated, however, that the importance of beauty probably had not been exaggerated.

In one study, for example, Polaroid pictures of a sample of college girls were rated for attractiveness. This rough index of each girl's beauty was compared to each girl's report of the number of dates she had had within the past year. We found an unexpectedly high correlation ($+.61$) between physical attractiveness and the woman's actual social experience. The girls in our sample represented a wide range of personality traits, social skills, intelligence, values and opinions, differences in inclination to date, and so on. Although in natural settings men do have the opportunity to know and appreciate such characteristics, physical attractiveness still had a major bearing on popularity.

Vulgarity. These findings contradict the self-reports of college students. A multitude of studies have asked students to list the characteristics they find most desirable in a date or mate ["Is It True What They Say About Harvard Boys?," PT, January]. Males almost always value physical attractiveness more than women, but both sexes claim that it is less important than such sterling characteristics as intelligence, friendliness and sincerity. What accounts for the discrepancy between

the reality and the self-report? Many students seem to believe that it is vulgar to judge others by appearance. They prefer to use such attributes as "soul" or warmth as bases for affection. Their apparent disregard for grooming seems to support their charge that it is only to members of the over-30 crowd that appearance matters.

Traits. Young adults may not be as inconsistent as it appears at first glance. There is evidence that students may prefer physically attractive individuals because they unconsciously associate

> *"Physical attractiveness may be the single most important factor in determining popularity among college-age adults."*

certain positive personality traits (traits which they value) with an attractive appearance. In a study conducted with Dion, we found that students thought good-looking persons were generally more sensitive, kind, interesting, strong, poised, modest, sociable, outgoing and exciting than less-attractive persons. Students also agreed that beautiful persons are more sexually warm and responsive than unattractive persons.

Lure. In addition to estimating the personality characteristics of attractive and unattractive persons, we asked the students to tell us what lay ahead for each individual. They expected that attractive persons would hold better jobs, have more successful marriages and happier and more fulfilling lives in general than less-attractive persons. They reversed their optimism on only one dimension—they did not believe that attractive individuals made better parents than did unattractive ones.

These findings suggest a possible reason for our nearly obsessive pursuit of suitably attractive mates. If we believe that a beautiful person embodies an ideal personality, and that he or she is likely to garner all the world's material benefits and happiness, the sub-

stantial lure of beauty is not surprising.

Sex. Is there any truth to these stereotypes? Is it true that attractive persons have better personalities or more successful marriages? It does seem possible that an attractive woman might have a happier marriage than a less-attractive woman. A beautiful woman has a wider range of social activity and consequently has a better chance of meeting a man who has similar interests and values—or any of the factors that appear to lead to stability in marriage.

It also seems possible that physically attractive women are in fact more responsive sexually than less-attractive females. Gilbert Kaats and Keith E. Davis found that good-looking college women were in love more often and had more noncoital sexual experience than girls of medium or low physical attractiveness. They also were more likely to have had sexual intercourse than girls of medium attractiveness. In almost any area of human endeavor, practice makes perfect. It may well be that beautiful women are indeed sexually warmer—not because of any innate difference—but simply because of wider experience.

Reversal. Do attractive coeds actually end up leading happier, more-fulfilling lives than less-attractive coeds? We examined interview data taken from women now in their late 40s and early 50s. We were able to locate early pictures of most of the women by looking through their college yearbooks. A panel of judges from a group of the same age (who presumably were familiar with the standards of beauty that prevailed 25 years ago) rated the pictures. We found that the physical attractiveness of each woman in her early 20s bears a faint but significant relationship to some of the life experiences she reports over two decades later.

Good looks in college seemed to have significant effect on marital adjustment and occupational satisfaction in older women, but the effect was exactly the opposite of what we expected. The more attractive the woman had been in college, the less satisfied, the less happy, and the less well-adjusted she was 25 years later.

Clifford Kirkpatrick and John Cotton have suggested why things do not go well with beautiful-but-aging women: "Husbands may feel betrayed and disillusioned in various ways and even disgusted with the reliance on charms which have faded with the passing of years." They neglect to mention how aging wives will feel about their once-handsome husbands.

Criterion. Love at first sight is the basis of song and story, but usually we get around to taking a second look. It is possible that time lessens the influence of our stereotyped images of beautiful persons. However, many of our interactions with other persons are once-only, or infrequent. We have limited exposure to job applicants, defendants in jury trials, and political candidates, yet on the basis of initial impressions we make decisions that affect their lives. In the case of political candidates, our decisions also affect our lives.

Our research indicates that physical attractiveness is a crucial standard by which we form our first impressions. There is reason to believe that Richard Nixon lost his first campaign for President at least in part because he did not have a good make-up man, while John Kennedy did not need one. Public figures eventually have to act, however, and handsome is is not always as handsome does. Mayor John Lindsay may well have been the most beautiful man in New York, but that apparently didn't solve the problems of subway travel, traffic, crime, or any of the other ills that bedevil New Yorkers.

Beholder. Our research has shown some of the ways we react to attractive persons. We still do not know what variables affect our perception of beauty. If we think that a person has a beautiful personality, do we also see him or her as physically more attractive than we ordinarily would? One study suggests that this may be so. Students took part in discussion groups with other students whose political views ranged from radical to conservative. We later asked the students to

> *"The more attractive the woman had been in college, the less satisfied, the less happy, and the less well-adjusted she was 25 years later."*

judge the physical attractiveness of the group members. We found that students thought that the persons who shared their political views were more physically attractive than those who didn't. Perhaps Republicans no longer think that John Lindsay is as beautiful, now that he is a Democrat.

We should point out that in each study we conducted, we used photographs drawn from relatively homogeneous socioeconomic samples, principally from the middle class. We excluded individuals of exceptional physical beauty and those of unusual unattractiveness, as well as those with noticeable physical handicaps or eyeglasses. Had we included the full range of beauty and ugliness it is possible that the effects of physical attractiveness would have been even more dramatic.

Health. Our research also does not tell us the source of our stereotyped images of beautiful persons. It seems possible that in earlier times physical attractiveness was positively related to physical health. Perhaps it still is. It might be the instinctive nature of any species to want to associate and mate with those who are the healthiest of that species. We may be responding to a biological anachronism, left over from a more primitive age.

Although social scientists have been slow to recognize the implications of our billion-dollar cosmetics industry, manufacturers may be quicker to capitalize upon the additional exploitation possibilities of beauty from early childhood through the adult years. Such exploitation could pour even more of our gross national product into the modification of the skins in which we are all confined—some of us more unhappily than others.

36

You Are What You Wear

Home economist Julia Ann Reed of the University of Texas seems to be unraveling a relationship between personality and clothing. Women's garments are much more revealing than they might suspect. It could be that, underneath it all, people are what they wear.

Last March, Reed questioned 400 Purdue University co-eds about their dressing habits and, on the basis of their answers, divided them into four groups. As a base line for comparison, Reed asked another group of students to scan photographs from magazines such as *Glamour* and *Mademoiselle* to identify fashions that were in or out on their campus.

Pacesetters. The "high fashion" dressers thus uncovered were those who chose the attire their classmates thought was the model of good taste. Pantsuits with flared or cuffed legs were a favorite among such stylish students.

Next in line were the "low fashion" women, who preferred the more low-keyed, normal casual wear of the season. A neat pair of casual pants or blue jeans and a fashionable blouse or sweater were the outfits they felt most at home in.

Stylishly somewhat behind these two groups (by about 10 years) were the "nonfashion" women, who apparently remained undaunted by the fact that the A-line skirt and the tight sweater are now used as costumes for nostalgia shows.

Finally, there were those who seemed to see well-pressed robes as the rags of materialism, and apparently were doing all they could to defy what their classmates considered good taste. Jeans appropriately tattered and patched and work shirts sufficiently wrinkled were the uniforms preferred by the "counterfashion" co-eds.

The Matching. After analyzing the responses to additional queries concerning the women's values, attitudes and personalities, Reed tried to predict which of these four clothing-style groups each subject would belong to.

On the basis of the 49 personality characteristics she investigated, she found she could place 72 percent of the young women at the appropriate clothing rack.

Stitching together the personality traits that best predicted a woman's clothing preferences, Reed offers the following profiles. Co-eds who dressed in high fashion were most attracted to a model dressed in high-fashion style, most interested in fashion, gave most importance to religious activities, spent most money on clothing, had the lowest grade-point averages and generally were majoring in the humanities. True to their expensive wardrobes, they thought of themselves as fashionable, formal and sophisticated; they considered themselves social climbers and also liked to think of themselves as the richest of the four groups. They were lowest among the groups in advocating New Left philosophy and disagreed least with their parents on social issues.

Personality Traits. To the low-fashion co-ed, money and social status were less important than her own good looks. These young women tended to be moderate on every trait except the extent to which they wanted to be more attractive.

The behind-the-times, nonfashion females were characterized by low socioeconomic background but high grade-point averages. They tended to be older than the women in the other groups and were more often enrolled in science majors. They were politically conservative, dogmatic and rarely used drugs. They were most attracted to a model dressed in non-fashion style, had high regard for Machiavellian tactics in human relations but were low in cynicism. Consistent with their conservative stance, they wanted to have constraints on their actions more than the others.

Unconventional Bent. The counter-fashion co-eds were considerably less keen on being hemmed in. They were the most liberal, most individualistic and most conscientious people in the study. On the other hand, they were the least status conscious, formal and sophisticated. These more tender-minded and apprehensive co-eds saw themselves as doing little social climbing and preferred to be most plain in terms of looks. They tended to be the youngest of the women studied and had least interest in the all-American subjects of fashion, athletics and religion. As the greatest advocates of New Left philosophy, these students most often disagreed with their parents on social issues. They were most attracted to a model dressed in counter fashion, displayed a low regard for Machiavellian tactics but were highly cynical, believing such tactics to be common. The counter-fashion co-eds indulged in drug taking more often than did the other groups and they generally expressed less dogmatism than the others.

The accuracy with which Reed was able to predict personality on the basis of wardrobe surprised her dissertation advisor, a psychologist who didn't think she would be able to tell a personality from its wrappings. Reed's results imply that clothing is indeed an outward symbol of personality. Most probably, she speculates, personality and dress are interwoven. That is, one's personality plays a part in determining the clothing one prefers, and the threads one wears help to sew up the personality. But Reed doesn't believe she has the matter completely covered yet and hopes there will be further investigations with more varied groups of subjects.

37

Funny, You Don't Look Cecil

by JAMES L. BRUNING and WILLIAM ALBOTT

Sticks and stones may break your bones, but what your parents choose to call you can give you a bad name for the rest of your life —or so say two experts who have examined the subject. James L. Bruning is professor and chairman of the Department of Psychology at Ohio University. William Albott is coordinator of institutional research and training at the Topeka State Hospital, Topeka, Kansas.

When a stranger asks, "Who are you?" you could legitimately answer by reeling off your occupation, age, sex, marital status or even your astrological sign. But, instead, most often you answer with a symbol, an abbreviation, representing all of the various and sundry characteristics that distinguish you from others. You answer by giving your name. And because names seem to amount to more than mere labels, researchers have looked into the power and influence wielded by the given names we answer to and have found that they manifest a very real effect on the way we see ourselves and each other.

The first attempts to discover how people feel about given names date back to the 1930s and 1940s. Handicapped by a complex rating system, those early studies asked only about preferences for a limited number of given names. But preferences did exist. Names such as Robert, Richard and Charles ranked highest among the male names while Vincent, Henry and Albert were often disliked. For female names, Jean, Jane, Virginia and Dorothy were best liked and, although none were consistently disapproved, those such as Mildred and Marie generally rated lower.

One somewhat surprising result turned up when individuals were asked about their own names. Men usually disliked what they were called only if it was uncommon—apparently having the same name as every Tom, Dick and Harry met with a man's approval. But women were different. They didn't care for their own names if they were either very uncommon or very common. And if sex made a difference, so did age. Older respondents favored formal names such as Harold or James, while the young usually voted for variants or nicknames such as Bill or Jim.

Yet the meanings of names can't be measured only by their popularity. Many common names, of course, have definitions and historical roots but, in America and most western European countries, such information doesn't count much—that Manfred means "peace among men" hasn't made it the pick of young parents who oppose war. Instead, the name that appears on the birth certificate, chosen from a long list of alternatives, seems to do more with what a name implies or connotes. So we turned our attention to the unwritten meanings of names.

Our first study, conducted by psychologist Barbara Buchanan now with Wooster College in Ohio, asked a group of college students to rule on 618 male and 442 female names. The students were to report not only how much they liked or disliked each one but also how much they thought each name suggested activity or passivity, as well as masculinity or femininity.

Again, the sexes saw things differently. Women apparently have clearer ideas about names than do men. While all of the students agreed more often on the inferences of male names than female names, the women consistently expressed the more extreme verdicts. Men and women also differed on what "activity" meant in a female name. While everyone saw most "flower" and "old-fashioned" names such as Pansy and Agnes as passive, the women rated only what they considered to be tomboy names such as Toby and Jody as active. The men, on the other hand, added Ursula, Bridget and Sophia to the active list. Unfortunately, Raquel wasn't on the roster but, more than likely, it, too,

would have sounded lively to the masculine ear.

In comparing our results with the earlier studies, popular male names had changed little. But as might have been expected, the female names had undergone fairly sizable changes in popularity with names such as Dorothy and Jean that were common and well liked in the '30s and '40s having dropped considerably.

The findings raised all sorts of questions about names. For example, could opinions about names affect how easily they're learned or remembered? If so, perhaps your inability to recall "good old what's-his-name" might have more to do with what he answers to than your faulty memory. And we found such a relationship. When subjects were asked to memorize a list of active, liked names to which the passive, disliked name Cecil was added, the disliked name stood out and was learned much faster than the others. Another group worked with photographs of men that had a name across the bottom of each. Again, Cecil led the rest in being remembered.

We also found in the latter study that subjects learned all of the names much easier when they were coupled with faces. When asked why, nearly everyone explained that they associated some feature in the photographs with the names. But they remembered Cecil either because the "guy in the picture looked like a Cecil" or "because the name didn't fit the face." Apparently a lot of people have a good idea about what a Cecil should look like.

So what does Cecil look like? Do common names really conjure up such definite stereotypes? When other subjects were to assign first names to photographs that varied in the degree of their masculine or feminine appearance, the names they chose clearly matched up. The man who looked strong and virile got a two-fisted name such as Bart or Mac while the more placid face was tagged Shelly or Carroll.

In another study, we had children decide which of a pair of stickmen, one with an active name and the other with a passive name, would be more likely to engage in either energetic or passive activities. The names used were nearly equal in their like-dislike ratings to avoid having active behavior given a popular name. While the kindergarten children performed at about chance level, the third and sixth graders easily identified stickmen with passive names such as Aldwin or Winthrop as more likely to spend their time coloring or reading while the stickmen with active names such as Sargent or Baxter would play ball or be able to run faster.

So, while elementary school children have apparently already learned the stereotypes names imply, it doesn't give any indication whether these stereotypes operate in real life. After all, there's so much more to a person than simply his name. To see just how much influence a name alone has, another study had a speaker give a short talk to a classroom of students who then evaluated him. The students had been given a vita showing his name, qualifications and background; however for half the class his name was shown as Mr. Adam Williams, while the rest read that he was Mr. Myron Williams. Although all of the differences weren't statistically significant, Mr. Adam Williams tended to be seen as consistently more active, masculine, dominating, competitive, cold and responsible than the same person who was introduced as Mr. Myron Williams.

A recent report by psychologists Herbert Harari of California State University at San Diego and John W. McDavid of Georgia State University showed that children with unusual names may actually suffer discrimination at the hands of teachers. In testing elementary school teachers with a median 10 years of classroom experience, essays supposedly written by Elmer, Hubert or Bertha were downgraded while comparable papers thought to have been written by David, Michael, Adelle, Lisa or Karen got higher scores.

Perhaps the most fundamental question remains unanswered: how much does a person learn to conform to his name? One of the major problems in trying to uncover the effect of a name on the individual is that parents not only assign the name but they also have expectations about the child's behavior. Does the behavior emerge because of the name or was the name chosen because it matched the parents' expectations?

McDavid and Harari also ran into this puzzle when they found that children's ratings of names corresponded closely to their opinions of peers who bore those names. The psychologists concluded that this could either mean that opinions about a person are influenced by his name or that experiences with that person affect evaluations of his name.

While the puzzle hasn't been solved, evidence does exist that names affect their bearer. Members of the Ashanti of West Africa believe that the day of the week on which a child is born determines his character. He is then named according to his day of birth. When arrest and criminal records were investigated, boys whose day names connoted quick tempers, aggressiveness and troublemaking were guilty much more often of offenses such as assault and murder than were children whose day names suggested passivity. It was concluded that the tribe's beliefs about the connotations between the day of birth and personality may effectively enhance certain traits that otherwise would remain latent. There is also evidence that unusual or disliked names can have definite deleterious effects. Two different studies found that boys with peculiar given names suffer emotional disturbances more often than boys with common names.

Although there has not been a great deal of systematic research into names, the findings clearly suggest that names have significant effects on behavior. What's in a name? A great deal more than most of us think!   HB

38 The Fallacy of Personal Validation: A Classroom Demonstration of Gullibility by Bertram R. Forer

Virtually every psychological trait can be observed in some degree in everyone. For the purpose of characterizing a particular individual, stipulation of those traits which he demonstrates is a meaningless procedure. It is not in the presence or absence of a trait that individuals differ. The uniqueness of the individual, as Allport *(1)* amply documents, lies in the relative importance of the various personality forces in determining his behavior and in the relative magnitude of these traits in comparison with other persons. Thus the individual is a unique configuration of characteristics each of which can be found in everyone, but in varying degrees. A universally valid statement, then, is one which applies equally well to the majority or the totality of the population. The universally valid statement is true for the individual, but it lacks the quantitative specification and the proper focus which are necessary for differential diagnosis. In a sense a universally valid statement is a description of a cultural group rather than a personal psychological datum.

A universally valid personality description is the type most likely to be accepted by a client as a truth about himself, a truth which he considers unique in him. Many, if not most, individuals are able to recognize the characteristics in themselves—when it is not to their disadvantage—while oblivious to their presence in others. An example is the tendency for students to perceive their own problems in textbooks of abnormal psychology. In such cases the individual lacks the quantitative frame of reference necessary for a critical comparison of the printed description and his own self-evaluation.

At times confirmation by a client or by some other person familiar with his history is used as a criterion in the validation of diagnostic inferences and procedures *(4)*. Test results may suggest certain problems and characteristic modes of behavior which therapists or the client, himself, can confirm or deny. Testing the correctness of inferences about a client by requesting his evaluation of them may be called "personal validation." When the inferences are universally valid, as they often are, the confirmation is useless. The positive results obtained by personal validation can easily lull a test analyst or a therapist into a false sense of security which bolsters his conviction in the essential rightness of his philosophy of personality or his diagnostic prowess. Such false validation increases his comfort in using what may have been a dubious instrument. A great danger arises when the confirmation of a prediction is extended uncritically to the instrument or conceptual system or person making the prediction. Such uncritical extensions occur too frequently in the clinical field.

Confirmation of a prediction does not necessarily prove the validity of the propositions from which the prediction was inferred. An identical prediction may be made from a group of propositions which contradict the original ones *(3,* p. 140). Taylor *(12)* has shown empirically that judges of case histories may arrive at identical predictions for different reasons. Confirmation of a variety of predictions which will differentiate among a number of clients is necessary if validation is to be accepted with any degree of confidence.

The crystal-gazer is likely to be aware of some of these points and other pseudo-diagnosticians, though they may be unaware of the fallacies inherent in their procedures, make effective use of "universal validity" and "personal validation" in deceiving their clients. Allport (1, p. 476) states that "one way in which character analysts secure a reputation for success is through the employment of ambiguous terms that may apply to any mortal person." A naive person who receives superficial diagnostic information, especially when the social situation is prestige-laden, tends to accept such information.[1] He is impressed by the obvious truths and may be oblivious to the discrepancies. But he does more than this. He also validates the instrument and the diagnostician. Crider's students *(4)* found surprisingly accurate the analyses they received from a pseudo-diagnostician. Crider, himself, seems to have been beguiled by the results and decries a priori rejection of the claims of these persons. While the use of matching procedures has revealed fairly high validity for inferences derived from projective

[1] D. G. Paterson, in a personal letter to the writer, describes and includes a universally valid personality sketch which he uses in luncheon club lectures. It is reproduced here with his permission.

"Above average in intelligence or mental alertness. Also above average in accuracy—rather painstaking at times. Deserves a reputation for neatness—dislikes turning out sloppy work. Has initiative; that is, ability to make suggestions and to get new ideas, open-mindedness.

"You have a tendency to worry at times but not to excess. You do get depressed at times but you couldn't be called moody because you are generally cheerful and rather optimistic. You have a good disposition although earlier in life you have had a struggle with yourself to control your impulse and temper.

"You are strongly socially inclined, you like to meet people, especially to mix with those you know well. You appreciate art, painting and music, but you will never be a success as an artist or as a creator or composer of music. You like sports and athletic events but devote more of your attention to reading about them in the sporting page than in actual participation.

"You are ambitious, and deserve credit for wanting to be well thought of by your family, business associates and friends. These ambitions come out most strongly in your tendency to indulge in day-dreams in building air-castles, but this does not mean that you fail to get into the game of life actively.

"You ought to continue to be successful so long as you stay in a social vocation. I mean if you keep at work bringing you in contact with people. Just what work you pick out isn't as important as the fact that it must be work bringing you in touch with people. On the negative side you would never have made a success at strictly theoretical work or in pure research work such as in physics or neurology."

tests by trained clinicians *(6, 7, 8, 9, 10)*, it has not supported the claims of persons employing non-standardized graphological techniques *(11)*.

Recently the writer was accosted by a night-club graphologist who wished to "read" his handwriting. The writer declined and offered to administer a Rorschach to the graphologist. An amiable discussion ensued, during which the graphologist ventured proof of the scientific basis of his work in that his clients affirmed the correctness of his interpretations. The writer suggested that a psychologist could make a blindfold reading and attain the same degree of verification.

EXPERIMENT

The following experiment was performed in the writer's class in introductory psychology to demonstrate the ease with which clients may be misled by a general personality description into unwarranted approval of a diagnostic tool. The writer had discussed his Diagnostic Interest Blank *(5)*[2] (hereafter referred to as DIB) in connection with the role of personal motivational factors in perceptual selectivity. Class members requested that they be given the test and a personality evaluation. The writer acquiesced. At the next meeting the 39 students were given DIB's to fill out, and were told that they would be given a brief personality vignette as soon as the writer had time to examine their test papers. One week later each student was given a typed personality sketch with his name written on it. The writer encouraged the expressed desire of the class for secrecy regarding the context of the sketches. Fortunately, this was the day on which a quiz was scheduled; hence it was possible to ensure their sitting two seats apart without arousing suspicion. From the experimenter's point of view it was essential that no student see the sketch received by any other student because all sketches were identical.[3] The students were unsuspecting.

The personality sketch contains some material which overlaps with that of Paterson, but consists of 13 statements rather than a narrative description. A further difference lies in the fact that this sketch was designed for more nearly universal validity than Paterson's appears to have been. The sketch consists of the following items.

1. You have a great need for other people to like and admire you.

2. You have a tendency to be critical of yourself.

3. You have a great deal of unused capacity which you have not turned to your advantage.

4. While you have some personality weaknesses, you are generally able to compensate for them.

5. Your sexual adjustment has presented problems for you.

6. Disciplined and self-controlled outside, you tend to be worrisome and insecure inside.

7. At times you have serious doubts as to whether you have made the right decision or done the right thing.

8. You prefer a certain amount of change and variety and become dissatisfied when hemmed in by restrictions and limitations.

[2] The DIB consists of a list of hobbies, reading materials, personal characteristics, job duties, and secret hopes and ambitions of one's ideal person. The test is interpreted qualitatively and personality dynamics are inferred along lines similar to projective tests.

[3] These statements came largely from a news-stand astrology book. The writer was not aware of Paterson's sketch at the time this problem was formulated and carried out.

9. You pride yourself as an independent thinker and do not accept others' statements without satisfactory proof.

10. You have found it unwise to be too frank in revealing yourself to others.

11. At times you are extroverted, affable, sociable, while at other times you are introverted, wary, reserved.

12. Some of your aspirations tend to be pretty unrealistic.

13. Security is one of your major goals in life.

Before the sketches were passed to the students, instructions were given first to read the sketches and then to turn the papers over and make the following ratings:

A. Rate on a scale of zero (poor) to five (perfect) how effective the DIB is in revealing personality.

B. Rate on a scale of zero to five the degrees to which the personality description reveals basic characteristics of your personality.

C. Then turn the paper again and check each statement as true or false about yourself or use a question mark if you cannot tell.

In answer to their requests students were informed that the writer had another copy of their sketch and would give it to them after the data were collected. After the papers had been returned to the writer students were asked to raise their hands if they felt the test had done a good job. Virtually all hands went up and the students noticed this. Then the first sketch item was read and students were asked to indicate by hands whether they had found anything similar on their sketches. As all hands rose, the class burst into laughter. It was pointed out to them that the experiment had been performed·as an object lesson to demonstrate the tendency to be overly impressed by vague statements and to endow the diagnostician with an unwarrantedly high degree of insight. Similarities between the demonstration and the activities of charlatans were pointed out. That the experience had meaning for them was indicated by the fact that at least one-third of the class asked for copies of the sketch so that they might try the trick on their friends.

RESULTS

The data show clearly that the group had been gulled. Ratings of adequacy of the DIB included only one rating below 4. Thus the instrument received a high degree of personal validation. In the evaluation of the sketch as a whole there were five ratings below 4 (Table 1). While a few students were most critical of the sketch than of the DIB, most of them were ready to admit that basic personality traits had been revealed.

The number of specific items accepted as true varied among the group from 8 to 13 except for one individual who accepted only 5 (Table 2). This same individual rated the test at 4 and the sketch at 2. Mean acceptance was 10.2 items.

No significant relationships were found between any of the ratings and sex, age, occupational background, or grades on the subsequent quiz.

TABLE 1
Distribution of ratings

Ratings	0	1	2	3	4	5	N
A (DIB)	0	0	0	1	25	13	39
B (Sketch)	0	0	1	4	18	16	39

TABLE 2
Distribution of "true" responses

Number True	5	6	7	8	9	10	11	12	13	N
Frequency	1	0	0	5	5	10	9	7	2	39

In addition to the high ratings of the DIB which indicate a degree of gullibility or fallacious judgment, further evidence can be seen in the degree to which ratings were made on other than evidential grounds or contrary to the evidence. If the individual accepts all of the items as applying to himself, he is somewhat justified in accepting the instrument; if he rejects all of the items in the sketch, he is justified in rejecting the DIB.

The chi-square test indicates a degree of association, significant at the 1-per-cent level, between ratings of the sketch (rating B) and the number of items checked as true. However, the operation of other factors in judgment from part to whole is clearly indicated. For some individuals the presence of 8 true statements among the 13 were considered sufficient evidence for acceptance of the sketch as perfect. For others, high, but imperfect, validity was indicated by the acceptance of 12 of the 13 items. It may be said, then, that among this group of students individuals varied in the degree to which they weighted the truth and falsity of the descriptive items in arriving at an overall evaluation.

Ratings of the DIB as a diagnostic instrument (rating A) and number of items accepted as true shown no significant relationship (the probability value of the chi-square is .4). On the one hand, estimation of the adequacy of the personality sketch was partially dependent upon the amount of confirmatory evidence. On the other hand, the degree of approval of the test was independent of the degree to which test results agreed with self-evaluations. That is, validation of the test instrument was an all-or-none affair depending on a certain minimum amount of evidence. The amount of confirmatory evidence set up as a standard varied among the students.

All of the students accepted the DIB as a good or perfect instrument for personality measurement. Most of them can be accused of a logical error in accepting the test on such scanty evidence. Those who accepted the test with a rating of 5 while accepting fewer than all of the 13 statements have demonstrated a disregard for the evidence of their own criticisms: The same can be said for those who rated the test higher than the personality sketch. It is interesting that the student most critical of the personality sketch, as indicated in an overall rating of 2 and acceptance of only 5 items, at the same time rated the DIB at 4.

TABLE 3
Group acceptance of sketch items

Response	Item Number												
	1	2	3	4	5	6	7	8	9	10	11	12	13
True	28	38	23	31	18	35	38	37	34	35	34	12	28
False	4	0	1	0	9	3	0	1	3	2	1	9	7
Uncertain	7	1	15	8	12	1	1	1	2	2	4	18	4

The degrees of group acceptance for the 13 items are indicated in Table 3. None of the items attained complete universal validity, though more than half of them were close to complete group acceptance. . . .

CONCLUSIONS

1. Claims of validity for their methods and results by pseudo-diagnosticians can be duplicated or surpassed in the laboratory without the use of a diagnostic instrument. Blindfold personality estimates can be shown to be valid when the method of personal validation (confirmation by the client) is used for descriptive items of approximate universal validity.

2. Validation of a test instrument or of a personality sketch by means of personal validation is a fallacious procedure which presupposes objectivity of self-evaluation and an understanding of other persons on the part of the client.

3. Using the method of personal validation, a fictitious personality sketch can easily deceive persons into approving a diagnostic device even when there is incomplete acceptance of the sketch itself. A minimum degree of correspondence between the sketch and self-evluation appears to engender an attitude of acceptance is carried uncritically to the test instrument.

4. The personal validation procedure is likely to yield more fallacious results in the case of overall evaluations of a personality sketch than when specific statements are evaluated individually. . . .

5. Clinical psychologists and others who make inferences about personality characteristics may be led into ascribing an excessively high degree of significance to these inferences. There is pressing need for clinicians to submit their own procedures, presuppositions, and, perhaps, projections to experimental scrutiny.

REFERENCES

1. ALLPORT, G. W. *Personality, a psychological interpretation.* New York: Holt, 1937.
2. BOBERTAG, O. Bemerkungen zum Verifikationsproblem. *Z. f. ang. Psychol.,* 1934, 46, 246–249.
3. COHEN, M. R., AND NAGEL, E. *Introduction to logic and the scientific method.* New York: Harcourt, Brace, 1934.
4. CRIDER, B. A study of a character analyst. *J. soc. Psychol.,* 1944, 20, 315–318.
5. FORER, B. R. *A diagnostic interest blank.* (In press.)
6. HARRISON, R. Studies in the use and validity of the Thematic Apperception Test with mentally disordered patients. II. A quantitative validity study. III. Validation by the method of "blind analysis." *Char. & Pers.,* 1940, 9, 122–133; 134–138.
7. HARRISON, R. The Thematic Apperception and Rorschach methods of personality analysis in clinical practice. *J. Psychol.,* 1943, 15, 49–74.
8. HARRISON, R., AND ROTTER, J. B. A note on the reliability of the Thematic Apperception Test. This *Journal,* 1945, 40, 97–99.
9. HERTZ, M. R., AND RUBINSTEIN, B. B. A comparison of three "blind" Rorschach analyses. *Amer. J. Orthopsychiat.,* 1939, 9, 295–314.
10. MURRAY, H. A., AND STEIN, M. Note on the selection of combat officers. *Psychosom. Med.,* 1943, 4, 386–391.
11. PASCAL, G. R., AND SUTTELL, B. Testing the claims of a graphologist. *J. Personality,* 1947, 16, 192–197.
12. TAYLOR, D. W. An analysis of predictions of delinquency based on case studies. This *Journal,* 1947, 42, 45–56.

VIII. Prejudice, Propaganda, and Persuasion

Gordon Allport once said, "The concept of attitudes is probably the most distinctive and indispensable concept in contemporary American social psychology." There has been more social psychological research on attitudes and attitude change than on any other issue.

A fair amount of research on attitudes seeks simply to discover whether people are favorably or unfavorably disposed toward other people. When people are unfavorably disposed to categories of people, we characterize them as prejudiced. We tend to think of prejudiced people as "authoritarian personalities" with all kinds of deep psychological hang-ups (see "The Authoritarian Personality by T. W. Adorno, et al.). There probably are people with authoritarian personalities, but ideas such as the authoritarian personality may also serve as stereotypes that reinforce the incorrect assumption that prejudice is characteristic of a small group of bad people. Gordon Allport, in "The Nature of Prejudice," makes it clear that the issue is more

Artwork by Martin Riskin.

complicated than this. Prejudice and stereotypes are natural products of the way in which we think. They involve prejudgments and overgeneralizations. We form prejudices in much the same way we form other inferences, extrapolating to specific cases (individual people) on the basis of general information (characteristics of people of the same sex, race, occupation, etc.). Prejudice is often a natural product of thinking, not a troubled exception.

Consider prejudice toward women, for example. Philip Goldberg ("Are Women Prejudiced Against Women?") shows that both men and women form expectations of what women can and cannot do that, although consistent with their experience (there *are* relatively few women in law, linguistics, and city planning), are nonetheless invalid. I believe that the inference that because most women *do not* work in various jobs or display particular skills, they *cannot* do the same things men do, is responsible for a great deal of injustice. However, the results of Goldberg's experiment are subject to alternative interpretations. Although he claims to have found that women consider themselves inferior in traditional feminine fields, the small differences he found do not warrant this conclusion (i.e., they were not statistically significant). Moreover, in Goldberg's experiment the subjects were asked to rate the quality of essays about occupations. If the subjects assumed that males were better writers than females, they would have rated all male essays of all occupations as superior to the female essays, without in any way believing that males could do the jobs any better. Whatever the criticisms of Goldberg's experiment, he does show how sexual biases can distort people's perceptions, which in turn can perpetuate empirically invalid and socially destructive attitudes.

People have strong investments in their attitudes, because they are a part of systems of understanding that define social reality. It is often difficult to change attitudes, because they can be justified in many different ways. The evidence that is relative to them is often open to countless interpretations. In the model that I have been advancing, the man on the street is like a social scientist, and the attitudes he possesses are hypotheses. In an interesting irony, the behavior of a social scientist provides us with an excellent example of ways in which we preserve our attitudes by selective interpretation of empirical facts. Wilhelm Wundt ("Cultivating the Conservative Stereotype") shows how a psychologist reinforces his political biases by slanting his interpretation of the results of an experiment.

One of the defining aspects of immaturity is egocentricity. I would expect people with poorly differentiated and poorly integrated conceptions of other people (and, incidentally, themselves) to be limited in their ability to see the essential ways in which they are similar to other people. It would follow, then, that the most prejudiced people (as I have represented the concept) would be most prone to emphasize the difference between members of out-groups and themselves. In a forceful demonstration, a school teacher shows how easy it is for children to create in-groups and out-groups, how quickly children can cultivate distorted perceptions of out-group members, and how much these perceptions affect the children's conception of themselves (see "Ghetto for Blue-Eyes in the Classroom," by John Leonard). However, in a set of studies on adults, Milton Rokeach and Louis Mezei ("Race and Shared Belief as Factors in Social Choice") show that membership in an out-group (in this case, a different race) is less important than the manifestation of differences in beliefs. When we get close enough to people to know more about them than their superficial characteristics, we make distinctions that supersede preliminary stereotypes.

I have placed the greatest emphasis on the cognitive component of attitudes (as opposed to the emotional and behavioral). The relationship between what people *think* about others and how they *react* toward them is not as straightforward as we might expect. Ronald Dillehay ("On the Irrelevance of the Classical Negative Evidence Concerning the Effect of Attitudes on Behavior") discusses some of the studies that seem to challenge the idea that there is a straightforward relationship between attitudes and behavior. Although the author shows that the studies he reviews do not really test the correspondence between attitudes and action, he does not explain why the relationship has been weak in studies that have supplied more valid tests. Is it possible that the idea of impression management could supply a positive explanation of the negative findings?

39 Reconsideration: The Authoritarian Personality

by Richard Christie

The Authoritarian Personality
by T. W. Adorno et al.
W. W. Norton & Co., 1950; paper, 1969,

Reconsidered by Richard Christie

The phenomenon of fascism, fed by the conflagration of World War II, made social scientists feel compelled to understand the holocaust, to predict whether it could happen again or would never happen in a democratic America. Fierce disagreements ensued among those who thought that fascism reflected some perverse strain in the German personality, or a unique concatenation of events in German history, or a fatal flaw in human nature that, given the right circumstances, could erupt anywhere.

One of the first major studies of this question, *The Authoritarian Personality*, was published in 1950 and provoked instant acclaim and controversy. The title was a catchy name for a seductive concept. The guiding premise of the book was "that the political, economic, and social convictions of an individual often form a broad and coherent pattern, as if bound together by a 'mentality' or 'spirit,' and that this pattern is an expression of deeplying trends in the personality." Potentially fascist individuals, the team of authors said, shared a constellation of predictable prejudices that reflected basic insecurities and conflicts deep in the personality. The personality-flaw theory of fascism turned up in other explanations at that time—notably in Wilhelm Reich's *Mass Psychology of Fascism* (1946), H. V. Dicks's interpretations of interviews with Nazi prisoners of war (1950), and Abraham Maslow's reflections on native fascists in America

("The Authoritarian Character Structure," 1943).

The Authoritarian Personality became one of the most important books ever published in the behavioral sciences; judging from the number of studies and debates it generated and from the opinions of the scientists themselves. In 1959 the Ford Foundation asked all present and former fellows of the Center for Advanced Study in the Behavioral Sciences to name the most influential book in the behavioral sciences in the previous 25 years. *The Authoritarian Personality* received the highest total score from the group of anthropologists, economists, historians, political scientists, psychologists, sociologists, and statisticians.

The conclusions of *The Authoritarian Personality* grew out of the neo-Freudian intellectual tradition that developed in Europe before the war. The germ of the book can be traced back to the Institute of Social Research at the University of Frankfurt, Germany, which in the 1920s

Agree or disagree?

"Present treatment of conscientious objectors, draft evaders, and enemy aliens is too lenient and mollycoddling. If a person won't fight for his country, he deserves a lot worse than just prison or a work camp."

received an endowment for the study of anti-Semitism. Members of the Frankfurt school—Erich Fromm, Herbert Marcuse, Theodore Adorno, Max Horkheimer—shared the Freudian conviction that politics and prejudice were determined more by unconscious conflicts within the nuclear family than by social or economic conditions.

The theory maintained that prejudice reflected a deep-seated psychological disturbance created in families that were marked by strong parental authority, especially by the dominance of the father and the submissive role of the mother. In such typical European bourgeois households, the Freudians thought, the instinctive needs of the children were thwarted and repressed. Instead of learning to accept and integrate the parts of the self that the parents punished or repudiated, the child repressed these elements and eventually came to displace them—or to project them, in Freudian terminology—onto minority groups such as the Jews. Was the bourgeois child forbidden to express sexual desires? Then Jews were regarded as oversexed, licentious, and lewd. Did the child have to be obsessively clean? Then Jews were filthy.

The Frankfurt researchers conducted interviews with hundreds of German citizens during the 1920s and confirmed their suspicions that anti-Semitism was rife in Germany and that the explosion of totalitarianism was imminent. When Hitler came to power the researchers were prepared. They left Germany; most came to the United States.

During the war, Horkheimer, who became director of research for the American Jewish Committee, persuaded the AJC to sponsor research along the lines begun in Germany. R. Nevitt Sanford, then a young faculty member at the University of California at Berkeley, and one of the pioneer group of academic psychologists trained by Henry Murray in the Psychological Clinic at Harvard, was in touch with Horkheimer, and the Berkeley Public Opinion Project came into being. Two other members of what was to become the most cited quartet in the field of personality and social psychology were Else Frenkel-Brunswik and Daniel J. Levinson. Frenkel-Brunswik had received her Ph.D. in psychology at the University of Vienna (yet another European connection) and was a research associate at Berkeley's famed Institute for Child Welfare. Levinson was a graduate student in personality and social psychology at the University of California.

When the Berkeley project began its research on the authoritarian personality, these three provided the uniquely American emphasis on quantitative methodology; their approach was grafted onto the qualitative work of the Frankfurt Institute, represented in the quartet by Theodore Adorno (who was never actually a member of the University of California faculty). When the research was completed, I was a graduate student at Berkeley and was quickly caught up in the whirlwind of excitement that the project generated. The fascist mentality was going to be dissected with

Agree or disagree?

"Patriotism and loyalty are the first and most important requirements of a good citizen."

the new techniques of personality measurement and assessment.

The Authoritarian Personality touched raw nerves with what seemed the cool hand of science. By bringing two intellectual traditions—the European philosophical and psychoanalytical school, and the pragmatic American concern with measurement—to one emotional topic, the research fitted its times perfectly.

The desire to find a scientific way to verify Freud's idea of the psychology of prejudice led to the development of a 30-item test known as the F-Scale (for fascist). This scale consisted of statements with which the test taker could agree or disagree strongly, somewhat, or slightly: "Obedience and respect for authority are the most important virtues children should learn," for instance. The results could be totaled to indicate whether the individual was high or low on authoritarianism. The researchers also designed other scales to measure a person's degree of anti-Semitism, racism, and prejudice in general (the E-, or Ethnocentrism, Scale), and the extent of his or her political and economic conservatism (the PEC-Scale).

The book was based primarily on the results of these questionnaires, which

were gathered from 2,000 people. (They were not a representative sample of the United States population, but an amalgam of college students, club members, and other groups available to the researchers, such as psychiatric patients at the Langley-Porter Neuropsychiatric Clinic in San Francisco and inmates at San Quentin prison.) In addition to such quantitative measures, the researchers fleshed out the statistics with clinical interviews with 80 people selected from the entire sample. For a qualitative analysis of authoritarianism they used a battery of psychoanalytically oriented tests that were thought to reveal unconscious desires and conflicts, including the Thematic Apperception Test (TAT), Projective Sentence Tests, and the Rorschach. Psychoanalysis had been an almost taboo subject in academic psychology prior to World War II, but after the war, as a result of the burgeoning number of graduate programs in clinical psychology, academia reached the apogee of its entrancement with Freudian theory and methods.

The final portrait of the authoritarian personality represented a mesh of techniques. The book's 990 pages contained more than 120 tables and figures, prolific quotations from the interviewees, and the subjective interpretations of the psychodynamic tests. The result was a rich mosaic of descriptive differences between prejudiced and unprejudiced people: The authoritarian person projected repressed hostility onto minority groups, was narrow-minded and rigid about rules and values, unquestioningly submissive to authority, sexually inhibited, intolerant of ambiguity, politically conservative—in short, ripe for fascism. The unprejudiced person, in contrast, was open-minded, liberal, independent, and kind—rather like the self-image of liberal intellectuals and psychologists.

The book was an immediate success with anyone who had a prejudice against prejudice. It was reassuring to believe that the Nazi terror occurred because good Germans had bad personalities.

But the book was also a success for its extraordinary scope, texture, and method. Given the brevity of the F-Scale, its ease of administration, and the enormous scientific and political significance of what it purported to measure, hundreds upon hundreds of researchers and students used the test, or variations of it, in their work. (See the Scarr and

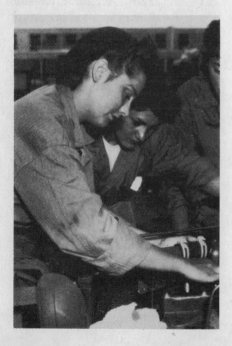

Weinberg article in this issue.) By 1974, at least 533 Ph.D. dissertations had dealt with various aspects of authoritarianism, along with untold numbers of studies by other social scientists.

Although *The Authoritarian Personality* burst upon psychology like a rocket, it fell to earth almost at once. In 1954 Marie Jahoda and I edited a book of essays and criticisms about the research. Sociologists objected to the authors' preoccupation with inner psychological workings as the primary cause of prejudice, rather than with historical, cultural, and situational causes. Others thought that the theoretical notion of an authoritarian personality might be correct but that the authors had not demonstrated it. The innovation of combining psychoanalysis and statistics, they felt, was doomed. "In the marriage of the two methodologies," wrote Herbert H. Hyman and Paul B. Sheatsley, "the quantitative statistical method is all too often cast in the role of the stodgy husband who just answers 'Yes, dear' to all the bright suggestions made by the wife."

As it happened, the wife's suggestions themselves became less popular throughout the decade. Many of the projective tests that were supposed to tap unconscious needs turned out to be technically deficient, useless as research tools. Social psychologists broke their romantic engagement with psychoanalysis and turned to their laboratories; the elegance of one's experimental design, not the collection of clinical tests and surveys, became the key to professional recognition and status.

A second attack on *The Authoritarian Personality* was directed at the F-Scale itself. Unfortunately, all of the items in the scale had been worded in such a way that agreement with them was the "authoritarian" answer. Later, researchers pointed out that, if they do not care much about the topic, some people can be counted on to agree with

---

Agree or disagree?

"Although women are necessary in the armed forces and in industry, they should be returned to their proper place in the home as soon as the war ends."

---

anything; further, most people will agree with vague statements about which they or anyone else have little knowledge on which to base a judgment ("The wild sex life of the ancient Greeks and Romans was tame compared to some of the goings-on in this country, even in places where people might least expect it"). Were high scores on the F-Scale due to authoritarian tendencies within the person, or were they due to simple agreement with ambiguous statements? And did this indiscriminate agreement reflect "submission to authority" or simply poor education? Or both?

Yet another serious blow to *The Authoritarian Personality* in the years after its publication came from the mood of McCarthyism across the country. The authors were blamed for focusing on authoritarianism of the political right and neglecting authoritarianism on the left. Now the argument turned to whether prejudiced people had a particular personality make-up and set of attitudes that attracted them to fascist politics, or whether prejudice was a matter of narrow-mindedness that could be found across the political spectrum. The F-Scale was duly redesigned and given new labels such as "dogmatism" and "rigidity," as psychologists sought to determine whether authoritarianism by any other name would smell as sour.

The authors of the original research had posited that the F-Scale was composed of nine personality characteristics, including conventional, conservative attitudes, submission to people in power, superstition and stereotypy, destructiveness and cynicism, and exaggerated concern with sex. After 30 years of statistical analysis of all the versions of the F-Scale, tested on different groups, it now appears that the original items do not fall into nine neat categories.

But some questions in the F-Scale have held up throughout all of the analyses: those dealing with general attitudes toward authority; with authoritarian submission ("Every person should have complete faith in some supernatural power whose decisions he accepts without question"); with conventionalism ("A person who has bad manners, habits, and breeding can hardly expect to get along with decent people"); and with what was called authoritarian aggression ("An insult to our honor should always be punished"). After close inspection of the hundreds of studies that had used the F-Scale, researchers have found that though many of the early experiments were inept and found no significant results, few actually contradicted the investigators' predictions about how authoritarian people would behave. Apparently the authoritarian personality was alive and well under the smoke screen of methods and politics.

In the past 10 years interest in the concept of authoritarianism has returned, fueled, I think, by the wave of political dissent in the 1960s. Cleaned-up, modernized versions of the F-Scale have enabled psychologists to predict people's attitudes and behavior in a range of real-life situations. My colleagues and I, for example, have used the F-Scale to help select unbiased juries for political trials. People with strongly conventional, law-and-order views are more likely than low authoritarians to assume that war protesters actually plotted to kidnap Henry Kissinger, that Joan Little planned to kill her prison guard in North Carolina, or that dissidents should be punished severely, no matter how slender the evidence.

Current laboratory experiments are also validating—and refining—the concept of authoritarianism. It is no longer enough to talk about simple dispositions of personality; the task is to define the conditions under which personal inclination is translated into behavior. The civil-rights story of the 1950s and 1960s taught the nation the difference between prejudice and discrimination. Plenty of people who would otherwise score high on tests of prejudice stopped their discriminatory actions when forced to by law; plenty of nonprejudiced liberals have discriminated against minorities because of social custom or pressure. Stanley Milgram's experiments in the early 1960s—which demonstrated that "good people" will obey authority and inflict pain on others even though they long not to—represented the new direction of social psychology in the study of

Agree or disagree?
"Negro musicians are sometimes as good as white musicians at swing music and jazz, but it is a mistake to have mixed Negro-white bands."

prejudice. The emphasis on personality shifted to emphasis on circumstance.

The current view of the authoritarian personality is that the creature exists, but it needs the proper conditions before it is lured from its lair. For example, in 1948 social psychologist Milton Rokeach did some experiments to show that ethnocentric, prejudiced individuals actually behaved more rigidly in experimental situations than nonprejudiced people did. This finding prompted a number of researchers to try to relate scores of authoritarianism and prejudice to other tests of rigidity. If one simply tallied up the hits and the misses in all their studies, one would become utterly confused.

An examination of the research shows that the connection between authoritarian attitudes and rigid behavior does not show up unless two conditions are met. First, a mental set, or expectation to behave a certain way, must be created. Second, high authoritarians are likely to behave inflexibly when they are under stress— when they have been frustrated in their goals or tasks, or when their self-esteem has been buffeted.

When both of these conditions are present, high scorers on the F-Scale do behave rigidly; they persist in inefficient and futile attempts to solve problems. If neither condition is present, there is rarely any predictable relationship between authoritarian attitudes and rigid behavior. When one condition is present and not the other, then high

authoritarians sometimes behave as expected and sometimes not.

Some parts of the book's path-finding research have fallen from current favor. The authors found strong relationships between F-Scale attitudes, anti-Semitism and racism, and political and economic conservatism. But in the last decade, few studies have bothered to see whether these relationships have lasted. One reason may be that because the original findings were so strong, some readers assumed that authoritarianism, prejudice, and conservatism are still closely connected. Another is that the prejudice and economic conservatism scales contained items specific to issues of the 1940s, and many of the items now seem outdated and heavy-handed ("Negro musicians are sometimes as good as white musicians at swing music and jazz, but it is a mistake to have mixed Negro-white bands").

Today, a quarter of a century since the original research, any effort to get people to reveal their true feelings must be sensitive to the sophisticated nuances of prejudice in the 1970s. It is baffling, though, that so few efforts have been made. A recent computer scan of research turned up only one contemporary version of a scale to measure anti-Semitism—most experimenters still use 40-year-old measures.

The authors of *The Authoritarian Personality* wanted to understand the roots of fascism and anti-Semitism. The F-Scale they created, especially in its modern forms, still identifies people who hold "conventional" opinions— those, for example, who oppose the ERA, welfare, legal support for abortion, negotiating a treaty on the Panama Canal, and legalizing the personal use of marijuana. But whether such people are any more likely than liberals to goose-step to their government's rules has not been resolved. Social scientists might like to think that liberalism is the best insulation against fascism, but they have not proved it.　□

Richard Christie, *professor of social psychology at Columbia University, has been studying variations of authoritarian attitudes and behavior since his graduate-school days. In recent years he has been using a modern version of the F-Scale to aid in jury selection for major political trials across the country.*

Reconsideration: The Nature of Prejudice

40

by Elliot Aronson

The Nature of Prejudice
by Gordon W. Allport
Addison-Wesley, 1954
Anchor Books, 1958, paper

Reconsidered by Elliot Aronson

The year was 1954. It was the year of the landmark Supreme Court decision in the case of Brown *vs.* the Board of Education of Topeka, Kansas. It was also the year of the publication of Gordon Allport's *The Nature of Prejudice*, the first scholarly synthesis of research and thinking about the social, personal, economic, and political causes of ethnic prejudice. These two events were not unrelated.

The 1954 decision overruled an 1896 Supreme Court decision, Plessy *vs.* Ferguson, that determined that a railroad was permitted to segregate its passengers racially as long as it provided equal facilities for both races. The impact of the 1896 decision, of course, extended far beyond railways, most seriously affecting black children who were being educated in segregated schools. In the Brown case the Court held that "separate but equal" was psychologically impossible because the mere fact of segregation implied to a segregated minority group that its members were inferior to the majority. Such an implication, the court said, could be damaging to the spirit of racial minorities.

The Brown case actually consisted of five separate cases that posed the same fundamental question: Does school segregation violate the equal protection under the laws guaranteed by the Fourteenth Amendment? This case may be the first instance in which the young science of social psychology significantly influenced the decision of the

Supreme Court. Social psychologists testified in all of the individual trials; moreover, in the actual Supreme Court case, three prominent social psychologists (representing a much larger group) filed an articulate amicus brief testifying to the harms of segregation. The brief read in part:

"Segregation, prejudice and discrimination and their social concomitants potentially damage the personality of all children. . . . Minority group children learn the inferior status to which they are assigned. . . . They often react with feelings of inferiority and a sense of personal humiliation. . . . Under these conditions the minority group child is thrown into a conflict with regard to his feelings about himself and his group. He wonders whether his group and himself are worthy of no more respect than they receive. This conflict and confusion leads to self-hate."

The Supreme Court ruling read in part:

"To separate [Negro children] from others of similar age and qualifications solely because of their race generates a feeling of inferiority as to their status in the community that may affect their hearts and minds in a way unlikely ever to be undone. . . . We conclude that in the field of public education the doctrine 'separate but equal' has no place. Separate educational facilities are inherently unequal."

Gordon Allport's book was both a harbinger and a reflection of the thinking that went into the Supreme Court decision. *The Nature of Prejudice* is a remarkable mixture of careful scholarship and humane values. Allport marshaled an impressive array of data and organized those data clearly and

passionately. The book has influenced an entire generation of social psychologists, and deservedly so; it is fair to say that in the quarter century since its publication, no better treatment of prejudice has appeared. I realize that that is a strong statement, given 25 years of frenzied research on prejudice and group conflict. But I do not imply that Allport's research is up to date or even that its thrust is absolutely right.

As I was rereading the book for the first time in 18 years, I was struck by two strong and apparently contradictory feelings. One was that *The Nature of Prejudice* is remarkably modern; the other was that it is hopelessly archaic.

What is modern about the book is Allport's perspective; he carefully chose among existing theories and data to come up with a brilliant and accurate statement of the eclectic causes and possible cures of prejudice. Indeed, with one notable exception (to be discussed later), the conclusions Allport drew are not noticeably different from the conclusions that a reasonable scholar would draw today. This is a tribute to the wisdom, scholarship, and judgment of a graceful mind. Allport avoided the twin pitfalls of championing one position to the exclusion of all others, or of giving each position equal status.

For example, he provided a good description of the prejudiced personality. But even as he acknowledged that the predisposition toward prejudice *could* be deeply ingrained in the personality of some individuals, Allport stopped short of granting this phenomenon the degree of universality and impact that other social scientists of the time did. By so doing, he avoided the pessimism to which many of his contemporaries fell victim: If prejudice is a deeply ingrained personality trait rooted in early childhood experiences, then its cure is unlikely without prolonged individual psychotherapy. This belief— like the position espoused around 1907

RECONSIDERATION: *THE NATURE OF PREJUDICE*, by Gordon W. Allport, written by Elliot Aronson, is taken from HUMAN NATURE Magazine, July 1978. Copyright © 1978 by Human Nature, Inc. Reprinted by permission of the publisher.

by sociologist William Graham Sumner that "stateways cannot change folkways"—was quite at odds with the spirit behind the 1954 Supreme Court decision and hardly encouraging to a social-action approach. Similarly, Allport acknowledged that prejudice can be affected by economic factors (e.g., competition for scarce jobs), but he thought that economic issues primarily aggravated prejudiced attitudes rather than being their primary cause.

Allport thought that the major causes of prejudice were conformity, social norms, and the conventional experience of living in a prejudiced society. Rather than trying to reduce the prejudice of the individual (through psychotherapy) or to eliminate economic competition, Allport concluded that it would be more effective to try to end segregation and discrimination and thus bring about contact between ethnic groups on an equal basis. If children hear their parents make offensive remarks about minority groups, see media stereotypes of minority groups, and deal only with minority-group members who have menial jobs, they are almost certain to share the prevailing stereotype. Allport confidently predicted that contact on an equal basis would reverse that trend. He advocated public policies that would provide better jobs for blacks; he refused to worry about the negative effect of economic competition, guessing that the benefits of equal contact would outweigh any temporary cost. Similarly, he bet heavily that school desegregation would ultimately reduce prejudice by bringing black and white children together under conditions of equal status.

Allport championed better jobs for blacks and the desegregation of schools not simply for economic or moral reasons, but also because he believed that if whites participated with blacks under conditions of equal status, their beliefs and prejudices would change. This was a psychologically important idea at a time when many researchers

This picture taken in a Tennessee classroom in 1961 seemed to justify Allport's hopes for racial harmony.

thought that the mere dispersal of information or "truth" about blacks was the best way to change attitudes. As early as 1954, Allport argued that participation and commitment were more important routes to attitude change. He wrote: "While preaching and exhortation may play a part in the process [of reducing prejudice], the lesson will not be learned at the verbal level alone. It will be learned in muscle, nerve, and gland best through participation." In addition, he recognized the fact that people tend to accept and make the best of an accomplished fact: "[Official policies] set models that once accepted, create habits and conditions favorable to their maintenance." It was not until 1959 that researchers began to find experimental support for these speculations. Allport was clearly ahead of his time.

This is not to say that Allport was entirely correct in his predictions. He erred in his belief that desegregation would by itself reduce prejudice. Allport's book brims with his confidence that school desegregation would eventually create understanding between ethnic groups and reduce conflict. At the time, Allport was not certain how the Brown *vs.* Board of Education case would be resolved. But he remained convinced that desegregation would occur, especially in the South, where the harm of segregation

appeared most flagrant. He reasoned that even if "separate but equal" remained the law of the land, communities would not be able to bear the financial burden of maintaining two sets of equal schools and inevitably they would desegregate.

It is now a quarter of a century since desegregation began, and many studies have assessed its effectiveness. One of the most thorough longitudinal studies of desegregation was published in 1975 by Harold Gerard and Norman Miller. Gerard and Miller, investigating the schools in Riverside, California, found that long after the schools were desegregated, black, white, and Mexican-American children tended not to integrate but to hang together in their own ethnic clusters. More disturbing, the children's anxiety increased and remained high long after desegregation had occurred. These depressing developments have been echoed in dozens of smaller studies across the nation.

Indeed, if one reads the most careful, scholarly reviews of the research on the effects of desegregation, such as those by Nancy St. John in 1975 and Walter Stephan in 1978, one must conclude that Allport's confidence was misplaced. The evidence is, at best, mixed; at worst, negative. No single study shows that desegregation brought a significant increase in the self-esteem of minority children; as a matter of fact, in fully 25 percent of the studies, desegregation is followed by a significant *decrease* in the self-esteem of the minority children. Because the Supreme Court had regarded low self-esteem among black children as one of the major harms of segregation, these results are ironic as well as tragic. Further, the weight of the evidence suggests that desegregation does not decrease the prejudice of white children toward black children and that desegregation *increases* the prejudice of blacks toward whites. Finally, although a few studies did find improvements in the academic performance of black children in desegrated schools, most do not show such trends.

What went wrong? The social psychologists who filed the original amicus brief in 1954 never meant to imply that the harmful effects of desegregation would be eliminated automatically, regardless of the conditions under which desegregation would be accomplished. Recent evidence supports their caution: Contact on an equal footing is not achieved simply by busing children of different ethnic groups to the same school. If the teacher indicates any prejudice or expects low performance from minorities, this attitude will be conveyed to the children and can adversely affect their self-esteem and achievement.

Then there is the problem of the atmosphere of the classroom. Allport specified that equality of contact would be most effective when individuals pursued common goals. What he apparently failed to realize is that American education does not promote the pursuit of common goals. The classroom structure in most schools is highly competitive, unintentionally encouraging the children to view each other as enemies. This system exacerbates whatever prejudices existed prior to desegregation. Too often, children find themselves locked in a win-lose situation where they must compete not only for good grades but also for the respect and affection of the classroom teacher, who is an extremely important person in the lives of young children. This competition can breed animosity even among children of similar interests and backgrounds. When tensions and stereotyping exist as a result of ethnic unfamiliarity, the competitiveness is particularly harmful and frequently manifests itself in name calling, jeering, and fistfights.

Moreover, because school facilities in black communities are almost never equal to those in middle-class white areas, children who spend their first years in ghetto schools tend to be handicapped by inadequate preparation. The result is that the performance of black and Mexican-American children may have been adequate in the ghetto school, but it falls woefully short of the class average in integrated schools. In short, minority children, following desegregation, frequently find themselves in a

highly competitive situation where they are almost certain to lose. Is it then any wonder that their self-esteem decreases and that their prejudice toward whites often increases? Allport's error was not in predicting that equal contact in pursuit of common goals could have beneficial effects, but in assuming that desegregation would bring equal contact and in ignoring the possibility that, under

Gordon W. Allport, American psychologist and author of The Nature of Prejudice.

existing classroom conditions, contact might be harmful.

We know more now than we knew in 1954 about making school desegregation work. In five years of research with the school systems of Austin, Texas, and Santa Cruz, California, my colleagues and I strove to change the nature of classroom contact and to equalize the status of elementary-school students by reducing the extent of the dog-eat-dog competitiveness and by teaching them the benefits of cooperating with one another. In our experiments children worked in groups of five; each child was given a unique and vital piece of the lesson. The only way that any child could retrieve all of the material (and do well on the impending quiz) was to work with, and listen hard to, the other four.

The black, white, and Mexican-American children in these classrooms grew to like one another more, felt a greater sense of self-esteem, tended to like

school more, and felt greater empathy for one another than the children in traditional, competitive classrooms. Although the test scores of white children were the same in cooperative groups as they were in traditional classes, the performance of minority children was significantly better in the cooperative groups. Similar findings have been reported by Stuart Cook in Colorado, David Johnson in Minnesota, and Robert Slavin in Maryland.

I said earlier that for all of the prescience of *The Nature of Prejudice*, its tone gives it a dated feeling, a sense that one is holding an elegant antique. Gordon Allport wrote as if he were above the battle, a fine fair-minded Christian gentleman who was extending his hand to the less fortunate Jews and Negroes. His style suggests noblesse oblige — prejudice is a problem for decent white Christian men to deal with. Of course it is easy for me to pick up this tone in 1978. Allport's naive paternalism, when viewed through the prism of the 1960s, seems both infuriating and touching.

Most of us were naively paternalistic in the early 1950s; reading this book provides exciting insights about the distance we have come. To those who were born in the late 1950s, like my children and my students, it seems outrageously naive to treat prejudice as a one-way street — whites being prejudiced against blacks. Black prejudice against whites was not being investigated in 1954 and was outside the experience of middle-class, educated, white gentiles of that era. Allport seems too insulated to imagine that the downtrodden might be seething with rage and hatred of *all* whites, even good and fair-minded whites. The shouts of "Honky" were yet to be heard in 1954 — at least in Harvard Yard.

When Allport was writing his book behind Harvard's cloistered walls, his university actively or passively committed acts of discrimination that were perfectly acceptable to the decision makers of our greatest private university. In 1954, if one saw a young black face in Harvard Yard, chances were that he was either a foreign student or had a broom in his hand. Harvard also had a severe quota for Jews. (A distinguished professor once unashamedly defended that system to me. "If we admitted un-

In 1949 a Baptist church in Arkansas provided the only school available for these black children.

dergraduates solely on the basis of SAT scores and grade-point averages," he said, "the place would begin to look like Brooklyn College." We obviously couldn't have that.) To the best of my knowledge, in 1954 there was only one Jewish full professor in Harvard's psychology department or its social relations department. And throughout the 1950s, the few female members of the faculty were required to enter the hallowed Harvard Faculty Club through the back door (literally) and to eat in a separate dining hall. Harvard's most eminent professors, Allport among them, were either unaware of the discrimination, did not think it mattered, felt powerless to change it, or tried to

change it and failed—I cannot be sure which.

I do not imply that Allport was behaving hypocritically. Far from it. Such an assertion would be the worst kind of Monday-morning quarterbacking. Allport was a man of his era, and while 1954 was a banner year in the fight against prejudice, it was still the dark ages in some ways. The events of the last decade—particularly the explosion of militant activism among blacks, women, and Hispanic and Native Americans—have sharpened our awareness.

It is a cliché nowadays to take a pessimistic stance about progress in the civil-rights movement, to despair that prejudice and discrimination are still

very much with us. My prescription for such pessimism: Read *The Nature of Prejudice.* For me, revisiting this book has been a powerful reminder of how much progress we have made and how much our consciousness has expanded in just a quarter of a century. Allport's magnificent book contributed mightily to that progress. It also serves as a time capsule of what it was like in 1954. We are doubly in his debt.   □

Elliot Aronson, *who spent the past year at the Center for Advanced Study in the Behavioral Sciences in Stanford, California, is professor of psychology at the University of California at Santa Cruz. He is author of* The Social Animal, *among other books, and has studied the nature of prejudice for many years.*

Are Women Prejudiced Against Women? PHILIP GOLDBERG

41

An attitude that predisposes a person to think, feel, or act in favorable or unfavorable ways toward a group or its individual members is commonly referred to as *prejudice*. In the following selection, Goldberg describes a study which was designed to determine whether women are prejudiced against women. A sample of female college students were asked to read excerpts of six articles written by six different authors in six different professional fields (art history, dietetics, education, city planning, linguistics, and law). For half the sample a given article was ascribed to a male author; for the other half it was attributed to a female author. After reading each excerpt, the subjects were asked to rate the articles for value, persuasiveness, and profundity, and to rate the authors for writing style, professional competence, professional status, and ability to sway the reader.

Goldberg's findings reveal an unmistakable tendency for women to be biased against women. That is, subjects consistently found an article more valuable and its author more competent when the article bore the name of a male than when the same article was ascribed to a female author. This tendency was stronger in those occupations that traditionally have been viewed as "masculine," but it was also present in traditionally "female" fields. In other words, "Women seem to think that men are better at *everything*."

These findings are curious in their own right, and they are of special interest in light of current discussions of sexism. If Goldberg's data are representative, anti-feminism is very pervasive in our society. While he does not address the question in this study, a determination of the causes of such prejudice would seem to warrant research attention.

"Woman," advised Aristotle, "may be said to be an inferior man."

Because he was a man, Aristotle was probably biased. But what do women themselves think? Do they, consciously or unconsciously, consider their own sex inferior? And if so, does this belief prejudice them against other women — that is, make them view women, simply because they *are* women, as less competent than men?

According to a study conducted by myself and my associates, the answer to both questions is Yes. Women *do* consider their own sex inferior. And even when the facts give no support to this belief, they will persist in downgrading the competence — in particular, the intellectual and professional competence — of their fellow females.

Over the years, psychologists and psychiatrists have shown that both sexes consistently value men more highly than women. Characteristics considered male are usually praised; those considered female are usually criticized. In 1957 A. C. Sheriffs and J. P. McKee noted that "women are regarded as guilty of snobbery and irrational and unpleasant emotionality." Consistent with this report, E. G. French and G. S. Lesser found in 1964 that "women who value intellectual attainment feel they must reject the woman's role" — intellectual accomplishment apparently being considered, even among intellectual women, a masculine preserve. In addition, ardent feminists like Simone de Beauvoir and Betty Friedan believe that men, in important ways, are superior to women.

Now, is this belief simply prejudice, or are the characteristics and achievements of women really inferior to those of men? In answering this question, we need to draw some careful distinctions.

Different or Inferior?

Most important, we need to recognize that there are two distinct dimensions to the issue of sex differences. The first question is whether sex differences exist at all, apart from the obvious physical ones. The answer to this question seems to be a unanimous Yes — men, women, and social scientists agree that, psychologically and emotionally as well as physically, women *are* different from men.

But is being different the same as being inferior? It is quite possible to perceive a difference accurately but to value it inaccurately. Do women automatically view their differences from men as *deficiencies?* The evidence is that they do, and that this value judgment opens the door to anti-female prejudice. For if someone (male or female) concludes that women are inferior, his perceptions of women — their personalities, behavior, abilities, and accomplishments — will tend to be colored by his low expectations of women.

As Gordon W. Allport has pointed out in *The Nature of Prejudice,* whatever the facts about sex differences, anti-feminism — like any other prejudice — *distorts perception and experience.* What defines anti-feminism is not so much believing that women are inferior, as allowing that belief to distort one's perceptions of women. More generally, it is not the partiality itself, but the distortion born of that partiality, that defines prejudice.

Thus, an anti-Semite watching a Jew may see devious or sneaky behavior. But, in a Christian, he would regard such behavior only as quiet, reserved, or perhaps even shy. Prejudice is self-sustaining: It continually distorts the "evidence" on which the prejudiced person claims to base his beliefs. Allport makes it clear that anti-feminism, like anti-Semitism or any other prejudice, constantly twists the "evidence" of experience. We see not what is there, but what we *expect* to see.

The purpose of our study was to investigate whether there is real prejudice by women against women — whether perception itself is distorted unfavorably. Specifically, will women evaluate a professional article with a jaundiced eye when they think it is the work of a woman, but praise the same article when they think its author is a man? Our hypotheses were:

Even when the work is identical, women value the professional work of men more highly than that of women.

But when the professional field happens to be one traditionally reserved for women (nursing, dietetics), this tendency will be reversed, or at least greatly diminished.

Some 140 college girls, selected at random, were our subjects. One hundred were used for the preliminary work; 40 participated in the experiment proper.

To test the second hypothesis, we gave the 100 girls a list of 50 occupations and asked them to rate "the degree to which you associate the field with men or with women." We found that law and city planning were fields strongly associated with men, elementary school teaching and dietetics were fields strongly associated with women, and two fields — linguistics and art history — were chosen as neutrals, not strongly associated with either sex.

Now we were ready for the main experiment. From the professional literature of each of these six fields, we took one article. The articles were edited and abridged to about 1500 words, then combined into two equal sets of booklets. The crucial manipulation had to do with the authors' names — the same article bore a male name in one set of booklets, a female name in the other set. An example: if, in set one, the first article bore the name John T. McKay, in set two the same article would appear under the name Joan T. McKay. Each booklet contained three articles by "men" and three articles by "women."

The girls, seated together in a large lecture hall, were told to read the articles in their booklets and given these instructions:

"In this booklet you will find excerpts of six articles written by six different authors in six different professional fields. At the end of each article you will find several questions. . . . You are not presumed to be sophisticated or knowledgeable in all the fields. We are interested in the ability of college students to make critical evaluations. . . ."

Note that no mention at all was made of the authors' sexes. That information was contained — apparently only by coincidence — in the author's names. The girls could not know, therefore, what we were really looking for.

At the end of each article were nine questions asking the girls to rate the articles for value, persuasiveness, and profundity — and to rate the authors for writing style, professional competence, professional status, and ability to sway the reader. On each item, the girls gave a rating of from 1 (highly favorable) to 5 (highly unfavorable).

Generally, the results were in line with our expectations — but not completely. In analyzing these results, we used three different methods: We compared the amount of anti-female bias in the different occupational fields (would men be rated as better city planners, but women as better dietitians?); we compared the amount of bias shown on the nine questions that followed each article (would men be rated as more competent, but women as more persuasive?); and we ran an overall comparison, including both fields and rating questions.

Starting with the analysis of bias by occupational field, we immediately ran into a major surprise. (See box below.) That there is a general bias by women against women, and that it is strongest in traditionally masculine fields, was clearly borne out. But in other fields the situation seemed rather confused. We had expected the anti-female trend to be reversed in traditionally feminine fields. But it appears that, even here, women consider themselves inferior to men. Women seem to think that men are better at *everything* — including elementary-school teaching and dietetics!

Scrutiny of the nine rating questions yielded similar results. On all nine questions, regardless of the author's occupational field, the girls consistently found an article more

---

Law: A Strong Masculine Preserve

| | MEAN | |
Field of article	Male	Female
Art History	23.35	23.10
Dietetics	22.05	23.45
Education	20.20	21.75
City Planning	23.10	27.30
Linguistics	26.95	30.70
Law	21.20	25.60

These are the total scores the college girls gave to the six pairs of articles they read. The lowest possible score—9—would be the most favorable; the highest possible score—54—the most critical. While male authors received more favorable ratings in all occupational fields, the differences were statistically significant only in city planning, linguistics, and—especially—law.

---

valuable — and its author more competent — when the article bore a male name. Though the articles themselves were exactly the same, the girls felt that those written by the John T. McKays were definitely more impressive, and reflected more glory on their authors, than did the mediocre offerings of the Joan T. McKays. Perhaps because the world has accepted female authors for a long time, the girls were willing to concede that the female professionals' writing styles were not *far* inferior to those of the men. But such a concession to female competence was rare indeed.

Statistical analysis confirms these impressions and makes them more definite. With a total of six articles, and with nine questions after each one, there were 54 points at which comparisons could be drawn between the male authors and the female authors. Out of these 54 comparisons, three were tied, seven favored the female authors — and the number favoring the male authors was 44!

Clearly, there is a tendency among women to downgrade the work of professionals of their own sex. But the hypothesis that this tendency would decrease as the "femaleness" of the professional field increased was not supported. Even in traditionally female fields, anti-feminism holds sway.

Since the articles supposedly written by men were exactly the same as those supposedly written by women, the perception that the men's articles were superior was obviously a distortion. For reasons of their own, the female subjects were sensitive to the sex of the author, and this apparently irrelevant information biased their judgments. Both the distortion and the sensitivity that precedes it are characteristic of prejudice. Women — at least these young college women — are prejudiced against female professionals and, regardless of the actual accomplishments of these professionals, will firmly refuse to recognize them as the equals of their male colleagues.

Is the intellectual double-standard really dead? Not at all — and if the college girls in this study are typical of the educated and presumably progressive segments of the population, it may not even be dying. Whatever lip service these girls pay to modern ideas of equality between men and women, their beliefs are staunchly traditional. Their real coach in the battle of the sexes is not Simone de Beauvoir or Betty Friedan. Their coach is Aristotle.

Cultivating the Conservative Stereotype

42

Wilhelm Wundt

Social scientists often criticize something they call stereotypic thinking. Negroes, they aver, were never obsessed by watermelon; Orientals are not necessarily inscrutable; and upper-class Englishmen are not all homosexual. Despite such worthy attempts to enlighten the bumpkins and hardhats, the social scientists have created some whopping stereotypes of their own (such as the Authoritarian Personality), which they defend with a cunning well beyond the means of the simple-minded bigots they love to condemn.

In 1958 a political scientist ironically named McClosky reported that a group of people he chose to call "conservatives" had scored high on Contempt for Human Weakness, high on Intolerance of Human Frailty, and low on Social Responsibility. Last year following in McClosky's wake an aspiring psychologist came along to illuminate this pseudometric stereotype of the hard-hearted, unsocial conservative on the very breeding ground of conservatism—New York City!

While a doctoral candidate at City University of New York, our budding behaviorist bothered 230 Liberal Party members and 217 registered Conservatives with an unexpected phone call for help from a (bogus) stranded motorist. Realizing the caller had a wrong number, 43 of the subjects hung up before finding out that they could have come to the rescue of the purported victim simply by phoning his tow service—since (so the story went) he had used up his last dime getting the wrong number. Those 404 who had enough patience to hear the caller out either gave "Help" by dialing the supposed tow-service number and talking unwittingly to a researcher or gave "No Help," by not dialing. In half of the pleas for help the bogus victim had a "white accent," in the other half a "black accent."

The investigator tested two hypotheses: 1) white victims would get more help from the liberals than from the hardhearted, unsocial conservatives, 2) black victims would be more discriminated against by the conservatives than by the liberals.

Studies like this one are advertised to scientists, scholars, journalists and students through the widely read *Psychological Abstracts*. Therefore, we should scrutinize our author's 103-word abstract to learn what impression he intended to give of his research.

"As expected," he wrote, "the extent to which blacks were helped less frequently than whites was greater for Conservative than Liberal Party members. Nevertheless, it seems that Liberal antiblack sentiment was observed when Liberals [hung up prematurely] more frequently for the black than white callers. Results suggest that Liberals may act in a less than egalitarian manner [when the rules of etiquette are not clear]."

Except for one additional sentence describing the method, this is the whole substance of the abstract. What does it tell us, and what does it not tell us?

CULTIVATING THE CONSERVATIVE STEREOTYPE, by Wilhelm Wundt. Reprinted by permission from NATIONAL REVIEW, 150 East 35 Street, N. Y., N. Y. 10016.

The abstract explicitly says that the conservatives discriminated white from black callers more than the liberals did; it implies that this difference arose when conservatives gave less help to blacks than liberals gave. The abstract says that this result was just what the author expected.

The abstract does *not* tell us which group gave more help to whites, although one of the author's two hypotheses had addressed that question. Instead, we are treated to an incidental finding of liberal antiblack prejudice along with some ad hoc speculation that serves to weaken the finding.

What is the box score at this point? The abstract has led us to believe that conservatives give less help to blacks than liberals do, though liberals sometimes slip when social prescriptions are vague. If we had no other information, we should have to go on believing that conservatives can never qualify as Good Guys. But let us look into the *Proceedings of the American Psychological Association 78th Annual Convention*, where the article itself gives a rather different picture—if one reads carefully and does not overlook the table.

Are you ready for this? All right. The table tells us that, while the sympathetic, responsible, egalitarian liberals helped the black caller 64 per cent of the time, the hardhearted, unsocial, ethnocentric conservatives helped the black caller 65 per cent of the time. There goes the trophy. And now I have a few words for the author.

Doctor, you have overlooked something, and so have the members of your dissertation committee—or have they? Presumably the committee members read this article almost as carefully as I did, since they knew it was to be published with their names appended. Men of their experience could quickly tell, as I did, that your conclusions grossly misrepresent your results. Even if you were carried away by an excess of gnostic afflatus, their wisdom should have restained you. It did not.

My friends, a strange kind of science is brewing at dear old CUNY. When the numbers turn out badly, the modern scientactivist simply nullifies them by non sequiturs in his discussion and omissions from his abstract. He could, of course, change the numbers themselves and escape detection altogether, but then he would have to admit to himself that he was no longer a scientist. Loss of the scientist role might severely damage his self concept. Today's scientactivist has learned to have his science and twist it too. Who can say, in a particular case, whether this perversion results from purposive dishonesty or foolish self-deception? Either way, it is pitiful.

Despite my reservations about the objectivity of the candidate (who, by the way, is now a university professor) or the ethics of his faculty committee, I would not leave the impression that this study is worthless. On the contrary, our informant planned well and no doubt executed his plan carefully. He observed actual political groups rather than the usual suspect hypothetical classes, and actual social behavior (dialing in the belief that one was helping) rather than mere questionnaire responses. I think this article says something important about the shop-worn myth of the Authoritarian Personality and the stale stereotype of the hard-hearted, unsocial conservative—though hardly what the author foolishly or deceptively suggests. As I read these results, they say:

1. If you are a white victim, you can expect more help from conservatives than from liberals, because conservatives are more sympathetic and responsible than liberals.

2. If you are black, you will fare no worse with a conservative who listens to you than with a liberal—and it will be easier to get a conservative to listen.

3. Whatever color you may be, if you pry the lid of CUNY and other similar establishments, you will see why Brand X (conservatism) never tests out ahead of Old Snake Oil (liberalism) no matter what the figures may say.

First, let me get the author's gratuitous remarks about social rules out of the way. What are the special, ambiguous circumstances in which liberals may be excused for hanging up on black callers? I must perforce condense the author's verbose argument, but I will not distort it. He says that familiar propositions asserting that liberals are comparative Good Guys must be set in a context of person and situation. Conservatives, being ethnocentric, are responsible and sympathetic to members of their own, white group. Liberals, on the other hand, are more egalitarian—though when the social prescription for good behavior is ambiguous, liberals may show antiblack sentiment. This fault, however, can be excused; after all, "is it appropriate or inappropriate to hang up after informing a person that he has reached the wrong number?"

A cute argument but a completely spurious one. The liberals, we learn, not only hung up on more *persons* than the conservatives did (liberals 29, conservatives 14), they also hung up on more *black* persons than *white* persons (numbers not revealed), while the conservatives hung up on

black and white equally. When it comes to hanging up, the liberals were clearly churls. No trumped up ambiguity nor even a *tu quoque* can be adduced to save them from disgrace. The last sentence of the abstract therefore stands exposed as a smoke screen obscuring the liberal hangup and distracting us from the author's failure to tell the fate of Hypothesis I.

What about Hypothesis II? Did it, like Hypothesis I, turn out just as the author expected? To our surprise we read: "It seems that conservatives, compared to liberals, tend to have greater social responsibility, feelings of sympathy, etc., toward others of their own "kind" [the whites, that is]. Surely, this is the essence of ethnocentrism." *Fascinating!* The conservatives treated the white caller better than the liberals did—and there goes Hypothesis I right down the drain. Best to say nothing about this unpleasant turn of events in the abstract, which will be read by so many.

But—pleads the author—the conservatives could pull this off only because they are so maddeningly ethnocentric. Very well. If the conservatives are more ethnocentric than the liberals (otherwise, why mention it?), they must have treated the black caller pretty shabbily. We would hardly accuse the conservatives of ethnocentrism just because they helped their own kind *more;* they would also have to show xenophobia by helping the outsiders *less,* would they not?

At long last, let us look at the author's table of results. There we find that the conservatives helped the white caller 92 per cent of the time, while the liberals helped the white caller only 76 per cent of the time. If the liberals are going to recoup their goodguyness, they will have to top the conservatives by at least 17 per cent in charity to the black caller; if they fail, the Good-Guy Trophy will have to be sent back to the conservatives.

43

Ghetto for blue-eyes in the classroom

by John Leonard

THE EYE OF THE STORM

For the third year in a row, Jane Elliott has introduced a little terror into the classroom where she teaches at the Riceville, Iowa elementary school. This time ABC cameramen were around to videotape that terror, thereby permitting it to visit with us all for a half hour in our living rooms.

The children of Riceville are, like the town, very white and very American. Most of the black faces they see are on television. How, then, was Mrs. Elliott to explain to her third-graders the assassination of Dr. Martin Luther King Jr. on April 4, 1968?

She conducted a simple experiment. She divided her class according to the color of each child's eyes. One day the blue-eyed children were declared to be superior. They sat where they preferred, went early to lunch, stayed late at recess, and were mightily encouraged in their work. The brown-eyed children wore collars, and were not permitted to eat with or play with the blue-eyed children. The next day Mrs. Elliott reversed the situation; brown eyes were now on top.

It began with giggles, but presently became serious. Mrs. Elliott knew her children and exploited their various vulnerabilities. Had a brown-eyed child been struck by his father for misbehaving? Brown-eyed children deserved it. Had a blue-eyed child forgotten his glasses? Dimwitted, typical. And the favored children did some exploiting of their own, proposing ingenious discriminations, affecting a lofty contempt, immensely enjoying their top-dog role, behaving in some instances viciously.

One significant result of the experiment was its effect on performance. On their day of inferiority, the brown-eyed children fared poorly on card-recognition tests; the blue-eyed ones surpassed themselves. The following day, the opposite occurred, with the "inferior" blue-eyed children admitting that they couldn't stop thinking about the collars around their necks or the taunts of their classmates.

GHETTO FOR BLUE-EYES IN THE CLASSROOM, by John Leonard, is reprinted by permission from the author.

All this is caught perfectly by the camera. The faces of the children are astonishing: on the playground, depressed and withdrawn; in the classroom, confused and fearful. Eyes of whatever color seem genuinely windows; inside the mind one sees cunning, wariness, doubt, glee. Even when Mrs. Elliott ended the experiment, and with enormous relief the whole class joined in song, one little girl was in tears and one little boy was wholly absorbed in ripping apart his collar before flinging it into the wastepaper basket.

I suppose some professional tsk-tskers will object to Mrs. Elliott's manipulation of young emotions; and some psychologist—who probably wrote his master's thesis on selecting the apposite color scheme for kindergarten furniture in the Swampscott public school system—will object that two days of role-playing can't inoculate a child against racism. But Mrs. Elliott, clearly an excellent teacher, can take care of those emotions; and of course there is no permanent vaccine for evil.

More to the point is what this quiet and effective television half hour reveals about the susceptibilities of our children. We know, or should have known unless we gave up reading after Rousseau three centuries ago, that children aren't innocent, any more than adults are; that decency, justice and morality are abstractions that must be communicated and sustained; that our condition is poor and solitary indeed, perhaps even "nasty, brutish and short," without a community to provide the mechanisms of interdependence and the means to protect individuality, otherness.

Unfortunately, not every elementary school is full of Mrs. Elliotts, although all of them are controlled environments. We had better stop thinking of schools as baby-sitters or factories for producing labor units, and start thinking about how vulnerable our children are when parked for six hours a day in a world they never made. Without a Mrs. Elliott, we might have to do something terribly unusual: actually raise our children.

44 Race and Shared Belief as Factors in Social Choice

Milton Rokeach · Louis Mezei

Several recent studies support the hypothesis that difference in belief on important issues are a more powerful determinant of prejudice or discrimination than differences in race or ethnic membership. White college students in the North and South[1] and white teen-agers in California[2] have been found in questionnaire-type studies to prefer Negroes with beliefs, values, and personalities perceived to be similar to their own (for example, a Negro who believes in God) to whites with beliefs, values, and personalities perceived to be dissimilar to their own (for example, a white atheist). More generally, these subjects are observed to rate less favorably those, regardless of race, whose belief systems are incongruent with their own than those, regardless of race, whose belief systems are congruent with their own. Rokeach, Smith, and Evans[3] have reported comparable results with Jewish children; the children of their study rated gentiles whose belief systems were seen as congruent with their own (for example, a gentile who is for Israel) more favorably than they did Jews whose belief systems were seen as incongruent with their own (a Jew who is against Israel). Stein[4] has recently reported confirmatory results in studies of Negro, Jewish and gentile teen-agers in a Northeastern city, as has Martin[5] in a study of the differential preferences of English Canadians for English Canadians, French Canadians, and Canadian Indians of varied beliefs.[6]

Generalization from these findings is, however, severely limited by the fact that in all these studies the social stimuli were "paper-and-pencil" stimuli and the discriminatory responses elicited were "paper-and-pencil" responses. To overcome this limitation, we conducted three experiments in which subjects were given the opportunity to discriminate on the basis of race or belief, or both, in real-life situations. These experiments are all alike in basic design. A naive subject engages four strangers, confederates of the experimenter, in a group discussion about an important or situationally relevant topic. Two of the confederates are white and two are Negro. One white and one Negro agree with the subject, and one white and one Negro disagree with him. The subject is then asked to state a preference for two of the four confederates.

In two of the experiments, conducted on a university campus, the subject chose two of the confederates to join him for a coffee break. In the third experiment, which was conducted in the natural field setting of an employment office, the subjects were actually applying for jobs; each chose two of four "job applicants" he would most like to work with. This third experiment provides the strongest test of our major hypothesis. For one thing, these subjects were unemployed workers (or, occasionally, employed workers seeking to change jobs), not college students. More important, they were under the impression that the procedures to which they were subjected were an integral part of a normal interview procedure, and they were totally unaware that they were participating in an experiment—a condition that can rarely be assured with college students participating in psychological experiments.

Within the basic framework of these experiments we were interested in three additional questions:

(1) *Comparison between white and Negro subjects.* The field experiment in the employment office included Negro as well as white applicants, and the results obtained from these two groups can be compared. This study was carried out during the winter of 1963–64, a period during which civil rights demonstrations and clashes provided

many daily headlines. In this charged atmosphere, would Negroes and whites pick working partners along race lines, or would beliefs relevant to the working situation be a more important determinant of interpersonal choice?

(2) *Comparison between subjects high and low in anti-Negro prejudice.* Rokeach, Smith, and Evans found that, "whether a person is high or low in prejudice against Jews and Negroes [as determined by scores on anti-Semitism and anti-Negro attitude scales], he responds to belief rather than racial or ethnic cues when given an opportunity to do so."[7] In our two campus experiments we also studied the extent to which racial attitudes predict social choice.

(3) *Comparison between public and private conditions.* If discrimination on the basis of race is institutionalized or if there exists extreme social pressure to discriminate along racial lines (as is most clearly the case in the South or in South Africa), there is virtually no likelihood that social discrimination will occur on the basis of similarity of belief. All the experiments to be reported here were conducted in the state of Michigan, where patterns of racial discrimination are less institutionalized and less subject to social pressure than they are in the South. Nevertheless, it is reasonable to assume that such pressures are far from absent in Michigan and consequently that our subjects would choose partners differently under public and private conditions. This assumption was tested in the two campus experiments.

Procedure in the Campus Experiments

Two virtually identical experiments were performed, one in 1961 with 20 white male subjects drawn from an introductory sociology class,[8] the second in 1963–64 with 48 white male subjects drawn from an introductory psychology class. At least 10 days before the respective experiments, instructors (not the experimenters) administered a six-item anti-Negro Scale.[9] "High-prejudice" subjects were defined as those who obtained plus scores and "low-prejudice" subjects as those who obtained minus scores on this scale.

The experiment was conducted in two adjacent rooms—one for receiving and interviewing the subjects, the other for group discussion—situated in an isolated wing of a campus building. To avoid suspicion, the confederates arrived separately. After all five participants had arrived, they were seated around a conference table and were told that their task was to discuss a controversial topic, to be selected from a list of five topics by their chairman, who was to be chosen by election. The topics were: (i) invasion of Cuba, (ii) elimination of fraternities from campus, (iii) allowing girls to visit men's dormitories, (iv) Bible reading in the schools, and (v) the grading system.

Each participant was first asked to introduce himself; then the subject, by prearrangement, was elected chairman. He selected the topic and then led a 15-minute discussion. One white and one Negro confederate agreed with the subject, and one white and one Negro disagreed. Identification was facilitated by printed name cards, as in TV panel shows. Personality effects on interpersonal choice was randomized by rotating the assignments of each confederate so that if he agreed with one subject he disagreed with the next. On terminating the discussion, the experimenter took the subject into the next room for a private interview. The experimenter displayed a seating chart of the participants and, under the guise of checking his written notes against the subject's judgment, asked the subject to identify the opinions expressed by the participants, thus assuring that the subject remembered their opinions as well as their names.

While the subject looked at the seating chart, the experimenter remarked that the participants would be interviewed individually and that therefore there would be enough time for several of them to take a coffee break; he then asked the subject, as chairman, to select two of the participants to join him for coffee. In half the cases the experimenter specified that they would be served coffee in a private room next door (the *private* condition), in the other half that they would go to the grill in the Student Union Building (the *public* condition), where the coffee would be paid for from research funds. After the subject made his choices he was asked how he had decided on them. The experimenter then explained the purpose of the experiment and pledged the subject to secrecy.

Procedure in the Field Experiment

The subjects in the field experiment were 26 Negro and 24 white male applicants for the positions of janitor, laundry worker, attendant, and recreational director at two mental hospitals in Michigan. The level of positions applied for was the same for Negro and white applicants. Experimental sessions were scheduled at the employment offices of the two hospitals on days when several job applicants were to appear for job interviews by prior appointment. All such applicants were included in the sample.

After an applicant had filled out the usual application form, the experimenter, posing as a staff member of the personnel office, accompanied him to a "waiting room" in which the four confederates, posing and dressed and previously trained to play their roles as job applicants, were already "waiting to be interviewed." As the experimenter and the subject entered, two confederates were looking intently at a mimeographed sheet entitled "Problems of working with mental patients," on which five topics were listed: what to do if a patient (i) misses dinner, (ii) refuses to shave because of a delusion, (iii) takes off his clothes, or (iv) asks to change his dining-room seat, and (v) what to do with juvenile offenders. In each case two specific courses of action were provided—one based on a rule, the other a more permissive alternative. The experimenter handed mimeographed sheets to the subject and to those confederates who did not already have them, explaining that "they are used in the training program" and suggesting that the applicants look at them while waiting their turns to be interviewed.

The experimenter then left the room, and the four confederates initiated a "spontaneous" discussion of at least three of the five topics. One white and one Negro confederate defended the permissive position, and one white and one Negro confederate defended the rule-oriented position. As in the campus experiments, confederates alternated positions from one applicant to another. The subject was gradually drawn into the discussion, his opinion being directly solicited if necessary. If the subject was not consistent in choosing either the rule or the permissive course of action in the several situations (and this was true of about half the subjects), the confederates tried to follow him, agreeing or disagreeing with him according to their predetermined assignments.

The experimenter returned after about 12 minutes, announcing that the interviewers were not quite ready yet. He then passed out 2 by 4 cards and asked each participant to write the names of the two people in the group whom he would most prefer to work with. Since the applicants did not yet "know" one another's names, they introduced themselves. The experimenter then assured the applicants that their choices would be kept confidential and that this part of the interview was "something new and has nothing to do with your employment interview." While the subject wrote down the two preferred names, each of the other four wrote down the names of the two confederates who agreed with the subject most of the time. This was done to check on whether there had been a slip-up in carrying out the assignments. (There were none.) The experimenter then collected the cards, thanked the applicants, and left. He or the personnel assistant returned shortly afterwards to escort the subject to his real interview.

The Choices

Under the experimental conditions described, there are six possible combinations of partners among which the subject can choose:

1) $S+O+$: two persons who agree with him, one of each race.
2) $S-O-$: two persons who disagree with him, one of each race.
3) $S+S-$: two persons of the same race (as the subject), one agreeing, the other disagreeing with him.
4) $O+O-$: two persons of the other race, one agreeing, the other disagreeing.
5) $S+O-$: one person of his own race who disagrees and a second person of the other race who disagrees.
6) $S-O+$: one person of his own race who disagrees and a second person of the other race who agrees.

It is reasonable to assume that the more frequently our subjects choose pattern 1 or 2 over the remaining patterns, the more probable it is that they are discriminating (that is, choosing preferentially) on the basis of belief criteria alone; the more frequently they choose pattern 3 or 4 over the remaining patterns, the more probable it is that they are discriminating on the basis of racial criteria alone; and the more frequently they choose pattern 5 or 6 over the remaining patterns, the more probable that they are not choosing preferentially on the basis of either race or belief criteria alone.

It is immediately obvious from Table 1 that the six patterns do not appear equally often. This is true for each of the three experiments considered separately, and when the data from all experiments are combined we see that patterns 1 through 6 were chosen by 47, 4, 7, 7, 22, and 31 subjects, respectively.

The most direct way of assessing the relative effects of congruence of belief and congruence of race, as determinants of personal choice, is to compare the number of subjects who chose two persons of the same belief (pattern 1) with the number who chose two persons of the same race (pattern 3). Pattern 1 (S+O+) was chosen twice as often as pattern 3 (S+S−) in the campus 1961 study, four times as often in the campus 1963–64 study, and 15 times as often in the field study. When the data from all three experiments are combined, we find that pattern 1 was chosen by 47 subjects and pattern 3 by only 7—a ratio of almost 7 to 1. Under the conditions described, similarity of belief is clearly a more powerful determinant of interpersonal choice than similarity of race.

Additional support for the initial hypothesis is obtained when we compare pattern 1 with pattern 2 and pattern 3 with pattern 4. Our subjects preferred two partners who agreed with them to two partners who disagreed with the 4 to 1, 13 to 0, and 30 to 3 in the three experiments, respectively. Of the 11 subjects in the three experiments, 47 chose two partners who agreed with them and only 4 chose two partners who disagreed with them. In contrast, 7 subjects (out of 118) preferred two partners of their own race (S+S−), and 7 preferred two partners of the other race (O+O−).

TABLE 1

FREQUENCY OF CHOICE OF VARIOUS RACE AND BELIEF PATTERNS IN THREE EXPERIMENTS. EACH PATTERN CONSISTS OF TWO PARTNERS S, SAME RACE AS SUBJECT; O, OTHER RACE +, AGREED WITH SUBJECT; − DISAGREED WITH SUBJECT.

| Experimental group | PATTERN | | | | | | |
	(1) S+O+	(2) S−O−	(3) S+S−	(4) O+O−	(5) S+O−	(6) S−O+	Total
Campus 1961	4	1	2	1	3	9	20
High prejudice	2	1	2	0	2	3	10
Low prejudice	2	0	0	1	1	6	10
Private	0	0	1	0	1	8	10
Public	4	1	1	1	2	1	10
Campus 1963–64	13	0	3	3	15	14	48
High prejudice	5	0	1	2	6	7	21
Low prejudice	8	0	2	1	9	7	27
Private	7	0	1	1	8	7	24
Public	6	0	2	2	7	7	24
Field 1963–64	30	3	2	3	4	8	50
Negro	15	3	1	2	3	2	26
White	15	0	1	1	1	6	24
All groups	47	4	7	7	22	31	118

Clearly, similarity of belief is a far more important basis for choosing partners than dissimilarity of belief; only 4 subjects out of 118 (instead of the 19 that would be expected by pure chance) chose two partners who disagreed with them (pattern 2). More surprising is that (i) only 14 subjects (instead of a theoretically expected 39) chose partners of one race (patterns 3 and 4), and (ii) of these 14, as many chose two partners from the other race as from their own.

Let us consider next the findings with respect to patterns 5 and 6. A sizable proportion of our subjects—53 of the 118—chose coffee- and work-partners varying in both belief and race, 22 chose pattern 5 (S+O−) and 31 chose pattern 6 (S−O+). But with respect to these two patterns we note an important difference between the two campus studies on the one hand and the field study on the other. In each of the campus studies, 60 percent apparently preferred partners differing from one another in both race and belief. But this was so of only 24 percent of the subjects in the field study; 60 percent in the field study chose two partners with beliefs congruent with their own, one white and one Negro. It is not possible to say whether these differences are due to sampling differences between college students and workers; or to the fact that choice of coffee-partners is a "one-shot deal," while choice of work partners has longer-range implications; or to the fact that the particular issues discussed were related to work in the one case but not in the other. Another interpretation which would seem to fit the data equally well is that while a majority of the work-applicants preferred partners with congruent beliefs (S+O+), a majority of the campus subjects preferred the mixed racial patterns 1, 5, and 6 (S+O+, S+O−, S−O+), their choices among these patterns being about evenly distributed. But this preference for SO patterns must be qualified by the fact that the campus subjects avoided pattern 2 (S−O−).

No matter how one chooses to state the differences between the subjects in the campus and field studies, it is clear that in all three expriments (i) similarity of belief is a considerably more frequent basis of choice than dissimilarity of belief; (ii) similarity of race is rarely a basis of choice—considerably less often even than chance, and no more frequently than dissimilarity of race; and (iii) similarity of belief is a considerably more frequent basis of choice than similarity of race.

In the campus 1963–64 and field studies, we obtained additional data on the order in which the two confederates were chosen. These data (Table 2) generally confirm the findings already presented. Considering first the campus 1963–64 results, note that, although a large proportion of the subjects chose a partner who disagreed as well as one who agreed, two-thirds of those who did so chose first the partner who agreed. In contrast, the first choices of all the subjects were exactly evenly divided between the two races. The comparable findings in the field study are even more decisively in favor of belief rather than race congruence as a determinant of choice. Here a much smaller proportion chose a disagreeing as well as an agreeing partner, and three-quarters of those who did so chose the agreeing partner first. Again, these results are in sharp contrast to those concerning race. All but a few subjects chose partners of both races, and only 40 percent of them chose the partner of their own race first. These findings are quite consistent for the Negro and white subjects considered separately.

TABLE 2

ORDER OF CHOICE OF PARTNERS IN TWO EXPERIMENTS

CHOICE		NO. OF SUBJECTS	
First	*Second*	*Campus study**	*Field study*
+	+	13	30
+	−	23	13
−	+	12	4
−	−	0	3
S	S	3	2
S	O	21	18
O	S	21	27
O	O	3	3

* 1963–64

Another interesting finding shown in Table 2 is that in both studies the proportion of choices on the basis of belief congruence decreases from the first to the second choice (in the campus 1963–64 study $x^2 = 4.50$, $P < .05$; in the field study $x^2 = 3.61$, $P < .10$). No such decreases are, of course, observed with respect to race in the campus study, since the racial choices, being exactly equal on the first choice, are already balanced. But in the field study we again note a tendency to balance out the unequal racial choices as the subjects proceed from the first to the second partner. These results enable us to understand better the choice patterns shown in Table 1. It would seem as if many of the subjects, especially the campus subjects, were somehow aware of the basis on which they made their first preferential choice, and motivated by considerations of fair-mindedness they were more likely to choose a second partner possessing both belief and racial characteristics opposite to those of the first partner. At the same time the results show that more of the subjects were fair-minded about race than about belief.

Comparison between white and Negro subjects. Under the experimental conditions described, that is, when a person possesses situationally relevant information about another person's beliefs, there is little evidence indeed that he will discriminate on the basis of race per se. The question may now be raised whether Negro subjects respond any differently from white subjects when choosing others. James Baldwin, perhaps the most eloquent spokesman of the Negro people today, has insisted that white people, even well-meaning liberal white people, cannot understand the perceptions, thoughts, feelings, and desires of the Negro who lives in a white society which oppresses him from birth; as a result of life-long oppression, the Negro's psychological processes are inevitably different from the white's. If Baldwin's contentions are correct we should find our Negro subjects choosing partners in ways which are significantly different from the ways whites choose.

But the results presented in Table 1 show that in this experimental situation, at least, Negroes chose partners in ways which were indistinguishable from whites. Fifteen Negro applicants (out of 26) and 15 white applicants (out of 24) chose two partners who agreed with them, one white and one Negro. Only three of the Negro subjects and only two of the white subjects chose two partners of one race, and these were not necessarily of their own race.

Comparison between subjects high and low in prejudice. In the two campus studies the subjects had been classified before the experiment as high or low in prejudice on the basis of an anti-Negro scale. The results of both studies are essentially the same for high- and low-prejudice groups (Table 1). It would seem that scores on an anti-Negro scale are not necessarily related to real-life discrimination.

Comparison between public and private conditions. In neither campus study did privacy appear to have an effect on racial choice. In 1961, only one out of 10 subjects in the private condition and two out of 10 in the public condition chose two partners of their own race or of the other race; in 1963–64, two out of 24 in the private condition and four out of 24 in the public condition chose two partners of their own race or of the other race. If we look further at the campus 1963–64 data, it is also evident that the frequency of choice of all six patterns is remarkably similar under the public and private conditions. But certain unanticipated differences in choice patterns appear between the two conditions in the campus 1961 study. Four subjects in the public condition but none in the private condition chose pattern 1—two partners who agreed with them; eight subjects in the private condition but only one in the public condition chose pattern 6—one partner of the same race who disagreed and one of the other race who agreed with the subject. The variability of patterns chosen is generally greater for the public than for the private condition, but it makes for a difference only in the belief choices, not the racial choices. While the difference between conditions is statistically significant ($x^2 = 7.27$), we are nevertheless inclined to discount this difference for methodological reasons[10] and to conclude tentatively that the social pressures in a northern campus community were not sufficiently great to produce consistent differences between public and private choices. In this connection and in support of this interpretation it should be pointed out that the naive subjects were undoubtedly aware that they were participating in interactions with the four others, within a university context or an employment-interview context in the State of Michigan (a state which took an early lead in developing nondiscriminatory laws and policies in employment and in education). This may have been sufficient to indicate to the subjects that there existed no strong external social pressures to discriminate along racial lines. In other words, the conditions under which the studies were conducted must have suggested to the subjects that they were more or less free to choose partners in any way they wanted to.

It is conceivable, of course, that, given the social context, the subjects may have felt some external pressure *not* to discriminate along racial lines. We had no way of determining which or how many subjects may have felt such pressure. In any event, our data show little or no discrimination along racial lines; and, whether or not external pressures not to discriminate along racial lines existed, the subjects were free to choose from among the remaining five patterns.

Our main interest in studying differences in discrimination patterns under public and private conditions stems from the assumption that the crucial social-psychological difference between them is the presence or absence of social pressures to coerce discrimination along racial lines. It is interesting to speculate about the results we might have obtained had we been able to replicate our studies in the deep South, An attempt by one of us to set up such a study in the deep South was unsuccessful, mainly because of anticipated reprisals toward research collaborators, confederates, and co-operating subjects. But had a study proven feasible we would have predicted results considerably different from those reported here, namely, that, because of greater social pressures existing under public than under private conditions, choice of coffee- and work-partners would have been more uniformly along racial rather than belief lines.

Regarding the role of belief versus race as a determinant of discrimination, Triandis[11] and Stein, Hardyck, and Smith[12] have raised the objection that in the vast majority of social situations where discrimination is practiced (for example, in employment, education, public transportation and accommodation, and housing) white people do not stop to inquire into the beliefs of Negroes in order to determine whether they are congruent or incongruent with their own. The person discriminated against is a total stranger whose belief system is unknown to the person doing the discriminating. We have already suggested that discrimination along racial lines can be expected to occur whenever there is sufficient social pressure or when it is institutionally sanctioned. Under such conditions beliefs are irrelevant as a basis for discrimination. What should be added is that white persons in general and prejudiced white persons in particular, as a result of living within a social system in which racial discrimination is socially reinforced, come to assume that Negro strangers possess beliefs, values, and personalities dissimilar to their own. Thus, Byrne and Wong[13] found in a group of white subjects in Texas that those with anti-Negro prejudice more frequently than those without assumed that Negroes' beliefs are dissimilar to their own. And Stein, Hardyck, and Smith have reported that "the correlations presented . . . seem to indicate that the inference made by most subjects about a Negro teenager, in the absence of other information, is that he is *unlike* them."[14]

A final point concerns the issue of equal-status social contacts. Brink and Harris's[15] public-opinion data show that whites who have had previous social contact with Negroes are less prejudiced and have fewer stereotypes than whites with no such contact. Many others have pointed out that racial prejudice can be overcome or eliminated if individuals get to know one another in equal-status contacts. Our studies lead to the same conclusion but with one important qualification. In the field study especially, all contacts were equal-status contacts, but not all individuals who interacted with one another had congruent beliefs. It should therefore be pointed out that the concept of "equal-status contacts" is not necessarily equivalent to the concept of "contact between individuals with congruent belief systems." And recent research by Stein[16] shows that the latter variable is more crucial than the former as a determinant of interpersonal choice.

Subjects' reports on reasons for choice. At the end of the campus 1963–64 study the subjects were invited to give their reasons for choosing as they did. Four types of reasons were given (Table 3). Since there were no differences between high- and low-prejudice subjects or between subjects in the public and private conditions, these breakdowns are not shown. The most frequent reason given—by 20 out of 48 subjects—was to "keep the discussion going" or some variant thereof ("interesting guys to talk with," "keep things going," "best talkers"). The majority of these 20 subjects had chosen patterns 5 and 6, combinations in which both race and belief are varied. Four additional subjects who had chosen patterns 5 and 6 said more or less explicitly that they chose one of each race and one of each belief. When asked why, they responded with such reasons as "because of my Army experience" or "I did not want to leave two Negroes" or "I picked one on color and one on belief."

A third type of reason was "Nice personality" or "I liked them." And a fourth type, which we have classified as "Other," may be interpreted as "evasive." The subject said he "didn't know" or "it didn't matter" or "I picked any two guys" or "I just picked two guys sitting next to me." It is interesting to note that 11 of the 13 subjects who chose pattern 1 (S+O+) but only 12 of the 29 who chose patterns 5 and 6 gave the third and fourth kinds of reason. This suggests that different processes underlie different choice patterns and, perhaps more important, that those who chose on the basis of belief con-

TABLE 3
REASONS FOR CHOICE IN CAMPUS 1963–64 STUDY, BY PATTERN OF CHOICE

			PATTERN			
Reason	*(1)*	*(2)*	*(3)*	*(4)*	*(5)*	*(6)*
	S+O+	S−O−	S+S−	O+O−	S+O−	S−O+
Quality of discussion	2	0	3	2	7	6
Race and belief	0	0	0	0	3	1
Personality	4	0	0	1	4	3
Other	7	0	0	0	1	4

gruence were generally more evasive about or unaware of the real reasons for their choices, possibly because choosing others on the basis of belief congruence violates religious and social ideals of tolerance toward those with opposing viewpoints.

Conclusion

Our three experiments and some of the others we have referred to suggest that the importance of racial attitudes per se as determinants of racial discrimination have been greatly overestimated and the importance of congruence of beliefs correspondingly underestimated. Whatever racial attitudes our subjects may have had seem to have exerted little or no influence on actual choices in social situations where external pressures to discriminate along racial lines were slight or absent (and pressures *not* to discriminate along racial lines possibly present). One of us has speculated elsewhere[17] on the basis of earlier findings with paper-and-pencil tests, now reinforced by the experiments here described, that "in those actions not subject to social sanction discrimination along racial or ethnic lines would not take place, not even in the South . . . the *locus* of racial and ethnic discrimination is to be sought in society, not in the individual's psyche. If society's constraints were altogether removed . . . man would still discriminate, if discriminate he must, not in terms of race or ethnic grouping, but in accord with his basic psychological predisposition, characteristic of all human beings, to organize the world of human beings in terms of the principle of belief congruence."

It remains to be seen whether the results of these experiments can be replicated with other kinds of subjects, in other kinds of situations, and in other kinds of cultural and subcultural contexts. And another task for future research is to explore in more detail the personal and social determinants of all the choice patterns we observed.

[1] M. Rokeach, P. W. Smith, R. I. Evans, *The Open and Closed Mind* (New York: Basic Books, 1960); D. Byrne and T. J. Wong, "Racial Prejudice, Interpersonal Attraction, and Assumed Dissimilarity of Attitudes," *Journal of Abnormal and Social Psychology* 65 (1962): 246; M. Rokeach and G. Rothman, "The Principle of Belief Congruence and the Congruity Principle as Models of Cognitive Interaction," *Psychological Review* 72 (1965): 128.

[2] D. D. Stein, J. A. Hardyck, M. B. Smith, "Race and Belief: An Open and Shut Case," *Journal of Personality and Social Psychology* 1 (1965): 281.

[3] Rokeach et al., *Open and Closed Mind.*

[4] D. D. Stein, "Similarity of Belief Systems and Interpersonal Preference: A Test of Rokeach's Theory of Prejudice," Ph.D. dissertation, University of California at Berkeley, 1965.

[5] Bette Mary Evans Martin, "Ethnic Group and Beliefs as Determinants of Social Distance," M.A. thesis, Department of Psychology, University of Western Ontario, 1964.

[6] The only exception to the cited findings is a study by H. C. Triandis, "A Note on Rokeach's Theory of Prejudice," *Journal of Abnormal and Social Psychology* 62 (1961): 184-86. For a critique of this study see M. Rokeach, "Belief versus Race as Determinants of Social Distance: A Comment on Triandis' Paper," *Journal of Abnormal and Social Psychology* 62 (1961): 187-88, and for a reconciliation of findings see Stein et al., "Race and Belief."

[7] Rokeach, *Open and Closed Mind,* p. 155.

[8] We thank Joe Smucker and Del Dyer, who conducted this experiment and analyzed the data.

[9] T. W. Adorno, E. Frenkel-Brunswik, D. J. Levinson, R. N. Sanford, *The Authoritarian Personality* (New York: Harper & Row, 1950), p. 142.

[10] It is tempting to suggest that these differences are somehow due to the existence of social pressures in the campus community in 1961 and to their disappearance in 1963–64, perhaps as a result of changing social norms concerning civil rights. If this interpretation were valid we would expect to find the campus 1963–64 results under both private and public conditions looking very much like the campus 1961 results found under private conditions. But this does not appear to be the case. A more likely possibility is that the differences between public and private conditions in the campus 1961 study are, because of the small number of cases, unreliable, despite the fact that they turn out to be statistically significant. We are inclined to discount these results because we determined the significance level by first looking at the data and then combining patterns 1–5 (in order to eliminate small frequencies) and, more important, because we have not been able to replicate them.

[11] See footnote 6.

[12] See footnote 2.

[13] See footnote 1.

[14] See footnote 2.

[15] W. Brink and L. Harris, *The Negro Revolution in America* (New York: Simon & Schuster, 1964).

[16] See footnote 4.

[17] Rokeach, "Comment on Triandis' Paper."

45

On the Irrelevance of the Classical Negative Evidence Concerning the Effect of Attitudes on Behavior

RONALD C. DILLEHAY   *University of Kentucky*[1]

Although the debate has been engaged in for a very long time, the question of the influence of attitudes on behavior has been particularly salient for the past several years. Perhaps heightened interest in behavior modification as a conceptual orientation that bypasses behavioral dispositions, at least in most forms, has recently raised new interest in the position that attitudes do not affect behavior. Whatever the reason, one now, more than previously, encounters in students and colleagues the conviction that attitudes either do not influence behavior significantly or are not a necessary consideration for the changing of behavior, the latter being a matter of identifying and manipulating the relevant environmental contingencies. Not infrequently, those who hold this conviction against the influence of attitudes on behavior cite the literature for support.

Three studies have come to be regarded as classical research on the relationship between attitudes and behavior. Whether they deal with them in a serious, interpretive fashion or only *pro forma*, most authors of textbooks in social psychology include in a prominent way the research by La Piere (1934), Kutner, Wilkins, and Yarrow (1952), and Minard (1952) in the section of their text on the relationship between attitudes and behavior (e.g., Collins, 1970; Cooper & McGaugh, 1963; Freedman, Carlsmith, & Sears, 1970; Hartley & Hartley, 1952; Hollander, 1971; Krech, Crutchfield, & Ballachey, 1962; Lindgren, 1969; McGinnies, 1970; Sampson,

1971; Sargent & Williamson, 1966; Sherif & Sherif, 1969; Watson, 1966). Indeed, it is typically the case that the only studies discussed in the treatment of the attitude–behavior issue are from this set of three. More specialized texts dealing with attitudes and attitude change (such as Dawes, 1972; Kiesler, Collins, & Miller, 1969; Triandis, 1971) and reference works on specialized topics in social psychology (e.g., Berger & Lambert, 1968; Harding, Kutner, Proshansky, & Chein, 1954, 1969; Marlowe & Gergen, 1969; McGuire, 1969; Scott, 1968) also deal seriously with one or several of these studies as empirical evidence that must be reckoned with against the thesis that attitudes affect behavior. In addition, numerous articles in psychological and sociological journals dealing with the relationship of attitudes to behavior cite and variously interpret these studies as serious examples of research on the effects of attitudes on behavior.

The reference to these studies seems to be unrelated to the inclination of the writer to save or discard the attitude concept. Occupants of all theoretical positions include discussion of one or more of these studies, although their predispositions apparently determine the treatment of them, as, for example, when some writers would save attitudes by identifying additional, companion determinants of behavior, while others would discredit the concept entirely. The accord displayed in these various points of view, then, lies in depicting these studies as classical research challenging the influence of attitudes on behaviors. For example, in discussing the La Piere study, Freedman et al. (1970) stated,

Some time later a letter was sent to the same motels asking whether they would accept Orientals as guests. Almost all those responding said they would not. The inconsistency between *their* behavior and *their* response to the letter . . . [p. 385, italics added].

[1] The author wishes to thank John Sensenig and Russell A. Jones for their comments on an earlier draft of this article.

Requests for reprints should be sent to Ronald C. Dillehay, Department of Psychology, University of Kentucky, Lexington, Kentucky 40506.

The thesis of this brief note is that these pieces of research, appropriate though they may be for other purposes, do not provide evidence on the question of the correspondence between attitudes and behavior. They should not, therefore, be used in the ever salient debate on this topic.

If an argument is to be informed by data, as it should be in a scientific enterprise, then the data should at least speak to the issue in debate. The data from these three studies do not, which is the first point of this article.

The bare essentials for examination of the way a person's attitudes are related to his behavior are an index of each concept in the stated relationship. None of these studies can be defended on this point. La Piere traveled around the western United States in the early 1930s with a young Chinese couple. They stopped at 251 places to eat or sleep and were refused service only once. Questionnaires were sent to the 250 accommodating places after a lapse of six months to inquire as to whether the establishments would serve Chinese. About half of the addressees responded to the mailed questionnaires; more than 90% of those responding said no, which of course did not fit the prior facts of accommodating service. In any case, the measure of attitude was supposedly the statement of policy as measured in the questionnaire after the behavior of serving the couple had occurred. How likely is it that the person who waited on La Piere and his friends was the same person as the one who answered the questionnaire? Probably not great at all, and certainly not great enough to merit the inference that these data represent a measure of behavior and attitude from the same person. A quote from La Piere (1934) will buttress this point:

> Accurate and detailed records were kept of all these instances. An effort, necessarily subjective, was made to evaluate the overt response of hotel clerks, bell boys, elevator operators, and waitresses to the presence of my Chinese friends [p. 232].

Surely these were not the respondents to the questionnaires.[2]

The same analysis of the Kutner et al. (1952) research produces a similar conclusion: The measure of attitude was very likely obtained from a different person than the actor furnishing the measure of behavior. In this study, which involved three women, two white and one black, visiting 11 restaurants in a northeastern United States city, the measure of behavior was service in the restaurant; the measure of attitude was obtained by telephone calls to the establishments, after letters had failed to elicit responses.

A second main criticism of these two pieces of research as relevant to the question of how much influence, if any, attitudes have on behavior, is that the elicited policy stand of the organization is less a measure of individual attitude than another kind of role behavior. In this view, the La Piere and the Kutner et al. studies compared role behavior of one kind with role behavior of another kind, probably entailing a different actor. There is no measure of attitude at all. What connects these behaviors is plainly seen when we note that the unit sampled is suprapersonal, the establishment rather than the individual. That is, these investigators examined the operation of the establishments through their role occupants' behaviors in two settings: performance of duties and statement of policies.

Note that this is not the argument that the expressions of one's attitude are modified by his role and that this is how we may interpret the behaviors of the respondents in these experiments, which is a frequently used explanation in the literature. The argument here is rather that attitude was not assessed, that we have no basis for saying individual consistency between attitudes and role behavior was shown in either the measure of action or the statement of policy. To argue that the respondents' attitudes were modified by role or situational influences in either of these studies would require that we substitute assumptions about the attitudes of the respondents for data about them, since we do not have the latter.

On these grounds alone, the two classic experiments by La Piere (1934) and Kutner et al. (1952) are not satisfactory as research on the relationship between attitudes and behavior. However, a further criticism can be raised which applies to these two experiments.

Both of these experiments appear to deal with

---

[2] Of all the references cited in the initial paragraph, Triandis (1971) alone raises this possibility, although he describes LaPiere's (1934) research and Kutner et al.'s (1952) experiment and deals with alternative explanations that preserve a possible relation between attitudes and behavior. The following is his entire statement on the first main point of the present article:

> Other weaknesses of this study include the fact that it is not known whether the same person admitted the Chinese couple and answered the letter, nor whether the 92% rejection rate would have been as high if the 49% of the institutions that did not answer La Piere's letter had answered it [p. 15].

Some other authors cited expressed reservations about these classical studies, but the reservations tended to be general and undeveloped and are not explicitly the points at issue in this article.

the experimental group half of the two-group, after-only design, a paradigm containing a treatment and a control group and commonly used in the attempt to study attitude change through experimental induction techniques. That is, in each study people at each establishment were caused to act in a certain way—serve the women customers or La Piere and his Chinese friends—and were later asked whether they would do that. If one had taken a random sample of establishments from the same population and not intervened (no visit to elicit service, the behavior sample), one would have a study designed to assess the influence of the experience of having served members of an ethnic minority on attitudes toward them. This assumes, of course, and gratuitously, as pointed out above, that the measure of attitude and the behavioral sample came in each case from the same individual. Unfortunately for the main intended and widespread actual use of the studies, this would suggest that they be classified as research on the influence of behavior on attitudes, and not the other way around. As a matter of fact, these pieces of research—La Piere's and Kutner et al.'s—take on the decided appearance of experimental treatment groups in a forced-compliance paradigm. But alas, they would not adequately serve to test the issue of the influence of behavior on attitudes, since the consistency prediction—that having served Chinese or blacks would induce positive attitudes toward them—is contradicted by the theoretical possibility that regardless of the prior attitude or policy, social recriminations might well have followed the highly visible action of serving Chinese or blacks. These social pressures might have easily sustained a previously negative policy ("attitude") or changed a positive policy ("attitude") to a negative one. Such conformity pressures are distinct possibilities since a considerable amount of time intervened between the "behavior" and the assessment of "attitude."

On this issue Kutner et al. (1952) reported comments made by the respondents they contacted by phone that contained explicit concern about the reaction of their other customers to the presence of blacks in the restaurant. La Piere (1934) stated the following: "From the woman proprietor of a small auto-camp I received the only 'yes,' accompanied by a chatty letter describing the nice visit she had had with a Chinese gentleman and his sweet wife during the previous summer [p. 234]."

Apparently concerned, perhaps as a result of this letter, that the experience with the Chinese couple had produced the negative questionnaire responses,

La Piere stated that "responses were secured from 32 hotels and 96 restaurants located in approximately the same regions, but uninfluenced by this particular experience with Oriental clients [p. 234]." He does not relate how many questionnaires had to be sent to establishments not visited to obtain this number of replies. This point may be critical, since the data do show that the distribution of responses is roughly comparable for both visited and nonvisited restaurants and hotels, but "subject loss" might well account for the similarity. Respondents whose establishments did (and would again) serve Chinese would likely be the very respondents who would not return the questionnaires, stating policies that would conflict with the assumed prevailing negative attitude toward Chinese in the general public. This latter point is speculative.

To sum up this point: These experiments likely did not have a measure of attitude and behavior from the same persons, a *sine qua non* of research on the influence of attitudes on behavior, nor did they use the individual as the unit of sampling, taking instead the establishment providing the service and studying two kinds of role behavior. Further, the measure of "behavior" is more plausibly regarded as an intervention, paralleling that in the typical experimental treatment group in a forced-compliance experiment. But unfortunately, the experiments were conducted under conditions, given the lag in measurement of "attitude," that do not allow predictions to consequences for "attitude" even if satisfactory measures were obtained from the same individuals, which is not likely. In addition, we cannot count on the failure of the "treatment" manipulation in La Piere's study since we do not know about the response rate to the mailed questionnaire by the "control" group, and known "subject loss" in the experimental group amounted to approximately 50%.

The inappropriateness of the research by Minard (1952) for the attitude and behavior controversy falls on grounds of the first point mentioned above, that behavior and attitude were not assessed for the respondents. Minard observed that the behavior of southern, white coal miners frequently varied over three categories of setting: the primary work setting (the mine), work-related activities (the industrial union hall, the miners' bus), and the residential setting. He made a statement about attitudes based on these behavioral observations. Campbell (1963) has already pointed out that to assume from the findings that attitudes and behavior are inconsistent requires that one deny or overlook the possibility of mediocre, that is, mid-range, attitudes and also situational differences in thresholds for discriminatory behavior. I wish here merely to make explicit the fact that all of Minard's measures dealt with behavior and that the requirement of a bare minimum of the measure of both attitude and behavior, independently assessed, was not met in this research. As such, it should not be used as empirical evidence that attitudes and behavior are not consistent. If a study provides data on only one concept in a two-concept relational statement, then it should not be counted as evidence for or against the relationship that is asserted. The assumptions required seem unwarranted.

Note that the thesis of this article is not that the features of these three oft-quoted studies are usually distorted from the original. The reports are typically accurate with the minor exceptions hardly substantive. Rather, the facts are misused. This is not a case, then, similar to that presented by Berkowitz (1971), dealing with the misreporting of an experiment by textbook authors. But both kinds of issues—the distortion in the reporting of facts and their misuse—speak out for cautions and critical use of research in presenting a case on issues of controversy. The scholar and textbook writer shoulder a special burden in this respect, one that requires their careful attention.

Neither is this an attempt to render a judgment of "worthless" on the research examined. While these studies should not be regarded as pertinent to the attitude–behavior consistency argument, which in Minard's case was never intended by him, they do seem relevant to other issues, for example, the relationship between the stated policy and actions of a business establishment, in the case of the La Piere and Kutner et al. studies, and the variation in behavior over situations, in the research by Minard (see, e.g., the discussion by Secord & Backman, 1964, pp. 436–437, 442). These studies should not, however, be included in the efforts to supply data in the controversy over the influence of attitudes on behavior.

REFERENCES

BERGER, S. M., & LAMBERT, W. W. Stimulus–response theory in contemporary social psychology. In G. Lindzey & E. Aronson (Eds.), *The handbook of social psychology.* (2nd ed.) Vol. 1. Reading, Mass.: Addison-Wesley, 1968.

BERKOWITZ, L. Reporting an experiment: A case study in leveling, sharpening, and assimilation. *Journal of Experimental Social Psychology,* 1971, 7, 237–243.

CAMPBELL, D. T. Social attitudes and other acquired behavioral dispositions. In S. Koch (Ed.), *Psychology: A study of a science.* Vol. 6. New York: McGraw-Hill, 1963.

COLLINS, B. E. *Social psychology.* Reading, Mass: Addison-Wesley, 1970.

COOPER, J. B., & McGAUGH, J. L. *Integrating principles of social psychology.* Cambridge, Mass.: Schenkman, 1963.

DAWES, R. M. *Fundamentals of attitude measurement.* New York: Wiley, 1972.

FREEDMAN, J. L., CARLSMITH, J. M., & SEARS, D. O. *Social psychology.* Englewood Cliffs, N.J.: Prentice-Hall, 1970.

HARDING, J., KUTNER, B., PROSHANSKY, H., & CHEIN, I. Prejudice and ethnic relations. In G. Lindzey (Ed.), *Handbook of social psychology.* (1st ed.) Cambridge, Mass.: Addison-Wesley, 1954.

HARDING, J., KUTNER, B., PROSHANSKY, H., & CHEIN, I. Prejudice and ethnic relations. In G. Lindzey & E. Aronson (Eds.), *The handbook of social psychology.* (2nd ed.) Vol. 5. Reading, Mass.: Addison-Wesley, 1969.

HARTLEY, E. L., & HARTLEY, R. E. *Fundamentals of social psychology.* New York: Knopf, 1952.

HOLLANDER, E. P. *Principles and methods of social psychology.* (2nd ed.) New York: Oxford University Press, 1971.

KIESLER, C. A., COLLINS, B. E., & MILLER, N. *Attitude change.* New York: Wiley, 1969.

KRECH, D., CRUTCHFIELD, R. S., & BALLACHEY, E. L. *Individual in society.* New York: McGraw-Hill, 1962.

KUTNER, B., WILKINS, C., & YARROW, P. R. Verbal attitudes and overt behavior involving racial prejudice. *Journal of Abnormal and Social Psychology,* 1952, 47, 647–652.

LA PIERE, R. T. Attitudes vs. actions. *Social Forces,* 1934, 13, 230–237.

LINDGREN, H. C. *An introduction to social psychology.* New York: Wiley, 1969.

MARLOWE, D., & GERGEN, K. J. Personality and social interaction. In G. Lindzey & E. Aronson (Eds.), *The handbook of social psychology.* (2nd ed.) Vol. 3. Reading, Mass.: Addison-Wesley, 1969.

McGINNIES, E. *Social behavior: A functional analysis.* Boston: Houghton Mifflin, 1970.

McGUIRE, W. J. The nature of attitudes and attitude change. In G. Lindzey & E. Aronson (Eds.), *The handbook of social psychology.* Vol. 3. Reading, Mass.: Addison-Wesley, 1969.

MINARD, R. D. Race relationships in the Pocahontas coal field. *Journal of Social Issues,* 1952, 8, 29–44.

SAMPSON, E. E. *Social psychology and contemporary society.* New York: Wiley, 1971.

SARGENT, S. S., & WILLIAMSON, R. C. *Social psychology.* (3rd. ed.) New York: Ronald Press, 1966.

SCOTT, W. A. Attitude measurement. In G. Lindzey & E. Aronson (Eds.), *The handbook of social psychology.* Vol. 2. Reading, Mass.: Addison-Wesley, 1968.

SECORD, P. F., & BACKMAN, C. W. *Social psychology.* New York: McGraw-Hill, 1964.

SHERIF, M., & SHERIF, C. W. *Social psychology.* New York: Harper & Row, 1969.

TRIANDIS, H. C. *Attitude and attitude change.* New York: Wiley, 1971.

WATSON, G. *Social psychology, issues and insights.* Philadelphia: Lippincott, 1966.

IX. Social Roles and Social Identity

The readings in this section portray social interaction as a complex pattern of rituals or "acts" that people play out in their everyday lives. Like actors, people dress up in costumes, and, with the world as their stage, they perform various roles. Sometimes, especially when people are in different cultures, they may misread the scripts for various performances. The experiences of the anthropologist Richard B. Lee ("Eating Christmas in the Kalahari") supply an interesting case in point.

Erving Goffman ("The Presentation of Self in Everyday Life") supplies finely tuned descriptions of the theatrical techniques we employ in our everyday lives. The model of social interaction created by Goffman is a complex one in which people are at once actors and members of the audience. The roles played by one person are evoked by the roles played by others. The situations people find themselves in create settings that call forth an almost ritualized series of exchanges. Implicit norms and unconscious social expectations supply the guidelines for social behavior.

But where is the individual in all of this? Where is the person behind the mask? According to some psychologists, we are, essentially, the roles we play. Kenneth Gergen ("Multiple Identity") argues that people change their identities in tune with the situations in which they find themselves. We are not as unified, internally consistent, and predictable as we like to believe; we become, in effect, the masks we wear. The sensational study by Philip Zimbardo ("Pathology of Imprisonment") supports and extends Gergen's characterization. When normal people were asked to play the role of prison guards, they *became* prison guards to a frightening degree. Zimbardo, like Gergen and Goffman, suggests that our behavior results from the playing out of social roles and from the demands of social situations. Ali Banuazizi and Siamak Movahedi accept the idea that Zimbardo's subjects played the roles and complied with social expectations, but they argue that the roles the subjects played were the roles of experimental subjects, not real life prison guards; and the expectations they fulfilled were the experimenter's.

Of central significance in social interaction is feedback from others. But if social behavior is viewed as role playing, of what relevance is this feedback to our identities? If somebody compliments you, does the compliment concern anything other than the facade you have created? And if everyone is an actor, the compliment may simply be part of the role your partner is playing—a script guided by norms of politeness, socially expected behavior, or even a tactic of ingratiation. Because of the ambiguity of voluntarily delivered feedback from others, people often place greater stock in more involuntary, nonverbal indications of how they are coming across. We base more on how people look at us, how close to us they stand, whether they are "busy" when we want to go out with them, and so on, than we do in what they say to us directly. It is for these reasons that third-person or overheard communications ("so-and-so said this or that about you") often have such a powerful impact on our self-esteem.

The subtlety and complexity of social feedback is well demonstrated by the research described in Robert Rosenthal's article, "Self-fulfilling Prophecy." As we interact with people, we communicate various expectations, which affect people's behavior in ways that tend to instigate the confirmation of the expectations. For example, we may expect to dislike a person, act unfriendly, and thereby evoke an unfriendly response. Rosenthal found that teachers' expectations affect the performance of their pupils, and that the expectations of social scientists affect the results of their experiments. Interestingly, no one yet knows how expectations are conveyed. Robert Rosenthal has turned to the study of nonverbal communication in search of an answer.

Just how powerful are the expectations we have about others? Powerful enough to cause trained professionals to believe that sane people who have been diagnosed as psychologically disturbed are, in fact, suffering from the disorder? David Rosenhan ("On Being Sane in Insane Places") explores a dramatic case of the ease with which people's identities are defined by their social roles and the expectations of others. The results of his study indicate that when sane people are placed in a context where people expect them to be insane, they are indistinguishable from other patients.

It is interesting to speculate about how people would act if they did not have to concern themselves with the give-and-take of self-presentation. Would they behave in unadulteratedly selfish and insensitive ways; or would they feel free to come forth with heartfelt affection toward others? Kenneth and Mary Gergen and William Barton ("Deviance in the Dark") created a situation in which concerns about social appearance were minimal and found, somewhat hopefully, that the major effect appeared to be to increase intimacy. As with most social psychological experiments, however, it is possible that the experimental situation—putting people in the dark with cohorts whom they would never see—created an implicit demand for affectionate reactions.

Eating Christmas in the Kalahari

by Richard Borshay Lee

46

The !Kung Bushmen's knowledge of Christmas is thirdhand. The London Missionary Society brought the holiday to the southern Tswana tribes in the early nineteenth century. Later, native catechists spread the idea far and wide among the Bantu-speaking pastoralists, even in the remotest corners of the Kalahari Desert. The Bushmen's idea of the Christmas story, stripped to its essentials, is "praise the birth of white man's god-chief"; what keeps their interest in the holiday high is the Tswana-Herero custom of slaughtering an ox for his Bushmen neighbors as an annual goodwill gesture. Since the 1930's, part of the Bushmen's annual round of activities has included a December congregation at the cattle posts for trading, marriage brokering, and several days of trance-dance feasting at which the local Tswana headman is host.

As a social anthropologist working with !Kung Bushmen, I found that the Christmas ox custom suited my purposes. I had come to the Kalahari to study the hunting and gathering subsistence economy of the !Kung, and to accomplish this it was essential not to provide them with food, share my own food, or interfere in any way with their food-gathering activities. While liberal handouts of tobacco and medical supplies were appreciated, they were scarcely adequate to erase the glaring disparity in wealth between the anthropologist, who maintained a two-month inventory of canned goods, and the Bushmen, who rarely had a day's supply of food on hand. My approach, while paying off in terms of data, left me open to frequent accusations of stinginess and hard-heartedness. By their lights, I was a miser.

The Christmas ox was to be my way of saying thank you for the cooperation of the past year; and since it was to be our last Christmas in the field, I determined to slaughter the largest, meatiest ox that money could buy, insuring that the feast and trance dance would be a success.

Through December I kept my eyes open at the wells as the cattle were brought down for watering. Several animals were offered, but none had quite the grossness that I had in mind. Then, ten days before the holiday, a Herero friend led an ox of astonishing size and mass up to our camp. It was solid black, stood five feet high at the shoulder, had a five-foot span of horns, and must have weighed 1,200 pounds on the hoof. Food consumption calculations are my specialty, and I quickly figured that bones and viscera aside, there was enough meat—at least four pounds—for every man, woman, and child of the 150 Bushmen in the vicinity of /ai/ai who were expected at the feast.

Having found the right animal at last, I paid the Herero £20 ($56) and asked him to keep the beast with his herd until Christmas day. The next morning word spread among the people that the big solid black one was the ox chosen by /ontah (my Bushman name; it means, roughly, "whitey") for the Christmas feast. That afternoon I received the first delegation. Ben!a, an outspoken sixty-year-old mother of five, came to the point slowly.

"Where were you planning to eat Christmas?"

"Right here at /ai/ai," I replied.

"Alone or with others?"

"I expect to invite all the people to eat Christmas with me."

"Eat what?"

"I have purchased Yehave's black ox, and I am going to slaughter and cook it."

"That's what we were told at the well but refused to believe it until we heard it from yourself."

"Well, it's the black one," I replied expansively, although wondering what she was driving at.

"Oh, no!" Ben!a groaned, turning to her group. "They were right." Turning back to me she asked, "Do you expect us to eat that bag of bones?"

"Bag of bones! It's the biggest ox at /ai/ai."

"Big, yes, but old. And thin. Everybody knows there's no meat on that old ox. What did you expect us to eat off it, the horns?"

Everybody chuckled at Ben!a's one-liner as they walked away, but all I could manage was a weak grin.

That evening it was the turn of the young men. They came to sit at our evening fire. /gaugo, about my age, spoke to me man-to-man.

"/ontah, you have always been square with us," he lied. "What has happened to change your heart? That sack of guts and bones of Yehave's will hardly feed one camp, let alone all the Bushmen around /ai/ai." And he proceeded to enumerate the seven camps in the /ai/ai vicinity, family by family. "Perhaps you have forgotten that we are not few, but many. Or are you too blind to tell the difference between a proper cow and an old wreck? That ox is thin to the point of death."

"Look, you guys," I retorted, "that is a beautiful animal, and I'm sure you will eat it with pleasure at Christmas."

"Of course we will eat it; it's food. But it won't fill us up to the point where we will have enough strength to dance. We will eat and go home to bed with stomachs rumbling."

That night as we turned in, I asked my wife, Nancy: "What did you think of the black ox?"

"It looked enormous to me. Why?"

"Well, about eight different people have told me I got gypped; that the ox is nothing but bones."

"What's the angle?" Nancy asked. "Did they have a better one to sell?"

"No, they just said that it was going to be a grim Christmas because there won't be enough meat to go around. Maybe I'll get an independent judge to look at the beast in the morning."

Bright and early, Halingisi, a Tswana cattle owner, appeared at our camp. But before I could ask him to give me his opinion on Yehave's black ox, he gave me the eye signal that indicated a confidential chat. We left the camp and sat down.

"/ontah, I'm surprised at you: you've lived here for three years and still haven't learned anything about cattle."

"But what else can a person do but choose the biggest, strongest animal one can find?" I retorted.

"Look, just because an animal is big doesn't mean that it has plenty of meat on it. The black one was a beauty when it was younger, but now it is thin to the point of death."

"Well I've already bought it. What can I do at this stage?"

"Bought it already? I thought you were just considering it. Well, you'll have to kill it and serve it, I suppose.

But don't expect much of a dance to follow."

My spirits dropped rapidly. I could believe that Ben!a and /gaugo just might be putting me on about the black ox, but Halingisi seemed to be an impartial critic. I went around that day feeling as though I had bought a lemon of a used car.

In the afternoon it was Tomazo's turn. Tomazo is a fine hunter, a top trance performer (*see* "The Trance Cure of the !Kung Bushmen," NATURAL HISTORY, November, 1967), and one of my most reliable informants. He approached the subject of the Christmas cow as part of my continuing Bushmen education.

"My friend, the way it is with us Bushmen," he began, "is that we love meat. And even more than that, we love fat. When we hunt we always search for the fat ones, the ones dripping with layers of white fat: fat that turns into a clear, thick oil in the cooking pot, fat that slides down your gullet, fills your stomach and gives you a roaring diarrhea," he rhapsodized.

"So, feeling as we do," he continued, "it gives us pain to be served such a scrawny thing as Yehave's black ox. It is big, yes, and no doubt its giant bones are good for soup, but fat is what we really crave and so we will eat Christmas this year with a heavy heart."

The prospect of a gloomy Christmas now had me worried, so I asked Tomazo what I could do about it.

"Look for a fat one, a young one . . . smaller, but fat. Fat enough to make us //gom ('evacuate the bowels'), then we will be happy."

My suspicions were aroused when Tomazo said that he happened to know of a young, fat, barren cow that the owner was willing to part with. Was Toma working on commission, I wondered? But I dispelled this unworthy thought when we approached the Herero owner of the cow in question and found that he had decided not to sell.

The scrawny wreck of a Christmas ox now became the talk of the /ai/ai water hole and was the first news told to the outlying groups as they began to come in from the bush for

the feast. What finally convinced me that real trouble might be brewing was the visit from u!au, an old conservative with a reputation for fierceness. His nickname meant spear and referred to an incident thirty years ago in which he had speared a man to death. He had an intense manner; fixing me with his eyes, he said in clipped tones:

"I have only just heard about the black ox today, or else I would have come here earlier. /ontah, do you honestly think you can serve meat like that to people and avoid a fight?" He paused, letting the implications sink in. "I don't mean fight you, /ontah; you are a white man. I mean a fight between Bushmen. There are many fierce ones here, and with such a small quantity of meat to distribute, how can you give everybody a fair share? Someone is sure to accuse another of taking too much or hogging all the choice pieces. Then you will see what happens when some go hungry while others eat."

The possibility of at least a serious argument struck me as all too real. I had witnessed the tension that surrounds the distribution of meat from a kudu or gemsbok kill, and had documented many arguments that sprang up from a real or imagined slight in meat distribution. The owners of a kill may spend up to two hours arranging and rearranging the piles of meat under the gaze of a circle of recipients before handing them out. And I also knew that the Christmas feast at /ai/ai would be bringing together groups that had feuded in the past.

Convinced now of the gravity of the situation, I went in earnest to search for a second cow; but all my inquiries failed to turn one up.

The Christmas feast was evidently going to be a disaster, and the incessant complaints about the meagerness of the ox had already taken the fun out of it for me. Moreover, I was getting bored with the wisecracks, and after losing my temper a few times, I resolved to serve the beast anyway. If the meat fell short, the hell with it. In the Bushmen idiom, I announced to all who would listen:

"I am a poor man and blind. If I have chosen one that is too old and too thin, we will eat it anyway and see if there is enough meat there to quiet the rumbling of our stomachs."

On hearing this speech, Ben!a offered me a rare word of comfort. "It's thin," she said philosophically, "but the bones will make a good soup."

At dawn Christmas morning, instinct told me to turn over the butchering and cooking to a friend and take off with Nancy to spend Christmas alone in the bush. But curiosity kept me from retreating. I wanted to see what such a scrawny ox looked like on butchering, and if there *was* going to be a fight, I wanted to catch every word of it. Anthropologists are incurable that way.

The great beast was driven up to our dancing ground, and a shot in the forehead dropped it in its tracks. Then, freshly cut branches were heaped around the fallen carcass to receive the meat. Ten men volunteered to help with the cutting. I asked /gaugo to make the breast bone cut. This cut, which begins the butchering process for most large game, offers easy access for removal of the viscera. But it also allows the hunter to spot-check the amount of fat on the animal. A fat game animal carries a white layer up to an inch thick on the chest, while in a thin one, the knife will quickly cut to bone. All eyes fixed on his hand as /gaugo, dwarfed by the great carcass, knelt to the breast. The first cut opened a pool of solid white in the black skin. The second and third cut widened and deepened the creamy white. Still no bone. It was pure fat; it must have been two inches thick.

"Hey /gau," I burst out, "that ox is loaded with fat. What's this about the ox being too thin to bother eating? Are you out of your mind?"

"Fat?" /gau shot back, "You call that fat? This wreck is thin, sick, dead!" And he broke out laughing. So did everyone else. They rolled on the ground, paralyzed with laughter. Everybody laughed except me; I was thinking.

I ran back to the tent and burst in just as Nancy was getting up. "Hey, the black ox. It's fat as hell! They were kidding about it being too thin to eat. It was a joke or something. A put-on. Everyone is really delighted with it!"

"Some joke," my wife replied. "It was so funny that you were ready to pack up and leave /ai/ai."

If it had indeed been a joke, it had been an extraordinarily convincing one, and tinged, I thought, with more than a touch of malice as many jokes are. Nevertheless, that it was a joke lifted my spirits considerably, and I returned to the butchering site where the shape of the ox was rapidly disappearing under the axes and knives of the butchers. The atmosphere had become festive. Grinning broadly, their arms covered with blood well past the elbow, men packed chunks of meat into the big cast-iron cooking pots, fifty pounds to the load, and muttered and chuckled all the while about the thinness and worthlessness of the animal and /ontah's poor judgment.

We danced and ate that ox two days and two nights; we cooked and distributed fourteen potfuls of meat and no one went home hungry and no fights broke out.

But the "joke" stayed in my mind. I had a growing feeling that something important had happened in my relationship with the Bushmen and that the clue lay in the meaning of the joke. Several days later, when most of the people had dispersed back to the bush camps, I raised the question with Hakekgose, a Tswana man who had grown up among the !Kung, married a !Kung girl, and who probably knew their culture better than any other non-Bushman.

"With us whites," I began, "Christmas is supposed to be the day of friendship and brotherly love. What I can't figure out is why the Bushmen went to such lengths to criticize and belittle the ox I had bought for the feast. The animal was perfectly good and their jokes and wisecracks practically ruined the holiday for me."

"So it really did bother you," said Hakekgose. "Well, that's the way they always talk. When I take my rifle and go hunting with them, if I miss, they laugh at me for the rest of the day. But even if I hit and bring one down, it's no better. To them, the kill is always too small or too old or too thin; and as we sit down on the kill site to cook and eat the liver, they keep grumbling, even with their mouths full of meat. They say things like, 'Oh this is awful! What a worthless animal! Whatever made me think that this Tswana rascal could hunt!'"

"Is this the way outsiders are treated?" I asked.

"No, it is their custom; they talk that way to each other too. Go and ask them."

/gaugo had been one of the most enthusiastic in making me feel bad about the merit of the Christmas ox. I sought him out first.

"Why did you tell me the black ox was worthless, when you could see that it was loaded with fat and meat?"

"It is our way," he said smiling. "We always like to fool people about that. Say there is a Bushman who has been hunting. He must not come home and announce like a braggard, 'I have killed a big one in the bush!' He must first sit down in silence until I or someone else comes up to his fire and asks, 'What did you see today?' He replies quietly, 'Ah, I'm no good for hunting. I saw nothing at all [pause] just a little tiny one.' Then I smile to myself," /gaugo continued, "because I know he has killed something big.

"In the morning we make up a party of four or five people to cut up and carry the meat back to the camp. When we arrive at the kill we examine it and cry out, 'You mean to say you have dragged us all the way out here in order to make us cart home your pile of bones? Oh, if I had known it was this thin I wouldn't have come.' Another one pipes up, 'People, to think I gave up a nice day in the shade for this. At home we may be hungry but at least we have nice cool water to drink.' If the horns are big, someone says, 'Did you think that somehow you were going to boil down the horns for soup?'"

"To all this you must respond in kind. 'I agree,' you say, 'this one is not worth the effort; let's just cook the liver for strength and leave the rest for the hyenas. It is not too late to hunt today and even a duiker or a steenbok would be better than this mess.'

"Then you set to work nevertheless; butcher the animal, carry the meat back to the camp and everyone eats," /gaugo concluded.

Things were beginning to make sense. Next, I went to Tomazo. He corroborated /gaugo's story of the obligatory insults over a kill and added a few details of his own.

"But," I asked, "why insult a man after he has gone to all that trouble to track and kill an animal and when he is going to share the meat with you so that your children will have something to eat?"

"Arrogance," was his cryptic answer.

"Arrogance?"

"Yes, when a young man kills much meat he comes to think of himself as a chief or a big man, and he thinks of the rest of us as his servants or inferiors. We can't accept this. We refuse one who boasts, for someday his pride will make him kill somebody. So we always speak of his meat as worthless. This way we cool his heart and make him gentle."

"But why didn't you tell me this before?" I asked Tomazo with some heat.

"Because you never asked me," said Tomazo, echoing the refrain that has come to haunt every field ethnographer.

The pieces now fell into place. I had known for a long time that in situations of social conflict with Bushmen I held all the cards. I was the only source of tobacco in a thousand square miles, and I was not incapable of cutting an individual off for noncooperation. Though my boycott never lasted longer than a few days, it was an indication of my strength. People resented my presence at the water hole, yet simultaneously dreaded my leaving. In short I was a perfect target for the charge of arrogance and for the Bushmen tactic of enforcing humility.

I had been taught an object lesson by the Bushmen; it had come from an unexpected corner and had hurt me in a vulnerable area. For the big black ox was to be the one totally generous, unstinting act of my year at /ai/ai, and I was quite unprepared for the reaction I received.

As I read it, their message was this: There are no totally generous acts. All "acts" have an element of calculation. One black ox slaughtered at Christmas does not wipe out a year of careful manipulation of gifts given to serve your own ends. After all, to kill an animal and share the meat with people is really no more than Bushmen do for each other every day and with far less fanfare.

In the end, I had to admire how the Bushmen had played out the farce—collectively straight-faced to the end. Curiously, the episode reminded me of the *Good Soldier Schweik* and his marvelous encounters with authority. Like Schweik, the Bushmen had retained a thoroughgoing skepticism of good intentions. Was it this independence of spirit, I wondered, that had kept them culturally viable in the face of generations of contact with more powerful societies, both black and white? The thought that the Bushmen were alive and well in the Kalahari was strangely comforting. Perhaps, armed with that independence and with their superb knowledge of their environment, they might yet survive the future.　∎

The Presentation of Self in Everyday Life by Erving Goffman

47

Introduction

When an individual enters the presence of others, they commonly seek to acquire information about him or to bring into play information about him already possessed. They will be interested in his general socio-economic status, his conception of self, his attitude toward them, his competence, his trustworthiness, etc. Although some of this information seems to be sought almost as an end in itself, there are usually quite practical reasons for acquiring it. Information about the individual helps to define the situation, enabling others to know in advance what he will expect of them and what they may expect of him. Informed in these ways, the others will know how best to act in order to call forth a desired response from him.

For those present, many sources of information become accessible and many carriers (or "sign-vehicles") become available for conveying this information. If unacquainted with the individual, observers can glean clues from his conduct and appearance which allow them to apply their previous experience with individuals roughly similar to the one before them or, more important, to apply untested stereotypes to him. They can also assume from past experience that only individuals of a particular kind are likely to be found in a given social setting. They can rely on what the individual says about himself or on documentary evidence he provides as to who and what he is. If they know, or know of, the individual by virtue of experience prior to the interaction, they can rely on assumptions as to the persistence and generality of psychological traits as a means of predicting his present and future behavior.

However, during the period in which the individual is in the immediate presence of the others, few events may occur which directly provide the others with the conclusive information they will need if they are to direct wisely their own activity. Many crucial facts lie beyond the time and place of interaction or lie concealed within it. For example, the "true" or "real" attitudes, beliefs, and emotions of the individual can be ascertained only indirectly, through his avowals or through what appears to be involuntary expressive behavior. Similarly, if the individual offers the others a product or service, they will often find that during the interaction there will be no time and place immediately available for eating the pudding that the proof can be found in. They will be forced to accept some events as conventional or natural signs of something not directly available to the senses. In Ichheiser's terms,[1] the individual will have to act so that he intentionally or unintentionally *expresses* himself, and the others will in turn have to be *impressed* in some way by him.

The expressiveness of the individual (and therefore his capacity to give impressions) appears to involve two radically different kinds of sign activity: the expression that he *gives,* and the expression that he *gives off.* The first involves verbal symbols or their substitutes which he uses admittedly and solely to convey the information that he and the others are known to attach to these symbols. This is communication in the traditional and narrow sense. The second involves a wide range of action that others can treat as symptomatic of the actor, the expectation being that the action was performed for reasons other than the information conveyed in this way. As we shall have to see, this distinction has an only initial validity. The individual does of course intentionally convey misinformation by means of both of these types of communication, the first involving deceit, the second feigning.

Taking communication in both its narrow and broad sense, one finds that when the individual is in the immediate presence of others, his activity will have a promissory character. The others are likely to find that they must accept the individual on faith, offering him a just return while he is present before them in exchange for something whose true value will not be established until after he has left their presence. (Of course, the others also live by inference in their dealings with the physical world, but it is only in the world of social interaction that the objects about which they make inferences will purposely facilitate and hinder this inferential process.) The security that they justifiably feel in making inferences about the individual will vary, of course, depending on such factors as the amount of information they already possess about him, but no amount of such past evidence can entirely obviate the necessity of acting on the basis of inferences. As William I. Thomas suggested:

> It is also highly important for us to realize that we do not as a matter of fact lead our lives, make our decisions, and reach our goals in everyday life either statistically or scientifically. We live by inference. I am, let us say, your guest. You do not know, you cannot determine scientifically, that I will not steal your money or your spoons. But inferentially I will not, and inferentially you have me as a guest.[2]

Let us now turn from the others to the point of view of the individual who presents himself before them. He may wish them to think highly of him, or to think that he thinks highly of them, or to perceive how in fact he feels toward them, or to obtain no clear-cut impression; he may wish to ensure sufficient harmony so that the interaction can be sustained, or to defraud, get rid of, confuse, mislead, antagonize, or insult them. Regardless of the particular objective which the individual has in mind and of his motive for having this objective, it will be in his interests to control the conduct of the others, especially their responsive treatment of him.[3] This control is achieved largely by influencing the definition of the situation which the others come to formulate, and he can influence this definition by expressing himself in such a way as to give them the kind of impression that will lead them to act voluntarily in accordance with his own plan. Thus, when an individual appears in the presence of others, there will usually be some reason

[1] Gustav Ichheiser, "Misunderstandings in Human Relations," Supplement to *The American Journal of Sociology,* LV (September, 1949); pp. 6-7.

[2] Quoted in E. H. Volkart, editor, *Social Behavior and Personality,* Contributions of W. I. Thomas to Theory and Social Research (New York: Social Science Research Council, 1951), p. 5.

[3] Here I owe much to an unpublished paper by Tom Burns of the University of Edinburgh. He presents the argument that in all interac-

for him to mobilize his activity so that it will convey an impression to others which it is in his interests to convey. Since a girl's dormitory mates will glean evidence of her popularity from the calls she receives on the phone, we can suspect that some girls will arrange for calls to be made, and Willard Waller's finding can be anticipated:

> It has been reported by many observers that a girl who is called to the telephone in the dormitories will often allow herself to be called several times, in order to give all the other girls ample opportunity to hear her paged.[4]

Of the two kinds of communication—expressions given and expressions given off—this report will be primarily concerned with the latter, with the more theatrical and contextual kind, the non-verbal, presumably unintentional kind, whether this communication be purposely engineered or not. As an example of what we must try to examine, I would like to cite at length a novelistic incident in which Preedy, a vacationing Englishman, makes his first appearance on the beach of his summer hotel in Spain:

> But in any case he took care to avoid catching anyone's eye. First of all, he had to make it clear to those potential companions of his holiday that they were of no concern to him whatsoever. He stared through them, round them, over them—eyes lost in space. The beach might have been empty. If by chance a ball was thrown his way, he looked surprised; then let a smile of amusement lighten his face (Kindly Preedy), looked round dazed to see that there *were* people on the beach, tossed it back with a smile to himself and not a smile *at* the people, and then resumed carelessly his nonchalant survey of space.
>
> But it was time to institute a little parade, the parade of the Ideal Preedy. By devious handlings he gave any who wanted to look a chance to see the title of his book— a Spanish translation of Homer, classic thus, but not daring, cosmopolitan too — and then gathered together his beach-wrap and bag into a neat sand-resistant pile (Methodical and Sensible Preedy), rose slowly to stretch at ease his huge frame (Big-Cat Preedy), and tossed aside his sandals (Carefree Preedy, after all).
>
> The marriage of Preedy and the sea! There were alternative rituals. The first involved the stroll that turns into a run and a dive straight into the water, thereafter smoothing into a strong splashless crawl towards the horizon. But of course not really to the horizon. Quite suddenly he would turn on to his back and thrash great white splashes with his legs, somehow thus showing that he could have swum further had he wanted to, and then would stand up a quarter out of water for all to see who it was.
>
> The alternative course was simpler, it avoided the cold-water shock and it avoided the risk of appearing too high-spirited. The point was to appear to be so used to the sea, the Mediterranean, and this particular beach, that one might as well be in the sea as out of it. It involved a slow stroll down and into the edge of the water—not even noticing his toes were wet, land and water all the same to *him!*—with his eyes up at the sky gravely surveying portents, invisible to others, of the weather (Local Fisherman Preedy).[5]

tion a basic underlying theme is the desire of each participant to guide and control the responses made by the others present. A similar argument has been advanced by Jay Haley in a recent unpublished paper, but in regard to a special kind of control, that having to do with defining the nature of the relationship of those involved in the interaction.

[4] Willard Waller, "The Rating and Dating Complex," *American Sociological Review*, II, p. 730.

[5] William Sansom, *A Contest of Ladies* (London: Hogarth, 1956), pp. 230-32.

The novelist means us to see that Preedy is improperly concerned with the extensive impressions he feels his sheer bodily action is giving off to those around him. We can malign Preedy further by assuming that he has acted merely in order to give a particular impression, that this is a false impression, and that the others present receive either no impression at all, or, worse still, the impression that Preedy is affectedly trying to cause them to receive this particular impression. But the important point for us here is that the kind of impression Preedy thinks he is making is in fact the kind of impression that others correctly and incorrectly glean from someone in their midst.

I have said that when an individual appears before others his actions will influence the definition of the situation which they come to have. Sometimes the individual will act in a thoroughly calculating manner, expressing himself in a given way solely in order to give the kind of impression to others that is likely to evoke from them a specific response he is concerned to obtain. Sometimes the individual will be calculating in his activity but be relatively unaware that this is the case. Sometimes he will intentionally and consciously express himself in a particular way, but chiefly because the tradition of his group or social status require this kind of expression and not because of any particular response (other than vague acceptance or approval) that is likely to be evoked from those impressed by the expression. Sometimes the traditions of an individual's role will lead him to give a well-designed impression of a particular kind and yet he may be neither consciously nor unconsciously disposed to create such an impression. The others, in their turn, may be suitably impressed by the individual's efforts to convey something, or may misunderstand the situation and come to conclusions that are warranted neither by the individual's intent nor by the facts. In any case, in so far as the others act *as if* the individual had conveyed a particular impression, we may take a functional or pragmatic view and say that the individual has "effectively" projected a given definition of the situation and "effectively" fostered the understanding that a given state of affairs obtains.

There is one aspect of the others' response that bears special comment here. Knowing that the individual is likely to present himself in a light that is favorable to him, the others may divide what they witness into two parts; a part that is relatively easy for the individual to manipulate at will, being chiefly his verbal assertions, and a part in regard to which he seems to have little concern or control, being chiefly derived from the expressions he gives off. The others may then use what are considered to be the ungovernable aspects of his expressive behavior as a check upon the validity of what is conveyed by the governable aspects. In this a fundamental asymmetry is demonstrated in the communication process, the individual presumably being aware of only one stream of his communication, the witnesses of this stream and one other. For example, in Shetland Isle one crofter's wife, in serving native dishes to a visitor from the mainland of Britain, would listen with a polite smile to his polite claims of liking what he was eating; at the same time she would take note of the rapidity with which the visitor lifted his fork or spoon to his mouth, the eagerness with which he passed food into his mouth, and the gusto expressed in chewing the food, using these signs as a check on the stated feelings of the eater. The same woman, in order to discover what one acquaintance (A) "actually" thought of another acquaintance (B), would wait until B was in the presence of A but engaged in conversation with still another person (C). She would then covertly examine the facial expressions of A as he regarded B in conversation with C. Not being in conversation with B, and not being directly observed by him, A would sometimes relax usual constraints and tactful deceptions, and freely express what he was "actually" feeling about B. This Shetlander, in short, would observe the unobserved observer.

Now given the fact that others are likely to check up on the more controllable aspects of behavior by means of the less controllable, one can expect that sometimes the individual will try to exploit this very possibility, guiding the impression he makes through behavior felt to be reliably informing.[6] For example, in gaining admission to a tight social circle, the participant observer may not only wear an accepting look while listening to an informant, but may also be careful to wear the same look when observing the informant talking to others; observers of the observer will then not as easily discover where he actually stands. A specific illustration may be cited from Shetland Isle. When a neighbor dropped in to have a cup of tea, he would ordinarily wear at least a hint of an expectant warm smile as he passed through the door into the cottage. Since lack of physical obstructions outside the cottage and lack of light within it usually made it possible to observe the visitor unobserved as he approached the house, islanders, sometimes took pleasure in watching the visitor drop whatever expression he was manifesting and replace it with a sociable one just before reaching the door. However, some visitors, in appreciating that this examination was occurring, would blindly adopt a social face a long distance from the house, thus ensuring the projection of a constant image.

This kind of control upon the part of the individual reinstates the symmetry of the communication process, and sets the stage for a kind of information game — a potentially infinite cycle of concealment, discovery, false revelation, and rediscovery. It should be added that since the others are likely to be relatively unsuspicious of the presumably unguided aspect of the individual's conduct, he can gain much by controlling it. The others of course may sense that the individual is manipulating the presumably spontaneous aspects of his behavior, and seek in this very act of manipulation some shading of conduct that the individual has not managed to control. This again provides a check upon the individual's behavior, this time his presumably uncalculated behavior, thus re-establishing the asymmetry of the communication process. Here I would like only to add the suggestion, that the arts of piercing an individual's effort at calculated unintentionality seem better developed than our capacity to manipulate our own behavior, so that regardless of how many steps have occurred in the information game, the witness is likely to have the advantage over the actor, and the initial asymmetry of the communication process is likely to be retained.

When we allow that the individual projects a definition of the situation when he appear before others, we must also see that the others, however passive their role may seem to be, will themselves effectively project a definition of the situation by virtue of their response to the individual and by virtue of any lines of action they intiate to him. Ordinarily the definitions of the situation projected by the several different participants are sufficiently attuned to one another so that open contradiction will not occur. I do not mean that there will be the kind of consensus that arises when each individual present candidly expresses what he really feels and honestly agrees with the expressed feelings of the others present. This kind of harmony is an optimistic ideal and in any case not necessary for the smooth working of society. Rather, each participant is expected to suppress his immediate heartfelt feelings, conveying a view of the situation which he feels the others will be able to find at least temporarily acceptable. The maintenance of this surface of agreement, this veneer of consensus, is facilitated by each participant concealing his own wants behind statements which assert values to which everyone present feels obliged to give lip service. Further, there is usually a kind of division of definitional labor. Each participant is allowed to establish the tentative official ruling regarding matters which are vital to him but not immediately important to others, e.g., the rationalizations and justifications by which he accounts for his past activity. In exchange for this courtesy he remains silent or non-committal on matters important to others but not immediately important to him. We have then a kind of interactional *modus vivendi*. Together the participants contribute to a single over-all definition of the situation which involves not so much a real agreement as to what exists but rather a real agreement as to whose claims concerning what issues will be temporarily honored. Real agreement will also exist concerning the desirability of avoiding an open conflict of definitions of the situation.[7] I will refer to this level of agreement as a "working consensus." It is to be understood that the working consensus established in one interaction setting will be quite different in content from the working consensus established in a different type of setting. Thus, between two friends at lunch, a reciprocal show of affection, respect, and concern for the other is maintained. In service occupations, on the other hand, the specialist often maintains an image of disinterested involvement in the problem of the client, while the client responds with a show of respect for the competence and integrity of the specialist. Regardless of such differences in content, however, the general form of these working arrangements is the same.

In noting the tendency for a participant to accept the definitional claims made by the others present, we can appreciate the crucial importance of the information that the individual *initially* possesses or acquires concerning his fellow participants, for it is on the basis of this initial information that the individual starts to define the situation and starts to build up lines of responsive action. The individual's initial projection commits him to what he is proposing to be and requires him to drop all pretenses of being other things. As the interaction among the participants progresses, additions and modifications in this initial informational state will of course occur, but it is essential that these later developments be related without contradiction to, and even built up from, the initial positions taken by the several participants. It would seem that an individual can more easily make a choice as to what line of treatment to demand from and extend to the others present at the beginning of an encounter than he can alter the line of treatment that is being pursued once the interaction is underway.

In everyday life, of course, there is a clear understanding that first impressions are important. Thus, the work adjustment of those in service occupations will often hinge upon a capacity to seize and hold the initiative in the service

---

[6] The widely read and rather sound writings of Stephen Potter are concerned in part with signs that can be engineered to give a shrewd observer the apparently incidental cues he needs to discover concealed virtues the gamesman does not in fact possess.

[7] An interaction can be purposely set up as a time and place for voicing differences in opinion, but in such cases participants must be careful to agree not to disagree on the proper tone of voice, vocabulary, and degree of seriousness in which all arguments are to be phrased, and upon the mutual respect which disagreeing participants must carefully continue to express toward one another. This debaters' or academic definition of the situation may also be invoked suddenly and judiciously as a way of translating a serious conflict of views into one that can be handled within a framework acceptable to all present.

relation, a capacity that will require subtle aggressiveness on the part of the server when he is of lower socio-economic status than his client. W. F. Whyte suggests the waitress as an example:

> The first point that stands out is that the waitress who bears up under pressure does not simply respond to her customers. She acts with some skill to control their behavior. The first question to ask when we look at the customer relationship is, "Does the waitress get the jump on the customer, or does the customer get the jump on the waitretss?" The skilled waitress realizes the crucial nature of this question. . . .
>
> The skilled waitress tackles the customer with confidence and without hesitation. For example, she may find that a new customer has seated himself before she could clear off the dirty dishes and change the cloth. He is now leaning on the table studying the menu. She greets him, says, "May I change the cover, please?" and, without waiting for an answer, takes his menu away from him so that he moves back from the table, and she goes about her work. The relationship is handled politely but firmly, and there is never any question as to who is in charge.[8]

When the interaction that is initiated by "first impressions" is itself merely the initial interaction in an extended series of interactions involving the same participants we speak of "getting off on the right foot" and feel that it is crucial that we do so. Thus, one learns that some teachers take the following view:

> You can't ever let them get the upper hand on you or you're through. So I start out tough. The first day I get a new class in, I let them know who's boss . . . You've got to start off tough, then you can ease up as you go along. If you start out easy-going, when you try to get tough, they'll just look at you and laugh.[9]

Similarly, attendants in mental institutions may feel that if the new patient is sharply put in his place the first day on the ward and made to see who is boss, much future difficulty will be prevented.[10]

Given the fact that the individual effectively projects a definition of the situation when he enters the presence of others, we can assume that events may occur within the interaction which contradict, discredit, or otherwise throw doubt upon this projection. When these disruptive events occur, the interaction itself may come to a confused and embarrassed halt. Some of the assumptions upon which the responses of the participants had been predicated become untenable, and the participants find themselves lodged in an interaction for which the situation has been wrongly defined and is now no longer defined. At such moments the individual whose presentation has been discredited may feel ashamed while the others present may feel hostile, and all the participants may come to feel ill at ease, nonplussed, out of countenance, embarrassed, experiencing the kind of anomy that is generated when the minute social system of face-to-face interaction breaks down.

In stressing the fact that the initial definition of the situation projected by an individual tends to provide a plan for the co-operative activity that follows — in stressing this action point of view — we must not overlook the crucial fact

that any projected definition of the situation also has a distinctive moral character. It is this moral character of projections that will chiefly concern us in this report. Society is organized on the principle that any individual who possesses certain social characteristics has a moral right to expect that others will value and treat him in an appropriate way. Connected with this principle is a second, namely that an individual who implicitly or explicitly signifies that he has certain social characteristics ought in fact to be what he claims he is. In consequence, when an individual projects a definition of the situation and thereby makes an implicit or explicit claim to be a person of a particular kind, he automatically exerts a moral demand upon the others, obliging them to value and treat him in the manner that persons of his kind have a right to expect. He also implicitly forgoes all claims to be things he does not appear to be[11] and hence forgoes the treatment that would be appropriate for such individuals. The others find, then, that the individual has informed them as to what is and as to what they *ought* to see as the "is."

One cannot judge the importance of definitional disruptions by the frequency with which they occur, for apparently they would occur more frequently were not constant precautions taken. We find that preventive practices are constantly employed to avoid these embarrassments and that corrective practices are constantly employed to compensate for discrediting occurrences that have not been successfully avoided. When the individual employs these strategies and tactics to protect his own projections, we may refer to them as "defensive practices"; when a participant employs them to save the definition of the situation projected by another, we speak of "protective practices" or "tact." Together, defensive and protective practices comprise the techniques employed to safeguard the impression fostered by an individual during his presence before others. It should be added that while we may be ready to see that no fostered impression would survive if defensive practices were not employed, we are less ready perhaps to see that few impressions could survive if those who receive the impression did not exert tact in their reception of it.

In addition to the fact that precautions are taken to prevent disruption of projected definitions, we may also note that an intense interest in these disruptions comes to play a significant role in the social life of the group. Practical jokes and social games are played in which embarrassments which are to be taken unseriously are purposely engineered.[12] Fantasies are created in which devasting exposures occur. Anecdotes from the past — real, embroidered, or fictitious — are told and retold, detailing disruptions which occurred, almost occurred, or occurred and were admirably resolved. There seems to be no grouping which does not have a ready supply of these games, reveries, and cautionary tales, to be used as a source of humor, a catharsis for anxieties, and a sanction for inducing individuals to be modest in their claims and reasonable in their projected expectations. The individual may tell himself through dreams of getting into impossible positions. Families tell of the time a guest got his dates mixed and arrived when neither the house nor anyone in it was ready for him. Journalists tell of times when an all-too-meaningful misprint occurred, and the paper's assumption of objectivity

---

[8] W. F. Whyte, "When Workers and Customers Meet," Chap. VII, *Industry and Society*, ed. W. F. Whyte (New York: McGraw-Hill, 1946), pp. 132-33.

[9] Teacher interview quoted by Howard S. Becker, "Social Class Variations in the Teacher-Pupil Relationship," *Journal of Educational Sociology*, XXV, p. 459.

[10] Harold Taxel, "Authority Structure in a Mental Hospital Ward" (unpublished Master's thesis, Department of Sociology, University of Chicago, 1953).

[11] This role of the witness in limiting what it is the individual can be has been stressed by Existentialists, who see it as a basic threat to individual freedom. See Jean-Paul Sartre, *Being and Nothingness*, trans. by Hazel E. Barnes (New York: Philosophical Library, 1956), p. 365 ff.

[12] Goffman, *op. cit.*, pp. 319-27.

or decorum was humorously discredited. Public servants tell of times a client ridiculously misunderstood form instructions, giving answers which implied an unanticipated and bizarre definition of the situation.[13] Seamen, whose home away from home is rigorously he-man, tell stories of coming back home and inadvertently asking mother to "pass the fucking butter."[14] Diplomats tell of the time a near-sighted queen asked a republican ambassador about the health of his king.[15]

To summarize, then, I assume that when an individual appears before others he will have many motives for trying to control the impression they receive of the situation. This report is concerned with some of the common techniques that persons employ to sustain such impressions and with some of the common contingencies associated with the employment of these techniques. The specific content of any activity presented by the individual participant, or the role it plays in the interdependent activities of an on-going social system, will not be at issue; I shall be concerned only with the participant's dramaturgical problems of presenting the activity before others. The issues dealt with by stagecraft and stage management are sometimes trivial but they are quite general; they seem to occur everywhere in social life, providing a clear-cut dimension for formal sociological analysis.

It will be convenient to end this introduction with some definitions that are implied in what has gone before and required for what is to follow. For the purpose of this report, interaction (that is, face-to-face interaction) may be roughly defined as the reciprocal influence of individuals upon one another's actions when in one another's immediate physical presence. *An* interaction may be defined as all the interaction which occurs throughout any one occasion when a given set of individuals are in one another's continuous presence; the term "an encounter" would do as well. A "performance" may be defined as all the activity of a given participant on a given occasion which serves to influence in any way any of the other participants. Taking a particular participant and his performance as a basic point of reference, we may refer to those who contribute the other performances as the audience, observers, or co-participants. The pre-established pattern of action which is unfolded during a performance and which may be presented or played through on other occasions may be called a "part" or "routine."[16] These situational terms can easily be related to conventional structural ones. When an individual or performer plays the same part to the same audience on different occasions, a social relationship is likely to arise. Defining social role as the enactment of rights and duties attached to a given status, we can say that a social role will involve one or more parts and that each of these different parts may be presented by the performer on a series of occasions to the same kinds of audience or to an audience of the same persons.

[13] Peter Blau, "Dynamics of Bureaucracy" (Ph.D. dissertation, Department of Sociology, Columbia University, University of Chicago Press), pp. 127-29.

[14] Walter M. Beattie, Jr., "The Merchant Seaman" (unpublished M.A. Report, Department of Sociology, University of Chicago, 1950), p. 35.

[15] Sir Frederick Ponsonby, *Recollections of Three Reigns* (New York: Dutton, 1952), p. 46.

[16] For comments on the importance of distinguishing between a routine of interaction and any particular instance when this routine is played through, see John von Neumann and Oskar Morgenstern, *The Theory of Games and Economic Behavior* (2nd ed., Princeton University Press, 1947), p. 49.

48

Multiple Identity

THE HEALTHY, HAPPY HUMAN BEING WEARS MANY MASKS

by Kenneth J. Gergen

POLONIUS UNDOUBTEDLY HAD GOOD INTENTIONS; his counsel to his son seems immanently reasonable. It has a ring of validity and it fits our religious and moral values. But it is poor psychology. I think we are not apt to find a single, basic self to which we can be true.

I came to this belief after writing letters to close friends one evening. When I read over what I had written, I was first surprised, then alarmed. I came across as a completely different person in each letter: in one, I was morose, pouring out a philosophy of existential sorrow; in another I was a lusty realist; in a third I was a lighthearted jokester; and so on.

I had felt completely honest and authentic as I wrote each letter; at no time was I aware of putting on a particular style to please or impress a particular friend. And yet, a stranger reading those letters all together would have no idea who I am. This realization staggered me. Which letter, if any, portrayed the true me? Was there such an entity—or was I simply a chameleon, reflecting others' views of me?

Parcels. Such questions I find are widespread in our culture. One young woman described the problem to her encounter group thus: "I feel like I'm contradictory . . . and people keep hitting me with the *you're-not-what-you-seem* issue, and it's really wearing me down . . . it's like I feel I can only give part here to one person and part there to another, but then I become a bunch of parcels. If I could just get all my reactions together . . ."

Her difficulties evoke Erik Erikson's classical description of identity diffusion: a state of bewilderment, typical of the young, at the lack of a firm sense of self. Other psychiatrists speak of self-alienation, a depressed feeling of estrangement from the masks of identity that society forces on the individual. Contemporary critics argue that rapid social and technological upheaval has created a crisis of identity: an individual no longer can develop and maintain a strong, integrated sense of personal identity. Writers from Alexander Pope to sociologist Erving Goffman have been alternately impressed and irritated at the use of masks in social life.

Bases. Such critics and psychologists have been working on two assumptions:

1) that it is normal for a person to develop a firm and coherent sense of identity, and

2) that it is good and healthy for him to do so, and pathological not to.

The first assumption underlies virtually all psychological research on the development of the self. Psychologists maintain that the child learns to identify himself positively (high self-esteem) or negatively (the inferiority complex); they have sought the origins of such feelings in different kinds of home environments and socialization styles. They believe that once the sense of self is fixed, it remains a stable feature of personality. Moreover, knowing a person's fixed level of self-esteem allows us to predict his actions: his neurotic or healthy behavior, his assertiveness in social relations, his academic performance, his generosity, and more.

The second assumption—that a unified sense of self is good and that inconsistency is bad—is so pervasive in our cultural traditions that it is virtually unquestioned. At the turn of the century William James said that the person with a divided sense of self had a "sick soul": he was to be pitied and redeemed. The psychologist Prescott Lecky argued that inconsistency of self was the very basis of neurotic behavior. And of course we are all apt to applaud the person of firm character who has self-integrity; we think of the inconsistent person as wishy-washy, undependable, a fake.

Doubt. My research over the past few years has led me to question both of these assumptions very seriously. I doubt that a person normally develops a coherent sense of identity, and to the extent that he does, he may experience severe emotional distress. The long-term intimate relationship, so cherished in our society, is an unsuspected cause of this distress because it freezes and constricts identity.

My colleagues and I designed a series of studies to explore the shifting masks of identity, hoping to document the shifts in an empirically reliable way. We wanted to find the factors that influence the individual's choice of masks; we were interested in both outward appearances and inward feelings of personal identity. To what extent are we changeable, and in what conditions are we most likely to change? Do alterations in public identity create a nagging sense of self-alienation? How do we reconcile social-role-playing with a unified personality?

Our studies dealt with the influence of the other person, the situation, or the individual's motives. In each experiment, we would vary one of these three factors, holding the other factors constant. We would thus assess their impact on the subject's presentation of himself; and when the whole procedure was over, we explored the participant's feelings of self-alienation and sincerity.

Selves. William James believed that one's close friends mold his public identity: "a man has as many different social selves as there are distinct groups of persons about whose opinion he cares." Our research supports this Jamesian hypothesis, and goes further. One's identity will change markedly even in the presence of strangers.

For instance, in one experiment a woman co-worker whom we identified as a clinical trainee interviewed 18 women college students. She asked each student a variety of questions about her background, then 60 questions about how she saw herself. Every time that the student gave a self-evaluation that was more positive than the norm, the interviewer showed subtle signs of approval: she nodded her head, smiled, occasionally spoke agreement. Conversely, she would disapprove of the student's negative self-evaluations: she would shake her head, frown, or speak disagreement. It became clear to the student that the trainee took a very positive view of her.

As a result of this procedure, the students' self-evaluation became progressively more positive. This increase was significantly greater than the minimal change that occurred in the control condition, where students received no feedback from the trainee.

This finding demonstrates that it is easy to modify the mask of identity, but it says little about underlying feelings. Did the young women think they were misleading the interviewer—telling her one thing while they secretly believed something else? To check on their private evaluations of themselves, after the interview we asked the students to undertake honest self-ratings that were not to be seen by the interviewer. We found significant increases in the self-esteem of students who had received the positive feedback; we found no such increases in the control condition. (We compared these self-ratings with those taken in other circumstances a month earlier.) One student in the experimental group told me later: "You know, it's very strange; I spent the rest of the day whistling and singing. Something about that interview really made me happy."

Our next experiment found that even this minimal amount of supportive reinforcement is not necessary to raise one's self-esteem. Sometimes another's outward characteristics are sufficient by themselves to change our self-concepts. Consider our response to the braggart, who spins glorious tales of success, and the whiner, who snivels and frets about his failures. My research with Barbara Wishnov suggests that these two types create entirely different identities in those around them.

Wishnov asked 54 pairs of young women college students to write descriptions of themselves. She explained that she would give the descriptions from one member to the other in each pair. Actually, instead, what she passed along to each was an evaluation that we had prepared in advance.

Each member of one group of students found herself reading the words of a braggart—a peer of impeccable character who described herself as being cheerful, intelligent and beautiful. She loved school, had had a marvelous childhood, and was optimistic about the future.

In contrast, each member of a second group read a description of a fellow student who might have been a dropout from psychotherapy: she was a whiner, unhappy, ugly, and intellectually dull; her childhood had been miserable; she hated school; and she was intensely fearful of the future.

The experimenter then asked each student to respond to this supposed partner by describing herself as honestly as possible in direct response to her.

Self-evaluations soared among the students who read positive evaluations of their peers; they found positive qualities in themselves that were nowhere in evidence in the self-appraisals they had made a month before; they hid negative characteristics. The braggart may produce a power imbalance that persons try to equalize by affirming their own virtues.

It is as if they are saying: *You think you're so great; well, I'm pretty terrific too.*

The whiner produced strikingly different results in the students who read the negative evaluations. These young women responded by admitting to an entire array of shortcomings that they had not previously acknowledged. They adopted a mask that seemed to say: *I know what you mean; I've got problems too.* Even so, they resisted admitting that they were just as unfortunate as the whiner: perhaps they sought to avoid budding friendships based on misery. Thus they did not conceal the virtues they had claimed for themselves a month earlier.

Under. Again we tried to explore beneath these masks. We asked the students a variety of questions after the interchange: *is it possible that anything the other [young woman] said about herself may have influenced you in any way? How honest did you feel you could be with her? Do you feel that your self-evaluations were completely accurate?*

About 60 percent of the subjects said that they felt completely comfortable with the selves they had presented to the partner. The partner had had no effect, they replied, and their own self-evaluations were completely honest and accurate. Moreover, they did not differ at all from the 40 percent who had felt alienated from their self-presentations. The young women shifted their masks with little conscious awareness that they were doing so.

Looks. A third experiment showed that we can induce changes in the way one presents oneself simply by varying the physical appearance of the other person.

In an experiment at the University of Michigan, Stanley J. Morse and I sought male applicants for an interesting summer job that paid well. As each volunteer reported in, we seated him alone in a room with a long table, and gave him a battery of tests to fill out. Among them, of course, was a self-evaluation questionnaire. We explained that his responses on this questionnaire would have nothing to do with his chances for being hired, but that we needed his honest answers to construct a good test. As the applicant sat there working, we sent in a stooge—supposedly another applicant for the job.

Stooges. In half of the cases, the stooge was our Mr. Clean. He was a striking figure: well-tailored business suit, gleaming shoes, and a smart attaché case, from which he took a dozen sharpened pencils and a book of Plato. The other half of the job applicants met our Mr. Dirty, who arrived with a torn sweat shirt, pants torn off at the knees, and a day's growth of beard. He had no pencils, only a battered copy of Harold Robbins' *The Carpetbaggers.* Neither stooge spoke to the real applicants as they worked on self-ratings.

We then compared the evaluations before and after the arrival of the stooge. Mr. Clean produced a sharp drop in self-esteem. Applicants suddenly felt sloppy, stupid and inferior by comparison; indeed, Mr. Clean was an intimidating character. But Mr. Dirty gave everyone a psychological lift. After his arrival, applicants felt more handsome, confident and optimistic. We might conclude that the slobs of the world do a great favor for those around them: they raise self-esteem.

Signals. The behavior and appearance of others inspire self-change, but the setting in which we encounter other persons also exerts an influence. For example, work situations consistently reward serious, steadfast, Calvinistic behavior. But for a person to act this way in all situations would be unfortunate, especially when the situation demands spontaneity and play. No one wants to live with the Protestant Ethic 24 hours a day, in this sense, the office door and the door to one's home serve as signals for self-transformation.

Margaret Gibbs Taylor and I showed how this transformation-by-setting occurs, in a study of 50 Naval-officer trainees. We told the trainees that they would be working in two-man teams on a task (their partners would be in an adjoining room). We put half of the trainees in the work condition, where they expected to have to solve a problem in fleet maneuvers. We showed them a large board on which we placed a variety of model ships. Their task, we said, would be to maneuver a model submarine out of danger in conditions of great stress. To succeed, the team would have to work with great precision in processing an array of complex information.

By contrast, we told the other half of the trainees that while they would be discussing fleet maneuvers with their partners, their primary aim should be to get along with each other as well as possible. We told them to pay special attention to each other's opinions and feelings, and to accommodate themselves to each other. We then asked all trainees to describe themselves to their partners in writing and, as accurately as possible, what they were really like as persons—in preparation for the actual interchange. We then compared these descriptions with those they had written about a month earlier.

Faces. The trainees in the hard-work condition described themselves in a way that would have made Calvin proud: they came across as significantly more logical, well-organized, and efficient than they had a month before. The trainees in the social-solidarity condition put on opposite masks: they described themselves as far more free and easy in disposition, more friendly and illogical, than they had earlier. Each group, in short, adopted the proper face for the occasion.

When the experiment was over, we asked the trainees how they had felt about their self-descriptions.

More than three quarters felt that they had been completely accurate and honest; and their self-evaluations did not differ from those of the 25 percent who had felt alienated from their self-presentations.

Lesson. Freudian theory awakened us to the motives that underlie behavior; for instance, we have become aware of the self-gratifying aspects of even the most altruistic behavior. I think that we can apply this lesson to the study of public identity. If someone appears open, warm and accepting, we may ask why that person adopts such a mask. We may inquire what the cold and aloof individual hopes to attain with that appearance. We should not, however, conclude that the mask is a sure sign of the person's deep-seated character. When motives change, conviviality may turn to coolness, the open man may become guarded.

We studied the relationship between masks and motives in several experiments, most of them based on approval-seeking. Carl Rogers pointed out that the warm regard of others is vital to feelings of self-regard and hence to feelings of personal worth. So we asked: *how do individuals present themselves when they want to gain the approval of others?*

In experiments designed to answer this question, we varied the characteristics of the other in systematic ways. He might be senior to our subject in authority, or junior; open and revealing, or closed and remote; a stern taskmaster or an easy-going boss. When an individual seeks approval from this diverse range of personalities, he adopts wholly different masks or public identities. When he is not seeking approval, self-presentation is much different in character.

Glow. I will use one of our experiments on authority figures as an illustration. A woman who was senior in age and status interviewed 18 undergraduate women. Before the session began, we took each student aside and asked if she would help us by trying as best as she could to gain the liking of the interviewer. We told her that she could do or say anything she wished to achieve this goal.

We observed the students' behavior in the interviews; all identified themselves to the interviewer in glowing terms. They indicated they were highly accepting of others, socially popular,

> ## "The loved one comes to see himself as passionate, poetic, vital, attractive, profound, intelligent, and utterly lovable."

perceptive, and industrious in their work. Students in the control condition, who had not been instructed to seek approval, showed no such change of masks.

So far, no surprise. What startled us was that this conscious role-playing had marked effects on the students' feelings about themselves. After the interview each student made a private self-appraisal, and we compared her rating to tests she had taken a month earlier. Apparently, in trying to convince the interviewer of their sterling assets, the students succeeded in convincing themselves. There was no such change in self-esteem in the control group.

In subsequent research we found that persons can improve their feelings about themselves simply by thinking about their positive qualities. It is not necessary to act the role; fantasizing about how they would act is sufficient.

Plastic. Taken together, our experiments document the remarkable flexibility of the self. We are made of soft plastic, and molded by social circumstances. But we should not conclude that all of our relationships are fake: subjects in our studies generally believed in the masks they wore. Once donned, mask becomes reality.

I do not want to imply that there are no central tendencies in one's concept of self. There are some lessons that we learn over and over, that remain consistent through life—sex-typing, for example. Men learn to view themselves as "masculine," women as "feminine." Some of us have been so rigorously trained to see ourselves as "inferior" or "superior" that we become trapped in these definitions. Often we cannot escape even when the self-concepts become inappropriate or unwanted.

But we have paid too much attention to such central tendencies, and have ignored the range and complexity of being. The individual has many potential selves. He carries with him the capacity to define himself, as warm or cold, dominant or submissive, sexy or plain. The social conditions around him help determine which of these options are evoked.

I believe we must abandon the assumption that normal development equips the individual with a coherent sense of identity. In the richness of human relations, a person receives varied messages about who he is. Parents, friends, lovers, teachers, kin, counselors, acquaintances all behave differently toward us; in each relationship we learn something new about ourselves and, as the relations change, so do the messages. The lessons are seldom connected and they are often inconsistent.

Worry. In this light, the value that society places on a coherent identity is unwarranted and possibly detrimental. It means that the heterosexual must worry over homosexual leanings, the husband or wife over fantasies of infidelity, the businessman over his drunken sprees, the commune dweller over his materialism. All of us are burdened by the code of coherence, which demands that we ask: *How can I be X if I am really Y, its opposite?* We should ask instead: *What is causing me to be X at this time?* We may be justifiably concerned with tendencies that disrupt our preferred modes of living and loving; but we should not be anxious, depressed, or disgusted when we find a multitude of interests, potentials and selves.

Indeed, perhaps our true concern should be aroused when we become too comfortable with ourselves, too fixed in a specific identity. It may mean that our environment has become redundant—we are relating to the same others, we encounter the same situations over and over. Identity may become coherent in this fashion, but it may also become rigid and maladaptive. If a man can see himself only as powerful, he will feel pain when he recognizes moments of weakness. If a woman thinks of herself as active and lively, moments of quiet will be un-bearable; if we define ourselves as weak and compliant we will cringe in-eptly when we are challenged to lead.

The social structure encourages such one-dimensionality. We face career al-ternatives, and each decision constricts the possibilities. Our social relation-ships stabilize as do our professional commitments; eventually we find our-selves in routines that vary little from day to day.

Intimacy. Many of us seek refuge from the confining borders and pres-sures of careers in long-term intimate relationships. Here, we feel, we can be liberated: we can reveal our true selves, give and take spontaneously, be fully honest.

Unfortunately, salvation through in-timacy usually is a false hope, based on Western romantic myth. Marriage, we are taught, soothes the soul, cures loneliness, and frees the spirit. It is true that at the outset, love and intimacy provide an experience in personal growth. The loved one comes to see himself as passionate, poetic, vital, at-tractive, profound, intelligent, and ut-terly lovable. In the eyes of his beloved, the individual becomes all that he would like to be: he tries on new masks, acts out old fantasies. With the security of love, identity may flower anew.

Rigidity. I have had a broad range of experience with young married cou-ples, and I observe that for most of them the myth of marriage dies quick-ly. In a matter of months they feel the pain of identity constriction; the role of mate becomes stabilized and rigid. I think that such stabilization occurs for at least three reasons:

1) *The reliance of each spouse on the other for fulfillment of essential needs.* To the extent that each partner needs the other for financial support, food-preparation, care of children, house-

keeping, and so on, stable patterns of behavior must develop. Each begins to hold the other responsible for certain things, and if these expectations are not met the violator is punished. *But you can't just quit your job,* one as-serts; *you call this dinner?* the other complains; and *How many times do I have to tell you not to make plans on Sunday when I'm watching the game?* Interdependency fosters standardized behavior. And along with standardized behavior comes a limited identity.

2) *Our general inability to tolerate inconsistencies in others.* From infancy we learn that, to survive, we must lo-cate the consistencies in our environ-ment and maintain them. If we could not predict from moment to moment whether a friend would respond to us with laughter, sadness, boredom or re-jection, we would rapidly become in-capable of action. Thus we reward consistent identity in others and punish variations. This process eases interac-tion, makes it predictable, and greases the wheels of social discourse. In an intimate relationship, it also constricts identity.

3) *Our inability to tolerate extreme emotional states for long periods of time.* The new identities that emerge in the early stage of a relationship de-pend in part on the emotional intensity of this period—an intensity fired by the discovery of another's love, the risk in trying new masks, the prospect of a major commitment, and sexual arou-sal. But it is seldom that we can sustain such grand passion, or tolerate the anger and depression that are its inevi-table counterparts. We weary of the emotional roller coaster, and replace passion with peace. It is difficult to restore intense feelings once we have quelled them, though some events may ignite them again temporarily.

Around. This picture is depressing, I realize. Probably most of us have friends who now settle for content-ment in place of joy, and we know others who ceaselessly search for ec-stasy in new relationships—only to see it vanish at the moment of capture. So-lutions are elusive, because the tight-ening of identity moves so slowly that only cumulative effects are visible.

But if we are aware of the process that limits identity, we can subvert it. We can broaden our experiences with others: the more unlike us they are, the more likely we are to be shaken from a rigid sense of identity. Lovers can pursue new experiences: confront a foreign culture, meet at odd times or places, drastically alter the schedule of who-does-what-and-when, develop individual interests. If each partner presents new demands, the stage is set for trying on new masks—and this in turn awakens new feelings about the self. Honest communication—*this is how I think you are now*—is essential. Once in the open, such images usually prove quite false; and as impressions are broken, expectations become more pliable and demands for consistency lose urgency. Finally, if playing a role does in fact lead to real changes in one's self-concept, we should learn to play more roles, to adopt any role that seems enjoyable—a baron, a princess, a secret agent, an Italian merchant—and, if the other is willing to play, a storehouse of novel self-images emerges.

The mask may be not the symbol of superficiality that we have thought it was, but the means of realizing our potential. Walt Whitman wrote: "Do I contradict myself? Very well then, I contradict myself. (I am large. I con-tain multitudes)." ◪

Pathology of Imprisonment
Philip G. Zimbardo

I was recently released from solitary confinement after being held therein for 37 months [months!]. A silent system was imposed upon me and to even whisper to the man in the next cell resulted in being beaten by guards, sprayed with chemical mace, blackjacked, stomped and thrown into a strip-cell naked to sleep on a concrete floor without bedding, covering, wash basin or even a toilet. The floor served as toilet and bed, and even there the silent system was enforced. To let a moan escape your lips because of the pain and discomfort . . . resulted in another beating. I spent not days, but months there during my 37 months in solitary. . . . I have filed every writ possible against the administrative acts of brutality. The state courts have all denied the petitions. Because of my refusal to let the things die down and forget all that happened during my 37 months in solitary . . . I am the most hated prisoner in [this] penitentiary, and called a "hard-core incorrigible."

Maybe I am an incorrigible, but if true, it's because I would rather die than to accept being treated as less than a human being. I have never complained of my prison sentence as being unjustified except through legal means of appeals. I have never put a knife on a guard's throat and demanded my release. I know that thieves must be punished and I don't justify stealing, even though I am a thief myself. But now I don't think I will be a thief when I am released. No, I'm not rehabilitated. It's just that I no longer think of becoming wealthy by stealing. I now only think of killing—killing those who have beaten me and treated me as if I were a dog. I hope and pray for the sake of my own soul and future life of freedom that I am able to overcome the bitterness and hatred which eats daily at my soul, but I know to overcome it will not be easy.

This eloquent plea for prison reform—for humane treatment of human beings, for the basic dignity that is the right of every American—came to me secretly in a letter from a prisoner who cannot be identified because he is still in a state correctional institution. He sent it to me because he read of an experiment I recently conducted at Stanford University. In an attempt to understand just what it means psychologically to be a prisoner or a prison guard, Craig Haney, Curt Banks, Dave Jaffe and I created our own prison. We carefully screened over 70 volunteers who answered an ad in a Palo Alto city newspaper and ended up with about two dozen young men who were selected to be part of this study. They were mature, emotionally stable, normal, intelligent college students from middle-class homes throughout the United States and Canada. They appeared to represent the cream of the crop of this generation. None had any criminal record and all were relatively homogeneous on many dimensions initially.

Half were arbitrarily designated as prisoners by a flip of a coin, the others as guards. These were the roles they were to play in our simulated prison. The guards were made aware of the potential seriousness and danger of the situation and their own vulnerability. They made up their own formal rules for maintaining law, order and respect, and were generally free to improvise new ones during their eight-hour, three-man shifts. The prisoners were unexpectedly picked up at their homes by a city policeman in a squad car, searched, handcuffed, fingerprinted, booked at the Palo Alto station house and taken blindfolded to our jail. There they were stripped, deloused, put into a uniform, given a number and put into a cell with two other prisoners where they expected to live for the next two weeks. The pay was good ($15 a day) and their motivation was to make money.

We observed and recorded on videotape the events that occurred in the prison, and we interviewed and tested the prisoners and guards at various points throughout the study. Some of the videotapes of the actual encounters between the prisoners and guards were seen on the NBC News feature "Chronolog" on November 26, 1971.

At the end of only six days we had to close down our mock prison because what we saw was frightening. It was no longer apparent to most of the subjects (or to us) where reality ended and their roles began. The majority had indeed become prisoners or guards, no longer able to clearly differentiate between role playing and self. There were dramatic changes in virtually every aspect of their behavior, thinking and feeling. In less than a week the experience of imprisonment undid (temporarily) a lifetime of learning; human values were suspended, self-concepts were challenged and the ugliest, most base, pathological side of human nature surfaced. We were horrified because we saw some boys (guards) treat others as if they were despicable animals, taking pleasure in cruelty, while other boys (prisoners) became servile, dehumanized robots who thought only of escape, of their own individual survival and of their mounting hatred for the guards.

We had to release three prisoners in the first four days because they had such acute situational traumatic reactions as hysterical crying, confusion in thinking and severe depression. Others begged to be paroled, and all but three were willing to forfeit all the money they had earned if they could be paroled. By then (the fifth day) they had been so programmed to think of themselves as prisoners that when their request for parole was denied, they returned docilely to their cells. Now, had they been thinking as college students acting in an oppressive experiment, they would have quit

PATHOLOGY OF IMPRISONMENT, by Philip G. Zimbardo, is published by permission of Transaction, Inc., from SOCIETY, Vol. 9, No. 6. Copyright © 1972 by Transaction, Inc.

once they no longer wanted the $15 a day we used as our only incentive. However, the reality was not quitting an experiment but "being paroled by the parole board from the Stanford County Jail." By the last days, the earlier solidarity among the prisoners (systematically broken by the guards) dissolved into "each man for himself." Finally, when one of their fellows was put in solitary confinement (a small closet) for refusing to eat, the prisoners were given a choice by one of the guards: give up their blankets and the incorrigible prisoner would be let out, or keep their blankets and he would be kept in all night. They voted to keep their blankets and to abandon their brother.

About a third of the guards became tyrannical in their arbitrary use of power, in enjoying their control over other people. They were corrupted by the power of their roles and became quite inventive in their techniques of breaking the spirit of the prisoners and making them feel they were worthless. Some of the guards merely did their jobs as tough but fair correctional officers, and several were good guards from the prisoners' point of view since they did them small favors and were friendly. However, no good guard ever interfered with a command by any of the bad guards; they never intervened on the side of the prisoners, they never told the others to ease off because it was only an experiment, and they never even came to me as prison superintendent or experimenter in charge to complain. In part, they were good because the others were bad; they needed the others to help establish their own egos in a positive light. In a sense, the good guards perpetuated the prison more than the other guards because their own needs to be liked prevented them from disobeying or violating the implicit guards' code. At the same time, the act of befriending the prisoners created a social reality which made the prisoners less likely to rebel.

By the end of the week the experiment had become a reality, as if it were a Pirandello play directed by Kafka that just keeps going after the audience has left. The consultant for our prison, Carlo Prescott, an ex-convict with 16 years of imprisonment in California's jails, would get so depressed and furious each time he

visited our prison, because of its psychological similarity to his experiences, that he would have to leave. A Catholic priest who was a former prison chaplain in Washington, D. C. talked to our prisoners after four days and said they were just like the other first-timers he had seen.

But in the end, I called off the experiment not because of the horror I saw out there in the prison yard, but because of the horror of realizing that *I* could have easily traded places with the most brutal guard or become the weakest prisoner full of hatred at being so powerless that I could not eat, sleep or go to the toilet without permission of the authorities. *I* could have become Calley at My Lai, George Jackson at San Quentin, one of the men at Attica or the prisoner quoted at the beginning of this article.

Individual behavior is largely under the control of social forces and environmental contingencies rather than personality traits, character, will power or other empirically unvalidated constructs. Thus we create an illusion of freedom by attributing more internal control to ourselves, to the individual, than actually exists. We thus underestimate the power and pervasiveness of situational controls over behavior because: a) they are often non-obvious and subtle, b) we can often avoid entering situations where we might be so controlled, c) we label as "weak" or "deviant" people in those situations who do behave differently from how we believe we would.

Each of us carries around in our heads a favorable self-image in which we are essentially just, fair, humane and understanding. For example, we could not imagine inflicting pain on others without much provocation or hurting people who had done nothing to us, who in fact were even liked by us. However, there is a growing body of social psychological research which underscores the conclusion derived from this prison study. Many people, perhaps the majority, can be made to do almost anything when put into psychologically compelling situations—regardless of their morals, ethics, values, attitudes, beliefs or personal convictions. My colleague, Stanley Milgram, has shown that more than 60 percent of the population will deliver what they think is a series of painful

electric shocks to another person even after the victim cries for mercy, begs them to stop and then apparently passes out. The subjects complained that they did not want to inflict more pain but blindly obeyed the command of the authority figure (the experimenter) who said that they must go on. In my own research on violence, I have seen mild-mannered co-eds repeatedly give shocks (which they thought were causing pain) to another girl, a stranger whom they had rated very favorably, simply by being made to feel anonymous and put in a situation where they were expected to engage in this activity.

Observers of these and similar experimental situations never predict their outcomes and estimate that it is unlikely that they themselves would behave similarly. They can be so confident only when they were outside the situation. However, since the majority of people in these studies do act in non-rational, non-obvious ways, it follows that the majority of observers would also succumb to the social psychological forces in the situation.

With regard to prisons, we can state that the mere act of assigning labels to people and putting them into a situation where those labels acquire validity and meaning is sufficient to elicit pathological behavior. This pathology is not predictable from any available diagnostic indicators we have in the social sciences, and is extreme enough to modify in very significant ways fundamental attitudes and behavior. The prison situation, as presently arranged, is guaranteed to generate severe enough pathological reactions in both guards and prisoners as to debase their humanity, lower their feelings of self-worth and make it difficult for them to be part of a society outside of their prison.

For years our national leaders have been pointing to the enemies of freedom, to the fascist or communist threat to the American way of life. In so doing they have overlooked the threat of social anarchy that is building within our own country without any outside agitation. As soon as a person comes to the realization that he is being imprisoned by his society or individuals in it, then, in the best American tradition, he demands liberty and rebels, accepting death as an alternative. The third alternative, however, is to allow oneself to become a good prisoner—docile, cooperative, uncomplaining, conforming in thought and complying in deed.

Our prison authorities now point to the militant agitators who are still vaguely referred to as part of some communist plot, as the irresponsible, incorrigible troublemakers. They imply that there would be no trouble, riots, hostages or deaths if it weren't for this small band of bad prisoners. In other words, then, everything would return to "normal" again in the life of our nation's prisons if they could break these men.

The riots in prison are coming from within—from within every man and woman who refuses to let the system turn them into an object, a number, a thing or a no-thing. It is not communist inspired, but inspired by the spirit of American freedom. No man wants to be enslaved. To be powerless, to be subject to the arbitrary exercise of power, to not be recognized as a human being is to be a slave.

To be a militant prisoner is to become aware that the physical jails are but more blatant extensions of the forms of social and psychological oppression experienced daily in the nation's ghettos. They are trying to awaken the conscience of the nation to the ways in which the American ideals are being perverted, apparently in the name of justice but actually under the banner of apathy, fear and hatred. If we do not listen to the pleas of the prisoners at Attica to be treated like human beings, then we have all become brutalized by our priorities for property rights over human rights. The consequence will not only be more prison riots but a loss of all those ideals on which this country was founded.

The public should be aware that they own the prisons and that their business is failing. The 70 percent recidivism rate and the escalation in severity of crimes committed by graduates of our prisons are evidence that current prisons fail to rehabilitate the inmates in any positive way. Rather, they are breeding grounds for hatred of the establishment, a hatred that makes every citizen a target of violent assault. Prisons are a bad investment for us taxpayers. Until now we have not cared, we have turned over to wardens and prison authorities the unpleasant job of keeping people who threaten us out of our sight. Now we are shocked to learn that their management practices have failed to improve the product and instead turn petty thieves into murderers. We must insist upon new management or improved operating procedures.

The cloak of secrecy should be removed from the prisons. Prisoners claim they are brutalized by the guards, guards say it is a lie. Where is the impartial test of the truth in such a situation? Prison officials have forgotten that they work for us, that they are only public servants whose salaries are paid by our taxes. They act as if it is their prison, like a child with a toy he won't share. Neither lawyers, judges, the legislature nor the public is allowed into prisons to ascertain the truth unless the visit is sanctioned by authorities and until all is prepared for their visit. I was shocked to learn that my request to join a congressional investigating committee's tour of San Quentin and Soledad was refused, as was that of the news media.

There should be an ombudsman in every prison, not under the pay or control of the prison authority, and responsible only to the courts, state legislature and the public. Such a person could report on violations of constitutional and human rights.

Guards must be given better training than they now receive for the difficult job society imposes upon them. To be a prison guard as now constituted is to be put in a situation of constant threat from within the prison, with no social recognition from the society at large. As was shown graphically at Attica, prison guards are also prisoners of the system who can be sacrificed to the demands of the public to be punitive and the needs of politicians to preserve an image. Social scientists and business administrators should be called upon to design and help carry out this training.

The relationship between the individual (who is sentenced by the courts to a prison term) and his community must be maintained. How can a prisoner return to a dynamically changing society that most of us cannot cope with after being out of it for a number of years? There should be more community involvement in these rehabilitation centers, more ties encouraged and promoted between the trainees and family and friends, more educational opportunities to prepare them for returning to their communities as more valuable members of it than they were before they left.

Finally, the main ingredient necessary to effect any change at all in prison reform, in the rehabilitation of a single prisoner or even in the optimal development of a child is caring. Reform must start with people—especially people with power—caring about the well-being of others. Underneath the toughest, society-hating convict, rebel or anarchist is a human being who wants his existence to be recognized by his fellows and who wants someone else to care about whether he lives or dies and to grieve if he lives imprisoned rather than lives free. ☐

"Reaction to the Stanford Prison Experiment: Letters to *American Psychologist*"

Another Look at Banuazizi and Movahedi's Analysis of the Stanford Prison Experiment

Ali Banuazizi and Siamak Movahedi (February 1975) presented a highly critical review of the now famous Stanford Prison Experiment conducted by Zimbardo and his associates (Haney, Banks, & Zimbardo, 1973). I do think a few general comments from someone not directly involved in that study are appropriate at this time.

Put simply, Banuazizi and Movahedi argued that the distressing behavior of the subjects in the prison study was not due to their response to a "psychologically compelling prison environment," as Haney et al. wished us to believe. Rather, their behavior was best viewed as a response to powerful demand characteristics in the experimental situation itself (Orne, 1962; Rosenthal, 1969). Not only was it possible that the experimenters successfully communicated their expectations to the subjects, but, more importantly, it seemed the subjects were "acting out their stereotypic images of a prison guard and, to a lesser extent, of a prisoner" (Banuazizi & Movahedi, 1975, p. 159). Ever since the "great awakening" produced by Orne and Rosenthal, such charges have been frequently leveled against social psychology research (e.g., Page, 1974; Schuck & Pisor, 1974). It is a serious charge. I do believe, however, that Banuazizi and Movahedi are incorrect in their assessment of the prison study.

Was the passivity, depression, helplessness, and even psychological dysfunction displayed by the prisoners only a remarkable performance offered in response to perceived experimental demand? It is not always clear why critics think such contamination would necessarily lead to confirmation of an experimental hypothesis, but the question must be answered.

First, it should be pointed out that the questionnaire data collected by Banuazizi and Movahedi show there is no single stereotype of prisoner behavior. No consensus emerged when their subjects were asked to predict how others behave in the role of "prisoner." Only one third of the respondents predicted prisoners would be passive or docile, while another third anticipated continual rebellion and defiance. Banuazizi and Movahedi are certainly aware of this fact, but seem to have overlooked it when devising their alternative explanation of the prison study results.

Second, the authors correctly pointed out in the first part of their article that Haney et al. did not have clearly defined hypotheses when they embarked upon their study. As Zimbardo (1973) has emphasized elsewhere, had the experimenters actually expected the severe apathy and psychological dysfunction eventually produced in some of the prisoners, the study would never have been run. Again, Banuazizi and Movahedi seem to have forgotten their earlier discussion of this point by the time their own conclusions are explicated. For the prisoners, at least, it seems unlikely that specific expectations could have been communicated to them by the experimenters. Banuazizi and Movahedi have themselves undermined this accusation.

The temporal flow of events during the 5-day prison study also seems to contradict Banuazizi and Movahedi's interpretation of the prisoners' behavior. If subjects were indeed "acting out" culturally defined roles, would it not be reasonable for them to show this in the first day of the study? I suggest that the violence and rebellion of the prisoners which occurred less than 2 days after the initiation of the experiment do reflect those subjects' stereotype of real prisoner behavior. Sporadic bursts of prison violence were frequently reported in the press even before Attica, reinforcing the impression that prisoners react to dehumanization and abuse of power with counterforce. The passivity and despondency of the prisoners in the study only occurred after the guards violently put down the rebellion using fire extinguishers, transformed the prisoner's rights into "privileges," played the prisoners against each other, and instigated systematic harassment of the prisoners.

Does this mean that the prisoners subsequently learned what their "role" should be? In a sense it does, but it means much more than play acting, for although severe emotional disturbance might be easily simulated, psychosomatic rashes are not. It must be remembered, furthermore, that after the first prisoner subject was released, the experimenters did, in fact, become suspicious that his symptoms were faked (Zimbardo, Haney, Banks, & Jaffe, 1972). To me, at least, this suggests that the symptoms shown by the prisoners released in later days must have been serious indeed, to convince the experimenters to release them.

If the prisoners' behavior cannot be dismissed as role playing, it is still conceivable that the "oppressive brutality" of the guards was only the acting out of a stereotype, and not a real response to the prison environment per se. What is the evidence on this second question?

First, the questionnaire data collected by Banuazizi and Movahedi do suggest that a single stereotype of guard behavior is widely held. Almost 90% of the respondents believed that other persons in the role of "guard" would be oppressive and hostile. This supports Banuazizi and Movahedi's interpretation of the guards' behavior during the actual prison study. Second, it is possible that the experimenters did, in fact, communicate specific expectations to all of the subjects concerning the guards' behavior. Before the subjects were randomly assigned to the role of guard or prisoner, all subjects were warned that "those assigned to the prisoner role should expect to be under surveillance, to be harassed, and to have some of their basic rights curtailed during their imprisonment, but not to be physically abused" (Haney et al., 1973). Thus, it is possible that the guards felt they had clear guidelines from both their cultural observations and the experimental instructions about how they should maintain order in the mock prison. Of course, it should be remembered that physical abuse did occur in spite of the experimenters' explicit instructions.

Haney et al. (1973) were aware that some might try to "explain away" the guards' behavior by attributing their conduct to good play-acting. What those authors sought to demonstrate, however, was that the behavior of the guards far exceeded what would be required of them were they merely responding to experimental demands. Although the evidence they offer in support of this contention might not sway Banuazizi and Movahedi, I find it persuasive: Harassment of the prisoners seemed to be greater when individual guards were alone with solitary prisoners, or out of range of recording equipment. Guards escalated their aggression against the prisoners even after the prisoners stopped resisting and complied with the commands issued to them. Some guards indicated a willingness to work extra shifts without pay (or is that, too, part of being a "good role-player"?). Unfortunately, Haney et al. did not report hard data to support their argument, so we must rely on their observational powers (and their integrity).

More importantly, we must ask ourselves what it means to say the guards were only "acting out" a common stereotype of how real guards treat real prisoners. In what sense is this different from saying the subjects were actually responding to a "psychologically compelling prison environment," as Haney et al. have wished to argue? I would suggest, in answer to this, that guards in a real penitentiary could also be said to be "playing a role" when they first begin their jobs. Like the guards in the prison study, real guards are given little or no training. Beyond what they have seen in films or heard from the more experienced guards, they really do not know what to expect. Just like the guards in the prison study, they only know that they must be "tough" with the prisoners in order to maintain order. In what way, then, is the subsequent behavior of the guards in the study any less "real" than the behavior of novice guards in actual penitentiaries? Certainly, a qualitative difference does not exist. Like real guards, the prison study guards began slowly but, once disinhibited, soon freely aggressed against the prisoners as a matter of routine.

I recognize that a difference of opinion on the interpretation of the Stanford Prison Experiment will persist, in spite of the arguments I have made. However, I have hoped to show that the findings of the prison study should not be discarded out of hand. Banuazizi and Movahedi have raised important issues, but I argue that they have not presented a strong case in support of their critical stance. Although the study is not an "experiment" in the more formal sense, it remains a powerful demonstration which should be taken seriously. I am sure there are others who will agree with me.

REFERENCES

Banuazizi, A., & Movahedi, S. Interpersonal dynamics in a simulated prison: A methodological analysis. *American Psychologist,* 1975, *30,* 152–160.

Haney, C., Banks, W. C., & Zimbardo, P. G. Interpersonal dynamics in a simulated prison. *International Journal of Criminology and Penology,* 1973, *1,* 69–97.

Orne, M. T. On the social psychology of the psychological experiment: With particular reference to demand characteristics and their implications. *American Psychologist,* 1962, *17,* 776–783.

Page, M. M. Demand characteristics and the classical conditioning of attitudes experiment. *Journal of Personality and Social Psychology,* 1974, *30,* 468–476.

Rosenthal, R. Interpersonal expectations: Effects of the experimenter's hypothesis. In R. Rosenthal & R. L. Rosnow (Eds.), *Artifact in behavioral research.* New York: Academic Press, 1969.

Schuck, J., & Pisor, K. Evaluating an aggression experiment by the use of simulating subjects. *Journal of Personality and Social Psychology,* 1974, *29,* 181–186.

Zimbardo, P. G. On the ethics of intervention in human psychological research: With special reference to the Stanford prison experiment. *Cognition: International Journal of Cognitive Psychology,* 1973, *2,* 243–256.

Zimbardo, P. G., Haney, C., Banks, W. C., & Jaffe, D. *Stanford prison experiment.* Stanford, Calif.: Philip G. Zimbardo, Inc., 1972. (Tape recording)

WILLIAM DeJONG
Stanford University

Demand Characteristics Are Everywhere (Anyway) A Comment on the Stanford Prison Experiment

In their recent criticism of the well-known Stanford Prison Experiment conducted by Zimbardo and his associates (Haney, Banks, & Zimbardo, 1973), Banuazizi and Movahedi (February 1975) contended that the prison experiment tapped only role-playing dispositions rather than any situationally elicited "strategic, coping responses to an asymmetrical power situation analogous to that of a real prison" (p. 159). Thus, Banuazizi and Movahedi attributed the oppressive and tormenting behavior of the student-"guards" and the passive and depressed behavior of the student-"prisoners," as observed in the Stanford Prison Experiment, to the demand characteristics inherent in the experimental role-playing situation.

As evidence for their methodological challenge they offered the results of a questionnaire administered to 185 college students from the Boston, Massachusetts, area which asked for predictions about how college students in general would behave if placed in the role of guard or prisoner in such an experiment. Additionally, respondents were asked about how they thought they, personally, would behave in the two experimental roles. Their results showed fairly strong consensus (roughly 90% agreement) that the students who played the *role* of guard would behave oppressively, aggressively, hostilely, etc. In contrast, predictions about student-prisoner behaviors were more variable and fell roughly into three different categories of (a) rebellious, defiant, etc. (48%); (b) passive, docile (47%); and (c) fluctuating, depending upon the behavior of the guards (46%). Banuazizi and Movahedi attributed the lack of consensus in predicting student-prisoner behavior to "the more diffuse nature of the popular conceptions of the role of prisoner" (p. 158). As for how the student-respondents felt that they personally would behave in the role of guard in a prison experiment, less than half predicted that they themselves would act aggressively or viciously toward the prisoners (47.1%), and only 14% predicted that they would act aggressively or rebelliously in the prisoner role.

Based on their questionnaire results, Banuazizi and Movahedi proposed an alternative interpretation of the outcome of the Stanford Prison Experiment. They wrote that:

In our view, the subjects responded to a number of demand characteristics in the experimental situation, acting out their stereotype images of a prison guard and, to a lesser extent, of a prisoner. (p. 159)

They emphasized that the stereotyped role expectations that subjects bring with them into an experimental situation are in fact "mental sets" that *dispose* the subjects to act out role-defined behavior, in this case, that of guards and prisoners. Furthermore, they contended that such dispositional mental sets influence the actual observed behavior even more strongly "when a concordance exists between these images of the subjects and the subjects and the demand characteristics of the experiment" (p. 159). They concluded that role playing, as an experimental strategy, is an inappropriate technique for testing situational versus dispositional hypotheses.

We find this a rather weak challenge to the results of the Stanford Prison Experiment. To this point, one could ask whether there is any difference between the dispositions or "mental sets" college research participants might bring to a simulated prison study and the dispositions and mental sets real-life novice guards and first-time prisoners might bring to a real prison situation, particularly so if these dispositions are functionally equivalent to highly sterotyped and emotionally laden role expectations, which Banuazizi and Movahedi assert they are. Surely, if culturally conditioned dispositions and mental sets exist for guard and prisoner role behaviors, these roles should, by definition, be shared by most members of the population, whether they are college students or novice guards and prisoners. Obviously it is possible for different segments of the population to hold different predisposing mental sets (or role expectations) — a possibility liable, of course, to empirical verification. However, to the extent that such mental sets are in fact widely shared, it may be just these dispositions along with an accompanying system of situational and social supports that are responsible for the kinds of behavior demonstrated by the participants in simulated *and* real situations, where some participants have been assigned the role of powerless, criminal penitents and others the role of powerful, moral monitors of their deviant charges.

In a word, to dismiss the results of the Stanford Prison Experiment as merely the consequence of demand characteristics is to ignore the equally real demand characteristics inherent in any number of real-life situations where predispositions are reinforced by group pressures, generated by peers who share the same stereotypes and predispositions.

Banuazizi, A., & Movahedi, S. Interpersonal dynamics in a simulated prison: A methodological analysis. *American Psychologist,* 1975, *30,* 152–160.
Haney, C., Banks, W., & Zimbardo, P. Interpersonal dynamics in a simulated prison. *International Journal of Criminology and Penology,* 1973, *1,* 69–97.

STEPHEN THAYER
City College of the
City University of New York
CAROLYN SAARNI
New York University
Movahedi and Banuazizi Reply:

A review of DeJong's comments indicates that he takes issue primarily with our interpretation of the prisoners' behavior in the Stanford Prison Experiment, and not so much with our interpretation of the behavior of the guards. Thus, he admits that "the violence and rebellion of the prisoners which occurred less than 2 days after the initiation of the experiment do reflect those subjects' stereotype of real prisoner behavior." On the other hand, with respect to the behavior of the guards, where he tries to qualify our interpretation, DeJong does not offer more than a trivial argument such which we have already dealt in our original article. While acknowledging that "Haney et al. did not report hard data to support their argument," DeJong insists that we should instead "rely on their observational powers (and their integrity)." Such criteria for the evaluation of scientific claims are not, of course, methodologically compelling.

DeJong maintains that a role-playing interpretation does not adequately explain the *reported* behavior of the prisoner subjects. But so do we maintain this. For the same reason, we played down such an explanation with respect to this group of subjects. A variety of other confounding variables or conditions — not fully described in a brief report of the experiment — could of course have provided the basis for other explanations. For example, we proceeded on the premise that the prisoner subjects could have obtained their release at any time by simply telling the experimenter that they no longer wished to remain as subjects in the experiment. Now, if this right had not been properly communicated to the subjects, the added frustration resulting from "real" imprisonment could provide a further clue for a fuller understanding of their so-called "pathological" reactions. Furthermore, our failure to adequately account for the psychosomatic rash of one of the prisoners, as suggested by DeJong, could hardly be construed as support for Haney et al.'s claim of having successfully simulated a prison environment. Psychosomatic rashes can occur in situations and for reasons that have very little to do with the social forces that operate in a stable prison structure.

DeJong's final argument contains the core of his, as well as Thayer and Saarni's, misunderstanding of our position. It represents, at the same time, a more general trend in the psychological studies of social behavior, one that the Stanford Prison Experiment in fact was designed to challenge. DeJong asks: In what sense is the proposition that "the guards were only 'acting out' a common stereotype of how real guards treat real prisoners . . . different from saying the subjects were actually responding to a 'psychologically compelling prison environment' "? The answer to this question depends entirely on how one chooses to interpret the expression "psychologically compelling prison environment." One can define this expression in such a way, of course, as to make a tautology out of the question, but that would not promote our understanding of the problem. The structural components of a real prison include not only its formal organization but a complex web of informal organizations that lie behind the facade of the formal one. The informal organizations determine and shape the implicit, but perhaps more significant, power structure of the institution, the inmates' system of stratification and leadership, the contingencies of reward and punishment, the mechanisms for the maintenance of order, and so forth. Explanations of the behavior of prisoners and guards — their responses to the psychologically compelling prison environment — should then be made with reference to these structures and processes. Viewed in such terms, there is a fundamental difference between saying that guards were simply "acting out their common stereotypes" and saying that the subjects were responding to a "psychologically compelling prison environment." Therefore, to argue that the behavior of real guards is the same as acting out common stereotypes, as have DeJong and Thayer and Saarni, is to advance a version of the dispositional hypothesis.

Continuing in his critique, DeJong asks, "In what way, then, is the subsequent behavior of the guards in the study any less 'real' than the behavior of novice guards in actual penitentiaries?" The use of the term *real* to predicate behavior in this context calls for a brief comment. It is difficult indeed to conceive of instances of behavior that are unreal, and hence even strict role playing is in no sense "unreal." Similarly, the behavior of guards in a role-playing study and the behavior of novice guards in an actual penitentiary are equally real. However, to posit that two behaviors, both of which are real, are equivalent responses to similar social psychological forces, is to commit the fallacy of assuming the identity of subjects based on the identity of their predicates.

REFERENCES
Banuazizi, A., & Movahedi, S. Interpersonal dynamics in a simulated prison: A methodological analysis. *American Psychologist,* 1975, *30,* 152–160.
DeJong, W. Another look at Banuazizi and

Movahedi's analysis of the Stanford prison experiment. *American Psychologist,* 1975, *30,* 1013–1015.

Doyle, C. L. Interpersonal dynamics in role playing. *American Psychologist,* 1975, *30,* 1011–1013.

Haney, C., Banks, W. C., & Zimbardo, P. G. Interpersonal dynamics in a simulated prison. *International Journal of Criminology and Penology,* 1973, *1,* 69–97.

Thayer, S., Saarni, C. Demand characteristics are everywhere (anyway): A comment on the Stanford prison experiment. *American Psychologist,* 1975, *30,* 1015–1016.

SIAMAK MOVAHEDI
Department of Sociology
University of Massachusetts, Boston
ALI BANUAZIZI
Boston College

SETTING:
A psychologist is
seated at his desk.

There is a knock
on his office door.

PSYCHOLOGIST:
Come in.
(A male student enters)
Sit down, please.

I am going to read you a set of
instructions. I am not permitted
to say anything which is not in the
instructions nor can I answer any
questions about this experiment.
OK? We are developing
a test of...

After the student
has completed the
experiment, he leaves.
    There is another
knock at the door.

The only difference
between the two
episodes is the smile!
    Can a smile affect
results of an experiment?
It not only can,
but probably does.
In the laboratory.
In the classroom.
And everywhere in life.

PSYCHOLOGIST:
Come in.
(A female student enters)
Sit down, please.
(The psychologist smiles)
**I am going to read you a set of
instructions. I am not permitted
to say anything which is not in the
instructions nor can I answer any
questions about this experiment.
OK? We are developing
a test of...**

50 Self-Fulfilling Prophecy

By Robert Rosenthal

Can a child become brighter because a teacher's special smile shows that he is expected to be smarter than he thought he was?

Let us look at what happens when the behavioral scientist, *seeking* absolute objectivity and fairness, approaches an experiment in social research.

Much of our scientific knowledge is based upon careful observation and recording of events. That the observer himself may have a biasing effect on his observations has long been recognized. There are two basic types of experimenter effects. The first operates without affecting the event or subject being studied. It occurs in the eye, the hand and the brain of the researcher. The second type is the result of the *interaction* between the experimenter and the subject of the experiment. And when the research deals with humans and animals, as it does in the behavioral sciences, this interaction actually can alter the responses or data that are obtained.

Quite unconsciously, a psychologist interacts in subtle ways with the people he is studying so that he may get the response he expects to get. This happens even when the person cannot see the researcher. And, even more surprisingly, it occurs when the subject is not human but a rat.

If rats became brighter when expected to by their researcher, isn't it possible that children become brighter when their teachers expect them to be brighter?

Lenore Jacobson, of the South San Francisco Unified School District, and I set out to see if this is so. Every child in an elementary school was given an intelligence test, a test described by us as one that would predict "intellectual blooming."

The school was in a lower socioeconomic neighborhood on the West Coast. There were three classrooms for each grade—one for children of above average ability, one for average ability, and one for below average ability. About 20 per cent of the children in each classroom were chosen at random to form the experimental group. The teachers were given the names of this group and told that these children had scored high on the test for intellectual blooming and would show remarkable gains in intellectual development during the next eight months.

In reality, the only difference between these children and their classmates was *in the minds* of their teachers.

At the end of the school year, all the children were again given the same I.Q. test. In the school as a whole, the children who had been designated as "bloomers" showed only a slightly greater gain in verbal I.Q. (two points) than their classmates. However, *in total* I.Q., the experimental group gained four points more on the average than their counterparts did, and in reasoning I.Q., the average gain was seven points more.

Usually, when educational theorists talk of improving scholastic achievement by improving teacher expectations, they are referring to children at the lower levels of achievement. It was interesting to find that teacher expectations affected children at the highest level of achievement as much as it did children at the lowest level.

At the end of the school year, we asked the teachers to describe the classroom behavior of all their pupils. The children in the group designated as the bloomers were seen as more interesting, more curious, and happier. The teachers also found "blooming" children slightly more appealing, better adjusted, and more affectionate, and with less need for social approval.

Many of the other children in the classes also gained in I.Q. during the year, but teachers reacted negatively to *unexpected* improvement. The more the undesignated children gained in I.Q. points, the more they were regarded as *less* well-adjusted, *less* interesting, and *less* affectionate. It appears that there may be hazards to unpredicted intellectual growth—at least in the eyes of the teacher. This is particularly true of children in the low-ability groups.

The effects of teacher expectation were most evident in reasoning I.Q. gains. But only the girls in the group designated as "bloomers" showed greater gains than the rest of the class. The boys designated as bloomers actually gained less than their classmates. Partly to check this finding, Judy Evans and I repeated the experiment with schoolchildren in a small Midwestern town. The children here were from substantial middle-class families.

Again we found that teacher expectations affected reasoning I.Q. gains in pupils. However, this time it was the boys who tended to show greater gains than girls. These results underline the effects of teacher expectations, but they also indicate the complexity of these effects as a function of the pupil's sex, social status, and very likely other variables as well.

In another study, conducted by Lane K. Conn, Carl N. Edwards, Douglas Crowne and me, we selected an East Coast school with upper-middle-class pupils. This time we also measured the children's accuracy in judging the emotion conveyed in tone of voice. The children who were more accurate in judging the emotional tone of an adult female's voice benefited most from favorable teacher expectations. And in this school, both the boys and girls who were expected to bloom intellectually showed greater reasoning I.Q. gains than their classmates.

W. Victor Beez of Indiana University conducted an experiment in 1967 which sheds some light on the phenomenon of teacher expectancy. His pupils were 60 preschoolers from a summer Head-Start program. Each child had one teacher who taught him the meaning of a series of symbols. Half of the teachers were led to expect good symbol learning, and the other half were led to expect poor learning.

Nearly 77 per cent of the children designated as good intellectual prospects learned five or more symbols. Only 13

---

per cent of the children designated as poor prospects learned five or more symbols. A researcher from the outside who did not know what the teachers had been told about the children's intellectual prospects assessed the children's actual performance.

What happened in this study was that the teachers with favorable expectations tried to teach more symbols to their pupils than did teachers who had unfavorable expectations. This indicates that the teacher's expectations may not only be translated into subtle vocal and visual nuances, but also may cause dramatic alterations in teaching style. Surprisingly, however, even when the amount of teaching was held constant, the children who were expected to learn more did learn more.

Teacher expectancy effects are not limited to the teaching of intellectual tasks. Recent research reported by J. Randolph Burnham and Donald M. Hartsough of Purdue University indicates that the teaching of motor skills also may be affected by teacher expectations. At a camp for underprivileged children from the Philadelphia area, Burnham administered a test to nonswimmers that ostensibly would predict psychological readiness to swim. He then randomly selected children from various age groups and gave their names to the waterfront counselors as those who were "ready" to swim. He found that the children designated as "ready" tended to pass more of the tests in the Red Cross beginning swimmer's course than the average for their peer group.

If the expectancy effect occurs in the laboratory and in the classroom, then it

is not surprising to find it occurring in everyday life. Your expectation of how another person will behave often may become a self-fulfilling prophecy. We know that nonverbal and unintentional communication between people does take place. What we don't know is *how* such communication occurs [see Communication Without Words, page 52]. Further research on the interaction of the experimenter and the subject may eventually teach us more about dyadic interactions in general.

The interaction of experimenter and his subject is a major source of knowledge in the behavioral sciences. Until recently, however, this interaction has been an uncontrolled variable in psychological research. But the demonstration of experimenter effects does not necessarily invalidate a great deal of behavioral research. It does mean, however, that we must take extra precautions to reduce "expectancy" and other unintended effects of the experimenter.

Just what does a behavioral scientist unintentionally do in gathering his data so that he unwittingly influences his sub-

jects' responses? This question must be answered satisfactorily if we want to have dependable knowledge in the behavioral sciences.

In our research, we have distinguished five categories of interactional effects between the experimenter and his subjects: the *Biosocial, Psychosocial, Situational, Modeling* and *Expectancy Effects*.

Biosocial Effects

The sex, age and race of investigators all have been found to affect the results of their research. It is tempting to assume that the subjects simply are responding to the biosocial attributes of the investigator. But the investigator himself, because of sex, age or race, may respond differently to male or female, young or old, white or Negro subjects. And even a slight change in behavior alters the experimental situation.

Our evidence suggests, for example, that male and female experimenters conduct the same experiment quite differently. The different results they obtain are not due to any error as such, but may well be due to the fact that they have unintentionally conducted different experiments.

In one study of the effect of the characteristics of subjects on the experimenter, the interaction between experimenters and subjects was recorded on sound film. Only 12 per cent of the investigators smiled even a little at male subjects, but 70 per cent smiled at female subjects. These smiles may well have affected the results of the experiment. It may be a heartening finding to know that chivalry is not dead, but as far as methodology is concerned it is a disconcerting finding. In general, the experimenter treated his male subjects and female subjects differently, so that, in a sense, men and women really were not in the same experiment at all.

Moreover, when we consider the sex of both the experimenter and the subject, other interaction effects emerge. In the study recorded on film, we found that the experimenters took more time to collect some of their data from subjects of the opposite sex than from subjects of the same sex.

The age of the investigator may also affect the subject's response. Studies suggest that young subjects are less likely to say "unacceptable" things to much older investigators, indicating that an "age-barrier" may exist in at least some behavioral studies.

The skin color of the investigator also may affect response, even when the response is physiological.

A number of studies have found that Negroes tend to control their hostility more when contacted by a white rather than a Negro experimenter and give more "proper" responses to white than black interviewers.

Psychosocial Effects

Experimenters are people, and so they differ in anxiety, in their need for approval, in personal hostility, authoritarianism, status and in personal warmth. Experimenters with different personalities tend to get different responses from their experimental subjects. For example, researchers higher in status—a professor as compared to a graduate student, or a captain as compared to a corporal —tend to obtain more responses that *conform* to the investigator's suggestions. And investigators who are warmer toward people tend to obtain more *pleasant* responses.

Situational Effects

Investigators experienced in conducting a given experiment usually obtain responses different from those of less experienced investigators. This may be because they behave differently. Also, experimenters who are acquainted with the people in the experimental group get results that differ from those obtained by researchers who have never met their subjects before.

What happens to the experimenter during the course of his experiment can influence his behavior, and changes in his behavior may lead to changes in the subjects' responses.

For instance, if the first few subjects respond as expected (*i.e.*, confirming the experimenter's hypothesis), the behavior of the researcher alters, and he influences subsequent subjects to respond in a way that supports his hypothesis.

Modeling Effects

Sometimes before an experimenter conducts a study, he first tries out the task he will have his research subjects perform. For example, if the task is to rate a series of 10 photos of faces according to how successful or unsuccessful the

persons pictured appear to be, the experimenters may decide to rate the photos themselves before contacting their subjects. Though evidence is not yet definite, it appears that at least sometimes the investigator's own ratings become a factor in the performance of his subjects. In particular, when the experimental stimuli, such as photos, are ambiguous, the subjects' interpretation may agree too often with the investigator's interpretation, even though the latter remains unspoken.

Some expectation of how the research might turn out is virtually a constant factor in all scientific experiments. In the behavioral sciences, this expectancy can lead the investigator to act unconsciously in such a way that he affects the responses of his subjects. When the investigator's expectancy influences the

responses in the direction of what the investigator expects to happen, we can appropriately regard his hypothesis as a *self-fulfilling prophecy*. One prophesies an event, and the expectation of the event then changes the behavior of the prophet in such a way as to make the prophesied event more likely.

In the history of psychology, the case of *Clever Hans* is a classic example of this phenomenon. Hans was a horse owned by a German mathematics instructor named Von Osten. Hans could perform difficult mathematical calculations, spell, read and solve problems of musical harmony by tapping his foot.

A panel of distinguished scientists and experts on animal behavior ruled that no fraud was involved. The horse was given no cues to tell him when to start or when to stop tapping his foot.

But, of course, there *were* cues. In a series of brilliant experiments reported in 1911, Oskar Pfungst showed that Hans could answer questions only when the questioner himself knew the answers and when the horse could see the questioner. Finally, Pfungst learned that a tiny forward movement of the experimenter's head was the signal for Hans to start tapping. A slight upward movement of the head, or even a raised eyebrow, was the signal for the horse to stop tapping.

Hans's questioners expected him to give the right answers, and their expectation was reflected in their unwitting signals to start and stop tapping. The horse had good eyesight, and he *was* a smart horse.

Self-fulfilling Prophecies

To demonstrate experimenter effects in behavioral research, we must have at least two groups of experimenters with different expectations. One approach is to take a survey of investigators in a certain area of research and ask those with opposite expectancies to conduct a standard experiment. But the differences in the results could be due to factors other than expectancy, and so a better strategy is required.

Rather than trying to find two groups of experimenters with different expectations, we could *create* such groups. In one experiment, we selected 10 advanced undergraduate and graduate students of psychology as our researchers. All were experienced in conducting research. Each was assigned a group of 20 participating students as his subjects. The experiment consisted of showing 10 photographs of people's faces one at a time to each subject. The participant was to rate the degree of success or failure reflected in the facial expression of the person in the photo. Each of the faces could be rated from −10 (extreme failure) to +10 (extreme success). The faces in the photos were actually quite neutral, and on the average the total ratings should have produced a numerical score of zero.

All 10 experimenters had identical instructions to read to their subjects, and they also had identical instructions on how to conduct the experiment. They were specifically cautioned not to deviate from these instructions.

Finally, we informed our researchers that the purpose of the experiment was to see how well they could duplicate results which were already well-established. We told half of the experimenters that the "well-established" finding was that people rated the faces in the photos as successful (+5). And we told the other half that people rated the faces in the photos as unsuccessful (−5). And thus informed, they began their research.

The results were clear-cut. Every researcher who was led to expect that the photographed people were successful obtained a higher average rating of success from his group than did any experimenter who expected low-success ratings.

We repeated this experiment twice with different groups with the same results. Research in other laboratories has shown much the same thing. Although not every experiment showed a significant effect, probability that results of all these experiments occurred by chance is less than one in a thousand billion.

Having found that what the experimenter expects to happen can affect the outcome of his research, we then began to look for some clues as to *how* the experimenter unwittingly communicates his expectancy to his subjects.

Through the use of accomplices who acted as subjects in an experiment, we learned how the responses of the first few subjects affected the experimenter's behavior to subsequent subjects. If the responses of the first few subjects confirmed the experimenter's hypothesis, his behavior to subsequent participants somehow influenced them also to confirm his hypothesis. But when the "planted" accomplices contradicted the expectations of the experimenter, the following subjects were affected by the experimenter's behavior so that they, too, tended to disconfirm his hypothesis. It seems, then, that the early returns of data in behavioral research can affect and possibly shape the final results.

Reverse Effects

In some of our experiments, when we offered too-obvious incentives or too-large rewards to investigators to bring in "good" data, the expectancy effect was reduced, and in some cases even reversed. Both the autonomy and the honesty of the researchers may have been challenged by the excessive rewards offered. It speaks well for the integrity of our student-researchers that they would not be bribed. In fact, they tended to bend over backwards to avoid the biasing effect of their expectation. But they often bent so far backward that the results of their experiments sometimes were the opposite of what they had been told to expect.

The process by which an experimenter unintentionally and covertly communicates instructions to his subjects is very subtle. For six years we have studied sound films of research interviews in an attempt to discover the cues that the experimenter unwittingly gives to the subject, and for six years we have failed, at least partly.

We know, however, that visual cues *are* important. Placing a screen between the investigator and the person he is interviewing reduces the investigator's influence on the results. But the expectancy effect is not eliminated completely, indicating that auditory cues are also important.

This was dramatically demonstrated by John G. Adair and Joyce Epstein of the University of Manitoba in their tape-recording experiment. They first duplicated the expectation effects study in which 10 photographs of people's faces are rated successful or unsuccessful. Half of the investigators were told to expect a success response and half a failure response. Adair and Epstein tape-recorded each of the sessions. The results matched those of the original studies.

Next, with a new group of subjects a second experiment was conducted. But instead of having live investigators, the subjects listened to the tape-recording of an investigator reading the standard instructions to the previous group. Again the results were much the same. Self-fulfilling prophecies, it seems, can come about as a result of the prophet's voice alone. Since in the experiment all prophets read standard instructions, self-fulfillment of prophecies may be brought about by the tone in which the prophet prophesies.

A dull rat

Early in our research on self-fulfilling prophecies, we thought that some form of operant conditioning might be the explanation. It could be that when the investigator obtained a response consistent with his expectations, he would look more pleasant, or smile, or glance at the subject approvingly. The investigator could be entirely unaware of these reinforcing responses. We analyzed many experiments to see if this type of operant conditioning was present. If indeed it was, then the subject's responses should gradually become more like those expected by the investigator—there would be a "learning curve" for subjects.

But no learning curve was found. On the contrary, it turned out that the first responses of the subject were about as much affected by the investigator's expectations as the last responses.

Further analysis revealed that while there was no learning curve for the subjects, there seemed to be a learning curve for the investigators. As the investigator interviewed more and more subjects, the expectancy effect grew stronger. It appeared possible that the subject's response was the reinforcing event. The subjects, then, may quite unintentionally shape the investigator's behavior. So not only does the experimenter influence his subjects to respond in the expected manner, but the subjects may well influence the experimenter to behave in a way that leads to fulfillment of his prophecies.

Perhaps the most significant implication of this research is that human beings can engage in highly effective and influential unintended communication with one another—even under controlled laboratory conditions.

But do expectancy effects occur when the experimental subjects are not human? We designed a study to find out. Twelve experimenters were each given five rats that were to be taught to run a maze with the aid of visual cues. Six of the experimenters were told that their rats had been specially bred for maze-brightness; the other six were told that their rats had been bred for maze-dullness. Actually, there was no difference between the rats.

At the end of the experiment, researchers with "maze-bright" rats found superior learning in their rats compared to the researchers with maze-dull rats.

A second experiment made use of the special training setup designed by B. F. Skinner of Harvard. Half the researchers were led to believe that their rats were "Skinner box bright" and half were told that their rats were "Skinner box dull." Initially, there were not really such differences in the rats, but at the end of the experiment the allegedly brighter animals *were* really brighter, and the alleged dullards *really* duller.

How can we reduce the expectancy effect in behavioral research?

One way is to design procedures that enable us to assess whether the expectancy effects have altered the results of an experiment. In addition, the experimenter could employ investigators who have not been told the purpose of the study, or automated data-collection systems could be used.

Perhaps a new profession of fulltime experimenters could be developed, who would perform others' experiments without becoming involved in setting up a hypothesis or interpreting the results. Precedents for such professionals are found in both medical research and public-opinion surveys.

Dependable Knowledge

Because of the general nature of expectancy and other experimenter effects, it would be desirable to use more experimenters for each study than we presently use. Having a larger number of returns we could assess the extent to which different experimenters obtained different results, and in any area of psychological research this is worth knowing.

Scientists have long employed control groups in their experiments. Usually the experimental group receives some kind of treatment while the control group receives no treatment. To determine the extent of the expectancy effect, we could add two special "expectancy control" groups to the experiment. In one of these special groups, the investigator would be told that the group's subjects had received some treatment, when in fact it had not. The experimenter in the other group would be told the subjects had not received treatment when in fact it had. Such a research design would permit us to assess the magnitude of the effect of experimenter's expectancy.

To the extent that we hope for dependable knowledge in the behavioral sciences, we must have dependable knowledge about the psychological ex-

periment and the interaction of experimenter and subject. We can no more hope to acquire accurate information for our disciplines without understanding the experimenter effect than astronomers or zoologists could hope to acquire accurate information without understanding the effects of their telescopes and microscopes. And behavioral scientists, being as scientifically self-conscious a group as they are, may one day produce a psychology of those psychologists who study psychologists.

Then, in the laboratory, in the classrooms, in every sector of our lives we will come closer to understanding the effect of a smile. ∩

51 On Being Sane in Insane Places

D. L. Rosenhan

If sanity and insanity exist, how shall we know them?

The question is neither capricious nor itself insane. However much we may be personally convinced that we can tell the normal from the abnormal, the evidence is simply not compelling. It is commonplace, for example, to read about murder trials wherein eminent psychiatrists for the defense are contradicted by equally eminent psychiatrists for the prosecution on the matter of the defendant's sanity. More generally, there are a great deal of conflicting data on the reliability, utility, and meaning of such terms as "sanity," "insanity," "mental illness," and "schizophrenia" (1). Finally, as early as 1934, Benedict suggested that normality and abnormality are not universal (2). What is viewed as normal in one culture may be seen as quite aberrant in another. Thus, notions of normality and abnormality may not be quite as accurate as people believe they are.

To raise questions regarding normality and abnormality is in no way to question the fact that some behaviors are deviant or odd. Murder is deviant. So, too, are hallucinations. Nor does raising such questions deny the existence of the personal anguish that is often associated with "mental illness." Anxiety and depression exist. Psychological suffering exists. But normality and abnormality, sanity and insanity, and the diagnoses that flow from them may be less substantive than many believe them to be.

At its heart, the question of whether the sane can be distinguished from the insane (and whether degrees of insanity can be distinguished from each other) is a simple matter: do the salient characteristics that lead to diagnoses reside in the patients themselves or in the environments and contexts in which observers find them? From Bleuler, through Kretchmer, through the formulators of the recently revised *Diagnostic and Statistical Manual* of the American Psychiatric Association, the belief has been strong that patients present symptoms, that those symptoms can be categorized, and, implicitly, that the sane are distinguishable from the insane. More recently, however, this belief has been questioned. Based in part on theoretical and anthropological considerations, but also on philosophical, legal, and therapeutic ones, the view has grown that psychological categorization of mental illness is useless at best and downright harmful, misleading, and pejorative at worst. Psychiatric diagnoses, in this view, are in the minds of the observers and are not valid summaries of characteristics displayed by the observed (3–5).

Gains can be made in deciding which of these is more nearly accurate by getting normal people (that is, people who do not have, and have never suffered, symptoms of serious psychiatric disorders) admitted to psychiatric hospitals and then determining whether they were discovered to be sane and, if so, how. If the sanity of such pseudopatients were always detected, there would be prima facie evidence that a sane individual can be distinguished from the insane context in which he is found. Normality (and presumably abnormality) is distinct enough that it can be recognized wherever it occurs, for it is carried within the person. If, on the other hand, the sanity of the pseudopatients were never discovered, serious difficulties would arise for those who support traditional modes of psychiatric diagnosis. Given that the hospital staff was not incompetent, that the pseudopatient had been behaving as sanely as he had been outside of the hospital, and that it had never been previously suggested that he belonged in a psychiatric hospital, such an unlikely outcome would support the view that psychiatric diagnosis betrays little about the patient but much about the environment in which an observer finds him.

This article describes such an experiment. Eight sane people gained secret admission to 12 different hospitals (6). Their diagnostic experiences constitute the data of the first part of this article; the remainder is devoted to a description of their experiences in psychiatric institutions. Too few psychiatrists and psychologists, even those who have worked in such hospitals, know what the experience is like. They rarely talk about it with former patients, perhaps because they distrust information coming from the previously insane. Those who have worked in psychiatric hospitals are likely to have adapted so thoroughly to the settings that they are insensitive to the impact of that experience. And while there have been occasional reports of researchers who submitted themselves to psychiatric hospitalization (7), these researchers have commonly remained in the hospitals for short periods of time, often with the knowledge of the hospital staff. It is difficult to know the extent to which they were treated like patients or like research colleagues. Nevertheless, their reports about the inside of the psychiatric hospital have been valuable. This article extends those efforts.

Pseudopatients and Their Settings

The eight pseudopatients were a varied group. One was a psychology graduate student in his 20's. The remaining seven were older and "established." Among them were three psychologists, a pediatrician, a psychiatrist, a painter, and a housewife. Three pseudopatients were women, five were men. All of them employed pseudonyms, lest their alleged diagnoses embarrass them later. Those who were in mental health professions alleged another occupation in order to avoid the special attentions that might be accorded by staff, as a matter of courtesy or caution, to ailing colleagues (8). With the exception of myself (I was the first pseudopatient and my presence was

The author is professor of psychology and law at Stanford University, Stanford, California 94305. Portions of these data were presented to colloquiums of the psychology departments at the University of California at Berkeley and at Santa Barbara; University of Arizona, Tucson; and Harvard University, Cambridge, Massachusetts.

known to the hospital administrator and chief psychologist and, so far as I can tell, to them alone), the presence of pseudopatients and the nature of the research program was not known to the hospital staffs (9).

The settings were similarly varied. In order to generalize the findings, admission into a variety of hospitals was sought. The 12 hospitals in the sample were located in five different states on the East and West coasts. Some were old and shabby, some were quite new. Some were research-oriented, others not. Some had good staff-patient ratios, others were quite understaffed. Only one was a strictly private hospital. All of the others were supported by state or federal funds or, in one instance, by university funds.

After calling the hospital for an appointment, the pseudopatient arrived at the admissions office complaining that he had been hearing voices. Asked what the voices said, he replied that they were often unclear, but as far as he could tell they said "empty," "hollow," and "thud." The voices were unfamiliar and were of the same sex as the pseudopatient. The choice of these symptoms was occasioned by their apparent similarity to existential symptoms. Such symptoms are alleged to arise from painful concerns about the perceived meaninglessness of one's life. It is as if the hallucinating person were saying, "My life is empty and hollow." The choice of these symptoms was also determined by the *absence* of a single report of existential psychoses in the literature.

Beyond alleging the symptoms and falsifying name, vocation, and employment, no further alterations of person, history, or circumstances were made. The significant events of the pseudopatient's life history were presented as they had actually occurred. Relationships with parents and siblings, with spouse and children, with people at work and in school, consistent with the aforementioned exceptions, were described as they were or had been. Frustrations and upsets were described along with joys and satisfactions. These facts are important to remember. If anything, they strongly biased the subsequent results in favor of detecting sanity, since none of their histories or current behaviors were seriously pathological in any way.

Immediately upon admission to the psychiatric ward, the pseudopatient ceased simulating *any* symptoms of abnormality. In some cases, there was a brief period of mild nervousness and anxiety, since none of the pseudopatients really believed that they would be admitted so easily. Indeed, their shared fear was that they would be immediately exposed as frauds and greatly embarrassed. Moreover, many of them had never visited a psychiatric ward; even those who had, nevertheless had some genuine fears about what might happen to them. Their nervousness, then, was quite appropriate to the novelty of the hospital setting, and it abated rapidly.

Apart from that short-lived nervousness, the pseudopatient behaved on the ward as he "normally" behaved. The pseudopatient spoke to patients and staff as he might ordinarily. Because there is uncommonly little to do on a psychiatric ward, he attempted to engage others in conversation. When asked by staff how he was feeling, he indicated that he was fine, that he no longer experienced symptoms. He responded to instructions from attendants, to calls for medication (which was not swallowed), and to dining-hall instructions. Beyond such activities as were available to him on the admissions ward, he spent his time writing down his observations about the ward, its patients, and the staff. Initially these notes were written "secretly," but as it soon became clear that no one much cared, they were subsequently written on standard tablets of paper in such public places as the dayroom. No secret was made of these activities.

The pseudopatient, very much as a true psychiatric patient, entered a hospital with no foreknowledge of when he would be discharged. Each was told that he would have to get out by his own devices, essentially by convincing the staff that he was sane. The psychological stresses associated with hospitalization were considerable, and all but one of the pseudopatients desired to be discharged almost immediately after being admitted. They were, therefore, motivated not only to behave sanely, but to be paragons of cooperation. That their behavior was in no way disruptive is confirmed by nursing reports, which have been obtained on most of the patients. These reports uniformly indicate that the patients were "friendly," "cooperative," and "exhibited no abnormal indications."

The Normal Are Not Detectably Sane

Despite their public "show" of sanity, the pseudopatients were never detected. Admitted, except in one case, with a diagnosis of schizophrenia (10), each was discharged with a diagnosis of schizophrenia "in remission." The label "in remission" should in no way be dismissed as a formality, for at no time during any hospitalization had any question been raised about any pseudopatient's simulation. Nor are there any indications in the hospital records that the pseudopatient's status was suspect. Rather, the evidence is strong that, once labeled schizophrenic, the pseudopatient was stuck with that label. If the pseudopatient was to be discharged, he must naturally be "in remission"; but he was not sane, nor, in the institution's view, had he ever been sane.

The uniform failure to recognize sanity cannot be attributed to the quality of the hospitals, for, although there were considerable variations among them, several are considered excellent. Nor can it be alleged that there was simply not enough time to observe the pseudopatients. Length of hospitalization ranged from 7 to 52 days, with an average of 19 days. The pseudopatients were not, in fact, carefully observed, but this failure clearly speaks more to traditions within psychiatric hospitals than to lack of opportunity.

Finally, it cannot be said that the failure to recognize the pseudopatients' sanity was due to the fact that they were not behaving sanely. While there was clearly some tension present in all of them, their daily visitors could detect no serious behavioral consequences— nor, indeed, could other patients. It was quite common for the patients to "detect" the pseudopatients' sanity. During the first three hospitalizations, when accurate counts were kept, 35 of a total of 118 patients on the admissions ward voiced their suspicions, some vigorously. "You're not crazy. You're a journalist, or a professor [referring to the continual note-taking]. You're checking up on the hospital." While most of the patients were reassured by the pseudopatient's insistence that he had been sick before he came in but was fine now, some continued to believe that the pseudopatient was sane throughout his hospitalization (*11*). The fact that the patients often recognized normality when staff did not raises important questions.

Failure to detect sanity during the course of hospitalization may be due to the fact that physicians operate with a strong bias toward what statisticians call the type 2 error (*5*). This is to say that physicians are more inclined to call a healthy person sick (a false positive, type 2) than a sick person healthy (a false negative, type 1). The reasons for this are not hard to find: it is clearly more dangerous to misdiagnose illness than health. Better to err on the side of caution, to suspect illness even among the healthy.

But what holds for medicine does not hold equally well for psychiatry. Medical illnesses, while unfortunate, are not commonly pejorative. Psychiatric diagnoses, on the contrary, carry with them personal, legal, and social stigmas (*12*). It was therefore important to see whether the tendency toward diagnosing the sane insane could be reversed. The following experiment was arranged at a research and teaching hospital whose staff had heard these findings but doubted that such an error could occur in their hospital. The staff was informed that at some time during the following 3 months, one or more pseudopatients would attempt to be admitted into the psychiatric hospital. Each staff member was asked to rate each patient who presented himself at admissions or on the ward according to the likelihood that the patient was a pseudopatient. A 10-point scale was used, with a 1 and 2 reflecting high confidence that the patient was a pseudopatient.

Judgments were obtained on 193 patients who were admitted for psychiatric treatment. All staff who had had sustained contact with or primary responsibility for the patient—attendants, nurses, psychiatrists, physicians, and psychologists—were asked to make judgments. Forty-one patients were alleged, with high confidence, to be pseudopatients by at least one member of the staff. Twenty-three were considered suspect by at least one psychiatrist. Nineteen were suspected by one psychiatrist *and* one other staff member.

Actually, no genuine pseudopatient (at least from my group) presented himself during this period.

The experiment is instructive. It indicates that the tendency to designate sane people as insane can be reversed when the stakes (in this case, prestige and diagnostic acumen) are high. But what can be said of the 19 people who were suspected of being "sane" by one psychiatrist and another staff member? Were these people truly "sane," or was it rather the case that in the course of avoiding the type 2 error the staff tended to make more errors of the first sort—calling the crazy "sane"? There is no way of knowing. But one thing is certain: any diagnostic process that lends itself so readily to massive errors of this sort cannot be a very reliable one.

The Stickiness of Psychodiagnostic Labels

Beyond the tendency to call the healthy sick—a tendency that accounts better for diagnostic behavior on admission than it does for such behavior after a lengthy period of exposure—the data speak to the massive role of labeling in psychiatric assessment. Having once been labeled schizophrenic, there is nothing the pseudopatient can do to overcome the tag. The tag profoundly colors others' perceptions of him and his behavior.

From one viewpoint, these data are hardly surprising, for it has long been known that elements are given meaning by the context in which they occur. Gestalt psychology made this point vigorously, and Asch (*13*) demonstrated that there are "central" personality traits (such as "warm" versus "cold") which are so powerful that they markedly color the meaning of other information in forming an impression of a given personality (*14*). "Insane," "schizophrenic," "manic-depressive," and "crazy" are probably among the most powerful of such central traits. Once a person is designated abnormal, all of his other behaviors and characteristics are colored by that label. Indeed, that label is so powerful that many of the pseudopatients' normal behaviors were overlooked entirely or profoundly misinterpreted. Some examples may clarify this issue.

Earlier I indicated that there were no changes in the pseudopatient's personal history and current status beyond those of name, employment, and, where necessary, vocation. Otherwise, a veridical description of personal history and circumstances was offered. Those circumstances were not psychotic. How were they made consonant with the diagnosis of psychosis? Or were those diagnoses modified in such a way as to bring them into accord with the circumstances of the pseudopatient's life, as described by him?

As far as I can determine, diagnoses were in no way affected by the relative health of the circumstances of a pseudopatient's life. Rather, the reverse occurred: the perception of his circumstances was shaped entirely by the diagnosis. A clear example of such translation is found in the case of a pseudopatient who had had a close relationship with his mother but was rather remote from his father during his early childhool. During adolescence and beyond, however, his father became a close friend, while his relationship with his mother cooled. His present relationship with his wife was characteristically close and warm. Apart from occasional angry exchanges, friction was minimal. The children had rarely been spanked. Surely there is nothing especially pathological about such a history. Indeed, many readers may see a similar pattern in their own experiences, with no markedly deleterious consequences. Observe, however, how such a history was translated in the psychopathological context, this from the case summary prepared after the patient was discharged.

This white 39-year-old male . . . manifests a long history of considerable ambivalence in close relationships, which begins in early childhood. A warm relationship with his mother cools during his adolescence. A distant relationship to his father is described as becoming very intense. Affective stability is absent. His attempts to control emotionality with his wife and children are punctuated by angry outbursts and, in the case of the children, spankings. And while he says that he has several good friends, one senses considerable ambivalence embedded in those relationships also. . . .

The facts of the case were unintentionally distorted by the staff to achieve consistency with a popular theory of the dynamics of a schizophrenic reaction (*15*). Nothing of an ambivalent nature had been described in relations with parents, spouse, or friends. To the extent that ambivalence could be inferred, it was probably not greater than is found in all human relationships. It is true the pseudopatient's relationships with his parents changed over time, but in the ordinary context that would hardly be remarkable—indeed, it might very well be expected. Clearly, the meaning ascribed to his verbalizations (that is, ambivalence, affective instability) was determined by the diagnosis: schizophrenia. An entirely different meaning would have been ascribed if it were known that the man was "normal."

All pseudopatients took extensive notes publicly. Under ordinary circumstances, such behavior would have raised questions in the minds of observers, as, in fact, it did among patients. Indeed, it seemed so certain that the notes would elicit suspicion that elaborate precautions were taken to remove them from the ward each day. But the precautions proved needless. The closest any staff member came to questioning these notes occurred when one pseudopatient asked his physician what kind of medication he was receiving and began to write down the response. "You needn't write it," he was told gently. "If you have trouble remembering, just ask me again."

If no questions were asked of the pseudopatients, how was their writing interpreted? Nursing records for three patients indicate that the writing was seen as an aspect of their pathological behavior. "Patient engages in writing behavior" was the daily nursing comment on one of the pseudopatients who was never questioned about his writing. Given that the patient is in the hospital, he must be psychologically disturbed. And given that he is disturbed, continuous writing must be a behavioral manifestation of that disturbance, perhaps a subset of the compulsive behaviors that are sometimes correlated with schizophrenia.

One tacit characteristic of psychiatric diagnosis is that it locates the sources of aberration within the individual and only rarely within the complex of stimuli that surrounds him. Consequently, behaviors that are stimulated by the environment are commonly misattributed to the patient's disorder. For example, one kindly nurse found a pseudopatient pacing the long hospital corridors. "Nervous, Mr. X?" she asked. "No, bored," he said.

The notes kept by pseudopatients are full of patient behaviors that were misinterpreted by well-intentioned staff. Often enough, a patient would go "berserk" because he had, wittingly or unwittingly, been mistreated by, say, an attendant. A nurse coming upon the scene would rarely inquire even cursorily into the environmental stimuli of the patient's behavior. Rather, she assumed that his upset derived from his pathology, not from his present interactions with other staff members. Occasionally, the staff might assume that the patient's family (especially when they had recently visited) or other patients had stimulated the outburst. But never were the staff found to assume that one of themselves or the structure of the hospital had anything to do with a patient's behavior. One psychiatrist pointed to a group of patients who were sitting outside the cafeteria entrance half an hour before lunchtime. To a group of young residents he indicated that such behavior was characteristic of the oral-acquisitive nature of the syndrome. It seemed not to occur to him that there were very few things to anticipate in a psychiatric hospital besides eating.

A psychiatric label has a life and an influence of its own. Once the impression has been formed that the patient is schizophrenic, the expectation is that he will continue to be schizophrenic. When a sufficient amount of time has passed, during which the patient has done nothing bizarre, he is considered to be in remission and available for discharge. But the label endures beyond discharge, with the unconfirmed expectation that he will behave as a schizophrenic again. Such labels, conferred by mental health professionals, are as influential on the patient as they are on his relatives and friends, and it should not surprise anyone that the diagnosis acts on all of them as a self-fulfilling prophecy. Eventually, the patient himself accepts the diagnosis, with all of its surplus meanings and expectations, and behaves accordingly (*5*).

The inferences to be made from these matters are quite simple. Much as Zigler and Phillips have demonstrated that there is enormous overlap in the symptoms presented by patients who have been variously diagnosed (*16*), so there is enormous overlap in the behaviors of the sane and the insane. The sane are not "sane" all of the time. We lose our tempers "for no good reason." We are occasionally depressed or anxious, again for no good reason. And we may find it difficult to get along with one or another person—again for no reason that we can specify. Similarly, the insane are not always insane. Indeed, it was the impression of the pseudopatients while living with them that they were sane for long periods of time—that the bizarre behaviors upon which their diagnoses were allegedly predicated constituted only a small fraction of their total behavior. If it makes no sense to label ourselves permanently depressed on the basis of an occasional depression, then it takes better evidence than is presently available to label all patients insane or schizophrenic on the basis of bizarre behaviors or cognitions. It seems more useful, as Mischel (*17*) has pointed out, to limit our discussions to *behaviors*, the stimuli that provoke them, and their correlates.

It is not known why powerful impressions of personality traits, such as "crazy" or "insane," arise. Conceivably, when the origins of and stimuli that give rise to a behavior are remote or unknown, or when the behavior strikes us as immutable, trait labels regarding the *behaver* arise. When, on the other hand, the origins and stimuli are known and available, discourse is limited to the behavior itself. Thus, I may hallucinate because I am sleeping, or I may hallucinate because I have ingested a peculiar drug. These are termed sleep-induced hallucinations, or dreams, and drug-induced hallucinations, respectively. But when the stimuli to my hallucinations are unknown, that is called craziness, or schizophrenia—as if that inference were somehow as illuminating as the others.

The Experience of Psychiatric Hospitalization

The term "mental illness" is of recent origin. It was coined by people who were humane in their inclinations and who wanted very much to raise the station of (and the public's sympathies toward) the psychologically disturbed from that of witches and "crazies" to one that was akin to the physically ill. And they were at least partially successful, for the treatment of the mentally ill *has* improved considerably over the years. But while treatment has improved, it is doubtful that people really regard the mentally ill in the same way that they view the physically ill. A broken leg is something one recovers from, but mental illness allegedly endures forever (18). A broken leg does not threaten the observer, but a crazy schizophrenic? There is by now a host of evidence that attitudes toward the mentally ill are characterized by fear, hostility, aloofness, suspicion, and dread (19). The mentally ill are society's lepers.

That such attitudes infect the general population is perhaps not surprising, only upsetting. But that they affect the professionals—attendants, nurses, physicians, psychologists, and social workers—who treat and deal with the mentally ill is more disconcerting, both because such attitudes are self-evidently pernicious and because they are unwitting. Most mental health professionals would insist that they are sympathetic toward the mentally ill, that they are neither avoidant nor hostile. But it is more likely that an exquisite ambivalence characterizes their relations with psychiatric patients, such that their avowed impulses are only part of their entire attitude. Negative attitudes are there too and can easily be detected. Such attitudes should not surprise us. They are the natural offspring of the

labels patients wear and the places in which they are found.

Consider the structure of the typical psychiatric hospital. Staff and patients are strictly segregated. Staff have their own living space, including their dining facilities, bathrooms, and assembly places. The glassed quarters that contain the professional staff, which the pseudopatients came to call "the cage," sit out on every dayroom. The staff emerge primarily for caretaking purposes—to give medication, to conduct a therapy or group meeting, to instruct or reprimand a patient. Otherwise, staff keep to themselves, almost as if the disorder that afflicts their charges is somehow catching.

So much is patient-staff segregation the rule that, for four public hospitals in which an attempt was made to measure the degree to which staff and patients mingle, it was necessary to use "time out of the staff cage" as the operational measure. While it was not the case that all time spent out of the cage was spent mingling with patients (attendants, for example, would occasionally emerge to watch television in the dayroom), it was the only way in which one could gather reliable data on time for measuring.

The average amount of time spent by attendants outside of the cage was 11.3 percent (range, 3 to 52 percent). This figure does not represent only time spent mingling with patients, but also includes time spent on such chores as folding laundry, supervising patients while they shave, directing ward cleanup, and sending patients to off-ward activities. It was the relatively rare attendant who spent time talking with

patients or playing games with them. It proved impossible to obtain a "percent mingling time" for nurses, since the amount of time they spent out of the cage was too brief. Rather, we counted instances of emergence from the cage. On the average, daytime nurses emerged from the cage 11.5 times per shift, including instances when they left the ward entirely (range, 4 to 39 times). Late afternoon and night nurses were even less available, emerging on the average 9.4 times per shift (range, 4 to 41 times). Data on early morning nurses, who arrived usually after midnight and departed at 8 a.m., are not available because patients were asleep during most of this period.

Physicians, especially psychiatrists, were even less available. They were rarely seen on the wards. Quite commonly, they would be seen only when they arrived and departed, with the remaining time being spent in their offices or in the cage. On the average, physicians emerged on the ward 6.7 times per day (range, 1 to 17 times). It proved difficult to make an accurate estimate in this regard, since physicians often maintained hours that allowed them to come and go at different times.

The hierarchical organization of the psychiatric hospital has been commented on before (20), but the latent meaning of that kind of organization is worth noting again. Those with the most power have least to do with patients, and those with the least power are most involved with them. Recall, however, that the acquisition of role-appropriate behaviors occurs mainly through the observation of others, with the most powerful having the most in-

Table 1. Self-initiated contact by pseudopatients with psychiatrists and nurses and attendants, compared to contact with other groups.

| Contact | Psychiatric hospitals | | University campus (nonmedical) | University medical center | | |
| | | | | Physicians | | |
	(1) Psychiatrists	(2) Nurses and attendants	(3) Faculty	(4) "Looking for a psychiatrist"	(5) "Looking for an internist"	(6) No additional comment
Responses						
Moves on, head averted (%)	71	88	0	0	0	0
Makes eye contact (%)	23	10	0	11	0	0
Pauses and chats (%)	2	2	0	11	0	10
Stops and talks (%)	4	0.5	100	78	100	90
Mean number of questions answered (out of 6)	*	*	6	3.8	4.8	4.5
Respondents (No.)	13	47	14	18	15	10
Attempts (No.)	185	1283	14	18	15	10

* Not applicable.

fluence. Consequently, it is understandable that attendants not only spend more time with patients than do any other members of the staff—that is required by their station in the hierarchy —but also, insofar as they learn from their superiors' behavior, spend as little time with patients as they can. Attendants are seen mainly in the cage, which is where the models, the action, and the power are.

I turn now to a different set of studies, these dealing with staff response to patient-initiated contact. It has long been known that the amount of time a person spends with you can be an index of your significance to him. If he initiates and maintains eye contact, there is reason to believe that he is considering your requests and needs. If he pauses to chat or actually stops and talks, there is added reason to infer that he is individuating you. In four hospitals, the pseudopatient approached the staff member with a request which took the following form: "Pardon me, Mr. [or Dr. or Mrs.] X, could you tell me when I will be eligible for grounds privileges?" (or " . . . when I will be presented at the staff meeting?" or ". . . when I am likely to be discharged?"). While the content of the question varied according to the appropriateness of the target and the pseudopatient's (apparent) current needs the form was always a courteous and relevant request for information. Care was taken never to approach a particular member of the staff more than once a day, lest the staff member become suspicious or irritated. In examining these data, remember that the behavior of the pseudopatients was neither bizarre nor disruptive. One could indeed engage in good conversation with them.

The data for these experiments are shown in Table 1, separately for physicians (column 1) and for nurses and attendants (column 2). Minor differences between these four institutions were overwhelmed by the degree to which staff avoided continuing contacts that patients had initiated. By far, their most common response consisted of either a brief response to the question, offered while they were "on the move" and with head averted, or no response at all.

The encounter frequently took the following bizarre form: (pseudopatient) "Pardon me, Dr. X. Could you tell me when I am eligible for grounds privileges?" (physician) "Good morning, Dave. How are you today?" (Moves off without waiting for a response.)

It is instructive to compare these data with data recently obtained at Stanford University. It has been alleged that large and eminent universities are characterized by faculty who are so busy that they have no time for students. For this comparison, a young lady approached individual faculty members who seemed to be walking purposefully to some meeting or teaching engagement and asked them the following six questions.

1) "Pardon me, could you direct me to Encina Hall?" (at the medical school: ". . . to the Clinical Research Center?").
2) "Do you know where Fish Annex is?" (there is no Fish Annex at Stanford).
3) "Do you teach here?"
4) "How does one apply for admission to the college?" (at the medical school: ". . . to the medical school?").
5) "Is it difficult to get in?"
6) "Is there financial aid?"

Without exception, as can be seen in Table 1 (column 3), all of the questions were answered. No matter how rushed they were, all respondents not only maintained eye contact, but stopped to talk. Indeed, many of the respondents went out of their way to direct or take the questioner to the office she was seeking, to try to locate "Fish Annex," or to discuss with her the possibilities of being admitted to the university.

Similar data, also shown in Table 1 (columns 4, 5, and 6), were obtained in the hospital. Here too, the young lady came prepared with six questions. After the first question, however, she remarked to 18 of her respondents (column 4), "I'm looking for a psychiatrist," and to 15 others (column 5), "I'm looking for an internist." Ten other respondents received no inserted comment (column 6). The general degree of cooperative responses is considerably higher for these university groups than it was for pseudopatients in psychiatric hospitals. Even so, differences are apparent within the medical school setting. Once having indicated that she was looking for a psychiatrist, the degree of cooperation elicited was less than when she sought an internist.

Powerlessness and Depersonalization

Eye contact and verbal contact reflect concern and individuation; their absence, avoidance and depersonalization. The data I have presented do not do justice to the rich daily encounters that grew up around matters of depersonalization and avoidance. I have records of patients who were beaten by staff for the sin of having initiated verbal contact. During my own experience, for example, one patient was beaten in the presence of other patients for having approached an attendant and told him, "I like you." Occasionally, punishment meted out to patients for misdemeanors seemed so excessive that it could not be justified by the most radical interpretations of psychiatric canon. Nevertheless, they appeared to go unquestioned. Tempers were often short. A patient who had not heard a call for medication would be roundly excoriated, and the morning attendants would often wake patients with, "Come on, you m-----f-----s, out of bed!"

Neither anecdotal nor "hard" data can convey the overwhelming sense of powerlessness which invades the individual as he is continually exposed to the depersonalization of the psychiatric hospital. It hardly matters *which* psychiatric hospital—the excellent public ones and the very plush private hospital were better than the rural and shabby ones in this regard, but, again, the features that psychiatric hospitals had in common overwhelmed by far their apparent differences.

Powerlessness was evident everywhere. The patient is deprived of many of his legal rights by dint of his psychiatric commitment (*21*). He is shorn of credibility by virtue of his psychiatric label. His freedom of movement is restricted. He cannot initiate contact with the staff, but may only respond to such overtures as they make. Personal privacy is minimal. Patient quarters and possessions can be entered and examined by any staff member, for whatever reason. His personal history and anguish is available to any staff member (often including the "grey lady" and "candy striper" volunteer) who chooses to read his folder, regardless of their therapeutic relationship to him. His personal hygiene and waste evacuation are often monitored. The water closets may have no doors.

At times, depersonalization reached such proportions that pseudopatients had the sense that they were invisible, or at least unworthy of account. Upon being admitted, I and other pseudopatients took the initial physical examinations in a semipublic room, where staff members went about their own business as if we were not there.

On the ward, attendants delivered verbal and occasionally serious physical abuse to patients in the presence of other observing patients, some of whom (the pseudopatients) were writing it all down. Abusive behavior, on the other hand, terminated quite abruptly when other staff members were known to be coming. Staff are credible witnesses. Patients are not.

A nurse unbuttoned her uniform to adjust her brassiere in the presence of an entire ward of viewing men. One did not have the sense that she was being seductive. Rather, she didn't notice us. A group of staff persons might point to a patient in the dayroom and discuss him animatedly, as if he were not there.

One illuminating instance of depersonalization and invisibility occurred with regard to medications. All told, the pseudopatients were administered nearly 2100 pills, including Elavil, Stelazine, Compazine, and Thorazine, to name but a few. (That such a variety of medications should have been administered to patients presenting identical symptoms is itself worthy of note.) Only two were swallowed. The rest were either pocketed or deposited in the toilet. The pseudopatients were not alone in this. Although I have no precise records on how many patients rejected their medications, the pseudopatients frequently found the medications of other patients in the toilet before they deposited their own. As long as they were cooperative, their behavior and the pseudopatients' own in this matter, as in other important matters, went unnoticed throughout.

Reactions to such depersonalization among pseudopatients were intense. Although they had come to the hospital as participant observers and were fully aware that they did not "belong," they nevertheless found themselves caught up in and fighting the process of depersonalization. Some examples: a graduate student in psychology asked his wife to bring his textbooks to the hospital so he could "catch up on his homework"—this despite the elaborate precautions taken to conceal his professional association. The same student, who had trained for quite some time to get into the hospital, and who had looked forward to the experience, "remembered" some drag races that he had wanted to see on the weekend and insisted that he be discharged by that time. Another pseudopatient attempted a romance with a nurse. Subsequently, he informed the staff that he was applying for admission to graduate school in psychology and was very likely to be admitted, since a graduate professor was one of his regular hospital visitors. The same person began to engage in psychotherapy with other patients—all of this as a way of becoming a person in an impersonal environment.

The Sources of Depersonalization

What are the origins of depersonalization? I have already mentioned two. First are attitudes held by all of us toward the mentally ill—including those who treat them—attitudes characterized by fear, distrust, and horrible expectations on the one hand, and benevolent intentions on the other. Our ambivalence leads, in this instance as in others, to avoidance.

Second, and not entirely separate, the hierarchical structure of the psychiatric hospital facilitates depersonalization. Those who are at the top have least to do with patients, and their behavior inspires the rest of the staff. Average daily contact with psychiatrists, psychologists, residents, and physicians combined ranged from 3.9 to 25.1 minutes, with an overall mean of 6.8 (six pseudopatients over a total of 129 days of hospitalization). Included in this average are time spent in the admissions interview, ward meetings in the presence of a senior staff member, group and individual psychotherapy contacts, case presentation conferences, and discharge meetings. Clearly, patients do not spend much time in interpersonal contact with doctoral staff. And doctoral staff serve as models for nurses and attendants.

There are probably other sources. Psychiatric installations are presently in serious financial straits. Staff shortages are pervasive, staff time at a premium. Something has to give, and that something is patient contact. Yet, while financial stresses are realities, too much can be made of them. I have the impression that the psychological forces that result in depersonalization are much stronger than the fiscal ones and that the addition of more staff would not correspondingly improve patient care in this regard. The incidence of staff meetings and the enormous amount of record-keeping on patients, for example, have not been as substantially reduced as has patient contact. Priorities exist, even during hard times. Patient contact is not a significant priority in the traditional psychiatric hospital, and fiscal pressures do not account for this. Avoidance and depersonalization may.

Heavy reliance upon psychotropic medication tacitly contributes to depersonalization by convincing staff that treatment is indeed being conducted and that further patient contact may not be necessary. Even here, however, caution needs to be exercised in understanding the role of psychotropic drugs. If patients were powerful rather than powerless, if they were viewed as interesting individuals rather than diagnostic entities, if they were socially significant rather than social lepers, if their anguish truly and wholly compelled our sympathies and concerns, would we not *seek* contact with them, despite the availability of medications? Perhaps for the pleasure of it all?

The Consequences of Labeling and Depersonalization

Whenever the ratio of what is known to what needs to be known approaches zero, we tend to invent "knowledge" and assume that we understand more than we actually do. We seem unable to acknowledge that we simply don't know. The needs for diagnosis and remediation of behavioral and emotional problems are enormous. But rather than acknowledge that we are just embarking on understanding, we continue to label patients "schizophrenic," "manic-depressive," and "insane," as if in those words we had captured the essence of understanding. The facts of the matter are that we have known for a long time that diagnoses are often not useful or reliable, but we have nevertheless continued to use them. We now know that we cannot distinguish insanity from sanity. It is depressing to consider how that information will be used.

Not merely depressing, but frightening. How many people, one wonders, are sane but not recognized as such in our psychiatric institutions? How many have been needlessly stripped of their privileges of citizenship, from the right to vote and drive to that of handling their own accounts? How many have feigned insanity in order to avoid the criminal consequences of their behavior, and, conversely, how many would rather stand trial than live interminably in a psychiatric hospital—but are wrongly thought to be mentally ill? How many have been stigmatized by well-intentioned, but nevertheless erroneous, diagnoses? On the last point, recall again that a "type 2 error" in psychiatric diagnosis does not have the same consequences it does in medical diagnosis. A diagnosis of cancer that has been found to be in error is cause for celebration. But psychiatric diagnoses are rarely found to be in error. The label sticks, a mark of inadequacy forever.

Finally, how many patients might be "sane" outside the psychiatric hospital but seem insane in it—not because craziness resides in them, as it were, but because they are responding to a bizarre setting, one that may be unique to institutions which harbor nether people? Goffman (4) calls the process of socialization to such institutions "mortification"—an apt metaphor that includes the processes of depersonalization that have been described here. And while it is impossible to know whether the pseudopatients' responses to these processes are characteristic of all inmates—they were, after all, not real patients—it is difficult to believe that these processes of socialization to a psychiatric hospital provide useful attitudes or habits of response for living in the "real world."

Summary and Conclusions

It is clear that we cannot distinguish the sane from the insane in psychiatric hospitals. The hospital itself imposes a special environment in which the meanings of behavior can easily be misunderstood. The consequences to patients hospitalized in such an environment—the powerlessness, depersonalization, segregation, mortification, and self-labeling—seem undoubtedly counter-therapeutic.

I do not, even now, understand this problem well enough to perceive solutions. But two matters seem to have some promise. The first concerns the proliferation of community mental health facilities, of crisis intervention centers, of the human potential movement, and of behavior therapies that, for all of their own problems, tend to avoid psychiatric labels, to focus on specific problems and behaviors, and to retain the individual in a relatively non-pejorative environment. Clearly, to the extent that we refrain from sending the distressed to insane places, our impressions of them are less likely to be distorted. (The risk of distorted perceptions, it seems to me, is always present, since we are much more sensitive to an individual's behaviors and verbalizations than we are to the subtle contextual stimuli that often promote them. At issue here is a matter of magnitude. And, as I have shown, the magnitude of distortion is exceedingly high in the extreme context that is a psychiatric hospital.)

The second matter that might prove promising speaks to the need to increase the sensitivity of mental health workers and researchers to the *Catch 22* position of psychiatric patients. Simply reading materials in this area will be of help to some such workers and researchers. For others, directly experiencing the impact of psychiatric hospitalization will be of enormous use. Clearly, further research into the social psychology of such total institutions will both facilitate treatment and deepen understanding.

I and the other pseudopatients in the psychiatric setting had distinctly negative reactions. We do not pretend to describe the subjective experiences of true patients. Theirs may be different from ours, particularly with the passage of time and the necessary process of adaptation to one's environment. But we can and do speak to the relatively more objective indices of treatment within the hospital. It could be a mistake, and a very unfortunate one, to consider that what happened to us derived from malice or stupidity on the part of the staff. Quite the contrary, our overwhelming impression of them was of people who really cared, who were committed and who were uncommonly intelligent. Where they failed, as they sometimes did painfully, it would be more accurate to attribute those failures to the environment in which they, too, found themselves than to personal callousness. Their perceptions and behavior were controlled by the situation, rather than being motivated by a malicious disposition. In a more benign environment, one that was less attached to global diagnosis, their behaviors and judgments might have been more benign and effective.

References and Notes

1. P. Ash, *J. Abnorm. Soc. Psychol.* **44**, 272 (1949); A. T. Beck, *Amer. J. Psychiat.* **119**, 210 (1962); A. T. Boisen, *Psychiatry* **2**, 233 (1938); N. Kreitman, *J. Ment. Sci.* **107**, 876 (1961); N. Kreitman, P. Sainsbury, J. Morrisey, J. Towers, J. Scrivener, *ibid.*, p. 887; H. O. Schmitt and C. P. Fonda, *J. Abnorm. Soc. Psychol.* **52**, 262 (1956); W. Seeman, *J. Nerv. Ment. Dis.* **118**, 541 (1953). For an analysis of these artifacts and summaries of the disputes, see J. Zubin, *Annu. Rev. Psychol.* **18**, 373 (1967); L. Phillips and J. G. Draguns, *ibid.* **22**, 447 (1971).
2. R. Benedict, *J. Gen. Psychol.* **10**, 59 (1934).
3. See in this regard H. Becker, *Outsiders: Studies in the Sociology of Deviance* (Free Press, New York, 1963); B. M. Braginsky, D. D. Braginsky, K. Ring, *Methods of Madness: The Mental Hospital as a Last Resort* (Holt, Rinehart & Winston, New York, 1969); G. M. Crocetti and P. V. Lemkau, *Amer. Sociol. Rev.* **30**, 577 (1965); E. Goffman, *Behavior in Public Places* (Free Press, New York, 1964); R. D. Laing, *The Divided Self: A Study of Sanity and Madness* (Quadrangle, Chicago, 1960); D. L. Phillips, *Amer. Sociol. Rev.* **28**, 963 (1963); T. R. Sarbin, *Psychol. Today* **6**, 18 (1972); E. Schur, *Amer. J. Sociol.* **75**, 309 (1969); T. Szasz, *Law, Liberty and Psychiatry* (Macmillan, New York, 1963); *The Myth of Mental Illness: Foundations of a Theory of Mental Illness* (Hoeber-Harper, New York, 1963). For a critique of some of these views, see W. R. Gove, *Amer. Sociol. Rev.* **35**, 873 (1970).
4. E. Goffman, *Asylums* (Doubleday, Garden City, N.Y., 1961).
5. T. J. Scheff, *Being Mentally Ill: A Sociological Theory* (Aldine, Chicago, 1966).
6. Data from a ninth pseudopatient are not incorporated in this report because, although his sanity went undetected, he falsified aspects of his personal history, including his marital status and parental relationships. His experimental behaviors therefore were not identical to those of the other pseudopatients.
7. A. Barry, *Bellevue Is a State of Mind* (Harcourt Brace Jovanovich, New York, 1971); I. Belknap, *Human Problems of a State Mental Hospital* (McGraw-Hill, New York, 1956); W. Caudill, F. C. Redlich, H. R. Gilmore, E. B. Brody, *Amer. J. Orthopsychiat.* **22**, 314 (1952); A. R. Goldman, R. H. Bohr, T. A. Steinberg, *Prof. Psychol.* **1**, 427 (1970); unauthored, *Roche Report* **1** (No. 13), 8 (1971).
8. Beyond the personal difficulties that the pseudopatient is likely to experience in the hospital, there are legal and social ones that, combined, require considerable attention before entry. For example, once admitted to a psychiatric institution, it is difficult, if not impossible, to be discharged on short notice, state law to the contrary notwithstanding. I was not sensitive to these difficulties at the outset of the project, nor to the personal and situational emergencies that can arise, but later a writ of habeas corpus was prepared

for each of the entering pseudopatients and an attorney was kept "on call" during every hospitalization. I am grateful to John Kaplan and Robert Bartels for legal advice and assistance in these matters.

9. However distasteful such concealment is, it was a necessary first step to examining these questions. Without concealment, there would have been no way to know how valid these experiences were; nor was there any way of knowing whether whatever detections occurred were a tribute to the diagnostic acumen of the staff or to the hospital's rumor network. Obviously, since my concerns are general ones that cut across individual hospitals and staffs, I have respected their anonymity and have eliminated clues that might lead to their identification.

10. Interestingly, of the 12 admissions, 11 were diagnosed as schizophrenic and one, with the identical symptomatology, as manic-depressive psychosis. This diagnosis has a more favorable prognosis, and it was given by the only private hospital in our sample. On the relations between social class and psychiatric diagnosis, see A. deB. Hollingshead and F. C. Redlich, *Social Class and Mental Illness: A Community Study* (Wiley, New York, 1958).

11. It is possible, of course, that patients have quite broad latitudes in diagnosis and therefore are inclined to call many people sane, even those whose behavior is patently aberrant. However, although we have no hard data on this matter, it was our distinct impression that this was not the case. In many instances, patients not only singled us out for attention, but came to imitate our behaviors and styles.

12. J. Cumming and E. Cumming, *Community Ment. Health* 1, 135 (1965); A. Farina and H. E. Freeman and O. G. Simmons, *The Mental Patient Comes Home* (Wiley, New York, 1963); W J. Johannsen, *Ment. Hygiene* 53, 218 (1969); A. S. Linsky, *Soc. Psychiat.* 5, 166 (1970).

13. S. E. Asch, *J. Abnorm. Soc. Psychol.* 41, 258 (1946); *Social Psychology* (Prentice-Hall, New York, 1952).

14. See also I. N. Mensh and J. Wishner, *J. Personality* 16, 188 (1947); J. Wishner, *Psychol. Rev.* 67, 96 (1960); J. S. Bruner and R. Tagiuri, in *Handbook of Social Psychology*, G. Lindzey, Ed. (Addison-Wesley, Cambridge, Mass., 1954), vol. 2, pp. 634–654; J. S. Bruner, D. Shapiro, R. Tagiuri, in *Person Perception and Interpersonal Behavior*, R. Tagiuri and L. Petrullo, Eds. (Stanford Univ. Press, Stanford, Calif., 1958), pp. 277–288.

15. For an example of a similar self-fulfilling prophecy, in this instance dealing with the "central" trait of intelligence, see R. Rosenthal and L. Jacobson, *Pygmalion in the Classroom* (Holt, Rinehart & Winston, New York, 1968).

16. E. Zigler and L. Phillips, *J. Abnorm. Soc. Psychol.* 63, 69 (1961). See also R. K. Freudenberg and J. P. Robertson, *A.M.A. Arch. Neurol. Psychiatr.* 76, 14 (1956).

17. W. Mischel, *Personality and Assessment* (Wiley, New York, 1968).

18. The most recent and unfortunate instance of this tenet is that of Senator Thomas Eagleton.

19. T. R. Sarbin and J. C. Mancuso, *J. Clin. Consult. Psychol.* 35, 159 (1970); T. R. Sarbin, *ibid.* 31, 447 (1967); J. C. Nunnally, Jr., *Popular Conceptions of Mental Health* (Holt, Rinehart & Winston, New York, 1961).

20. A. H. Stanton and M. S. Schwartz, *The Mental Hospital: A Study of Institutional Participation in Psychiatric Illness and Treatment* (Basic, New York, 1954).

21. D. B. Wexler and S. E. Scoville, *Ariz. Law Rev.* 13, 1 (1971).

22. I thank W. Mischel, E. Orne, and M. S. Rosenhan for comments on an earlier draft of this manuscript.

Letters

D. L. Rosenhan's article "On being sane in insane places" (19 Jan., p. 250), while full of important observations, is seriously flawed by methodological inadequacies and by conclusions that are inconsistent with—indeed, that directly contradict—the data he presents. . . . When Rosenhan's pseudopatients faked a history and were subsequently "misdiagnosed" by physicians at the psychiatric hospitals where they presented themselves, they established nothing about the accuracy of diagnosis per se, but merely reaffirmed the critical role of history-taking in medicine. Most physicians do not asume that patients who seek help are liars; they can therefore, of course, be misled. The so-called "Munchausen syndrome," of people who fake medical illness and may be admitted to hospitals repeatedly and receive years of extended treatment, is documented in the literature, as is, of course, simple effective malingering. It would be quite possible to conduct a study in which patients trained to simulate histories of myocrdial infarction would receive treatment on the basis of history alone (since a negative electrocardiogram is not diagnostic), but it would be preposterous to conclude from such a study that physical illness does not exist, that medical diagnoses are fallacious labels, and that "illness' and "health" reside only in doctors' heads.

More misleading than Rosenhan's false conception of how diagnoses are reached, and his inaccurate conclusion thereform that psychiatric diagnoses are empty labels, is his apparent total ignorance of the definitions of "insanity," "psychosis," "schizophrenia," and "schizophrenia in remission." Insanity is a legal term. It is not a psychiatric diagnosis. Though its exact definition varies among the states, it usually entails "the inability to decide right from wrong." This is a legal definition applied by *courts*. No psychiatrist ever "diagnoses" a patient as sane or insane. People legally insane at one point in time may be in general nonpsychotic (seizure disorder), and many, in fact most, people who are psychotic are never declared insane.

Most shocking, however, is Rosenhan's conclusion that "the normal are not detectably sane," by which he evidently means "not detectably nonpsychotic." In fact, all the pseudopatients were discharged with the diagnosis of "schizophrenia *in remission*," which means that they were clearly seen by the doctors to be nonpsychotic in the hospitals where they were observed but had been psychotic during the period described by their "history." Thus, Rosenhan's study demonstrates that despite false historical data and the set of the hospital environment, 12 nonpsychotics were observed by their psychiatrists to be nonpsychotic—a record of 100 percent accuracy.

In the rest of this article, Rosenhan poignantly describes neglect and abuses in psychiatric hospitals. He rightly reopens the door to this storehouse of bad practice and demands that the psychiatric professions enter, take responsibility, and change. But faulty application of concepts does not invalidate those concepts. The concept "psychosis" (Rosenhan refers mostly to "insanity") is eminently justifiable not only by such symptoms as hallucinations, or by such responses to medication as one sees with lithium, but by the entire thrust of modern biology: how surprising it would be if the central nervous system of man —alone among all living tissue—were immune to biochemical or psysiological pathology. . . .

Rosenhan might have summarized his important observations as follows: that given our current ignorance of biochemical and physiological parameters, psychiatric diagnoses may be inaccurate; that the psychiatric professions persist in overinterpretation and thereby increase the risk of type-2 errors; that given the ease with which histories of symptoms can be faked, coupled with the absence of positive chemical-biological diagnostic tests, the relationship between psychiatric diagnoses and the law needs reexamination and revision; and that the practice of psychiatry deviates disgracefully from accurate application of its concepts and ideals.

Unfortunately, through the publicity attracted by his methods, conclusions, and rhetoric. Rosenhan may have provided society with one more excuse for pursuing the current trend of vilifying psychiatric treatment and neglecting its potential beneficiaries.

PAUL R. FLEISCHMAN

Department of Psychiatry,
Yale University,
New Haven, Connecticut 06520

. . . What Rosenhan must wish to conclude is that the criteria for distinguishing sane from insane are not clear or unambiguous. This of course is a well-known fact. The question is, just how vague are the criteria? That in none of 12 cases was the phony patient spotted by the authorities gives the erroneous impression that these criteria are very, very vague. However, this is not necessarily borne out by the "data."

While it is true that psychosis is thought to "reside in" the patient (that is, the adjective "psychotic" is applied to a person), it is generally understood that the psychosis manifests itself only under certain conditions. The psychotic is not expected to be bizarre in everything he says or does. . . . The conditions on the ward are designed (rightly or wrongly) to make the patients manageable (hence to appear sane). Those whose psychosis is not suppressed are transferred from the admitting ward. Accordingly, a much more impressive demonstration of his point could be made by Rosenhan if he were to take obviously insane persons and, by giving them a new name and releasing them to a community where they were not known, successfully pass them off as sane.

That the pseudopatients were not diagnosed as sane is not surprising. These pseudopatients were not just sane persons; they were sane persons feigning insanity. From the experiment, then, the only accurate conclusion to be drawn is that presumably competent judges cannot distinguish the insane from the sane-feigning-insanity when the judges are not aware of a possible reason for faking. While malingering is a diagnostic possibility, "researching" is not. A proper "control" condition would be to repeat the study with a regular medical problem. Send pseudopatients with "low back pain" or "severe headaches" to physicians and see how many of them are detected as "researchers." . . .

LEWIS R. LIEBERMAN

Columbus College,
Columbus, Georgia 31907

52 Deviance in the Dark

by Kenneth J. Gergen, Mary M. Gergen
and William H. Barton

Wanted:
subjects for a psychology experiment.

THE STUDENT SEES THE NOTICE on a bulletin board and on a whim decides to volunteer. He or she learns nothing about the experiment beforehand except that it is about "environmental psychology." He arrives at the appointed hour at an address given over the phone. A man ushers him into an empty room, and leaves him with a series of written tasks to complete. Twenty minutes later, the man reappears and says he is taking the student to a chamber that is absolutely dark. The only light in the chamber will be a pinpoint of red over the door, he says, so the student can find his way out should that be necessary. "You will be left in the chamber for no more than an hour with some other people," the man says. "There are no rules... as to what you should do together. At the end of the time period you will each be escorted from the room alone, and will subsequently depart from the experimental site alone. There will be no opportunity to meet the other participants."

The man asks the student to slip off his or her shoes, empty all pockets and leave whatever he or she is carrying behind. Then he takes the student through a set of double doors into the chamber and leaves him on his own in the pitch black.

Spatial disorientation sets in. Visual contact with the other people is impossible. Perhaps a childhood fear of the dark looms up. The student has no name or face. Conversely, he is freer to project on to others in the chamber the characteristics he chooses. The purpose of this experiment is to find out what the student will do in this environment and what sort of relationships will evolve in this setting. What do people do under conditions of extreme anonymity?

Almost 50 persons participated in our initial exploration. They were between the ages of 18 and 25, and primarily students from colleges and universities in a 10-mile radius of Swarthmore College. They were divided into groups of approximately eight persons, half males and half females. The chamber itself was 10 feet wide and 12 feet long. The floor and walls were padded. The ceiling was above arm's reach.

We tape-recorded all voice communication during each hour's session and used infrared cameras to record how our subjects dispersed themselves around the room. After each hour was over, we asked our subjects to write down their impressions of the experience. We then ran the experiment three more times, but this time we left the lights on. By comparing the behavior of the groups in the darkened chamber with the behavior of groups in the lighted chamber, we hoped to find out what people will do to and with each other when cut away from the normal sanctions governing their lives. Will they try to reestablish life as usual? Or will they willingly forsake the sanctions for another way of interacting?

The logic of our experiment was simple. If it is true, as sociologist Erving Goffman argues, that society channels most of an individual's energy into set patterns as a result of rewards or punishments, then it follows that the behavior of most individuals is routinized. We all come to act in more or less expected ways. During an hour with six or seven strangers in a padded room in the dark, we thought, our subjects would be free from the expectations of friends, family and so on *not* to act as usual. Even if someone tried to introduce society's norms into the chamber, the dark would make it difficult to reward or punish our subjects appropriately for their behavior. The fact that participants knew they would never meet face to face

provided a final guarantee that they could interact the way they wanted to.

The Deafening Silence. The differences in behavior between students in the darkroom and light-room groups proved enlightening. Subjects in the lighted room kept a continuous, focused stream of conversation going from start to finish of the session. In the dark room, talk slacked off dramatically after the first 30 minutes. At one point in a dark-room session that included a very talkative boy, the conversation had become muted, disjointed, and faltering. Finally, the boy said in a loud voice, "Why isn't anybody talking?" A voice returned the answer softly, "Why don't you shut up?"

Verbal inactivity in the dark chamber, however, was not matched by inactivity at other levels of interaction. Subjects entering the lighted room quickly found a place to sit (seldom closer than three feet to any other subject); and remained seated in the same positions throughout the session. Using photographs, we could predict with better than 90 percent accuracy the individual placement of each subject during the last five minutes of a session from his position during the first five minutes. But in the dark room subjects moved about fluidly. It was difficult to predict with greater than 50 percent accuracy where subjects would be from one five-minute period to the next.

All dark-room participants accidentally touched one another, while less than five percent of the light-room subjects did. More to the point, almost 90 percent of the dark-room participants touched each other on purpose, while almost none of the light-room subjects did. Almost 50 percent of the dark-room participants reported that they hugged another person. Almost 80 percent of the dark-room subjects said they felt sexual excitement, while only 30 percent of the light-room subjects said they did.

The impressions of the hour written by the dark-room subjects give a less cut and dried idea of what went on. "There was tension and nervousness at the beginning," wrote one girl. "A lot of movement.

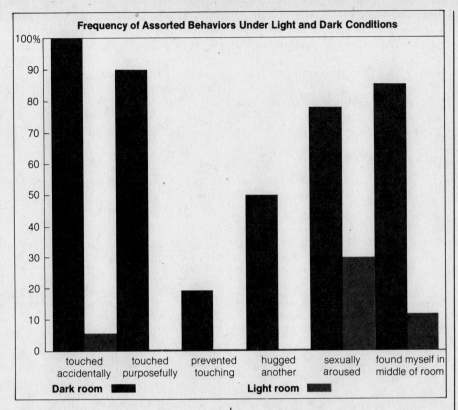

Frequency of Assorted Behaviors Under Light and Dark Conditions

Dark room · Light room

touched accidentally · touched purposefully · prevented touching · hugged another · sexually aroused · found myself in middle of room

Gradually, a significant change took place. People sat down in smaller groups, a large portion were silent, the darkness no longer bothered me. The last group of us sat closely together, touching, feeling a sense of friendship and loss as a group member left. I left with a feeling that it had been fun and nice. I felt I had made some friends. In fact I missed them."

A boy wrote, "As I was sitting Beth came up and we started to play touchy face and touchy body and started to neck. We expressed it as showing love' to each other. Shortly before I was taken out, we decided to pass our 'love' on, to share it with other people. So we split up and Laurie took her place. We had just started touchy face and touchy body and kissed a few times before I was tapped to leave."

Another boy wrote, "Felt joy over the possibility of not having to look at people in clichéd ways. Enjoyed feeling of a self-awareness surrounded by a rich environment . . . Enjoyed the wantonness of just crawling around and over other people to get from one place to another." Others wrote they felt more "free" during the session yet more "serious" than normal. The dark-room subjects indicated they were less anxious to be known by others and less anxious to know the identity of others. With the simple subtraction of light, a group of perfect strangers moved within approximately 30 minutes to a

stage of intimacy often not attained in years of normal acquaintanceship.

Intimacy Is Natural. The results of these experiments suggested to us that when freed from normative constraints, people, at least people between the ages of 18 and 25, develop very immediate and close relations. To check this observation, we joined with Caroline Curtis to run a second set of experiments. We repeated the dark-room sessions with 22 more people, and extended the time in the chamber to an hour and a half. Given the emotional intensity reached in the chamber after 60 minutes, we wanted to see what would happen in 90 minutes.

Our second group of dark-room subjects emulated the behavior of the first group. In the extra 30 minutes, subjects became even more open with each other. Fifteen percent more subjects in the 90-minute sessions said they talked about "important" things. Reports of boredom from the 90-minute subjects dropped by the same percent. In effect, we got the same behavior in the longer sessions that we got in the shorter, but more of it.

We next contrasted the behavior of the three 90-minute groups with three additional 90-minute groups who were told they *would* meet after the session. The purpose was to see what would happen when we reduced the amount of anonymity our subjects could expect, thus in-

creasing the chances that they would be punished or ridiculed for their behavior.

Compared with the subjects who were guaranteed anonymity, the subjects who were told they would be introduced after the session were less likely to explore the chamber, more likely to feel bored, less likely to introduce themselves, less likely to hug, less likely to "feel close to another person," and more likely to feel panicky. By pulling back the cloak of anonymity, we reduced the intensity of relations in the chamber.

The behavior of our subjects in the dark room suggests that we must think anew the question of anonymity. Supposedly, we live in the "Age of Anonymity." Large-scale accounting systems replace our names with numbers. We use mechanical means to select people impersonally for college entrance, career placement and even marriage. Urban living is so complex that personal idiosyncrasy cannot be tolerated. We are in danger, say the critics, of becoming anonymous creatures with no individual significance.

Psychologists such as Leon Festinger, Albert Pepitone and Philip Zimbardo have added a significant dimension to these ideas. Both laboratory and field studies have demonstrated that when a person is without markers of personal identity, when he or she becomes *deindividuated* in the researchers' terms, the stage is set for increased aggression. Faceless people are more likely to harm each other, a finding with important implications for the high incidence of crime in the anonymous setting of the inner city.

Yet few of our subjects found anything displeasing about the experience of anonymity. Most gained deep enjoyment and volunteered to return without pay. Anonymity itself does not seem to be a social ill. Rather, the state of anonymity seems to encourage whatever potentials are most prominent at the moment— whether for good or for ill. When we are anonymous we are free to be aggressive or to give affection, whichever expresses most fully our feelings at the time. There is liberation in anonymity.

Why did our subjects chose to be so affectionate in the dark room? They were faced with an immense number of alternatives for action, and yet, almost all chose some form of closeness. Were these intimacies based on fear of the unknown threat—an attempt to band together to ward off danger? None of our data support this explanation, and in fact, analysis revealed that those who were most un-settled by the circumstance were least likely to form close relationships. We are struck, instead, by what seemed an essen-tial desire for intimate alliance among our subjects. Of course, our samples were young, and the numbers not large. But it does seem that if the social norms govern-ing our relationships did not keep dis-tance among us—as they did in the case of our light-room subjects—the sharing of in-timacy such as in the dark room, would be widespread.

It appears that people share strong yearnings to be close to each other. How-ever, our social norms make it too costly to express these feelings. Our traditions appear to keep us at a distance. Perhaps these traditions have outlived their usefulness.

X. Self-Concept and Social Development

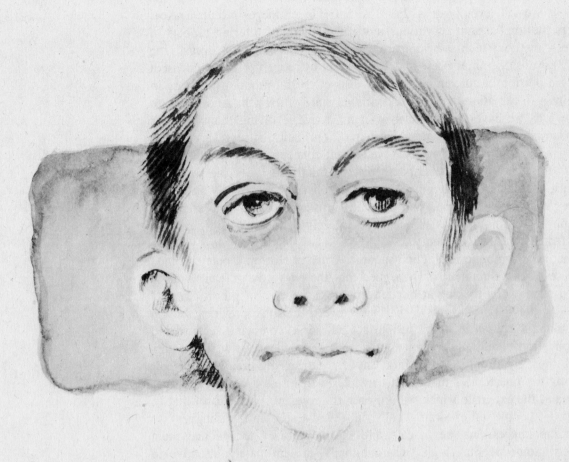

The self has received surprisingly little attention from social psychologists in spite of its obvious significance in social relations. What people think of themselves (their self-concept) and the type of people they would like to become (their *ideal-self*, or *ego-ideal*) affect virtually every aspect of their lives. But like so many important constructs, the self-concept is hard to define and difficult to assess. It does not lend itself easily to social psychological research.

Perhaps the most salient aspect of ourselves is our physical form—our faces and bodies. At birth, of course, infants have no real sense of self. One of the first indications that they have developed a self-concept is their ability to recognize themselves, which usually occurs before 2 years of age. A fascinating series of studies by Gordon Gallup, Jr., and others has indicated that chimpanzees and orangutans (species of great apes), but not monkeys and other lower primates, are able to recognize themselves. (The method used to test this ability is to paint a stripe on the face of animals who have been looking at themselves in a mirror, and see whether they try to wipe it off.) Moreover, in support of two theoretical assumptions—(1) that social experience is necessary to the development of a sense of self, and (2) that we see ourselves through the eyes of others—Gallup and others have found that chimpanzees reared in social isolation do not develop the ability to recognize themselves.

The essential physical source of our sense of self is our brains. Unlike the cells in other parts of our bodies, the neural cells in our brain do not replenish themselves throughout our lives. In effect, we are born with all the brain cells we will ever possess. In "The Self Under Siege," Reuben Abel considers the implications of various modern methods of altering aspects of ourselves—methods such as brain stimulation, brainwashing, and drugs. One response to the dilemmas presented by Abel is to recognize that at least a substantial portion of our sense of self consists of the information we store in our brains—information that is in a continual state of growth. Another is to treat the idea we have about ourselves as an active, evolving theory, rather than as a static concept. Seymour Epstein ("The Self-Concept Revisited") suggests that people do not really develop self-concepts; they develop self-*theories*. They learn to understand themselves in much the same way that they learn to understand other people and the physical world—by gathering data, organizing information, and drawing inferences. It is interesting to contemplate the implications of making the seemingly small and semantic change from "concept" to "theory."

The early symbolic interaction theorist, Charles Horton Cooley, coined the phrase "looking-glass self." He argued that the *only* way we can come to know ourselves is by looking at our reflections in the eyes of others: the "I" of our identities cannot perceive the "me" directly. In the previous section we examined the ways in which people act out social roles and scripts, and the implications these performances have for their identities. "The Many Me's of the Self-Monitor," by Mark Snyder, carries this analysis further, addressing the question of the extent to which we possess a consistent inner identity and the extent to which we are only the roles we play. According to the author, people differ dramatically in their desire and willingness to manage the impressions they create and in their ability to manage them effectively. Some people—high "self-monitors"—are intimately attentive to the way they (and others) come across. They change their personalities to match the situation. I have a good friend whose ability to take on different roles is phenomenal. He is able to change his identity as quickly as he changes his clothes. Other people—low "self-monitors"—perhaps more principled, perhaps more rigid, are much the same wherever they are.

Feelings of *shyness* and *jealousy* are closely associated with how people feel about themselves. Social psychologists are just beginning to investigate these social-emotional reactions. As is often the case, early research on topics such as these is broad-reaching and exploratory. The selections included here, an excerpt from a book called *Shyness*, by Philip Zimbardo, and the recent article "Getting at the Heart of Jealous Love," by Virginia Adams, report the results of survey research—the number of people who feel shy and jealous, whether these feelings are more characteristic of males than females, young people than old people, those with a little versus those with a lot of education, and so on. Although feelings of shyness and jealousy clearly are reflections of the way people feel about themselves, and although they both indicate the importance to the self-concept of relations with others, social psychological research has not, as yet, gone very far in explaining their origins or the conditions that control them.

How people feel about others and how others feel about them exert a powerful effect on how they feel about themselves. The strongest of all positive interpersonal emotions is love. "The Love Research," by Zick Rubin, is in an early stage, but already it has produced some interesting findings. Consider for example the finding that contrary to popular opinion, females tend to fall in love less easily than males and to break off relationships more readily. Although the author of the article on love interprets this sex difference in terms of cultural variables, the difference also ties in with a basic biological difference between the sexes: males produce many more sex cells and can reproduce many more children than females. Thus, early in our evolutionary history at least, it should have been more in females' than males' best interests, genetically speaking, to elect the best possible males to father their children. Because females must carry children during pregnancy, and because they typically assume primary responsibility for them after they are born, they should be more concerned with who the fathers of their children are. Zick Rubin's overview of research on love paves the way for the article by Elaine Walster on passionate love. Evoking a classic theory of emotion, Elaine Walster puts forth a simple but counterintuitive proposition—any type of arousal, even anger, fear, or disgust, may heighten the experience of "Passionate Love."

If you ask the average person what he or she strives for most in life, the answer is liable to be *happiness*. As with shyness, jealousy, and love, there has been little research on this emotion in social psychology; and what data there are have come from responses to questionnaires. However, unlike Zimbardo and Clanton and Smith, Jonathan Freedman analyzes happiness in terms of a number of social psychological theories. Any number of things can make people happy—a good meal, a new car, a stiff drink—but as Freedman implicitly shows, (1) the central source of happiness for most people lies in what they think of themselves, and (2) what people think of themselves is intimately connected with the reactions of others.

53

The Self Under Siege

by Reuben Abel

What is the self? The question surely seems bizarre. What could be more obvious to me than my own self—my own body, my own headaches, my own habits, my memories, my food preferences, my fears and hopes and purposes? Surely I know that it is I, myself, who am now sitting at a typewriter, trying to clarify these ideas, but getting hungry and wishing I were somewhere else. And no one would dispute the wisdom of Socrates' advice—"Know thyself!"— or of Shakespeare's—"To thine own self be true!" But the growth of science, although it has strengthened some of our common-sense opinions, has brought into question many of our firmest beliefs about the nature of the self.

On the positive side, immunologists have pointed out that bodily organs can not always be successfully transplanted from one person to another, even

Vermont rock maple dolls made by Joel Ellis and his Cooperative Manufacturing Company about 1873. In the Margaret Woodbury Strong Museum, Rochester, New York.

© H. Landshoff

though there seems to be no reason for the rejection. The limits of acceptance seem to be set idiosyncratically by the body itself. When my body accepts the transplant of some foreign tissues, but rejects others, those decisions may be characterized as delineating the contours of my self—distinguishing my self from the rest of the world. (Could this ability to preserve the uniqueness of the self have evolutionary survival value? Could it be biologically adaptive for the species?)

Also (on the positive side) biochemistry and genetics have explained the self-maintenance of the self in terms of the unchanging genotype: I continue to be my own self—despite the fact that every molecule of my phenotype is replaced in the course of time by something that comes from outside of me, despite the fact that my body never stops changing—because of the constancy of my genotype. The particular arrangement of my DNA, fixed once and for all at the moment I was conceived, continues to replicate itself. Regardless of what I eat, drink, and breathe, regardless of the alterations of metabolism, regardless of illness and the vicissitudes of ceaseless interaction with the environment, my invariant DNA continues to proclaim the unimpaired integrity of my self.

The Erosion of the Self

On the negative side, however, science has badly eroded the simple concept of the self. Cloning, for example, can be considered a direct contradiction of the uniqueness of the self. Biologists have already been able to take a cell from an adult frog, and place its nucleus so that it can be nurtured in another egg. The single nucleus contains all the genetic material required to make the adult individual what it is. The new independent creature thus grown will be a genetic duplicate of the original. There is no theoretical reason why this cloning can not be performed on human beings, although it is of course far from feasible now. When the cloned creature matures, will it be another "self"?

Then there is the challenge to the ancient truism that all people are mortal. It is surely part of our accepted wisdom that the self—the bodily self, at any rate!—comes to an end in the fullness of its days. But new life-extension techniques, recently exemplified in dramatic ways, seem to indicate that a person can be kept alive indefinitely. The heart can be kept beating (and the brain will continue to send out impulses) by artificial means: electrical cardiac stimulators, nutrients and drugs delivered intrave-

nously by tubes, blood transfusions, respirators, organ transplants, dialysis machines, resuscitators, and the like. Moreover, new cryogenic techniques can maintain a level of life (apparently indefinitely) in freezers. Do you continue to be "the same self" while you persist in such endless mindless senseless vegetable existence?

Are you the same person if you have had your sex changed surgically?

Inherent in the traditional view is the assumption that the self is an agent, a spontaneous initiator of actions, one who does things, or causes them to be done. But it is now possible to manipulate the self and its actions to an extraordinary degree. Electrical stimulation of specific regions of the brain can induce hunger, or pleasure, or sexual desire, or curiosity, or anxiety. Electrodes planted in your head can stimulate your aggressiveness or friendliness, can enlarge or diminish your productivity, can put you to sleep or wake you up. In the famous experiment performed by Yale's José Delgado, a fighting bull was stopped in the midst of a charge by a signal transmitted by radio to an electrode implanted in its brain. Scientists have been able to control animals as if they were toys, making them fight, play, run, sleep, and mate. If this is done on human beings, what will have happened to the self that makes such decisions?

Brain-washing by sophisticated techniques can alter your memories: make you "remember" what never happened, make you "forget" selectively any single fact about yourself. Your conception of who and what you are, your memory of an unalterable past, can be edited and reconstituted, almost *ad lib*. Will you still be the same self?

Drugs and Personality

From another viewpoint, pharmacology has undermined the simple idea of the self as the possessor of personality traits or character. The variety of drugs, and the extent to which they can predictably alter the "self," is quite remarkable. Although no drug usually has a single action, sedatives will relax you, hypnotics will make you go to sleep, anesthetics will make you lose sensation in selected areas. Analgesics, such as morphine or aspirin, will make you feel less pain; convulsants, such as strychnine, will produce a convulsion; anti-convulsants, dilantin for example, will stop it. Ataractics will tranquilize you; euphoriants, like amphetamine, will make you feel good; anti-depressants will relieve your unhappiness; and psychedelics, LSD for example, will alter your very perception of yourself and the world. The drug dimethyl tryptamine (DMT), which is chemically related to LSD, will produce visual and auditory hallucinations and may induce psychosis. A cer-

Reuben Abel is chairman of the Division of Humanities at The New School for Social Research in New York. He is also adjunct professor of Philosophy at the Graduate Faculty of The New School. His most recent book is MAN IS THE MEASURE *(Free Press, 1976).*

tain amount of DMT is produced naturally within the brain; normal persons cope with it by generating a regulator chemical; but schizophrenics apparently lack that ability. Now it seems possible to supply this regulator chemical, so that, if this hypothesis is verified, schizophrenia (by far the most common form of mental illness) may be wiped out. There is also some evidence that manic depression may be alleviated by lithium carbonate.

Thus it does not appear altogether fanciful to suppose that most (perhaps all) of our psychoses, even our mental quirks and psychological idiosyncrasies, may be largely eliminated by psycho-pharmacological means, just as dental caries are now being prevented by fluorides in the water supply.

We are thus confronted with a shattering assault on the concept of the Self. If your self can be duplicated by cloning; if it can be maintained indefinitely in suspended animation; if your sex can be changed; if your behavior, temperament, and motivations can be manipulated; if your memories can be reconstituted; if your character and personality can be chemically transformed; if your perception of your self can be altered—what remains of the self which Socrates commanded us to know?

Our answer must be: such intellectual crises are often entailed by significant advances in knowledge. They are among the hazards encountered by imperfect human beings in coping with a world not made for us. We sometimes have to reformulate even our most basic concepts. The self as we have understood it is not more firmly entrenched as a datum of our experience than (as we discovered only the other day) *Homo sapiens* is a fixed species, or than time, space and matter are independent entities. The human endeavor to apprehend the world is an open-ended process. When Socrates said "Know thyself!" he did not mean, discover thyself! but, create thyself!   □

The Self-Concept Revisited

Or a Theory of a Theory

54

SEYMOUR EPSTEIN   *University of Massachusetts* [1]

Is there a need for a self-concept in psychology? Almost from the beginning, the field has been divided on this question. From a behavioristic viewpoint, the self-concept has an aura of mysticism about it, appearing not far removed from the concept of a soul. One can neither see a self-concept, nor touch it, and no one has succeeded as yet in adequately defining it as a hypothetical construct. Definitions that are offered tend to lack meaningful referents or to be circular. Thus, the self has been defined in terms of the "I" or the "me," or both, or as the individual's reactions to himself. Some authors, apparently having despaired of providing an adequate definition, dispense with the matter by an appeal to common sense and by asserting that everyone knows he has a self as surely as he knows what belongs to him and what does not. Allport (1955), in an attempt to make a fresh start, coined a new word, the "proprium," which he defined as "all the regions of our life that we regard as peculiarly ours [p. 40]." The difficulty here is that one cannot identify the proprium until one identifies what people regard as essentially theirs, which, in effect, requires identification of the self. One occasionally detects a note of authoritative assertiveness in place of logical analysis when an author feels certain he knows what the self is, but finds it a slippery concept whose adequate definition is irritatingly elusive. Thus, Sullivan (1953) stated,

[1] Invited address presented at the meeting of the Canadian Psychological Association, Montreal, June 1972.

The preparation of this article was supported by National Institute of Mental Health, United States Public Health Service Grant MH-01293.

The author wishes to acknowledge his appreciation to James Averill and Ervin Staub for their helpful comments upon reading an earlier version of this article.

Requests for reprints should be sent to Seymour Epstein, Psychology Department, University of Massachusetts, Amherst, Massachusetts 01002.

When I talk about the self-system, I want it clearly understood that I am talking about a *dynamism* which comes to be enormously important in understanding interpersonal relations. This dynamism is an explanatory conception; it is not a thing, a region, or what not, such as superegos, egos, ids, and so on [p. 167].

It is encouraging to know that a dynamism, unlike an ego, is a concept that can be understood without specifying its referents.

If the self is not a thing and cannot be defined as a concept, then perhaps it can be dispensed with altogether. It is noteworthy that Allport, one of the proponents of the self-concept, essentially agrees with this conclusion. He noted that everything that has been explained by reference to a self-concept can be explained as well without it, and the only advantage in retaining the word is that it draws attention to important areas of psychology that otherwise would be ignored. He stated,

If the horizons of psychology were more spacious than they are I venture to suggest that theories of personality would not need the concept of self or of ego except in certain compound forms, such as *self-knowledge, self-image, ego-enhancement, ego-extension* [Allport, 1955, p. 56].

Despite the above arguments, there are a number of behavioral scientists, representing a variety of schools of thought, who believe that the self-concept is not only a useful explanatory construct, but a necessary one. Included among these are James, Cooley, Mead, Lecky, Sullivan, Hilgard, Snygg and Combs, and Rogers. To make matters more interesting, those self-theorists identified as phenomenologists consider the self-concept to be the most central concept in all of psychology, as it provides the only perspective from which an individual's behavior can be understood. From such a position, behavioristic attempts to develop an objective, scientific psychology that does not include a self-concept can represent nothing more than a futile exercise in mimicking the physical sciences.

Although there is disagreement about the value of the self-concept as an explanatory concept, there can be no argument but that the subjective feeling state of having a self is an important empirical phenomenon that warrants study in its own right. Like many other phenomena, the subjective feeling of self tends to be taken for granted until it is absent. When the latter involuntarily occurs, the individual reports an overwhelming feeling of terror. This is well illustrated in the following description by Lauretta Bender (1950) of the reactions of a schizophrenic girl on meeting her psychiatrist:

> Ruth, a five year old, approached the psychiatrist with "Are you the bogey man? Are you going to fight my mother? Are you the same mother? Are you the same father? Are you going to be another mother?" and finally screaming in terror, "I am afraid I am going to be someone else" [p. 135].

Granting that there need be no argument about the existence of a feeling state of having a self, the issue remains as to whether there must be divergent viewpoints on the value of the self-concept as an explanatory construct. Is psychology destined to remain with two schools of thought, a subjective one in which the self-concept is central, and an objective one in which it is superfluous? Hopefully, it is possible to integrate the two approaches within a broader framework. It is the aim of this article to do just this. I submit that the difficulty has been that the self-concept is not really a self-concept at all, but something similar. When the proper concept is substituted for the self-concept, the pieces of the jigsaw puzzle that thus far have eluded assembly will be found to fit neatly into place and form a picture that should be satisfactory to behaviorists and phenomenologists alike. Let me anticipate that, as with many integrations of familiar material, you probably will react to the solution, once presented, as absurdly self-evident.

The Nature of the Self-Concept

THE SELF-CONCEPT AS VIEWED BY OTHERS

As a beginning, it will be helpful to consider the views of others on the nature of the self-concept. Perhaps its identity can then be determined by establishing a composite photograph.

William James (1910), one of the first psychologists to have written extensively on the self, identified two fundamentally different approaches, one in which the self is regarded as a knower, or has an executive function, and the other in which it is regarded as an object of what is known. James saw no value to the self as a knower for understanding behavior and felt that it should be banished to the realm of philosophy. The self as an object of knowledge he identified as consisting of whatever the individual views as belonging to himself. This includes a material self, a social self, and a spiritual self. The material self is an extended self which contains, in addition to the individual's own body, his family and possessions. The social self includes the views others hold of the individual. The spiritual self includes the individual's emotions and desires. All aspects of the self are capable of evoking feelings of heightened self-esteem and well-being, or lowered self-esteem and dissatisfaction. James, apparently, viewed the self as having a unity as well as being differentiated, and as being intimately associated with emotions as mediated through self-esteem.

Cooley (1902) defined the self as "that which is designated in common speech by the pronouns of the first person singular, 'I,' 'me,' 'my,' 'mine,' and 'myself' [p. 136]." He noted that what is labeled by the individual as self produces stronger emotions than what is labeled an nonself, and that it is only through subjective feelings that the self can be identified. He believed that the feeling state is produced by the belief that one has control over events, or by cognitive discrimination, such as in noting that one's own body is different from other people's bodies. He introduced the concept of the "looking-glass self," which refers to an individual perceiving himself in the way that others perceive him. Cooley, apparently, assumed greater prevalence of this process than the poet, Robert Burns (1897, p. 43), who, upon observing the twitching and squirming of a genteel woman to an undetected louse crawling on her in church, wrote:

> O wad some Power the giftie gie us
> To see oursels as ithers see us!
> It wad frae monie a blunder free us,
> an' foolish notion.
> What airs in dress an' gait wad lea'e us,
> an ev'n devotion!

George Mead (1934) expanded upon Cooley's looking-glass self. He noted that the self-concept arises in social interaction as an outgrowth of the individual's concern about how others react to him. In order to anticipate other people's reactions so that he can behave accordingly, the individual learns to perceive the world as they do. By incorporating estimates of how the "generalized other" would respond to certain actions, the individual acquires a source of internal regulation that serves to guide and stabilize his behavior in the absence of external pressures. According to Mead, there are as many selves as there are social roles. Some of the roles are relatively broad and of considerable significance for the individual, whereas others are specific to particular situations, and of little significance as personality variables.

For Sullivan (1953), as for Cooley and Mead, the self arises out of social interaction. However, unlike Cooley and Mead, Sullivan emphasized the interaction of the child with significant others, particularly the mother figure, rather than with society at large. Sullivan identified the self-system as "an organization of educative experience called into being by the necessity to avoid or to minimize incidents of anxiety [p. 165]." Elaborating on this, he noted that the child internalizes those values and prohibitions that facilitate the achievement of satisfaction in ways that are approved of by significant others. Subsystems of approved-of and disapproved-of tendencies are organized within frameworks of "the good me" and "the bad me." It is evident that, for Sullivan, the need to avoid unpleasant affect is a major function of the self-system.

Lecky (1945) identified the self-concept as the nucleus of the personality. He defined personality, in turn, as an "organization of values that are consistent with one another [p. 160]." The organization of the personality is considered to be dynamic, as it involves a continuous assimilation of new ideas and rejection or modification of old ideas. It is assumed that all concepts are organized within a unified system, whose preservation is essential. The self-concept, as the nucleus of the personality, plays a key role in determining what concepts are acceptable for assimilation into the overall personality organization. There is one major motive, the striving for unity. A threat to the organization of the personality produces feelings of distress.

The views of Snygg and Combs (1949) are similar to those of Lecky. They defined the self-concept as "those parts of the phenomenal field which the individual has differentiated as definite and fairly stable characteristics of himself [p. 112]." Thus, they viewed the self-concept as the nucleus of a broader organization which contains incidental and changeable as well as stable personality characteristics.

Hilgard (1949), in a Presidential Address to the APA, identified three types of evidence that provide support for the concept of an inferred self. These are continuity of motivational patterns, genotypical patterning of motives, and the interpersonal nature of important human motives. The continuity of motivational patterns refers to people regarding themselves as essentially the same people they were a year ago, despite superficial changes. The genotypical patterning of motives refers to the observation that different actions can satisfy the same motive, and that certain motives can be substituted for others. Hilgard also noted that the existence of defense mechanisms provides strong evidence for a self-concept, as in order for there to be a defense mechanism, there has to be some aspect of the self that requires being defended. Unfortunately, despite having made an interesting case for postulating a self-concept, Hilgard made no attempt to identify it.

Rogers (1951) defined the self as "an organized, fluid, but consistent conceptual pattern of perceptions of characteristics and relationships of the 'I' or the 'me,' together with values attached to these concepts [p. 498]." He stated that the self-concept includes only those characteristics of the individual that he is aware of and over which he believes he exercises control. There is a basic need to maintain and enhance the self. Threat to the organization of the self-concept produces anxiety. If the threat cannot be defended against, catastrophic disorganization follows. His views have, obviously, a great deal in common with those of Lecky and Snygg and Combs.

Allport (1955), as already noted, preferred the term *proprium* to *self*. The proprium consists of those aspects of the individual which he regards as of central importance, and which contribute to a sense of inward unity. The proprium thus draws attention to the importance of what others regard as ego involvement. Accordingly, it is not surprising that a theme in Allport's writing is that research in psychology is often trivial because subjects are not sufficiently ego-involved. The proprium has the following eight attributes: (*a*) awareness of a bodily self, (*b*) a sense of continuity over time, (*c*) ego enhancement, or a need for self-esteem, (*d*) ego extension, or the identification of the self beyond the borders of the body, (*e*) rational process, or the synthesis of inner needs with outer reality, (*f*) self-image, or the person's perception and evaluation of himself as an object of knowledge, (*g*) the self as knower, or as executive agent, (*h*) "propriate striving," or the motivation to increase rather than decrease tension, and to expand awareness and seek out challenges. In a later work, Allport (1961), in apparent agreement with James, decided that the self as knower did not belong in the realm of psychology.

Sarbin (1952) noted that behavior is organized around cognitive structures. One such important structure is the structure of the self. Like other structures, the self is hierarchically organized, and is subject to change, usually in the direction from lower order to higher order constructs. Among the substructures of the self are empirical selves, including a somatic self and a social self. An "I" or "Pure Ego" is represented as the cross section of the individual's total cognitive organization, including his different empirical selves, at a moment in time.

Having reviewed a variety of positions on the nature of the self-concept, we are now in a position to summarize the characteristics that others have attributed to it. These include the following:

1. It is a subsystem of internally consistent, hierarchically organized concepts contained within a broader conceptual system.

2. It contains different empirical selves, such as a body self, a spiritual self, and a social self.

3. It is a dynamic organization that changes with experience. It appears to seek out change and exhibits a tendency to assimilate increasing amounts of information, thereby manifesting something like a growth principle. As Hilgard (1949) noted, it is characterized more aptly as integrative than integrated.

4. It develops out of experience, particularly out of social interaction with significant others.

5. It is essential for the functioning of the individual that the organization of the self-concept be maintained. When the organization of the self-concept is threatened, the individual experiences anxiety, and attempts to defend himself against the threat. If the defense is unsuccessful, stress mounts and is followed ultimately by total disorganization.

6. There is a basic need for self-esteem which relates to all aspects of the self-system, and, in comparison to which, almost all other needs are subordinate.

7. The self-concept has at least two basic functions. First, it organizes the data of experience, particularly experience involving social interaction, into predictable sequences of action and reaction. Second, the self-concept facilitates attempts to fulfill needs while avoiding disapproval and anxiety.

IDENTIFICATION OF THE SELF-CONCEPT AS A SELF-THEORY

Having laid out the pieces of the jigsaw puzzle, it should now be possible to determine the nature of the overall picture. Or, for those who prefer rid-dles, the problem can be presented as follows: What is it that consists of concepts that are hierarchically organized and internally consistent; that assimilates knowledge, yet, itself, is an object of knowledge; that is dynamic, but must maintain a degree of stability; that is unified and differentiated at the same time; that is necessary for solving problems in the real world; and that is subject to sudden collapse, producing total disorganization when this occurs? The answer, by now, should be evident. In case it is not, I submit that *the self-concept is a self-theory*. It is a theory that the individual has unwittingly constructed about himself as an experiencing, functioning individual, and it is part of a broader theory which he holds with respect to his entire range of significant experience. Accordingly, there are major postulate systems for the *nature of the world, for the nature of the self, and for their interaction*. Like most theories, the self-theory is a conceptual tool for accomplishing a purpose. The most fundamental purpose of the self-theory is to *optimize the pleasure/pain balance of the individual over the course of a lifetime*. Two other basic functions, not unrelated to the first, are to *facilitate the maintenance of self-esteem*, and to *organize the data of experience in a manner that can be coped with effectively*. These functions were derived from the assumption that, at its most basic level, human behavior is organized biologically according to a pleasure/pain principle, and from an analysis of the conditions that produce total, sudden disorganization of the personality, as in acute schizophrenia.

The position I am advocating has obviously much in common with Kelley's (1955) view that the individual, as he goes about the business of attempting to solve the problems of everyday living, proceeds in a manner similar to that of the scientist who is attempting to solve more impersonal problems. Both continuously make and test hypotheses and revise their concepts accordingly. Both organize their observations into schemata which then are organized into a network of broader schemata called theories. If experience were not so arranged, it would be impossible to behave effectively in a complex world with innumerable conflicting demands. Further, without such a system, the individual would be overwhelmed by innumerable isolated details that would have to be recalled to guide behavior.

While Kelley does not postulate a self-concept, given the value of a distinction between self and nonself it can be surmised that a universal higher order postulate in an individual's overall conceptual system is that the data of experience can be organized into a self-system and a world system. Not only are the cues for differentiating self and non-self ubiquitous and salient to the point that they are normally impossible to ignore, but there are overwhelming advantages to making the distinction. For one, to act within a world of shared reality, it is necessary to distinguish what is subjective from what is common experience. Second, the distinction between self and nonself is useful for the individual to exercise control of his behavior. Third, for humans to live harmoniously in social communities, it is necessary to have a concept of responsibility, and such a concept would be meaningless without a distinction between self and nonself. It is thus apparent that in everyday living, as well as in science, it is important to distinguish the subjective world of self from the objective world of nonself. However, where man, the scientist, needs the distinction to study the objective world for its own sake, for man, the human being, the distinction is important only to the extent that it contributes to the satisfaction of his personal needs and happiness. Thus, the theory I am proposing differs from Kelly's theory in that Kelly assigns little significance to emotion, while in the present theory emotion occupies a position of central importance.

Structure of the Self-Theory

ATTRIBUTES IN COMMON WITH ALL THEORIES

All theories can be evaluated by the degree to which they are extensive, parsimonious, empirically valid, internally consistent, testable, and useful. Accordingly, it should be of interest to examine self-theories of individuals with respect to each of these attributes.

Extensivity

All other things being equal, the more extensive a theory, the better the theory. This holds for an individual's self-theory as well as for other theories. An individual with an extensive self-theory will have concepts available for coping with a wide variety of situations. He will be aware of more facets of his feelings, abilities, and personality characteristics than an individual with a narrow self-theory. Accordingly, he should be more flexible and open to new experience. A person with a narrow self-theory will experience life in a relatively simplified fashion. Things for him should tend to be black or white, and he characteristically should exhibit repression and rigidity.

Good theories are expansive. They become more differentiated and extensive as additional data are made available. Poor theories are not only restricted, they are restrictive. Put otherwise, an individual with a narrow self-theory will tend to avoid drawing inferences that disturb the stability he has achieved through limiting his ways of construing the world and himself.

There are at least three reasons why individuals may have excessively restricted self-theories. One is that the individual lacks the cognitive capacity to differentiate and generalize adequately, as in the case of children and mental defectives. A second is that under stress, all theories tend to become restricted as this protects the theory against disorganization. Thus, individuals who are highly threatened, particularly if they have a low threshold for disorganization, can be expected to have restricted self-theories. It should be considered that individuals who, at one time, were highly anxious and learned to react to threat by restricting their self-theories may continue to react to minor threats with constriction, even though they no longer are highly anxious. As the self-theory is derived from experience, it follows that the diversity of experience that an individual is exposed to is a critical factor in determining the complexity and range of his self-theory. It can be expected that the person whose self-theory is narrow because of limited exposure will not be as resistant to change as the person who is defending against anxiety and disorganization.

Parsimony

Holding other factors constant, the more parsimonious a theory, the better the theory. Parsimony is achieved by a theory having both broad, integrative postulates and an efficiently organized set of subpostulates. A theory totally lacking in parsimony would require a separate postulate for each item of behavior to be predicted. Such a theory, in fact, would be an absence of theory. Within the realm of personality, an individual with a self-theory low in parsimony would lack stability. As the result of an absence of general guiding principles, or values, his behavior would be completely situationally determined. The opposite would be expected of an individual with a parsimonious self-theory. He would exhibit stability as a consequence of the presence of basic values, or highly general postulates, and, at the same time, would be flexible and discriminating due to the contribution of lower order postulates.

Of considerable interest is the situation in which

parsimony is achieved at the sacrifice of other requirements, such as empirical validity or testability. This is well illustrated in cases of paranoia, where a single untestable postulate is used to account for a wide variety of conflicting evidence. Thus, a paranoid individual with delusions of persecution may see in a friendly gesture an attempt to deceive him. Obviously, an unqualified postulate that attempts to explain too much is a bad postulate.

Empirical Validity

Higher order postulates assimilate lower order constructs that are generalizations derived from experience. Given that the theory is essentially an inductive one, how is it possible for it to fail to represent reality? For one, inferences extend beyond data, and the process of inference may be incorrect. Second, much human learning is based on vicarious, rather than direct, experience. That is, the child is taught values, attitudes, and consequences of actions independent of its direct experiences. When vicarious experience conflicts with direct experience, it is the latter that may lose out, depending on circumstances. Sullivan (1953) and Rogers (1951) both emphasized the manner in which significant others use the child's dependence upon them to teach the child to misrepresent his own experience. Thus, if labeling anger toward a mother or sibling is reacted to with withdrawal of affection, the child may learn to not label the emotion for what it is, and may even learn to substitute the word love for hate, if this is a precondition for acceptance. Finally, it should be noted that experience, whether direct or vicarious, is not the only factor that determines whether a concept will be assimilated into an individual's self-theory. Among other factors that have to be considered are a need for internal consistency and a need to maintain the organization of the self-system. To satisfy these other conditions, it is at times necessary to sacrifice empirical validity.

No theory, whether a scientific theory or a self-theory, is ever completely valid. The most that can be hoped for is that it will be self-correcting. Accordingly, a more important question than why some self-theories are low in validity is why some theories are not self-correcting. One reason is that when the organization of a self-theory is under stress, it becomes important for the individual to defend whatever organization exists and to avoid jeopardizing it by attempting to assimilate new information. Thus, individuals who are in a state of high stress or anxiety can be expected to avoid assimilating new information. Second, a self-theory may not be self-correcting because of repression. If an individual has learned to reduce anxiety

by failing to make certain observations or to use certain labels, he has, in effect, shut himself off from having experiences that could correct his faulty concepts. That is, repression insulates the individual from the corrective experiences necessary for him to change his invalid concepts.

I have observed elsewhere, in a discussion of research on anxiety in parachuting conducted by Fenz and myself (Epstein, 1967), that maximum reality awareness is not always desirable. In order for mastery of anxiety to proceed at an optimal rate, it is necessary for awareness of threat to be paced properly. It is by attending to new aspects of a stressful situation as old aspects are mastered that the individual ultimately masters the entire situation. If there is no selective shutting out to begin with, the individual may be overwhelmed with anxiety and disorganization will occur. This observation is consistent with the conclusion that the self-theory can assimilate data only up to a certain rate without provoking excessive anxiety. Accordingly, an effective defense system is one that allows awareness of reality to progress according to the rate at which it can be assimilated. This can be contrasted with an inadequate defense system which has an all-or-none quality, either shutting out awareness of reality completely, or allowing the individual to be overwhelmed.

Internal Consistency

The most effective way to destroy a theory is to demonstrate contradictions within its own postulate system. Case histories of schizophrenics demonstrate that total disorganization of the self-theory may be brought about by the emergence into awareness of some aspect of the self previously denied, such as homosexual impulses or feelings of hostility to a loved one (cf. Kaplan, 1964). Apparently, it is not the inconsistency itself that produces the disorganization, but *awareness* of the inconsistency. An individual's self-theory can contain considerable inconsistency even with regard to relatively basic postulates without the individual experiencing stress, as long as he is able to deny the inconsistency. Of course, such inconsistency represents a potential source of stress and disorganization, as there is always the possibility that conditions will arise where denial is no longer possible.

Testability

A self-theory, if it is to be useful in coping with real events, must, like a scientific theory, be testable. As previously noted, a good self-theory is one that increases in validity with increasing experience. It is obvious that concepts that are not testable cannot be improved by experience. The question may be raised as to why, then, should individuals entertain concepts that are not open to testing. The answer is that such concepts are protected from invalidation. It is assumed that the disconfirmation of a concept in the self-theory produces anxiety; the more significant the concept for maintaining the self-theory, the greater the anxiety. Individuals who have reason to suspect that reality may invalidate a postulate important to their self-theory will thus have strong motivation to insulate that concept from the test of reality. Put otherwise, under certain circumstances, illusion may be preferable to reality, and when this is so, the individual will avoid subjecting his concepts to testing. In less dramatic ways, all people, to some extent, shield their significant concepts from being invalidated, as all people are motivated to avoid anxiety.

Usefulness

A self-theory does not exist for its own sake but, like other theories, is developed for the purpose of solving problems. It has already been noted that the basic functions of the self-theory are to maintain a favorable pleasure/pain balance, to maintain self-esteem, and to assimilate the data of experience. A good self-theory is one that carries out these functions effectively, while a poor self-theory does so inadequately. A failure of the self-theory to carry out any one of its functions places it under stress, and if the stress is great enough, the theory ultimately collapses. The corresponding subjective experience is a state of disorganization. Case histories of schizophrenics (cf. Kaplan, 1964) support the above analysis by indicating that states of mounting stress and ultimate disorganization often are preceded by unassimilable experiences, feelings of failure and inadequacy, or a prolonged period of unhappiness with no hope for the future. Collapse of a self-theory under stress, although it is a consequence of maladaption, can, in itself, be adaptive as it provides an opportunity for a more effective reorganization. The terror and incapacity that follow the collapse of the self-structure in schizophrenia, as well as the desperate need schizophrenics exhibit to establish a new structure, even if an unrealistic one, provide strong evidence for the importance of a self-theory in human behavior.

THE NATURE OF THE POSTULATES

Postulates Inferred from the Structure of a Self-Theory

Given the assumption that individuals have self-theories which contain postulates that direct their

behavior, it follows that if an individual's behavior is to be understood, it is necessary to reconstruct his postulate system. How is one to undertake this task? It is assumed that there are certain domains in which all people have postulates and other domains in which some people have postulates. Some of the more general domains can be identified by an analysis of the functions of the self-theory, namely, the maintenance of a favorable pleasure/pain balance, the assimilation of the data of experience, and the maintenance of self-esteem. Accordingly, it can be surmised that every individual will have postulates that are assessments of where he stands on each of these variables. Organized under these postulates will be a hierarchical arrangement of postulates of lesser generality. For example, under a postulate evaluating overall self-esteem, there will be second-order postulates relating to general competence, moral self-approval, power, and love worthiness. These postulates are presumably common to all people, at least in Western society. Lower order postulates organized under competence include assessments of general mental and physical ability. The lowest order postulates under competence include assessments of specific abilities. As one moves from lower order to higher order postulates, the postulates become increasingly important to the maintenance of the individual's self-theory. It is assumed that the sum of the appraisals of the individual's ability to derive pleasure from life, to assimilate experience, and to maintain self-esteem determines the overall stability of his self-theory. Thus, a self-theory under minimum stress would be expected to contain higher order postulates such as the following: "I am basically a worthwhile human being"; "I know where I am going and what is expected of me"; "I expect to lead a happy life"; "I am a highly competent person"; "I like myself and consider myself to be a decent person"; "People who matter to me care a great deal about me." The corresponding postulate system for someone with a self-theory under a great deal of stress, and therefore subject to disorganization, might read as follows: "I am a worthless human being"; "Life is meaningless, and has nothing to offer me"; "I will never know happiness"; "I am incompetent, a total failure"; "I am a despicable human being"; "No one whom I respect could ever care for me."

Postulates Inferred from Emotions

One approach to identifying the concepts that organize an individual's experience is to ask him about them. Rogers and his colleagues (cf. Rogers & Dymond, 1954) have used a Q-sort technique in which individuals rate themselves on self-descriptive statements by distributing them in a quasi-normal distribution. Kelley (1955) analyzed the concepts that individuals employ to identify likenesses and differences among triads of people they are asked to compare, such as mother, teacher, and close friend. Both approaches require the individual to be able to identify consciously the concepts he uses. Neither approach is satisfactory from the viewpoint proposed here, which assumes that individuals are not necessarily aware of the significant postulates in their self-theories. Fortunately, the relationship between emotion and cognition provides an indirect means of identifying an individual's significant concepts. There are two ways in which emotions can be used to infer cognitions. One follows from the assumption that human emotions, at least for the main part, depend on interpretation of events (cf. Arnold, 1960; Epstein, 1967, 1972; Lazarus, 1966; Schachter, 1964). Thus, if I make the interpretation that someone has wronged me and deserves to be punished, I feel anger. If I interpret a situation as one that is threatening, and that I would like to escape from, I feel fear. If I make the interpretation that I am deprived of love or the satisfaction of some other need vital to my happiness, and have no hope that it will ever be fulfilled, I feel depressed. If I make the interpretation that love, or something else important to me, is being given to someone else instead of me, I feel jealousy. The point I wish to make is that, as each emotion implies an underlying cognition, by knowing a person's emotional dispositions, it should be possible to reconstruct some of his major postulates. This, of course, presupposes sufficiently detailed knowledge about the relationship of cognition to emotion, an area that has been receiving increasing attention.

The second, and probably more fruitful way of using emotions to infer postulates, follows from the assumption that for an emotion to occur, a postulate of significance to the individual must be implicated. It is assumed further that negative emotions arise when any of the functions of the self-theory is interfered with or is threatened. Included are threats to the assimilative capacity of the self-system, to self-esteem, and to a favorable pleasure/pain balance. Positive emotions occur when any of these functions are facilitated or when it is anticipated that they will be. It is assumed that the stronger the positive or negative emotion, the more significant is the postulate that is implicated for maintaining a function of the self-theory of the individual. Thus, if a woman is found to register strong anticipatory anxiety before a beauty contest

and considerable unhappiness after not winning it, but little reaction before and after failing an important examination, it can be inferred that, within her self-system, beauty is more important than academic achievement. This, of course, may appear to be self-evident, but the point is that if one were to ask her, she might well report having the opposite values. I believe that a systematic study of emotions in everyday life, including the situations that produce the emotions, provides a promising approach for advancing knowledge of human behavior, in general, and one that can be used effectively by individuals to advance their own self-knowledge. My students and I have recently begun a research program in which people keep records of their emotions on a day-to-day basis on specially constructed forms over a protracted period of time. Although the data have not yet been formally analyzed, preliminary results are dramatically exciting. Not only does the technique provide interesting new information on the relationship between emotions and underlying implicit cognitions, in general, but we have observed that awareness of such relationships in their own data by individuals can be highly therapeutic.

THE EMPIRICAL SELVES

In considering the structure of an individual's postulate system, I have thus far discussed the nature of some general postulates that relate to the overall self-system. However, as noted earlier, the self-system is differentiated as well as integrated. It follows that, in considering structure, it is necessary to consider the subsystems, or different empirical selves, which retain a degree of independence despite being influenced by as well as influencing the generic self-system. Thus, the same overall level of self-esteem may be achieved by high appraisal of the body self and low appraisal of the inferred inner self, as by the reverse. Further, in order to examine the development of the self-system, it is necessary to consider the sequential emergence of the subsystems of a body self, an inferred inner self, and a moral self.

By the body self, I mean the individual's biological self, his possessions, and those individuals, groups, and symbols he identifies with. The inferred inner self refers to all aspects of the individual's psychological self, or personality. It includes the individual's cognitions, conscious and unconscious, that relate to his abilities, traits, wishes, fears, and other motivational and emotional dispositions. Expressed otherwise, the inferred inner self represents the bulk of the self-theory.

It includes the moral self, which is a subdivision that contains the self-evaluative reactions of the individual, including an overall appraisal of himself as a worthwhile human being as well as evaluative reactions to individual aspects of himself.

Time will not permit a systematic discussion of the postulates with reference to the different subsystems of the self. My aim, for the moment, is simply to note one of the directions in which a more extensive analysis would have to proceed.

Developmental Aspects of the Self-Theory

DEVELOPMENT OF A BODY SELF

For the child to learn that he has a body self requires a relatively simple act of concept formation in which he must recognize that his own body is a subset of one in a broader set of all human bodies. The level of abstract thinking that is required apparently lies within the capacity of the chimpanzee. In a series of interesting experiments, Gallup (1968) demonstrated that after a few exposures to a mirror, a chimpanzee exhibited self-directed as opposed to other-directed behavior to the mirror. That is, the chimpanzee reacted as if he recognized that the mirror image was a representation of himself and that it was not another chimpanzee. Lower order animals, children below the age of 10 months, and older mental defectives exhibit other-directed behavior in response to a mirror (Gallup, 1968).

An example of how direct the training that one has a body self like other body selves can be was provided by a recent visit of my two-year-old niece. Donna was seated at the dining room table with the entire family. In order to occupy her, her mother would say something such as, "Where is Aunt Alice? Point to Aunt Alice," after which Donna would point and everyone would applaud. Having made the rounds several times, and all errors having long since been eliminated, to liven things up, someone said, "Point to Donna; where is Donna?" This turned out to be not so simple a task. Donna looked around the table, could find no Donna, and began to point randomly. At this point, the mother said, "You know who Donna is. Point to the little girl everyone calls Donna," whereupon Donna, with an apparent flash of insight, unhesitatingly pointed to herself. Such a task is as clearly an example of training in concept formation as if one were to use blocks with labels on them.

The body self is, of course, not learned only by direct training. It can be assumed that it is inferred from a variety of cues which are capable of indicating that one has characteristics in common with other people, yet differs from them, just as they differ from one another. Thus, it is evident to the child that he has hands and feet that look more like other people's than like those of the dog or cat who inhabit the same household. Although there are parts of one that one cannot see, such as eyes and nose, there are mirrors, and even without mirrors it does not take much of an inference to recognize that if one corresponds to people in all ways one can see, one probably corresponds to them in ways that one cannot see. Moreover, what cannot be seen can be detected by other senses, or otherwise inferred. Thus, one can identify the nose by touch, and the presence of two eyes can be inferred by opening and closing one at a time. In addition to evidence that one has a body like other people's, there is also evidence that one's body is uniquely one's own. Among the factors that contribute to this conclusion are: (*a*) *saliency*—it hurts more when one's own arm is pinched than when someone else's is; (*b*) *continuity*—no one's body is with one as much as one's own; (*c*) *control*—one can make one's own limbs respond to one's wishes more easily and dependably than anyone else's; and (*d*) *double sensation*—when one touches oneself, the part doing the touching and the part being touched receive sensation, whereas when one touches someone else, only the part doing the touching receives sensation.

Not only are there a multitude of cues available to support the inference of a body self, but there is also strong reinforcement for formulating the concept. For one, there is social approval and disapproval to consider. A child who thought he was something he was not, such as a boy who thought he was a dog, would be subjected to untold ridicule. Second, the distinction between self and nonself is necessary if experience is to be organized into a stable and predictable system. Third, the distinction is necessary for exercising effective control.

DEVELOPMENT OF AN INFERRED INNER SELF

Once a body self has been developed, it facilitates the development of an inferred inner self, which is assumed to proceed in an analogous manner. While the level of conceptual ability required for the development of the inferred inner self can be assumed to be greater than that for the body self, as the elements are more abstract, the level of inference is still not very great.

Just as it is evident that some people are short and others tall, that some have loud voices and others soft voices, and that some wear their hair short and others long, it is evident that people differ in behavioral characteristics, such as friendliness, aggressiveness, and helpfulness. In identifying people physically, one does not add up their separate characteristics, but recognizes a configuration. It is assumed that the same is true for identifying people's personalities. Now, if one recognizes that people have stable patterns of underlying personality attributes inferred from their repetitive behavior, then there is as much reason to assume that people have a personality identity as that they have a body identity. It follows, if others have personality identities and if one is a person, that one must have a personality identity also. Other sources for inferring an inner self include a feeling of continuity of experience, ego involvement, awareness of the need to defend some inner aspect of one's being against threat, awareness of underlying motives that need not be expressed, awareness of a tendency to automatically evaluate oneself, and awareness of emotions associated with self-esteem. All of these imply the existence of an inner self that is different from the body self, invisible to the perception of others, yet very real.

Consider the experience that an individual has when his self-esteem is severely injured, such as when he is humiliated in the presence of people he wishes to impress. Such an experience is apt to be acutely distressing, to prevent the individual from sleeping nights, and to reverberate for months, years, and possibly a lifetime. Where in the body does the hurt reside? Since it cannot be located in the body self, such experiences suggest the existence of some nonphysical aspect of the self that is more significant than the body self. The same argument can be made for positive experiences. When an individual has a feeling of joy because he has accomplished something important to him, where in the body self does the pleasurable feeling reside? Unlike pleasant physical stimulation, it cannot be attributed to the body self. Accordingly, it suggests the existence of a nonphysical self. Given the existence of a body image, the proclivity of people to think in concrete imagery, and the observation that there is something within the body that appears to have an identity of its own, it is not surprising that it is conceptualized as a spiritual homunculus rather than as a hierarchical organization of concepts that assimilates experience and guides behavior. This accounts for why belief in a soul has been so prevalent throughout human history.

The question may be raised as to what conditions impede the development of an inferred inner self. It can be assumed that one such condition is an absence of a feeling of control, as such a feeling provides one of the important sources for inferring an inner self. Further, since the inferred inner self has as its functions assimilating the data of experience, maintaining a favorable pleasure/pain balance, and maintaining self-esteem, it follows that any conditions that prevent the individual from achieving these functions should impede the development of an inferred inner self. Under certain circumstances, an inferred inner self might be a detriment to the individual as it could contribute to an unfavorable pleasure/pain balance. Consider the case of a child who is unconsciously, if not consciously, hated and who, if he were to internalize the values of significant others, would hate himself. Consider, further, that the only attention he could hope to obtain would be when he failed in something. We are considering a situation in which the self-system, were it to develop, would have to be turned against the welfare of the individual, contributing to low self-esteem and to an unfavorable pleasure/pain balance. It is hypothesized that under such circumstances, if extreme enough, a self-system would not develop at all, while under less extreme circumstances, the development of a restricted or distorted self-system would occur.

DEVELOPMENT OF A MORAL SELF

The body self and the inferred inner self developed because of their utility as conceptual tools for organizing the data of experience. They would have value even in a world in which individuals did not judge each other, and in which there was no reason to seek approval and avoid disapproval. The moral self, on the other hand, is presumed to develop only because of the need to obtain approval and to avoid disapproval. The child initially labels behavior that pleases him as good and behavior that displeases him as bad, much in the way that he labels sweet-tasting food as good and bitter-tasting food as bad. Up to this point, he has no moral self; his only concern is with his own pleasure. This state of affairs, obviously, does not last very long. In order to fit into a society, he must be taught to take into account the wishes of others. The parents, as the carriers of the culture, have the task of redefining what is good and what is bad, so that the child will feel that he is good when his behavior coincides with socially accepted mores and that he is bad when it does not. Whether they do so consciously or unconsciously, directly or indirectly, parents tend to withhold affection following behavior they disapprove of, and to bestow affection following behavior they approve of. Before long, the child receives the message that, operationally defined, good means what the parents approve of and bad means what the parents disapprove of. Further, good is associated with a feeling of being loved, and bad with a feeling of being unworthy of love. The child is now able to avoid open conflict with and disapproval from others, as he has internalized the parents' values and can correct himself. He has become his own evaluator, feeling pleased with himself and loveworthy when he behaves according to his internalized standards, and guilt ridden and unworthy of love when he violates these standards. Thus, he has developed a moral self which appears to him to have an identity of its own as it is not under his conscious control.

A problem which warrants special consideration in any treatment of the moral self is the existence of intense, irrational self-belittlement or self-hatred. It is known, for example, that people confess to serious crimes they could not have committed, and that in every mental hospital there are patients who complain of being the most despicable individuals who ever existed and who do not deserve to live. Freud accounted for this phenomenon by attributing it to hostility turned inward. More specifically, he believed the depressed person has unacceptable hostile feelings toward a figure who denied him love, either purposely or unintentionally. By identifying with, or internalizing, this lost love object, the individual maintains the relationship, in a sense, and can then acceptably express his hostility toward the other person by directing it at himself. Its very complexity makes me doubt the generality of this explanation. I would like to suggest a simpler one, which rests on the assumption that a sudden drop in self-esteem is more distressing than a chronically low level of self-esteem. If this is true, then individuals who anticipate that their self-esteem will be lowered by others will tend to chronically devaluate themselves in order to prevent a greater discomfort. In more dramatic cases, such as in psychotic depression, I believe that Freud is correct in assuming that an unconscious component is also involved. My explanation, however, is that the unacceptable feelings, which need not necessarily be hostile, produce an anticipation of disapproval or loss of love from a significant other. However, the internalized values of the significant other define the individual's own values. Accordingly, the individual withdraws approval from himself and treats himself as unworthy of love. Further, by retaining his self-evaluation

at a low level, he is saved from concern over the greater pain of having it further lowered. This can account for why depressed people resist efforts to increase their self-esteem.

I believe the mechanism just described is of highly general significance, and can account for the relative stability of people's self-esteem if it is assumed that there are two fundamental tendencies that work in opposition to each other, thereby affecting a balance. One tendency is for the individual to wish to raise his self-esteem, as high self-esteem feels good. The other is for the individual to wish to avoid a drop in self-esteem, as a drop in self-esteem feels particularly bad. Accordingly, the individual avoids evaluating himself unrealistically highly, as this would expose him to decreases in self-esteem. As a result, it can be expected that even under the most favorable circumstances, self-esteem will tend to increase only gradually.

Implications

What is accomplished by the statement that the self-concept is identified more properly as a self theory? Does it contribute anything more than Sullivan's statement that the self is not an ego or an id, but a dynamism? I believe it solves a number of problems that could not be resolved by previous theories of the self, and that it has other significant implications as well.

1. By recognizing that individuals have implicit theories about themselves as functioning individuals, it is possible to assimilate the views of phenomenologists on the nature of the self-concept into a broader framework that should be acceptable to all psychologists. When the self-concept is redefined as a self-theory, it can no longer be dismissed as unscientific, or as a reincarnation of the soul, unless one is also willing to dismiss theory, in general, as unscientific.

2. The recognition that the self-theory is a theory solves the problem of how the self can be both the subject and object of what is known. All theories contain knowledge, yet influence the acquisition of new knowledge. Expressed otherwise, theories influence, as well as are influenced by, the acquisition of data. Accordingly, there is no need to banish the executive function of the self to philosophy, as James and Allport have exhorted us to do. The executive self can live comfortably within psychology and even make highly respectable contributions to it, as long as it is willing to renounce its previous confused notions about being

a self-concept, and recognize that it is, in fact, one important attribute of a self-theory.

3. The concept of an inherent growth principle, postulated according to acts of faith and goodwill by phenomenologists and humanists, becomes comprehensible once it is recognized that individuals have self-theories, for it is a characteristic of theories, at least good ones, to increase in scope with exposure to new data.

4. The relationship of emotion to the self-system, identified as a cognitive structure, is elucidated when it is recognized that the self-theory is a working theory whose most general function is to make life livable, meaning emotionally satisfying. Thus, the self-theory, as described, does not exist apart from the emotions, and to a large extent the opposite is also true.

5. The recognition that an individual's self-theory, like any other theory, is a hierarchically organized conceptual system for solving problems, can explain its total disorganization when a basic reason, the theory is incapable of fulfilling its functions. It also indicates that drastic disorganization can serve a constructive function, as it permits drastic reorganization.

6. The need for people to defend desperately certain concepts or values, no matter how unrealistic they are, can be comprehended readily once it is recognized that a self-theory is necessary in order to function, and that any theory is better than none.

In conclusion, I have presented a theory which attempts to incorporate phenomenological views on the self-concept within an objective framework. Assuming that what I have said is essentially true, it has broad implications for an understanding of human behavior. If the theory of a theory that I have presented does not rate highly, in your judgment, on the attributes by which all theories can be judged, namely, extensivity, parsimony, empirical validity, internal consistency, testability, and usefulness, I can but hope that it at least has had heuristic value, and has stimulated your thinking about your own assumptions.

REFERENCES

ALLPORT, G. W. *Becoming.* New Haven: Yale University Press, 1955.

ALLPORT, G. W. *Pattern and growth in personality.* New York: Holt, Rinehart & Winston, 1961.

ARNOLD, M. B. *Emotion and personality.* New York: Columbia University Press, 1960. 2 vols.

BENDER, L. Anxiety in disturbed children. In P. H. Hoch & J. Zubin (Eds.), *Anxiety.* New York: Grune & Stratton, 1950.

BURNS, R. To a louse. In, *The complete poetical works of Robert Burns.* New York: Houghton Mifflin, 1897.

COOLEY, C. H. *Human nature and the social order.* New York: Scribner's, 1902.

EPSTEIN, S. Toward a unified theory of anxiety. In B. A. Maher (Ed.), *Progress in experimental personality research.* Vol. 4. New York: Academic Press, 1967.

EPSTEIN, S. The nature of anxiety with emphasis upon its relationship to expectancy. In C. D. Spielberger (Ed.), *Anxiety: Current trends in theory and research.* New York: Academic Press, 1972.

GALLUP, G. G. Mirror-image stimulation. *Psychological Bulletin,* 1968, **70**, 782–793.

HILGARD, E. R. Human motives and the concept of the self. *American Psychologist,* 1949, **4**, 374–382.

JAMES, W. *Psychology: The briefer course.* New York: Holt, 1910.

KAPLAN, B. *The inner world of mental illness.* New York: Harper & Row, 1964.

KELLEY, G. A. *The psychology of personal constructs.* New York: Norton, 1955. 2 vols.

LAZARUS, R. S. *Psychological stress and the coping process.* New York: McGraw-Hill, 1966.

LECKY, P. *Self-consistency: A theory of personality.* Long Island, N.Y.: Island Press, 1945.

MEAD, G. H. *Mind, self, and society.* Chicago: University of Chicago Press, 1934.

ROGERS, C. R. *Client-centered therapy.* New York: Houghton Mifflin, 1951.

ROGERS, C. R., & DYMOND, R. F. (Eds.) *Psychotherapy and personality change: Coordinated studies in the client-centered approach.* Chicago: University of Chicago Press, 1954.

SARBIN, T. R. A preface to a psychological analysis of the self. *Psychological Review,* 1952, **59**, 11–22.

SCHACHTER, S. The interaction of cognitive and psychological determinants of emotional state. In L. Berkowitz (Ed.), *Advances in experimental social psychology.* Vol. 1. New York: Academic Press, 1964.

SNYGG, D., & COMBS, A. W. *Individual behavior.* New York: Harper & Row, 1949.

SULLIVAN, H. S. *The interpersonal theory of psychiatry.* New York: Norton, 1953.

THE MANY ME'S OF THE SELF-MONITOR

55

BY MARK SNYDER

Is there a "true self" apart from the social roles we play? Perhaps not for people identified in studies as high self-monitors, who are keenly aware of the impression they are making and constantly fine-tuning their performance.

"The image of myself which I try to create in my own mind in order that I may love myself is very different from the image which I try to create in the minds of others in order that they may love me."

—W. H. Auden

The concept of the self is one of the oldest and most enduring in psychological considerations of human nature. We generally assume that people are fairly consistent and stable beings: that a person who is generous in one situation is also likely to be generous in other situations, that one who is honest is honest most of the time, that a person who takes a liberal stance today will favor the liberal viewpoint tomorrow.

It's not always so: each of us, it appears, may have not one but many selves. Moreover, much as we might like to believe that the self is an integral feature of personal identity, it appears that, to a greater extent, the self is a product of the individual's relationships with other people. Conventional wisdom to the contrary, there may be striking gaps and contradictions—as Auden suggests—between the public appearances and private realities of the self.

Psychologists refer to the strategies and techniques that people use to control the impressions they convey to others as "impression management." One of my own research interests has been to understand why some individuals are better at impression management than others. For it is clear that some people are particularly sensitive to the ways they express and present themselves in social situations—at parties, job interviews, professional meetings, in confrontations of all kinds where one might choose to create and maintain an appearance, with or without a specific purpose in mind. Indeed, I have found that such people have developed the ability to carefully monitor their own performances and to skillfully adjust their performances when signals from others tell them that they are not having the desired effect. I call such persons "high self-monitoring individuals," and I have developed a 25-item measure—the Self-Monitoring Scale—that has proved its ability to distinguish high self-monitoring individuals from low self-monitoring individuals. (See box on page 34.) Unlike the high self-monitoring individuals, low self-monitoring individuals are not so concerned about taking in such information; instead, they tend to express what they feel, rather than mold and tailor their behavior to fit the situation.

My work on self-monitoring and impression management grew out of a long-standing fascination with explorations of reality and illusion in literature and in the theater. I was struck by the contrast between the way things often appear to be and the reality that lurks beneath the surface—on the stage, in novels, and in people's actual lives. I wanted to know how this world of appearances in social relationships was built and maintained, as well as what its effects were on the individual personality. But I was also interested in exploring the older, more philosophical question of whether, beneath the various images of self that people project to others, there is a "real me." If we are all actors in many social situations, do we then retain in any sense an essential self, or are we really a variety of selves?

Skilled Impression Managers

There are striking and important differences in the extent to which people can and do control their self-presentation in social situations: some people engage in impression management more often—and with greater skill—than others. Professional actors, as well as many trial lawyers, are among the best at it. So are successful salespeople, confidence artists, and politicians. The onetime mayor of New York, Fiorello LaGuardia, was particularly skilled at adopting the expressive mannerisms of a variety of

THE MANY ME'S OF THE SELF-MONITOR, by Mark Snyder. Parts of this article appear in the chapter "Impression Management" by Mark Snyder in the book SOCIAL PSYCHOLOGY IN THE EIGHTIES, 3rd Edition, by Lawrence S. Wrightsman and Kay Deaux (Monterey, Calif.: Brooks/Cole, 1981). Reprinted by permission.

Studies show that high self-monitors are most adept at detecting impression management by others.

---

ethnic groups. In fact, he was so good at it that in watching silent films of his campaign speeches, it is easy to guess whose vote he was soliciting.

Of course, such highly skilled performances are the exception rather than the rule. And people differ in the extent to which they can and do exercise control over their self-presentations. It is the high self-monitoring individuals among us who are particularly talented in this regard. When asked to describe high self-monitoring individuals, their friends say that they are good at learning which behavior is appropriate in social situations, have good self-control of their emotional expression, and can effectively use this ability to create the impression they want. They are particularly skilled at intentionally expressing and

---

MONITOR YOUR SELF

On the scale I have developed to measure self-monitoring, actors are usually high scorers, as are many obese people, who tend to be very sensitive about the way they appear to others. For much the same reason, politicians and trial lawyers would almost certainly be high scorers. Recent immigrants eager to assimilate, black freshmen in a predominantly white college, and military personnel stationed abroad are also likely to score high on the scale.

The Self-Monitoring Scale measures how concerned people are with the impression they are making on others, as well as their ability to control and modify their behavior to fit the situation. I believe that it defines a distinct domain of personality that is quite different from the traits probed by other standard scales.

Several studies show that skill at

self-monitoring is not associated with exceptional intelligence or with a particular social class. Nor is it related, among other things, to being highly anxious or extremely self-conscious, to being an extravert, or to having a strong need for approval. They may be somewhat power-oriented or Machiavellian, but high self-monitoring individuals do not necessarily have high scores on the "Mach" scale, a measure of Machiavellianism developed by Richard Christie of Columbia University. (Two items from the scale: "The best way to handle people is to tell them what they want" and "Anyone who completely trusts anyone else is asking for trouble.") The steely-eyed Machiavellians are more manipulative, detached, and amoral than high self-monitoring individuals.

The Self-Monitoring Scale describes a unique trait and has proved to be both statistically valid and reliable, in tests on various samples.

At left is a 10-item abbreviated version of the Self-Monitoring Scale that will give readers some idea of whether they are low or high self-monitoring individuals. If you would like to test your self-monitoring tendencies, follow the instructions and then consult the scoring key.   —**M.S.**

These statements concern personal reactions to a number of different situations. No two statements are exactly alike, so consider each statement carefully before answering. If a statement is true, or mostly true, as applied to you, circle the T. If a statement is false, or not usually true, as applied to you, circle the F.

1. I find it hard to imitate the behavior of other people.   T F
2. I guess I put on a show to impress or entertain people.   T F
3. I would probably make a good actor.   T F
4. I sometimes appear to others to be experiencing deeper emotions than I actually am.   T F
5. In a group of people I am rarely the center of attention.   T F
6. In different situations and with different people, I often act like very different persons.   T F
7. I can only argue for ideas I already believe.   T F
8. In order to get along and be liked, I tend to be what people expect me to be rather than anything else.   T F
9. I may deceive people by being friendly when I really dislike them.   T F
10. I'm not always the person I appear to be.   T F

SCORING: Give yourself one point for each of questions 1, 5 and 7 that you answered F. Give yourself one point for each of the remaining questions that you answered T. Add up your points. If you are a good judge of yourself and scored 7 or above, you are probably a high self-monitoring individual; 3 or below, you are probably a low self-monitoring individual.

High self-monitors may prefer as friends those who avoid strategic posturing—in others words, low self-monitors.

accurately communicating a wide variety of emotions both vocally and facially. As studies by Richard Lippa of California State University at Fullerton have shown, they are usually such polished actors that they can effectively adopt the mannerisms of a reserved, withdrawn, and introverted individual and then do an abrupt about-face and portray, just as convincingly, a friendly, outgoing, and extraverted personality.

High self-monitoring individuals are also quite likely to seek out information about appropriate patterns of self-presentation. They invest considerable effort in attempting to "read" and understand others. In an experiment I conducted with Tom Monson (then one of my graduate students), various cues were given to students involved in group discussions as to what was socially appropriate behavior in the situation. For example, some of them thought that their taped discussions would be played back to fellow students; in those circumstances, I assumed they would want their opinions to appear as autonomous as possible. Others believed that their discussions were completely private; there, I assumed they would be most concerned with maintaining harmony and agreement in the group. High self-monitoring individuals were keenly attentive to these differences; they conformed with the group

when conformity was the most appropriate behavior and did not conform when they knew that the norms of the larger student audience would favor autonomy in the face of social pressure. Low self-monitoring individuals were virtually unaffected by the differences in social setting: presumably, their self-presentations were more accurate reflections of their personal attitudes and dispositions. Thus, as we might have guessed, people who are most skilled in the arts of impression management are also most likely to practice it.

Although high self-monitoring individuals are well skilled in the arts of impression management, we should not automatically assume that they necessarily use these skills for deceptive or manipulative purposes. Indeed, in their relationships with friends and acquaintances, high self-monitoring individuals are eager to use their self-monitoring abilities to promote smooth social interactions.

We can find some clues to this motive in the way high self-monitoring individuals tend to react to, and cope with, unfamiliar and unstructured social settings. In a study done at the University of Wisconsin, psychologists William Ickes and Richard Barnes arranged for pairs of strangers to spend time together in a waiting room, ostensibly to wait for an experiment to begin. The researchers then recorded the verbal and nonverbal behavior of each pair over a five-minute period, using video and audio tapes. All possible pairings of same-sex undergraduates at high, moderate, and low levels of self-monitoring were represented. Researchers scrutinized the tapes for evidence of the impact of self-monitoring on spontaneous encounters between strangers.

In these meetings, as in so many other aspects of their lives, high self-monitoring individuals suffered little or no shyness. Soon after meeting the other person, they took an active and controlling role in the conversation. They were inclined to talk first and to initiate subsequent conversational sequences. They also felt, and were seen by their partners to have, a greater need to talk. Their partners also viewed them as having been the more directive member of the pair. It was as if high self-monitoring individuals were particularly concerned about

WILLIAM JAMES ON THE ROLES WE PLAY

A man has as many social selves as there are individuals who recognize him and carry an image of him in their mind . . . . But as the individuals who carry the images form naturally into classes, we may practically say that he has as many different social selves as there are distinct *groups* of persons about whose opinions he cares. He generally shows a different side of himself to each of these different groups. Many a youth who is demure enough before his parents and teachers swears and swaggers like a pirate among his 'tough' young friends. We do not show ourselves to our children as to our club companions, to our masters and employers as to our intimate friends. From this there results what practically is a division of the man into several selves; and this may be a discordant splitting, as where one is afraid to let one set of his acquaintances know him as he is elsewhere; or it may be a perfectly harmonious division of labor, as where one tender to his children is stern to the soldiers or prisoners under his command."

—William James
The Principles of Psychology, 1890

For a defendant on trial, it may take as much work to present a truthful image to the jury as a deceptive one.

---

managing their behavior in order to create, encourage, and maintain a smooth flow of conversation. Perhaps this quality may help self-monitoring people to emerge as leaders in groups, organizations, and institutions.

Detecting Impression Management In Others

High self-monitoring individuals are also adept at detecting impression management in others. To demonstrate this finely tuned ability, three communications researchers at the University of Minnesota made use of videotaped excerpts from the television program "To Tell the Truth." On this program, one of the three guest contestants (all male in the excerpts chosen for the study) is the "real Mr. X." The other two who claim to be the real Mr. X are, of course, lying. Participants in the study watched each excerpt and then tried to identify the real Mr. X. High self-monitoring individuals were much more accurate than their low self-monitoring counterparts in correctly identifying the real Mr. X. and in seeing through the deception of the other two contestants.

Not only are high self-monitoring individuals able to see beyond the masks of deception successfully but they are also keenly attentive to the actions of other people as clues to their underlying intentions. E. E. Jones and Roy Baumeister of Princeton University had college students watch a videotaped discussion between two men who either agreed or disagreed with each other. The observers were aware that one man (the target person) had been instructed either to gain the affection or to win the respect of the other. Low self-monitoring observers tended to accept behavior at face value. They found themselves attracted to the agreeable person, whether or not he was at-

tempting to ingratiate himself with his discussion partner. In contrast, high self-monitoring observers were acutely sensitive to the motivational context within which the target person operated. They liked the target better if he was disagreeable when trying to ingratiate himself. But when he sought respect, they were more attracted to him if he chose to be agreeable. Jones and Baumeister suggest that high self-monitoring observers regarded agreeableness as too blatant a ploy in gaining affection and autonomy as an equally obvious route to respect. Perhaps the high self-monitoring individuals felt that they themselves would have acted with greater subtlety and finesse.

Even more intriguing is Jones's and Baumeister's speculation—and I share their view—that high self-monitoring individuals prefer to live in a stable, predictable social environment populated by people whose actions consistently and accurately reflect their true attitudes and feelings. In such a world, the consistency and predictability of the actions of others would be of great benefit to those who tailor and manage their own self-presentation in social situations. From this perspective, it becomes quite understandable that high self-monitoring individuals may be especially fond of those who avoid strategic posturing. Furthermore, they actually may prefer as friends those comparatively low in self-monitoring.

How can we know when strangers and casual acquaintances are engaged in self-monitoring? Are there some channels of expression and communication that are more revealing than others about a person's true, inner "self," even when he or she is practicing impression management?

Both scientific and everyday observers of human behavior have suggested that nonverbal behavior—facial expressions, tone of voice, and body movements—reveals meaningful in-

formation about a person's attitudes, feelings, and motives. Often, people who engage in self-monitoring for deceptive purposes are less skilled at controlling their body's expressive movements. Accordingly, the body may be a more revealing source of information than the face for detecting those who engage in self-monitoring and impression management.

More than one experiment shows how nonverbal behavior can betray the true attitude of those attempting impression management. Shirley Weitz of the New School for Social Research reasoned that on college campuses where there are strong normative pressures supporting a tolerant and liberal value system, all students would avoid saying anything that would indicate racial prejudice—whether or not their private attitudes supported such behavior. In fact, she found that among "liberal" white males at Harvard University, the most prejudiced students (as determined by behavioral measures of actual attempts to avoid interaction with blacks) bent over backwards to *verbally* express liking and friendship for a black in a simulated interracial encounter. However, their *nonverbal* behaviors gave them away. Although the prejudiced students made every effort to say kind and favorable things, they continued to do so in a cool and distant tone of voice. It was as if they knew the words but not the music: they knew *what* to say, but not *how* to say it.

Another way that prejudice can be revealed is in the physical distance people maintain between themselves and the target of their prejudice. To demonstrate this phenomenon, psychologist Stephen Morin arranged for college students to be interviewed about their attitudes toward homosexuality. Half the interviewers wore "Gay and Proud" buttons and mentioned their association with the As-

High self-monitoring people may pay a price: they may be unable to communicate their private feelings.

sociation of Gay Psychologists. The rest wore no buttons and simply mentioned that they were graduate students working on theses. Without the students' knowledge, the distance they placed their chairs from the interviewer was measured while the interviews were going on. The measure of social distance proved to be highly revealing. When the student and the interviewer were of the same sex, students tended to establish almost a foot more distance between themselves and the apparently gay interviewers. They placed their chairs an average of 32 inches away from apparently gay interviewers, but only 22 inches away from apparently nongay interviewers. Interestingly, most of the students expressed tolerant, and at times favorable, attitudes toward gay people in general. However, the distances they chose to put between themselves and the interviewers they thought gay betrayed underlying negative attitudes.

Impression Managers' Dilemmas

The well-developed skills of high self-monitoring individuals ought to give them the flexibility to cope quickly and effectively with a diversity of social roles. They can choose with skill and grace the self-presentation appropriate to each of a wide variety of social situations. But what happens when the impression manager must effectively present a true and honest image to other people?

Consider the case of a woman on trial for a crime that she did not commit. Her task on the witness stand is to carefully present herself so that everything she does and says communicates to the jurors clearly and unambiguously her true innocence, so that they will vote for her acquittal. Chances are good, however, that members of the jury are somewhat skeptical of the defendant's claims of

innocence. After all, they might reason to themselves, the district attorney would not have brought this case to trial were the state's case against her not a convincing one.

The defendant must carefully manage her verbal and nonverbal behaviors so as to ensure that even a skeptical jury forms a true impression of her innocence. In particular, she must avoid the pitfalls of an image that suggests that "she doth protest her innocence too much and therefore must be guilty." To the extent that our defendant skillfully practices the art of impression management, she will succeed in presenting herself to the jurors as the honest person that she truly is.

It often can take as much work to present a truthful image as to present a deceptive one. In fact, in this case, just being honest may not be enough when facing skeptical jurors who may bend over backwards to interpret any and all of the defendant's behavior—nervousness, for example—as a sign of guilt.

The message from research on impression management is a clear one. Some people are quite flexible in their self-presentation. What effects do these shifts in public appearance have on the more private realities of self-concept? In some circumstances, we are persuaded by our own appearances: we become the persons we appear to be. This phenomenon is particularly likely to occur when the image we present wins the approval and favor of those around us.

In an experiment conducted at Duke University by psychologists E. E. Jones, Kenneth Gergen, and Keith Davis, participants who had been instructed to win the approval of an interviewer presented very flattering images of themselves. Half the participants (chosen at random) then received favorable reactions from their interviewers; the rest did not. All the participants later were asked to esti-

mate how accurately and honestly their self-descriptions had mirrored their true personalities.

Those who had won the favor of their interviewers considered their self-presentations to have been the most honest of all. One interpretation of this finding is that those people were operating with rather pragmatic definitions of self-concept: that which produced the most positive results was considered to be an accurate reflection of the inner self.

The reactions of other people can make it all the more likely that we become what we claim to be. Other people may accept our self-presentations at face value; they may then treat us as if we really were the way we pretend to be. For example, if I act as if I like Chris, chances are Chris will like me. Chris will probably treat me in a variety of friendly ways. As a result of Chris's friendliness, I may come to like Chris, even though I did not in the first place. The result, in this case, may be beneficial to both parties. In other circumstances, however, the skilled impression manager may pay an emotional price.

High self-monitoring orientation may be purchased at the cost of having one's actions reflect and communicate very little about one's private attitudes, feelings, and dispositions. In fact, as I have seen time and again in my research with my former graduate students Beth Tanke and Bill Swann, correspondence between private attitudes and public behavior is often minimal for high self-monitoring individuals. Evidently, the words and deeds of high self-monitoring individuals may reveal precious little information about their true inner feelings and attitudes.

Yet, it is almost a canon of modern psychology that a person's ability to reveal a "true self" to intimates is essential to emotional health. Sidney Jourard, one of the first psychologists

For high self-monitors, a person may have not one but many selves: "I am me, the me I am right now."

to hold that view, believed that only through self-disclosure could we achieve self-discovery and self-knowledge: "Through my self-disclosure, I let others know my soul. They can know it, really know it, only as I make it known. In fact, I am beginning to suspect that I can't even know *my own soul* except as I disclose it. I suspect that I will know myself "for real" at the exact moment that I have succeeded in making it known through my disclosure to another person."

Only low self-monitoring individuals may be willing or able to live their lives according to Jourard's prescriptions. By contrast, high self-monitoring individuals seem to embody Erving Goffman's view of human nature. For him, the world of appearances appears to be all, and the "soul" is illusory. Goffman defines social interactions as a theatrical performance in which each individual acts out a "line." A line is a set of carefully chosen verbal and nonverbal acts that express one's self. Each of us, in Goffman's view, seems to be merely the sum of our various performances.

What does this imply for the sense of self and identity associated with low and high self-monitoring individuals?

I believe that high self‑monitor-

ing individuals and low self-monitoring individuals have very different ideas about what constitutes a self and that their notions are quite well-suited to how they live. High self-monitoring individuals regard themselves as rather flexible and adaptive people who tailor their social behavior shrewdly and pragmatically to fit appropriate conditions. They believe that a person is whoever he appears to be in any particular situation: "I am me, the me I am right now." This self-image fits well with the way high self-monitoring individuals present themselves to the world. It allows them to act in ways that are consistent with how they believe they should act.

By contrast, low self-monitoring individuals have a firmer, more single-minded idea of what a self should be. They value and strive for congruence between "who they are" and "what they do" and regard their actions as faithful reflections of how they feel and think. For them, a self is a single identity that must not be compromised for other people or in certain situations. Indeed, this view of the self parallels the low self-monitoring individual's consistent and stable self-presentation.

What is important in understanding oneself and others, then, is not the

elusive question of whether there is a quintessential self, but rather, understanding how different people define those attributes of their behavior and experience that they regard as "me." Theory and research on self-monitoring have attempted to chart the processes by which beliefs about the self are actively translated into patterns of social behavior that reflect self-conceptions. From this perspective, the processes of self-monitoring are the processes of self—a system of operating rules that translate self-knowledge into social behavior.   Ω

Mark Snyder is professor of psychology at the University of Minnesota in Minneapolis, where he teaches a graduate-level course called "The Self." In addition to his research on self-monitoring, he is studying stereotypes and the effect of stereotypes on social relationships.

For further information, read:

Gergen, Kenneth. *The Concept of Self*, Holt, Rinehart & Winston, 1971, paper, $4.50.

Goffman, Erving. *The Presentation of Self in Everyday Life*, Doubleday (reprint of 1959 edition), paper, $2.50.

Snyder, Mark. "Self-Monitoring Processes," in *Advances in Experimental Social Psychology, Vol. 12*, Leonard Berkowitz, ed:, Academic Press, 1979, $24.

Snyder, Mark. "Cognitive, Behavioral, and Interpersonal Consequences of Self-Monitoring," in *Advances in the Study of Communication and Affect, Vol. 5: Perception of Emotion in Self and Others*, Plenum, 1979, $24.50.

Snyder, Mark. "Self-Monitoring of Expressive Behavior," *Journal of Personality and Social Psychology*, 30(1974): 526-537.

Shyness

by Philip G. Zimbardo

56

I remember as far back as 4 years old, some of the stuff I use to do to avoid seeing people that came to visit us. They were people I knew, like cousins, aunts, uncles, friends of the family, and even my brothers and sister. I hid in clothes baskets, hampers, closets, in sleeping bags, under beds and there's probably an endless list, all because I was scared of people.

As I grew up, things got worse.

Worse? It's hard not to chuckle at what sounds like the start of a Woody Allen routine. But our laughter is clearly a defense against empathizing too closely with this painful memory of a high-school student. We'd like to believe she's exaggerating; life just couldn't be that bad. But for many shy people, it clearly is.

My brother, who had to wear leg braces to correct the damage of infantile paralysis, developed this same morbid fear of people. Whenever there was a knock at the door, George would quickly count to see if all family members were present and accounted for. If they were, he would scurry to his post under the bed or to an even safer retreat behind the locked bathroom door. Only after much begging and pleading would he relent and come out to be greeted by a neighbor or visiting relative from out of town.

My mother, a compassionate woman gifted with insights into the workings of human nature, decided that she must help George before his shyness got completely out of hand. His agonies had persisted even after he no longer had to wear the leg braces. Convinced that he should be with other children his own age, she persuaded the public school to enroll George, although he was only four-and-a-half years old and it was already the middle of the term. As my mother relates:

He cried and sobbed nonstop for nearly that whole first day, clinging to my dress in near terror. Whenever the teacher or another child looked his way, he'd bury his head in my lap or look at the ceiling. But when the class was being told a story or playing musical toys, his curiosity got the better of him and he couldn't help but look and listen.

The idea came to me that George would not be so self-conscious if he could become invisible, if he could watch and join in the action but not be watched by the other children. Obviously he couldn't disappear; but he could do the next best thing—become a masked man like his hero on the radio, the Lone Ranger.

After dinner I encouraged George to help me make a hooded mask out of a brown paper shopping bag. We cut out eyes, a nose, and a mouth and colored it a little to make it attractive. He tried it on, liked it, and made me repeat over and over, "Who is that masked child?" Gleefully he'd reply, "The Lone Ranger," or "Mr. Nobody," or "None of your business," or he'd just roar like a lion. Sometimes he'd remove the hood to reassure me it was still him.

His teacher agreed to give my plan a try; in fact, she did more than that, she made it work. She told the other children that the new child would be wearing a special mask and they were not to try to remove it, but just to enjoy playing with this masked child. Surprisingly, this unusual approach worked. George could be part of the class, though set apart. He could imagine being unrecognized when he wanted to be without having to hide himself. Gradually he moved closer to the other children and eventually, in a few weeks, was lured into play.

He stayed on in kindergarten for another year, and his confidence grew as the classroom routine became more familiar. But still the mask—on every morning before class and off only when his brother arrived to take him home.

Then the big day came at the end of the year when the class circus was to be presented for the parents of the graduating kindergartners. Since George had been through it last year, he was an old hand at the festivities. "Would you like to be circus master?" the teacher asked him. He jumped up and down with joy. "George, you know that the circus master wears a top hat and a fancy costume, but not a mask," she wisely continued, "so, if you want to be the circus master, you'll have to exchange your mask for this outfit. Okay?"

And there George was, not only part of the group, but leading the circus. Shouting to look here and for everyone to notice that! No need for the mask any longer, he was on his way to becoming a happier, healthier child. Although he was never totally outgoing, he did develop close friendships with boys and girls, and was later elected to class office in junior and senior high school.

George's need to wear a paper bag over his head for a year and a half might seem bizarre. But this ingenious solution enabled him gradually to relate effectively to others and led to the day when he could take off the mask and be himself. The paper bag was a successful solution for an extremely shy child. Others aren't so lucky. They grow into adulthood without ever learning to deal with this agonizing problem.

Shyness can be a mental handicap as crippling as the most severe of physical handicaps, and its consequences can be devastating:

- Shyness makes it difficult to meet new people, make new friends, or enjoy potentially good experiences.
- It prevents you from speaking up for your rights and expressing your own opinions and values.
- Shyness limits positive evaluations by others of your personal strengths.
- It encourages self-consciousness and an excessive preoccupation with your own reactions.
- Shyness makes it hard to think clearly and communicate effectively.
- Negative feelings like depression, anxiety, and loneliness typically accompany shyness.

To be shy is to be afraid of people, especially people who for some reason are emotionally threatening: strangers because of their novelty or uncertainty, authorities who wield power, members of the opposite sex who represent potential intimate encounters. George and the young girl whose comments opened the chapter both felt threatened by virtually everyone. They provide rather dramatic examples of shyness. But the everyday garden variety of this problem quietly intrudes itself into all of our lives.

Have you ever arrived at a party in full swing and discovered that the only person you know is the hostess —and she's not in sight? "Who are *you*?" someone asks and only invisible butterflies come out of your mouth, "Let's get to know one another better by telling our names and something personal about ourselves." Immediately you're into full dress rehearsal: "My name is . . . (damn it, oh yes) . . . Phil Zimbardo. I am a . . . a . . . person (no that's not personal enough— why didn't I go to the movies?)." Once again, without gusto, "My name is, uh . . . ! !" Such common experiences make it possible for those people who are not shy to at least appreciate some of the agonies that shy people go through.

Despite the negative consequences and the intensity of shyness, the problem can be overcome. But to do so, it's necessary to recognize the basis of the shyness and then tailor an appropriate program to alter its foundation.

Shyness is a fuzzy concept; the closer we look, the more varieties of shyness we discover. So before we can even begin to consider what to do about it, we have to know more about what shyness is. The Oxford English dictionary tells us that the word's earliest recorded use was in an Anglo Saxon poem written around 1000 A.D., in which it meant "easily frightened." "To be shy" is to be "difficult of approach, owing to timidity, caution or distrust." The shy person is "cautiously averse in encountering or having to do with some specified person or thing." "Wary in speech or action, shrinking from self-assertion; sensitively timid," the shy individual may be "retiring or reserved from difference" or from a different mold, "of questionable character, disreputable, 'shady.' " Webster's defines shyness as being "uncomfortable in the presence of others."

But somehow such definitions don't seem to add much to common-sense knowledge. No single definition can be adequate, because shyness means different things to different people. It is a complex condition that has a whole range of effects—from mild discomfort to unreasonable fear of people to extreme neurosis. To begin to understand better this phenomenon, we gave the Stanford Shyness Survey to nearly 5000 people.

Do you presently consider yourself to be a shy person?

_____ yes _____ no

(Well, *do* you?)

If you answered "no," was there ever a period in your life during which you considered yourself to be a shy person?

_____ yes _____ no

In our survey, we sidestepped the issue of providing a specific definition of shyness. Instead, we allowed each person to adopt his or her own definition. First, we asked people to accept or reject the shy label. Then we wanted to know what went into that decision. We asked what kinds of people and situations make them feel shy, and what thoughts, feelings, actions, and physical symptoms were associated with their shyness.

IT'S A UNIVERSAL EXPERIENCE

The most basic finding of our research establishes that shyness is common, widespread, and universal. More than 80 percent of those questioned reported that they were *shy at some point in their lives*, either now, in the past, or always. Of these, over 40 percent considered themselves *presently shy*—that means four out of every ten people you meet, or 84 million Americans!

For some people, shyness has long been a regular intruder in their everyday lives. About a quarter reported themselves *chronically shy*, now and always. Of these, a lonely 4 percent—*true blue shys*—told us that their self-definition of shyness was based on the fact that they were shy *all* of the time, in *all* situations, and with virtually *all* people.

The prevalence of shyness varies from culture to culture and with different types of people. However, we have never found a group of people where fewer than a quarter declared themselves presently shy, and, in fact, with some groups of people, like junior-high-school girls and students from some Oriental cultures, that statistic jumps to 60 percent. The percentage of true-blue shys is never less than 2 percent of any group we have studied, and may go as high as 10 percent in some groups, like the Japanese.

In deciding whether or not to call themselves shy, people who answered the survey used as one index how *often* they felt shy. About a third of the people had a sense of feeling shy at least half the time, in more situations than not. Over 60 percent reported being shy only occasionally, but they viewed these times as being sufficiently significant to label themselves shy. For example, you might be shy only in public speaking, but that could be enough to cause serious problems if you have to give reports in public, as many students and business people must do.

Fewer than 20 percent answering the survey reported that they do not label themselves as shy. Whatever shyness meant to each of them, they felt it didn't apply as a personal trait. But interestingly, most of these people acknowledged reacting with such symptoms of shyness as blushing, heart pounding, and "butterflies in the stomach" in certain social settings. In other words, some people and some situations made them react with the kind of thoughts, feelings, and actions that characterize the shy person. These *situationally* shy people do not see themselves as shy, but rather see certain external events, such as walking into a room of strangers, as causing temporary discomfort. This distinction between those who are ready to label *themselves* as shy and those who label only their *reactions to some situations* as shy is an important one, which we will explore more in a subsequent chapter.

To say shyness is a universal experience is a rather broad generalization, but one with a solid basis. Only about 7 percent of all Americans sampled reported that they have never, ever experienced feelings of shyness. Similarly, in other cultures, only a small minority of people claim to have never personally experienced shyness.

Shyness is more prevalent among schoolchildren than adults, for many currently not-shy adults have managed to overcome their childhood shyness. Nevertheless, our research emphatically rejects the myth that shyness is only a childhood affliction. It may be more obvious to us in children, because they generally are under closer daily scrutiny than are adults. But a substantial portion of the adult population continues to be shy. Robert

Young, TV's beloved Dr. Marcus Welby, is among those.

> I've always been shy. As a kid, I was even afraid of the teacher. Later I grew to be one of those tall, skinny youngsters who don't have the looks or the weight for football and thus weren't automatic high-school heroes. In my teens, that was important.

Some provocative evidence suggests that adolescence may generate more shyness among girls than boys. In a sample of elementary-school youngsters from the fourth, fifth, and sixth grades, the average prevalence of those who were presently shy was 42 percent—like the original survey. These boys and girls were equally likely to label themselves as shy. But, when we look at seventh and eighth graders, not only does the average level of shyness escalate to 54 percent, but it is the teenage girls who account for this increase. It may be that the need to be popular in school and to be considered physically (sexually) attractive by the opposite sex is programmed more forcefully into our teenage girls than boys. A fourteen-year-old girl writes of her self-conscious anguish:

> I get very nervous and my head starts to itch very badly and I just keep scratching it like a fool. I don't know how to act around people. I act differently at home than I do at school. I don't even dress the way I want to.

And, from a letter to Ann Landers, we see the plight of the "mixed-up" teenage girl who feels "different" from her peers and longs to become just like them—yet maybe a little more special.

> Dear Ann Landers: I hope you won't throw my letter away just because it's from a mixed-up teenager. I really feel yucky and need help. My main problem is I don't like my personality—I try to be overly friendly to cover up my shyness and then I act loud. I'm jealous of certain girls and wish I was like them but when I try to be, it doesn't come off.
>
> Some days I feel popular just because a certain guy says hello or smiles at me. The next day I'm miserable because a group of girls are huddled in a corner and I think they are laughing at me behind my back. My grades are O.K. but they could be better. Mom says I'm disorganized. She yells because I pay so much attention to my hair instead of my homework. This is my fourth letter to you. I've thrown all the others away, but this one is going into the mail no matter what. Signed, Different.

More women are shy than men, right? Wrong! Another false generalization, probably based on observations that men tend to be more assertive, aggressive, and obvious in social encounters. Our information indicates no difference between the sexes in prevalence of shyness. In fact, a slightly higher percentage of college men than college women report being shy, but this slight sex difference is in the other direction for some noncollege groups, and varies according to the culture investigated.

Shyness moves in mysterious ways, afflicting even those who have never been shy before. Newcomers to shyness make up slightly less than half of all those who are presently shy. Many of these are young adults who have not been shy as children, but for some reason have recently turned shy.

Still, shyness can be conquered, set aside, or outgrown. Some 40 percent reported that they used to be shy but are no longer so, a reassuring indication. Based in part on the experience of these shyness "has beens," we may be able to offer useful advice to the chronically and presently shy.

HOW DOES SHYNESS AFFECT PEOPLE?

We are slowly beginning to gain some understanding of shyness. Although we can't define exactly what it is, we do know that it is prevalent. Another clue to this complex condition may be uncovered by examining how shyness affects different people. Shyness spans a wide psychological continuum: it can vary from occasional feelings of awkwardness in the presence of others all the way to traumatic episodes of anxiety that totally disrupt a person's life. For some people, shyness seems to be a chosen, preferred style of life: for others, it is an imposed life sentence without possibility of parole.

At one end of the continuum are those who feel more comfortable with books, ideas, objects, or nature than with other people. Writers, scientists, inventors, forest rangers, and explorers might well have chosen a life's work that enables them to spend much of their time in a world only sparsely populated with humans. They are largely introverts, and association with others holds limited appeal compared to their needs for privacy and solitude. Like Greta Garbo, they would rather be alone.

Indeed, many people today are rediscovering the attractive quality of Thoreau's solitary life at Walden Pond. But even within this narrow slice of the shyness continuum, there are gradations from those who can easily relate to people when necessary, to others who find interaction difficult, because they don't know how to make small talk, address a group of people, dance, or handle a formal dinner with ease.

The middle range of shyness includes the bulk of shy people, those who feel intimidated and awkward in certain situations with certain types of people. Their discomfort is strong enough to disturb their social lives and inhibit their functioning, making it difficult or impossible to say what they think or do what they'd like to do.

This type of anxiety may take the form of blushing and obvious embarrassment, as a young business executive describes:

> Throughout my thirty-three years I have been subject to excessive blushing as an especially incapacitating symptom of shyness. Although my drive and persistence has resulted in a Masters in Business Administration and a position as Assistant Vice President of a large, multibank holding company, the energy diverted by the shyness/blushing syndrome has undoubtedly prevented my movement into still higher responsibility.

Or this discomfort may be concealed behind an offensive attack that puts people off, as a writer reports:

> I barge in, hog conversations, rattle on endlessly making an ass and nuisance of myself, appearing to be insensitive to others, all for the same reasons others attempt to fade into the woodwork. My underlying terror of being in public is no less, and my problems are no less serious than those of wall flowers.

Even San Francisco lawyer Melvin Belli, who is noted for his dramatic courtroom tactics, admits that not only has he "often been shy," but that he "became flamboyant to hide shyness."

Since the same source of shyness—a fear of people—produces such different reactions, a person's outward behavior is not always a reliable indicator of how shy he or she really feels. Shyness often has an impact on the way we act, but not necessarily in obvious or direct ways. Ultimately, you are shy if you *think* you are, regardless of how you act in public.

People in the middle range of the shyness continuum generally are shy because they lack social skills, and/or they lack confidence in themselves. Some don't have the social skills essential for keeping the machinery of human relationships functioning smoothly. They don't know how to start a conversation or ask for a raise or speak up in class. Others don't have the confidence to do what they know is right. What this lack of self-confidence can do even to a very intelligent person is illustrated by the account of a young woman whose shyness forced her to drop out of law school:

> I started law school in September, after scoring highly on the law board exams and maintaining a 3.94 [near straight A] grade-point average in college and being accepted to three law schools with no difficulty. But I withdrew before the first quarter was over. I didn't quit because I was afraid of putting in the many study hours, but because I am so shy that I could not take sitting in class and hoping (praying) that I would not be called on. This is true despite the fact that I prepared the work and knew the answers!

At the far end of the shyness continuum are those individuals whose fear of people knows no bounds—the chronically shy. They experience extreme dread whenever called on to do something in front of people, and are rendered so helpless by their overwhelming anxiety that their only alternative is to flee and hide. These incapacitating consequences of extreme shyness are not limited to the young or to students. Nor do they dissipate over time. A sixty-four-year-old woman writes:

> I have lived a whole lifetime of shyness. It was years before I could accept myself enough to believe that some person would think I was worthy of being his wife. I felt inadequate. I felt I wasn't good enough. I was considered antisocial. I couldn't relax with people. I never entertained my husband's friends. I was afraid of being no good, poor sport, anything. So if I didn't entertain them, I wouldn't be known. Finally, I was a cast-off, nobody liked me, including my husband. He divorced me and that was the end.

At its worst, shyness may become a severe form of neurosis, a mind paralysis that can result in depression and may eventually be a significant influence in suicide. A businesswoman who describes herself as an attractive, young-looking fifty-year-old responded to a radio talk-show discussion on shyness with this shattering glimpse into her psyche:

> I am lonely beyond belief. I live in complete solitude without a friend in the world, neither male nor female. I have been betrayed many times over and my experiences in life have left me very unhappy and bitter. I spend the holidays in complete solitude. It is a period of great sadness and depression for me and I dread each approaching holiday more and more, because of the intensifications of my loneliness at a time when most people are in the company of friends and relatives. I often think of ending my life, but lack the guts to go through with it.

For these people and for people in every segment of the continuum, shyness is a personal problem. Not a little irritation, not a minor perturbation, but a real problem.

THE POSITIVE SIDE OF SHYNESS

Although many of these stories and statistics are distressing, we need to remember that shyness has many favorable aspects, too. Between 10 and 20 percent of all those who are shy *like* it. They prefer shyness because they have discovered its positive side.

"Reserved," "retiring," "unassuming," "modest" are all descriptions of shy people which carry a favorable connotation. Moreover, when polished, such a demeanor is often considered "sophisticated" or "high class." David Niven, Prince Charles, Katherine Hepburn, and Jacqueline Onassis come to mind as typical of this "I'd rather be somewhat shy" type.

A British psychologist writing in 1927 offers us a most delightful view on the virtues of shyness:

> Shyness is so common, at least in this country, that we tend to accept it as something inborn, as a characteristic part of the charm of youth, and as evidence, when it persists into later years, of a certain fineness of character; it seems even to be a trait, perhaps not wholly to be deplored, in the national temperament.

Shyness makes one appear discreet and seriously introspective. It also increases one's personal privacy and offers pleasures that only solitude can bring. Shy people do not intimidate or hurt others as overbearing, more forceful people may do. Isaac Bashevis Singer, the author, puts it eloquently:

> I don't think that people should get over being shy. It is a blessing in disguise. The shy person is the opposite of the aggressive person. Shy people are seldom the great sinners. They allow society to remain in peace.

Another advantage of shyness is that one can be more selective in relating to others. Shyness offers an opportunity to stand back, observe, and then act cautiously and deliberately. Shy people can also feel secure in the knowledge that they will never be considered obnoxious, overaggressive, or pretentious. Similarly, the shy person can easily avoid interpersonal conflicts and, in some cases, may be valued as a good listener.

A particularly interesting positive outcome of being shy is the anonymity and protection it provides. Shyness itself can serve as a mask to keep a person from being noticed, from standing out in the crowd. Under conditions of anonymity, people often feel liberated from the restraints of what they "ought" and "should" do. Behavior is freed from the limitations usually imposed by social convention. The Mardi Gras and Halloween offer vivid examples of the marked changes in personality that the anonymity of masks and costumes encourages.[8]

In putting my shy brother behind a mask, my mother intuitively knew that he, too, would feel freer to act. Of course, to the other children he was anything but anonymous. But their perspective was not his. And it is the subjective view that is most important in understanding shyness.

In questioning people about shyness, we have let them do the defining—telling it as they see it. We now know that shyness is prevalent, often a problem full of anxiety and grief, but for some a sought-after state of being.

57

Getting at the heart of
JEALOUS LOVE

BY VIRGINIA ADAMS

A central theme of myth, art, and psychoanalysis,
jealousy has lately come under closer scrutiny by social
psychologists. Recent studies clarify its symptoms, the circumstances
that trigger it, the link to self-esteem, and why men and
women behave differently under its influence.

Their names are Way, Azo, Laf, Lil, Tip Tye, Geo Logical, Brother Jud, and Even Eve. Calling themselves a Best Friend Identity Cluster (B-FIC), or the Purple Submarine, the five women and three men live together in two old Victorian houses in the Haight-Ashbury section of San Francisco. Nonmonogamous in their relationships, they pair off nightly according to a fixed sleeping schedule they describe as "nonpreferential" and "rotational." Members of the Purple Submarine—all heterosexual—are sexually faithful to one another, and they believe that through their experiment in group living, they have eliminated, or at least transcended, the age-old problem of sexual jealousy.

If so, their achievement is remarkable, for sexual jealousy was the undoing of numerous failed Utopias in the past and is assumed by many to be an all-but-universal emotion. "It is a tragic characteristic of all people, to be unable to share," the Viennese psychoanalyst Wilhelm Stekel once wrote. Or, as Jeff B. Bryson, a social psychologist at San Diego State University in California, says, "Jealousy is at least as common as chicken pox."

The Purple Submarine is one of two such groups that together form Kerista Village in San Francisco. An organization, not a place, Kerista Village is held together by the ideal of "polyfidelity," a word the Keristans coined to express their goal of loyalty to the group rather than to any one person (see box on page 308). Behavioral science has begun to take an interest in the nine-year-old Keristan venture, but knowledge about sexual jealousy is as yet too limited to explain how the crew of the Purple Submarine has routed jealousy—if, indeed, they have really done so.

Theories about jealousy abound. Most were derived from on-the-spot observations by anthropologists, armchair speculation by sociologists, or conclusions reached by psychoanalysts treating emotionally disturbed patients. "Unfortunately," a University of Maryland social psychologist named Gregory L. White wrote not long ago, "this theoretical fire has not produced much research heat." In fact, Bryson told the American Psychological Association a couple of years ago, "Some future historian, reviewing our scientific literature, would feel justified in presuming that jealousy was either nonexistent in our

society or, at most, experienced by an isolated subset of pathological individuals."

Finally, in the late 1970s, Bryson, White, Robert G. Bringle of Indiana-Purdue University at Indianapolis, and a few other social psychologists brought the rigor of the laboratory to bear on the study of sexual, or romantic, jealousy. They began by trying to define it, and soon found that there were almost as many definitions of jealousy as there were writers about it. It has been described, somewhat pretentiously, as "a cry of pain," "the fear of annihilation," and "the shadow of love." Almost certainly, it is not one emotion but many; definitions mention anger and anxiety; hatred and humiliation; shame, sorrow, and suspicion. Rather like love, Bryson suggests, jealousy is whatever a person chooses to label jealousy.

For research purposes, that is not very useful. Today, most social psychologists accept as basic the distinction psychoanalysts and sociologists have long made between envy, felt when a person covets what someone else has but claims no right to it, and jealousy, distinguished by fear of losing to someone else what rightfully belongs to the jealous person. Most psychologists also believe that jealousy entails a threat to self-esteem as well as to a valued relationship. It is agreed, too, that the threat may be actual, potential, or entirely imaginary.

Jealous people are unhappy people. They report more overall dissatisfaction with their lives than others do.

What the pioneers of jealousy research wanted to know was what kinds of people are most vulnerable to sexual jealousy; what circumstances are most likely to provoke it; what jealousy actually feels like; and what specific behavior stems from it. Several studies confirm the link between romantic jealousy and self-esteem. Others reveal marked sex differences. Women, for instance, are more likely than men are to try to make their partners jealous. And when an interloper threatens an intimate relationship, women generally react by trying to save the relationship, while men more often concentrate on saving face.

Who Gets Jealous? A New Study

The newest findings about sexual jealousy are just now being reported by the social psychologists Elliot Aronson of the University of California at Santa Cruz and Ayala Pines of the University of California at Berkeley. Their work relies chiefly on a "Sexual Jealousy Inventory," a compilation of more than 200 questions chosen by the researchers to elicit data on almost every conceivable aspect of jealousy and its presumed or possible antecedents and effects. The inventory includes numerous yes-or-no queries, such as, "Would you experience jealousy if you are at a party and don't know where your mate is?" Most questions, however, are answered by circling the number, on a scale of 1 to 7, that most nearly corresponds to the subject's attitude or experience.

So far, about 100 men and women ranging in age from their late 20s to their early 50s have filled out the inventory. Many were students; others were participants in a two-day discussion of romantic jealousy conducted by the researchers last year.

Statistical analysis of one sample of 53 subjects has yielded "correlations" between jealousy and certain personal characteristics, circumstances, and events. A correlation between two factors means that they occur together frequently; it does not prove that one causes the other. Aronson and Pines say the correlations are "highly significant," meaning they are probably not due to chance.

To begin with, the study supports the impression of other investigators (Bringle among them) that jealousy goes with feelings of insecurity and an unflattering self-image. The study also shows that the less education people have, the more often they feel jealous, conceivably because educational deficiencies may lower self-esteem.

If the Aronson and Pines findings are to be believed, people who feel jealous because of a mate's real or imagined infidelity may themselves be faithless. Subjects who admitted that they had betrayed their current sexual partner were very likely not only to feel insecure about their relationship but also to suffer often from jealousy. A possible explanation is that a person's own tendency to stray may lead to a suspicion that the partner is capable of yielding to similar tendencies.

Jealous people seem to be unhappy people. The men and women who reported the greatest overall dissatisfaction with their lives were those who felt jealous most often. People who said they were not happy with their partners were nevertheless very often jealous. That correlation struck Aronson and Pines as ironic, because a person in an unhappy relationship might be expected to feel indifferent toward a mate's dalliance. On the other hand, the causal sequence—if there is *any* causal connection between the two factors—may go in the other direction: perhaps jealousy makes a relationship unhappy, not the reverse.

Happy or not, jealous people apparently feel bound to their mates, no matter what alternatives might be open to them. According to Aronson and Pines, jealousy was most frequently experienced by the men and women who gave the most emphatic no's when asked, "If you found another person you could be intimate with, would you leave your present sexual partner?" A response of 1 stood for "definitely not," while 4 was labeled "perhaps," and 7 denoted "definitely." The ratings chosen by the most jealous subjects clustered at the low end of the scale.

Staying in a relationship a long time was strongly linked to an absence of jealous feelings. Subjects who rated themselves as very jealous people had been with their present partner an average of 58 months, while those who did not think of themselves as jealous had been with the same mate for 110 months. Like Bringle, Aronson and Pines found that a partner's own chronological age was important; younger people reported jealousy more often than did older ones.

Notably, it doesn't take much to stir up jealousy in a jealous person. The men and women who reported feeling jealous most often were those who replied yes to the question, "Would you experience jealousy when you call your mate and the phone is busy?" The often-jealous were also likely to admit that they felt pangs of jealousy when their telephone rang and the person on the other end either hung up without a word or else said, "Sorry, wrong number."

Yet another finding that may give jealous people pause: It is very difficult to conceal jealousy. Men and women who conceded that they were often jealous also reported that they knew their friends considered them so.

Gregory White has been studying jealousy since 1976, longer than Aronson and Pines. He is a highly prolific

POLYFIDELITY:
The Kerista Village Ideal

Don't bother looking up "polyfidelity" in the dictionary; it's not there. Ask Even Eve, one of the founders of Kerista Village, an egalitarian, Utopian community in San Francisco.

Even Eve is a native of Vermont, a writer, an artist, and the editor of two Kerista periodicals, *Utopian Eyes*, a magazine, and *Storefront Classroom*, a newspaper. She will explain that the coined word polyfidelity "describes a group of best friends, highly compatible, who live together as a family unit, with sexual intimacy occurring equally between all members of the opposite sex, no sexual involvement outside the group, an intention of lifetime involvement, and the intention to raise children together with multiple parenting."

Geo Logical, a former psychiatric nurse from Georgia, outlines the most sensational-sounding feature of Keristan life, the "balanced rotational sleeping pattern." All members of B-FICs, the Best Friend Identity Clusters that make up Kerista Village, follow such a cycle.

"It's simply a *sleeping* pattern, *not* a sex schedule," Geo says. "Having sexual intercourse or not having it is a private decision made by two individuals who are spending their night's horizontal time together. Such a decision is based on many variable factors—level of tiredness, wellness or illness, whether or not people have decided they will or will not have sexual intercourse during a woman's menstrual period."

"Polyfidelity: Beyond Jealousy and Possessiveness," reads the headline for an article in *Utopian Eyes*. The piece conveys the belief of the Keristans that their experiment in group living is successful.

"When we announce to people that we have lived for years without jealousy or possessiveness, most people think we must surely be exaggerating," Eve told *Psychology Today*. "Yet it is true. This is not to say we don't deal with problems of a psy-chological or interpersonal nature from time to time. . . . We do, but jealousy has not been one of them."

There are no twosomes in Kerista Village. "We feel it is humanly possible to have many primary relationships running simultaneously," Eve says. "To me, the erotic fantasy of sleeping with a variety of delightful men—all of whom I love—and living with a number of other marvelous female partners who are sleeping with the same people is extremely exciting. It is also very 'homey'; it is a family unit involving trust, fidelity, raising children." (So far, Kerista Village has one child, Eve's, with the biological father's identity presumably uncertain and all members of Eve's B-FIC acting as psychological parents. Another child was due this spring.)

Trying to make outsiders understand their multiple, "nonpreferential, rotational" relationships, Keristans like to draw analogies and to ask Socratic questions: "What if someone said to you that out of all the fruits that exist—bananas, pears, oranges, apples, strawberries, papa-ya, mangoes—you must choose *one* to eat to the exclusion of all others for the rest of your life. Which *one* would you choose?" And then: "You don't believe that nature's rotational fruit-production cycle interferes with your spontaneity?"

The Keristans range in age from 20 to 57, with most about 30. About half finished college, but few (apart from the nurse, an elementary school teacher, and an auditor) have ever pursued conventional careers.

The villagers have won few converts. Their maximum strength was 20, and now there are only 15 of them. Two have been with the organization since it was formed nine years ago; others have belonged for periods of six months to seven years.

What the Keristans call their "social laboratory" or "live-in test-tube" brings to mind nonmonogamous Utopias of the past that foundered after a few months or a few years: Oneida in the 19th century, which lasted for some 30 years, and some of the hippie communes of the 1960s. Why should Kerista Village succeed where they failed?

The new collectivists say the important factors are their devotion to Utopian ideals, their sharing of living space, their efforts to break with

Illustration by Jo Teodorescu

"To me, the erotic fantasy of sleeping with a variety of delightful men—all of whom I love—is extremely exciting."

the past, and, above all, their avoidance of romantic love.

Their ideals of sharing and equality reach beyond the sexual, and Keristans try to express them in a multiplicity of activities. They work at regular jobs or in Village-owned enterprises such as publishing, carpentry, gardening, home services, and repairs. They write and produce plays, make speeches, conduct seminars. They swim and prepare gourmet meals for themselves. In addition, Geo writes: "We keep our dishes washed and our laundry done." What they consider to be their uniqueness derives partly from the fact that, as the Kerista Village Handbook asserts, "judgment, morality, evaluation, and intellectuality are not dirty words in Kerista Village." Many similar-sounding but failed communes were "more into hedonism," Eve says.

The Best Friends are "not angry revolutionaries," do not feel alienated, and are by no means ascetics. "One of our mottoes, and the name of one of our oldest songs," the handbook says, "is 'If it ain't fun, it won't git done.'" Summing up, the handbook affirms that "we love our ideals above all else, and this is what makes all of our different love relationships, sex, and home lives so cozy, so indescribably delicious."

Eve also stresses the importance of the new beginning the Keristans believe they have made: "Ours is an alternative approach involving a complete restructuring of sexual attitudes, not to speak of attitudes toward many other things, and works best for people who are making a fresh, clean start in lifestyle. You begin a process of psychological transformation and preparation *before* entering into sexual relationships."

Still, the past can get in the way of the present; but the Keristans have found a remedy. Eve speaking again: "We do a lot of Gestalt work among

ourselves (we use our own term for it, Gestalt-O-Rama), some of which is aimed at learning more about past conditioning, so that we can become conscious of what's going on inside ourselves, and, eventually, overcome the pull of those parts of it that we don't like. In this process we've found that jealousy is inextricably interwoven with romantic love."

She goes on to explain why the group is opposed to romantic love and what they mean when they use the term. "I'm referring to the exclusive 'zap' sort of relationship so often depicted on film or TV. Those relationships are personality-centered rather than based on shared ideals and interests, and the pattern is that there can only be one primary involvement of this sort happening at a time. Since everyone believes this, people are naturally going to get worried when a partner strikes up a relationship with anyone else, since this implies that one person or the other is going to be in first place, and the original person might be replaced. Jealousy and possessiveness are thus obvious outcomes."

Elliot Aronson, a social psychologist who has met with members of Kerista, likes them, respects their sincerity ("They're not kooks"), and hopes to study the group to further his understanding of jealousy. But he does not think they have gone "beyond" jealousy and possessiveness. "I believe that preferentiality is part of the human condition," he says.

Skeptics, of course, might add that among human beings, romantic love is inevitable. On one occasion, the Keristans were trying to explain polyfidelity to a group of Russians: "But what about falling in love?" one of the visitors asked. "Isn't that just a natural, irrational happening between *two* people? How do you deal with this?"

The Keristans were doing their best to get their ideas across, and they were failing. But they weren't about to give up. "Falling in love," they said, "is the opiate of the people."   —V. A.

researcher who has written some half-dozen papers based on different aspects of one of the widest-ranging studies of jealousy ever made.

White devised a 35-page "Relationships Questionnaire" that asks subjects to rate themselves on 9-point scales measuring jealousy and a host of personality traits, attitudes, and actions that could be correlated with it. Jealousy itself was assessed by posing six queries: "How jealous do you get of your partner's relationship with members of the opposite sex?" "In general, how jealous a person do you think you are?" "Have you ever seriously thought about breaking up with your partner because of his/her attraction to someone else of the opposite sex?" "My relationship with my partner has made me (much more to much less) jealous than I usually am." "How often do you get jealous of your partner's relationship with members of the opposite sex?" "How much is your jealousy of your partner a problem in your relationship?"

White recruited 150 couples for what he described as a study of "heterosexual romantic relationships" through newspaper advertisements, posters, and announcements to college classes. Most of the subjects—84 percent, to be exact—were white, their average age was just under 22, and 91 percent were students at the University of California in Los Angeles. Of the total, 21 percent considered themselves casual daters; at least one partner in a relationship went out with other people. Of the rest, 50 percent rated themselves serious daters who did not see others; 13 percent were living together; and 16 percent were either engaged or married. The unmarried couples had been together an average of nearly a year.

Since the Aronson-Pines and the White questionnaires are not identical, conclusions drawn from them are not precisely comparable. Nevertheless, White's findings support the Aronson-Pines impression that jealousy goes along with both a sense of dependence on a relationship and with a person's feeling that he or she is in some way lacking.

On one point, White's results did seem to contradict those of the California researchers. He found that chronic low self-esteem *as such* corre-

Jealous men try to repair damaged self-esteem; jealous women concentrate on repairing the damaged relationship.

lated with jealousy only for men, not for women. (White measured self-esteem with self-ratings on items such as, "I take a positive attitude toward myself" and "I feel useless.")

But on items measuring other aspects of self-esteem, White found a correlation with jealousy for both sexes. People who reported that their self-esteem depended heavily on what their partners thought of them usually scored high on the jealousy items. Thus the most jealous people ranked themselves toward the upper end of the scale on items such as, "I would feel terrible about myself if my partner didn't respect me." Not-so-jealous people responded with a high rating on items like this one: "I find that I am pretty happy with myself regardless of what my partner thinks of me."

In a related finding, White noted that jealous people were apt to consider themselves inadequate as mates, as measured by responses to such questions as, "Would you agree that you are the type of person your partner is looking for?" The most jealous men and women rated themselves more deeply involved in their relationship than their partners were. Going beyond the usual techniques for figuring out correlations, White analyzed "perceived inadequacy" and "relative involvement" and concluded that these two characteristics not only occur in jealous people but actually *cause* jealousy. His explanation is that both qualities make people consider their relationship fragile, in part because a person who thinks himself or herself inadequate is acutely aware of "a greater potential for attraction between partner and a rival who may or may not yet exist."

Men versus Women: Who's More Jealous?

On the always controversial question of sex differences, Aronson and Pines

have much to contribute. Nobody will be surprised to learn that results are inconclusive when it comes to the question of which sex has the greater propensity to jealousy—that is, which has more of a personality trait that Bringle calls "dispositional jealousy." But men and women *feel* differently when they are jealous, and on some occasions they *act* differently.

Popular wisdom holds that women are more jealous than men, and in March, newspaper reporters speculated that the woman suspected of shooting diet doctor Herman Tarnower had acted out of jealousy. But a 1976 survey of 143 murders committed in jealous rage found only 20 of the perpetrators to be women. Of course, jealous rage, especially when it ends in murder, is not typical of what most people experience, and researchers have generally discovered no significant sex differences in disposition to jealousy.

Aronson and Pines asked 54 adults, "Who are more jealous—men or women?" and instructed their subjects to pick a number from 1 ("men much more jealous") to 7 ("women much more jealous"), with 4 standing for "equally jealous." The average verdict was 4.4. Thus the consensus was that women are more jealous. But when the researchers assessed the self-reports of actual jealousy (not opinions about other people's jealousy) in the men and women who completed their questionnaire, they found no significant sex differences.

Bringle did find such differences, but only in one group of subjects. He constructed a "Self-Report Jealousy Scale" to appraise jealousy in social, family, and work situations. The scale includes just 20 items, each describing a situation that would make some people jealous. An example or two shows what it is like: "You are stood up and then learn that your date was out with another person," and "Your spouse or steady looks at another."

The idea is for subjects to rate their emotional reaction to such a situation on a 9-point scale, from "not very jealous" at one end to "very jealous" at the other. Bringle has administered his test to several groups of people and has generally found that the sexes rack up similar scores. On one occasion, however, when his subjects were 131 married couples between the ages of 20 and 40, women did report more intense jealous reactions. Bringle himself suggests that the finding could be "just an accident of the sample."

Turning to the way it feels to be jealous and to the behavior evoked by jealousy, Aronson and Pines found several statistically significant sex differences. Women scored higher than men when asked how jealous they would feel in the face of a mate's infidelity. (It could be argued that these higher scores show women to be the jealous sex, but Aronson does not interpret them that way, believing that the scores measure particular experiences of jealousy rather than jealousy as a personality trait.) One question took this form: "Would you experience jealousy if you discovered that your mate was having a love affair, but your mate is very discreet, no one else knows about it, and your mate doesn't know that you know?" With 7 indicating extreme jealousy on the scale, women averaged 6.1, and men, 5.

The result was a bit different when subjects were asked if they would feel jealous about an affair when "everybody but you has known about it for a long time." In that case, the average woman's score was 6.4, in contrast to 5.5 for men.

Other findings suggest that jealousy causes women greater suffering than it does men. All subjects were asked to remember "the situation which produced your most extreme experience of jealousy," and to rate the degree to which they had had each of 20

In a society that values private property and perfect relationships, the chances of eliminating jealousy are poor.

possible physical reactions, such as nausea or headaches. For women, the average score was 2.1, compared with 1.5 for men. On 30 possible emotional reactions, such as humiliation and confusion, the women rated themselves at 2.5, as against 2 for men.

Scores for both sexes were higher when the questions were theoretical rather than personal—that is, when subjects were asked, in effect, "What does jealousy do to people in general?" rather than, "What does it do to you?" Women then rated physical distress at 6.2 and emotional suffering at 6.3. For men, the comparable figures were 4.8 and 5.4.

Given the intensity of the women's physical and psychological response to betrayal, it is surprising that they did not often translate their response into action. Here the important question was, "Have any of your intimate relationships ended because of your jealousy?" A rating of 1 on the answer scale meant never, while 7 indicated that all relationships had ended for that reason. Women's average response was 1.3; men's was 2.2. Men, in short, were more likely to get out of an alliance that made them jealous.

When an Old Flame Shows Up

That finding seems consistent with studies by Jeff Bryson and his colleagues at San Diego State. Bryson's group have found that men try to repair their damaged self-esteem, while women, perhaps swallowing their pride, concentrate on repairing the damaged relationship.

One thing the Bryson group wondered about was whether or not an interloper's attractiveness has any bearing on the way the injured partner reacts. The key research tool was a set of four specially made videotapes depicting a hackneyed but undeniably jealousy-inducing situation: an old ri-

val breaks in on a current relationship.

This is the scenario the research team dreamed up, as outlined by Bryson: "The scene opened with a scan of a party, stopping on a couple sitting on a couch. After a 45-second segment during which the couple cuddled, kissed, and toasted each other, one member of the couple got up and left the room, apparently to refill the wine glasses. Approximately 15 seconds after this, the interloper, the old boyfriend or girlfriend of the partner remaining on the couch, entered the picture. The partner jumped up, hugged the interloper briefly, and the two of them sat down on the couch. During the next 60 seconds, they performed progressively more intimate actions, including touching each other and exchanging one brief kiss. Shortly after the kiss, the absent partner returned, looking down at the two people on the couch." On that dramatic high note, the tape ended.

The scene came in one of four versions. In two tapes, the female partner left for more wine, and the interloper was female (attractive in one tape and unattractive in the other). In the second pair of tapes, the male partner left the room and returned to confront the woman and her "old boyfriend," who was in one case appealing, in the other, decidedly otherwise.

Forty female subjects were randomly assigned to watch either the attractive or the unattractive "old girlfriend" do her interloping best. An equal number of male subjects viewed one or the other of the "old boyfriend" films. After the screening, the subjects rated the likelihood that each of 36 described feelings or actions would correspond to their own behavior.

Analysis of the ratings showed that men were much more likely than women to say they would begin going out with others or become "more sexually aggressive with others." Women were more apt to say they would put

on a show of indifference, or try to make themselves more attractive to their partners. The sex differences were particularly marked when the old flame was attractive. "If we assume that an attractive interloper is seen as more threatening to the relationship," the researchers said, "then males become more likely to bolster their egos by pursuing alternative relationships. Females, on the other hand, become less likely to engage in behaviors that might accent the threat to the existing relationship." What may account for the sex difference is the fact that actively seeking new relationships is still socially more acceptable for men than it is for women.

The Bryson males, so ready to abandon a jealousy-provoking relationship, may be compared with men Kinsey studied years ago. Of Kinsey's divorced male subjects, 51 percent gave the wife's infidelity as a major reason for the breakup, in contrast to 27 percent of his divorced female subjects. The Bryson females, who hoped to patch things up, are like the Aronson-Pines women, of whom so few had ever ended a relationship because they were jealous. Bryson's women also recall Theodor Reik's idea of the female sex. Women, the noted psychoanalyst said, characteristically fight to win back a lost lover instead of giving up the relationship as a lost cause.

Inadequacy in Romance

Gregory White has also found some interesting sex differences in jealousy-related behavior. In one phase of his many-faceted study, he gave a new twist to research on the low self-esteem/jealousy connection. His interest was in a particular kind of diminished self-esteem, a person's belief that he or she is inadequate as a romantic partner. What White had in mind was a chicken-and-egg sort of question: which comes first, the experience of jealousy or the self-perception of inadequacy? As it turns out, there are two right answers, one for men and one for women.

White's findings are based on his original questionnaire and on a retest of as many of his original subjects as possible (126, as it turned out) after a nine-month lag to be sure that the connection between jealousy and inadequacy was really there and not just an artifact of a single test situation.

This time the relevant parts of the questionnaire were the six queries about feelings of jealousy, along with several questions probing the subjects' ideas about themselves as romantic partners. On that theme, a typical question read, "Have there ever been times when you felt no matter how hard you tried, you couldn't make your partner happy?"

On the basis of complicated statistical procedures, White concluded that in the women, feelings of inadequacy appeared first and lead to jealousy, while in men, the reverse was true. *After* the men felt they had reason to be jealous, they then began to worry that something was wrong with them.

To explain this sex difference, White cited previous research showing that women, perhaps because of the way they are brought up, are more likely than men to "monitor" their relationships—that is, to pay attention to the details of them and to be conscious of the impact of their personalities on their partners. Long before a rival appears, women may look for things in themselves that might disappoint their partners. Men, presumably preoccupied with the outside world, may pay little attention to a relationship, or to qualities in themselves that might disturb it, until things have actually gone wrong.

Testing the Relationship

In another phase of his project, White studied a phenomenon that Jessie Bernard, a sociologist, had described in 1971: the deliberate provocation of jealousy. "The husband," Bernard wrote, "pretends to be interested in other women in public—makes passes at every pretty girl, leers at other women, pretends excitement at the touch of the hostess—all in an ostentatious manner that calls attention to

him, but only when the wife is there to observe and suffer. Or the wife flirts with other men in an equally open and provocative way. The idea is to publicly humiliate the spouse."

Women, White learned, behave that way more often than men do. He also discovered that the motives of the jealousy-inducers, and the techniques they employed, were more various than Bernard had suggested.

Again, White's data came from his Relationships Questionnaire. Now the significant questions were these: "Have you ever tried to get your partner jealous over your relationship with someone else on purpose? If yes, please outline your reasons. If yes, how did you try to make your partner jealous?" And then: "Who would you say is more involved in your relationship, you or your partner? Rate yourself as much more, more, equally, less, or much less involved."

Analysis of the responses revealed five jealousy-inducing techniques. The commonest, reported by more than half the 300 subjects, was to discuss or exaggerate the appeal of some third person. The next most popular method was flirting (cited by 28 percent), dating others (24 percent), fabricating another attachment (14 percent), and talking about a previous partner (11 percent).

Reasons given broke down into five groups. When subjects said things like, "I wanted him to spend more time with me," White labeled their motive *Increase Rewards*. The other categories were *Bolster Self-Esteem* ("I was feeling low and needed to remind him that I'm special to him"); *Test Relationship* ("To see if he still cared"); *Revenge* ("Out of anger because he was going out"); and *Punishment* ("We were having a fight").

More than 38 percent of White's female subjects were motivated by the desire for a reward, compared with 15 percent of the men. In the group as a whole, the attempt to get a reward of some sort motivated 30 percent of the subjects. The commonest motive, though, was to test the relationship; it appeared in almost 40 percent of all cases.

Degree of involvement in the relationship did not seem to have anything to do with whether or not men tried to provoke jealousy, but it was

an important factor among the women. Female subjects who considered themselves more involved than their partners were almost twice as likely to report inducement as were the rest of the women. Overall, 73 subjects said they had deliberately induced jealousy. Of these, 31 percent were women; only 17 percent were men.

Why that great dissimilarity? White thinks it reflects not any immutable personality difference between men and women, but the imbalance in power that seems to mark the entire relationship of the sexes, not just romantic or sexual aspects. For women, especially for those who feel more involved than their mates, provoking jealousy may be a way of trying to gain control and of redressing the balance of power. It is as if a woman delivered an ultimatum: "You'd better care as much as I do, or I'll leave you."

High-Jealousy Cultures

As interesting as sex differences in jealousy are cross-cultural variations. Ralph B. Hupka, a social psychologist at California State University in Long Beach, recently surveyed two centuries of anthropological reports and found great differences both in the prevalence of jealousy and in the way it was expressed. So consistent were the quantitative distinctions that Hupka found he could characterize particular societies as either "low-jealousy cultures," like the Todas of Southern India, or "high-jealousy cultures," like the Apache Indians of North America.

According to Hupka, jealousy was rare among the Todas because their culture did not encourage possessiveness toward either things or people, placed few restrictions on sexual gratification, and did not make marriage or progeny a condition for social recognition. In short, there was not much to be jealous about. It was otherwise with the Apache. "Sexual pleasure was something to be earned after a long period of deprivation and to be jealously guarded thereafter against intruders," Hupka said. To the Apache man, an "unsullied" wife, and children he knew to be his, were so important for status reasons that when he planned to be away from home he had a close relative keep secret watch over his wife and report on her behavior when he returned.

Remarking that "there is no one universal way of being jealous," Hupka assembled some illustrations. A jealous Samoan woman used to bite her rival in the nose, while a Zuñi wife in New Mexico got back at her straying husband by refusing to wash his clothes. Among the Plateau tribes of Northern Rhodesia, the whole community avenged a jealous husband by impaling his wife and her lover on stakes. A Hidatsa Indian in North America had a right to kill his faithless wife if he felt like it, but the most admired course he could take was to present the wife formally to her new lover. If a husband wanted to show how glad he was to be rid of her, he might throw in a horse or other valuable gift.

As for the origins of jealousy, Hupka says it "is not inborn; it is intrinsic to the process of socialization; i.e., learning what is valued in our society and protecting it against a rival." Kinsey and other biologically oriented scientists disagree, pointing to evidence of jealousy in mammals as proof that the emotion is inherited. Freud was convinced that adult jealousy stems from the Oedipal period; developmental psychologists look for the beginnings of jealousy in rivalry between brothers and sisters; sociologists often blame monogamy. That institution, the sociologist Kingsley Davis has suggested, in what was surely one of the understatements of all time, perhaps "causes adultery to be resented and therefore creates jealousy."

The reasons for so much uncertainty about the roots and characteristics of jealousy lie partly in the complexity of the emotion itself—and partly in research difficulties. Aronson and Pines point out that "experimental social psychologists are undoubtedly discouraged by the fact that 'real' jealousy is almost impossible to observe systematically," yet to induce it in the laboratory is usually considered unethical. (However, Aronson and Pines are planning a "research-encounter" project in which couples troubled by jealousy will try to learn something about the emotion by provoking it in their partners during a workshop. The researchers hope to learn something,

too, and they believe they can protect participants by warning them of risks in advance and by gaining fully informed consent.)

The safest research approach, Aronson and Pines observe, "is to ask a wide range of people about their experiences of jealousy in much the same way that Kinsey asked people about their sexual experiences." The trouble with that is the unreliability of "self-report." With jealousy often labeled immature and unattractive, some subjects may just plain lie about it. Some may deny it honestly, in the sincere belief that they are really free of it—but they may be the most jealous people of all. And what about the people who readily tell a researcher that, yes, they often feel jealous? Those people, some scientists suggest, may really be far less jealous than men and women who cannot bring themselves to such an admission.

At least until the experimenters find some way around these difficulties, the writings of the psychoanalysts, who were among the first of the behavioral scientists to pay attention to jealousy, are still among the best sources of information about the origins and characteristics of jealousy.

Beginning with Freud, analysts have stressed that the difference between normal and pathological jealousy is one of degree, and that even normal jealousy is not entirely rational—an observation about the basic nature of jealousy that few contemporary investigators would deny. No less instructive is the assertion of Theodore Isaac Rubin, a neo-Freudian psychoanalyst in New York, that "Jealousy is born of feeling that we have so little to give compared to someone else." An equally provocative hint that the jealous person might do well to look into his or her own psychic state is Otto Fenichel's suggestion that the basis of jealousy is often "an unconscious tendency toward infidelity which is projected onto the partner." The jealous person, that is, may concentrate on a partner's real or imagined faithlessness in order not to worry about his or her own.

As for descriptions of jealousy, some of the best are to be found in the psychoanalytic literature. Take this sketch of the "eye of jealousy" by

psychoanalyst William Evans: "It is furtive because it is frightened. It is covert rather than overt. From its hiding place, it sees innumerable facts but never gets its facts right. It can, at its most flagrant, build up a case on insufficient evidence, so that 'trifles light as air become confirmations strong as proofs of holy writ.' More generally, the jealous man cuts a ridiculous figure. . . . He observes minutely and misses the mark monumentally."

Still, the psychoanalysts leave unanswered the question of whether jealousy can be abolished, as the inhabitants of Kerista Village believe it can. In American society as a whole, Jessie Bernard maintains, "Marital jealousy is declining as our conception of the nature of the marital bond itself is changing. . . . If monogamic marriage is changing, there may be less and less need for jealousy to buttress it, and less socialization of human beings to experience jealousy."

Aronson and Pines are not optimistic about the prospects for doing away with jealousy in the United States. "America is a paired, family-oriented society," they say. "It is a society that emphasizes ownership and private property. It is characterized by competition and by a strong desire to have a perfect relationship. All these aspects of contemporary American society tend to aggravate the feeling and expression of jealousy."

The inevitability of jealousy—to Aronson and Pines, it *is* inevitable—goes deeper than that, to the very nature of love and intimacy. "It may be," the two California researchers say, "that precisely what we most value about certain relationships is what also makes them essentially nonreplicable and nonshareable, and hence leaves a place for jealousy."

Virginia Adams is an associate editor of Psychology Today. She is the author of *Crime*, a volume in the Time-Life Books *Human Behavior* series.

For further information, read:
Bernard, Jessie. "Jealousy in Marriage," in *Medical Aspects of Human Sexuality*, 5(1971):200-215.
Bringle, Robert G. and Scott Evenbeck. "The Study of Jealousy as a Dispositional Characteristic," in *Love and Attraction*, Mark Cook and Glenn Wilson, eds., Pergamon Press, 1979, $62.
Evans, William N. "The Eye of Jealousy and Envy," in *The Psychoanalytic Review*, 63(1975):481-493.
Kerista Village Handbook. Obtainable from Kerista Village, P.O. Box 1174, San Francisco, Calif. 94101.
Robbe-Grillet, Alain. *Jealousy*, Grove Press, 1959; paper, 1978, $2.95.

58

For centuries, poets have been trying to capture the essence of whatever it is that makes the world go around. Now behavioral scientists are having their turn.

Zick Rubin, PhD, is professor of social psychology at Brandeis University and the author of *Liking and Loving: An Invitation to Social Psychology.*

Love has always been one thing, maybe the only thing, that seemed safely beyond the research scientist's ever-extending grasp. With an assist from Masters and Johnson, behavioral scientists have, to be sure, dug rather heavily into the topic of human sexual behavior. But whereas sex might now be explored scientifically, love remained sacrosanct.

Or so we thought.

Love was a taboo topic for researchers as recently as 1958, when the president of the American Psychological Association, Dr. Harry F. Harlow, declared in faintly mournful tones, "So far as love or affection is concerned, psychologists have failed in their mission. The little we know about love does not transcend simple observation, and the little we write about it has been written better by poets and novelists." Since the poets and novelists had always been notoriously contradictory about love, defining it as everything from "a spirit all compact of fire" to "a state of perceptual anesthesia," this was a pretty severe indictment.

But the psychologists did not take this charge lying down. Instead, they rallied to the call and started a quiet revolution. Over the past dozen years, and at a positively accelerating pace, behavioral scientists have begun to study love. They have done so on their own terms, with the help of such tools of the trade as laboratory experiments, questionnaires, interviews and systematic behavioral observation. And although the new love research is still in its early stages, it has already made substantial progress. The research has proceeded on several fronts, including explorations of the psychological origins of love, its links to social and cultural factors and the ways in which it deepens—or dies—over time.

Recent studies of falling in love have indicated that there is a sense in which love is like a Brooks Brothers suit or a Bonwit dress. For one person's feelings toward another to be experienced as "love," they must not only feel good and fit well, they must also have the appropriate label. Sometimes a sexual experience contributes to such labeling. One college student told an interviewer that she was surprised to discover that she enjoyed having sex with her boyfriend, because until that time she had not been sure that she loved him. The pleasant surprise helped to convince her that she was actually "in love."

Paradoxically, however, people sometimes label as "love" experiences that seem to be negative rather than positive. Consider the rather interesting case of fear. Ovid noted

The Love Research

by ZICK RUBIN

in *The Art of Love,* written in first-century Rome, that an excellent time for a man to arouse passion in a woman is while watching gladiators disembowel one another in the arena. Presumably the emotions of fear and repulsion stirred up by the grisly scene would somehow be converted into romantic interest.

Ovid himself did not conduct any controlled experiments to check the validity of the fear-breeds-love principle, but two psychologists at the University of British Columbia, Drs. Donald L. Dutton and Arthur P. Aron, recently did so. They conducted their experiment on two footbridges that cross the Capilano river in North Vancouver. One of the bridges is a narrow, rickety structure that sways in the wind 230 feet above the rocky canyon; the other is a solid structure upriver, only 10 feet above a shallow stream. An attractive female experimenter approached men who were crossing one or the other bridge and asked if they would take part in her study of "the effects of exposure to scenic attractions on creative expression." All they had to do was to write down their associations to a picture she showed them. The researchers found that the men accosted on the fear-arousing bridge were more sexually aroused than the men on the solid bridge, as measured by the amount of sexual imagery in the stories they wrote. The men on the high-fear bridge were also much more likely to telephone the young woman afterward, ostensibly to get more information about the study.

The best available explanation for these results comes from a general theory of emotion put forth by Dr. Stanley Schachter of Columbia University. Schachter's experiments suggested that the experience of emotion has two necessary elements. The first is physiological arousal—a racing heart, heightened breathing, sweating and the like. These symptoms tend to be more or less identical for any intense emotion, whether it be anger, fear or love. The second necessary element, therefore, is the person's subjective labeling of his or her arousal. In order to determine which emotion he or she is experiencing, the person must look around and determine what external stimulus is causing the inner upheaval.

This labeling is a complicated process, and (as Ovid apparently knew some 2,000 years ago) mistakes can happen. In the Capilano Canyon study, subjects apparently relabeled their inner stirrings of fear, at least in part, as sexual arousal and romantic attraction. This sort of relabeling is undoubtedly encouraged by the fact that the popular stereotype of falling in love—a pounding heart, shortness of breath, trembling hands—all bear an uncanny resemblance to the physical symptoms of fear. With such traumatic expectations of what love should feel like, it is no wonder that it is sometimes confused with other emotions. As the Supremes put it in a song of the 1960s, "Love is like an itching in my heart."

In the case of the Capilano Canyon study, of course, one cannot say that the subjects actually "fell in love" with the woman on the bridge. But the same sort of labeling process takes place in more enduring romantic attachments. In the process, social pressures also come crashing into the picture. Young men and women are taught repeatedly that love and marriage inevitably go together, and in the large majority of cases they proceed to act accordingly on this assumption.

Americans are more likely than ever to get married (well over 90 percent do so at least once), and all but a minuscule proportion of people applying for marriage licenses will tell you that they are in love. It is not simply that people who are in love decide to follow their hearts' dictates and get married. It also works the other way around. People who are planning to get married, perhaps for economic reasons or in order to raise a family, invariably follow their culture's dictates and decide that they are "in love."

The pressure to label a promising relationship as "love" seems especially strong for women. Sociologist William Kephart of the University of Pennsylvania asked over a thousand Philadelphia college students the following question: "If a boy (girl) had all the other qualities you desired, would you marry this person even if you were not in love with him (her)?" Very few of the respondents (4 percent of the women and 12 percent of the men) were so unromantic as to say yes. But fully 72 percent of the women (compared with only 24 percent of the men) were too practical to answer with a flat no and, instead, pleaded uncertainty.

One of Dr. Kephart's female respondents put her finger on the dilemma, and also on the resolution of it. She wrote in on her questionnaire, "If a boy had all the other qualities I desired, and I was not in love with him—well, I think I could talk myself into falling in love."

Whereas women may be more highly motivated than men to fall in love with a potential spouse, men tend to fall in love more quickly and less deliberately than women. In a study of couples who had been computer-matched for a dance at Iowa State University, men were more satisfied than women with their dates, reported feeling more "romantic attraction" toward them and even were more optimistic about the possibility of a happy marriage with their machine-matched partners. In a study of dating couples at the University of Michigan, I found that among couples who had been dating briefly—up to three months— boyfriends scored significantly higher than their girlfriends did on a self-report "love scale." These men were more likely than their partners to agree with such statements as "It would be hard for me to get along without———," "One of my primary concerns is———'s welfare" and "I would do almost anything for———." Among couples who had been together for longer periods of time the male-female difference disappeared.

The idea of measuring love on a paper-and-pencil scale is, incidentally, not an entirely new one. When Elizabeth Barrett Browning wrote, "How do I love thee? Let me count the ways," she was, as any mathematician can tell you, referring to the most basic form of measurement. Six years ago, when I was searching for an unspoiled topic for my doctoral dissertation, I decided to take Browning's advice. ("Why do you want to measure *that*?" my dissertation committee asked me. "Why not measure something more conventional like cognitive dissonance or identity diffusion?" I looked down at the rocky canyon

230 feet below and answered, voice trembling, "Because it's there.") The items on the scale that emerged refer to elements of attachment (the desire to be near the other), caring (the concern for the other's well-being) and intimacy (the desire for close and confidential communication with the other). The ancient Greeks had a similar conception of love. Where they went wrong was in never asking the masses to put their *eros* and *agape* for one another on nine-point scales.

Skeptics may point out, of course, that a paper-and-pencil love scale does not really measure how much people love each other, but simply how much they *say* they love each other. But there is some corroborating behavioral evidence for the scale's validity. For example, scores on the scale checked out with the well-known folk wisdom that lovers spend a great deal of their time gazing into each other's eyes. Surreptitious laboratory observation through a one-way mirror confirmed that "strong lovers" (couples whose members received above-average scores on the love scale) made significantly more eye contact than "weak lovers" (couples whose scores on the love scale were below average). Or, as the popular song puts it, "I only have eyes for you."

Whereas men seem to fall in love more quickly and easily than women, women seem to fall out of love more quickly and with less difficulty than men, at least in the premarital stages. For the past several years, my coworkers and I have been conducting an extensive study of student dating couples in the Boston area. We found, to our initial surprise, that women were somewhat more likely to be "breaker-uppers" than men were, that they saw more problems in the relationship and that they were better able to disengage themselves emotionally when a breakup was coming. Men, on the other hand, tended to react to breakups with greater grief and despair.

These tendencies run counter to the popular stereotypes of women as star-struck romantics and men as aloof exploiters. In fact, women may learn to be more practical and discriminating about love than men for simple economic reasons. In most marriages, the wife's status, income and life chances are far more dependent on the husband's than vice versa. As a result, the woman must be discriminating. She cannot allow herself to fall in love too quickly, nor can she afford to stay in love too long with "the wrong person." The fact that a woman's years of marriageability tend to be more limited than a man's may also contribute to her need to be selective. Men, on the other hand, can better afford the luxury of being "romantic."

Sociologist Willard Waller put the matter most bluntly when he wrote, some 40 years ago, "There is this difference between the man and the woman in the pattern of bourgeois family life: a man, when he marries, chooses a companion and perhaps a helpmate, but a woman chooses a companion and at the same time a standard of living. It is necessary for a woman to be mercenary." As more women enter business and professional careers, and as more men make major commitments to homemaking and childrearing, it is likely that this difference will diminish.

In spite of these culturally based sex differences, the usual course of love is probably pretty much the same for human beings of both sexes. A key task for love researchers is to explore the stages and sequences through which love develops. To this end, Drs. L. Rowell Huesmann of the University of Illinois at Chicago Circle and George Levinger of the University of Massachusetts recently developed a unique computer program, called RELATE, that simulates the development of close relationships. Given information about the personalities of the two partners and following a built-in set of rules and assumptions, RELATE is able to generate a "scenario" of the likely course of their relationship. In its maiden effort along these lines, RELATE simulated the relationship of two hypothetical sweethearts, John (who was described to RELATE in the computer-language equivalent of "attractive, but shy") and Susan (introduced to RELATE as "outgoing and popular").

After a few minutes of whirring and clicking, RELATE came up with its prediction. It hypothesized that after a period of time during which they interacted at a superficial level, "John learns that Susan is willing to disclose intimacies in response to his disclosures, and he confides in her completely. This leads the pair into active striving for a deep romantic involvement." By the end of RELATE's love story, John and Susan were both oriented toward a permanent relationship, although neither had yet proposed marriage. Erich Segal, eat your heart out!

Since John and Susan are only hypothetical, it is impossible to know how accurate RELATE's scenario really is. Moreover, Drs. Huesmann and Levinger freely acknowledge that at present the simulations are greatly oversimplified, providing at best pale reflections of the events of real-life relationships. But the computer-matchmaker has already proved to be of value to researchers in refining their models of the development of love in real life.

Note, for example, that John and Susan's romance did not get very far until John learned that Susan would reciprocate his disclosures. My study of Boston couples, conducted in collaboration with Drs. Letitia Anne Peplau (now at UCLA) and Charles T. Hill (now at the University of Washington) has confirmed RELATE's working assumption along these lines, to wit: love is most likely to flourish when the two partners are *equally involved* in their relationship. In our study of 231 dating couples, 77 percent of the couples in which both partners reported that they were equally involved in 1972 were still going together (or, in some cases married) in 1974, as compared with only 45 percent of unequally involved couples.

The importance of equal degrees of involvement makes it clear that love, like water, seeks its own level. As Columbia University sociologist Peter M. Blau explains, "If one lover is considerably more involved than the other, his greater commitment invites exploitation and provokes feelings of entrapment, both of which obliterate love. . . . Only when two lovers' affection for and commitment to one another expand at roughly the same pace do they mutually tend to reinforce their love."

Because of this mutual reinforcement, love will sometimes beget love—provided that the first person's love is communicated to the second. To help make the point, Dr. Paul Rosenblatt of the University of Minnesota sifted through anthropologists' reports of "love magic" in 23 primitive societies, from the Chaga of East Africa to the Kwoma of New Guinea. He came to the conclusion that although love magic often works, it isn't really magic. Instead, such exotic practices as giving one's "victim" a charmed coconut, flashing a mirror at her or blowing ashes in her face all serve to heighten the woman's love by indirectly communicating the man's love for her. When love magic is practiced without the victim's knowledge, it is not nearly so effective. (Other studies have made it clear, however, that expressions of love must also be well-timed. If too much affection is expressed too soon, equity is undermined and the tactic will backfire.)

Dr. Rosenblatt's study illustrates quite directly what some observers fear most about the new love research— that it will rob love of its magic and mystery. Sen. William Proxmire is one of those who takes this point of view. In a much-publicized statement last year, Sen. Proxmire identified a study of romantic love sponsored by the National Science Foundation as "my choice for the biggest waste of the taxpayer's money for the month of March. I believe that 200 million Americans want to leave some things in life a mystery, and right at the top of the things we don't want to know is why a man falls in love with a woman and vice versa."

Dr. Ellen Berscheid, the University of Minnesota researcher whose work was singled out by the senator, responded vigorously to the attack: "I assume the senator has some knowledge of the divorce rate in this country and understands that the absence of love is the basis on which many divorces are instigated. I believe he has been divorced and recently was reconciled with his second wife [in February, 1975]. He ought to realize better than most people why we should know all we can about the determinants of affection."

Writing in the *New York Times*, columnist James Reston also defended the love researchers. "Mr. Proxmire is a modern man," Reston wrote, "who believes that government should help people with their problems. He is a land-grant college man and will vote any amount of money for basic research on the dangers of natural selection in animals, and on how to get the best bulls and cows together on the farms of Wisconsin, but he is against basic research on the alarming divorce rate or breakup of the human family in America. You have to assume he was kidding."

But, of course, the senator was not kidding, and his sentiments are undoubtedly shared by a large number of Americans, even if not by the entire 200 million claimed in his statement. Even some psychologists themselves share his viewpoint. At a symposium sponsored by the American Psychological Association Convention several years ago, one panelist declared that "the scientist in even attempting to interject love into a laboratory situation is by the very nature of the proposition dehumanizing the state we call love."

My view of the matter, and that of other love researchers, is rather different. We are quite aware of the difficulties inherent in the attempt to study love, and we have no illusion that we will ever unlock all of love's mysteries. But we also believe that especially at a time when many people are terribly confused about what love is or should be, the scientific study of love can make a positive contribution to the quality of life. To shun this task is no more justified than the taboo until several centuries ago against scientific study of the human body, on the grounds that such research would somehow defile it. In the words of one of the most humane of modern psychologists, the late Dr. Abraham H. Maslow, "We *must* study love; we must be able to teach it, to understand it, to predict it, or else the world is lost to hostility and to suspicion."

Passionate Love

59

by Elaine Walster

Definitions

Liking has been defined by a number of researchers (e.g., Newcomb, 1961; Homans, 1950) as "a positive attitude toward another, evidenced by a tendency to approach and interact with him." Theorists generally agree on the genesis of liking: individuals like those who reward them.*

Researchers have spent little time defining or investigating *passionate love*. Many theorists simply assume that passionate love is nothing more than very intense liking. We would argue, however, that passionate love is a distinct emotional state. We would argue that a person will experience love only if 1) he is physiologically aroused, and 2) he concludes that love is the appropriate label for his aroused feelings.

Passionate Love: A Taboo Topic

Most of us would agree that passion is more fascinating than friendship. However, a multitude of researchers have conducted experiments on liking, while very few have explored passionate love.

What accounts for this imbalance?

1) First, scientists who wanted to investigate romantic attraction found it very difficult to secure research funds. Granting agencies, sensitive to the feelings of legislators and the public, were nervous about even considering proposals whose titles contained the offensive words "Love" or "Sex." Even today, whenever a researcher is ill-mannered enough to affix such a title to his proposal, alert bureaucrats quickly expurgate the offensive term and substitute the euphemism, "social affiliation."

2) Psychologists did not themselves acknowledge the legitimacy of investigating passionate love. They often ridiculed colleagues who began conducting experiments on this taboo topic. To study love was to be "soft-headed," "unscientific," or to possess a flair for the trivial. It is interesting to note that early in their careers some of our most eminent social psychologists conducted one — and only one — study on romantic attraction. Professional reaction to their research uniformly led them to decide to investigate other topics.

3) Psychologists tend to assume that in the laboratory one can only study mild and quickly developing phenomena. Although poets argue that love may occur "at first sight," psychologists have had less confidence that one can generate passionate love in a two-hour laboratory experiment. Thus, many researchers erroneously assumed that passionate love could only be studied in the field.

This report was financed by National Institute of Mental Health Grant MH 16661 and National Science Foundation Grant GS 2932. The theoretical framework I present was developed in collaboration with Dr. Ellen Berscheid, University of Minnesota.
* We use the term *companionate love* to indicate unusually intense *liking* between two persons.

Suddenly, the situation changed. The humanists invaded psychology, and the study of tender emotions became respectable. Masters and Johnson's (1966) impressive research demonstrated that even sex could be examined in the laboratory. (Ironically, these pioneers were attacked by the public for failing to investigate love as well as sex.) In the last five years more psychologists have begun to study romantic love than investigated the phenomenon in the history of psychology.

The problem now is not finding respectability but finding out some facts. Presently, when faced with requests for information about love and sex, chagrined psychologists must admit that "they really don't know love at all." Hopefully, in this conference we can gain a better understanding about this vital — and entertaining — topic. In this lecture, I will propose a theoretical framework which may give us a better understanding of passionate love.

"What Is This Thing Called Love?"

Interpersonal attraction and companionate love seem like sensible phenomena. One can predict quite well how much a person will like another, if he knows to what extent the other rewards or punishes the person. Reward has so predictable an impact on liking that Byrne et al (1968) could with confidence propose an exact correspondence between reinforcement and liking: ("Attraction towards X is a positive linear function of the proportion of positive reinforcements received from X or expected from X.") Data support their formulation.

Sometimes passionate love seems to operate in a sensible fashion. Some practical people have been known to fall in love with those beautiful, wise, entertaining, and kind people who offer affection or material rewards to them. Generally, however, passionate love does not seem to fit so neatly into the reinforcement paradigm. Individuals do *not* always feel passionate about the person who provides the most rewards with the greatest consistency. Passion sometimes develops under conditions that would seem more likely to provoke aggression and hatred than love. For example, reinforcement theorists argue that "we like those who like us and reject those who dislike us." Yet individuals experience intense love for those who have rejected them.

A woman discovers her husband is seeing another. The pain and suffering the jealous wife experiences at this discovery cause her to realize how much she loves her husband.

Lovers pine away for the girls who spurn their affection. For example, a recent Associated Press release reports the desperate excuse of an Italian lover who kidnapped his former sweetheart: " 'The fact that she rejected me only made me want and love her more,' he tearfully explained."

Reinforcement theorists tell us that "frustration always breeds aggression." Yet, inhibited sexuality is assumed to be the foundation of romantic feelings. Freud (1912) even argued that:

Some obstacle is necessary to swell the tide of libido to its height; and at all periods of history whenever natural barriers in the way of satisfaction have not sufficed, mankind has erected conventional ones in order to enjoy love.

The observation that passionate love flourishes in settings which would seem to thwart its development has always been puzzling to social scientists. Poets attribute such inexplicable phenomena to the essential illogic of love. Scientists, who refuse to acknowledge that anything is inexplicable, do not have such an easy way out.

Happily, we believe that a theoretical framework exists which makes the "illogical" phenomena of passionate love explicable and predictable.

Schachter's Two-Component Theory

On the basis of an ingenious series of experiments, Schachter (1964) proposed a paradigm for understanding human emotional response. He argues that in order for a person to experience true emotion, two factors must coexist: 1) The individual must be physiologically aroused, and 2) It must be reasonable to interpret his stirred-up state in emotional terms. Schachter argued that neither physiological arousal nor appropriate cognitions *alone* is sufficient to produce an emotional experience.

It is possible to manipulate an individual's physiological arousal artificially. A drug, adrenalin, exists whose effects mimic the discharge of the sympathetic nervous system. Shortly after one receives an injection of adrenalin, systolic blood pressure increases markedly, heart rate increases somewhat, cutaneous blood flow decreases, muscle and cerebral blood flow increase, blood sugar and lactic acid concentration increase, and respiration rate increases slightly. The individual who has been injected with adrenalin experiences palpitation, tremor, and sometimes flushing and accelerated breathing. These reactions are identical to the physiological reactions which accompany a variety of natural emotional states.

An injection of adrenalin will not, by itself, however, engender an emotional response in a person. When an individual is injected with adrenalin and asked to introspect, he will report either no emotional response or, at best, report feeling "as if" he might be experiencing some emotion (Marañon, 1924). Individuals make statements such as "I feel *as if* I were afraid." The person who has been injected with adrenalin perceives that something is not quite authentic about his reactions. Something is missing.

Schachter argues that what is missing is an appropriate label for the physiological reactions one is experiencing. If one could lead the drugged individual to attribute his stirred-up state to some emotion-arousing event (rather than attributing it to the injection of adrenalin which he received), Schachter argues that he would experience a "true" emotion.

The researcher who wishes to test the notion that physiological arousal and appropriate cognitions are separate and indispensable components of a true emotional experience, is faced with the challenging task of separately manipulating these two components. In a classic study, Schachter and Singer (1962) conceived of a way to do just that. Volunteers were recruited for an experiment which the experimenters claimed was designed to investigate the effects of a new vitamin compound, Suproxin, on vision.

Manipulating Physiological Arousal: Volunteers were injected with a substance which was identified as Suproxin. Actually, one half of the students were injected with epinephrine (½ cc of a 1.1000 solution of Winthrop Laboratory's Suprarenin). Such an injection causes the intense physiological reactions described earlier. One half received a placebo (½ cc of saline solution).

Manipulating an Appropriate Explanation: Schachter wished to lead some of the volunteers to correctly attribute their physiological state to a nonemotional cause (the injection). He wished to lead others to attribute their stirred-up state to an emotional cause.

Thus, in one condition, (the *Non-Emotional Attribution* condition), individuals were given a complete explanation of how the shot would affect them. They were warned that in 15 to 20 minutes the injection of "Suproxin" would cause palpitation, tremor, etc. Presumably, when students began to experience these symptoms, they could properly attribute their stirred-up state to the shot and would *not* attribute their excitement to the activities in which they were engaging at the time the adrenalin began to take effect.

In the *Emotional Attribution* conditions, things were arranged to *discharge* students from attributing their stirred-up state to the shot. One group of volunteers was given no information about possible side effects of the shot. A second group of volunteers was deliberately misled as to the potential side effects of the shot. It was assumed that volunteers who received either no information or incorrect information would be unlikely to attribute their tremors and palpitations to the shot. After all, these symptoms took 20 minutes to develop. Instead, the authors hoped that volunteers would attribute their arousal to whatever they happened to be doing when the drug took effort. The authors then arranged things so that what volunteers "happened to be doing" was participating in either a gay, happy, social interaction or participating in a tense, explosive interaction.

If the subject had been assigned to the *Euphoria* condition, his fellow student (who was actually a confederate) had been trained to generate excitement while they waited 20 minutes for the experiment to begin. As soon as the experimenter left the room, the confederate began "acting up." He shot paper wads into the wastebasket, built a paper tower which he sent crashing to the floor and generally kidded around.

In the *Anger* setting, the confederate had been trained to make the subject angry. The confederate first complained about the experimental procedures. He became especially indignant on encountering the questionnaire they had been asked to fill out (and which admittedly asked stupid and offensive questions). Finally, the confederate slammed his questionnaire to the floor and stomped out.

The authors assessed subject's emotional reactions to the confederate's behavior in two ways. Observers stationed behind a one-way mirror assessed to what extent the subject caught the stooge's euphoric or angry mood; secondly, subjects were asked to describe their moods and to estimate how euphoric and angry they felt.

Schachter and Singer predicted that those subjects who had received an adrenalin injection would have stronger emotional reactions than would subjects who had received a placebo or had received an adrenalin injection but had been warned of exactly what physiological changes they should expect. The data supported these hypotheses. The experiment thus supported the contention that both physiological arousal and appropriate cognitions are indispensable components of a true emotional experience. Schachter and Wheeler (1962) and Hohmann (1962) provide additional support for this contention.

The Two-Component Theory and Passionate Love

The discovery that almost any sort of intense physiological arousal — if properly interpreted — will precipitate an emotional experience has intriguing implications. We were particularly intrigued by the possibility that Schachter's "two-component" theory might help explain a heretofore inexplicable phenomenon — passionate love.

As long as researchers were busily absorbed in figuring out how passionate love could be integrated into the reinforcement paradigm, we made little progress. The observation that negative experiences often lead to increased evaluation remained inexplicable.

A sudden insight solved our dilemma. Two components are necessary for a passionate experience: arousal and appropriate cognitions. Perhaps negative experiences do not increase love by somehow improving one's evaluation of the other (beneficially altering his cognitions). Perhaps negative experiences are effective in inducing love because they intensify the second component — arousal.

We would suggest that perhaps it does not really matter how one produces an agitated state in an individual. Stimuli that usually produce sexual arousal, gratitude, anxiety, guilt, loneliness, hatred, jealousy, or confusion may all increase one's physiological arousal, and thus increase the intensity of his emotional experience. As long as one attributes his agitated state to passion, he should experience true passionate love. As soon as he ceases to attribute his tumultuous feelings to passion, love should die.

Does any evidence exist to support our contention? Some early observers noticed that any form of strong emotional arousal breeds love (although not, of course, interpreting this relationship in Schachterian terms). Finck (1891), an early psychologist, concluded:

Love can only be excited by strong and vivid emotions, and it is almost immaterial whether these emotions are agreeable or disagreeable. The Cid wooed the proud heart of Diana Ximene, whose father he had slain, by shooting one after another of her pet pigeons. Such persons as arouse in us only weak emotions or none at all, are obviously least likely to incline us toward them. . . . Our aversion is most likely to be bestowed on individuals who, as the phrase goes, are neither 'warm' nor 'cold'; whereas impulsive, choleric people, though they may readily offend us, are just as capable of making us warmly attached to them (p. 240).

Unfortunately, experimental evidence does not yet exist to support the contention that almost any form of high arousal, if properly labeled, will deepen passion. There are, however, a few studies designed to test other hypotheses, which provide some minimal support for our contention.*

Since it was the juxtaposition of misery and ecstasy in romantic love that we initially found so perplexing, let us first examine the relation between negative experiences and love.

Unpleasant Emotional States: Facilitators of Passion?

That negative reinforcements produce strong emotional reactions in all animals is not in doubt (see Skinner, 1938). There is some evidence that under the right condition such unpleasant, but arousing, states as fear, rejection, and frustration do enhance romantic passion.

* These studies are only "minimally supportive" because the authors investigate only liking, not passionate loving — a phenomenon we have argued is unique. Whether or not the same results would occur in a romantic context must yet be determined.

Fear: A Facilitator of Passion

Frightening a person is a very good way of producing intense psychological arousal for a substantial period of time (see Ax, 1953; Wolf and Wolff, 1947; and Schacter, 1957).

An intriguing study by Brehm et al (1970) demonstrates that a frightened man is a romantic man. Brehm et al tested the hypothesis that "a person's attraction to another would be multiplied by prior arousal from an irrelevant event." In this experiment, some men were led to believe that they would soon receive three "pretty stiff" electrical shocks. Half of the men, "Threat" subjects, were allowed to retain this erroneous expectation throughout the experiment. Half of the men, "Threat-Relief," were frightened and then, sometime later, were told that the experimenter had made an error; they had been assigned to the control group and would receive no shock. The remainder of the men were assigned to a control group, in which the possibility of their receiving shock was not even mentioned.

Men were then introduced to a young co-ed, and asked how much they liked her.

The Threat subjects who expected to be shocked in the future should be quite frightened at the time they meet the girl. The Threat-Relief subjects who had just learned they would not be shocked should be experiencing vast relief when they meet the girl. Both the frightened and the frightened-relieved men should be more aroused than are men in the control group. Brehm predicted, as we would, that Threat and Threat-Relief subjects would like the girl more than would control subjects. Brehm's expectations were confirmed; threatened men experienced more liking for the girl (and did not differ in their liking) than did control group men, who had never been frightened. An irrelevant frightening event, then, does seem to facilitate attraction.

Rejection: An Antecedent of Passion

Rejection is always disturbing. And generally when a person is rejected he has a strong emotional reaction. Usually he experiences embarrassment, pain, or anger. Although it is probably most reasonable for a rejected person to label his agitation in this way, if our hypothesis is correct, it should be possible, under the right conditions, to induce a rejected individual to label his emotional response as "love" as well as "hate."

Some slight evidence that passionate love *or* hate may emerge from rejection comes from several laboratory experiments designed to test other hypotheses (Dittes, 1959; Walster, 1965; and Jacobs et al, 1971).

Let us consider one of these experiments and the way a Schachterian might reinterpret these data.

The experiment of Jacobs et al was designed to determine how changes in the self-esteem of college students affected their receptivity to love and affection. First, students took a number of personality tests (the *MMPI*, Rorschach, etc.). A few weeks later, a psychologist returned an analysis of his personality to each student. Half of the students were given a flattering personality report. The reports stressed their sensitivity, honesty, originality, and freedom of outlook. (Undoubtedly this flattering personality report confirmed many of the wonderful things the students already thought about themselves.) Half of the students received an insulting personality report. The report stressed their immaturity, weak personality, conventionality, and lack of leadership ability. This critical report was naturally most upsetting for students.

Soon after receiving their analyses, the males got acquainted individually with a young female college student (actually, this girl was an experimental confederate). Half of the time the girl treated the boy in a warm, affectionate, and accepting way. Under such conditions, the men who had received the critical personality evaluation were far more attracted to her than were their more confident counterparts. (Presumably, the previous irrelevant arousal engendered by rejection facilitated the subsequent development of affection.)

Half of the time the girl was cold and rejecting. Under these conditions, a dramatic reversal occurred; the previously rejected men disliked the girl more than did their more confident counterparts. (Presumably, under these conditions, the low self-esteem individual's agitation was transformed to hatred.)

An irrelevant, painful event, then, can incite various strong emotional reactions toward others. Depending on how he labels his feelings, the individual may experience either intensive attraction or intense hostility.

Frustration and Challenge: Facilitators of Passion

Socrates, Ovid, Terence, the Kama Sutra and "Dear Abby" are all in agreement about one thing; the person whose affection is easily won will inspire less passion than the person whose affection is hard to win.

Vassilikos (1964) poetically elucidated the principle that frustration fuels passion while continual gratification dims it:

Once upon a time there was a little fish who was a bird from the waist up and who was madly in love with a little bird who was a fish from the waist up. So the Fish-Bird kept saying to the Bird-Fish: "Oh, why were we created so that we can never live together? You in the wind and I in the wave. What a pity for both of us." And the Bird-Fish would answer: "No, what luck for both of us. This way we'll always be in love because we'll always be separated" (p. 131).

Some provisional evidence that the hard-to-get person may engender unusual passion in the eventually successful suitor comes from Aronson and Linder (1965). These authors tested the hypothesis that: "A gain in esteem is a more potent reward than invariant esteem." They predicted that a person would be better liked if his positive regard was difficult to acquire than if it was easily had.

This hypothesis was tested in the following way: Subjects were required to converse with a confederate (who appeared to be another naive subject) over a series of seven meetings. After each meeting, the subject discovered (secretly) how her conversation partner felt about her. How the confederate "felt" was systematically varied. In one condition the girl expressed a negative impression of the subject after their first meetings. (She described the subject as being a dull conversationalist, a rather ordinary person, not very intelligent, as probably not having many friends, etc.) Only after the partners had become well acquainted did she begin expressing favorable opinions of the subject. In the remaining conditions, from the first, the confederate expressed only positive opinions about the subject.

As Aronson and Linder predicted, subjects liked the confederate whose affection was hard to win better than they liked the confederate whose high opinion was readily obtained.

The preceding evidence is consistent with our suggestion that under the right conditions, a hard-to-get girl should generate more passion than the constantly rewarding girl.

The aloof girl's challenge may excite the suitor; her momentary rejection may shake his self-esteem. In both cases, such arousal may intensify the suitor's feelings toward her.

The preceeding analysis lends some credence to the argument that the juxtaposition of agony and ectasy in passionate love is not entirely accidental. (The original meaning of "passion" was, in fact, "agony" — for example, as in Christ's passion.) Loneliness, deprivation, frustration, hatred, and insecurity may in fact supplement a person's romantic experiences. Passion requires physiological arousal, and all of the preceding states are certainly arousing.

Pleasant Emotional States: Facilitators of Passion?

We would like to make it clear that, theoretically, passion need not include a negative component. The positive reinforcements of discovery, excitement, companionship, and playful-joy can generate as intense an arousal as that stirred by fear, frustration, or rejection. For example, in many autobiographical accounts, entirely joyful (albeit brief) passionate encounters are described (e.g., Duncan, 1968).

Sexual Gratification: A Facilitator of Passion

Sexual experiences can be enormously rewarding and enormously arousing. Masters and Johnson (1966) point out that sexual intercourse induces hyperventilation, tachycardia, and marked increases in blood pressure. And, religious advisors, school counselors, and psychoanalysts to the contrary — sexual gratification has undoubtedly generated as much passionate love as has sexual continence.

Valins (1966) demonstrated that even the erroneous belief that another has excited one (sexually or aesthetically) will facilitate attraction. Valins recruited male college students for a study of males' physiological reactions to sexual stimuli. The sexual stimuli he utilized were ten semi-nude *Playboy* photographs. The subjects were told that while they scrutinized these photographs, their heart rate would be amplified and recorded. They were led to believe that their heart rates altered markedly to some of the slides but that they had no reaction at all to others. (Valins assumed that the subjects would interpret an alteration in heart rate as sexual enthusiasm.)

The subjects' liking for the "arousing" and "nonarousing" slides was then assessed in three ways. Regardless of the measure used, the men markedly preferred the pin-ups they thought had aroused them to those that had not affected their heart rate. 1) They were asked to rate how "attractive or appealing" each pin-up was. They preferred the pin-ups they believed were arousing to all others. 2) They were offered a pin-up in remuneration for participating in the experiment. They chose the arousing pin-ups more often than the nonarousing ones. 3) Finally, they were interviewed a month later (in a totally different context) and they still markedly preferred the arousing pin-ups to the others.

Need Satisfaction: A Facilitator of Passion

Although psychologists tend to focus almost exclusively on the contribution of sex to love, other rewards can have an equally important emotional impact. People have a wide variety of needs, and at any stage of life many of one's needs must remain unsatisfied. When any important unsatisfied need is recognized or met, the emotional response which accompanies such reinforcement could provide fuel for passion. To the adolescent boy who has been humored, coddled, and babied at home, the girl who finally recognizes his masculinity may be an over-powering joy. The good, steady, reliable, hard-working father may be captivated when an alert lady recognizes that he has the potential to be a playful and reckless lover.

To the person who has been deprived of such rewards, an intelligent, artistic, witty, beautiful, athletic, or playful companion may prove a passionate and absorbing joy.

Labeling

We are proposing a two-factor theory of passionate love. Yet the preceding discussion has focused almost exclusively on one factor. We have concentrated on demonstrating that physiological arousal is a crucial component of passionate love, and that fear, pain, and frustration as well as discovery and delight may contribute to the passionate experience.

We should now at least remind the reader that according to our theory an individual will be incapable of experiencing "love" unless he's prepared to define his feeling in that way.

Cultural Encouragement of Love

In our culture, it is expected that everyone will eventually fall in love. Individuals are strongly encouraged to interpret a wide range of confused feelings as love. Linton makes this point in a somewhat harsh observation:

All societies recognize that there are occasional violent emotional attachments between persons of the opposite sex, but our present American culture is practically the only one which has attempted to capitalize on these and make them the basis for marriage. The hero of the modern American movie is always a romantic lover, just as the hero of an old Arab epic is always an epileptic. A cynic may suspect that in any ordinary population the percentage of individuals with capacity for romantic love of the Hollywood type was about as large as that of persons able to throw genuine epileptic fits (p. 175).

Individuals are often encouraged to interpret certain confused or mixed feelings as love, because our culture insists that certain reactions are acceptable if one is madly in love. For example, the delightful experience of sexual intercourse can be frankly labeled as "sexual fun" by a man. Such an interpretation of what she is experiencing is probably less acceptable to his partner. She (and her parents) are undoubtedly happier if she attributes her abandoned behavior to love.

Margaret Mead interprets jealousy in one way:

Jealousy is not a barometer by which the depth of love may be read. It merely records the degree of the lover's insecurity. It is a negative, miserable state of feeling, having its origin in a sense of insecurity and inferiority.

Jealous people, however, usually interpret their jealous reactions in quite another way; jealous feelings are taken as evidence of passionate love rather than inferiority. Thus, in this culture, a jealous man is a loving man rather than an embarrassed man.

Thus, whether or not an individual is susceptible to "falling in love," should depend on the expectations of his culture and his reference groups.

Individual Expectations

An individual's own expectations should also determine how likely he is to experience love.

The individual who thinks of himself as a nonromantic person should fall in love less often than should an individual who assumes that love is inevitable. The nonromantic may experience the same feelings that the romantic does, but he will code them differently.

Similarly, individuals who feel they are unlovable should have a difficult time finding love. Individuals convey their expectations in very subtle ways to others, and these expectations influence the way one's partner labels *his* reactions. The insecure girl who complains to her boyfriend: "You don't love me, you just think you do. If you loved me you wouldn't treat me this way," and then itemizes evidence of his neglect, may, by automatically interpreting her boyfriend's actions in a damaging way, effect an alteration in his feelings for her. Alternately, a girl with a great deal of self-confidence, may (by her unconscious guidance) induce a normally unreceptive gentleman to label his feelings for her as love.

REFERENCES

Aronson, E., & Linder, D. Gain and loss of esteem as determinants of interpersonal attractiveness. *Journal of Experimental Social Psychology*, 1965, *1*, 156-171.

Ax, A. F. Fear and anger in humans. *Psychosomatic Medicine*, 1953, *15*, 433-442.

Brehm, J. W., Gatz, M., Goethals, G., McCrimmon, J., & Ward, L. Psychological arousal and interpersonal attraction. Mimeo, 1970. Available from authors.

Byrne, D., London, O., & Reeves, K. The effect of physical attractiveness, sex, and attitude similarity on interpersonal attraction. *Journal of Personality*, 1968, *36*, 269-271.

Dittes, J. E. Attractiveness of group as function of self-esteem and acceptance by group. *Journal of Abnormal and Social Psychology*, 1959, *59*, 77-82.

Duncan, I. *Isadora*. New York: Award Books, 1968.

Finck, H. T. *Romantic love and personal beauty: Their development, causal relations, historic and national peculiarities*. London. Macmillan, 1891.

Freud, S. The most prevalent form of degradation in erotic life. In E. Jones (ed.), *Collected papers, 4*. London: Hogarth, 1925, pp. 203-216.

Hohmann, G. W. The effect of dysfunctions of the autonomic nervous system on experienced feelings and emotions. Paper read at Conference on Emotions and Feelings at New School for Social Research, New York, 1962.

Homans, G. C. *The human group*. New York: Harcourt, Brace, and World, 1950.

Jacobs, L., Walster, E., & Berscheid, E. Self-esteem and attraction. *Journal of Personality and Social Psychology*, 1971, *17*, 84-91.

Linton, R. *The study of man* (1936). New York: Appleton-Century, 1964.

Maranon, G. Contribution a l'etude de l'action emotive de l'adrenaline. *Revue Francaise Endocrinalogia*, 1924, *2*, 301-325.

Masters, W. H., & Johnson, V. E. *Human sexual response*. Boston: Little, Brown and Company, 1966.

Mead, M. In A. M. Krich, *The anatomy of love*. New York: Dell, 1960.

Newcomb, T. N. *The acquaintance process*. New York: Holt, Rinehart, and Winston, 1961.

Schachter, J. Pain, fear and anger in hypertensives and normotensives: A psychophysiological study. *Psychosomatic Medicine*, 1957, *19*, 17-24.

Schachter, S. The interaction of cognitive and physiological determinants of emotional state. In Berkowitz (ed.), *Advances in experimental social psychology, 1*. New York: Academic Press, 1964, pp. 49-80.

Schachter, S., & Singer, J. Cognitive, social and physiological determinants of emotional state. *Psychological Review*, 1962, *69*, 379-399.

Schachter, S., & Wheeler, L. Epinephrine, chlorpromazine, and amusement. *Journal of Abnormal Social Psychology*, 1962, *65*, 121-128.

Valins, S. Cognitive effects of false heart-rate feedback. *Journal of Personality and Social Psychology*, 1966, *4*, 400-408.

Vassilikos, V. *The plant; the well; the angel: A trilogy*. Translated from Greek.

60

Happy People

A psychologist unveils the 5 theories of happiness

By Jonathan Freedman

Illustrations by Debby Young

Are you happy?'' psychologist Jonathan Freedman began asking people back in the fall of 1975. ''If so, why? If not, why not?'' he wanted to know.

But when the inquiring professor interviewed individuals face to face about their personal happiness, they just couldn't answer him freely. Time after time they would clam up. It was almost as if he wanted to know intimate details about their sex lives. He had stumbled onto something quite fascinating. In fact, as Archbishop Whatley of Dublin said over 100 years ago, ''This happiness is no laughing matter.'' It is very serious business.

Freedman, however, was determined to get answers. What is happiness? Who has it? How do you get it? And how can you measure it? So he tried to get his information by mail; through his surveys, he questioned, pushed and prodded. It was then that he found he wasn't alone in his fascination with this most basic human condition. Almost a hundred thousand people took the

If you are doing better than someone else is, you are happy; if you are doing worse, you are unhappy.

time and energy and used their own postage stamps to reply to his questionnaire. Then, he compared his results with research done by other psychologists, sociologists and survey experts. We think you'll find his work fascinating and helpful. If you just generally feel happy, you may discover why. And if you're unhappy, you may learn how to do something about it.

There is no simple formula for producing happiness. I just can't list a set of requirements and say that these, or some proportion of these, are necessary; that you will be happy if you have them and unhappy if you do not. Yes, certain elements are very closely related to happiness. For example, married people are happier than unmarrieds on the average. Sex, good health, an above-poverty income, friends and a job each makes happiness easier to attain. Also, there is evidence that people who have confidence in their own guiding values, who believe that there is meaning and direction in life, and who feel they have control over the good and bad things that happen to them are generally happier than people who do not.

But not one of these factors is either necessary or sufficient. You can lack any one of them and still be happy—and you can have all of them and still be miserable.

I cannot provide a recipe—like a cup of love and a teaspoon of guiding values. Perhaps that's because happiness depends on something more complex than a combination of ingredients. It depends less on the mixture of elements than on how the individual responds to them.

In lieu of supplying you with a ''no-bake, quick-cake'' recipe for happiness, what I can do is provide you with five basic theories of what makes an individual happy.

Comparison to Others

The comparison theory is a compelling one, widely discussed and simple to understand. It goes like this: If you are doing better than someone else is, you are happy; if you are doing worse, you are unhappy. There is no set level of anything—money, sex, love, whatever. Rather, you look around at other people and get some idea of how much of each important element they seem to have. You are satisfied if you have about as much, and delighted if you have more.

Take, for example, the college graduate and the less-educated man who both earn the same salary. The college graduate compares himself to other college graduates, so his income might not seem very good. In fact, it might seem low. In contrast, the high school graduate compares himself to other high school graduates. If he finds that he is making more than most of them, he feels good about it.

The Ten Pillars Of Happiness

RANK	SINGLE MEN	SINGLE WOMEN	MARRIED MEN	MARRIED WOMEN
1.	*Friends and social life*	*Friends and social life*	*Personal growth*	*Being in love*
2.	*Job or primary activity*	*Being in love*	*Being in love*	*Marriage*
3.	*Being in love*	*Job or primary activity*	*Marriage*	*Partner's happiness*
4.	*Recognition, success*	*Recognition, success*	*Job or primary activity*	*Sex life*
5.	*Sex life*	*Personal growth*	*Partner's happiness*	{ *Recognition, success*
6.	*Personal growth*	*Sex life*	*Sex life*	{ *Personal growth*
7.	*Finances*	*Health*	*Recognition, success*	{ *Job or primary activity*
8.	*House or apartment*	*Body and attractiveness*	*Friends and social life*	{ *Friends and social life*
9.	{ *Body and attractiveness*	*Finances*	*Being a parent*	*Health*
10.	{ *Health*	*House or apartment*	*Finances*	*Being a parent*

(Bracketed items were rated equal in importance.)

Although this makes sense and, I suspect, is true some of the time for some people, it is not the whole story. For one thing, I did not find that sexual satisfaction was related to one's notion of others' sexual behavior. Most people think (wrongly) that others are more sexually active than themselves; but those who thought others were more active were just about as likely to be happy themselves as anyone else. In other words, happiness with sex depended not on number of sex partners, only somewhat on frequency, and not at all on what one thought others were doing. It depended on whether one was in love, and how "good" the sex was, whatever that meant to them.

My guess is that the comparison theory works in the realm of your achievement of goals set by society, but a more *absolute* happiness scale is in play concerning certain crucial, personal elements of your life. In other words, society says it is good to make money, be successful, get recognition and have a good job; and society also defines what each of these terms mean. How much money is a lot? We can only tell by comparing ourselves to others similar to us.

In contrast, other crucial elements in our lives are evaluated without comparisons and without the definitions of society. We experience and judge them directly. For instance, I don't much care whether Craig Claiborne or any other famous gourmet likes a particular restaurant. I may use his judgment in deciding whether to try the place, but once I'm there, I can taste the food for myself; if I like it, that's all that matters.

The absolute scale seems to me to work for internal states that contribute to happiness: sexual pleasure, love, satisfaction with marriage and family. Also, self-confidence, feelings of control and a sense of meaning in life all depend mainly on the

---

Jonathan Freedman is a professor of psychology at Columbia University in New York City, and author of Crowding and Behavior.

Some expectations are realistic. Others are based on ignorance, Hollywood and comic books.

individual himself or herself, and comparisons to others are largely irrelevant.

Expectations vs. Achievements

A related theory is that happiness depends on the comparison between what we expect and what we get. Instead of comparing ourselves to others, we ask ourselves what we want (or expect) and are happy when we achieve as much and particularly when we get more. Under these terms, what other people are doing matters only insofar as they have influenced our goals and expectations. If I make half a million dollars and that's what I expected to make, I'm happy—even if everyone else makes a million. In the same way, if a comedy movie gets rave reviews from the critics and from our friends, but it turns out that we only laugh or smile a few times, we are disappointed. But if we had heard nothing about the movie and simply wandered in on impulse, the few laughs and smiles may be enough to give us a good time.

This process operates in many aspects of life. Unexpected success brings pleasure and happiness; unexpected failure brings dissatisfaction and leads to unhappiness. And, attaining what you expect may bring a more or less neutral reaction. For example, if you confidently expect to make $30,000 a year by the age of 35, earnings of $30,000 will give you only modest satisfaction. It is, after all, just what you expected. And I'm not talking about dreams and fantasies that are fulfilled. If you *fantasize* about making a million dollars or even $30,000, that's entirely different from truly expecting such an income. When a dream is achieved,

presumably that is very satisfying and may give great happiness.

Many kinds of interpersonal, social aspects of life also are affected in part by our expectations. What do we think marriage will be like? How many friends should one have? What is it like to have a new baby? How often should you fall in love, and how wonderful will it be when it happens? We all have expectations about these things, some of them reasonable, probably some of them entirely unrealistic, based on ignorance, Hollywood and comic books. If we expect to have total and unleavened joy from the arrival of a newborn baby, we will be very disappointed by diaper changes, three o'clock feedings and colic. Similarly, if we expect love and marriage to be endlessly ecstatic, we are in for some surprises.

Even strong physical pleasures such as sex may be heightened or reduced by expectations. If you assume you will have sex twice a day throughout marriage, you will usually be disappointed and may be unhappy even though you are having as much as you *really* want. But there's one group of people who probably still won't be pleased by reaching their goals, or even by occasionally surpassing them. These are the people who have decided, for one reason or another, that life is miserable and that nothing good will ever happen to them. Their expectations are so low that they are almost always reached or exceeded. Yet, these people typically derive little satisfaction from anything. They continue to view life as an unhappy state, and occasional successes do not mean much. These may be extreme cases, but they are examples of the fact that our attitudes toward life also determine how much we enjoy what happens to us, and what we achieve. If you expect to be unhealthy, unloved and unemployed, being right will not make you less unhappy.

Adaptation Level
(or, What You Are Used To)

All organisms tend to get accustomed to any level of stimulation they experience for a long period. This is called adaptation, and the amount of stimulation to which they become accustomed is called their "adaptation level."

Adaptation occurs in virtually all aspects of our lives. We get used to a certain level of income, a life-style, a quiet or busy social life, the kind of community we live in, a certain amount of sex, the number of friends we have and how intimate we are with them, a certain amount of success, the work we do and just about everything else. The key point of all of this is that we barely notice these things as long as we are at our adaptation level. Only when our lives change, when we deviate from this level, do we feel a real impact. In terms of happiness, one theory is that we derive satisfaction and happiness only when we surpass our adaptation level and unhappiness when we sink below it.

This process works for all of the important elements that contribute to happiness. If we are usually perfectly healthy, any sickness makes us unhappy. But if we are usually in very poor health, a slight improvement makes us happy.

This theory explains why people who seem to have everything are not necessarily happy. After a while they get used to having "everything" and only getting more will have a substantial effect on their happiness. However, adapting to a particular level doesn't necessarily eliminate all of the good that is derived from that level. We get used to having lots of friends yet still enjoy seeing them all.

Hierarchy of Needs

Here's another question, unanswered by the three above-mentioned theories: Why do two people who seem very similar in most respects, who have the same kinds of lives, the same level of material and social goods, and maybe even the same degree of optimism and sense of control often differ enormously in their satisfaction with life and their happiness?

Abraham Maslow, a leading humanistic psychologist, suggested some years ago that people have a hierarchy of needs that range from the most basic, physiological needs to higher, more humane, complex, creative ones. He believed that it was necessary to satisfy those needs lower on the hierarchy before one could begin satisfying the higher ones. In particular, the highest need, which he called self-actualization—a complete

expression of one's potential and feeling—could be fulfilled only after all the lower ones were satisfied. Presumably, happiness comes from taking care of all these needs.

The twist, however, is that each time you satisfy one need, a higher one comes to the fore. When you are hungry, you don't worry too much about being creative. When you are without love, you may not worry too much about expressing your need to understand the world. When you are worrying about gaining recognition and increasing your self-esteem, you may not be concerned with realizing your full potential. Thus, at each stage, almost as we discussed in terms of adaptation level, a new series of needs becomes important. This means that people move up the ladder, become fuller, more

There is no one best way to respond to the world to attain happiness.

actualized people, but do not necessarily become happier because they are always trying to fulfill *some* need.

Another way of looking at this is that as we ascend the ladder, as we satisfy more needs or just get more out of life, our standards and sights change. I think that many people do follow Maslow's scenario: They constantly expand their horizons, constantly want more. In many ways this is good, but it may also mean that happiness is never achieved. This theory may explain why happiness can be so elusive; once attained for a moment, it seems to slip from one's grasp and be just around the bend, just beyond one's grip.

Talent for Happiness

Finally, there is the idea that some people have a "talent" for happiness that others lack. We all know that some people enjoy life more than others, make the most of what they have, while others are exactly the opposite—always complaining, never seeming to experience joy, looking at the sour side of everything. Such divisions in people do exist, and to some extent this "talent" or capacity plays a role in happiness. Unfortunately, we just don't know what constitutes this talent or how one gets

it. Perhaps there are complex personality traits or combinations of them that allow or encourage happiness and others that do the opposite, but we don't know what they are. I don't think it's true, as some have suggested, that happiness comes from asking very little from life. Some of the happiest people have asked a lot; some of the unhappiest have asked little. Nor is there any reason to believe that true happiness comes from passively accepting whatever happens to you. Under some circumstances presumably this would help, but many of the happiest people fight constantly for what they want, accept nothing at face value, constantly strive for more.

Having looked at a great many answers to questions concerning happiness, it seems clear that there is no one best way to respond to the world in order to attain happiness. Overall, however, these theories of happiness can help a great deal in understanding the phenomenon. Taken together, they give a fairly good picture of who is happy and perhaps what determines happiness. The major conclusion is that happiness is an enormously complex concept and feeling, and that the quest for happiness is inevitably constant and dynamic for most people. We change, the world changes, our needs change and our requirements for happiness change—all the time.

One final thought. While it is true that happiness is elusive and that the pursuit must continue for our entire lives, it is also true that at no point is the quest hopeless. One of the clearest findings from my research is that almost nothing in one's past makes happiness unattainable in the future. People who led very unhappy childhoods, whose parents divorced or died, who were treated coldly, who had physical and psychological problems, still manage to be happy adults. People who have unsuccessful marriages, get divorced and remarry are just as likely to be happy as those in a first marriage. People who are unhappy where they live and move to another city, are just as likely to be happy in their new location as people who were there in the first place. And people who are 65 and older are just as likely—perhaps even a little *more* likely—to be happy as younger people.

The pursuit of happiness is difficult and chancy, but you are never eliminated from the game. ■

XI. Toward Moral Maturity

The readings in this volume are organized in a rough hierarchy that extends from the evolutionarily most basic, natural determinants of social behavior to those that are mediated by the higher cognitive processes unique to humans. The selections in this final section relate to what is commonly considered the epitome of human development—the acquisition of morality.

Morality involves the rules that prescribe rights and duties. Most social psychology texts discuss the acquisition of morality in terms of socialization. They assume that parents, teachers, and other members of society teach children to behave morally. The articles included in this section take a quite different tack. They assume that children are far from passive recipients of moral indoctrination; rather, they actively construct their moral principles. This assumption stems from Jean Piaget's theory of cognitive development.

Early in Piaget's career, in 1932, he published an engaging and insightful book—*The Moral Judgment of the Child*. The central problem it dealt with was to explain how, if children acquire a sense of morality from adults and other socializing agents, they can ever become morally autonomous, that is,

Artwork by Martin Riskin.

develop their own moral values. Piaget observed children and found that young children do, in fact, orient almost exclusively to adults. However, he also found that as children get older, they become increasingly oriented to their relations with peers, and, in a context of "mutual respect," they construct their own rules, regulations, and principles of justice. Thus, ultimately, most people derive their moral principles from their own experience. They figure out what is right and wrong in much the same way they figure out why, for example, some things float on water and other things do not.

In the mid 1950s, a young graduate student at the University of Chicago, Lawrence Kohlberg, became interested in Piaget's theory of moral development. He developed a test of moral judgment that he believed improved on Piaget's tests, and gave it to some 72 subjects. Kohlberg has followed these subjects, testing their ideas about morality approximately every three years for 30 years. The results of this long-term study (see "The Child as a Moral Philosopher") indicate that people may pass through as many as six stages of moral development, defined in terms of qualitatively different ways of thinking about moral issues. By the early 1970s Kohlberg's theory had become the most influential in the field.

The work of cognitive-developmental theorists such as Lawrence Kohlberg and Jean Piaget is controversial because it makes value statements. Kohlberg's theory is attempting to decipher the logic of the moral decisions made by people at different stages of cognitive and social maturity. He is not concerned with *what* people believe is right or wrong (the content of moral thought, or moral attitudes); he is concerned with the rules they use to arrive at conclusions about what is right and wrong (the structure of thought). It is of more interest to Kohlberg to learn that one person believes it is wrong to steal because it violates a law and another person believes that it is wrong to steal because he doesn't want people to think that he is a bad person than it is to learn that both people believe that stealing is wrong. Similarly, there is no one-to-one relationship between moral reasoning and moral action. There are many reasons for performing the same act; and knowing what is right is no guarantee that a person will do what is right.

In recent years Kohlberg has turned his attention to the practical task of fostering moral maturity. At first he devoted his attention to moral discussion groups; then he decided that a full-scale restructuring of the moral environment was necessary to promote major changes in moral orientation. He attempted to create "just communities" in schools and prisons (see "Moral Thinking: Can It Be Taught?" by Howard Muson).

Kohlberg's theory has been severely criticized, as has the success of his just communities. He has dismissed some of the criticisms as misconceptions, has made changes in his theory to accommodate to others, and is wrestling with those that are more trenchant. At present it is unclear how much of Kohlberg's theory of moral development is a reflection of his own values and ingeniousness, and how much is a reflection of a universal truth.

When we think of morality, we are often disposed to use people as the unit of analysis. We believe that there are moral and immoral people. Kohlberg does not encourage us to employ his stages as defining characteristics of people. He insists that they describe ways of thinking about moral issues, not by types of motivation, behavior, or personality. Yet, ways of thinking about moral issues are associated with ways of thinking about other issues, such as politics. Charles Hampden-Turner and Phillip Whitten ("Morals

Left and Right") suggest that political conservatives generally employ mid-level conventional moral reasoning (Stages 3 and 4), that liberals generally employ utilitarian moral reasoning (Stage 5), and that political radicals can be divided into two groups—those who have immature hedonistic conceptions of morality (Stage 2) and those who are principled, at the top of the scale (Stage 6).

Research on moral development is often considered to fall within the confines of developmental psychology, not social psychology. I believe that social psychology would benefit by rooting many of its studies in a developmental context. Social psychologists generally employ subjects in their experiments who are easiest to acquire and most cooperative—students in their classes, or elementary school children. This procedure may result in the production of a "social psychology of sophomores" that says little about people at other stages of development. Moreover, in considering behavior as an end product, rather than tracing its development, social psychologists sacrifice information about its origins that could help define it and give it meaning. The developmental perspective that characterizes this final section parallels the evolutionary perspective of earlier sections. We understand phenomena in relief. We can understand human social behavior by casting it in the context of nonhuman social behavior and by casting it within the context of the life span of individuals.

In the final article in this volume, "Some Issues of Ethics in Social Psychology," by Stephen G. West and Steven P. Gunn, we return to conventional social psychology and examine the social psychologist as ethical philosopher. Conducting research on human (and nonhuman) subjects requires difficult moral decisions. To what extent is it right to jeopardize people's welfare in order to contribute to knowledge? In what ways can we keep the costs to a minimum?

61 Reconsideration: The Moral Judgment of the Child

by Dennis Krebs

The Moral Judgment of the Child
by Jean Piaget
The Free Press, 1932

Reconsidered by Dennis Krebs

If you had visited the elementary schools of Geneva or Neuchâtel during the early 1930s, you might have observed a young Swiss scholar playing marbles with children. You could not have been blamed if you found his behavior frivolous, or even strange; but you would not have had to watch for long to see that he took the matter seriously—interacting with the children with intensity and respect, asking them for advice, and quizzing them about the rules of the game. Although you might have suspected that the reason the scholar gave the children for his interest in the game—to relearn how to play marbles— was less than forthright, it is unlikely that you would have guessed that the purpose of his endeavor was nothing less ambitious than to discover the origins of morality, and that the information he acquired would form part of the basis for his fifth book, *The Moral Judgment of the Child*.

The young scholar, of course, was Jean Piaget. Today, 46 years and more than two dozen books later, he is the world's best-known child psychologist. But what does playing marbles have to do with morality? According to Piaget, "All morality consists in a system of rules, and the essence of all morality is to be sought for in the respect which the individual acquires for these rules." Games like marbles are microcosms. They take place in societies of children and are governed by rules that are created and enforced by children. Adult influence is minimal. What better place to observe the development of concepts of right and wrong, fairness and cheating, justice and injustice?

Piaget published only one book on moral development, in 1932, and never returned to the topic. The rest of his work has dealt almost exclusively with intellectual development. He considered his early study of moral development as a preliminary piece of work and said that he hoped it would "supply a scaffolding" for later researchers and theorists. By now the edifice Piaget inaugurated has changed in many ways, but it owes its origins to the ingenious design of an exceptionally creative architect.

Piaget followed up his observations of marble players by interviewing children extensively about a number of moral issues, usually exploring their responses to little stories he had created. In the second section of *The Moral Judgment of the Child* he presents and analyzes children's responses to pairs of stories in which characters commit minor transgressions. The best-known and most thoroughly investigated pair was designed to test children's concepts of responsibility:

"A little boy who is called John is in his room. He is called to dinner. He goes into the dining room. But behind the door there was a chair, and on the chair there was a tray with fifteen cups on it. John couldn't have known that there was all this behind the door. He goes in, the door knocks against the tray, bang go the fifteen cups and they get all broken.

"Once there was a little boy whose name was Henry. One day when his mother was out he tried to get some jam out of the cupboard. He climbed up onto a chair and stretched out his arm. But the jam was too high up and he couldn't reach it and have any. But while he was trying to get it he knocked over a cup. The cup fell down and broke."

Are these children equally guilty? Which is the naughtier, and why?

Piaget believed that choosing the child in the first story as the naughtier indicated an *objective* sense of responsibility; choosing the child in the second story indicated a *subjective* sense. He found that young children tend to display an objective sense of responsibility; older children, a subjective sense. These responses, when combined with responses to pairs of stories dealing with other moral issues, led Piaget to conclude that children typically pass through two phases of morality. He called the first phase the "morality of constraint," or "heteronomy," to indicate that it consisted of ideas that appeared to have been imposed from the outside by authorities. He called the second phase "the morality of cooperation," or "autonomy." Piaget was careful to indicate that, although the morality of cooperation generally followed the morality of constraint in a child's development, they could not be considered clear-cut "stages."

Within the context of his broad conclusions, Piaget drew several more specific ones. Young children believe that rules are unchangeable and absolute; that children with good intentions who do a lot of damage (break 15 cups) are naughtier than children with bad intentions who do less damage (break one cup); that when people transgress they should be punished severely; and that obedience to authority is more important than loyalty to friends. Older children, on the other hand, believe that rules are flexible; that intentions are more important than consequences; that punishments should foster restitution rather than vindictiveness; and that loyalty to peers is more important than obedience to adults.

Piaget suggested that the evolution from the morality of constraint to the morality of cooperation was the result of the interaction of social, emotional, and intellectual forces. He believed that societies of young children are characterized by "unilateral respect" for adults and that children's thought processes are limited by "egocentricity" (the inability to take another's point of view) and "realism." Young children believe that "right is to obey the will of the adult; wrong is to have a will of one's own," and that rules are like real things that should not be broken. Because young children are not disposed to take the role of others, they fail to consider fully people's intentions when evaluating their actions.

As children grow older they develop more sophisticated thought processes and acquire greater independence from adults, and thus more autonomy. The social relationships of older children are more cooperative; they give respect to their peers and demand it in return. Ultimately, unilateral respect gives way to "mutual respect," and children discover moral principles like equality, reciprocity, and fairness. Moral autonomy is achieved only "when mutual respect is strong enough to make the individual feel from within the desire to treat others as he himself would wish to be treated."

In all likelihood, the specific conclusions reached by Piaget are erroneous, or at best limited. I would not recommend reading *The Moral Judgment of the Child* to learn about the causes and course of moral development. Its major value lies in Piaget's introduction of a new and ingenious way of looking at and investigating morality.

Piaget began by recognizing that everybody is an amateur ethical philosopher, each developing his or her own ideas about right and wrong. Instead of debating whether one theory is better than another, as philosophers of ethics do, Piaget set out to investigate them scientifically. Most of the scientific work on morality available to Piaget was sociological. He was particularly aware of the writings of the French sociologist Emile Durkheim. But instead of comparing the complex moral systems of adults in different societies, as Durkheim and other sociologists had done, Piaget searched for their origin in children. He agreed that moral concepts are influenced by society, but argued that it is not necessary to turn to different cultures to find different social systems; he looked within his own culture and compared the societies of children with the societies of adults. It was this assumption that led him to observe children playing marbles.

The advantages of the methods introduced by Piaget are obvious. Observing children is much more practical than observing societies, and the developmental method permits an investigator to assess not only differences in the concepts of morality possessed by different people or different societies, but also how the concepts change with development. However, it must be said that Piaget's research did not live up to the developmental ideal. He substituted the cross-sectional comparison of children of different ages for the observation of long-term changes within the same individuals, and he interviewed only a small sample of working-class children from a limited age range. Yet the application of an empirically oriented developmental perspective to the investigation of children's concepts of morality was an innovation of major importance.

The ideas and findings in *The Moral Judgment of the Child* have been widely criticized, but many of the criticisms are based on misrepresentations of Piaget's work. Some critics have identified Piaget with positions he does not endorse, supposing that Piaget saw two clear-cut, invariant stages of moral judgment, and that he held that the ideas of children consistently stem from one stage or the other. Investigators have conducted experiments showing that children often give both heteronomous and autonomous judgments, depending on the issue, and that adults can quite easily induce children to change the type of judgment they make through example and attention, praise, or reward.

But Piaget plainly stated that the two phases of morality he outlined can exist side by side and that the same child will judge sometimes one way, sometimes the other. He stressed that the phases of moral development were not proper stages, and he was aware that children tend to give adults the answers they are looking for. Indeed, he considered young children's dependence on authority the defining aspect of their heteronomous morality. Piaget felt that the good interviewer could separate superficial answers that were the result of suggestion from responses that reflected the child's general point

Piaget still watches children to discover the way the mind develops.

Yves de Braine—Black Star

of view. He argued that "a conviction having real solidarity with a given structure will resist suggestion."

The most prevalent criticisms of Piaget's work on morality relate to his neglect of behavior and his use of the clinical method. Piaget made no pretense of explaining behavior. Although it is unfortunate that Piaget neglected what many believe to be the most important aspect of moral development, it is only fair to recognize that he stated explicitly that he intended to limit his investigation to the development of moral *judgment*.

Piaget neglected behavior, but he did attend to a related issue—the nature of the relationship between the hypothetical answers children gave to his imaginary stories and the practical reasoning they used in their everyday lives. He entertained the possibility that the ethical theories of children and adults are simply "a sort of rambling chatter . . . whose contents may be devoid of any intelligible meaning." He considered three possible relationships between "storybook" morality and the morality of life: (1) The answers given by children to the investigator are the same ones they would give in practice; (2) there is a time-lag between the children's theoretical evaluations and their real judgments, with the former progressively becoming a conscious realization of the latter; and (3) there is no connection between the two types of judgment. Piaget favored the second alternative, but he considered the question open. It is interesting to note that he only briefly considers a fourth possibility, the one that would readily occur to most of us—we easily learn to make high-level judgments about hypothetical situations but fail to apply them consistently in real life.

Only recently have psychologists begun to investigate this important issue, and the findings are mixed. When, for example, William Damon gave children a hypothetical problem involving the distribution of 10 candy bars, he found that about half the children showed the same level of reasoning for both the problem and a similar life situation; slightly more than a third used more sophisticated reasoning in the hypothetical task than in a real situation; and the rest used more sophisticated reasoning in the actual situation. A task involving authority showed a much closer correspondence between the two types of reasoning.

Piaget's use of the interview has also come under fire, but Piaget gave considerable thought to the costs and benefits of this method. He argued persuasively that it should be used only by trained interviewers and that interviewers would have to spend at least a year in daily practice before they could hope to use it proficiently. He set out in detail the requirements for an adequate interview. Few modern researchers would meet the standards set by Piaget, and most don't even try.

Psychologists have done extensive research on Piaget's theory of morality, especially in the past decade. Most of it involves highly controlled laboratory experiments. These studies provide interesting and useful information but often fail to test Piaget's central ideas. The forces of concern to Piaget were broad and basic, but most of the experiments test the effect of small, almost infinitesimal, influences on children's responses to pairs of stories. Piaget's goal was to produce an overall sketch of the *structure* of children's concepts of morality. He was more concerned with the reasons behind the decisions the children made (their answers to his "why" questions) than with the choices themselves (which typically serve as the "responses" that are investigated in experiments today). He explored their concepts at length in his interviews, seeking elaborations, pursuing implications, challenging conclusions.

Some recent controlled experiments have shown that influences other than those identified by Piaget affect children's responses to pairs of stories. Others have shown that children can understand intentions at a much earlier age and are less egocentric than Piaget supposed. But many of the problems unearthed by these studies simply reflect inadequacies in the way the children who served as subjects in other studies were interviewed; they do not alter the basic conclusions Piaget reached, for example the idea that objective responsibility diminishes and the consideration of intention increases as a child grows older. They do not disprove Piaget's overriding theory.

In recent years a growing number of studies have been conducted by psychologists who are basically sympathetic to Piaget's point of view and whose goal is to elaborate and refine his conclusions. Piaget's studies of moral judgment inspired the work of Lawrence Kohlberg of Harvard University, whose theory of moral judgment and development now overshadows Piaget's in the attention it receives.

Kohlberg ties moral development much more exclusively to intellect than does Piaget, and this emphasis on the structure of thought has led him to redefine the "stages" of moral development described by Piaget. He argues that Piaget failed to distinguish among different forms of heteronomy and autonomy. There is a vast difference between the idea that it is right to obey authority because authorities have the power to inflict punishment and the idea that we should obey the law because law and order are essential to our social system. Similarly, an apparently autonomous attitude such as "I have the right to do whatever I want" is quite different from an attitude such as "I have the duty to oppose forces that violate my moral principles."

By continuing to test people into adulthood, Kohlberg concluded that there are *six* types of moral orientation, not two; that they constitute universal *stages* of moral development; and that people move through them one at a time in an invariant sequence. Kohlberg's theory is controversial and there is dispute about whether his stages are genuine, exclusive, or universal. But no matter how one assesses current theory, it is obvious that the study of moral development has come a long way since the days Piaget played marbles with children.

Dennis Krebs *is associate professor of psychology at Simon Fraser University in Burnaby, British Columbia. He has written widely on altruism, empathy, and moral development.*

The Child as a Moral Philosopher

By Lawrence Kohlberg

62

How can one study morality? Current trends in the fields of ethics, linguistics, anthropology and cognitive psychology have suggested a new approach which seems to avoid the morass of semantical confusions, value-bias and cultural relativity in which the psychoanalytic and semantic approaches to morality have foundered. New scholarship in all these fields is now focusing upon structures, forms and relationships that seem to be common to all societies and all languages rather than upon the features that make particular languages or cultures different.

For 12 years, my colleagues and I studied the same group of 75 boys, following their development at three-year intervals from early adolescence through young manhood. At the start of the study, the boys were aged 10 to 16. We have now followed them through to ages 22 to 28. In addition, I have explored moral development in other cultures — Great Britain, Canada, Taiwan, Mexico and Turkey.

Inspired by Jean Piaget's pioneering effort to apply a structural approach to moral development, I have gradually elaborated over the years of my study a typological scheme describing general structures and forms of moral thought which can be defined independently of the specific content of particular moral decisions or actions.

The typology contains three distinct levels of moral thinking, and within each of these levels distinguishes two related stages. These levels and stages may be considered separate moral philosophies, distinct views of the socio-moral world.

We can speak of the child as having his own morality or series of moralities. Adults seldom listen to children's moralizing. If a child throws back a few adult cliches and behaves himself, most parents—and many anthropologists and psychologists as well—think that the child has adopted or internalized the appropriate parental standards.

Actually, as soon as we talk with children about morality, we find that they have many ways of making judgments which are not "internalized" from the outside, and which do not come in any direct and obvious way from parents, teachers or even peers.

Moral Levels

The *preconventional* level is the first of three levels of moral thinking; the second level is *conventional*, and the third *postconventional* or autonomous. While the preconventional child is often "well-behaved" and is responsive to cultural labels of good and bad, he interprets these labels in terms of their physical consequences (punishment, reward, exchange of favors) or in terms of the physical power of those who enunciate the rules and labels of good and bad.

This level is usually occupied by children aged four to 10, a fact long known to sensitive observers of children. The capacity of "properly behaved" children of this age to engage in cruel behavior when there are holes in the power structure is sometimes noted as tragic (*Lord of the Flies, High Wind in Jamaica*), sometimes as comic (Lucy in *Peanuts*).

The second or *conventional* level also can be described as conformist, but that is perhaps too smug a term. Maintaining the expectations and rules of the individual's family, group or nation is perceived as valuable in its own right. There is a concern not only with *conforming* to the individual's social order but in *maintaining*, supporting and justifying this order.

The *postconventional* level is characterized by a major thrust toward autonomous moral principles which have validity and application apart from authority of the groups or persons who hold them and apart from the individual's identification with those persons or groups.

Moral Stages

Within each of these three levels there are two discernable stages. At the preconventional level we have:

Stage 1: Orientation toward punishment and unquestioning deference to superior power. The physical consequences of action regardless of their human meaning or value determine its goodness or badness.

Stage 2: Right action consists of that which instrumentally satisfies one's own needs and occasionally the needs of others. Human relations are viewed in terms like those of the marketplace. Elements of fairness, of reciprocity and equal sharing are present, but they are always interpreted in a physical, pragmatic way. Reciprocity is a matter of "you scratch my back and I'll scratch yours" not of loyalty, gratitude or justice.

And at the conventional level we have:

Stage 3: Good-boy—good-girl orientation. Good behavior is that which pleases or helps others and is approved by them. There is much conformity to stereotypical images of what is majority or "natural" behavior. Behavior is often judged by intention —"he means well" becomes important for the first time, and is overused, as by Charlie Brown in *Peanuts*. One seeks approval by being "nice."

Stage 4: Orientation toward authority, fixed rules and the maintenance of the social order. Right behavior consists of doing one's duty, showing respect for authority and maintaining the given social order for its own sake. One earns respect by performing dutifully.

At the postconventional level, we have:

Stage 5: A social-contract orientation, generally with legalistic and utilitarian overtones. Right action tends to be defined in terms of general rights and in terms of standards which have been

"Virtue-words like honesty point approvingly to certain behaviors but give us no guide to understanding them."

critically examined and agreed upon by the whole society. There is a clear awareness of the relativism of personal values and opinions and a corresponding emphasis upon procedural rules for reaching consensus. Aside from what is constitutionally and democratically agreed upon, right or wrong is a matter of personal "values" and "opinion." The result is an emphasis upon the "legal point of view," but with an emphasis upon the possibility of *changing* law in terms of rational considerations of social utility, rather than freezing it in the terms of Stage 4 "law and order." Outside the legal realm, free agreement and contract are the binding elements of obligation. This is the "official" morality of American government, and finds its ground in the thought of the writers of the Constitution.

Stage 6: Orientation toward the decisions of conscience and toward self-chosen *ethical principles* appealing to logical comprehensiveness, universality and consistency. These principles are abstract and ethical (the Golden Rule, the categorical imperative); they are not concrete moral rules like the Ten Commandments. Instead, they are universal principles of *justice*, of the *reciprocity* and *equality* of human rights, and of respect for the dignity of human beings as *individual persons*.

Up to Now

In the past, when psychologists tried to answer the question asked of Socrates by Meno "Is virtue something that can be taught (by rational discussion), or does it come by practice, or is it a natural inborn attitude?" their answers usually have been dictated, not by research findings on children's moral character, but by their general theoretical convictions.

Behavior theorists have said that virtue is behavior acquired according to their favorite general principles of learning. Freudians have claimed that virtue is superego-identification with parents generated by a proper balance of love and authority in family relations.

The American psychologists who have actually studied children's morality have

tried to start with a set of labels—the "virtues" and "vices," the "traits" of good and bad character found in ordinary language. The earliest major psychological study of moral character, that of Hugh Hartshorne and Mark May in 1928-1930, focused on a bag of virtues including honesty, service (altruism or generosity), and self-control. To their dismay, they found that there were *no* character traits, psychological dispositions or entities which corresponded to words like honesty, service or self-control.

Regarding honesty, for instance, they found that almost everyone cheats some of the time, and that if a person cheats in one situation, it doesn't mean that he *will* or *won't* in another. In other words, it is not an identifiable character trait, *dis*honesty, that makes a child cheat in a given situation. These early researchers also found that people who cheat express as much or even more moral disapproval of cheating as those who do not cheat.

What Hartshorne and May found out about their bag of virtues is equally upsetting to the somewhat more psychological-sounding names introduced by psychoanalytic psychology: "superego-strength," "resistance to temptation," "strength of conscience," and the like. When recent researchers attempt to measure such traits in individuals, they have been forced to use Hartshorne and May's old tests of honesty and self-control and they get exactly the same results —"superego strength" in one situation predicts little to "superego strength" in another. That is, virtue-words like honesty (or superego-strength) point to certain behaviors with approval, but give us no guide to understanding them.

So far as one can extract some generalized personality factor from children's performance on tests of honesty or resistance to temptation, it is a factor of ego-strength or ego-control, which always involves non-moral capacities like the capacity to maintain attention, intelligent-task performance, and the ability to delay response. "Ego-strength" (called "will" in earlier days) has something to do with moral action, but it does not take us to the core of morality or to the definition of virtue. Obviously enough, many of the greatest evil-doers in history have been men of strong wills, men strongly pursuing immoral goals.

Moral Reasons

In our research, we have found definite and universal levels of development in moral thought. In our study of 75 American boys from early adolescence on, these youths were presented with hypothetical moral dilemmas, all deliberately philosophical, some of them found in medieval works of casuistry.

On the basis of their reasoning about these dilemmas at a given age, each boy's stage of thought could be determined for each of 25 basic moral concepts or aspects. One such aspect, for instance, is "Motive Given for Rule Obedience or Moral Action." In this instance, the six stages look like this:

1. Obey rules to avoid punishment.
2. Conform to obtain rewards, have favors returned, and so on.
3. Conform to avoid disapproval, dislike by others.
4. Conform to avoid censure by legitimate authorities and resultant guilt.
5. Conform to maintain the respect of the impartial spectator judging in terms of community welfare.
6. Conform to avoid self-condemnation.

In another of these 25 moral aspects, the value of human life, the six stages can be defined thus:

1. The value of a human life is confused with the value of physical objects and is based on the social status or physical attributes of its possessor.
2. The value of a human life is seen as instrumental to the satisfaction of the needs of its possessor or of other persons.
3. The value of a human life is based on the empathy and affection of family members and others toward its possessor.
4. Life is conceived as sacred in terms of its place in a categorical moral or religious order of rights and duties.
5. Life is valued both in terms of its relation to community welfare and in terms of life being a universal human right.
6. Belief in the sacredness of human life as representing a universal human value of respect for the individual.

I have called this scheme a typology. This is because about 50 per cent of most people's thinking will be at a single stage, regardless of the moral dilemma involved. We call our types *stages* because they seem to represent an *invariant developmental sequence*. "True" stages come one at a time and always in the same order.

All movement is forward in sequence, and does not skip steps. Children may move through these stages at varying speeds, of course, and may be found half in and half out of a particular stage. An individual may stop at any given stage and at any age, but if he continues to move, he must move in accord with these steps. Moral reasoning of the conventional or Stage 3-4 kind never occurs before the preconventional Stage-1 and

Stage-2 thought has taken place. No adult in Stage 4 has gone through Stage 6, but all Stage-6 adults have gone at least through 4.

While the evidence is not complete, my study strongly suggests that moral change fits the stage pattern just described. (The major uncertainty is whether all Stage 6s go through Stage 5 or whether these are two alternate mature orientations.)

How Values Change

As a single example of our findings of stage-sequence, take the progress of two boys on the aspect "The Value of Human Life." The first boy Tommy, is asked "Is it better to save the life of one important person or a lot of unimportant people?". At age 10, he answers "all the people that aren't important because one man just has one house, maybe a lot of furniture, but a whole bunch of people have an awful lot of furniture and some of these poor people might have a lot of money and it doesn't look it."

Clearly Tommy is Stage 1: he confuses the value of a human being with the value of the property he possesses. Three years later (age 13) Tommy's conceptions of life's value are most clearly elicited by the question, "Should the doctor 'mercy kill' a fatally ill woman requesting death because of her pain?". He answers, "Maybe it would be good to put her out of her pain, she'd be better off that way. But the husband wouldn't want it, it's not like an animal. If a pet dies you can get along without it—it isn't something you really need. Well, you can get a new wife, but it's not really the same."

Here his answer is Stage 2: the value of the woman's life is partly contingent on its hedonistic value to the wife herself but even more contingent on its instrumental value to her husband, who can't replace her as easily as he can a pet.

Three years later still (age 16) Tommy's conception of life's value is elicited by the same question, to which he replies: "It might be best for her, but her husband—it's a human life—not like an animal; it just doesn't have the same relationship that a human being does

to a family. You can become attached to a dog, but nothing like a human you know."

Now Tommy has moved from a Stage 2 instrumental view of the woman's value to a Stage-3 view based on the husband's distinctively human empathy and love for someone in his family. Equally clearly, it lacks any basis for a universal human value of the woman's life, which would hold if she had no husband or if her husband didn't love her. Tommy, then, has moved step by step through three stages during the age 10-16. Tommy, though bright (I.Q 120), is a slow developer in moral judgment. Let us take another boy, Richard, to show us sequential movement through the remaining three steps.

At age 13, Richard said about the mercy-killing, "If she requests it, it's really up to her. She is in such terrible pain, just the same as people are always putting animals out of their pain," and in general showed a mixture of Stage-2 and Stage-3 responses concerning the value of life. At 16, he said, "I don't know. In one way, it's murder, it's not a right or privilege of man to decide who shall live and who should die. God put life into everybody on earth and you're taking away something from that person that came directly from God, and you're destroying something that is very sacred, it's in a way part of God and it's almost destroying a part of God when you kill a person. There's something of God in everyone."

Here Richard clearly displays a Stage-4 concept of life as sacred in terms of its place in a categorical moral or religious order. The value of human life is universal, it is true for all humans. It is still, however, dependent on something else, upon respect for God and God's authority; it is not an autonomous human value. Presumably if God told Richard to murder, as God commanded Abraham to murder Isaac, he would do so.

At age 20, Richard said to the same question: "There are more and more people in the medical profession who think it is a hardship on everyone, the person, the family, when you know they are going to die. When a person is kept alive by an artificial lung or kidney it's

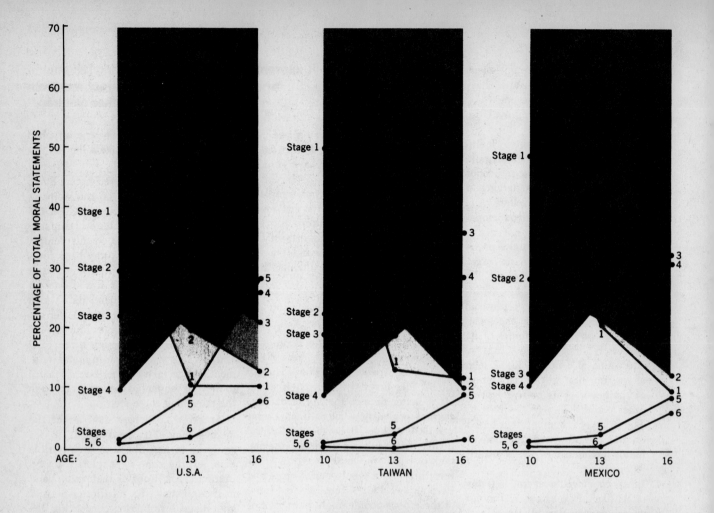

1. Middle-class urban boys in the U.S., Taiwan and Mexico (*above*). At age 10 the stages are used according to difficulty. At age 13, Stage 3 is most used by all three groups. At age 16 U.S. boys have reversed the order of age 10 stages (with the exception of 6). In Taiwan and Mexico, conventional (3-4) stages prevail at age 16, with Stage 5 also little used.

2. Two isolated villages, one in Turkey, the other in Yucatan, show similar patterns in moral thinking. There is no reversal of order, and preconventional (1-2) thought does does not gain a clear ascendancy over conventional stages at age 16.

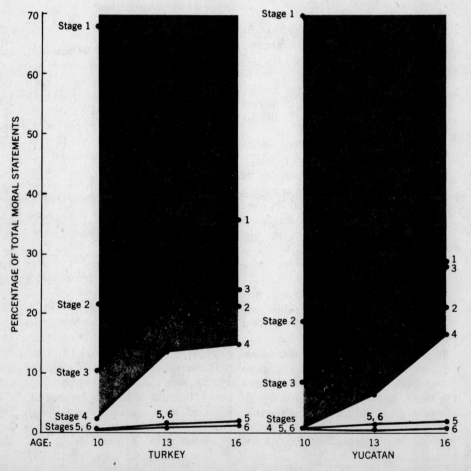

more like being a vegetable than being a human. If it's her own choice, I think there are certain rights and privileges that go along with being a human being. I am a human being and have certain desires for life and I think everybody else does too. You have a world of which you are the center, and everybody else does too and in that sense we're all equal."

Richard's response is clearly Stage 5, in that the value of life is defined in terms of equal and universal human rights in a context of relativity ("You have a world of which you are the center and in that sense we're all equal"), and of concern for utility or welfare consequences.

The Final Step

At 24, Richard says: "A human life takes precedence over any other moral or legal value, whoever it is. A human life has inherent value whether or not it is valued by a particular individual. The worth of the individual human being is central where the principles of justice and love are normative for all human relationships."

This young man is at Stage 6 in seeing the value of human life as absolute in representing a universal and equal respect for the human as an individual. He has moved step by step through a sequence culminating in a definition of human life as centrally valuable rather than derived from or dependent on social or divine authority.

In a genuine and culturally universal sense, these steps lead toward an increased *morality* of value judgment, where morality is considered as a form of judging, as it has been in a philosophic tradition running from the analyses of Kant to those of the modern analytic or "ordinary language" philosophers. The person at Stage 6 has disentangled his judgments of—or language about—human life from status and property values (Stage 1), from its uses to others (Stage 2), from interpersonal affection (Stage 3), and so on; he has a means of moral judgment that is universal and impersonal. The Stage-6 person's answers use moral words like "duty" or "morally right," and he uses them in a way implying universality, ideals, impersonality: He thinks and speaks in phrases like "regardless of who it was," or ". . . I would do it in spite of punishment."

Across Cultures

When I first decided to explore moral development in other cultures, I was told by anthropologist friends that I would have to throw away my culture-bound moral concepts and stories and start from scratch learning a whole new set of values for each new culture. My first try consisted of a brace of villages, one Atayal (Malaysian aboriginal) and the other Taiwanese.

My guide was a young Chinese ethnographer who had written an account of the moral and religious patterns of the Atayal and Taiwanese villages. Taiwanese boys in the 10-13 age group were asked about a story involving theft of food. A man's wife is starving to death but the store owner won't give the man any food unless he can pay, which he can't. Should he break in and steal some food? Why? Many of the boys said, "He should steal the food for his wife because if she dies he'll have to pay for her funeral and that costs a lot."

My guide was amused by these responses, but I was relieved: they were of course "classic" Stage-2 responses. In the Atayal village, funerals weren't such a big thing, so the Stage 2-boys would say, "He should steal the food because he needs his wife to cook for him."

This means that we need to consult our anthropologists to know what content a Stage-2 child will include in his instrumental exchange calculations, or what a Stage-4 adult will identify as the proper social order. But one certainly doesn't have to start from scratch. What made my guide laugh was the difference in form between the children's Stage-2 thought and his own, a difference definable independently of particular cultures.

Illustrations number 1 and number 2 indicate the cultural universality of the sequence of stages which we have found. Illustration number 1 presents the age trends for middle-class urban boys in the U.S., Taiwan and Mexico. At age 10 in each country, the order of use of each stage is the same as the order of its difficulty or maturity.

In the United States, by age 16 the order is the reverse, from the highest to the lowest, except that Stage 6 is still little-used. At age 13, the good-boy, middle stage (Stage 3), is not used.

The results in Mexico and Taiwan are the same, except that development is a little slower. The most conspicuous fea-

ture is that at the age of 16, Stage-5 thinking is much more salient in the United States than in Mexico or Taiwan. Nevertheless, it *is* present in the other countries, so we know that this is not purely an American democratic construct.

Illustration 2 shows strikingly similar results from two isolated villages, one in Yucatan, one in Turkey. While conventional moral thought increases steadily from ages 10 to 16 it still has not achieved a clear ascendency over preconventional thought.

Trends for lower-class urban groups are intermediate in the rate of development between those for the middle-class and for the village boys. In the three divergent cultures that I studied, middle-class children were found to be more advanced in moral judgment than matched lower-class children. This was not due to the fact that the middle-class children heavily favored some one type of thought which could be seen as corresponding to the prevailing middle-class pattern. Instead, middle-class and working-class children move through the same sequences, but the middle-class children move faster and farther.

This sequence is not dependent upon a particular religion, or any religion at all in the usual sense. I found no important differences in the development of moral thinking among Catholics, Protestants, Jews, Buddhists, Moslems and atheists. Religious values seem to go through the same stages as all other values.

Trading Up

In summary, the nature of our sequence is not significantly affected by widely varying social, cultural or religious conditions. The only thing that is affected is the *rate* at which individuals progress through this sequence.

Why should there be such a universal invariant sequence of development? In answering this question, we need first to analyze these developing social concepts in terms of their internal logical structure. At each stage, the same basic moral concept or aspect is defined, but at each higher stage this definition is more differentiated, more integrated and more general or universal. When one's concept of human life moves from Stage 1 to Stage 2 the value of life becomes more differentiated from the value of property, more integrated (the value of life enters an organizational hierarchy where it is "higher" than property so that one steals property in order to save life) and more universalized (the life of any sentient being is valuable regardless of status or property). The same advance is true at each stage in the hierarchy. Each step of development then is a better cognitive organization than the one before it, one which takes account of everything present in the previous stage, but making new distinctions and organizing them into a more comprehensive or more equilibrated structure. The fact that this is the case has been demonstrated by a series of studies indicating that children and adolescents comprehend all stages up to their own, but not more than one stage beyond their own. And importantly, *they prefer this next stage*.

We have conducted experimental moral discussion classes which show that the child at an earlier stage of develop-ment tends to move forward when confronted by the views of a child one stage further along. In an argument between a Stage-3 and Stage-4 child, the child in the third stage tends to move toward or into Stage 4, while the Stage-4 child understands but does not accept the arguments of the Stage-3 child.

Moral thought, then, seems to behave like all other kinds of thought. Progress through the moral levels and stages is characterized by increasing differentia-tion and increasing integration, and hence is the same kind of progress that scientific theory represents. Like accept-able scientific theory—or like *any* theory or structure of knowledge—moral thought may be considered partially to generate its own data as it goes along, or at least to expand so as to contain in a balanced, self-consistent way a wider and wider experiential field. The raw data in the case of our ethical philosophies may be considered as conflicts between roles, or values, or as the social order in which men live.

The Role of Society

The social worlds of all men seem to contain the same basic structures. All the societies we have studied have the same basic institutions—family, econ-omy, law, government. In addition, how-ever, all societies are alike because they *are* societies—systems of defined complementary roles. In order to *play* a social role in the family, school or society, the child must implicitly take the role of others toward himself and toward others in the group. These role-taking tendencies form the basis of all social institutions. They represent vari-ous patternings of shared or comple-mentary expectations.

In the preconventional and conven-tional levels (Stages 1-4), moral content or value is largely accidental or culture-bound. Anything from "honesty" to "courage in battle" can be the central value. But in the higher postconventional levels, Socrates, Lincoln, Thoreau and Martin Luther King tend to speak with-out confusion of tongues, as it were. This is because the ideal principles of any social structure are basically alike, if only because there simply aren't that many principles which are articulate, comprehensive and integrated enough to be satisfying to the human intellect. And most of these principles have gone by the name of justice.

Behavioristic psychology and psycho-analysis have always upheld the Philis-tine view that fine moral words are one thing and moral deeds another. Morally mature reasoning is quite a different matter, and does not really depend on "fine words." The man who understands justice is more likely to practice it.

In our studies, we have found that youths who understand justice act more justly, and the man who understands justice helps create a moral climate which goes far beyond his immediate and personal acts. The universal society is the beneficiary.

Moral Thinking: Can It Be Taught?

63

By Howard Muson

Illustrations by Jim Harter

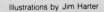

Stage One: Punishment-Obedience Orientation

Stage Two: Instrumental-Exchange Orientation

As democracies go, this one is ragged, restless, and properly irreverent toward authority: 35 teenagers, black and white, street kids and middle class, with a half-dozen teachers and two consultants, all arranged in a rough circle, draped over desks, chairs, windowsills, at Cambridge High School in Massachusetts. They are called a Just Community, and they meet in a garishly orange schoolroom with graffiti on the back wall and paint peeling from the ceiling—hardly the setting, it would seem, for a revival of the Periclean ideal.

Their guiding light, watching from a lonely angle near a blackboard, attired in a drab gray wool shirt and blue trousers, is Professor Lawrence Kohlberg of Harvard University, the elite Ivy League institution down the street. The 51-year-old psychologist, who is best known for his six-stage theory of development in moral judgment, has invested much of his time for the past five years in the Cambridge Cluster School. The Cluster School operates as a separate en-

clave within the high school for half of every day and lets kids and teachers settle their own problems and make their own rules on a one-person, one-vote basis.

The kids seem to have learned their lessons well. As soon as the meeting is called to order, a few of them propose to ask the two visitors to leave—an editor from *Psychology Today* and a man who runs homes for juvenile offenders in Massachusetts, whom Kohlberg has brought along to observe. One young woman complains that too often visitors to the community meetings are less interested in the students than in writing about Kohlberg's work (which they know just helps "Larry" get grant money, a teacher confides to me later). Another says the students resent being looked upon as "guinea pigs," but a third, a cool-looking blonde in the front of the room, quips, "We're all guinea pigs of nature!" Everyone breaks up, no one presses the issue, and the guests are allowed to stay, proving, perhaps, that democ-

racy can be gracious as well as ornery.

Kohlberg's Just Community resembles a lively encounter group, but it is less concerned with emotional catharsis than with the development of moral judgment toward issues of "justice and fairness." As such, it represents a small but significant experiment in what is called moral education, a relatively recent movement, a revival of interest, really, in the notion that moral issues are a proper part of the school curriculum.

Though moral instruction has always been regarded as the job of parents and churches, the schools have inevitably had a role in passing on the values of the larger culture. They strenuously pursued that mission in the 19th century when the *McGuffey's Readers* were teaching generations of school kids how to behave as well as how to read—or trying to teach them. But educators have been skeptical about all such lessons in virtue ever since a classic investigation was made by two psychologists, Harthorne and May, in the 1920s. Harthorne and May evaluated a variety of school programs designed to instill honesty, altruism, and self-control in the pupils through "moral urging" and rewards for desirable conduct. Their conclusion was that indoctrina-

Stage Three: Good Boy-Nice Girl Orientation

Stage Four: System-Maintaining Orientation

In the wake of complaints about declining standards
of public and private conduct, psychologists have become increasingly
interested in how people learn to think about moral issues.
The dominant theorist has been Harvard's Lawrence Kohlberg,
whose perspectives have changed considerably since he
began putting his ideas into action in schools and prisons.
(The illustrations represent Kohlberg's famous "stages" of moral reasoning.)

tive programs of this kind had little appreciable effect on the kids' subsequent behavior.

The reasons for the revival of interest in moral education are not hard to find. It began during the Vietnam war and the campus upheavals of the 1960s and gathered momentum during the 1970s, when many people saw a decline in standards of both public and personal conduct—from Watergate and other scandals in high public office and in American business to the breakdown of family loyalties, sexual experimentation, widespread drug use, and increasing youth crime, including the destruction of school property and assaults on teachers.

A Gallup poll in 1975 showed that 79 percent of the Americans queried were willing to turn over some of that responsibility for moral training to the schools. Hundreds of schools have thus experimented with some form of instruction in moral values, and a lively interest remains, despite the back-to-basics movement, and even though parents and educators are still suspicious of any teaching that smacks of religious indoctrination or,

indeed, promotes political views that are not to their liking.

Kohlberg brought to the revival a theory, formulated in the late 1950s, which not only seemed to match, in its elegance, the real complexities of moral issues themselves, but also stressed the development of conscious processes of "moral reasoning," which could, presumably, be stimulated and advanced in the classroom. Moreover, since the aim of the method was to enhance the *capacity* for moral reasoning, it did not teach any particular set of values and was therefore not, Kohlberg emphasized, indoctrinative. Finally, Kohlberg conceived a series of hypothetical "moral dilemmas" that were clever and provocative, even if they sounded a little like fairy tales.

There was, for instance, the famous case of Heinz, whose wife is dying and can only be saved by a rare drug; the drug has been discovered by the local pharmacist, who is the sole owner and is charging an exorbitant price that Heinz cannot pay. Should Heinz steal the drug? Does the pharmacist have a right to charge so much for it?

(There are no "right" answers, but for a few responses that are typical of different stages of moral reasoning, see box on page 340.)

Another popular Kohlberg story is the dilemma of Sharon, who goes shopping one day with her best friend, Jill. Jill tries on a sweater, and walks out of the store wearing it under her coat, leaving Sharon to face a security officer who demands that she tell him the name of the other girl. The owner of the store tells her she will be in serious trouble if she does not report her friend, who, he is sure, has been shoplifting. Should Sharon protect her friend and not reveal her name? Does she really owe anything to Jill, who has walked out and left her in this dilemma?

Kohlberg's hypothesis has inspired countless studies, doctoral theses, workshops, seminars, conference papers, and journal articles. It has also inspired a rather fierce controversy. Critics argue that, far from being value free, his work reflects a liberal, Ivy League emphasis on social conscience that has nothing whatsoever to do with the way most people view

Stage Five: Social-Contract Orientation

Stage Six: Universal Ethical-Principles Orientation

the world. In recent years, more empirically minded researchers have questioned whether there really are six distinct stages of development, whether the evidence is convincing, and whether children can actually be stimulated to climb the stage ladder by discussions of moral dilemmas in the classroom.

Such have been the methodological criticisms of the theory that some researchers are beginning to believe there is nothing much left of it. "I suspect the system is beginning to fall apart," said Joseph Adelson, an expert on adolescence, in a recent paper. Adelson, a clinician and professor of psychology at the University of Michigan, says of Kohlberg's cognitive theory: "Many of its early propositions are not easily replicable by others, producing, as it so often does, a sense of being beleaguered and an even greater insularity."

While his theory is under attack, however, Kohlberg himself has been moving in a much more pragmatic direction. Today, he speaks almost disparagingly of "science fiction" dilemmas that, he feels, have little to do with kids' real concerns. In the Just Community, he seeks to promote individual development through group action. Kohlberg thinks of himself as more of an educator than a psychologist, believing that only by teaching others is he ethically justified in experimenting on them. (He is professor of education and social psychology in the Harvard Graduate School of Education.) He even admits that his approach is now "indoctrinative," by which he means that he is openly trying to instill an appreciation of demo-

cratic processes and a sense of community in the kids.

The Just Community is rooted in the idea, shared by many educators since John Dewey, that the most important values taught in school derive from the very way the schools are organized and governed. In this "hidden curriculum," the argument goes, the students learn not democracy but obedience to authority and to arbitrary rules made by adults. Kohlberg and his colleagues have introduced Just Communities at high schools in Pittsburgh, Pa., Brookline, Mass., and Scarsdale, N.Y., as well as in Cambridge; they have also tried establishing them in two prison programs at the Connecticut Correctional Institution in Niantic, and have taught the techniques to prison administrators from Iowa to Nevada.

But this, the most recent emphasis in Kohlberg's work, has already earned one devastating critique from a researcher named Roy Feldman, who was hired by the state of Connecticut in 1974—with Kohlberg's approval—to do a three-year evaluation of the Niantic programs. Feldman also interviewed senior school administrators in Cambridge about the high school project and concluded that the democracy in all three programs was a sham: "It appears that the pseudo-democratic means and procedures of Kohlberg's Just Communities are among the most important features of their operation to institutional administrators. This does not mean that social control is the only reason [they] have supported Just Communities. Some do believe that the program does or might produce more justice

than prior alternatives. Nevertheless, virtually all the senior administrators interviewed by the author perceived that the Just Community . . . is a fundamental management technique of social control which utilized peer pressure to urge conformity to middle-class values."

Legend and Theory

The controversy over Kohlberg is likely to influence future research into moral development as well as the teaching about moral values in the schools. For his approach remains the most fully developed (over a period of 20 years) and sophisticated one around, and to understand the issues, it is essential to go back to the beginning of Kohlberg's odyssey.

As a doctoral candidate in clinical psychology at the University of Chicago, Kohlberg was fascinated by the work of Jean Piaget, particularly *The Moral Judgment of the Child* (1932), in which the Swiss psychologist described how children from the ages of about two to 12 grew in their reasoning about the rules of playing marbles. Kohlberg interviewed a group of 75 youths from 10 to 16, probing their responses to dilemmas drawn from old books of casuistry and from works like *Les Miserables* (*Psychology Today*, September 1968). From their responses and his own study of ideas about moral stages, from Plato to John Dewey, Kohlberg identified six types of moral reasoning, which he unveiled in his doctoral thesis in 1958.

Piaget believed that children progressed from a heteronomous stage of moral reasoning, in which their values were largely dictated by others, to an autonomous phase, when they began to make their own choices. Kohlberg came to believe that children moved to higher stages of moral judgment as their capacity for more sophisticated logical "operations" emerged and as their ability to empathize with others grew in their social interactions. He saw the stages as unfolding in an invariant sequence, in response to internal pressures and challenge from the environment.

At Stage One, the "punishment-and-obedience orientation," the child defers to the superior position and power of the parent. In Stage Two, the "instrumental-relativist orientation," he agrees to a rule or does a favor only if he conceives it will bring him some benefit in return. Stage Three is the "good boy–nice girl orientation," in which the child seeks the approval of others and conforms in order to please. Stage Four was originally defined as the "law-and-order orientation," characterized by adherence to rules for the sake of maintaining social order. (Kohlberg now sees it as being an enlargement of horizons away from one's narrow group and toward a concern for the wider community.) Stage Five was the "social-contract, legalistic orientation," in which justice flows from a contract between the governors and governed that assures equal rights for all.

At the summit of the hierarchy was the highly abstract Stage Six, in which the individual chooses according to ethical principles that, like Kant's categorical imperative, appeal to logical comprehensiveness, universality, and consistency. Borrowing from the philosophy of John Rawls, Kohlberg has said about this stage that "personally chosen moral principles are also principles of justice, the principles any member of society would choose for that society if he did not know what his position was to be in the society and in which he might be the least advantaged." What that means, to take a practical example, is that in deciding one's position on capital punishment, a person would have to view the issue from the standpoint of one sentenced to death as well as from that of the murder victim.

Everyone familiar with the Kohlberg legend knows what happened

A MORAL DILEMMA: THE CASE OF HEINZ

Probably the most widely debated of Kohlberg's dilemmas is the story of Heinz. It is discussed in classrooms and in standard Kohlberg interviews that determine the stage level of moral reasoning achieved by people, according to his theory. The theory concerns the *ways* people think about moral values, not the actual choices they make. So, technically, there are no right or wrong answers to the question of whether Heinz should or should not steal in order to save his dying wife. However, Kohlberg hastens to add that in this particular case, all Stage Five people (the most principled stage, in Kohlberg's current schema) agree that the right to life takes priority over the right to property.

Here are the details of the dilemma, along with one young subject's responses in interviews over a period of several years:

In Europe, a woman was near death from a special kind of cancer. There was one drug that the doctors thought might save her. It was a form of radium that a druggist in the same town had recently discovered. The drug was expensive to make, but the druggist was charging 10 times what the drug cost him to make. He paid $200 for the radium and charged $2,000 for a small dose of the drug. The sick woman's husband, Heinz, went to everyone he knew to borrow the money, but he could only get together about $1,000, which is half of what it cost. He told the druggist

that his wife was dying, and asked him to sell it cheaper or let him pay later. But the druggist said, "No, I discovered the drug and I'm going to make money from it." So Heinz gets desperate and considers breaking into the man's store to steal the drug for his wife.

Tommy at Age 10 (Stage One)

Heinz shouldn't steal; he should buy the drug. If he steals the drug, he might get put in jail and have to put the drug back anyway.

But maybe Heinz should steal the drug because his wife might be an important lady, like Betsy Ross; she made the flag.

Tommy at Age 13 (Stage Two)

Heinz should steal the drug to save his wife's life. He might get sent to jail, but he'd still have his wife.

(**Interviewer:** "Tommy, you said he should steal the drug for his wife. Should he steal it if it were a friend who was dying?")

That's going too far. He could be in jail while his friend is alive and free. I don't think a friend would do that for him.

Tommy at Age 16 (Stage Three)

If I was Heinz, I would have stolen the drug for my wife. You can't put a price on love, no amount of gifts make love. You can't put a price on life either.

Tommy at Age 21 (Stage Four)

When you get married, you take a vow to love and cherish your wife. Marriage is not only love, it's an obligation. Like a legal contract.

Kohlberg with his "Just Community" friends at Cambridge High.

next. Along came Moshe Blatt, a graduate student of Kohlberg's at the University of Chicago, who in 1968 tried to raise stage levels of moral reasoning in a Jewish Sunday-school class by vigorous debate of hypothetical dilemmas. In his doctoral thesis, Blatt reported success: after a year, the pupils had advanced by an average of one-third of a stage.

Further studies by Kohlberg followers confirmed that it was possible: classroom discussions of moral dilemmas, guided by an active, probing teacher, brought the students into contact with higher stages of moral reasoning than their own, and, through the cognitive conflict that occurred, stimulated stage advances. The assessment of stage level was done in interviews that scored the subject on his or her responses to questions about standard dilemmas.

But in one large study of 957 individuals, more than 45 percent could not be placed in one stage or another; most of the group were in transition between two stages, but some gave responses that straddled three stages. And how meaningful, after all, were the one-third or one-half stage advances the Kohlbergites were claiming, when dealing with such elusive categories?

In response, Kohlberg and his associates kept revising and redefining their stage criteria. But critics like William Kurtines of Florida International University and Esther Greif of Boston University, who did an extensive review of the research literature

in 1974, concluded that the "scale" used to measure the stages lacked standardization in administration and scoring. Others complained about fudging in the scoring manual, arguing that the use of labels such as "transitional," or "ambiguous," or even "guess" to classify some responses revealed the shaky foundation of the whole edifice. To make matters worse, the manuals were not easy to get hold of, and researchers reported having to apply to Kohlberg personally to get one.

A fundamental reservation about the theory was that it concerned moral judgment, and was of little use in predicting behavior. Two people at the same level of reasoning might very well act quite differently under the pressure of circumstance. Or two people at different stages might make the same moral choice, as was demonstrated dramatically by a study at the University of California of students who participated in the Free Speech Movement in 1968: disproportionately large numbers of people at Kohlberg's highly principled Stages Five and Six took part in the sit-in; but so did a large percentage of students who were judged to be at the relatively primitive Stage Two.

Kohlberg himself stressed that the theory had to do with the form and not the substance of moral decision-making; the scoring manual, for instance, diligently describes possible reasons for which Heinz should and should *not* steal the drug, without endorsing either of the choices. On the

other hand, Kohlberg clearly believes that his higher stages lead to more principled behavior, and he often cites anecdotes of improvements in behavior by those who have been exposed to his method.

Another anomaly was discovered several years ago by Kohlberg and his associate Richard Kramer, when they tested the stage levels of his original group of subjects. (Kohlberg has interviewed them every three years since he wrote his original thesis, and most are now in their 30s.) At the time, he and Kramer found that many who had been Stage Four in previous interviews had inexplicably regressed to Stage Two—a revelation that challenged the very assumption on which the theory was based: that stage change proceeds only upwards, to ever-higher levels.

Soon the Kohlberg camp came up with an intriguing explanation. They had been looking at their subjects during the 1960s, when many were college sophomores trying to make the difficult transition to the most principled levels of moral reasoning. In breaking out of the conventional mold of Stage Four, they were questioning every standard of morality and passing through a phase in which all values not based on instinct were distrusted. (Some people referred to the transition as Stage Four-and-a-half, but Kohlberg says it is not considered a stage.)

It was a theory that helped to explain what was going on at campuses like Harvard in those days; indeed, undergraduates showed up at Kohlberg lectures with buttons that read, "Stage Two— and Proud of It!" Looking back, Kohlberg says, "This transitional state led to a susceptibility to a variety of ideologies which mixed Stage Two instrumental hedonism with radical moral ideologies, as suggested by the famous [Stokely Carmichael] slogan that the proper revolutionary position for a woman was prone."

Patching a Leaky Boat

Today, to those critics like Kurtines and Greif who question his "scale," Kohlberg says that he never had one. He has had scoring systems that tried to describe the data adequately, he says, but he never claimed they were standardized enough to provide consistent measurements. Last year, however, Kohlberg and his colleagues completed a five-part manual that is based on interviews and testing with the original Ph.D. subjects. Kohlberg says the new manual, based on five years of "painfully boring work," can be considered a scale and will provide the consistency and reliability his critics have demanded.

Whether or not the manual will satisfy them remains to be seen. Even if it does not, Kohlberg's cognitive theory remains the most exciting one around. Many experts will agree with Piaget that moral judgment does seem to unfold in a developmental pattern, and Kohlberg's theory has provided the most comprehensive effort to describe it to date. Defending it before the American Psychological Association last summer, Kohlberg used an analogy from Charles Peirce, the noted empiricist philosopher. "Peirce compared scientific theory to a leaky boat: you patch in one place and then stand in another place while you patch or revise elsewhere," Kohlberg said. "Sometimes patching doesn't work and the boat sinks. But not, as Thomas Kuhn points out, until another boat comes along the scientist can move to. I'd be happy to stop patching up Piaget's assumptions if I could see another boat on the horizon."

Some of the "patching" Kohlberg has done turns out to be quite extensive. For one thing, Stage Six has been dropped from the manual entirely. It had always been criticized as elitist and culturally biased. Kohlberg estimated from field studies that only about 7 percent of 16-year-olds in America and Mexico used Stage Six reasoning; but less than 1 percent of that age group on Taiwan employed it, and none of those he studied in Turkey or Yucatan had even reached Stage Five.

Many who felt Kohlberg's theory was merely a scientific justification for libertarian values saw Stage Six as making moral heroes of people like Daniel Ellsberg whose consciences brought them into conflict with society. Kohlberg argues that, far from exalting the individual, Stage Six described individuals who appeal to a higher community. "Martin Luther King was trying to speak for an ideal community of some sort, one that

would embody brotherhood, and so forth," he says. Pointing out that none of his longitudinal subjects had achieved Stage Six by 1976, Kohlberg lamented at a recent symposium: "Perhaps all the Sixth Stage persons of the 1960s had been wiped out, perhaps they had regressed, or maybe it was all my imagination in the first place."

A colleague named Carol Gilligan raised another argument that brought a significant revision in Kohlberg's

"Critics felt Kohlberg's theory was merely a scientific justification for libertarian values."

stages. Gilligan discovered that, in a few studies of comparable groups of men and women, more women ended up in Stage Three and more men in Stage Four. She then pointed out that Stage Three qualities of pleasing others and mercy enabled women to play a useful social role in smoothing tensions and bringing people together. Why should that stage be regarded as inferior to Stage Four? (As Portia says to Shylock in *The Merchant of Venice*: ". . . though justice be thy plea, consider this, that in the course of justice none of us should see salvation. We do pray for mercy.")

But Kohlberg found the discrepancy between men and women was due to an error in his stage criteria—an initial tendency to put men with an Archie Bunker mentality in Stage Four, which had described a law-and-order mentality. Bunker belongs in Stage Three, Kohlberg now thinks, because he is not concerned with the larger society; rather, his reasoning is a "law-and-order within-our-group sort of thing." That would explain why in some studies more men than women have ended up in Stage Four, Kohlberg asserts; more recent work, he says, shows no significant sex differences. "Carol Gilligan would also make the

claim that there's male bias built into our scale by the kind of moral dilemmas we choose to look at, which emphasize justice, property, and conflicts in rights," Kohlberg adds. "She would argue that some other kind of dilemmas, which involve issues of caring and responsibility toward the community—for example, how much you should sacrifice for the community—might show more women at the upper end of the scale. I would agree."

Moral Education in Prison

The language suggests the new emphasis in Kohlberg's thinking, which is on community rather than on abstract justice. In the symposium at the University of Illinois, he said: "Our Cluster approach is not merely Socratic and developmental, it is indoctrinative. Its goal is not attainment of the Fifth Stage, but a solid attainment of the Fourth Stage commitment to being a good member of a community or a good citizen."

In a prison setting, even that was an ambitious goal. Kohlberg and two doctoral candidates, Joseph Hickey and Peter Sharf, began working with about 20 male juveniles and 20 controls at the Cheshire reformatory in Connecticut in 1970. A few months later, after a riot at the state correctional institution for women in Niantic, they agreed to start a second project for about 20 inmates there. (A later group of the male offenders were moved from Cheshire to a more agreeable residence at the Niantic prison.)

Both programs were conceived as experiments in rehabilitating prisoners through discussions of moral dilemmas, which in the case of the women inmates were drawn from their lives in the prison. But after a couple of years, the consultants decided that individual progress depended on more basic changes in what they called the "moral atmosphere" of the prison. Thus was born the concept of the Just Community, in which guards and inmates were to settle, by democratic means, all major issues of rules and policy arising out of the group—within the limits of the law and state penal policy.

In their community meetings, the inmates were to discuss solutions based on fairness and morality; they were to be encouraged to engage in "role-taking"—putting themselves in the shoes of others in order to understand their thinking and feelings.

The kinds of issues that came before the two groups ranged from curfews and tampering with the prison security system to incidents of physical violence. In one videotape I saw, a small group sitting around a living room listened as one woman who was refusing to do her work assignment read a little essay she was required to write to explain her reasons. She said, in effect, that she simply did not feel like working. As the discussion went on, the other women gave her emotional support (tears were frequent at the women's meetings, evidently) and reminded her of what would happen if everyone in the cottage refused to work. Gradually, the woman revealed that she was resentful because her lover, another inmate, had been suspended by the group and forced to leave the cottage.

In his extremely critical report on the prison programs, Roy Feldman concedes that the meetings did encourage inmates and guards to speak openly with one another. Feldman, who taught political science at MIT for several years before becoming a research associate at Harvard, also grants that supervisors and staff were personally concerned with fairness.

But Feldman goes on to report that there was very little talk of concepts of fairness or justice at the meetings; the staff had difficulty introducing discussions of moral dilemmas; further, many decisions relating to the rules of the prison were made unilaterally by staff. When behavior was viewed as intolerable, administrators would, on occasion, suspend the workings of democracy, and might remove an inmate from the program—a decision that was supposed to be left to the community.

The only thing that seemed to unite the community, Feldman suggests, was a strong desire to keep it going. (The inmates certainly preferred it to the regular prison.) As a result, the guards seem to have used the meetings for investigating infractions that might have led to criticism of the program—for instance, when a hypodermic syringe or illicit drug had been found on the premises and the au-

thorities wanted to find out who was responsible.

Feldman both examined the results of the moral-judgment interviews with the inmates undertaken by Kohlberg's associates and conducted interviews of his own. He concluded that the program did nothing to raise levels of moral reasoning or to lower the recidivism rate. He charges that those scorers who did report improvement often knew the dates of the interviews—which could bias

---

"There was little talk of fairness and justice at the prison meetings, charges Roy Feldman, a Kohlberg critic."

---

them in judging stage changes over time—and that he was under pressure from one of the consultants to the program to produce positive results.

Kohlberg got into a hassle with Feldman over the renewal of his contract—the dispute concerned the adequacy of the first year's results—and has never seen the final report or the paper on it Feldman gave recently at Rutgers, though Kohlberg's office is on the third floor of Larson Hall at the Graduate School of Education and Feldman's is on the fourth. (Feldman's paper will be published this fall by Praeger in *Moral Development and Politics*, edited by Richard Wilson and Gordon Schochet.)

Reflecting on the prison experience, Kohlberg cites the difficult circumstances under which it was carried out. The majority of the inmates were at the lowest levels of moral reasoning, Stages One and Two. The early meetings at the Cheshire reformatory took place in a room filled with noise from the rest of the prison; on one occasion, Kohlberg mentioned, a guard was beating an inmate and the discussion of moral issues was punctuated with screams.

The Just Community for male inmates was shut down in 1977, when

it was discovered that one of the night guards was being blackmailed by the men after he had made sexual propositions; he was smuggling dope into the prison for them. But the women's community continues. "I think the fact that it has stayed open is pretty impressive testimony," Kohlberg says. "I don't know if it's getting any stage change or if it's affecting recidivism—that would have required really heroic measures in terms of following those people when they got out and helping them adjust to their communities.

"But I know that some of those inmates were remarkably touched, as they might have been by any program that appealed to their better moral natures—the Black Muslims, Daytop, Synanon—but those are all indoctrinative and undemocratic. At least the Just Community idea had the virtue of fairness."

The Birth of the Cluster School

Although Kohlberg visited the prisons every few weeks, he says the program was really in the hands of two consultants. He has a larger stake in the Cluster School, which he believes has a much better chance of success, in part, because he is working with teachers who are more dedicated and intellectually sophisticated than prison guards.

The Cluster School grew out of an "alternative school" started at Cambridge High School in the 1960s, one of those experiments that enabled some students to develop their own ways of learning outside the impersonal curriculum of the larger school. The school couldn't handle all the students who wanted to get in, so another was set up in 1974, with Kohlberg's help, to govern itself as a Just Community.

The students were to be a cross-section of the high school, chosen from among volunteers, by neighborhood and race; they would spend half the day in a designated corridor of the building, where they would hold their community meetings and take English and social studies classes, in which discussions of moral issues would be encouraged, along with a few elective courses. The big question, of course, was whether the kids would govern themselves responsibly, or, intoxicated by their power, would make Stage Two decisions based on narrow self-interest.

The risks were soon evident. During the second week of school, while discussing a list of electives that were to be offered in the afternoons, a student said that he did not like any of them, would not vote for any, and proposed that students not have to attend classes. "Before the faculty quite knew what was happening, a vote was taken, compulsory afternoon school abolished, and the bell rang," Kohlberg recalls. "I yelled that it was only a straw vote, and the next day the teachers explained that the school could not vote to violate a state law."

By the second year, the community was wrestling with fundamental moral and social problems. Blacks in the group raised a fairness issue, and called for more equal representation in the community. There were 47 whites, 18 blacks, and six openings to be filled at the time. Only one of the six students on the waiting list was black. The blacks, explaining their feelings of isolation as a minority, proposed that all six places be given to blacks. One white student said he wanted more black kids in the community but confessed that he didn't know what the community was going to tell the whites on the waiting list.

Another student provided a justification: "All you have to do is explain to them that the community decided it was the best idea to take all blacks this time for the community's sake, and from now on, every June we're going to admit more kids, we'll admit half black, half white."

The community voted to admit six blacks. (The current group of 45 students is evenly divided racially.) But the vote raised an issue of reverse discrimination that, in turn, may illuminate Kohlberg's current priorities. In the winter issue of *The Public Interest*, William J. Bennett of the National Humanities Center and Edwin J. Delattre of the National Humanities Faculty argue that the discussion made a mockery of the notion that the students should develop "reasons" for their actions. Bennett and Delattre conclude: "At the end, the result is a pronunciamento of a 'general will of the democracy' class—a tyranny of a particular majority over students who ask questions (and over

their rights) and over those on the waiting list who have a reasonable expectation to have themselves and their rights 'treated equally.'"

A Case of Theft

When I visited the Cluster School, the issue was stealing. "Due to a recent rash of thefts," announced the agenda for the community meeting on Friday, "it seems we're back to square one on theft." In the early

> "'Our approach is not merely developmental,' Kohlberg has said about his school democracy, 'it is indoctrinative.'"

months of the Cluster School, when a theft occurred on the premises, students tended to reason that anyone foolish enough to bring something valuable to school had to expect theft to occur. But in later incidents, the community assumed more responsibility and made a rule that if a member of the group was the culprit, he should come forward, make restitution, and apologize to the group.

In the spring, the community had gone on an outing to a camp in New Hampshire and some stereo equipment had been stolen from the grounds and put aboard the bus that took the group back to Cambridge. Now, a teacher named Diane Tabor is talking about money stolen from her handbag during a more recent community trip to a roller rink. The teacher has her suspicions about the identity of the thief or thieves. She suspects others in the group know who is responsible as well, but won't "squeal"; they had discussed it in their small-group meetings the previous day "I don't want to be a bad guy any more than anyone else," Diane says. "Should I speak out?"

The issue is what everyone refers to as "community trust." A white girl asks how the members can trust one

another if a member of their group is ripping them off. Reluctantly, Diane, who is also white, reveals her suspicions. She names a black student, Keith (the students' names are changed), as possibly responsible in both cases. Keith is not present, but another black, Ray, reports that Keith told him he had taken the stereo on the bus because he thought it was Ray's (the equipment had been returned).

"I don't believe that!" says the pert, gum-chewing blonde in the front.

Then, when a black student remarks, "It's beginning to sound like only the black kids are thieves," the issue explodes into a discussion of racial stereotypes and prejudice that is rough-and-tumble but under control. Kohlberg and the teachers intervene only to focus the issue, which is whether the blacks, whose code calls on them to protect their own, will be more loyal to the thief or to the community. In Kohlberg's terms, it is a choice between Stage Three devotion to one's narrow group and a Stage Four commitment to the rules of the wider community.

"If someone was a friend of the thief's and a member of the community," says Kohlberg, "it seems to me—and maybe I am way out—that what is good for whoever stole is to return the money and be reinstated in the community. There's not going to be a drastic punishment. But that would be what is best for that person, and that is what a friend would help the person do."

"Do you think there's enough trust in this community so that you could be honest and not automatically protect another black kid?" asks Arthur Lipkin, an English teacher, addressing a tall black, Bobby, who happens to be a relative of the suspected thief and is a leader in the discussion.

"Let me tell you something, Arthur," he answers. "Personally, I would try to protect anyone in here that I didn't think did anything ridiculous. That is how I feel, that is what I think, that is what I was taught, that is what I believe."

What Kohlberg and the staff are suggesting is that the students bring "peer pressure" on the thief. Later on, Kohlberg's research associate Ann Higgins tells me that Bobby, after the meeting, has promised to produce the suspected boy, Keith, at the next session on Monday. Keith did show up, and denied everything, Ann Higgins reported. But after further coaxing from his friends, who told him he was blowing his opportunity, he did admit stealing the stereo equipment and apologized for it at a third meeting on Tuesday.

Believing as they do in the worth of their community, Kohlberg and the teachers saw trust, which had taken so much effort to build in this heterogeneous group, as the important issue. Viewed through another lens, however, the heat on Keith could be interpreted as an insistence on group conformity that, under other circumstances, could turn ugly.

Was it really essential that he confess to the group and make a public apology? Couldn't a face-saving way be found for Keith to restore the stolen goods and be accepted back into the group's good graces? Perhaps a way could be found, Kohlberg and Ann Higgins agreed, but they did think that some sort of publicized apology was needed.

Asked if majority rule could turn into tyranny, Kohlberg replied: "In all the schools I've worked in, the first issue is whether the group has the right to make any rules at all. The issue doesn't come up in an authoritarian country. As soon as you have a democracy, particularly with the more sophisticated kids, you get the issue of whether it's desirable to make any rules that limit the rights of individuals. At the Just Community in Scarsdale, the majority voted a rule that the students couldn't come to class high. Some of the kids protested that this was a violation of their rights, that smoking pot was one of the Rights of Man, so to speak.

"If the majority could lawfully impose such a ban, one girl said, why could it not also make a rule against, say, picking one's nose? The kids' response was that, while picking one's nose might be offensive to some, coming to class high would be highly disruptive to learning, which was why they were all there. It is intrinsically disruptive, in that it prevents participation.

"Tyranny may occur when there is un-thought out conformity to the group rather than a highly rational dialogue on what are the limits of the group. Some of the things we do bear a

resemblance to things I've seen on the kibbutz. I was heavily influenced by research some of my students and I did on the kibbutz. The kibbutz convinced me that the collectivist tradition could be combined with the democratic tradition."

From my brief visit to the Cluster School, I would say the discussions are open and surprisingly uninhibited. You can't tell kids they have a democracy and then urge them to keep their mouths shut. The students seemed to

---

"'Today,' Kohlberg says, 'participation is an educational response to the growing privatism of youth.'"

---

care for one another, to understand their differences, and to talk about them forcefully and honestly.

They are also weighing issues that are less academic than the normal social studies curricula and more momentous than those that have come before student governments in the past. (One teacher commented that in his own high school experience, the students usually had power to decide little more than the date of the senior prom.)

But do adults unfairly influence the dialogue, and do school administrators pull strings from behind the scenes? In other words, is there anything to Roy Feldman's charge that the Cluster School is a pseudodemocracy?

A Tender Experiment

As adults, Kohlberg and the teachers no doubt have a disproportionate influence. They do not see their role as being exclusively laid-back "facilitators" of discussion in the Rogersian mold; they believe in strong advocacy, when the issue warrants it.

It also appears that, on occasion,

fearing their tender experiment might not survive, staff members have brought pressure on the kids to see things their way. Feldman, who is on the advisory commitee that oversees a Ford Foundation grant to study the Cluster School, says that one senior administrator used the term "blackmail" to describe how the staff had gotten the community to agree not to permit pot-smoking—a politically sensitive issue—at a school event.

William Lannon, superintendent of schools, who has a son in the program, and Elsa Wasserman, the school counselor who helped set up the school, strenuously disputed Feldman's judgment that senior administrators see it as a means of social control. Wasserman says the few instances when the staff tried to pressure the kids occurred in the first years. "In the beginning, we wanted to survive," Wasserman says. "But as the community grew, and we learned to care about each other, pressure was no longer necessary. . . . I know this program is good; it makes sense, and I've seen how it can change the kids' way of thinking about moral issues."

The students are given the moral-judgment interview when they first enter the school, each fall, and again when they graduate. Kohlberg has publicly stated that though most are at Stage Two when they enter, almost all are Stages Three and Four when they graduate. (Fifteen of 17 graduates went on to college last year.) But he admits that only a small portion of the three years' worth of data from the tests has actually been scored as yet.

"I don't think moral education ought to be based on Kohlberg's theory necessarily," Kohlberg says. "I would be happy for people to take an eclectic approach. I welcome working with a behavior modifier or anyone else." Nevertheless, theory may very well influence practice in one essential respect. If you believe, as Kohlberg does, that people like the students at the Cluster School start at a lower level of moral reasoning, and that a sense of community represents a higher stage, you might then believe that whatever serves the community is good and justifies any action, even if it ignores the rights of individuals. The argument resembles, in a way, Nixon's attempts to justify all manner of violations in the name of "national security."

Kohlberg still sees his Just Communities as stimulating individual stage development in the students, but he is increasingly concerned with how the progress of the group—the "moral atmosphere"—influences that development. Indeed, he now sees communities as evolving in stages that depend on how the members succeed in living up to their own "collective norms." He and his colleagues are studying the process, with Ford money, in both the Cambridge and Brookline Just Communities. "At the moment," he explains, "there's clearly a norm in the Cluster School of maintaining trust around property issues. But there's uncertainty about whether the norm has developed to the point, in terms of strength, where the kids are willing to force it on one another."

A great deal of loving attention has been lavished on the Cluster School, but can the experiment be duplicated elsewhere? Not easily. When I came across biographies of the teachers in the school, I was as dazzled by their qualifications as I was impressed, watching them in action, by their dedication: for example, Bill Ford, a black, has a B.A. from Columbia and an M.A. from the Harvard Graduate School of Education; Diane Tabor has a B.A. from Mount Holyoke, an M.A. in English literature from Middlebury, and a Ph.D. from the Harvard Graduate School of Education; Brian Mooney, a Vietnam veteran, has studied in Spain and Panama, spent a year in religious studies at a Catholic monastery, and is now a Ph.D. candidate at Boston University.

Guiding a Just Community seems to require teachers who are not only open-minded and caring, but have a real appreciation of the subtleties of participatory democracy and Kohlbergian dialectics. Educators will admit that not all teachers fit the description. "After five years of democracy at the Cluster School," Kohlberg says, "the staff still can't relax too much. That's probably why democracy doesn't spread more. You can make mistakes, as we do day after day, but you simply can't fall back on mechanical formulas."

The Just Community experiment provides a showcase for those who would try to keep democratic ideals alive in the post-Watergate generation. "Periodically," says Kohlberg, "someone comes along who rediscovers what John Dewey was trying to do in the schools or what Thomas Osborne was trying to do at Sing Sing in 1914. Somehow I'd like to keep those experiments in democracy alive and progressing, instead of having to rediscover them in each generation."

In adolescents who are leaving their families and who have a great deal of idealism, Kohlberg says, the desire for some kind of community is particularly strong—especially today. Kohlberg's work is, in part, a response to the loss of community trust he sees in the larger society, as he made plain in his paper at the University of Illinois:

"Today, participation represents an educational response to the growing privatism of youth. The opposite of participation, the back-to-basics movement, is just the symptom of the current national disease of privatism which afflicts the youth even more than their elders.

"Behind the back-to-basics movement is the basic of California's Proposition 13, money. Behind money is the true basic expressed by the title of Robert Ringer's book at the top of the best-seller list, *Looking Out for No. 1*. In our stage system, by the way, if you look out for No. 1, you are probably Stage Two. In terms of outcomes of education, the recent Gallup poll indicates that the most endorsed educational outcome is the ability to write a job application letter with correct grammar and spelling. In terms of educational input, the most endorsed input is not spending money.

"The new privatism unites the cynical or the disillusioned liberal with the cynical or the disillusioned conservative." **∩**

Howard Muson is managing editor of *Psychology Today*.

For further information, read:

Benson, George C. S. and Thomas S. Engeman. *Amoral America*, Hoover Institution Press, 1975, $8.95.

Hickey, Joseph and Peter Scharf. *Democratic Justice and Prison Reform*, Jossey-Bass, in press.

Hersh, Richard, Joseph Reimer, and Diana Pritchard Paolitto. *Promoting Moral Growth*, Longman, 1979, $12.50, paper, $6.95.

Kurtines, William and Esther Blank Greif. "The Development of Moral Thought: Review and Evaluation of Kohlberg's Approach," *Psychological Bulletin*, Vol. 81, No. 8, 1974.

Scharf, Peter, ed. *Readings in Moral Education*, Winston Press, 1978, $7.95.

Sprinthall, Norman A. and Ralph L. Mosher, eds. *Value Development As the Aim of Education*, Character Research Press, Union College, Schenectady, N.Y., 1978, $4.25.

"If I had sabotaged the order of the onetime Führer of the German Reich, Adolf Hitler, I would have been not only a scoundrel but a despicable pig, like those who broke their military oath to join the ranks of the anti-Hitler criminals in the conspiracy of July 20, 1944." —ADOLF EICHMANN

Morals Left & Right

by Charles
Hampden-Turner
& Phillip Whitten

ALL RESPONSIBLE LAW-ABIDING CITIZENS resemble one another; every outlaw is responsible in his own fashion. In the past decade the wanted poster replaced the campaign poster as the official portrait of the American hero. Test cases turned the courtroom into a forum for national issues; members of conspiracies received more attention than members of Congress. Henry David Thoreau was a household word, along with his doctrine of civil disobedience. Commitment was defined by one's willingness to be arrested, political experience by the length of one's police record. The "Group W Bench" (those selected for prosecution by the State) included such diverse figures as Martin Luther King and Abbie Hoffman, Dr. Spock and Bobby Seale.

The national campaign for law and order has since produced a new dictionary of household words, and a new American hero. Those who take the brunt charge political repression, claiming that blind enforcement of the legal code threatens an important and legitimate source of social change. It has become critical that we understand the fashions of responsible outlaws, as well as those of ordinary citizens, in terms that will allow their politics to remain constructive. We cannot accept the simple analysis of an Agnew speech or a Weatherman bomb threat.

Split. Recent research indicates that the polarization of Americans into political camps—left-wing vs. right-wing, militant vs. pacifist, the movement vs. the system—can be traced to the levels of moral development that guide individuals through most of their daily activity. Certain moral perspectives impel "radical" thinking, while certain other moral perspectives impel "conservative" interpretations of reality.

Studies comparing the moral judgments made by political conservatives, liberals and radicals have confirmed some of the stereotypes each group uses to describe the others as well as those they use to describe themselves. There is evidence to support the conservative's notion that the radical movement consists of starry-eyed idealists "infiltrated" by Machiavellian opportunists. The same evidence, however, also justifies the radical's claim of moral superiority over both liberals and conservatives.

64

In which conservatives, radicals and liberals are examined and graded on the extent to which their values have developed.

MORALS LEFT AND RIGHT, by Charles Hampden-Turner and Phillip Whitten. Copyright © 1974 by Ziff-Davis Publishing Company. Reprinted by permission from **PSYCHOLOGY TODAY** Magazine.

There are also indications that the confrontation tactics developed by the radical movement, and so violently condemned by law-and-order advocates, can actually increase the moral awareness of the young. Not surprisingly, these tactics are less effective with older generations. Radical education tends to accelerate the polarization of Americans into political camps—the armed camps of the revolution.

Research conducted in the San Francisco Bay Area and Boston offers four keys to an understanding of the recent political and cultural turmoil in the United States.

1. Different levels of moral judgment tend to discriminate radicals from liberals—at least among middle-class Americans.

2. College activists typically are found at the highest and lowest stages of moral development.

3. A person seldom can comprehend judgments more than one level above the one in which he usually is found.

4. Growth in the capacity for moral judgment can be induced by creating conflicts between two or more stages and by dramatizing the issues.

Stages. This research incorporates the model of sequential stages of moral growth developed by Lawrence Kohlberg of the Harvard Graduate School of Education. He found that moral perspective progresses through as many as six stages during a person's life. To determine a subject's stage of development Kohlberg would ask him to explain his solutions to a variety of moral dilemmas that had no "right" answers. For example, a subject might be asked to imagine that his wife will die of a disease unless she takes a certain drug. The sole supplier of the drug demands so great a profit that the subject cannot find the money. The typical solution in this case is theft, but the justifications offered by subjects vary according to their levels of moral development.

Moral value in the first two preconventional states is defined in terms of self-centered needs. At Stage 1, the individual is primarily motivated by desire to avoid punishment by a superior power: *God would punish me if I let my wife die. My father-in-law would make trouble for me.*

At Stage 2, concern has shifted to the satisfaction of quasi-physical needs. The individual develops an awareness of the relative value of each person's needs as his own drives are frustrated by demands for exchange and reciprocity: *I have a right to the services of my wife, and naturally this is more important than whatever rights the druggist may claim. No one is going to look out for my interest or my wife's unless I do.*

The conventional orientation of Stages 3 and 4 involves conformity to traditional role expectations and maintenance of existing social and legal order. The Stage-3 individual is motivated to avoid social disapproval for nonconformity and would like to be judged by his intentions: *I'd do what any half-decent husband would do—save his family and carry out his protective function.*

The Stage-4 person understands how his role fits into larger constellations of roles, the institutions approved by others. He seeks to perform his duty—to meet the expectations of society: *My wife and I submitted ourselves to a higher law, the institution of marriage. The fabric of our society is held together by this institution. I know my lawful duty when I see it.*

The two postconventional stages represent the most advanced levels of moral development. Decisions are based on consideration of shared values rather than on self-centered interests or blind conformity to external standards. The Stage-5 individual perceives his duty in terms of a social contract, recognizing the arbitrary nature of rules made for the sake of agreement. He avoids infringing on the rights of others, or violating the welfare of the majority: *My wife and I promised to love and help one another, whatever the circumstances. We chose to make that commitment and in our daily lives together it is constantly renewed. I am therefore committed to saving her.*

The Stage-6 person relies heavily on his own conscience and the mutual respect of others. He recognizes the universal principles that underlie social commitments and seeks to apply them as consistent principles of moral judgment: *No contract, law, obligation, private gain or fear of punishment should impede any man from saving those he loves. For the sake of my wife I will steal the drug; for the sake of others who might share my experience, I will steal the drug publicly, so that society may cease to sacrifice human relationships to the profit motive.*

Height. People progress from stage to stage, but most never advance beyond Stages 3 and 4. It is primarily college-educated, middle-class youth who have attained high levels of moral judgment in recent years. And even they are inclined, when their formal education has been completed, to backslide on the scale.

At each level, the person takes into consideration the logic of each of the lower steps, with the highest level taking precedence. The Stage-6 man is aware of the demands made upon him in a situation by roles, laws and previous commitments—and he may undergo much agony if these considerations conflict with his conscience.

We found in the research that young adults who thought of themselves as political conservatives consistently referred to law, order, authority maintenance (Stage 4) and conformity to stereotyped roles

(Stage 3) in making their moral judgments. Self-professed liberals and moderates tended to make Stage-5 judgments. Radicals, however, showed an interesting division. Although most radicals had Stage-6 consciences and principle orientation, a large minority made egocentric Stage-2 judgments.

These findings correspond to the image of a fairly homogenous silent majority of conservative Americans confronting a disparate array of left-of-center idealists (Stage 6) and opportunists (Stage 2). Between these poles are the Stage-5 liberals, desperately urging the two groups at least to agree on the methods of disagreement.

Levels. If the U.S. faced dilemmas no more complex than whether or not poor men should steal drugs to save their wives, most political partisans would probably agree. The levels of rationale used to arrive at a solution to the problem would then concern only philosophers. Unfortunately, it is not that simple.

Conservatives, liberals and radicals use moral judgments to justify actions that affect the lives of millions. Different levels of moral development are intimately associated with different political positions on such issues as race relations and the Vietnam war. For instance, radicals attack Asian policy on grounds of conscience (Stage 6), or on grounds that it is detrimental to the personal economic or domestic interests of American citizens (Stage 2). Conservatives in Stages 3 and 4 defend the war. They praise "our boys" for meeting role expectations so well, especially by comparison with "campus bums." They exhort patriotic citizens to support the lawful authority of the Commander in Chief, who knows much more about the situation than those who try to legislate in the streets. This polarity tears apart the moral hierarchy and discourages commitment to a rational dialogue.

Wings. The cleavages between stages of development can be understood on a deeper level by using Silvan Tomkins' distinction between left-wing and right-wing ideology. Tomkins asks:

"Is man the measure, an end in himself, an active, creative, thinking, desiring, loving force in nature (Left)? or, must man realize himself, attain his full stature, only through struggle towards, participation in, conformity to, a norm, a measure, an ideal essence, basically independent of man (Right)?"

The Stage-6 man whose conscience shrieks at the barbarity of the Vietnam war perceives *himself* as an "active, creative, thinking, desiring, loving" arbiter of right and wrong. He is undaunted by charges of treason or unAmericanism because he has an ideal of a nobler America yet to be created by people like him. At a more primitive level, the Stage-2 radical objects to the war because it threatens to delay satisfaction of his own personal needs and impulses. The war constrains and frustrates him in a dozen different

"The quest for self may require many of the things conservatives abhor: permissiveness, experimentation, incompleteness, frankness, criticism, skepticism and contradictions."

ways and confronts him with obligations beyond his will and, perhaps, beyond his ability to fulfill.

Fabric. Conservatives express concern that the war is eroding patriotism and respect for authority (Stages 3 and 4). They fear that disrespect for authorities and the breaking down of order are tarnishing America's reputation and undermining its position in the world. Duty, honor, patriotism, loyalty, the flag, the free world and our national mission help define our proper roles (Stage 3) and constitute the symbolic fabric of lawful authority (Stage 4).

The Stage-5 liberal objects to the war because it disregards social contracts of negotiation and agree- and academic freedom can survive only if dissenters and authorities respect implied agreements on the limits of dissent, the need to work for change within the system by peaceful means, and the necessity for rational dialogue. As a result the liberal regards virtually no act by those in authority as base enough to merit opposition that violates the social contract. When Robert McNamara went to Harvard to speak as Secretary of Defense, the academic community apparently was more shocked by the students who shouted him down than they were by the saturation bombing and killing of civilians that his policy brought about. These Harvard liberals wanted polite discussion of wholesale slaughter confined to the question-and-answer period.

Laps. The race issue also has polarized conservatives and radicals at their different levels of moral judgment. Law and order (Stage 4) has, of course, become a rallying cry for resistance to black demands. But the cultural stereotypes typical of Stage-3 thinking—Miss America, the Wild West, our boys, red-blooded Americans, etc.—are more subtly racist. The images are those of the dominant culture, a culture ostensibly dedicated to individualism, but actually demanding a conformity some can never achieve. Those who are already several laps behind in the Great American Race are absurdly handicapped, while those who maintain the system with their own preferences in mind have a distinct advantage.

Radicals and many liberals have become convinced that the black and the poor must be given the right to define their own needs and shape their own institutions and norms. This can happen only in a society that permits the disadvantaged to create and implement Stage-6 judgments and Stage-5 contracts, which in turn can become laws (Stage 4), roles (Stage 3), and instrumentalities (Stage 2) infused with their creators' consciousness. In short, the disadvantaged can never "catch up." They must instead be encouraged to *originate.*

Virtue. Young people have been forced to create a counterculture in order to transcend cultural values that are dominated by the conservative, rule-centered

"College activists typically are found at the highest and lowest stages of moral development."

Stages 3 and 4 and to move through Stage 5 into the fully person-centered Stage 6. The old culture's external symbols of virtue—status, high income, private property, good grades, winning the ball game—were amenable to relatively precise measurement and linear ordering. A man was only as good as his credit rating. Now virtue is being attributed to the self. This sort of virtue must be uncovered and shaped from a thousand jumbled ideas and feelings deep within the person. The quest for self may require many of the things conservatives abhor: permissiveness, experimentation, incompleteness, frankness about previously taboo topics, criticism of and skepticism toward the inherited truths, and the recognition of contradictions.

Growth beyond Stage 4 requires the creation of

voluntary commitments to others as well as acts of conscience in which *authenticity* is crucial to communication and agreement. Those who deviate from well-worn roles and traditions risk total alienation, unless their humanity and sensitivity can evoke others' humanity to create new bonds.

Impact. For those at Stages 3 and 4, authenticity is at best a qualified good. They see the self as lacking intrinsic worth, able to achieve value only by conformity to a norm, a measure, an ideal essence, basically independent of man. Conservative Americans believe that the self-centered strivings typical of Stage-2 behavior must be harnessed and controlled by imposed roles (Stage 3) and due respect for authority (Stage 4). It is considered safer, and indeed more civilized, to make a calculated impact or good impression. The well-groomed, self-conscious, respectable aspects of the personality should be revealed to others selectively. President Nixon embodies this type of control; having learned that his temper gets him into trouble, he will be silent for days—even months—after a setback before he counterattacks with carefully rehearsed indignation. Although people at Stages 5 and 6 may regard this attribute as inauthentic, those at Stages 3 and 4 regard it as essentially civilized. The President checks himself, keeps himself in control, and personifies the lawful restraint of potentially dangerous impulses.

An individual must like and trust his unvarnished self before he can give authenticity a free rein. Unbridled and confident, kids let their hair fly free, their beards grow wild and their bodies go unsupported. Their love is expressed openly; their indignation is combustible. Their quest for self-discovery frustrates and provokes the authorities determined to squeeze the young into conservative molds. The old culture believes that the spontaneous self betrays the individual, causes trouble, impedes the installation of new technology, weakens moral imperatives, undermines social control, and is bad for business.

The people of the conservative old culture (Stages 3 and 4) live with perpetual psychological scarcity—the assumption that there is never enough, materially or spiritually, to satisfy everyone's needs. There is always a shortage—of status, authority, wealth, property and school marks that are ordered hierarchically for purposes of envious competition and comparison. Profiteers push their ideals safely beyond the reach of most persons, and those who fall just short in an atmosphere of contrived scarcity never feel adequate to question those ideals.

Plenty. Radicals and liberals are perplexed by the contradictions of the old culture. They know there is enough to go around. They attack the system that the old culture designed to protect the resources—a system that maintains itself at the cost of abandoning millions

---

Political Stamping Grounds

Three psychologists from Millikin University in Decatur, Ill., hunting behavioral measures of political attitudes, recently dropped "lost letters"—addressed but unstamped—in parking lots outside churches in a small city. Most churchgoers dutifully posted the letters, and many went the second mile: they added stamps.

But that's where religious and political differences showed up: 89 per cent of the Catholics and 88 per cent of the liberal Protestants added the postage, but only 43 per cent of the persons attending conservative Protestant churches did so.

The fascinated researchers—Gordon Forbes, R. Kent Tevault and Henry F. Gromoll—then studied car locking as a possible index of protectiveness, often related to political attitudes. Even though all the churches were in low-crime areas, the results were significant if less dramatic than the stamp findings: only 32.47 per cent of the liberal churchgoers—but 40.67 per cent of the conservatives—locked their car doors before going in to worship.

---

of its own citizens to malnutrition, infant mortality and death from easily preventable diseases.

It is significant that the radical counterculture originated among some of the brightest students at the best universities. Having won the glittering prizes, these students denounced the whole rat race as worthless and unjust. They formed an uncertain alliance with those who rejected the race because they missed the shining prizes by a mile. Both groups increasingly reject marks, hierarchies and competitiveness, as they insist on sharing and communal festivals of life, and are determined to create an abundance of sights, sounds, experiences and the necessities of life.

Head-on. The drawback to a morality that adheres to cultural stereotypes and law and order is that such guidelines are national rather than international. In the absence of international law and order such moral judgments steer rival nations into collision courses.

Paradoxically, the only way to create international law-and-order and world-citizen stereotypes is through the preliminary exercise of conscience (Stage 6) and contracts between nations (Stage 5). These initially would conflict with the patriotic structure of each nation. In the absence of world authority or roles by which Stage-3 and Stage-4 persons can be guided, we are stuck in an international jungle where our national authority and our boys struggle for dominion.

The crucial flaw in the radical morality can be seen in the Janus-faced character of college protest movements. Studies by Norma Haan and her associates at the University of California at Berkeley and Irvin Doress in Boston have found that both the highly moral Stage 6 and the essentially premoral Stage 2 were heavily represented in the radical population, along with a few Stage-5 allies.

Researchers who compared persons in these highest and lowest groups found that they are outwardly very similar. Many members of both groups had interrupted their college careers, moved off-campus, disagreed with their parents and involved themselves intensely in politics, assumed the dress and speech of the counterculture, and begun to pursue creative and artistic endeavors.

Highly moral radicals, however, valued sensitivity, empathy and altruism far more than did the premoral subjects, who prided themselves on being aloof, reserved, stubborn and uncompromising. Whereas the Stage-6 radicals seem capable of replacing outdated structures by pouring in their creative energies and capacities and building anew, Stage-2 radicals are essentially adolescents who mimic, misinterpret and misrepresent the principled thinkers.

Slips. Elliot Turiel's recent discovery of "Temporary 2s" complicates any neat distinction between 6s and 2s. Unlike the typical premoral individual, the Temporary 2 comprehends higher levels of judgment but refuses to use them. This could be interpreted as a regression in the service of the ego, or it might be that such students do not oppose roles or authorities in general, but merely the particular roles and the particular authorities they are confronting. It could also mean, however, that the transition from Stage 4 to the more person-centered Stages 5 and 6 has miscarried, with the result that the individual slips back into premoral judgment.

Sharing. These findings suggest that the characteristics commonly regarded as symptoms of person-centered growth—the communal, experiential trappings of the counterculture—might equally well be interpreted as a regression to an egocentric state. Indeed, there is some evidence that hippies and street people are mostly 2s with some stereotyped beautiful 3s. Radicalism became fashionable, a local convention, and many adopted the style of the revolution without the awareness of the revolutionary. The harsh truth is that crime spreads and drug addiction reaches epidemic proportions as the constituency of conscience grows. Chase N. Peterson, Harvard's Dean of Admissions, speaks of "kids, searching earnestly for a magical mystery tour as they share despair, hope, marijuana and gonorrhea."

Given this ambiguity in which those who are moral run in harness with those who are amoral, we can begin to understand the conspiracy theories so prevalent on the American Right. The Right accuses radicals of putting up an idealistic front of wishy-washy, starry-eyed, bleeding-heart do-gooders and dupes, behind which all manner of sinister and criminal elements gnaw at the nation's moral fiber.

To many conservatives the Left seems conspiratorial and treacherous for yet another reason. Practitioners of Stage-3 and Stage-4 judgments can easily understand the rationale of Stage-2 leftists, but they cannot comprehend the judgments of Stage-6 radicals. Kohlberg found that people cannot generally comprehend more than one level above their own. Conservatives know that conscience is somehow good. The liberal (Stage-5) media may frequently have stressed how high-minded was the disobedience of such men as Daniel and Philip Berrigan, William Sloane Coffin and Martin Luther King, but individuals at Stages 3 and 4 can never accept the wisdom or sincerity of such men. Rather, it sounds to them like typical liberal rhetoric that covers the advance of dangerous elements whose Stage-2 behavior conservatives recognize clearly.

Grow Up. One of the more predictive items on the California F Scale, which discriminates between conservative and liberal tendencies, is the statement that *Young people sometimes get rebellious ideas, but as they grow up they ought to get over them and settle down.* The statement describes precisely the experiences of Stage-3 and Stage-4 individuals who have grown out of the self-assertive, premoral Stage 2.

Both the Left and the Right, therefore, have good reason to see each other in terms of their own immoral pasts. While conservatives at Stages 3 and 4 see the Stage-2 radical as occupying a level morally beneath them, Stage-6 radicals and Stage-5 liberals see conservatives as being in a condition from which they have emancipated themselves. Each partisan feels that in attacking the other he is burning the effigy of his own moral infancy.

Finally, we come to the difficult problem of how maturity might best be induced in moral judgment. One hypothesis, implicit in Kohlberg's model of moral development, holds that congruence between the different levels will enhance growth. For example, if authorities are fair-minded, then persons will swiftly pass through the law-and-order orientation to share the conscience of the authorities themselves. Research indicates that children with Stage-6 mothers reach and transcend Stage 4 at a relatively early age, suggesting that conservative and radical levels of judgment are potentially synergistic.

But a second hypothesis, also supported by research, suggests another conclusion. When disputes are dramatized in a classroom and higher-level judgments clash with lower-level ones in dialectic, students learn to prefer the higher-level judgments. From this we might infer that the shortcomings of lower-level judgments must be demonstrated before they are discarded.

Fair. Our two hypotheses are, perhaps, reconcilable. Growth is enhanced by congruence between the different levels of judgment. For example, Kenneth Keniston found that young radicals are oriented to conscience and commitment, partly because fair-minded parents explained rules to them when they were children. This kind of progress is blocked, however, when the different levels move *out* of harmony, when there is a credibility gap between the explanations of the authorities and the perceptions of the young. At this point growth proceeds from conflict rather than from cooperation.

This pattern parallels many college uprisings in the late '60s. Students seized buildings on issues of conscience (Stage 6). Administrators responded with law-and-order arguments (Stage 4). Liberal faculties desperately tried to mediate (Stage 5).

Persons who witnessed police violence were shocked away from conventional thinking, either rising to Stage 5, Stage 6, or backsliding to Stage 2.

Such confrontations can promote moral growth by dramatizing the conflict between higher and lower stages of development. Even when the conflict fails to produce immediate reform, it gathers more recruits for what promises to be a long and continuing struggle.

In any society the Stage-6 individuals, and to a lesser extent the Stage-5 ones, are the experimenters, the innovators, the dynamic segment of society. But the conventional elements in society, represented by Stages 4 and 3, function to salvage the conventional social system when experimental morality miscarries.   ♫

Some Issues of Ethics in Social Psychology

by Stephen G. West and Steven P. Gunn

ABSTRACT: *In a review of the implications for social psychology of tightening ethical standards, we contend that there is a current shift in the field toward investigating neutral or positive, rather than negative, aspects of human behavior. The major methodological approaches (laboratory experiments, field experiments, role playing, and complex correlational methods) are discussed with respect to the issues of validity of causal inference, ecological validity, and ethics. Finally, it is argued that there is a fundamental difference in the perception of the nature of man on the part of humanistic critics and traditional experimental social psychologists which leads to different assessments of the long-term effects of deception research on subjects. Long-term follow-up studies are proposed as a source of empirical information on which investigators and ethics committees may base decisions about the acceptability of the level of risk associated with experimental manipulations.*

During the past few years, the community of academic psychology has been engaged in a process of critical self-examination regarding the ethics of psychological research with human subjects. The manifestations of this process have taken several different forms. First, the American Psychological Association in 1973 published a revision of the *Ethical Principles in the Conduct of Research with Human Participants*. The revised guidelines discuss in detail a number of ethical issues that arise in research; new emphasis is placed on several problems, including possible long-term effects of research on the subject, deceptive research practices, and the impact of research on society. Second, a number of journals, particularly the *American Psychologist*, have published articles on ethical issues in research. Some of these have been favorable or unfavorable comments on the current APA ethical guidelines; others have attempted to assess empirically subjects' perceptions of and reactions to psychological research procedures. Third, research proposals seem to be receiving increased scrutiny with refer-

ence to the ethical treatment of subjects at both the federal and university levels. A number of researchers have reported that this increased ethical scrutiny has had a direct impact on their programs of research. To take one instance, some researchers in the area of aggression (e.g., Baron, Note 1) have reported difficulty in gaining the approval of their respective research committees for the use of anger manipulations that have been traditionally utilized in aggression research. These researchers have reported that they have had to utilize a less severe anger manipulation than they have employed in their past research.

Many researchers, including ourselves, consider the stricter ethical standards now being applied to research proposals to be an immutable fact of life. In designing research, we find ourselves adopting new procedures and sometimes new methodologies in order to avoid confrontation on ethical grounds. This article outlines some of the implications of this trend for the nature of the field of social psychology. In discussing these implications, we feel it is instructive to juxtapose the shape of the emerging field against the desires of social psychology's humanistic critics. It is our contention that many of the current trends in the field of social psychology are direct or indirect reflections of humanistic concerns.

In our consideration of the impact of ethical issues on the methods and findings of social psychology, we first describe the ways in which the content of social psychology appears to be changing in a manner consistent with the recommendations of one of the more influential humanistic critics, Sidney Jourard (1968). A review of the criticisms of traditional social psychological methods as advocated

A portion of this paper was presented in the symposium "Ethical Issues in Social Psychology: Some Current Thoughts" (B. Latané, Chair) at the meeting of the American Psychological Association, Washington, D.C., September 1976.

We would like to thank Richard Archer, Nancy Avis Rosen, Lee Sechrest, and Robert Wicklund for their thoughtful comments on an earlier version of this manuscript.

Requests for reprints should be sent to Stephen G. West, who is now at the Department of Psychology, Florida State University, Tallahassee, Florida 32306.

by Jourard (1967) and Kelman (1967, 1968, 1972) is then followed by a discussion of the ethical and empirical advantages and disadvantages of several strategies of research currently being employed in social psychology. Finally, we offer some brief observations and discuss possible advantages of collecting empirical data with which to assess the effect, if any, that participation in social psychological research may have on subjects.

The Content of Social Psychology

In his book *Disclosing Man to Himself*, Jourard (1968) argued for a shift in the areas of inquiry of the field.

How odd it seems that psychology has learned more about man at his worst than at his best . . . We need psychologists with the most informed imaginations and talent for ingenious experimentation to wrestle with such questions as, "What are the outer limits of human potential for transcending biological pressures, social pressures, and the impact on a person of his past conditioning? What developmental and interpersonal and situational conditions conduce to courage, creativity, transcendent behavior, love, laughter, commitment to truth, beauty, justice, and virtue?" (pp. 6–7)

Has social psychology taken heed of Jourard's advice? From our perception, the answer to this question is yes. There seems to be an increasing number of articles being published which address the positive aspects of human behavior. While a systematic study has yet to be conducted, the number of articles on positive aspects of human behavior (e.g., impression formation, attribution) seem to be increasing, with no concurrent increase in articles on negative aspects of human behavior (e.g., aggression, cheating). Research areas that address topics which represent limitations to man's freedom of choice, such as social influence and conformity, also seem to have lost favor. Some evidence for this argument can be found in Capasso and Hendrick's (1976) bibliography of articles in social psychology. For example, there were nearly three times as many articles published during the second half of 1975 on altruism and helping behavior as on aggression. The cause of these changes in research activity in social psychology is, of course, uncertain. On the one hand, these changes may reflect historical fluctuations in the topics of interest to social psychologists. On the other hand, they may reflect increased humanistic concerns on the part of many social psychologists. While social psychologists have traditionally neglected some of the more positive forms of human behavior, it now seems as if the situation has been reversed. Some

colleagues do not want to discuss negative aspects of human behavior; they prefer to focus exclusively on the more positive side of humanity. In addition, there is some evidence that people evaluate the ethics of research accentuating the negative aspects of human behavior more stringently than research addressing the positive forms of human behavior. For example, Schlenker and Forsyth (1977) found that subjects judged the ethicality of two different obedience experiments (Milgram, 1963; West, Gunn, & Chernicky, 1975) solely as a function of the proportion of participants who were reported to have been obedient. The proportion of participants who were described as having been "psychologically upset" by the procedure did not affect the subjects' ethical judgments. Bickman and Zarantonello (Note 2) reported similar results. This bias, if it is shared by ethics committees and journal editors, is particularly troublesome. It will tend to discourage research in potentially important areas that involve negative aspects of the human character. Research should be evaluated on the basis of its potential scientific contribution and the total amount of risk to which subjects may be potentially exposed, but not on the likelihood that the research will support a positive view of mankind.

Social Psychological Methods

Now let us consider the methods of social psychology. Humanistic critics have questioned both the validity and the ethics of some of the traditional methods used in the field of social psychology, particularly the deception experiment. As an alternative, they offer methods that attempt to take advantage of more positive human motives. For example, Jourard (1967) argued that traditional social psychological research methods were failing, citing demand characteristics (Orne, 1962) and experimenter bias (Rosenthal, 1963) as fatal flaws of the laboratory experiment. As an alternative, Jourard argued for the use of a research methodology in which the experimenter would be open and honest with the subject; he even encouraged disclosures of actual aspects of personal life by the experimenter.

Another critic, Kelman (1967, 1968, 1972), has also argued for a different approach to research. While Kelman has not ruled out the use of deception per se, he has objected to its pervasiveness in social psychological research. "What concerns me most is not so much that deception is used, but precisely that it is used without question. It has now become standard operating procedure in the social psychologist's laboratory" (Kelman, 1967, p. 3). This use of deception in the social psychological research of the early 1960s has been documented by Seeman (1969), who found that nearly 40% of the articles published in the *Journal of Personality* and the *Journal of Abnormal and Social Psychology* involved some sort of deception. Kelman (1967) pointed out some of the possible dangers of deception experiments: long- or short-term harmful consequences to the subject, the denigration of the experimenter–subject relationship, and addition to the "already considerable degree of deceit and irrationality that pervades modern life." Like Jourard, Kelman (1967) raised questions about the methodological advantages of deception experiments, also citing the potentially limiting effects of demand characteristics and experimenter bias. As a solution, he called for "participatory research," which would be designed to

involve the subject as an active participant in a joint effort with the investigator. The procedures would depend on the subject's positive motivations to contribute to the research enterprise—because he has been persuaded of the importance of the research, or because he feels that he has a unique contribution to make, or because he has a special stake in the outcome of the investigation. (Kelman, 1972, p. 1003)

With the preceding humanistic commentary as background, let us review the ways in which the methods of social psychology have changed. The methodology of social psychology seems to be in a state of radical evolution. Students and faculty have discovered that Volume 2 of the *Handbook of Social Psychology* contains more than Aronson and Carlsmith's (1968) chapter on experimental methodology. No longer is the laboratory deception experiment the only way to conduct research. Indeed, although we like to consider ourselves experimental social psychologists, we have employed such foreign methodologies as systematic observation, computer simulation, archival analysis, content analysis, and interviewing in our research. Sometimes these methods have been used in conjunction with an experimental manipulation, sometimes they have not. We believe that the current broadening of methods in social psychology may yield great potential benefits to the field in terms of the quality and the ecological validity of its results. The methods are often complimentary in their advantages and disadvantages, and generalizations based on multiple methodologies will, for the most part, be better than generalizations based on a single methodology. At the same time, some social psycholo-

gists apparently have been overwhelmed by the new methodology of the field, arguing that the use of experimental methodology is no longer necessary. We believe that attempts to phase out experimental methods can only result in a precipitous decrease in the quality of social psychological data. As a means of clarifying this position, we will now briefly discuss the ethical and empirical advantages and disadvantages of four alternative strategies: (a) traditional laboratory experiments, (b) role playing, (c) field experiments, and (d) complex correlational methods.

LABORATORY EXPERIMENTS

Traditional laboratory experiments are the foundation upon which the field has been built. Laboratory experiments have great advantages over other techniques in terms of control over extraneous influences and the ability of the investigator to make causal statements about his or her results. What are the disadvantages? First, as discussed in a prior section, humanistic critics have cited the problem of deception, which is often, but not necessarily, a component of laboratory experiments. (This issue is briefly addressed in the final section of this article.) Second, humanistic and other critics have cited the problems of experimenter bias and subject artifacts (motivations) such as demand characteristics and evaluation apprehension. Let us briefly consider these problems.

The problems of experimenter bias and subject motivations, like any other experimental artifacts, need to be considered seriously by the investigator. However, we do not share the pessimism of some social psychologists that all laboratory research is so tainted by these problems as to be meaningless. Considering first the problem of experimenter bias, two conclusions may be reached: (a) The extent of the problem is unknown, since the research that has demonstrated this effect has normally utilized naive experimenters who conducted only one condition of the experiment. Such procedures are not representative of those used in laboratory experiments in social psychology (Aronson, 1968). (b) This problem, when it does exist, can be eliminated easily through the use of appropriate control procedures such as keeping the experimenter blind to the subject's condition or using automated instructions (cf. Aronson & Carlsmith, 1968).

A similar set of arguments may be presented with regard to the problem of subject artifacts. Weber and Cook (1972) point out that two necessary conditions must take place for subject artifacts to be a problem in social psychological research: (a) The motive to adopt some sort of subject role must be aroused, and (b) the subject must perceive situational cues that guide behavior so that he or she can alter it to be consistent with the aroused motive. In certain types of research, such as personality inventories, attitude surveys, and interviews, both conditions may easily be present, permitting subject motivations to become a serious potential artifact. However, in experiments, there is an additional condition that must be fulfilled before subject motivations become problematic: The cues must differ across the experimental treatment conditions. If subject motivation is aroused to the same degree across conditions, it is not a confounding. Only when it differs between experimental treatments, thus altering the obtained pattern of treatment means, does it become a serious problem. Finally, it should be noted that subject motivations do not pose a problem unless the subject has control over the dependent variable. For example, if the dependent variable is an unobtrusive measure or a physiological measure, it is unlikely that subject motivations will affect the results. In light of the above qualifications, it appears that the problem of subject motivation is probably less serious than some critics have maintained. Supporting this analysis, Kruglanski's (1975) recent review of the subject-artifact literature reaches the following conclusion:

There has been a remarkable paucity of instances in which the straightforward test on an alleged artifact was executed. Only straightforward experimental tests may yield unambiguous evidence regarding the prevalence of artifacts among the reported findings. Therefore, the absence of such tests renders rather unsupported the pessimism of some authors regarding the validity of conclusions emerging out of the experimental laboratory. (p. 140)

Subject motivations and experimenter bias have been presented as potential challenges to the internal validity of laboratory experiments (cf. Aronson & Carlsmith, 1968). The *external* validity or generalizability of laboratory findings represents yet another set of potential limitations or disadvantages of that methodology. Use of noncollege subject populations is difficult in laboratory experimentation, the range of experimental manipulations may be too narrow or the gradations too great, and the laboratory environment may be too unique or too artificial to permit generalization to other settings. These and other potential threats to external validity are characteristic of virtually any *single* experiment. However, single experiments with extended

replications, and replications by different investigators in different labs in different localities, serve to minimize lingering doubts about the external validity of an observed relationship. If a laboratory experiment is skillfully constructed and executed, the internal validity of the findings may be accepted with a reasonable degree of certainty. Given data that are internally valid, further research will determine the limits of their generalizability. Although the data may be qualified, reinterpreted, or reaffirmed by subsequent investigations, the original findings will remain as one solid bit of information in the data base of the science.

In conclusion, traditional laboratory experiments are subject to a number of problems. They are admittedly inefficient in generating hypotheses and are not well adapted to testing ideas about longterm or intimate interpersonal relationships. In addition, multiple replications in diverse settings may be necessary to establish the generalizability of laboratory findings. However, laboratory experimentation is a remarkably powerful and efficient way of testing deductive hypotheses and making causal inferences; laboratory experiments have served us well over the years for these purposes. It is our hope that social psychologists do not become so infatuated by the new, young, and attractive methodologies that have recently arrived on the scene that they divorce their faithful methodology of many years, the laboratory experiment.

ROLE PLAYING

The methodology most frequently advocated by humanistic social psychologists is role playing. This method has distinct ethical advantages over the laboratory experiment in that it avoids the use of deception and it takes advantage of the subject's positive motivations to make a contribution to science. However, role playing also has several distinct disadvantages. Freedman (1969) raises serious epistemological questions about the usefulness of role playing as a method of testing hypotheses:

The argument comes down to the simple truth that data from role-playing studies consist of what some group of subjects guesses would be their reaction to a particular stimulus. The subjects are giving their estimates, their intuitions, their insights, and their introspections about themselves or others. (p. 111)

Miller (1972), in a review of experiments that directly compared the outcomes of role-playing experiments and laboratory-deception experiments, found that role-playing subjects were able to replicate only the most obvious results of deception experiments.

Theoretical considerations also lead to the prediction that role-playing subjects will process information differently than will subjects involved in a deception experiment. First, several authors (e.g., Easterbrook, 1959; Kahneman, 1973) have argued that arousal decreases the subject's attention to peripheral cues in the environment. In studies involving motivation or emotion, for example, role-playing subjects and involved subjects would be expected to be attending to different sets of cues. Second, Mandler (1975) has noted that the procedure of examining the contents of consciousness changes the contents of consciousness. Thus, when the subject is thinking about how he or she would act in a given situation, the thought process will be different than when his or her attention is focused on the situation.

Supporting this argument, Nisbett and Wilson (1977) have reviewed a wide variety of data which strongly suggest that subjects have little direct awareness of their higher order mental processes. Different cognitive structures apparently mediate higher order mental processes, such as complex judgments, and subjects' introspections concerning these processes. Thus, taken together, the empirical, theoretical, and epistemological problems of role playing lead us to conclude with Freedman (1969) that "role playing is not a substitute for experimental research" (p. 114).

To summarize, role playing is not, in general, a valid method of testing hypotheses about human behavior. It is, however, an excellent method of generating hypotheses that can then be tested using an alternative methodology or data source. In situations that are familiar to the subject, that are highly specific, and in which emotional and motivational processes are not involved, role playing may lead to results that parallel those of experiments in the laboratory or in natural settings. However, in situations that do not satisfy these criteria, it is unlikely that the results of typical role-playing experiments can accurately represent the complex interplay of personal and environmental forces observed in a well-executed, and perhaps deceptive, experiment.

FIELD EXPERIMENTS

In the course of the past 5 years, there has been an increased interest in and utilization of field experimental methods (cf. Mark, Cook, & Diamond, 1976). In comparison with the laboratory experiment, field experiments offer a number of advantages: (a) the elimination of the potential problem of subject artifacts, since the subjects are usually unaware that they are participating in an experiment, (b) the use of more representative subject populations than college sophomores, (c) an increased certainty that the experimental situations are representative of those found in the real world, and (d) the ability to study important or stressful events in the real world that would be unethical to study in the laboratory (Bickman & Henchy, 1972; McGuire, 1967, 1969). As an example of this final advantage, Helmreich, Kuiken, and Collins (1968) studied attitude change in Navy recruits who were about to be subjected to a highly stressful experience as a part of their regular Navy training. However, field experiments also have several disadvantages relative to laboratory experiments. Unless the investigator chooses the field situation carefully, a large number of potential confounding or interfering influences can arise (Ellsworth, 1977; Sommer, 1971). Field experiments also have a number of ethical disadvantages relative to laboratory experiments. In laboratory experiments, the subjects know they are subjects; in field experiments, the subjects often are unaware that their behavior is being observed for scientific purposes. The loss of control over the subject's behavior also raises ethical problems: Should the subject have an extreme negative reaction during the course of the experiment, it may be difficult or impossible for the experimenter to intervene in the situation. Often, as Campbell (1969) points out, adequate debriefing to restore the subject to his or her original state may be impossible in the field. Finally, as a result of the above problems, field experiments are also subject to legal scrutiny (cf. Nash, 1975; Silverman, 1975). Although the problems we have cited are extreme and although most field experiments involve innocuous manipulations (e.g., finding a dime in a phone booth) and the observation of public behavior (e.g., donation to charity), field experiments may be considered to be ethically risky and should continue to be subjected to more stringent ethical review than laboratory experiments.

COMPLEX CORRELATIONAL METHODS

During the past few years, some social psychologists have advocated a radically different research strategy. This involves the collection of naturalistic data that are then analyzed using modern statistical methods, including regression analysis, time-series analysis, time-lagged correlational analysis, and path analysis (McGuire, 1973). This method of collecting data has some distinct advantages over the laboratory experiment. Subjects are studied under naturalistic conditions, so there is no concern that the experimental situations and subject populations are not representative of the real world. In addition, ethical problems in collecting data can often be minimized: In most cases, there is no deception, and informed consent can be obtained from the subject prior to participation. Finally, long-term and intimate relationships can, with the consent of the subject, be easily investigated (cf. Rubin, Peplau, & Hill, Note 3). While so far this strategy of research has not been advocated by humanistic social psychologists, it would seem that the use of these methods represents a potential return to grace for social psychology.

Alas, returns to grace are always somewhat chimerical. In the present case, the return to grace would at best be at the expense of the beautiful simplicity of results that characterizes a number of experiments in our field; at worst it would be at the expense of the ability to make causal inferences from our data. In particular, all of the complex correlational methods are subject to the third-variable problem that an unidentified factor outside the analysis may be causing the results. In contrast, whenever we conduct an experiment and obtain significant differences between the treatment groups, we know what caused the results: It is most certainly the manipulation. An equally strong causal statement cannot be made using any non-experimental method.

In addition, stringent assumptions underlie the use of complex correlational techniques. Correlations are profoundly affected by any unreliability or restriction of range of the variables. Significant intercorrelations among predictor variables lead to tremendous instability in the obtained effects and to problems in the interpretation of the results. Most of these techniques assume that a very large sample is used. Finally, some of the techniques demand a priori specification of either the nature of the effect (time series) or the causal relationships of an entire network of variables (path analysis). In the absence of a priori specification, replication of the results on a second sample of data becomes essential. Social psychologists have often failed to consider these important assumptions in using these techniques, while sociologists, who have

been involved in the development of the techniques, have usually been more conservative. Indeed, it sometimes seems as if social psychologists are rushing in to analyze data sets where sociologists have feared to tread.

In summary, the complex correlational techniques have advantages over simple correlation, although the causal inferences that can be made using these techniques may be more equivocal than those that can be made on the basis of a well-designed experiment.[1] These techniques do allow us to investigate certain topics, such as long-term and intimate relationships, to which experiments are poorly adapted. These techniques are powerful methods of analyzing naturalistic data, provided the assumptions underlying their use are satisfied.

ETHICS AND METHODOLOGY

From the foregoing discussion of the relative advantages and disadvantages of various research methodologies, it appears that the choice of a particular methodology should be based on a weighing of the relative merits of (a) strong causal inferences on the side of laboratory experiments and (b) ecological validity on the side of complex correlational methods. Field experiments fall somewhere in between the laboratory and correlational approaches as a combination of relatively good ecological validity and poor control of the experimental process. Role playing and similar neointrospectionist methodologies are frequently unacceptable due to their tenuous epistemological and empirical status. The complex correlational and experimental methods are truly complementary; to have a viable field of social psychology we must have both the strong demonstration of cause and effect provided by experiments and the ecological validity provided by complex correlational methods.

However, when considering research questions that may involve threats to the self-esteem of subjects and, thus, the necessity of deception in the laboratory approach, the degree to which a given investigator feels comfortable as the perpetrator of a potentially threatening deception will lead some researchers to choose the correlational approach while others will pursue the deception experiment.

---

[1] Sechrest (Note 4) has recently pointed out that in spite of enormous expenditures of money and the use of large, well-collected data sets, complex correlational analyses have not succeeded in establishing a causal link between smoking and lung cancer that is convincing to everyone.

Such a self-selection process would, therefore, maintain a healthy balance between the two methodologies and their associated data. But the current trend toward more stringent ethical standards poses a threat to the balance between laboratory and correlational research and restricts the degree of choice in investigator may exercise in selecting a research strategy for a given topic. Investigators may be forced to abandon powerful, well-designed, and well-controlled experiments in favor of correlational approaches or weaker laboratory manipulations. Alternatively, researchers may simply turn their attention to other topic areas that ethics committees and review boards find less objectionable. It is our contention that the stricter standards for treatment of experimental subjects have been advanced in the absence of supportive data and that the possible consequences of a bowdlerized approach to experimentation may have a number of deleterious effects on the field of social psychology.

We are not suggesting that the deception experiment be reinstituted as the "standard operating procedure" of social psychology. Rather, it is our view that ethics committees should not institute rejection of powerful deception experiments as their standard operating procedure. That a deception experiment and its findings violate the philosophical sensitivities of one branch of the field is insufficient justification for the abolition of the practice.

One final comment about the methodological status of the deception experiment. Critics of deception research have warned that by the year 2000, no naive subjects will be available for social psychologists to deceive. What then will be the fate of the field? However, even a casual reading of the research literature fails to confirm the ensuing expectation that the proportion of subjects classified as suspicious of experimental procedures has evidenced a significant increase in recent years. Once again, the rhetoric of the laboratory's critics may appear convincing, but supportive data are nowhere to be found.

Conclusion

We have reviewed some of the trends in the content and the methods of social psychology in relation to the position of the humanistic critics. We conclude with two final observations. First, to the extent that stricter ethical standards are applied to research proposals, we can expect that milder, less deceptive manipulations will be used in social psychological experiments. This has some interesting

implications: (a) The trend toward nonmotivational theories in social psychology is likely to be accelerated. If researchers are prevented from using manipulations that are capable of arousing motives, then it is unlikely that they will obtain results that support a motivational interpretation. (b) Social psychologists who use the milder, less deceptive manipulations will probably have to run more subjects in order to demonstrate differences between their treatment conditions. For example, if the strength of the manipulation is decreased by one half, four times as many subjects will have to be used to maintain the same power of the statistical test as in the original design. This leads to the following ethical question: Is it worse to deceive four times as many subjects half as much or to use the present experimental procedure? The answer to this question is a function of the investigator's personal theory of the relation between the level of deception (and/or stress) and the corresponding risk to the subject.

Second, the commentary by the ethical critics and the rebuttal by the traditional experimental social psychologists on deception experiments closely parallel these groups' respective views of the human animal. To the humanistic critics, people are relatively fragile creatures who can experience long-term positive growth only as a result of positive experiences. Deception experiments, then, can only have long-term negative effects on the participants. To the traditional experimental social psychologist, the individual in a deception experiment experiences short-term tensions that are then reduced in some manner. These psychologists view the effects of deception as transitory, with the subject being returned to his original state prior to the completion of the experiment. According to this view, debriefing ensures that any tensions aroused during the experiment will be reduced so that the subject will not experience any long-term ill effects as a result of his or her participation. Thus, a fundamental difference in the perception of human nature on the part of the humanistic critics and the experimental social psychologists leads to different assessments of the long-term effects of deception.

It may be possible to collect data concerning the degree of long-term risk to the subjects. Follow-ups of experiments that have employed highly stressful and deceptive procedures (Clark & Word, 1974; Milgram, 1974; Ring, Wallston, & Corey, 1970; Zimbardo, 1974) have uniformly failed to demonstrate long-term negative consequences of the experimental manipulations (see Holmes, 1976a, 1976b, for a review). The current APA ethical guidelines (APA, 1973) recommend such follow-ups in cases where unusually stressful or deceptive manipulations have occurred, in order to detect and ameliorate any long-term negative aftereffects. Data from such long-term follow-ups might also be used as input in our decisions concerning the ethics of proposed research. For example, in areas such as aggression, where the experimental procedures are relatively standardized, follow-up data from subjects in the anger conditions could be compared with those from subjects in the control conditions in a true experimental design. Alternatively, follow-up data from deception experiments might be compared with data from nondeception experiments in a quasi-experimental design. These investigations would provide the researcher with empirical data on the level of risk of his or her manipulations. It is hoped that the use of empirical information as an input in making ethical decisions will help to provide a more rational basis for such decisions than will relying entirely on one's personal view of the human condition.

REFERENCE NOTES

1. Baron, R. A. *Effects of victim's pain cues, victim's race, and level of prior instigation upon physical aggression.* Unpublished manuscript, Purdue University, 1976.
2. Bickman, L., & Zarantonello, M. *The effects of deception and level of obedience on subjects' ratings of the Milgram study.* Unpublished manuscript, Loyola University (Chicago), 1976.
3. Rubin, Z., Peplau, L. A., & Hill, C. T. *Becoming intimate: The development of male–female relationships.* Book in preparation, 1976.
4. Sechrest, L. B. Discussion. In B. Latané (Chair), *Ethical issues in social psychological research: Some current thoughts.* Symposium presented at the meeting of the American Psychological Association, Washington, D.C., 1976.

REFERENCES

American Psychological Association. *Ethical principles in the conduct of research with human participants.* Washington, D.C.: Author, 1973.

Aronson, E. Running and pushing the experimental subject. *Contemporary Psychology,* 1968, *13,* 5–7.

Aronson, E., & Carlsmith, J. M. Experimentation in social psychology. In G. Lindzey & E. Aronson (Eds.), *Handbook of social psychology* (Vol. 2). Cambridge, Mass.: Addison-Wesley, 1968.

Bickman, L., & Henchy, T. *Beyond the laboratory: Field research in social psychology.* New York: McGraw-Hill, 1972.

Campbell, D. T. Reforms as experiments. *American Psychologist,* 1969, *24,* 409–429.

Capasso, D. R., & Hendrick, C. Bibliography of journal articles in social psychology: Second half 1975. *Personality and Social Psychology Bulletin,* 1976, *2,* 191–206.

Clark, R. D., III, & Word, L. E. Where is the apathetic bystander? Situational characteristics of the emergency. *Journal of Personality and Social Psychology,* 1974, *29,* 279–287.

Easterbrook, J. A. The effect of emotion on cue utilization and the organization of behavior. *Psychological Review,* 1959, *66,* 183–201 .

Ellsworth, P. C. From abstract ideas to concrete instances: Some guidelines for choosing natural research settings. *American Psychologist,* 1977, *32,* 604–615.

Freedman, J. L. Role playing: Psychology by consensus. *Journal of Personality and Social Psychology,* 1969, *13,* 107–114.

Helmreich, R., Kuiken, D., & Collins, B. Effects of stress and birth order on attitude change. *Journal of Personality,* 1968, *36,* 466–473.

Holmes, D. S. Debriefing after psychological experiments: I. Effectiveness of postdeception dehoaxing. *American Psychologist,* 1976, *31,* 858–867. (a)

Holmes, D. S. Debriefing after psychological experiments: II. Effectiveness of postexperimental desensitizing. *American Psychologist,* 1976, *31,* 868–875. (b)

Jourard, S. M. Experimenter–subject dialogue: A paradigm for a humanistic science of psychology. In J. F. T. Bugenthal (Ed.), *Challenges of humanistic psychology.* New York: McGraw-Hill, 1967.

Jourard, S. M. *Disclosing man to himself.* Princeton, N.J.: Van Nostrand, 1968.

Kahneman, D. *Attention and effort.* Englewood Cliffs, N.J.: Prentice-Hall, 1973.

Kelman, H. C. Human use of human subjects: The problem of deception in social psychological experiments. *Psychological Bulletin,* 1967, *67,* 1–11.

Kelman, H. C. *A time to speak: On human values and social research.* San Francisco: Jossey-Bass, 1968.

Kelman, H. C. The rights of the subject in social research: An analysis in terms of relative legitimacy. *American Psychologist,* 1972, *27,* 989–1016.

Kruglanski, A. W. The human subject in the psychology experiment: Fact and artifact. In L. Berkowitz (Ed.), *Advances in experimental social psychology* (Vol. 8). New York: Academic Press, 1975.

Mandler, G. *Mind and emotion.* New York: Wiley, 1975.

Mark, M. M., Cook, T. D., & Diamond, S. S. Fourteen years of social psychology: A growing commitment to field experimentation. *Personality and Social Psychology Bulletin,* 1976, *2,* 154–157.

McGuire, W. J. Some impending reorientations in social psychology: Some thoughts provoked by Kenneth Ring. *Journal of Experimental Social Psychology,* 1967, *3,* 124–139.

McGuire, W. J. Theory-oriented research in natural settings: The best of both worlds for social psychology. In M. Sherif & C. Sherif (Eds.), *Interdisciplinary relationships in the social sciences.* Chicago: Aldine, 1969.

McGuire, W. J. The yin and yang of progress in social psychology: Seven koan. *Journal of Personality and Social Psychology,* 1973, *26,* 446–456.

Milgram, S. Behavioral study of obedience. *Journal of Abnormal and Social Psychology,* 1963, *67,* 371–378.

Milgram, S. *Obedience to authority.* New York: Harper & Row, 1974.

Miller, A. G. Role playing: An alternative to deception? A review of the evidence. *American Psychologist,* 1972, *27,* 623–636.

Nash, M. M. "Nonreactive methods and the law." Additional comments on legal liability in behavioral research. *American Psychologist,* 1975, *30,* 777–780.

Nisbett, R. E., & Wilson, T. D. Telling more than we can know: Verbal reports on mental processes. *Psychological Review*, 1977, *84*, 231–259.

Orne, M. T. On the social psychology of the psychological experiment: With particular reference to demand characteristics and their implications. *American Psychologist*, 1962, *17*, 776–783.

Ring, K., Wallston, K., & Corey, M. Mode of debriefing as a factor affecting subjective reaction to a Milgram-type obedience experiment—An ethical inquiry. *Representative Research in Social Psychology*, 1970, *1*, 67–88.

Rosenthal, R. On the social psychology of the psychological experiment. *American Scientist*, 1963, *51*, 268–283.

Schlenker, B. R., & Forsyth, D. R. On the ethics of psychological research. *Journal of Experimental Social Psychology*, 1977, *13*, 369–396.

Seeman, J. Deception in psychological research. *American Psychologist*, 1969, *24*, 1025–1028.

Silverman, J. Nonreactive methods and the law. *American Psychologist*, 1975, *30*, 764–769.

Sommer, R. Some costs and pitfalls in field research. *Social Problems*, 1971, *19*, 162–166.

Weber, S. J., & Cook, T. D. Subject effects in laboratory research: An examination of subject roles, demand characteristics, and valid inference. *Psychological Bulletin*, 1972, *77*, 273–295.

West, S. G., Gunn, S. P., & Chernicky, P. Ubiquitous Watergate: An attributional analysis. *Journal of Personality and Social Psychology*, 1975, *32*, 55–65.

Zimbardo, P. G. On the ethics of intervention in human psychological research: With special reference to the Stanford prison experiment. *Cognition*, 1974, *2*, 243–256.

We need your advice

Because this book will be revised on a regular basis, we would like to know what you

think of it. Please fill in the brief questionnaire on the reverse of this card and mail it to us.

Business Reply Mail

Social Psychology
2nd Edition

SOCIAL PSYCHOLOGY: CONTEMPORARY PERSPECTIVES

I am a ___ student ___ instructor

Term used _____ 19 ____

Name _____

School _____

Address _____

City _____ State _____ Zip _____

How do you rate this book?

1. Please list (by number) the articles you liked best.

_____   _____   _____   _____   _____

Why? _____

_____

2. Please list (by number) the articles you liked least.

_____   _____   _____   _____   _____

Why? _____

_____

3. Please evaluate the following:

	Excell.	Good	Fair	Poor	Comments
Organization of the book	____	____	____	____	_____
Section introductions	____	____	____	____	_____
Overall Evaluation	____	____	____	____	_____

4. Do you have any suggestions for improving the next edition?

_____

_____

_____

5. Can you suggest any new articles to include in the next edition?

_____

_____

_____

_____

_____

_____

_____

Thank you very much